MW01036824

LUKAN
AUTHORSHIP
OF
HEBREWS

OTHER BOOKS IN THIS SERIES:

NAC STUDIES IN BIBLE & THEOLOGY

LUKAN AUTHORSHIP
OF
HEBREWS

DAVID L. ALLEN

SERIES EDITOR: E. RAY CLENDENEN

ACADEMIC

NASHVILLE, TENNESSEE

Lukan Authorship of Hebrews

Copyright © 2010 by David Allen

All rights reserved.

ISBN: 978-0-8054-4714-9

Published by B&H Publishing Group
Nashville, Tennessee

Dewey Decimal Classification: 227.87
Subject Heading: BIBLE. N.T. HEBREWS—COMMENTARY \ LUKE, PHYSICIAN

Scripture quotations are from the *Holman Christian Standard Bible* ® Copyright ©
1999, 2000, 2002, 2003, 2009 by Holman Bible Publishers. Used by permission.

Printed in the United States of America

1 2 3 4 5 6 7 8 9 10 11 12 • 17 16 15 14 13 12 11 10

BP

To

Suzanne Allen

my godly mother who taught me to love Jesus,

His Word, and His Church.

She is the Proverbs 31 woman.

In Memoriam:

Lewis Allen

my father, who went home to be with the Lord earlier this year.

Dad served as an usher in my home church for 45 years.

"I had rather be a doorkeeper in the house of my God,

than dwell in the tents of wickedness." Psalm 84:10, KJV

TABLE OF CONTENTS

LIST OF ABBREVIATIONS

AB	Anchor Bible
ABRL	Anchor Bible Reference Library
ACNT	Augsburg Commentaries on the New Testament
AGJU	Arbeiten zur Geschichte des antiken Judentums und des Urchristentums
AJT	*Asia Journal of Theology*
AnBib	Analecta biblica
ANQ	*Andover Newton Quarterly*
ANRW	*Aufstieg und Niedergang der römischen Welt: Geschichte und Kultur Roma im Spiegel der neueren Forschung.* Edited by H. Temporini and W. Haase
ASNU	Acta seminarii neotestamentici upsaliensis
AThR	*Anglican Theological Review*
BBB	Bonner biblische Beiträge
BDAG	Bauer, W., F. W. Danker, W. F. Arndt, and F. W. Gingrich, *Greek-English Lexicon of the New Testament and Other Early Christian Literature.* 3rd ed.
BECNT	Baker Exegetical Commentary on the New Testament
BETL	Bibliotheca ephemeridum theologicarum lovaniensium
BFCT	Beiträge zur Förderung christlicher Theologie
Bib	*Biblica*
BJRL	*Bulletin of the John Rylands University Library of Manchester*
BNTC	Black's New Testament Commentary
BR	*Biblical Research*
BRev	*Bible Review*
BSac	*Bibliotheca Sacra*
BTB	*Biblical Theology Bulletin*
BWA(N)T	Beiträge zur Wissenschaft vom Alten (und Neuen) Testament
BZ	*Biblische Zeitschrift*
BZNW	Beihefte zur Zeitschrift für die neutestamentliche Wissenschaft und die Kunde der älteren Kirche
CBQ	*Catholic Biblical Quarterly*
CGTSC	Cambridge Greek Testament for Schools and Colleges
ConBNT	Coniectanea biblica: New Testament Series
CQR	*Church Quarterly Review*
CR	*Currents in Research*
CurBS	*Currents in Research: Biblical Studies*
EBib	*Etudes bibliques*

EKKNT	Evangelisch-Katholischer Kommentar zum Neuen Testament
EvQ	*Evangelical Quarterly*
ExpTim	*Expository Times*
FBBS	Facet Books, Biblical Series
GNS	Good News Studies
GOTR	*Greek Orthodox Theological Review*
GTA	Göttinger Theologische Arbeiten
Her	Hermeneia
HeyJ	*Heythrop Journal*
HTKNT	Herders theologischer Kommentar zum Neuen Testament
HNT	Handbuch zum Neuen Testament
HTA	Historisch Theologische Auslegungsreihe
HTR	*Harvard Theological Review*
HTS	Harvard Theological Studies
HUCA	*Hebrew Union College Annual*
IBS	*Irish Biblical Studies*
ICC	International Critical Commentary
IEJ	*Israel Exploration Journal*
Int	*Interpretation*
JBL	*Journal of Biblical Literature*
JETS	*Journal of the Evangelical Theological Society*
JOTT	*Journal of Translation and Textlinguistics*
JQR	*Jewish Quarterly Review*
JSJSup	Journal for the Study of Judaism Supplement Series
JSNT	*Journal for the Study of the New Testament*
JSNTSup	Journal for the Study of the New Testament: Supplement Series
JTS	*Journal of Theological Studies*
KEK	Kritisch-exegetischer Kommentar über das Neue Testament
KNT	Kommentar zum Neuen Testament
LQ	*The Lutheran Quarterly*
LXX	Septuagint
MT	Masoretic Text
NA^{27}	Novum Testamentum Graece, Nestle-Aland, 27th ed.
NAC	New American Commentary
NACSBT	New American Commentary Studies in Bible and Theology
NCBC	New Century Bible Commentary
Neot	*Neotestamentica*
NICNT	New International Commentary on the New Testament

NIDNTT	New International Dictionary of New Testament Theology
NIGTC	New International Greek Testament Commentary
NKZ	*Neue kirchliche Zeitschrift*
NOT	*Notes on Translation*
NovT	*Novum Testamentum*
NovTSup	Novum Testamentum Supplement Series
NSBT	New Studies in Biblical Theology
NTC	New Testament Commentary
NTS	*New Testament Studies*
OBT	Overtures to Biblical Theology
OPTAT	*Occasional Papers in Translation and Textlinguistics*
ÖTK	Ökumenischer Taschenbuch-kommentar
RevQ	*Revue de Qumran*
RevThom	*Revue Thomiste*
SANT	Studien zum Alten und Neuen Testaments
SBLDS	Society of Biblical Literature Dissertation Series
SBLMS	Society of Biblical Literature Monograph Series
SBLSBS	Society of Biblical Literature Sources for Biblical Study
SBLSCS	Society of Biblical Literature Septuagint and Cognate Studies
SBLSP	*Society of Biblical Literature Seminar Papers*
SBT	Studies in Biblical Theology
SE	*Studia evangelica*
SJT	*Scottish Journal of Theology*
SNTSMS	Society for New Testament Studies Monograph Series
SNTSU	*Studien zum Neuen Testament und seiner Umwelt*
Str-B	Strack, H. L., and P. Billerbeck, *Kommentar zum Neuen Testament aus Talmud und Midrasch,* 6 vols.
StPatr	*Studia patristica*
Su	*Studia theologica varsaviensia*
SVTQ	*St. Vladimir's Theological Quarterly*
SwJT	*Southwestern Journal of Theology*
TBT	*The Bible Today*
TDNT	*Theological Dictionary of the New Testament,* ed. G. Kittel and G. F,, trans. G. W. Bromiley. 10 vols. (Grand Rapids: Eerdmans, 1964–74)
THKNT	Theologischer Handkommentar zum Neuen Testament
TNTC	Tyndale New Testament Commentaries
TRu	*Theologische Rundschau*
TynBul	*Tyndale Bulletin*
WBC	Word Biblical Commentary

WTJ	*Westminster Theological Journal*
WUNT	Wissenschaftliche Untersuchungen zum Neuen Testament
ZNW	*Zeitschrift für die neutestamentliche Wissenschaft und die Kunde der älteren Kirche*
ZTK	*Zeitschrift für Theologie und Kirche*

SERIES PREFACE

We live in an exciting era of evangelical scholarship. Many fine educational institutions committed to the inerrancy of Scripture are training men and women to serve Christ in the church and to advance the gospel in the world. Many church leaders and professors are skillfully and fearlessly applying God's Word to critical issues, asking new questions, and developing new tools to answer those questions from Scripture. They are producing valuable new resources to thoroughly equip current and future generations of Christ's servants.

The Bible is an amazing source of truth and an amazing tool when wielded by God's Spirit for God's glory and our good. It is a bottomless well of living water, a treasure-house of endless proportions. Like an ancient tell, exciting discoveries can be made on the surface, but even more exciting are those to be found by digging. The books in this series, NAC Studies in Bible and Theology, often take a biblical difficulty as their point of entry, remembering B. F. Westcott's point that "unless all past experience is worthless, the difficulties of the Bible are the most fruitful guides to its divine depths."

This new series is to be a medium through which the work of evangelical scholars can effectively reach the church. It will include detailed exegetical-theological studies of key pericopes such as the Sermon on the Mount and also fresh examinations of topics in biblical theology and systematic theology. It is intended to supplement the New American Commentary, whose exegetical and theological discussions so many have found helpful. These resources are aimed primarily at church leaders and those who are preparing for such leadership. We trust that individual Christians will find them to be an encouragement to greater progress and joy in the faith. More important, our prayer is that they will help the church proclaim Christ more accurately and effectively and that they will bring praise and glory to our great God.

It is a tremendous privilege to be partners in God's grace with the fine scholars writing for this new series as well as with those who will be helped by it. When Christ returns, may He find us "standing firm in one spirit, with one mind, working side by side for the faith of the gospel" (Phil 1:27).

E. Ray Clendenen
B&H Publishing Group

AUTHOR'S PREFACE

As a sophomore in a small Christian college in 1976, I took the required Creative Writing course. One of the assignments included writing a 10-page paper supposedly exemplifying our ability to write creatively. The professor provided a list of topics from which we could choose. I chose "the Authorship of Hebrews." I had never studied this subject before, but the topic intrigued me. After class, the professor met me at the door and said: "I see, Mr. Allen, that you have chosen the topic 'the Authorship of Hebrews.' I have always had a sneaking suspicion that Luke was somehow involved in Hebrews as I have noted several similarities in the Greek New Testament between it and Luke's writings. Why don't you explore that option in your paper?" I did. Over the next seven years, I continued to research the matter.

When I entered the Ph.D. program at the University of Texas at Arlington in 1983, I did so to study under the linguist Robert Longacre. When I approached Dr. Longacre about accepting me as his student, I informed him I had already made the decision to write on the authorship of Hebrews and wanted to know if he would be willing to direct such a dissertation. With his dry wit, he responded with a grin: "Why would you want to write on that? I can tell you who wrote it." I thought to myself, "Oh great, he probably thinks either Paul, or Apollos, or Barnabas wrote it, and then when I tell him I would be arguing for Luke, he would give me the standard old tired line why it is impossible that Luke wrote it." To my utter surprise, he said: "Luke wrote it." You could have knocked me over with a feather! Professor Longacre had noticed, throughout his long career as a linguist, some similarities between Hebrews and the Lukan writings, leading him to suspect that Luke may have played a role in authorship. When I responded that was my own theory I would be arguing in the dissertation, he was surprised and pleased. Four years later, I successfully defended my dissertation with Dr. Longacre as my major supervisor and J. Harold Greenlee (renowned New Testament textual critic and secretary to the committee that had produced the UBS Greek New Testament) serving as one of the outside readers who approved it.

Over the next twenty plus years of additional research and writing, through two pastorates and two professorships, that dissertation gradually morphed into this book. Additionally, my work with Hebrews also led to the opportunity, kindly afforded me by Broadman & Holman, to write the New American Commentary on Hebrews (forthcoming later this year). My hope and prayer is that this work will reopen the question of the authorship of Hebrews in New Testament studies.

Zech 4:10 asks the question "Who despises the day of small things?" It was a small thing that day in Creative Writing class when I chose to write on the authorship of Hebrews. Little did I realize that the subject would become something of an "obsession," to quote my wife. I will be forever grateful to the professor that day, who also happened to be the president of the college, who nudged me in the direction of the possibility of Lukan authorship. His name: Paige Patterson, current president of Southwestern Baptist Theological Seminary.

I also had the privilege of attending a university with a fellow Christian gentleman whose spirit and demeanor always reminded me of our Savior. We shared a love for linguistics and both studied under Robert Longacre, he with a focus on the Old Testament and I with a focus on the New Testament. In more recent years, my friend paved the way for this work to be published by Broadman & Holman. Additionally, because of his clear thinking, his equally clear editing skills, and his judicious advice, this work is in far better shape than it ever would have been without him. For his keen eye and countless hours of labor, I am truly grateful. Thank you, Ray Clendenen.

David L. Allen

INTRODUCTION

For the past 35 years, the question of the authorship of Hebrews has intrigued me. The more I have studied the issue, the more I have become convinced of the viability of the theory of Lukan authorship.[1] Questions of authorship can seldom be established with certainty, and I do not make such an ambitious claim for this project. The discovery of an early manuscript of Hebrews with the words "Luke the Physician . . . to the church at . . ." would be helpful to the case. My purpose is to suggest there is sufficient evidence to warrant a new presentation of an old theory, namely that Luke, the companion of the apostle Paul and author of Luke–Acts, is the independent author of Hebrews.[2]

The suggestion that Luke had something to do with the writing of Hebrews finds early support among the church fathers. Eusebius quoted Origen as saying that some believed the epistle could have been the work of Luke. Throughout church history, a few scholars have suggested, though none has argued extensively for it, that Luke was (or could have been) the author of Hebrews. On this list are such prominent names as John Calvin and Franz Delitzsch. However, modern New Testament studies are content to leave the question unanswered; since 1976 there have been no new theories concerning the provenance of Hebrews combining authorship, recipients, and date. Hughes is simply summing up the attitude of most when he says that "as things are, the riddle of the authorship of Hebrews is incapable of solution."[3]

---

[1] This work is a substantial revision and expansion of my 1987 doctoral dissertation on Lukan authorship of Hebrews. I argued that Luke was Jewish, that he wrote his Gospel and Acts to a converted former Jewish high priest named Theophilus, who served AD 37–41, and that Luke wrote Hebrews to a group of the converted priests mentioned in Acts 6:7 who had fled Jerusalem after the Stephanic persecution (Acts 8:1) and who had relocated in Antioch of Syria.

[2] Arguments for the traditional view that Luke was a contemporary of Paul are well known and will not be rehearsed here. Likewise the arguments for a dating of Luke–Acts prior to AD 70 are well known and will be discussed only insofar as they impact the theory of Lukan authorship of Hebrews.

[3] P. E. Hughes, *A Commentary on the Epistle to the Hebrews* (Grand Rapids: Eerdmans, 1977), 19.

Before I offer a summary of the theory to be presented, the reader should be cautioned to keep in mind several things throughout the discussion. First, any theory that pretends to be able to answer all questions and to neatly categorize all data so that everything fits snugly into place is immediately suspect. As in the realm of scientific investigation, a new hypothesis need not answer all questions in order to be considered viable. A good theory is one that accounts for most of the available data but, like the periodic chart of the elements, does not fit everything neatly into the system, nor does it have to do so. One must simply live with the anomalies.

Second, because the text does not name the author, the historical testimony is inconclusive, and the internal evidence does not provide enough information to determine authorship, the most fruitful approach is to consider theories that provide other textual data with which to compare Hebrews in terms of lexical choice, style, and conceptual framework. This is an argument against considering either Barnabas or Apollos as the author, in that as far as we know, there are no extant texts written by these men to compare with Hebrews.[4] Of course this does not mean it could not have been written by one of them. (Matthew, Mark, James, and Jude each authored only one book in the New Testament.) It merely means there is no way of making any comparative study.

Third, in a study of this nature, one should be cautious about selectively presenting evidence of similarity between two writers or texts while minimizing their differences. Some who argue for Pauline authorship appear to have fallen into this trap. We must seek balance in treatment of the issue. We must avoid the Scylla of superficial treatment of the evidence and the Charybdis of dogmatism. As James Swetnam is reported to have remarked, "Fresh investigations are always to be welcomed if they are really fresh and really investigations."

Fourth, the unavoidable uncertainty that plagues the attempt to identify the author of Hebrews is magnified by the number of first-century details that elude our knowledge. Although the attempt to identify the author is worth the effort, one should not imagine that we tread on *terra firma* for most of this journey. While venturing beyond information found in the book itself concerning the author poses a

---

[4] The so-called *Epistle of Barnabas* is probably a second-century Alexandrian work wrongly attributed to Barnabas. Eusebius included it among the spurious books (*Ecclesiastical History*, 3.25).

danger of entering "into the uncharted realm of conjecture and idio-syncratic reconstruction,"[5] the voyage is well worth the taking, with proper precautions. After all, history is replete with discoveries that result from such intrepidity.

Fifth, although it is possible that Hebrews was written by an unknown author in the first century, the most helpful place to begin our search should be with the New Testament authors themselves, and then major figures in first-century Christianity who are mentioned in the New Testament (such as Apollos and Barnabas). This was the approach of the church fathers. One should first examine the possibility that the author is among the known New Testament authors. When this is done, two candidates emerge as front-runners: Paul and Luke. As Michael Goulder humorously put it when he asserted that Luke made use of Mark and Matthew as sources (while rejecting Q and other unknown sources): "We certainly ought to consider the devil we know before opting for the devil we don't know."[6]

The following is an abstract of a holistic theory of Lukan authorship that will be argued in this study. By holistic I mean that I shall present a theory regarding the authorship and background, including recipients and date, for Luke–Acts and Hebrews. The author of Luke–Acts was Luke the physician, who traveled with the apostle Paul and who wrote the Gospel of Luke (c. AD 60–61), and Acts (c. AD 62–63). Acts was written in Rome during Paul's first Roman imprisonment. Luke's intended reader of his two-volume work was Theophilus, a former Jewish high priest who served in Jerusalem from AD 37–41 and was deposed by Herod Agrippa. The grounds for this deposition are not known. Herod may have wanted to ensure that the high priest was firmly committed to his new leadership, and perhaps Theophilus was too lenient on the Christians to suit Herod, or had become a Christian himself.

Luke was the independent author of Hebrews, which he wrote from Rome c. AD 67–69, probably after the death of Paul. The letter was written to former priests of the Jerusalem temple, the first group of whom had been converted to Christianity during the early years of the Jerusalem church before the Stephanic persecution (Acts 6:7).

---

[5] I. Salevao, *Legitimation in the Letter to the Hebrews: The Construction and Maintenance of a Symbolic Universe*, JSNTSup 219 (London: Sheffield Academic Press, 2002), 104.

[6] M. Goulder, *Luke: A New Paradigm*, JSNTSup 20 (Sheffield, England: Sheffield Academic Press, 1989), 88.

These former priests constituted a segment of the church in Syrian Antioch, where they had fled as a result of this persecution. Once relocated in Antioch, they lived in relative safety and became part of the Antiochene church. Luke was probably a member of this church or, at the very least (since both Scripture and tradition link Luke with Antioch) probably had contact with these former priests on numerous occasions.

Chapter 1 surveys the history of the question of authorship with a focus on the history of the theory of Lukan authorship. Chapter 2 evaluates the evidence for Barnabas, Apollos, and Paul as authorial candidates. Chapter 3 considers the linguistic argument and evaluates the similarities between Luke–Acts and Hebrews, including lexical, stylistic, and textlinguistic similarities. Chapter 4 compares the purposes of Luke–Acts and Hebrews. Chapter 5 surveys the theological viewpoints of Luke–Acts and Hebrews. Here, the conceptual theological framework that undergirds the three works will be evidenced. Chapter 6 adduces evidence for the Jewish background and milieu of Luke–Acts. I will suggest that Luke was Jewish and, even if not, capable of writing a work such as Hebrews. Chapter 7 provides a historical reconstruction of the circumstances surrounding the writing of Hebrews. Here, I will synthesize matters of authorship, recipients, location of recipients, date, and other relevant background material into a holistic framework.

These chapters carry varying degrees of evidential weight. To borrow an analogy from architecture, chaps. 3–5 comprise the "load-bearing walls" of the structure (argument). These chapters in the aggregate produce the most salient evidence of vocabulary and stylistic comparisons, theme/purpose comparisons, and theological comparisons, which serve to identify Luke as the author of Hebrews. The two chapters that propose Luke's Jewishness and offer a plausible historical reconstruction of background and provenance are not as crucial for the overall theory. Luke may have been the author but may not have been Jewish, may not have written from Rome, may not have written to former priests living in Antioch, and may not have written prior to AD 70, as I have suggested. I trust the reader will judge the case on the merits of the linguistic, textlinguistic, and theological evidence, and not on some of my conjectures in other areas.

To employ another analogy to make an important point about this work, what I am attempting to do, with a few exceptions, is aerial photography as opposed to crop-dusting. In this age of specialization, there is still a need and a place for the bird's-eye view of things lest we lose the ability to see the forest for the trees. This work is an effort to get the big picture. In many places the evidence has been presented in broad sweeps, simply because covering every "field" minutely would require time, space, and expertise that I do not possess. Luke–Acts comprises 28 percent of the entire New Testament, Hebrews another 4 percent; hence, these three books together comprise almost 33 percent of the New Testament. Whole monographs have been written on individual aspects of Lukan theology as well as the theology of Hebrews, but are treated in this text in only a few pages or paragraphs. The past forty years have witnessed an endless stream of books, commentaries, articles, and monographs in studies of Luke as well as Hebrews. The burgeoning pile of literature is so enormous that one would have to do nothing but read just to keep abreast of it. To go into detailed comparison in each major area of the chapter on theology alone, much less other chapters, would be a Herculean task. We hope enough is presented to show that the similarities between Luke–Acts and Hebrews are significantly greater than previously noted, and that the Lukan authorship of Hebrews is a viable, even preferable, theory.

On occasion, however, we will abandon our aerial mapping of the lay of the land and swoop down to a particular field for some row-by-row crop-dusting. This will occur, for example, in chap. 2 when we engage William Leonard's arguments for Pauline authorship, in chap. 3 when we look at certain linguistic evidences, and so on throughout each chapter.

This leads to a third and final analogy: the courtroom. This work is an attempt to prosecute the case for Lukan authorship by presenting a preponderance of evidence, the cumulative effect of which becomes difficult to deny. When enough physical evidence from the "crime scene" is collected and evaluated; when the field of "suspects" is narrowed to include two or three individuals; when the historical, textual, and other witnesses have been interrogated, the crucial question becomes, "Which suspect is most implicated by the evidence?"

When all the clues are assembled and appropriate deducing is done, a compelling case can be made for Luke.

The importance and uniqueness of the theory presented here lie in the fact that no one has argued for independent Lukan authorship by collating the evidence particularly in the area of linguistics and presenting it in a systematic fashion as I have attempted. Previous comparisons of the vocabulary of Luke–Acts with Hebrews have often miscounted words unique to the three works. In addition, I have charted a number of stylistic data unique to Luke–Acts and Hebrews, which have not previously been presented. Second, no one has sought to argue for the Jewishness of Luke as further evidence of his authorship of Hebrews. Third, no one has synthesized the evidence into the particular theory of authorship and background that I seek to present through historical reconstruction in chap. 7.[7]

As Hughes remarks with regard to the authorship of Hebrews, "Failing the discovery of fresh and positive evidence . . . we must be content with our ignorance. To say this is not to imply that the offering of conjectures is out of place . . . ."[8] It is not only the synthesis of evidence for Lukan authorship that can be gleaned from others, but also the "fresh and positive evidence" which I am presenting here that merits renewed consideration for the theory of Lukan authorship.

In my estimation, the primary reason Luke has not been considered seriously is the presumption he was a Gentile, while the author of Hebrews was apparently a Jew. For centuries, the paradigm in New Testament studies that Luke was a Gentile has been axiomatic, as can be seen by any cursory reading of commentaries on Luke–Acts.[9] However, within Lukan studies today, there is no such consensus regarding Luke's background.[10] As will be demonstrated, there is much

---

[7] The closest theory to my own of which I am aware was suggested by J. V. Brown in a little-known article in 1923, but he opted for collaborate authorship by Luke and Paul ("The Authorship and Circumstances of 'Hebrews'–Again!" *BSac* 80 [1923]: 505–38). Brown was the first to suggest that the recipients were former Jewish priests, not Bornhäuser (as usually cited by scholars). Others who have argued for former Jewish priests as the recipients include K. Bornhäuser, *Empfänger und Verfasser des Briefes an die Hebräer*, BFCT 35/3 (Gütersloh, Germany: Bertelsmann, 1932); C. Spicq, *L'Épître aux Hébreux*, 2 vols. EBib (Paris: Gabalda, 1952–53); and C. Sandegren, "The Addressees of the Epistle to the Hebrews," *EvQ* 27 (1955): 221–24.

[8] P. E. Hughes, *Hebrews*, 19.

[9] After noting that most commentators still posit a Gentile background for Luke, Bock comments: "In sum, it seems very likely that Luke was a Gentile, though it is unclear whether his cultural background was Semitic." D. L. Bock, *Luke 1:1–9:50*, BECNT (Grand Rapids: Baker, 1994), 6–7. The Gentile background paradigm continues to dominate.

[10] In his work on the theology of Acts, J. Jervell categorically states regarding Luke, "He was

evidence to suggest Luke was a Hellenistic Jew whose writings exhibit both Jewish and Greek characteristics.

Sometimes interpretative communities become locked into viewing the world from a particular grid, so new ways of looking at things often are dismissed or simply do not come to mind. How true is the axiom that a way of seeing is also a way of not seeing. Many in New Testament studies today see the Lukan situation through the twin lenses of Gentile background and post-Pauline time frame. This latter focus has always troubled me in that the straightforward testimony of the Scriptures and early church history clearly locates Luke within the Pauline circle. The internal and external evidence for such a perspective is quite strong.

The practice of picking up the stick from the other end often results in new solutions to old problems, i.e., the construction of a new paradigm, to put it in Kuhn's terms.[11] My theory on the authorship of Hebrews is the result of such an approach. If Luke were Jewish, then authoring Hebrews becomes both possible and plausible and is supported by other corroborating factors. In addition, with regard to the date of Luke–Acts, I am picking up the stick from the pre-AD 70 end. This well-worn tradition was for a time seldom advanced, but in more recent days is experiencing a revival among certain scholars.

I hope to make several contributions with this study. First, the issue of the authorship of Hebrews needs to be reopened. A trickle of articles and one colloquium on this subject in the last few years may be an indication that this issue may be reexamined. With the advent of more sophisticated language tools and the computer, we are able to compare the vocabulary and style of other New Testament books with Hebrews in a much more detailed and accurate way.

Second, approaching the question of Lukan authorship of Hebrews and the background of Luke from a somewhat different perspective (by offering a holistic theory undergirded by linguistic, theological, literary, and historical evidence) will, I hope, provide a viable explanatory paradigm.[12] Unlike a single hypothesis, a paradigm is more

---

a Jewish Christian." J. Jervell, *The Theology of the Acts of the Apostles* (Cambridge: University Press, 1996), 5.

[11] Thomas Kuhn, *The Structure of Scientific Revolutions*, 2nd revised ed. (Chicago: University of Chicago Press, 1970).

[12] William Lane does something similar to this on a smaller scale in that he interprets Hebrews from the paradigm of a house church setting located in Rome. *Hebrews 1–8*, WBC 47A (Dallas: Word, 1991), lx–lxii.

like a cluster or complex of hypotheses. I am suggesting more than Lukan authorship of Hebrews, although that is indeed the primary argument. I am approaching the entire subject from a paradigm composed of several hypotheses: Luke wrote Luke–Acts; he was a traveling companion of Paul; he wrote Luke–Acts prior to AD 70; his ethnic background is Jewish; the recipient of Luke–Acts was Theophilus, a former Jewish high priest who served in Jerusalem from AD 37–41 and was deposed by Herod Agrippa; and the recipients of Hebrews were former Jewish priests who converted to Christianity and fled to Syrian Antioch during the persecution following Stephen's martyrdom. Virtually all of these hypotheses, with the exception of the first, could be proven wrong and yet Luke still be the author of Hebrews. The merits of the case for Lukan authorship should be judged primarily on the more tangible linguistic and theological evidence presented in chaps. 3–5.

Third, if there is merit to this theory, then exegetical/interpretative insights may be gained that will deepen our understanding of Hebrews. If the author were one of the New Testament writers, then from a hermeneutical perspective Hebrews could be interpreted in the light of his other writing(s), and perhaps new light could be shed on certain exegetical questions. For example, the translation of *machairan* as "sword" in Heb 4:12 might be better translated as "scalpel," a secondary but nonetheless legitimate meaning of the Greek word. Both the context and the suggestion of Lukan authorship would make this interpretation and translation of the word much more likely than "sword." If the recipients were indeed Jewish priests, then perhaps the word refers to the double-edged knife used by the priests to prepare sacrifices. Such a meaning is within the semantic realm of possibility and has much within its context to commend it even if the recipients were not former priests.

A fourth contribution is theological. Again, if the author is a New Testament writer, this fact would allow us to interpret Hebrews against the backdrop of his other writing(s). Conversely, Hebrews might furnish a helpful perspective that would allow us to clarify a certain theological motif in a given author's work. For example, Lukan studies since Conzelmann have generally held that Luke attributes no direct soteriological significance to the suffering and death of Jesus on the cross. Recently, a number of Lukan scholars have broken with this interpretation. If Hebrews were the work of Luke, then clearly Conzelmann's thesis would not only need the recent modification it has undergone, but would have to be rejected.

Fifth, this work furnishes additional data to the growing body of evidence that Luke's ethnic background was Jewish. Chapters 5 and 6 collate this evidence, which has been difficult to find elsewhere in a single work. Those interested in this aspect of Lukan studies will find food for thought.

Sixth, chap. 1 is the only place I know where one can trace the history of the theory of Lukan authorship for Hebrews from Origen to the present day. I trust this material will be helpful to all interested in the subject and will provide at least some background to the discussion over the past two thousand years of Christian history.

If the paradigm suggested here elicits new insights and leads to a new understanding of the problem of the authorship of Hebrews, or a new or at least broader understanding of Luke's writings, then this work will have fulfilled its purpose. To this end, perhaps New Testament studies will benefit from this modest contribution.

Chapter 1

HISTORICAL SURVEY OF THE AUTHORSHIP QUESTION: DEVELOPMENT OF THE LUKAN THEORY

The question of the authorship of Hebrews has been the source of much speculation throughout church history.[1] Most recent commentaries on Hebrews do not spend a great deal of time discussing matters of authorship and recipients. This is understandable in light of the multitude of theories available. The prescript "to the Hebrews" was a second-century scribal addition that was most likely deduced from the letter's content. In and of itself, the title offers no help in identifying the recipients of the letter.[2] Unlike the Pauline Epistles, there is no formal salutation naming author or readers. However, the conclusion of Hebrews is reminiscent of Paul's style and has led many to argue for Pauline authorship. Some have suggested the author deliberately omitted the introduction, but this is doubtful. Those who suggest Paul omitted any reference to his name because he was the apostle to the Gentiles (and was writing a letter to Jewish Christians) overlook that the letter itself makes it clear that the readers knew the author's identity.[3] Furthermore, if one wanted to pass the letter off as Pauline for canonical purposes, an alteration of the introduction by adding the

---

[1] For the state of research on Hebrews as a whole, especially including matters of background and provenance, H. Feld's extensive surveys of Hebrews up to 1985 are unparalleled (*Der Hebräerbrief*, Erträge der Forschung [Darmstadt: Wissenschaftliche Buchgesellschaft, 1985], and "Der Hebräerbrief: Literarische Form, religionsgeschichtlicher Hintergrund, theologische Fragen," ANRW 2.25.4 [1987]: 3522–601). C. Spicq's two-volume commentary in French is still valuable for covering the field through the early 1950s. The best surveys in English include the introductory material in W. L. Lane, *Hebrews 1–8*, WBC 47a (Dallas: Word, 1991), xlvii–clvii; P. Ellingworth, *The Epistle to the Hebrews*, NIGTC (Grand Rapids: Eerdmans, 1993), 3–80; and C. R. Koester, *Hebrews*, AB 36 (New York: Doubleday, 2001), 19–131, with Koester covering material through the end of the twentieth century.

[2] See the discussion on the title in relationship to the epistle's canonicity in B. Childs, *The New Testament as Canon: An Introduction* (Philadelphia: Fortress, 1985), 413–15. F. S. Marsh, "Hebrews, Epistle to the," *Dictionary of the Apostolic Church*, ed. J. Hastings (New York: Charles Scribner's Sons, 1919), 1:539, offered the interesting conjecture: "It is easy to imagine how the Epistle became connected with St. Paul's name. When once an anonymous letter bearing the simple title προς Εβραιους was appended to a collection of acknowledged Pauline Epistles, the addition to the heading of the words του Παυλου would only be a matter of time."

[3] Against E. Gräßer who argued that the author wanted to remain anonymous because he was a second generation Christian as implied in Hebrews 2:3 (*An die Hebräer*, EKKNT 17/1 [Zürich: Benziger, 1990], 1:22).

name of Paul would seem more likely than a total excision. The current scholarly consensus is there never was a salutation or introduction. The beautifully balanced literary sentence with which Hebrews begins has all the earmarks of the original introduction to the work.

Equally unconvincing are the theories of pseudonymity posited by Overbeck, Wrede, Goodspeed, and more recently by Rothschild. Overbeck's elaborate scheme in viewing the conclusion of Hebrews as a part of the church's effort to ensure canonization of the letter by attributing it to Paul is totally unnecessary.[4] Wrede argued that the author added a postscript in Pauline style so that Hebrews would appear to be a Pauline prison letter.[5] Today these theories rarely resurface. Goodspeed suggested that Hebrews may have been originally pseudonymous rather than anonymous[6] and Gräßer argued that Hebrews was composed as an anonymous letter from the outset.[7] However, if the letter originally contained any ascription to Paul, Guthrie argued: "it is impossible to envisage any situation in which it would lose its ascription and still continue to be regarded with some favor. There are no parallels to this kind of thing among the pseudepigrapha."[8] Another minority view is that the postscript was not penned by the author, but was a later interpolation to provide additional (apostolic) authority for the text. Rothschild has more recently argued that the postscript (Heb 13:20–25 in her view) "not only exhibits literary reliance on Paul's undisputed corpus, but also, as an aspect of this reliance, *appropriates Paul's identity as the author of Hebrews's own*."[9] Rothschild argued that the author of Hebrews composed the postscript as a deliberate echo of Paul's style so that Hebrews would be seen as Pauline and "published as part of an existing *corpus Paulinum*."[10] Amazingly, Rothschild argued that such an effort "is not only consistent with the personality behind Hebrews, but is its necessary correlative and that Hebrews's reception history attests the overwhelming success of this

---

[4] F. Overbeck, *Zur Geschichte des Kanons: Zwei Abhandlungen* (Chemnitz: E. Schmeitzner, 1880; repr., Wissenschaft: Buchgesellschaft, 1965), 30–70.

[5] W. Wrede, *Die literarische Rätsel des Hebräerbriefs* (Göttingen: Vandenhoeck & Ruprecht, 1906), 3–5.

[6] E. J. Goodspeed, *An Introduction to the New Testament* (Chicago: University of Chicago Press, 1937), 257.

[7] Gräßer, *Hebräer 1–6*, 22.

[8] D. Guthrie, *New Testament Introduction*, 4th rev. ed. (Downers Grove: InterVarsity, 1990), 682.

[9] C. Rothschild, *Hebrews as Pseudepigraphon: The History and Significance of the Pauline Attribution of Hebrews*, WUNT 235, ed. J. Frey (Tübingen: Mohr Siebeck, 2009), 4.

[10] Ibid.

deception up until the Reformation."[11] Pseudonymity for Hebrews falters on many linguistic, stylistic, and conceptual links between Hebrews 13 and the rest of the letter and serves to illustrate the authenticity of the letter's conclusion.[12]

The theory of a Greek translation of Hebrews from a Hebrew or Aramaic original (as suggested by Clement of Alexandria) cannot be sustained in light of the evidence. The many examples of Greek *paranomasia* and other stylistic devices make it clear that Hebrews is not a translation of a Hebrew original. The author's exclusive use of the LXX for quotations also argues against the translation theory, especially when it is recognized, for example, that the Greek word *hupotassō* used in Heb 2:8 does not occur in the Hebrew original of the Psalm quotation (yet the author's argument is built upon this Greek word itself).

The inconclusive nature of the internal and external evidence for authorship coupled with the historical obscurity surrounding its provenance has provided scholars with a fertile field for further theorizing. Many have conjectured, some have conjured, but very few have been convinced in the search for the author of Hebrews.

A succinct presentation of the major theories relative to the authorship of Hebrews is necessary before the case for Lukan authorship can be championed. I have presented in a chart below the major theories of authorship in chronological order. It is not my intention to discuss thoroughly each theory, as one can find this information elsewhere.[13] The name of the scholar who suggested a theory will appear in the left column, followed by the "Proposed Author" in the right column. This will show the wide-ranging theories of authorship.

---

[11] Ibid., 5.

[12] This has been demonstrated by F. Filson (*'Yesterday.' A Study of Hebrews in the Light of Chapter 13*, SBT 4, ed. C. F. B. Moule, P. Ackroyd, F. V. Filson, and G. E. Wright [London: SCM, 1967], and Attridge, *Hebrews*, 384–410.

[13] The reader should consult the footnotes and bibliography for works by authors listed in this chart. Helpful surveys and summaries of the various theories can be found in the following: F. F. Bruce, "Recent Contributions to the Understanding of Hebrews" *ExpTim* 80 (1969): 260–64; and his *Hebrews*, rev. ed., NICNT (Grand Rapids: Eerdmans, 1990), 14–20; G. W. Buchanan, "The Present State of Scholarship on Hebrews," in *Judaism, Christianity and Other Greco-Roman Cults*, ed. M. Smith and J. Neusner, vol. 1 (Leiden: Brill, 1975), 299–330; J. C. McCullough, "Some Recent Developments in Research in the Epistle to the Hebrews," *IBS* 2 (1980–81): 141–65; J. C. McCullough, "Hebrews in Recent Scholarship," *IBS* 16 no. 2 (1994): 66–86; 108–20); D. Guthrie, *New Testament Introduction*, rev. ed. (Downers Grove: InterVarsity, 1990), 668–82; H. Weiss, *Der Brief an die Hebräer*, KEK 13 (Göttingen: Vandenhoeck & Ruprecht, 1991), 61–66; Ellingworth, *Hebrews*, 3–21; and Koester, *Hebrews*, 42–54, whose summary of authorship, recipients, destination, and date would be especially helpful to pastors.

Table 1: Theories on Authorship of Hebrews

Scholar	Proposed Author
Pantaenus	Paul (but noted no salutation as common with Paul)
Clement of Alexandria	Paul (translated by Luke)
Origen[a]	Unknown (but some said that Clement of Rome wrote it and others that Luke did)
Tertullian[b]	Barnabas
Augustine	Paul (tentatively)
Jerome	Paul (tentatively)
Aquinas	Paul (Hebrew original translated by Luke)
Luther[c]	Apollos
Calvin[d]	Luke (or Clement of Rome)
Grotius	Luke (independently)
Boehme[e]	Silas
Welch	Peter
A. Harnack	Priscilla and Aquila
J. Chapman	Aristion
William Ramsay	Philip
W. Leonard[f]	Paul
A. M. Dubarle	Jude
C. P. Anderson	Epaphras
L. Herrmann	John the Apostle
Legg	Timothy
Ruth Hoppin[g]	Priscilla
J. M. Ford	Mary (Mother of Jesus), assisted by Luke and John

[a] Quoted by Eusebius. Origen pointed out that the thoughts were Pauline but the style was un-Pauline.
[b] Tertullian may have confused Hebrews with the spurious *Epistle of Barnabas*. Riggenbach, Windisch and W. Manson argued for Barnabas in the twentieth century.
[c] Luther was the first to suggest Apollos as the author. He has been followed by many since. See T. W. Manson, W. F. Howard, C. Spicq, F. Lo Bue, H. W. Montefiore, and G. Guthrie.
[d] Calvin noted the stylistic similarities of Luke's writings and Hebrews, but he did not argue the case in depth. He seems to posit Lukan authorship independent of Pauline influence, however.
[e] Boehme (in the introduction to his commentary on Hebrews in 1825) and Mynster (in the *Studien und Kritiken*, 2, 344). Boehme builds on the resemblance of Hebrews with 1 Peter and theorizes that Silas wrote both works. Mynster proposed a Galatian audience and speculated that Hebrews was written by Silas in company with Paul and sent to that region. (See Moses Stuart, *Hebrews*, 259). T. Hewitt later defended Silas in his 1960 commentary on Hebrews.
[f] Leonard's work constitutes the best 20th century presentation of the Pauline authorship theory.
[g] Hoppin, following Harnack, provides the most elaborate and best argument available for Priscilla as the author. See Zahn's critique (*Introduction*, 2:365–66); also D. A. DeSilva, *Perseverance in Gratitude: A Socio-Rhetorical Commentary on the Epistle to the Hebrews* (Grand Rapids: Eerdmans, 2000), 25.

Three observations emerge from this. First, from the church fathers until the present, at least sixteen possible authors have been proposed. Sometimes joint authorship has been suggested, as, for example, Priscilla and Aquila. Second, the options offered by the patristics, medieval, and Reformation scholars almost always involved well known apostles or individuals who were associated with the apostles in some close fashion. For example, Paul could have been proposed as the author because his apostolic authority was necessary to make Hebrews a part of the canon.[14] Canonicity may have been important in the theories of authorship among the church fathers, but it is still significant that suggestions for possible authorship consistently included members of the apostolic group. Third, though not specified in the chart above, matters of provenance, recipients, and date are likewise as diverse as the proposals of authorship. This is of course due to the fact that nowhere does the book of Hebrews locate itself or specify its recipients.

The historical testimony[15] regarding the authorship of Hebrews begins in the Western Church with Clement of Rome's clear use of the letter in his letter to the Corinthians. In fact, Clement quotes or alludes to Hebrews more frequently than to any other canonical book. If Clement's letter to the Corinthians can be successfully dated near the end of the first century (as has been the traditional view), then the historical testimony concerning the authorship of Hebrews pre-dates the second century.[16] Too much should not be made of Clement's proposal since chronological and stylistic considerations would mitigate against it.[17] Clement's silence regarding authorship may indicate

---

[14] On the question of the canonicity of Hebrews, particularly as it relates to authorship, see J. Thayer, "Authorship and Canonicity of the Epistle to the Hebrews," *BSac* 24 (1867): 681–722; and C. Spicq, *L'Épître aux Hébreux* (Paris: Librairie Lecoffre, 1952–53), 1:169–96; C. P. Anderson ,"The Epistle to the Hebrews and the Pauline Letter Collection," *HTR* 59 (1966): 429–38; C. P. Anderson, "Hebrews among the Letters of Paul," *SR* 5 (1975–76): 258–66; W. H. P. Hatch, "The Position of Hebrews in the Canon of the New Testament," *HTR* 29 (1936): 133–51, who has one of the best discussions on the position of Hebrews in the New Testament canon. N. Lardner, *The Works of Nathaniel Lardner* (London: William Bell, 1838), 4:88–91, cites Greek and Latin testimonies from AD 107 to AD 1070, and is the most comprehensive study of the issue.

[15] Helpful surveys include A. Lincoln, *Hebrews: A Guide* (Edinburgh: T&T Clark, 2006), 2–8; P. E. Hughes, *A Commentary on the Epistle to the Hebrews* (Grand Rapids: Eerdmans, 1977), 19–30; and Koester, *Hebrews*, 19–63, who in addition to questions of authorship, provided the most comprehensive survey of the history of interpretation of the letter.

[16] Clement's letter to the Corinthians has been dated c. AD 70 as well, which if true would indicate a pre-70 AD date for Hebrews.

[17] J. Conder, *A Literary History of the New Testament* (London: Seeley, Burnside & Seeley,

that he did not consider Paul to be the author. Furthermore, since Clement's citation of Hebrews proves the letter was known in Rome by the end of the first century, how can one explain the silence of the Roman church if Clement indeed were or could have been considered the author? These are valid questions, but one should not make too much of an argument from silence.

Hebrews is not cited by any of the earlier Latin fathers except Tertullian, who ascribed authorship to Barnabas. Eusebius noted that Irenaeus quoted Hebrews in a work that is not extant; Eusebius also indicated that Irenaeus did not accept Pauline authorship.[18] Caius, according to Eusebius, affirmed thirteen Pauline Epistles, and thus did not consider Hebrews to be Paul's.[19] Hippolytus likewise denied Pauline authorship. The general testimony of the Western Church through the third century is that Hebrews was not from the pen of Paul.[20]

Written historical testimony concerning the authorship of Hebrews actually begins with statements attributed to Pantaenus, head of the Alexandrian school. He assigned Hebrews to the apostle Paul, but observed that contrary to Paul's custom in other epistles, there is no salutation identifying him as the author. At the end of the second century, Eusebius cited Clement of Alexandria (student of Pantaenus), who said that Paul wrote Hebrews originally in Hebrew and that Luke translated it into Greek for a Hellenistic Jewish audience. Clement stated that this fact (Luke's translation) accounted for the stylistic similarities between Hebrews and Luke-Acts.

> The epistle to the Hebrews is the work of Paul, and that it was written to the Hebrews in the Hebrew language; but that Luke translated it carefully and published it for the Greeks, and hence the same style of expression is found in this epistle and in the Acts. But he says that the words, Paul the Apostle, were probably not prefixed, because, in sending it to the Hebrews, who were prejudiced and suspicious of him, he wisely did not wish to repel them at the very beginning by giving his name.[21]

1845), 443, argued that the difference between the canonical epistles and the earliest church fathers' writings warrants the conclusion that Hebrews could not have been written by Clement, Barnabas (assuming Barnabas is the author of the *Epistle of Barnabas*), or Polycarp.

[18] Eusebius, *Ecclesiastical History* 5.26.

[19] Ibid. 6.26.

[20] Ibid. 6.20.

[21] Clement of Alexandria, quoted by Eusebius, from Clement's *Hypotyposes*, in *Ecclesiastical History* 6.14.

By the middle of the third century, Origen detected Pauline influence on the thoughts of the letter, but he attributed the style and actual writing to someone else.

> That the verbal style of the epistle entitled 'To the Hebrews', is not rude like the language of the apostle, who acknowledged himself rude in speech, that is, in expression; but that its diction is purer Greek, any one who has the power to discern differences of phraseology will acknowledge. Moreover, that the thoughts of the epistle are admirable, and not inferior to the acknowledged apostolic writings, any one who carefully examines the apostolic text will admit . . . If I gave my opinion, I should say that the thoughts are those of the apostle, but the diction and phraseology are those of someone who remembered the apostolic teachings, and wrote them down at his leisure what had been said by his teacher. Therefore, if any church holds that this epistle is by Paul, let it be commended for this . . . . But who wrote the epistle, in truth, God knows. The statement of some who have gone before us is that Clement, bishop of the Romans, wrote the epistle, and of others that Luke, the author of the Gospel and the Acts, wrote it.[22]

From Origen's statement the following may be surmised. First, he judged the style to be unlike Paul, and he considered this to be incontrovertible. Second, he attributed the "thoughts" to Paul, but not the actual composition. Origen posited a Pauline disciple, who jotted down Paul's ideas and then elaborated on them; in this way Hebrews was linked to Paul. Third, Origen offered no theory of authorship. Fourth, he cited tradition that Clement of Rome or Luke wrote it.

Several matters concerning Origen's statement need to be explored further. There are three possible meanings of the articular participle translated "wrote" in Origen's statement. The first option refers to someone who wrote as Paul's amanuensis. The second option is "who wrote down what Paul said and then edited it for final production." The third option is "who wrote as the independent author." Origen clearly denied that the actual composition of the letter was Paul's. In attributing the thoughts to Paul, Origen disavowed any form of translation or dictation since he claimed that the author wrote "at his leisure" what he "remembered" Paul saying. How much time elapsed between the original hearing of Paul's words and writing them down is anyone's guess. Furthermore, he did not specify that a disciple developed Paul's ideas with his knowledge or at his direction. Origen's

---

[22] Origin, as quoted by Eusebius, *Ecclesiastical History* 6.25. The oldest extant text of Hebrews is found in $\mathfrak{P}^{46}$ (c. AD 200) where it occurs immediately following Romans (most likely due to its length) in a fourteen-letter Pauline collection.

comments, however, have at times been interpreted in this way. Bleek interpreted Origen's remarks to mean "in its matter it is not inferior to the acknowledged apostolical writings, being in his opinion indebted for its argument to Paul, but for its style and finish to some disciple who jotted down his master's ideas, and then drew them out still further, and wove them together into a sort of commentary."[23]

Origen's theory actually raises more problems than it solves. For example, how are we to construe the relation of Paul to his so-called disciple who wrote down Paul's thoughts? The author of Hebrews was not a translator, nor did he receive the letter by dictation (at least in the sense that Paul used an amanuensis in his other letters). If Luke or Clement collected Paul's thoughts and recorded them in their own hand, would they not then be considered the actual author of the letter? The fact that Paul used an amanuensis for most if not all of his letters, coupled with the fact that using such a person did not appreciably affect his style (with the exception of the Pastorals if they are considered Pauline)[24] argues against Origen's hypothesis as well as those who advance similar hypotheses.

Those like J. Hug, S. Davidson, and more recently David Black,[25] who argued that Origen's statement "as to who wrote the epistle . . . " meant who wrote it down for Paul (i.e., who functioned as his amanuensis or translator) find themselves swimming upstream against the context and usage of the Greek *ho grapsas*. Both Hug and Black render the participle in Greek as "who wrote down" in an effort to maintain Pauline authorship and they assert the context justifies such a translation. In fact, the opposite is the case. In the sentence immediately following, Origen refers to "Luke, who wrote [*ho grapsas*] the Gospel," clearly meaning authorship and not "who wrote down" the gospel as an amanuensis or translator. The critique of this interpretation by Bleek and Thayer is, in my view, difficult if not impossible to overcome.[26] Mitchell noted many instances in Eusebius's *Ecclesiastical*

---

[23] J. F. Bleek, *Introduction to the New Testament*, 2nd ed., trans. W. Urwick (Edinburgh: T&T Clark, 1869), 2:105.

[24] I consider all 13 letters to be genuinely Pauline.

[25] See J. L. Hug, *Introduction to the New Testament*, trans. from the 3rd German edition by D. Fosdick (Andover: Gould & Newman, 1836), 590; S. Davidson also supports this view in *An Introduction to the Study of the New Testament*, 2nd rev. ed. (London: Longmans, Green, & Co., 1882), 1:190. See also D. A. Black, "On the Pauline Authorship of Hebrews (Part 2): The External Evidence Reconsidered," *Faith and Mission* 16 (1999): 80–81.

[26] See Bleek, *Introduction*, 2:106; J. H. Thayer, "Authorship and Canonicity of the Epistle to the Hebrews," *BSac* 24 (1867): 707–8. B. Weiss stated emphatically "Origen himself has no

History where the Greek verb "to write" "refers both to authorship and to actual penning" and thus concluded "Black's distinction between author and amanuensis cannot be maintained in light of this evidence."[27]

Origen was the first to suggest the theory that the thoughts were from Paul, but the composition was from someone else. In this way he sought to reconcile the two disparate views which came down to him, namely, some who said Paul was the author and others that a different Christian teacher wrote it. Thus, when Origen says that the tradition handed down to him included the possibility of Lukan authorship, it is clear that he means independent Lukan authorship and not that Luke was a translator, amanuensis, or collector of Paul's thoughts, since Origin himself was the first to suggest such a theory. Hug, Black, and others who attempt to translate *ho grapsas* as "who wrote down" fail to see this point.[28] When Origen says "but who wrote it, only God knows," he meant to indicate uncertainty as to which of Paul's disciples developed his ideas, and was thus the actual author.

W. H. Goold, the editor of John Owen's seven-volume commentary on Hebrews, raised serious objections to Origen's view. First, it leaves undefined the relation between Paul and his assistant. Neither an amanuensis, a translator, nor an editor can account for the differences which led to the suggestion of this theory. Second, it proves too much. If Luke did all that is claimed according to this theory, he is entitled to be called the author. This point is not adequately recognized or dealt with by those who want to maintain Pauline authorship, but give Luke credit for its "composition." Third, the separation of thought from language, which this view proposes, creates a greater difficulty than the theory proposed to deal with it in the first place. Fourth, it is not more difficult to suppose that Paul polished his own sentences in writing to the Hebrew Christians than it is to suppose that someone else was employed to do it.[29] These points by Goold are

---

doubt whatever that the epistle cannot possibly have proceeded from Paul on account of its language (*A Manual of Introduction to the New Testament,* trans. A. J. K. Davidson [New York: Funk & Wagnalls, 1889], 2).

[27] A. C. Mitchell, *Hebrews,* SP 13 (Collegeville, MN: Liturgical, 2007), 3–4.

[28] P. Maier's translation of Eusebius supports the traditional understanding of ὁ γραψας (*Eusebius: The Church History, A New Translation with Commentary* [Grand Rapids: Kregel, 1999], 227).

[29] J. Owen, *An Exposition of the Epistle to the Hebrews,* ed. W. H. Goold (Edinburgh: Ritchie, 1812), 1:95.

well taken. Given the fact that Luke has clearly presented, in edited form, many of Paul's sermons in Acts, on what grounds can we deny at least the possibility that Luke may have taken an even more significant role in the composition of Hebrews?

The Alexandrian tradition regarding authorship continued to grow so that by the fourth century Paul was regarded as the author (either directly or indirectly) of the letter. However, from the very beginning of this tradition, Hebrews was usually attributed to Paul in a tentative, indirect fashion.[30]

In the ancient Syrian church, Ephraem (c. AD 378) appears to indicate that Rom 2:16, Eph 5:15, and Heb 10:31 were all written by Paul. In Western Syria the Antiochian Synod (c. AD 264) issued a letter to Paul of Samosata which quoted statements by Paul in his Corinthian letters and Heb 11:26, implying that all were written by the same apostle. In the Peshitta, Hebrews appears at the end of the Pauline Epistles before the General Epistles. Delitzsch argued it was put there because of its anonymity, not because it was thought to proceed from someone other than Paul.[31] By the middle of the fourth century, Pauline authorship was well attested in the Eastern Church, yet immediate Pauline composition was primarily asserted in the late third and fourth centuries.

Turning to the Western Church, no tradition regarding Pauline authorship apparently existed. Rather, in the late second and early third centuries, Tertullian believed the letter had been written by Barnabas.[32] In the Roman Church, there was likewise no tradition of Pauline authorship until very late. Clement of Rome made the first reference to the epistle in his letters to the Corinthians, but he did not posit Pauline authorship. The Muratorian Canon (c. AD 170–210) referred to the thirteen epistles of Paul but did not list Hebrews, thus

---

[30] Davidson, *Introduction*, 1:216, noted: "If it be said that the difficulties of style, etc. increase the force of the external evidence in favor of Paul, since nothing but an authentic tradition could have survived these difficulties, we reply the difficulties changed the tradition by compelling those who followed it to resort to an indirect Pauline authorship. Instead of enhancing the strength of the external testimony by suggesting the thoughts are Paul's, the composition and language another, they actually weaken it."

[31] F. Delitzsch, "Über Verfasser und Leser des Hebräerbriefs mit besonderer Berucksichtigung der neuesten Untersuchungen Wieseler's und Thiersch's," in *Zeitschrift für die gesammte lutherische Theologie und Kirche* (Leipzig: Dorffling und Franke, 1849), 510.

[32] Tertullian, *On Modesty*, 20. B. Pixner, "*The Jerusalem Essenes, Barnabas and the Letter to the Hebrews*" in *Qumranica Mogilanensia*, ed. Z. J. Kapera (Krakow, Poland: Enigma Press, 1992), 6:167–78, is a recent champion of Barnabas.

indicating that the Roman church did not regard Paul as the author. The Shepherd of Hermas, Justin Martyr, Irenaeus, Gaius of Rome, and Hippolytus all make use of Hebrews, but none ascribe authorship to Paul. It was only toward the end of the fourth century that Pauline authorship began to be accepted in the Western Church. What brought this about we do not know. Davidson suggested four causes. First, the ecclesiastical dialogue which began to take place between the East and the West may have encouraged Pauline authorship in the West. Second, the prominence of Jerome and Augustine influenced the formation of the opinion. Third, the use of Hebrews in the Arian controversy for the orthodox position may have helped to establish its apostolicity. Fourth, the study of Origen's writings may have been persuasive. Clearly Hilary and Ambrose were familiar with them.[33]

In the fourth century, Eusebius informed us that there were fourteen well-known and undisputed Pauline Epistles (including Hebrews) but he also pointed out that some rejected Hebrews as canonical on the grounds that the Roman church disputed its Pauline authorship.[34] Athanasius likewise included Hebrews among the Pauline Letters, placing it after the letters addressed to churches but before letters addressed to individuals. Hebrews is found in this position in Sinaiticus, Alexandrinus, and Vaticanus, all of which appear in the fourth and fifth centuries AD. The Greek Church in the fourth century placed Hebrews tenth among the Pauline Epistles, whereas the Syrian and Western Church placed it fourteenth.[35]

Toward the close of the fourth century, Jerome tied together several strands of information which he had received. First, Hebrews was disputed as Pauline on stylistic grounds. Second, Tertullian considered Barnabas to be the author. Third, others had suggested Luke or Clement of Rome as the author, perhaps as the arranger of Paul's ideas, or even as translator of Paul's Hebrew original into the polished Greek of the letter. Fourth, Paul may have omitted his name since he

---

[33] Davidson, *Introduction*, 1:194. Weiss, *A Manual of Introduction*, 2:2, concurs.

[34] Eusebius, *Ecclesiastical History* 3.3.5; 6.20.3. For a complete presentation of the patristic evidence on authorship, see F. Bleek, *Der Brief an die Hebräer* (Berlin: Dümmler, 1828), 1:81–90.

[35] See D. Trobisch, *Paul's Letter Collection: Tracing the Origins* (Philadelphia: Fortress, 1994), 10–21; and Gamble, "The New Testament Canon: Recent Research and the Status Quaestionis," in *The Canon Debate: On the Origins and Formation of the Bible*, ed. L. McDonald and J. Sanders (Peabody, MA: Hendrickson, 2002), 282–86.

was held in low regard by the readers.[36] Jerome in the Latin Vulgate identified Hebrews as Pauline, as did Augustine, although only tentatively by both writers.[37] Hebrews was firmly embedded in the list of canonical books by the time of the Synods of Hippo (AD 393) and Carthage (AD 397 and 419), where it was located at the end of the 13 Pauline Epistles, a fact which confirms the uncertainty over Pauline authorship. The gradual reception of the Alexandrian tradition by the end of the fourth century may have led to this "silent transfer" of Hebrews from the tenth place in the Greek canon of Paul's epistles to the fourteenth position.

This tradition prevailed throughout the Middle Ages. For example, in the prologue to his commentary on Hebrews, Aquinas clearly accepted Pauline authorship along with the theory of a Hebrew original, which was then translated into Greek by Luke.[38] Pauline authorship was held during the medieval period; when this was questioned, however, Luke was usually suggested as the likely translator of Paul or even as the independent author.[39]

With the dawn of the Reformation came a return to the skepticism of the Patristic era concerning Pauline authorship. In the sixteenth century, Luther championed Apollos while Calvin preferred Luke or Clement of Rome. In the seventeenth century, Hugo Grotius was the first to put forth linguistic evidence for Lukan authorship of Hebrews. His evidence only consisted of similarities among ten words and phrases.[40] The seventeenth, eighteenth, and nineteenth centuries witnessed a tug-of-war over Pauline authorship, but the twentieth century (even after Leonard's 1939 masterpiece in favor of Paul) was increasingly skeptical about the Pauline theory and offered a flurry of theories regarding other possible authors. Oddly enough, the century dawned with the suggestion by Harnack[41] that Priscilla was the author. The last new theory to be proposed was in 1976 by J. Ford who

---

[36] Jerome, *Lives of Illustrious Men*, 5.

[37] Jerome, *Epist.* 53.8; 129.3; Augustine, *On Christian Doctrine*, 2.8; *Civ.* 16.22. See the evidence for this presented by Davidson, *Introduction*, 1:223–26.

[38] T. Aquinas, *Commentary on the Epistle to the Hebrews*, trans. C. Baer (South Bend, IN: St. Augustine's Press, 2006), 7. See also the Latin edition, *Super Epistolas Sancti Pauli Lectura: ad Hebraeos lectura*, 8th rev. ed., ed. P. Raphael Cai (Rome: Marietti, 1953), 2:356.

[39] So Spicq, *L'Épître aux Hébreux*, 1:197–219.

[40] H. Grotius, *Annotationes in Epistolam ad Hebraeos*, in *Opera Omnia Theologica* (Amstelodamum: Apud Heredes Joannis Blaev, 1732), 2:1010.

[41] A. Harnack, "Probabilia über die Addresse und den Verfasser des Hebräerbriefs," *ZNW* 1 (1900): 16–41.

argued that Mary the mother of Jesus was the author, assisted by Luke and John.[42] These are the only two women who have been proposed as potential authors.

From this brief survey of the historical testimony concerning authorship in general, we are now in a position to survey the history of scholarship concerning Lukan authorship in particular.[43] It has been fashionable for some time now to dismiss the possibility of the Lukan authorship of Hebrews by parroting previous commentators without so much as a second look at the historical or linguistic evidence.[44] This is true for both German and English commentators with rare exception. For example, note Iutisone Salevao's remark against Lukan authorship: "differences of style—outweigh the points of affinity between Hebrews and Luke-Acts." Yet not ten pages later he quoted approvingly F. F. Bruce who said that Hebrews is stylistically closer to Luke-Acts than any of the other New Testament writers.[45] Granted there are other factors beyond style to consider and Salevao has perhaps taken this into consideration.

The suggestion that Luke was in some way responsible for Hebrews in its present form (either as translator, amanuensis, or independent author), goes back to the time of the church fathers. Clement of Alexandria (c. AD 155–220), quoted by Eusebius, made the suggestion that Paul was the author, but that Luke translated Hebrews into Greek.[46] Origen (c. AD 185–254), quoted by Eusebius, said that the thoughts were Pauline, but the diction and composition was by someone who recorded from memory Paul's teaching.[47] Origen reported that some believed Clement of Rome had written it, while others assigned it to Luke. Origen's statements clearly imply more than just the possibility that Luke translated the text. Eusebius (c. AD 265–339) took a similar position as Clement of Alexandria, suggesting that Hebrews was written by

---

[42] J. M. Ford, "The Mother of Jesus and the Authorship of the Epistle to the Hebrews," *TBT* 82 (1976): 683–94. She actually suggested a tripartite authorship with Mary, John, and Luke. She had earlier suggested the author of Hebrews was a "Paulinist" who was responding to the activity of Apollos in Corinth (J. M. Ford, "The First Epistle to the Corinthians or the First Epistle to the Hebrews?" *CBQ* 28 [1966]: 402–16).

[43] A chronological survey of the history of research on this issue is helpful since one cannot find this information elsewhere in any commentary or work on New Testament introduction.

[44] O'Brien, XXX.

[45] I. Salevao, *Legitimation in the Letter to the Hebrews: The Construction and Maintenance of a Symbolic Universe*, in JSNTSup 219, ed. S. Porter (New York: Sheffield Academic Press, 2002), 98, 107.

[46] *Ecclesiastical History* 6.14.

[47] Ibid., 6.25.

Paul in Hebrew and translated by Clement of Rome or by Luke.[48] By the end of the fifth century, Hebrews was recognized as a part of the canon of Scripture and Pauline authorship was generally accepted, although the possibility of Lukan involvement was also an accepted position.

As noted above, throughout the Middle Ages, writers on the subject in general continued to believe that Paul was the author. If Hebrews was considered to be a translation, Luke was the preferred translator over Clement of Rome. This is illustrated by Aquinas's comments in his preface to Hebrews. He accepts Pauline authorship but suggests that Hebrews was translated by Luke.[49] Others during this period who believed the letter to have been written by Luke under Pauline superintendence include Luculentius (6th century), Primasius (6th century), and Haymo and Maurus (9th century).[50]

The time of the Reformation brought new challenges to the Pauline authorship theory. Calvin suggested Luke or Clement of Rome as the independent author of Hebrews.[51] Over a century later, Grotius argued for independent Lukan authorship.[52]

By the nineteenth century, some were beginning to look more carefully at the position of Grotius and his advocacy for Lukan authorship. Some took the position that Luke was the independent author with or without the influence of Paul; others suggested that Luke wrote at Paul's behest, with differing views on the amount of liberty granted Luke. In 1830, Köhler suggested that Luke had a hand in the writing of Hebrews,[53] while at the same time Stein noted in his commentary on Luke that the style of Hebrews was closer to Luke's two volumes than to any other New Testament writer.[54] Writing eight years later

---

[48] Ibid., 3.38.

[49] T. Aquinas, *Commentary on the Epistle to the Hebrews*, trans. C. Baer (South Bend, IN: St. Augustine's Press, 2006), 336.

[50] Cited by F. Delitzsch, *Hebrews Commentary on the Epistle to the Hebrews*, trans. T. L. Kingsbury (Edinburgh: T&T Clark, 1872; repr., Grand Rapids: Eerdmans, 1952), 1:24 and H. Alford, "Prolegomena and Hebrews," *Alford's Greek Testament: An Exegetical and Critical Commentary*, vol. 4, part 1, 5th ed. (Boston: Lee & Shepard, 1878; repr., Grand Rapids: Guardian, 1976), 53. See also the bibliographical data in Spicq, *L'Épître aux Hébreux*, 2:381.

[51] J. Calvin, *The Epistle of Paul the Apostle to the Hebrews and the First and Second Epistles of St. Peter*, ed. D. W. Torrance and T. F. Torrance, trans. W. B. Johnston (Grand Rapids: Eerdmans, 1963), 216.

[52] Grotius, *Annotationes in Epistolam ad Hebraeos*, 2:1010.

[53] J. F. Köhler, *Versuch über die Abfassungszeit: der epistolischen Schriften im Neuen Testament und der Apokalypse* (Leipzig: J. A. Barth, 1830), 206–9.

[54] K. Stein, *Kommentar zu dem Evangelium des Lucas: nebst einem Anhänge über den Brief an die Laodiceer* (Halle: Schwetschke & Sohn, 1830), 293–95.

in his commentary on Hebrews, Stein accepted the possibility that Luke was the independent author based upon the stylistic similarities which had been noticed by Grotius, Köhler, and others.[55] Likewise the Catholic scholar Hug argued for Pauline authorship, but suggested Luke had a hand in the phraseology.[56] In 1842 Stier suggested that Luke had written Hebrews under Pauline influence; in 1845 Conder argued for Luke as the author.[57] Lutterbeck suggested Paul wrote the last nine verses of Hebrews 13, while the rest of the letter was composed by Apollos with the help of Luke, Clement, and other companions of Paul.[58] Ebrard (1853) suggested that the thoughts were Pauline but Luke was the independent author.[59]

In 1857 Franz Delitzsch's classic two-volume commentary on Hebrews appeared. This commentary was an important advance for the theory of independent Lukan authorship.[60] Suggesting that Luke wrote in Paul's name, but nonetheless independently of him, Delitzsch brought forth new linguistic evidence to link the three works. He believed Luke had adopted the thoughts of Paul and remodeled them. His evidence mostly consisted in lexical and stylistic data which he pointed out frequently in his commentary. Also significant was the medical language which Delitzsch noticed in Hebrews, especially in

---

[55] K. Stein, *Der Brief an die Hebräer: theoretisch-practisch erklärt und in seinem grossartigen Zusammenhange dargestellt* (Leipzig: Carl Heinrich Reclam, 1838), 5.

[56] Hug, *Introduction to the New Testament*, 601.

[57] J. Conder speculated that Silas and Luke are the same individual. "The close connection between Paul and Luke has been considered as imparting an Apostolic sanction to the writings of the Evangelist; and this ancient opinion would have appeared to rest upon far stronger grounds, had the identity of that Evangelist with Paul's chosen colleague, Silas, been understood. In like manner, the tradition, that the Epistle to the Hebrews was composed by Luke, would have seemed to carry with it a higher degree of probability, had it come down to us in another shape, the name Silvanus being substituted for that of Luke, or rather the true character of Luke having been recognized." *A Literary History of the New Testament* (London: Seeley, Burnside & Seeley, 1845), 466.

[58] A. Lutterbeck, *Die neutestamentlichen Lehrbegriffe: oder, Untersuchungen über das Zeitalter der Religionswende, die Vorstufen des Christenthums und die erste Gestaltung desselben: ein Handbuch fur alteste Dogmengeschichte und systematische Exegese des neuen Testamentes.* (Mainz: Florian Kupferberg, 1852), 103.

[59] J. H. A. Ebrard, *Exposition of the Epistle to the Hebrews*, trans. and rev. A. C. Kendrick, *Biblical Commentary on the New Testament*, ed. H. Olshausen (New York: Sheldon, Blakeman & Co., 1858), 6:428–29.

[60] F. Delitzsch had written a previous article on the authorship and recipients of Hebrews ("Über Verfasser und Leser des Hebräerbriefs mit besonderer Berucksichtigung der neuesten Untersuchungen Wieseler's und Thiersch's." *Zeitschrift fur die gesammte lutherische Theologie und Kirch* [Leipzig: Dorffling und Franke, 1849], 250–85) in which he briefly advocated the possibility of Lukan authorship. See also his *Hebrews*, 2:409–17.

three places: 4:12–13, 5:12–14, and 12:11–13. His statements regarding Lukan authorship of Hebrews appear at the end of his second volume.

> Taking into account the observations made in the course of the exposition from the beginning to the end, we consider it in the highest degree probable that Luke composed the epistle from statements made to him by the apostle [Paul], being commissioned by the latter thereto. We esteem it possible that Luke was the independent author of it . . . .[61]

There can be little doubt that Delitzsch's advocacy of independent Lukan authorship caused many to reexamine this particular theory.

Delitzsch accepted the traditional paradigm of Luke's Gentile background, but was open to the possibility that Luke was Jewish. Only a few scholars during the nineteenth century (like Tiele [1858] and Hoffman [1873]) made that suggestion. It is unclear what effect this had on the way influential scholars like Godet and Delitzsch viewed the likelihood of Lukan authorship, but it certainly did not hurt the cause. In all probability it gave the theory greater credibility.

Some of the similarities between Luke and Hebrews noted by Delitzsch along with some additional similarities were put forth by Carl Weizsacker in a rather lengthy 1862 journal article.[62] Kurtz argued against Lukan authorship in his commentary on Hebrews a few years later by noting that the heads of churches were called *presbuteroi* by Luke in Acts but were called *hēgoumenoi* in Hebrews. (He also noted Luke's use of *baptisma* whereas Hebrews uses *baptismos*.[63]) Kurtz's point about the Lukan use of *hēgoumenoi* is inaccurate, because Luke uses it substantively in the sense of "ruler" in Luke 22:26, Acts 7:10, 14:12, and 15:22 (in fact, *hēgoumenoi* refers to church leaders in Acts 14:12 and 15:22, and *presbuteroi* is also used in 15:22). Furthermore, *hēgoumenoi* is used in the sense of church leaders *only* by Luke and Hebrews.

In 1869, the first edition of a now classic commentary on Luke's Gospel appeared by the French scholar F. Godet. It has since been translated and reprinted numerous times. At the end of his second volume, Godet makes a comment about the relationship of Luke's writings to Hebrews, noting their "features of agreement which are highly

---

[61] Delitzsch, *Hebrews*, 2:416–17.

[62] C. Weizsacker, "Die Johanneische Logoslehre," *Jahrbucher fur Deutsche Theologie* 7 (1862): 619–708.

[63] J. H. Kurtz, *Der Brief an die Hebräer* (Mitau: Neumann, 1869), 18.

remarkable."[64] In a footnote to this sentence, Godet remarked that he believed Luke was the author of Hebrews. He then compared four passages in Luke's Gospel which are analogous to passages in Hebrews. He also noted a similar transformation taking place in the Gospel of Luke and in Hebrews: in Luke, the Mosaic system is transformed into spiritual obedience; in Hebrews, the Levitical *cultus* is transformed into a spiritual *cultus*. Finally, Godet noted that in both Luke's Gospel and Hebrews the human development of Jesus forms the foundation of the Christology.[65] Godet accepted the traditional paradigm regarding Luke's Gentile background, so his promotion of Lukan authorship of Hebrews is all the more interesting and significant.

G. Lünemann collated Delitzsch's evidence which was scattered throughout his two-volume commentary and presented it in six pages of his own commentary on Hebrews.[66] The only valid critique of Delitzsch by Lünemann is his occasional point that some of Delitzsch's evidence is not unique to the Lukan writings and Hebrews but may occur elsewhere in the New Testament. However, when this adjustment is made, even Lünemann admits there is still a sizeable body of linguistic and stylistic evidence linking Luke with Hebrews.

Lünemann countered the arguments of Tiele and Hoffman that Luke was Jewish and asserted that Luke's Gentile status was "fully decisive" against his having written Hebrews.[67] Lünemann's rather caustic[68] critique of Delitzsch's evidence for Lukan authorship has

---

[64] F. Godet, *A Commentary on the Gospel of Luke*, 4th ed., trans. E. W. Shalders and M. D. Cusin (New York: Funk & Wagnalls, 1887), 2:421.

[65] Ibid., 422.

[66] G. Lünemann, *The Epistle to the Hebrews*, trans. from the 4th German ed. by M. Evans, *Meyer's Critical and Exegetical Handbook to the New Testament*, ed. H. A. W. Meyer, 11 vols. (New York: Funk & Wagnalls, 1885), 356–63. The first edition of Lünemann's commentary on Hebrews appeared in 1855, two years prior to Delitzch's commentary. In subsequent editions, Lünemann's critique of Delitzsch appeared.

[67] Ibid., 363.

[68] Lünemann's abrasive remarks regarding Delitzsch's lack of critical acumen in the evidence he puts forward for Luke include comments such as Delitzsch's attempt to connect Luke with Hebrews was "predestined to failure." "The evidence for his assertion has been scattered by Delitzsch through his whole commentary; and it almost seems as though this, for the reader and critic highly inconvenient mode of proceeding, has been chosen under the unconscious feeling that the evidence was not in a position to admit of synoptical classification, without in such case at once being laid bare in all its weakness. For so soon as we critically sift that which has been uncritically piled together by Delitzsch . . . " (*Hebrews*, 356). Another example occurs on page 363: "all these are arguments which ought not to have been found at all, in a work which lays claim to a scientific character." These remarks, which in their intensity and critical nature cross the boundary of scholarly disagreement, may perhaps be traceable to a comment made by Delitzsch about Lünemann in the preface to his commentary: "There is then, in the first place,

been influential in dissuading many from this hypothesis. This can be seen from a cursory reading of various commentaries on Hebrews and volumes on New Testament introduction since that time.

Although Alford did not argue for Lukan authorship of Hebrews, his comments on the matter are significant enough to include here. Alford's fourth volume of his *Greek New Testament: An Exegetical and Critical Commentary* originally appeared in the same year as Delitzsch's commentary (1857), and was revised by the author prior to his death in 1871. The fifth edition appeared in 1875 and included all of Alford's revisions. His bibliography cited Lünemann's first edition only and may explain why Alford made no mention of Lünemann's critique of Delitzsch's evidence for Lukan authorship.

Alford listed eight companions of Paul whom he considered capable of writing Hebrews, devoting most of the discussion to Luke, Barnabas, and Apollos. He stated that if Col 4:10–14 is evidence that Luke was a Gentile then "it would be impossible to allot him more than a subordinate share in the composition."[69] Then follows this interesting admission:

> Could we explain away the inference apparently unavoidable from Col. iv. 14, such a supposition [Luke's authorship of Hebrews] would seem to have some support from the epistle itself. The students of the following commentary will very frequently be struck by the verbal and idiomatic coincidences with the style of St. Luke. The argument, as resting on them, has been continually taken up and pushed forward by Delitzsch, and comes on his reader frequently with a force which at the time it is not easy to withstand.[70]

Here Alford acknowledged the evidence which Delitzsch amassed for Lukan authorship, but in the next paragraph denies the possibility by noting that the "tone" of Luke-Acts is so "essentially different"

---

one department—the theological—in the interpretation of this epistle, in which not a little still remains to be accomplished, as even those who have done the most in this line themselves (Such as Bleek and Tholuck) would hardly be disposed to question. Nor would, I think, even Lünemann wish to do so, since his own performances in this respect might have been far more considerable, had he not so entirely left out of view the valuable contributions to theological exegesis furnished by Prof. v. Hofmann in his *Schriftbeweis*" (1871:viii). However, in his introduction, Delitzsch moderately praised Lünemann's commentary calling it "worthy to form a part of Meyer's complete commentary on the New Testament. It is founded for the most part on Bleek, though with real independence" (Ibid., 33). Delitzsch's commentary appeared only two years after Lünemann's work, and Lünemann's acrimonious remarks included in later editions of his work may be an example of a bruised ego lashing out.

[69] Alford, "Hebrews," 53.
[70] Ibid.

from the spirit of the writer of Hebrews. Lukan studies within the past 50 years have shown that Alford's negative assessment of Luke's lack of "rhetorical balance" was inaccurate. What does it mean for Alford to say that Luke is the "polished Christian civilian" while the author of Hebrews was a "fervid and prophetic rhetorician"? Luke could be "fervid and prophetic" even in narrative writing. In light of the many comparisons that can be made between the prologues of Luke and Hebrews, his statement that "no two styles can be more distinct, than that of this preface, and of any equally elaborated passage in the Epistle to the Hebrews" is surely wide of the mark. Alford concluded this rather lengthy paragraph in a way that would, in light of modern Lukan (not to mention psychological) studies, be an evident overstatement: " . . . it would shake our confidence in the consistency of human characteristics . . . were we to believe Luke . . . to have become so changed, in the foundations and essentials of personal identity, as to have written this Epistle to the Hebrews."[71]

Alford chalked up the similarities between Luke and Hebrews to a common Alexandrian training (which is now highly debatable for the author of Hebrews, not to mention Luke) and a common source, namely, Paul. Like Lünemann, Alford believed that if Luke were a Gentile, then he could not have been the independent author of Hebrews. But this supposition, along with his other reasoning against Luke, does not seem to me to be able to bear the weight put upon it.

In the introduction to his Hebrews commentary (1878) Cowles presented an excellent case for Lukan authorship with some Pauline involvement. Especially significant is his argument for Caesarea[72] as the location of the recipients and his dating of the letter not later than AD 64. Cowles posited Luke as "mainly the responsible author of this epistle in the sense that the style is his, and to some extent, the course of argument and the prominence given to points of doctrine, as well as also the personal allusions; while yet he may have written under the eye of Paul, with his most entire concurrence and endorsement, and with perhaps large aid from Paul's suggestions."[73] Cowles essentially posited independent Lukan authorship.

---

[71] Ibid., 54.

[72] Among past and present commentators on Hebrews, H. Cowles (in my opinion) produces the most persuasive argument in favor of Caesarea. Spicq's arguments for Caesarea are also worthy of note (Hébreux, 1:247–50).

[73] H. Cowles, The Epistle to the Hebrews; with Notes, Critical, Explanatory and Practical, Designed for both Pastors and People (New York: Appleton & Co., 1878), 11.

Evidence in favor of Luke adduced by Cowles included the following: (1) personal allusions in Hebrews, (2) style, including modes of thought, style of speech, and choice of words and phrases, (3) use of the LXX, (4) frequent reference to the ministry of angels, (5) prominence given to the incarnation and humanity of Christ, and (6) the Holy Spirit as embodying the power of the gospel age.[74] Cowles has one of the better arguments for Lukan authorship of Hebrews, yet he is seldom referenced in any of the twentieth-century commentaries or introductions on the subject, either by those who support the theory or by those who argue against it.[75]

Lukan involvement in Hebrews was also suggested by Zenas. He believed that Paul was behind the letter, but that authorship should be ascribed to a collaboration between Luke and Timothy.[76] Timothy was suggested as a possible author by Legg in 1968, but the inclusion of his name within the text of Hebrews itself (not to mention other factors) excludes him from serious consideration.

Gardiner (1887) wrote a very influential article that had important ramifications for both Pauline and Lukan authorship theories. He investigated the lexical evidence in Hebrews in order to see if any new light could be cast upon the matter of authorship. Gardiner catalogued the length of the New Testament books (i.e., the number of lines of Greek text) and combined that with a word list based on their frequency of use by each writer. His approach was statistically based, but as he admitted there was a certain "fallacy in this process," since vocabulary varies with an author's subject matter.[77]

Gardiner's greatest error, however, was in his total of the number of words unique to the Lukan writings and Hebrews. He placed this number at thirty-four. As I will demonstrate, there are actually fifty-three such words unique to Luke-Acts and Hebrews. Gardiner's miscount led him to say: "This fact tends, of course, to connect this epistle with both S. Luke and S. Paul, but especially with the latter." Since there are fifty-three words unique to Luke and Hebrews and

---

[74] Ibid., 11–17.

[75] H. Attridge, *The Epistle to the Hebrews*, Her (Philadelphia: Fortress, 1989); W. Lane, *Hebrews 1–8*; and Ellingworth, *Hebrews*, make no mention of him.

[76] Zenas, *Apologia ad Hebraeos: The Epistle (and Gospel) to the Hebrews* (Edinburgh: T&T Clark, 1887), 239.

[77] F. Gardiner, "The Language of the Epistle to the Hebrews as Bearing upon its Authorship," *JBL* 7 (1887): 1–27.

fifty-six words unique to Paul and Hebrews, the relationship among the three is virtually identical in terms of unique vocabulary.

Gardiner's conclusion is illuminating. He thought his investigation would confirm the hypothesis that Hebrews reflected Pauline thoughts and reasoning but Lukan phraseology, and therefore that Hebrews was written by Luke to express ideas and arguments received from Paul. The result of his investigation caused him to change his views. He rejected Pauline and Lukan authorship and opted for Barnabas as the most likely candidate. A final point about Gardiner's article should be made. If his figures for non-content words such as conjunctions, prepositions, and the like are compared throughout his article, the results show that Luke is statistically much closer to Hebrews than Paul. Since an author's use of non-content words would tend to be more demonstrative of personal writing style, this evidence further supports the contention noticed as early as the Patristics that Hebrews is much closer to the Lukan writings than to Paul—a fact which is highly significant for authorship.

Gardiner's egregious error in miscounting the number of words unique to Luke and Hebrews should restrain anyone from making such statements as Marcus Dods who footnoted his statement of the "insufficiency" of the Lukan authorship hypothesis, "The similarities to the usage of Luke in the vocabulary of the Epistle have been examined with *final thoroughness* [emphasis mine] by Prof. Frederic Gardiner in the *Journal of Soc. of Bibl. Lit. and Exegesis* for June 1887."[78] There are precious few matters in New Testament studies that can be said to have been examined with final thoroughness.

Just two years after Gardiner's article, B. F. Westcott's commentary on Hebrews appeared. Westcott's erudition is known to all and although he did not support Lukan authorship of Hebrews, he considered it a possibility. His comments relative to Luke are significant and therefore a rather lengthy quotation follows.

> It has already been seen that the earliest scholars who speak of the Epistle notice its likeness in style to the writings of Luke; and when every allowance has been made for coincidences which consist in forms of expression which are found also in the LXX. or in other writers of the N.T., or in late Greek generally, the likeness is unquestionably remarkable. No one can work independently at the Epistle without observing it. But it is not possible to establish any sure conclusion on such a resemblance. The author of the Epistle

---

[78] Dods, "Hebrews," 227.

may have been familiar with the writings of St Luke themselves, or he may have been in close connexion with the Evangelist or with those whose language was moulded by his influence. In any case the likeness of vocabulary and expression is not greater than that which exists between I Peter and the Epistles of St Paul. If indeed it were credible that the Epistle was originally written in 'Hebrew,' then the external and internal evidence combined would justify the belief that the Greek text is due to St Luke. If that opinion is out of the question, the historical evidence for St Luke's connexion with the Epistle is either destroyed or greatly weakened, and the internal evidence gives no valid result . . . We are left then with a negative conclusion. The Epistle cannot be the work of St Paul, and still less the work of Clement. It may have been written by St Luke. It may have been written by Barnabas, if the "Epistle of Barnabas" is apocryphal. The scanty evidence which is accessible to us supports no more definite judgment.[79]

There are several comments which need to be made in the light of research presented in this book. Westcott's statement that the similarities between Luke and Hebrews is no greater than that between 1 Peter, Paul, and Hebrews cannot be sustained on the basis of the evidence. While there are similarities between 1 Peter and Hebrews, it is clear that the similarities between the Lukan writings and Hebrews are far greater. Furthermore, the only place where Paul's similarities to Hebrews are greater than Luke's is vocabulary, and the difference is only three words (53 for Luke and 56 for Paul). In the areas of style and doctrine Hebrews is clearly closer to Luke than to Paul.

Westcott commented that the author of Hebrews may have been familiar with the writings of Luke, may have been closely connected to Luke, or may have been affiliated with people whose thinking and language was influenced by Luke. Could the many similarities, especially in style, be accounted for on the supposition that the author was either familiar with Luke's writings or spent some time in Luke's company? No one spent more time with Paul than Luke, yet their styles are clearly distinguishable. It is even more unlikely that an author of Hebrews "twice removed" from Luke would reflect a style so similar to him. Unless the author were deliberately imitating Lukan style (and it must be asked why would anyone do this?), such similarities as do exist would be difficult to account for apart from Luke's involvement in its composition.

---

[79] B. F. Westcott, *The Epistle to the Hebrews* (London: Macmillan, 1892; repr., Grand Rapids: Eerdmans, 1955), lxxvi–lxxvii.

Westcott considered it likely that if Hebrews were originally written in Hebrew, then the external and internal evidence pointed to Luke as the translator. What does not follow is Westcott's next statement: if that possibility were out of the question, the historical evidence linking Luke with Hebrews is "destroyed or greatly weakened." It is certainly not destroyed (although the church fathers' testimony in favor of Paul would be slightly stronger than that for Luke). The historical evidence for the strongest candidates—Paul, Barnabas, and Luke—is, on the whole, rather weak.

Westcott concluded that Hebrews "cannot be the work of Paul." "Cannot" is a strong word; one I think should not be used regarding Paul and Hebrews. Hebrews could be the work of Paul if we could account for the radical stylistic shift. But most modern scholars agree that it is very unlikely that Hebrews was written by Paul. Finally, Westcott concluded that Hebrews "may have been written by Luke." This is a rather surprising admission given his previous statements! Obviously, Westcott considered Lukan authorship a viable possibility.

In 1898 two other scholars came out in support of Luke as the author of Hebrews (as opposed to being a translator or amanuensis). W. Lewis theorized that Hebrews was the joint production of Paul and Luke, with Luke acting not as an amanuensis but as a redactor of (or commentator on) Paul's thoughts. He argued that Hebrews was written by Luke from Caesarea while Paul was imprisoned there c. AD 58–60. Lewis did not present any additional linguistic evidence for Lukan authorship; instead, he suggested that Paul's defense before Festus and Herod Agrippa (Acts 26) furnished Luke with the material for the book of Hebrews. Lewis based this proposal on certain similarities between Paul's defense and the themes in Hebrews. In particular, Lewis believed that in prison Paul studied and reflected on the relationship between the temple cultus and the Christian faith. This study formed the basis of Paul's defense and produced, through Luke, the letter to the Hebrews.[80]

Lewis' reconstruction is certainly possible and if Luke were indeed the independent author of Hebrews, he could have written it at this time. Such a date would, of course, put the writing of Hebrews be-

---

[80] W. Lewis, "Bringing the First-Begotten Into the World." *Biblical World* 12 (1898): 109–10; W. Lewis, "St. Paul's Defense Before King Agrippa, in Relation to the Epistle to the Hebrews," *Biblical World* 13 (1899): 244–48.

fore Luke and Acts on a conventional dating table. Lewis was later followed in his reconstruction by G. Campbell Morgan in 1924.[81]

William Alexander was the other scholar in 1898 who supported Lukan authorship of Hebrews. Originally published in 1872, the third revised edition of his *Leading Ideas of the Gospels* contained considerably more information on Luke's Gospel as well as an appendix which highlighted Lukan linguistic parallels to Hebrews. Alexander considered the statement in Heb 5:2 ("he can deal gently with the ignorant and misguided") to be "a lovely summary of St. Luke's Gospel . . . by the evangelist's own hand."[82] The linguistic similarities between Luke and Hebrews which had been presented by Delitzsch and discussed by Lünemann were collated by Alexander in an appendix. Whereas Delitzsch drew attention to these similarities in his commentary and Lünemann collated them (yet presented the material in paragraph form, which made it difficult for the reader to really see the comparisons), Alexander presented the linguistic collations side by side for easy study.

In addition, he presented new evidence for Lukan authorship not cited by Delitzsch, some of which was furnished him by W. K. Hobart. Some of this evidence consisted of vocabulary unique to the Lukan writings and Hebrews; other evidence was vocabulary which occurs mostly in Luke-Acts and Hebrews, but only rarely in other New Testament books. Hobart also furnished Alexander with a list of medical words found in Hebrews. Alexander's study of this evidence led him to conclude that the author of Hebrews had a better-than-average knowledge of medical terminology (which would not be surprising if the author were Luke).[83] Finally, Alexander noted other conceptual similarities between Luke and Hebrews. His summary of the evidence and conclusion follows.

> (i) There is quite a flight of words, expressions, and constructions in the Epistle to the Hebrews, commonly (not seldom exclusively) used by St. Luke. After all deductions for a common source in the LXX., or in the current Greek of the Church and of society in that age, the coincidence is, to say the least, remarkable. (ii.) There are in the Epistle to the Hebrews various traces of the results of a medical training, and of psychological power, whether in analysis of modes of thought and feeling, or in delineations of character. These indications also point in the direction of St. Luke. (iii.) To this we may add–(A) Common Christological conceptions, notably of the ascended

---

[81] G. C. Morgan, *The Acts of the Apostles* (New York: F. H. Revell Co., 1924), 506.
[82] W. Alexander, *The Leading Ideas of the Gospels*, 3rd rev. ed. (London: Macmillan, 1892), 8.
[83] Ibid., 313–19.

Christ in heaven. (B) Common notes of ecclesiastical and spiritual life. (1) The Christian life one of continuing sanctification. (2) A life characterized by Confirmation as the complement of Baptism, and by participation in the Holy Eucharist. (3) One in which the angels have a part, and to which (in the entirest subordination as of the finite to the Infinite, of the created to the Uncreated) they afford certain gleams of help and beauty. To us it seems that, while no demonstration is attainable, the advance of critical study points to some modification of the view advanced by Clement of Alexandria and Origen.[84]

Just what "modification" Alexander had in mind he did not specify. Clearly he believed Luke to have been more than an amanuensis or translator for Paul. He maintained that the letter was authored by Luke, with perhaps some Pauline influence or input.

Nineteenth century Catholic scholars who joined with Hug in suggesting that Luke, under Pauline influence, played some role in the authorship of Hebrews were Dollinger,[85] Zill and Huyghe.[86] Their views were mostly based on linguistic and stylistic data linking the works. Lukan advocacy was unusual in that the Catholic Church had clearly adopted Pauline authorship, placing greater weight on the testimony of the church fathers.

The nineteenth century came to a close with Milligan's work on the theology of Hebrews. Milligan spent several pages at the beginning of his work discussing theories of authorship and other matters of provenance. Regarding Luke's involvement, he was quite clear about the options as he saw them: if Hebrews was a Greek translation of a Hebrew original, then Luke would be the likely author; if not, Luke could not have been the author since he was a Gentile.[87] The first half of Milligan's statement is based on the evidence of the Patristics and many who followed them throughout church history. The second half of his statement is clearly repudiated by the available evidence. Luke may not have been a Gentile, and even if he were, that does not preclude his authorship of Hebrews.

[84] Ibid., 324.

[85] J. J. Dollinger, *The First Age of Christianity*, 4th ed., trans. H. Oxenham (London: Wm. H. Allen & Co., 1866; repr., London: Gibbings & Co., 1906), 85. He noted the most probable view was, "that St. Luke wrote the Epistle under St. Paul's inspiration."

[86] L. Zill, *Der Brief an die Hebräer übersetzt und erklärt* (Mayence: Franz Kirchheim, 1879); C. Huyghe, *Commentarius in epistolam ad Hebraeos* (Gandavi: Excudebant A. Huyshauwer et. L. Scheerder succ. C. Poelman, 1901).

[87] G. Milligan, *The Theology of the Epistle to the Hebrews with a Critical Introduction* (Edinburgh: T&T Clark, 1899), 27–28.

The assessment by Lünemann, Alford, Milligan, and many others that Luke could not be the author of Hebrews (because in their view he was not Jewish) became the dominant position that virtually every twentieth-century writer on the subject would assert. Luke's Gentile background was presupposed at the dawn of the twentieth century. Ironically, as the twenty-first century has begun, no such certainty exists in Lukan studies. As a matter of fact, the view that Luke was Jewish gained significant ground in the last half of the twentieth century, so much so that Jervell could state with dogmatic certainty, "Luke was a Jew,"[88] and Rebecca Denova, in one of the latest studies on a narrative-critical reading of Luke-Acts, concluded that Luke-Acts was written by a Jew and for a Jewish readership.[89]

Early in the twentieth century, two articles by A. Eagar appeared which gave the Lukan authorship theory renewed relevance.[90] Eagar suggested Luke was the independent author of Hebrews. His argument included a comparison of the prologues of Luke and Hebrews, which had been hitherto undeveloped. He also discovered that the Pauline Letters most similar in style to Luke's writings were the letters Paul wrote while Luke was with him. Several points that shed new light on the issue are worth noting:

> First, several of the arguments used in favor of the Pauline authorship are quite as strongly in favour of S. Luke . . . .Secondly, we have seen that there are special reasons which make it practically impossible to refer the Epistle to the Hebrews to S. Paul. Now, none of these objections applies to S. Luke . . . .From these two considerations we see that all such arguments for the Pauline authorship of an Epistle as may also be applied to S. Luke become arguments for the Lucan authorship, since they are not affected, in his case, by the objections that make it impossible to apply them to S. Paul . . . .The case from a comparison of our Epistle with the Third Gospel and Acts seems to me extremely strong. It is worth mentioning that it becomes even stronger when we compare the Epistle to the Hebrews with the secondary Lucan works [by which Eagar means those Pauline epistles written by Paul while Luke was in his company: 2 Corinthians, Colossians, and the Pastorals.][91]

This last point needs further investigation to determine how much more linguistic similarity exists with these works compared to

---

[88] J. Jervell, *The Theology of the Acts of the Apostles* (Cambridge: University Press, 1996), 5.

[89] R. Denova, *The Things Accomplished Among Us: Prophetic Tradition in the Structural Pattern of Luke-Acts*, JSNTSup 141 (Sheffield: Sheffield Academic Press, 1997), 230–31.

[90] A. Eagar, "The Authorship of the Epistle to the Hebrews." *Expositor* 10 (1904): 74–80, 110–23.

[91] Ibid., 77, 120.

Hebrews than, for example, Romans and Hebrews. Greater similarity between the Pastorals and Hebrews is indisputable since this has been explored at some length within the last two centuries. Similarities to Colossians have also been noticed, but additional research on Colossians and 2 Corinthians in comparison with Luke-Acts and Hebrews would be helpful.

In 1922, Clarke noticed the similarity between Luke-Acts, Hebrews and the Maccabean writings. He concluded:

> When allowance has been made on the one hand for the smaller extent of Hebrews, and on the other for the number of common words which must inevitably be found in every book, the degree of affinity evinced by Lk-Acts and Hebrews towards 2 and 3 Maccabees seems substantially the same. . . . These figures suggest that Luke may have read 2 and 3 Maccabees before writing Acts. . . . It was no doubt known to the author of Hebrews who belonged to the same literary circles as Luke.[92]

In 1923, J. V. Brown argued for the collaborate authorship of Luke and Paul, with Luke editing the work and giving it its final form. In this way, the many correlations in style and vocabulary are accounted for. For example, Brown noted several significant parallels between Hebrews and Stephen's speech in Acts 7. This area of research would continue to grow throughout the twentieth century as many scholars highlighted these parallels.[93] In addition, Brown was the first to suggest that the group of former Jewish priests mentioned in Acts 6:7 were the likely recipients of Hebrews.

The following year, G. Campbell Morgan briefly argued for the Lukan authorship of Hebrews, essentially following the theory of W. Lewis discussed above. He argued that Luke had written "what Paul had taught."[94] Morgan was known more as a preacher than a theologian, which perhaps explains why he is never cited in commentaries or other works as one who promoted Lukan authorship of Hebrews.

In 1930, Narborough discussed analogies between Hebrews and Luke-Acts. He concluded that the most that can be said for Lukan authorship of Hebrews is the comparison between Stephen's speech in Acts 7 with Hebrews. "These parallelisms are noteworthy; but Lucan authorship of Hebrews would be a bold and precarious inference to

---

[92] A. C. Clarke, *Acts of the Apostles* (Oxford: Clarendon Press, 1933), 74–75.
[93] Brown, "Authorship," 135.
[94] Morgan, *Hebrews*, 506.

draw from them."[95] Of course Narborough did not take into account all the other evidence that can be marshaled for Luke, but his point linking Acts 7 with sections of Hebrews would be further refined by others.

Badcock put an interesting twist to the Lukan hypothesis when he suggested that the voice of Hebrews was Barnabas's but the composition was Luke's.[96] The basis for this theory, according to Badcock, is the following: (1) Luke's statements about Barnabas in Acts, (2) Barnabas's Levitical background, and (3) Luke's association with Paul and Barnabas.

In 1955, Lukan authorship was bolstered, albeit unintentionally, by C. P. M. Jones's important article, "The Epistle to the Hebrews and the Lukan writings." This new angle was the theological angle. Jones succeeded in establishing a clear kinship between Luke-Acts and Hebrews in three major areas: (1) similarity of language, (2) similarity of facts or interest, and (3) theological similarity, especially in the areas of Christology and eschatology. He focused most of his discussion on the third point, particularly the eschatological connections between Luke-Acts and Hebrews.[97]

Jones's other significant point was to challenge the prevailing paradigm that Luke-Acts was the work of a Gentile with an anti-Jewish bias, while Hebrews was clearly the work of someone of Jewish background. One purpose of his article was to show that these attitudes unqualified do not do full justice to the facts and that even if true (i.e., if Luke turned out to be a Gentile), are not incompatible. This is an important point to be made, having significant ramifications for the Lukan hypothesis. Even if Luke had been a Gentile, he still could have written a letter like Hebrews.

Similarly, in his New Testament theology L. Goppelt placed his treatment of Luke and Hebrews in the same chapter since he considered their theological kinship, especially in the area of eschatology.[98] A short article by T. Jelonek argued that based on the similarities

---

[95] F. D. V. Narborough, *The Epistle to the Hebrews* (Oxford: Clarendon Press, 1930), 10–11.

[96] F. J. Badcock, *The Pauline Epistles and the Epistle to the Hebrews in Their Historical Setting* (New York: Macmillan, 1937), 198.

[97] C. P. M. Jones, "The Epistle to the Hebrews and the Lukan Writings," in *Studies in the Gospels: Essays in Memory of R. H. Lightfoot*, ed. D. E. Nineham (Oxford: Basil Blackwell, 1955), 113–43.

[98] L. Goppelt, *Theology of the New Testament*, ed. J. Roloff, trans. J. Alsup (Grand Rapids: Eerdmans, 1982), 2:265–66.

between Stephen's speech (Acts 7) and Hebrews, Luke wrote Hebrews in Paul's name.[99] My doctoral dissertation submitted in 1987 at the University of Texas at Arlington argued for the independent Lukan theory primarily on linguistic, stylistic, and theological grounds. Two years later, I suggested that further evidence for Luke could be adduced by comparing the purposes of Luke-Acts and Hebrews.[100] Two additional articles that summarized some of my arguments appeared in 1996 and 2001.[101]

A recent commentator on Hebrews dismisses the possibility of Lukan authorship, claiming that differences in style, vocabulary, and theology "outweigh the points of affinity between Hebrews and Luke-Acts. Some of the more noticeable differences include the absence from Luke-Acts of the motif of Christ as high priest and the kind of theological speculation that is characteristic of Hebrews."[102] I will attempt to show in this study that such statements are entirely wide of the mark.

Several conclusions can be drawn from this survey. First, Luke was an early candidate for independent authorship. Second, linguistic similarities between Luke-Acts and Hebrews, along with Luke's association with Paul, were the primary bases for Luke's suggested authorship. Third, Delitzsch's commentary in 1871 was the first argument for Lukan authorship where substantive linguistic evidence was presented. Fourth, Gardiner's error in vocabulary tabulation of words unique to Luke-Acts and Hebrews, often repeated subsequently by others, contributed to the tacit dismissal of Lukan authorship. Fifth, many scholars assume that Luke was a Gentile and, thus, could not be the author of Hebrews. Sixth, Eagar's article advanced the Lukan hypothesis in a fresh way by emphasizing the close relationship that existed between Luke and Paul. Eagar also discussed, from a stylistic perspective, how Luke's presence (or absence) can be detected in the Pauline Epistles. Seventh, the theological ties between Luke and Hebrews (observed by Jones and Goppelt in the twentieth century) gave the theory of Lukan authorship additional weight. Finally, the present state of Lukan

---

[99] T. Jelonek, "Chrystologia listu do Hebrajezykow." *Analecta Cracoviensia* 17 (1985): 253–57.

[100] D. Allen, "The Purposes of Luke-Acts and Hebrews Compared: an Argument for the Lukan Authorship of Hebrews," in *The Church at the Dawn of the 21st Century*, ed. P. Patterson, J. Pretlove, and L. Pantoja (Dallas: Criswell Publications, 1989), 123–35.

[101] D. Allen, "The Lukan Authorship of Hebrews: A Proposal," *JOTT* 8 (1996): 1–22; D. Allen, "The Authorship of Hebrews: The Lukan Proposal," *Faith and Mission* 18 (2001): 27–40.

[102] Salevao, *Legitimation in the Letter to the Hebrews*, 98.

studies on his possible Jewish background renders ineffective the "Gentile" theory against Lukan authorship. Among the many theories in the past two centuries concerning the authorship of Hebrews, the Lukan theory still has much to commend it.[103]

---

[103] Recent 21st century commentaries waste no space in their rejection of the possibility of Lukan authorship of Hebrews. C. Koester, *Hebrews: a New Translation with Introduction and Commentary*, AB 36 (New York: Doubleday, 2001), 43, states: "The problem is that nothing in Hebrews points particularly to Luke, and the general similarities in style indicate only that both came from a similar Hellenistic environment." Likewise, P. O'Brien, *The Letter to the Hebrews*, Pillar New Testament Commentary (Grand Rapids: Eerdmans, 2010), 6, dispatches the Lukan option in one sentence: "Luke has been proposed as a candidate, but the points of connection between him and Hebrews are too slight to support a theory that he wrote the latter." The following chapters will, I believe, show the case to be otherwise.

Chapter 2

BARNABAS, APOLLOS, AND PAUL

O f all candidates for the authorship of Hebrews, three seem to have gained the most support in modern times (though the Pauline theory gradually waned in the twentieth century to the point that it is seldom argued by scholars today): Barnabas, Apollos, and Paul. Evidence for and against each will be considered.

The Argument for Barnabas[1]

Barnabas has had the support of scholars ancient and modern. Tertullian presented this hypothesis, writing in such a way as to imply that he had no doubt about it.

> For there is extant withal an Epistle to the Hebrews under the name of Barnabas—a man sufficiently accredited by God, as being one whom Paul has stationed next to himself in the uninterrupted observance of abstinence: Or else, I alone and Barnabas, have not we the power of working? And, of course, the Epistle of Barnabas is more generally received among the Churches than that apocryphal Shepherd of adulterers.[2]

Additional support for Barnabas is found in the fourth century *Tractatus Origenis* by Gregory of Elvira who wrote: "The most holy Barnabas says, Through him we offer to God the sacrifice of lips that acknowledge his name."[3] This is an allusion to Heb 13:15, and thus Gregory attributes Hebrews to Barnabas. Filaster, the fourth century bishop of Brescia, also speaks of Hebrews as a letter from Barnabas.[4] Jerome (c. AD 345–c. 419) pointed out that Hebrews was believed to be

---

[1] Cf. G. Salmon, *Introduction to the New Testament*, 3rd ed. (London: John Murray, 1888), 446–48; E. Riggenbach, *Der Brief an die Hebräer*, KNT, ed. T. Zahn (Leipzig: A. Deichert, 1913); G. Edmundson, *The Church in Rome in the First Century* (London: Longmans, Green & Co., 1913); K. Bornhäuser, *Empfänger und Verfasser des Briefes an die Hebräer*, BFCT 35/3 (Gütersloh: Bertelsmann, 1932); and H. Mulder, "Barnabas en de Gemeente te Jeruzalem," *Homileticaen Biblica* 24 (1965): 198–200; id., "De Schrijver van de Brief aan de Hebreeen," *Homileticaen Biblica* 24 (1965): 110–14. J. A. T. Robinson, *Redating the New Testament* (London: SCM, 1976), 217–20, appears to believe that Barnabas should be given serious consideration as the author. Mulder argued that Tertullian's suggestion of Barnabas as the author was mostly ignored by early Christian writers (because Barnabas lost favor in the Church when he broke ranks with Paul), but this is hardly likely. More recently, see the arguments in favor of Barnabas by P. E. Hughes, *A Commentary on the Epistle to the Hebrews* (Grand Rapids: Eerdmans, 1977), 28–29.

[2] Tertullian, *On Modesty*, 20.

[3] Cited in Hughes, *Hebrews*, 25.

[4] Augustine, *Haeresibus*, 89.

Paul's letter, yet many considered it to be the work of either Barnabas, Luke, or Clement.[5] The sixth century Codex Claromantus lists "the Epistle of Barnabas" among the canonical books. The stichometric figures for this epistle are very close to Hebrews; as a result Westcott suggested that it is likely they are one and the same.[6]

While certainly not significant or conclusive, there is evidence among the early church fathers that suggests Barnabas was the author. This evidence is definitely identified with the Western (Latin) tradition, a tradition that had strongly denied Pauline authorship. Other evidence to support Barnabas adduced by scholars includes the following: (1) He was a Levite of Cyprus (Acts 4:36), hence his interest in the Old Testament ritual and sacrificial system (as is found in Hebrews) would be understandable. (2) Barnabas was a member of the Pauline circle and would probably have associated with Timothy (since Timothy came from the area evangelized by both Barnabas and Paul; cf. Acts 16:1).[7] (3) The Hellenistic perspective in Hebrews suggests to some scholars that Barnabas was the author. When the Antiochene Hellenists were evangelized, the church at Jerusalem sent Barnabas to coordinate this new thrust (Acts 11:19–26). (4) Barnabas is called the "son of exhortation" (Acts 4:36), and the epistle to the Hebrews is called by its author a "word of exhortation" (Heb 13:22). (5) The Pauline tone of the epistle could result from Barnabas, being Paul's traveling companion on his first missionary journey, sharing Paul's perspective and conceptual framework. Thiersch argued that Hebrews was jointly authored by Paul and Barnabas. He believed Barnabas was the primary author, who consented to the conclusion written by Paul, who in this way adopted the whole document.[8]

Barnabas's high profile in Acts, coupled with his Levitical background, makes him an attractive candidate for the author of Hebrews—especially if it were written to the Jerusalem church. However, the major weakness of this suggestion is that we have no extant writings

---

[5] Jerome, *Lives of Illustrious Men*, 5.

[6] B. F. Westcott, *The Epistle to the Hebrews* (London: Macmillan, 1892; repr., Grand Rapids: Eerdmans, 1955), xxviii–xxix.

[7] J. Owen, *An Exposition of the Epistle to the Hebrews* (Edinburgh: Ritchie, 1812), 1:70, puts a question mark beside this evidence. He noted that Timothy was the companion of the writer and was unknown to Barnabas, since Timothy joined Paul after he and Barnabas separated.

[8] H. Thiersch, *De Epistola ad Hebraeos: Commentatio historica* (Marburgi: Sumtibus Elwerti Bibliopolae Et Typographi Academici, 1848), 1–13, cited in F. Bleek, *Introduction to the New Testament*, 2nd ed., translated by W. Urwick (Edinburgh: T&T Clark, 1869), 2:112.

of Barnabas to compare with Hebrews; the so-called *Epistle of Barnabas* is considered spurious. Bleek considers Tertullian's view "an accidental oversight on Tertullian's part," which arose from his confusion of Hebrews with the *Epistle of Barnabas*. Of course, this does not mean that Barnabas could not possibly be the author of Hebrews; it merely means that we have no additional material with which to conduct comparative studies.

Guthrie,[9] following McNeile-Williams,[10] argued against Barnabas on the basis that if he had been the acknowledged author, how did Pauline authorship become a viable option? The suggestion that Paul's name would have been appended to the epistle in order for it to gain canonicity is not, according to Guthrie, "conceivable." Another argument against Barnabas may be the way in which the author addresses the issue of Levi and the tithe in Hebrews 7. The historical debates that existed in the first century between the priests and the Levites on this subject cannot be dealt with here,[11] but it is clear that a Levite would not have approached the subject in a priestly fashion as appears to be the case here.

Bargil Pixner recently supported Barnabas as the author, and he believed that the recipients were Qumranian priests who converted to Christianity in Acts 6:7 (Spicq and others agreed with this view of the recipients). Since Barnabas was a Levite, he would have had both the knowledge and the motivation to write Hebrews to such a group.[12] Dan Wallace has suggested that Hebrews was co-authored by Barnabas and Apollos; Barnabas was the main author and Apollos served as his assistant.[13]

The contrast in style and general tone between Hebrews and the so-called *Epistle of Barnabas* would virtually rule out Barnabas as the author of Hebrews if it could be proven that Barnabas was the *Epistle's*

[9] D. Guthrie, *New Testament Introduction*, 4th rev. ed. (Downers Grove: InterVarsity, 1990), 675.

[10] A. H. McNeile, *Introduction to the New Testament*, 2nd ed., rev. C. S. C. Williams (Oxford: Clarendon, 1953), 237.

[11] See Horbury, "The Aaronic Priesthood in the Epistle to the Hebrews," *JSNT* 19 (1983): 43–71.

[12] B. Pixner, "The Jerusalem Essenes, Barnabas and the Letter to the Hebrews," in *Qumranica Mogilanensia*, ed. Z. J. Kapera (Krakow, Poland: Enigma Press, 1992), 6:167–78. Pixner noted that Qumran's opposition to the temple was directed against the Hasmonean high priests, whom they considered to be illegitimate.

[13] "Hebrews," *Biblical Studies Foundation*, (http://bible.org/seriespage/hebrews-introduction-argument-and-outline.htm).

author. Stuart's point is well taken: "The difference between this writer and him who wrote the epistle to the Hebrews . . . is heaven-wide." Stuart calls it "a hopeless case."[14]

The Argument for Apollos

The suggestion, which is perhaps the most popular in modern New Testament studies, is that Apollos wrote Hebrews.[15] Luther was the first to make this suggestion[16]; it is therefore important to note that none of the church fathers considered him—not even the Alexandrian school (which claimed Apollos as its primary leader). It is curious that the fathers never mentioned Apollos as a possible author, though they had numerous opportunities to do so.

Those who argue for Apollos do so based on Luke's description of him in Acts and by Paul's description in First Corinthians. He was apparently a great orator and "powerful in the use of the Scriptures" (Acts 18:24), two characteristics apparently true of the author of

---

[14] M. Stuart, *A Commentary on the Epistle to the Hebrews* (Andover: Warren F. Draper, 1854), 237.

[15] See F. Bleek, *Der Brief an die Hebräer erlautert durch Einleitung, Übersetzung und fortlaufenden Kommentar* (Berlin: F. Dümmler, 1828), 1:395–430; T. W. Manson, "The Problem of the Epistle to the Hebrews," *BJRL* 32 (1949): 1–17; C. Spicq, *L'Épître aux Hébreux* (Paris: Librairie Lecoffre, 1952–53), 1:211–19; id., "L'Épître aux Hébreux, Apollos, Jean-Baptiste, les Hellénistes et Qumran," *RevQ* 1 (1958–59): 365–90; H. Montefiore, *A Commentary on the Epistle to the Hebrews* (New York: Harper; London: Black, 1964), 9–28; H. Attridge, *The Epistle to the Hebrews*, Her (Philadelphia: Fortress, 1989), 4 (n. 28); R. Nash, "The Notion of Mediator in Alexandrian Judaism and the Epistle to the Hebrews," *WJT* 40 (1978): 89–115; and G. Guthrie, "The Case for Apollos as the Author of Hebrews," *Faith and Mission* 18 (2002): 41–56. Guthrie has the best argument in modern scholarship for Apollos, which includes an historical survey through the twentieth century of the proposal. Montefiore's argument that Hebrews was written in Ephesus by Apollos to the Corinthian church in AD 52 has been thoroughly critiqued by L. D. Hurst in "Apollos, Hebrews, and Corinth: Bishop Montefiore's Theory Examined," *SJT* 38 (1985): 505–13. T. W. Manson's thesis (that Apollos wrote Hebrews from Corinth to the churches in the Lycus valley to address the Colossian heresy) has been thoroughly critiqued by Guthrie, "The Case for Apollos as the Author of Hebrews." *Faith and Mission* 18 (2002): 41–56. D. H. Appel, *Der Hebräerbrief: ein Schreiben des Apollos on Judenchristen Gemeinde* (Leipzig: A. Deichert'ssche Verlagsbuchhandlung, 1918), argued that Apollos wrote Hebrews in Ephesus to Corinth between AD 64 and AD 70. This theory was also argued by F. L. Bue, "The Historical Background of the Epistle to the Hebrews," *JBL* 75 (1958): 52–57.

[16] See Luther, *WA* 10.I.1.143.13–20. See also C. R. Koester, *Hebrews*, AB 36 (New York: Doubleday, 2001), 35, n. 53 for detailed information on Luther's proposal and bibliography. He notes that Luther's proposal actually first appeared in a sermon on Hebrews 1:1–4 which was published in 1522 (*Sermons*, vol. 7, 167). See also Luther's 1545 *Commentary on Genesis* (LW, 178). Luther attributed authorship to Apollos based on the supposed Alexandrian influence on Hebrews. The fact that this has been shown to be vastly overrated in recent years weakens the case for Apollos significantly.

Hebrews. He was a member of Paul's circle, which would explain the Pauline influences in the letter. He was also associated with Timothy (1 Cor 16:10–12), as was the author of Hebrews (Heb 13:23).

Apollos' connection with Alexandria would seem to explain the so-called Alexandrian tone of the book.[17] However, scholars have increasingly called this point into question. R. Williamson has brought the most serious challenge against the alleged Platonism of the author of Hebrews, as well as the so-called influence of Philo.[18] He has shown that the Old Testament Levitical cultus and typological milieu furnish a better explanation for the author's approach than any supposed Alexandrian influence.[19] He goes on to list a number of differences between Alexandrian thought and the epistle. D. Runia's study of this brought him to a moderate position. He noted the linguistic, hermeneutical, and thematic correspondences are "impressive," and indicates that the author of Hebrews must have been familiar with the Philonic heritage, but there remains a demonstrable difference in the thought worlds. "The antitheses ontological versus eschatological dualism and allegory versus typology sum up much of the difference." He also noted a crucial point of divergence in the area of Christology.[20] Consequently, what was once considered a strong argument in favor of Apollos has since been severely weakened.[21]

---

[17] So Spicq, "L'Épître aux Hébreux," 1:211–19; W. F. Howard, "The Epistle to the Hebrews," *Int* 5 (1951): 82–84; and A. M. Hunter, "Apollos the Alexandrian," in *Biblical Studies*, ed. J. R. McKay and J. F. Miller (Philadelphia: Westminster, 1976), 147–56.

[18] See R. Williamson, *Philo and the Epistle to the Hebrews* (Leiden: Brill, 1970).

[19] See also W. Horbury, "The Aaronic Priesthood in the Epistle to the Hebrews," *JSNT* (1983): 43–71: "The author's closeness to Josephus rather than Philo on the issue of Levi and the tithe might suggest a 'marginal consideration' in favor of a Palestinian rather than an Alexandrian authorship." The same could be said for the recipients as well.

[20] D. Runia, *Philo in Early Christian Literature: A Survey*, vol. 3, in *Compendia Rerum Iudaicarum ad Novum Testamentum*, Section III, *Jewish Traditions in Early Christian Literature* (Minneapolis: Fortress, 1993), 78. Runia's conclusion is that the two authors came from the same milieu "in a closer sense than was discovered in the case of Paul." The thought worlds are "markedly different," especially with respect to Christology (p. 78). See also H. Weiss, *Der Brief an die Hebräer*, KEK 13 (Göttingen: Vandenhoeck & Ruprecht, 1991), 103, who likewise noted the divergence in Christology between Philo and Hebrews.

[21] B. Lindars concurs: "The exhaustive study of R. Williamson has shown conclusively that Hebrews owes no direct debt to Philo" (B. Lindars, *The Theology of the Letter to the Hebrews* [Cambridge: Cambridge University Press, 1991], 24). G. Sterling's "Ontology Versus Eschatology: Tensions Between Author and Community in Hebrews" in *In the Spirit of Faith: Studies in Philo and Early Christianity in Honor of David Hay*, ed. D. Runia and G. Sterling, vol. 13 (Providence: Brown Judaic Studies, 2001), 190–211, is an excellent current assessment of Philo and Hebrews. He concludes that both the author and recipients of Hebrews betray knowledge of Platonizing exegetical traditions which were current among some first-century Jewish and

Narborough suggested "if Apollos was the author a puzzling phenomenon in 6:2 becomes at once intelligible." "Baptisms" in the plural is included among the fundamentals of Christian instruction since Apollos knew the baptism of John before he was taught the baptism of Jesus (Acts 18:25).[22] Such a connection is, however, so thin as to be virtually invisible.

Two major reasons seem to militate against Apollos as the author. First, the lack of any support from early church tradition, and second, the fact that there are no extant works of Apollos to which we may compare Hebrews.[23] Of course, many others have been suggested as author, but space prohibits discussion of each theory. The bibliography contains references for further detailed reading.

The Argument for Paul

A growing consensus against Pauline authorship developed in the twentieth century. However, the Patristic evidence for Paul, though inconclusive, should not be so easily dismissed. As shown above, of the three major traditions of authorship that circulated in the first four centuries, the Alexandrian tradition regarded Hebrews in some sense as the work of Paul. Pantaenus, mentor of Clement, suggested that Paul did not use his name in this epistle out of reverence for the Lord and to avoid suspicion (since he was known as the apostle to the Gentiles). The Pauline tradition continued to grow in Alexandria so that by the fourth century it was accepted, but often not without question.

Christian communities, but that there is no need to posit direct dependence (pp. 209–10). On this line of thought, see also Nash, "The Notion of Mediator in Alexandrian Judaism," 98–115. It is now generally recognized that Hebrews is not dependent on or indebted to Philo, nor does it exhibit any real Platonizing tendencies.

[22] F. D. V. Narborough, *The Epistle to the Hebrews* (Oxford: Clarendon Press, 1930), 14–15.

[23] A. Harnack's theory of Priscillian authorship is intertwined with the role which Priscilla and Aquila played in Apollos' Christian instruction in Acts. See his, "Probabilia über die Addresse und den Verfasser des Hebräerbriefs," *ZNW* 1 (1900): 16–41. See also F. Schiele, "Harnack's 'Probabilia' Concerning the Address and the Author of the Epistle to the Hebrews," *AJT* 9, no. 1 (1905): 290–308. Schiele attempted to advance Harnack's hypothesis by arguing, as Harnack did, that the letter was written to a Roman destination. He concluded, "It will not, therefore, seem a wholly groundless conjecture that, the lost address of the Epistle to the Hebrews may have run [*Priska kai 'Akulas, hoi adelphoi,] tois eklektois parepidemois episunagoges 'Hbraion, tois ousin en 'Roma, kletois hagiois…*" (p. 308). See the excellent critique of Harnack's position in C. C. Torrey, "The Authorship and Character of the So-Called 'Epistle to the Hebrews'," *JBL* 30 (1911): 137–56.

Pauline authorship began to be questioned again during the time of the Renaissance and Reformation, and doubt continues to the present time. Some have attempted to retain Paul's involvement in the writing of Hebrews, but in such a reduced and modified role that he could scarcely be called the author. For example, it has been suggested that Paul wrote only the final chapter, or the epistolary epilogue or conclusion (13:22–25).[24]

The inclusion of Hebrews in $\mathfrak{P}^{46}$, an Egyptian codex dated as early as AD 200 that contains a collection of Paul's writings, reveals that Hebrews was considered by some to be a part of the Pauline corpus at that time.[25]

William Leonard ably defended Pauline authorship of Hebrews in his classic *Authorship of the Epistle to the Hebrews*.[26] Roman Catholic scholars appear to be the largest group who still support the Pauline hypothesis (although departure from the Church's traditional position has become more frequent in recent years).[27] Christos Voulgaris argued for Pauline authorship in a 1999 article.[28] A three-part article by Eta Linnemann was published in German in 2000 and in English in 2002. She demonstrated that commentators have often overstated the case against Paul. David A. Black's three articles in 1999 and 2001 constitute the best argument for Pauline authorship today.[29]

---

[24] For the view that Paul wrote only the last chapter (Hebrews 13), see C. R. Williams, "A Word Study of Hebrews 13," *JBL* 30 (1911): 128–36, and E. D. Jones, "The Authorship of Hebrews XIII," *ExpTim* 46 (1934–35): 562–67. For Paul as the author of the epistolary benediction only, see J. Héring, *The Epistle to the Hebrews*, trans. A. W. Heathcote and P. J. Allcock (London: Epworth, 1970), 126.

[25] B. Metzger, *The Text of the New Testament* (New York and Oxford: Oxford Univ. Press, 1968), 37–38, 252.

[26] W. Leonard, *Authorship of the Epistle to the Hebrews* (Rome: Vatican Polyglot Press, 1939).

[27] The best discussion of the history of Catholic scholarship from the beginning of the 19th century to the sixth decade of the 20th century regarding the Pauline hypothesis is J. Frankowski's "Problemy autorstwa Listu do Hebrajczykow i etapy egzegezy katolickiej w dobie wspolczesnej," *Su* 6 (1968–69): 201–33.

[28] Christos Sp. Voulgaris, "Hebrews: Paul's Fifth Epistle from Prison," *GOTR* (1999): 199–206.

[29] E. Linnemann, "Wiederaufnahme-Prozess in Sachen des Hebräerbriefes," in *Fundamentum* 2 (2000): 102–12 (Part 1), 52–65 (Part 2), and 88–110 (Part 3), later appearing as "A Call for a Retrial in the Case of the Epistle to the Hebrews," trans. D. E. Lanier, *Faith and Mission* 19/2 (2002): 19–59; D. A. Black, "On the Pauline Authorship of Hebrews (Part 1): Overlooked Affinities between Hebrews and Paul." *Faith and Mission* 16 (Spring 1999): 32–51; "On the Pauline Authorship of Hebrews (Part 2): The External Evidence Reconsidered," *Faith and Mission* 16 (Summer 1999): 78–86; "Who Wrote Hebrews: The Internal and External Evidence Reexamined," *Faith and Mission* 18 (2002): 3–26.

Voulgaris supported Pauline authorship based on "new evidence," namely, the connection between Heb 13:23, Phil 2:19–24, and Phlm 22. A comparison of the information given in these three passages indicates that they are identical. Voulgaris believes *apolelumenon* in Heb 13:23 cannot mean "release from prison." Rather, Paul had sent Timothy on an unnamed mission, not mentioning either its intent or destination for security reasons. When Paul wrote to Philippi he expressed his desire to send Timothy (2:19–24). Paul also said he planned to visit Philippi (2:24).[30] All prison letters, including Hebrews, were written by Paul in Rome during his house arrest in AD 60–62.[31] After Timothy left for Philippi, Paul decided to write Hebrews to the church at Jerusalem. Paul wrote for two reasons: (1) to strengthen their faith and prevent a relapse into Judaism, and (2) Paul wanted to reconcile with the Christians in Jerusalem who were zealous for the law and to improve his relations with them. Paul informs them that Timothy is on his way to a mission (in Philippi) and as soon as he returns to Paul in Rome, both will come to Jerusalem.[32] The reason Paul does not allude to his imprisonment in Hebrews as he does in the other prison epistles is due to his imminent release (which he expected before the epistle reached its destination).[33]

Unfortunately, according to Voulgaris, Paul never made it back to Jerusalem. The time of his release coincided with the unexpected death of Porcius Festus, the Roman Governor of Judea in early AD 62. Jewish rioting followed, James was killed, and the surrounding area fell into political and social disorder. When Paul returned to Rome from Spain, he was forced to cancel his trip to Jerusalem. After a few years of freedom, he was imprisoned again in Rome and executed.[34]

This entire outline is quite speculative. However, it is plausible that Hebrews was written to the Jerusalem church after the death of James to reassure believers in the face of renewed persecution. On this dating, Hebrews would predate the beginning of the Jewish War by only a few years. Although I prefer to place its composition after AD 66, Voulgaris' suggestion relative to the date (and even its Jerusalem destination) is within the realm of possibility.

---

[30] Voulgaris, "Hebrews: Paul's Fifth Epistle from Prison," 200–3.
[31] Ibid., 204.
[32] Ibid., 205.
[33] Ibid.
[34] Ibid., 206.

David Black advanced the case for Paul by retracing the evidence of the church fathers and showing that many during that time considered Pauline authorship to be possible. He interpreted Origen's *ho grapsas* to mean "who served as Paul's amanuensis" and thus concluded that Origen affirmed Pauline authorship. Black also presented an accessible reading of the linguistic and theological evidence that had been offered by William Leonard more than 60 years ago.[35]

Eta Linnemann sought to bolster the case for Paul by lexical, stylistic, and literary comparison. Reviving the excellent work of C. Forster, she offered no new evidence as far as I can discern, but her article served to highlight the fact that Paul was not unaccustomed to using literary niceties and lexical similarities that were common to both the Pauline Letters and Hebrews. Linnemann's article is surprising in many ways. First, after acknowledging its anonymity, she wrongly concluded that "critical theologians," with their speculation over the authorship question, have "impaired" the authority of the epistle.[36] But how can that be? Critical theologians may impair biblical authority when they question what is clearly affirmed in Scripture, but how can that be the case when they speculate about the authorship of a book that is clearly anonymous?

Second, her statement, "up until the year AD 200, the Epistle to the Hebrews was generally considered to be a Pauline epistle," will come as a surprise to some scholars. Who in the second century considered it to be Pauline? The only name that can be produced is Pantaenus, whom Clement of Alexandria (quoted by Eusebius) reported as affirming that Hebrews was written by Paul. This hardly justifies the statement that Hebrews is "generally considered to be a Pauline epistle."

Third, her reference to Origen's dictum ("as to who wrote the epistle, only God knows") and those today who agree with it as "pseudopious" and "hindering lest the arguments against Pauline authorship of Hebrews be perceived in their inadequacy and decisively rejected,"[37] will simply raise smiles among scholars today. Such sweeping remarks deliberately ignore some 1,800 years of study which reach a near-unanimous conclusion that considerable evidence exists against Pauline authorship. While some of the arguments against Paul are

---

[35] Black, "Who Wrote Hebrews?" 3–26.
[36] Linnemann, "Call for a Retrial," 19.
[37] Ibid.

weak and inconclusive, it is myopic to assert that the body of evidence against Pauline authorship is inadequate and should be decisively rejected.

Despite these caveats, however, Linnemann reiterated the arguments of C. Forster, Moses Stuart, and William Leonard and made a good case for Pauline authorship. Her article is divided into six sections: manuscript evidence, the testimony of the early church, style, vocabulary, particularities of Hebrews used against Paul, and the line of argument in Hebrews. We shall briefly evaluate each section.

Linnemann surveyed the manuscript evidence, concluding that Hebrews is as well-attested as Romans. She then makes a leap in logic by asking if it is conceivable that an anonymous writing like Hebrews could have been canonized.[38] We are left to infer that Paul was the author, and that this explains the manuscript evidence and its acceptance into the canon. In evaluating the testimony of the early church fathers, she offered the surprising suggestion that Hebrews' absence from the Muratorian canon (c. AD 200) actually supports Pauline authorship. She quoted from the canon that Paul " . . . only writes to seven congregations with authorial attestation," and concluded that this "raises the possibility that Paul wrote to the Hebrews *without authorial attestation. —*if there *were* no letter without attestation, it would not have been necessary to point out that the subsequently named epistle had been written *with* authorial attestation."[39] Such reasoning appears to be very thin.

Linnemann's assessment of Origen's views is somewhat negative. She wondered how, if Paul was assumed to be the author, other possibilities (like Clement of Rome or Luke) were considered at that time. How could the testimony of Pantaenus remain hidden from them or from Origen? In light of this, she concluded that what Origen considered to be the tradition handed down was actually "an earlier collection of speculations" which Origen's contemporaries had circulated. Of course, this is itself sheer speculation. For Linnemann, the belief of Pauline authorship "was not so much condemned" as it was set aside on the basis that the thoughts were Paul's, but not the actual writing.[40]

---

[38] Ibid., 20.
[39] Ibid., 21 (emphasis original).
[40] Ibid., 23.

Her assessment of Tertullian's statement that Barnabas wrote Hebrews fares better. Her critique of Zahn's support of Barnabas as the possible author is valid in that Tertullian probably erroneously identified Hebrews with the *Epistle of Barnabas.*[41]

Linnemann devoted two short paragraphs to the possibility of Lukan authorship. She notes that not more than twenty words are unique to Acts and Hebrews and nine others are unique to Luke and Hebrews. She mentioned "some" words unique to Luke, Acts, and Hebrews. She then noted that 37 words are unique to both Hebrews and Romans, and 11 more words are unique to Hebrews, Romans, and 1 Corinthians, "yielding a total of 48 as compared to 27 for Luke and Hebrews.[42] Like so many before her, Linnemann's calculations are incomplete. As shown in chap. 3, there are 56 words unique to the Pauline Epistles (including the Pastorals) and Hebrews, and 53 words unique to Luke-Acts and Hebrews. On this basis alone, it would be impossible to argue against Lukan authorship. One might at least be able to argue for collaborate authorship.

She concluded there are no sufficient grounds for denying Pauline authorship from the Patristic evidence. This would appear to be a somewhat truncated view of the evidence. Nevertheless, she should be applauded for pointing out that some Patristic evidence exists for Pauline authorship, though it is not as strong as she asserts. One should also heed her comment that anonymity "makes it necessary to exercise ever greater care in consideration of all available facts."[43]

In evaluating the style of Hebrews, Linnemann criticized those who make "wholesale assertions" about Paul's inferior style. In fact, she entitled a subsection "Defamation," and castigated Donald Guthrie who "would presume to dress down the apostle Paul—as one would an ignorant grammar school pupil."[44] At this point, in spite of her strident language, I find myself in partial agreement with her. At times modern authors exaggerate the stylistic differences between Paul and Hebrews to the point of concluding the "impossibility" of Pauline authorship. While the stylistic argument against Paul is formidable—perhaps even devastating—it does not render the view "impossible." As judicious scholars note, it is merely "highly unlikely."

---

[41] Ibid., 24. See my previous discussion of Barnabas.
[42] Ibid., 26.
[43] Ibid.
[44] Ibid., 27.

Linnemann's section on style makes a more substantial case. She examined Harold Attridge's assertions in his commentary's section, "Literary Characteristics of Hebrews: Language and Style."[45] Linnemann succeeded in countering virtually all of Attridge's examples of Hebrews' so-called "better Greek" with similar examples from the Pauline Epistles, especially Romans. She considered 14 figures of speech in Hebrews, ranging from alliteration to paronomasia, and found Pauline examples for each. She admitted that there is a greater vocabulary range in Hebrews than in the Pauline Epistles of comparable length. She concluded that none of the characteristics of elevated Greek in Hebrews is absent from the Pauline Epistles and thus Attridge's claim is disproved. However, merely showing that such literary characteristics are not absent in Paul should not be turned into evidence for Pauline authorship in light of other stylistic differences that Linnemann does not address.

With respect to the vocabulary of Hebrews, Linnemann noted that 69.1% of the vocabulary occurs in the Pauline Epistles. She also indicated that 58 words occur only in Hebrews and the Pauline Letters.[46] She listed eight pronouns and particles occurring only in Hebrews and Paul. While this is perhaps the strongest evidence for Pauline authorship, Linnemann has not presented the total picture. As I shall demonstrate in chap. 3, there are no less than 53 words unique to Luke-Acts and Hebrews, only three less than the number of words unique to Paul and Hebrews. Nevertheless, Linnemann's work in this area shows that Hebrews has more in common with Paul's writings than many commentators care to admit.

Next Linnemann dealt with scholars who dispute Pauline authorship based on Hebrews' anonymity since this was not Paul's habit. She asks whether anonymity is ever a question of style. Rather, it is a question of necessity. "Whoever writes anonymously has grounds for so doing."[47] She accepted Clement of Alexandria's thesis that Paul wrote anonymously for the Jewish readers because of their strong prejudice against him. The lack of apostolic authority in Hebrews is another consequence of anonymous authorship. Finally, she noted that Barnabas, Apollos, Luke, or Clement of Rome had no reason to

---

[45] Ibid., 28–35; Attridge, *Hebrews*, 13–21.
[46] Ibid., 35. The count is actually 56.
[47] Ibid., 37.

write anonymously, so the letter's anonymity argues against their authorship and in favor of Paul.

This line of reasoning, however, faces a formidable problem. Internal evidence shows that the recipients knew who the author was. Furthermore, as Jewish Christians, the recipients would have welcomed a letter from Paul (unlike an audience of non-Christian Jews). These two facts, especially the first, significantly weakens her argument.

Her position is stronger when she deals with standard arguments against Paul, such as the lack of the Pauline "spiritual experience," the lack of numerous Pauline themes (including the High Priest theme), the author's use of the LXX, the inclusion of names referring to Jesus, and other theological differences.[48] She mostly succeeds in showing that the evidence is often overstated or overrated. She also offers a persuasive argument that Heb 2:3 does not automatically preclude Pauline authorship of the letter.

Linnemann has difficulty dealing with the absence of the phrase *en christō* in Hebrews when it occurs so frequently in the Pauline Epistles. Her hypothesis is that Paul avoids it to preserve his anonymity since the phrase might announce to the recipients that he was the author.[49] This is skating on very thin ice.

Her last section traces the line of argument in Hebrews to show that Paul could be the author. She makes periodic comparisons with Romans (the Pauline Epistle most like Hebrews in vocabulary, style, and theology) to show the similarity of Hebrews to Paul's thinking.[50]

She concluded there is no serious evidence against Pauline authorship. Unsubstantiated claims (beginning with Origen and passed down through history) have created a disposition against Paul that most scholars view with virtual certainty today. As her title indicates, she calls for a retrial in the case of the Pauline authorship of Hebrews.

We will now consider the arguments for Pauline authorship. They are based primarily upon three factors: (1) similarity in vocabulary, (2) some theological similarity, and (3) the historical testimony from the church fathers. It is striking that not one commentator on the Book of Hebrews actually engages Leonard's arguments in favor of Pauline authorship. Before any other theory can be reasonably considered, Leonard's work must be met head-on. For more than 400

---

[48] Ibid., 38–45.
[49] Ibid., 44.
[50] Ibid., 50–52.

pages (including appendices) he not only presents detailed evidence for Pauline authorship, but also produces an analysis of the epistle.

Space does not permit a page-by-page engagement of Leonard's arguments, nor is this necessary since much of his work analyzes the epistle without specific comparisons to Paul's Letters. The greatest concentration of evidence for similarity to the Pauline Letters is found in the latter part of chap. 1 (pp. 23–42), where Leonard carefully analyzes Hebrews and notes the Pauline parallels. I shall concentrate on this internal investigation and evaluate the strength of his evidence, and then critique each chapter.

Leonard begins by noting that the skillful interweaving of exposition and paraenesis in this epistle is unlike anything we have in the Pauline Letters.

> No greater contrast to the manner of Romans and Galatians and even of some other Pauline letters could well be imagined. It is, perhaps, in the matter of knitting arguments together logically and artistically rather than in vocabulary, or sentence-building that Hebrews is felt to be so different from the Pauline letters.[51]

Leonard contradicts Black, a contemporary defender of the Pauline hypothesis, on this issue. Black said that the paraenetic-dogmatic plan of Hebrews cannot be declared to be un-Pauline since, for example, Paul inserts Rom 6:12–14 and Gal 4:12–20 in doctrinal sections of those two books. Yet a careful study of Romans reveals how unlike Hebrews the first 11 chapters are. One has to read all the way to 6:12 in Romans to find the first imperative in the book! Black correctly identified Gal 4:12–20 as a paragraph unit, but only one imperative occurs in it (v. 12): "I beseech you, become as I am." This paragraph hardly functions as a paraenetic section like the warnings or other hortatory passages in Hebrews. There is no "parallel" between the Pauline writings and Hebrews on the alternating use of exposition and exhortation.[52]

However, Leonard reminds us that this should not sway our thinking against Paul since quite severe contrasts can sometimes be observed within an author's literary production. While we can agree with this explanation as far as it goes, the point is that the Pauline Letters taken together still betray a considerable difference of thought flow

---

[51] Leonard, *Authorship*, 23.
[52] Black, "Who Wrote Hebrews?" 4.

when compared to Hebrews, and the weight of this evidence certainly makes it less probable that Hebrews came from the pen of Paul.

Leonard admits that the "exquisite symmetry" found in the prologue to Hebrews has nothing to rival it in the Pauline Letters.[53] Again Leonard and Black are in contradiction: Black said, "It [the prologue] compares nicely with Paul's eulogy to love in I Corinthians 13, a passage that most scholars consider to be a literary masterpiece."[54] He does not mention the Lukan prologue, which is usually cited by grammarians and commentators as "parallel" in literary beauty. In fact, the Lukan prologue is a far more appropriate comparison than is 1 Corinthians 13.

Leonard notes that Paul, like the author of Hebrews, is fond of citing the Psalter. He cites no less than two- dozen Psalms (but some of these are from his Acts speeches and hence the Lukan choice of material must come into play). Three of the ten Psalms cited in Hebrews also occur in the Pauline Letters or in his speeches in Acts.

Hebrews 2:1–4 is introduced by the typically Pauline *dia touto*, "on account of this," or "therefore." Yet no special status can be granted to this argument in light of the fact that the same connecting phrase is found in Matthew, Mark, Luke, John, Acts, and the Johannine Epistles. In fact, Leonard observes that the connective phrases in Hebrews are "rather different from those of St. Paul."[55] Black pointed out that the adverb *perissoteros* occurs twice in Hebrews (6:17; 7:15) and 10 times in Paul but nowhere else in the New Testament, and *endikos* likewise occurs only in Heb 2:2 and Rom 3:8. These examples furnish genuine evidence in favor of Paul.[56]

The reference in 2:1–4 to angels being mediators of the law and to the charismatic signs are said to find striking parallels in Galatians 3 and 1 Corinthians 12.[57] Yet the same could be said for Stephen's speech in Acts 7 (where angels as mediators of the law are mentioned), and in Acts 2 and *passim* (where the charismatic signs occur). Indeed, Acts 2 is a much closer parallel to Heb 2:1–4 than the Corinthian passage. Again, no special status can be claimed for Paul here.

---

[53] Leonard, *Authorship*, 25.
[54] Black, "Who Wrote Hebrews?" 4–5.
[55] Leonard, *Authorship*, 25.
[56] Black, "Who Wrote Hebrews?" 5.
[57] Leonard, *Authorship*, 25.

Hebrews 2:3 (the word first spoken by the Lord and then "confirmed unto us by them that heard him") is usually taken as an argument against Pauline authorship since Paul does not class himself as one who heard the gospel from someone else. Leonard, followed by Black, countered this argument by pointing out that the writer is referring to Christ's public preaching during his earthly ministry which Paul had not heard.[58] While this may be a plausible solution to the problem, it is not the attitude we find in the Pauline Epistles where Paul magnifies his apostleship. Most scholars have not accepted Leonard's solution and Heb 2:3 remains a major obstacle for the Pauline authorship hypothesis.

In the same paragraph, Leonard notes that the term *sōtēria*, "salvation," is characteristic of Paul and Hebrews, although it is not exclusively Pauline (since it occurs 14 times in Luke-Acts and seven in Hebrews). It also occurs once in Mark, once in John, twice in Jude, and three times in Revelation. It is as much a characteristic word of Luke-Acts as it is of Paul and Hebrews.

In Heb 2:5–18 Leonard argues that the incarnation and passion of Christ prove the superiority of Jesus over the angels in an "eminently Pauline way."[59] The quotation of Psalm 8 here (and in 1 Cor 15:27) supports this view as well as the use of the expression "flesh and blood," which occurs only in Matthew, the Pauline Letters, and Hebrews.

The phrase *theou zōntos*, "living God," in Heb 3:12 reminds one of the Pauline Letters where it occurs six times. The phrase occurs four times in Hebrews, once in Acts, once in 1 Peter, and twice in Revelation.[60] While the phrase is most characteristic of Paul and Hebrews, it is not unique to them.

The lexical item *epaggelias*, "promise," is associated with the gospel in 4:1 and is paralleled in Acts 13:32 in Paul's Pisidian discourse. In both places it is associated with the verb *euaggelizō*, "to declare the glad tidings." Leonard observes that the word occurs often in the Pauline Letters and occurs no less than thirteen times in Hebrews.[61] It also occurs nine times in Luke-Acts and five times in the Petrine Letters. Thus, it is by no means a purely Pauline word. Furthermore,

---

[58] Ibid., 26.
[59] Ibid.
[60] Ibid., 28.
[61] Ibid.

the parallel between Heb 4:1 and Acts 13:32 in the use of this word actually links Hebrews more with Luke than it does with Paul.

In Heb 4:14–16, Leonard sees four parallels with the Pauline Letters as follows. First, the Greek word *homologia,* "confession," is a purely Pauline word occurring three times in Hebrews. Second, the noun *astheneia,* "weakness," is largely but not exclusively a Pauline word. Third, the son of God who possesses human nature without sin is said to be reminiscent of 2 Cor 5:20 (in that passage Christ's sinless nature is mentioned, though His humanity is not). The similarity in view here is conceptual, not verbal. Fourth, "although the verbal expression is considerably different and altogether more liturgical," the phrase "approach with confidence the throne of grace" calls to mind Rom 5:2; Eph 2:18; 3:12.[62] Again, the similarity is conceptual. These four examples serve as evidence that Hebrews is not as unlike the Pauline Letters in some places as we have often been led to believe.

Hebrews 5:12–10:18 is what Leonard calls the "sacerdotal center" of the epistle and contains fewer Pauline parallels since its subject matter is nowhere else so treated in Scripture. Nevertheless, 5:12–14 furnishes a strong parallel with 1 Cor 3:1–3 both in vocabulary (with the repetition of the words "babe," "milk," and "perfect"), and in the concept of spiritual immaturity.[63] Furthermore, the use of the phrase "having their senses exercised" (4:14) is Pauline in that only he speaks of exercising toward godliness (1 Tim 4:7). These are true Pauline parallels. However, the use of *trophē* 'food' is not found in the Pauline Letters, but is used eight times in Luke-Acts, twice in Hebrews (Heb 5:12,14), and four times in Matthew.

Leonard notes that the noun *teleiotēs,* "perfection," (Heb 6:1) occurs elsewhere only in Col 3:14. The expression *eanper epitrepē ho theos,* "if God permits" finds a very close verbal parallel in 1 Cor 16:7 with the phrase "if the Lord permits."[64] This latter example counts as a true Pauline comparison. However, the verb *epitrepō,* "to allow, permit," occurs six times in Luke-Acts and only three times in the Pauline Letters.

In the same paragraph Leonard points out that while the noun *metochos* is absent from the Pauline Letters (it occurs only in Luke and Heb 1:9; 3:1,14; 6:4; 12:8), the verb form is unique to Hebrews and

---

[62] Ibid., 29.

[63] Ibid., 30.

[64] Ibid., 31.

the Pauline Letters. He further notes that while the verb *anakainizō* is unique to Hebrews, the similar words *anakainoō*, *anakainōsis*, and *ananeoomai* are exclusively Pauline. The verb *geōrgeō*, "to cultivate," and the noun *geōrgion*, "field," are used respectively in Heb 6:7 and 1 Cor 3:9 but nowhere else in the New Testament.[65]

Leonard observes that in 6:9–12 the particular form of *peithō* (*pepismetha*) occurs only here and four times in the Pauline Letters.[66] He fails to note, however, that this particular form also occurs in Luke 20:6. The use of the triad faith, hope, and love is a Pauline concept that occurs twice in Hebrews: here and in 10:19–25, and this is a true Pauline parallel. Furthermore, the word *mimētēs* "to imitate" is also primarily Pauline in the New Testament (1 Cor 6:16; 11:1; Eph 5:1; 1 Thess 1:6; 2:14). However, the cognate *mimeomai* used in Heb 13:7 also occurs in 3 John 11 as well as 2 Thess 3:7,9.

In Heb 6:16–20, the notation that "God cannot lie" is paralleled in Titus 1:2 and is semantically equivalent to the positive statement in Rom 3:2, "let God be true, but every man a liar." Leonard argues that the use of *bebaiōsis* ("confirmation") and *bebaios* ("certain, secure") in 6:16,19 though not uniquely Pauline (occurring in Mark and Peter), does have a Pauline ring (i.e., Paul uses it eight times).[67]

Leonard observes that the subject in Heb 7:1–10:18 is so unique that parallels with the Pauline Letters are "necessarily few." However, it is possible, according to Leonard, to show that the author's views are not "remote from the fund of ideas contained in the Pauline Epistles."[68] Such concepts as the weakness of the law and the distinction of the two covenants are Pauline in nature, but certainly not exclusively so in the New Testament. Finally, Leonard argues that only Hebrews (five times) and Paul (twice, Rom 15:16; Eph 5:2) refer to Christ's voluntary death as *thusia* ("sacrifice") and *prosphora* ("offering"). But *prosphora* also occurs twice in Acts, and the cognate *prospherō* is used twenty times in Hebrews, but not once by Paul.

In Heb 10:19–25, Leonard observes, the second occurrence of the triad faith, hope, and love occurs, which is otherwise a Pauline trilogy. He further points out that the use of *suneidēsis*, "conscience," occurs five times in Hebrews and is a characteristically Pauline word. But it

---

[65] Ibid.
[66] Ibid., 32.
[67] Ibid.
[68] Ibid.

also occurs three times in 1 Peter and twice in Acts (both in Pauline speeches).[69] According to Leonard, Heb 10:26–31 is another passage with strong similarities to Pauline material. For example, Deut 32:35 is quoted in v. 30 and in Rom 12:19, but the wording (which is the same in both verses) does not correspond either to the Hebrew text or to the LXX.[70] Hebrews 10:32–39 shares two parallels with Pauline material. The term *theatrizomenoi* "to make a spectacle" reminds one of the corresponding noun *theatron* "a spectacle" in 1 Cor 4:9.[71] The only other writer to use this noun is Luke in Acts 19:29,31 but there it has the meaning of "a place for public shows."

The quotation of Hab 2:4, "the just shall live by faith," in v. 38 is paralleled by Paul in Rom 1:17 and Gal 3:11. These two examples constitute valid evidence for Pauline similarity.

Hebrews 11 also exhibits several Pauline lexical parallels. Leonard notes,

> The knowledge of the origin of the world, which rests on faith in the creative word of God (11.3), is set forth in the same intellectual terminology as the rational knowledge of God's existence and nature in Romans 1.20 (νοοῦμεν [*nooumen*] and νοοῦμεν κατηρτίσθαι [*nooumen katērtisthai*]) while the use of βλεπόμενα [*blepomena*] and βλεπόμενα [*blepomena*] in verse 3 recalls Romans 8.24, 1 Cor. 13.12, and especially 2 Cor. 4.18.[72]

The description of Abraham's faith in Hebrews 11 is echoed in Rom 4:19 with the use of *nenekrōmenon*. In the same vein the citation of Gen 21:12 in Heb 11:18 is also found in Rom 9:7. Finally, twice in Hebrews we read of the "reproach of Christ" and this is semantically similar to Paul's quotation of Ps 69:9 in Rom 15:3.[73]

Here also Leonard has presented valid evidence to show similarity to the Pauline literature. Most of the passages he cites to show a link between Hebrews and Paul are from Romans. If the thesis of Lukan authorship is correct, then it could be argued that Luke was quite familiar with a number of Pauline themes in Romans and later incorporated them when writing Hebrews. Luke was with Paul in Corinth when Romans was written (see Acts 20:4,5).

---

[69] Ibid., 33.
[70] Ibid., 34.
[71] Ibid.
[72] Ibid.
[73] Ibid., 35.

Hebrews 12:1–13 employs the athletic imagery that is common to the Pauline vocabulary. The use of *agōn,* "race," for the concept of the Christian life is unique to Paul and Heb 12:1.[74] In 12:22 Leonard notes the reference to the "heavenly Jerusalem," a phrase which corresponds to the "Jerusalem above" of Gal 4:26.[75] Leonard points out that the chapter concludes (12:29) with a short sentence or dictum characteristic of Paul's style.[76] However, it is difficult to give much weight to this argument because such dicta can be found in other New Testament writings such as James or the Johannine Letters. It may be a Pauline characteristic, but it is not exclusively Pauline.

Leonard found a number of Pauline parallels in both form and content in Hebrews 13, where Hebrews is perhaps most like the Pauline Letters. While Hebrews does not begin like an epistle, it certainly concludes like one. Hebrews 13 contains a series of short exhortations that are reminiscent of Rom 12:9–21. The epilogue (with its attendant doxology in 13:20,21) and the double concluding salutation in 13:24 (*aspasasthe...aspazontai*) are both Pauline in form (although both 1 Peter and 3 John also possess this closing double salutation). Finally, the concluding benediction "Grace be with you" is likewise Pauline.

There are similarities in content as well. The word *philadelphia,* "brotherly love," is used by Peter, Paul, and Hebrews, but only Paul and the writer of Hebrews connect it with *philoxenia* "hospitality" (Rom 12:13; Heb 13:2).[77] Leonard believes the phrase "let brotherly love remain" echoes Paul, but this phrase might be too generic to be restricted to Paul and Hebrews. The adjective *philarguros* "without love of money" occurs only in 1 Tim 3:3 and Heb 13:5. Furthermore, the verb *tharreō* "to speak boldly" occurs only in 2 Corinthians (five times) and Heb 13:6.[78] The use of the anarthrous (without the definite article) phrase *en sōmati* "in the flesh" occurs only in Heb 13:3 and 2 Cor 12:2,3.[79] The phrase *phagein ouk echousin* "they have no authority to eat" in Heb 13:10 is parallel in form to 1 Cor 9:4–6 but not parallel in reference.[80]

---

[74] Ibid.
[75] Ibid.
[76] Ibid., 36.
[77] Ibid.
[78] Ibid., 37.
[79] Ibid.
[80] Ibid., 39.

The call to *mnēmoneuō,* "remember," in 13:7 is Pauline in style, but not exclusively so since it is also found in Acts 20:31,35 (albeit in a Pauline speech). In addition, appeals to "remember" are made by Jesus in the Gospels as well as in Revelation. The noun "remembrance," which is used by Paul six times, never occurs in Hebrews. Leonard sees another Pauline parallel in the use of *peripateō,* "walk," in Hebrews.[81] This argument, however, lacks credibility since the metaphor is found elsewhere in the New Testament (especially in the Johannine Letters).

Leonard sums up all of this evidence and concludes there is "a cumulative series of internal indications which support the tradition of its Paulinity."[82] While Leonard has amassed a considerable amount of lexical evidence to support his position, many of his examples are not unique to Paul and Hebrews; therefore, they have limited value in determining the authorship of Hebrews. Furthermore, a critical reading of Leonard's book (especially pp. 23–43) could lead to the conclusion that his evidence of similarity points to other New Testament writers as possible authors of Hebrews—especially Luke. But his case does not end here. In the next section of his work, he moves to a discussion of the theology of Hebrews.

Leonard argues for Pauline likeness to Hebrews in the following nine areas: God and the angels, man, the preparation of salvation, the person of Christ, Christ's salvific work, subjective salvation, faith, the Holy Spirit and the Church, and eschatology.[83]

God and the Angels.   The doctrine of God in Hebrews shows no real divergence from Paul according to Leonard, but neither does he note any specific lexical or semantic parallels. In fact, Leonard notes that the description of God in Hebrews as the "father of spirits" is "remote from Pauline usage."[84]

Likewise, the angelology of Hebrews does not appear to be at variance with the Pauline Letters, but again neither does Leonard present any specific lexical or semantic comparisons. Rather than presenting evidence that would link Hebrews to Paul's Letters (over against other New Testament writings), Leonard appears to conclude that the lack of major theological differences between the two is sufficient to prove

---

[81] Ibid.
[82] Ibid., 43.
[83] Ibid., 46–106.
[84] Ibid., 47.

his point. Actually, it can be shown that Hebrews is much closer to Luke-Acts in its treatment of angels than any other New Testament writing (see chap. 5).

Man. A survey of the anthropology of Hebrews again does not reveal any unique doctrinal parallel to the Pauline Letters; in fact, as Leonard notes (quoting Westcott) the moral sense of *sarx,* "flesh," which is prominent in the Pauline Letters, but does not occur in Hebrews.[85] Hebrews also does not describe man as a "spirit" (as well as body and soul), while all three terms are used in Paul's anthropology. The one lexical parallel which Leonard uncovers is in Heb 13:17 and 2 Cor 12:5, where we find the phrase *huper tōn psuchōn humōn,* "for your souls."[86]

Preparation of Salvation. The concept of salvation history found in Hebrews is according to Leonard "not at variance with Paulinism."[87] He cites Rom 15:9, which refers to the promises made to the patriarchs. Once again, the same connection could be made to other New Testament writers, especially Luke. In fact, Hebrews shares a much closer conceptual framework and emphasis on the continuity/discontinuity of salvation history with Luke than with Paul or any other writer of the New Testament (see chap. 5).

Person of Christ. Certain facets of the Christology of Hebrews are somewhat akin to Pauline thought. Both present Christ as being in the image of God (Heb 1:3; Col 1:15), and both present him as the agent and sustainer of all creation (Heb 1:2,3; Col 1:16–17).[88] Yet there are considerable differences between Hebrews and Paul as well.

After a survey of the Christological titles found in Hebrews, Leonard admits:

> A comparison of the Messianic nomenclature in Hebrews and the Pauline letters certainly reveals some remarkable differences. Our author never uses the combination 'Christ Jesus' which is so frequent with St. Paul that over a dozen examples can be cited from Romans alone. Also noteworthy is the relative

---

[85] Ibid., 49.

[86] Ibid., 50.

[87] Ibid., 52.

[88] In addition, E. Ellis has noted: "There is, between Hebrews and Paul, an agreed Christological understanding of salient Old Testament passages" (*The Making of the New Testament Documents,* in Biblical Interpretation Series, ed. R. A. Culpepper and R. Rendtorff, vol. 39 [Leiden: Brill, 1999], 287).

infrequency of the name Jesus Christ (three examples as against seventeen [sic] in Romans).[89]

Additional differences are cited in this section. Hebrews does not make use of the Pauline terms *eikōn* (although the term is used in Heb 10:1) and *morphē* in describing the substantial essence shared by the Son and the Father.[90] It is striking that the Pauline emphasis on the resurrection of Christ, a doctrine occurring in nearly all his epistles, is not mentioned (although it is certainly assumed) in Hebrews (except in Heb 13:20).

Christ's Salvific Work.   Leonard notes that the redemptive work through Christ's physical body is common to the Pauline Letters and Hebrews (cf. Rom 7:4 and Heb 10:10).[91] But this is also a common theme in Peter's writings. The Christology of Hebrews is in fact much closer to Luke-Acts than to Paul in that an enthronement Christology is emphasized over against the two-foci Christology of the Pauline Letters (see chap. 5).

From a soteriological perspective, Leonard notes, "The essential redemptive work of offering sacrifice is here [in Hebrews] surrounded with a wealth of sacerdotal detail which is only very slightly paralleled in the Pauline Epistles."[92] He attempts to vitiate this evidence by an appeal to the fact that the two soteriologies are not mutually exclusive. Again, the mere fact that they are not mutually exclusive does not provide one with a good argument in favor of Pauline authorship. Hauck points out that Paul never used the verb *hupomenō,* "persevere," for Jesus' sufferings.[93] The differing conceptual emphases in Hebrews and the Pauline Letters certainly make it less likely that Paul was the author.

Subjective Redemption.   Under the rubric of "subjective redemption" Leonard discusses the mode by which believers appropriate Christ's sacrificial death. The concept of justification that is so prominent in the Pauline Letters "is only very slightly touched upon by the author of Hebrews."[94] Furthermore, we might add that the Pauline phrase *en Christō,* "in Christ," which occurs almost 170 times in his

---

[89] Leonard, *Authorship*, 55.
[90] Ibid., 62.
[91] Ibid., 63.
[92] Ibid., 66.
[93] *TDNT*, 4:588
[94] Leonard, *Authorship*, 78.

Letters is not once used in Hebrews. Once again, we can agree with Leonard that there is no contradiction between Paul and Hebrews on this aspect of theology, but we must disagree that this proves Pauline authorship.

Faith. The concept of faith in Hebrews is approached in a significantly different way than in the Pauline Letters. Where Paul often uses the verb *pisteuo*, "to believe," Hebrews uses it only twice. In addition, Pauline phrases like *pistis, Iēsou, eis Iēsoun, en Iēsou, pistis christou* and *eis christon* are totally absent from Hebrews.[95] Leonard asserts that the noun "faith" is just as common in Hebrews as in the Pauline Letters; but the emphases are different, making Pauline authorship less probable. Otto Betz has noted a "shift of emphasis" in Hebrews with regard to faith when compared to the Pauline Epistles. In Paul, faith primarily looks back, while in Hebrews it primarily looks forward. Yet Betz rightly notes similarities between Paul and Hebrews on the subject of faith. Paul indeed does have a concept of faith looking to the future as in 2 Cor 5:7 and Gal 3:22. Betz notes that Paul describes a failure of faith "in a way similar to that of Heb. 10:37–39" when he refers to Peter's lapse at Antioch in Gal 2:12,16.[96] Thus, it cannot be argued that the concept of faith in Hebrews is so different from Paul as to exclude him from authorship, but it should be noted that the focus in Hebrews is clearly different from Paul.

Holy Spirit. The doctrine of pneumatology in Hebrews is mentioned only briefly. Twice in Hebrews we find the citation formula "the Holy Spirit says," a phrase not found in the Pauline Letters. Leonard notes that the concept of Christ acting under the impulse of the Spirit "cannot have been unfamiliar to St. Paul, since it is so prominent in the Gospel of Luke and the Acts."[97] Again, this discussion provides no additional support for Pauline authorship.

Church. With respect to ecclesiology, Hebrews is not nearly as developed as the Pauline Letters. In Paul the dominant image for the church is the body of Christ; in Hebrews it is viewed as a house (Heb 3:1–6).

---

[95] Ibid., 84.

[96] O. Betz, "Firmness in Faith: Hebrews 11:1 and Isaiah 28:16," in *Scripture: Meaning and Method, Essays Presented to A. T. Hanson for His Seventieth Birthday,* ed. B. Thompson (North Yorkshire: Hull University Press, 1987), 109.

[97] Ibid., 92.

Eschatology. Finally, eschatology is also not as developed in Hebrews as in the Pauline Letters. Yet there are some similarities to be found. For example, "the day" refers to eschatological judgment in Heb 10:25 and in the Pauline Letters.[98] But by and large the eschatology of Hebrews is closer to the eschatology of Luke-Acts than to any other New Testament writing (see below).

Leonard's treatment of the theology of Hebrews succeeds in showing a number of parallels to the Pauline Epistles and thus provides valid evidence for the Pauline hypothesis. However, to argue for Paul on the grounds that no *significant* differences can be found between the Pauline Letters and Hebrews fails to give due weight to the differences that do exist as well as to the fact that New Testament writers exhibit different theological emphases.

For example, Anderson's excellent discussion of the theological significance of Abraham in Paul and Hebrews is instructive for the question of authorship.[99] Abraham plays a significant role in the theology of both authors. He is introduced at Heb 2:16 ("the descendants of Abraham"), and He appears in 6:13–20 as an example of those who inherit the promises through endurance. Two Abrahamic promises are of special interest to the author of Hebrews: his progeny (Gen 15:4–5) and his inheriting the land (Gen 15:7). In Hebrews, the promise of the land, eschatologically interpreted (Heb 11:9–16) has yet to be fulfilled. Another passage in Hebrews with ties to the Abrahamic promises in Genesis is Heb 6:13–20. Here the focus is on the oath God swears by His name to Abraham; it is a clear reference to Gen 22:16–17 (which is the only passage in Genesis where God swears an oath). The oath is particularly significant in Hebrews; it occurs two other times: in 4:3 (quoting Psalm 95) and in 7:21 (quoting Psalm 110). As Anderson rightly concludes: "God's oath is associated with three of the key teachings of the epistle: the blessing of Abraham regarding progeny, the priesthood and cultic activity of Jesus, and the availability of entrance into the 'rest.'"[100]

Hebrews 11:8–12 and 11:17–19 are the second and third Abrahamic passages (vv. 17–19 clearly refer to Genesis 22 as well). What is

---

[98] Ibid., 100.

[99] C. P. Anderson, "Who are the Heirs of the New Age in the Epistle to the Hebrews?" in *Apocalyptic and the New Testament: Essays in Honor of J. Louis Martyn*, ed. J. Marcus and M. Soards, JSNTSup 24 (Sheffield: Sheffield Academic Press, 1989), 255–77.

[100] Ibid., 260.

interesting and indicative for Anderson is "that despite the importance given the story of the sacrifice of Isaac, nowhere in Hebrews is any interest shown in that part of Genesis 22 which refers to Gentiles . . . (22:18). If Paul had quoted this passage (which he does not), surely that is one part he would have quoted—with emphasis added!"[101] Paul's favorite Abrahamic text is Gen 15:6 which furnished the foundation for his doctrine of justification by faith (see Rom 4:3). Abraham's faith preceded circumcision; therefore, Abraham was justified by faith before God while he was still a Gentile. Unlike portions of Genesis 15 and 17, which Paul quotes in Romans 4 and Galatians 3, Genesis 22 is the only passage of the three to mention Gentiles. However, Paul studiously avoids the entire passage. Why? It is damaging to his position. It could be wrongly interpreted by Paul's readers that Abraham was justified on the basis of his obedient act in Genesis 22 (and thus on the basis of a "work," not faith). Anderson therefore notes, "Unlike Hebrews . . . Paul looks to Genesis 15 rather than Genesis 22 for the promise of descendants to Abraham."[102] The upshot of all this illustrates the different focus of Paul and the author of Hebrews and thus furnishes an example of why theologically it is unlikely that Paul wrote Hebrews.[103]

Like Anderson, Marie Isaacs laments a reading of Hebrews that interprets it against a Pauline background and a Pauline approach to the relationship of Jews and Gentiles in the church. Hebrews does not seek to answer the problem of an emerging Gentile Christianity within a predominantly Jewish-Christian church. Such an approach is "wholly misleading." She also sees that Abraham is depicted in Hebrews differently than in Paul.[104]

---

[101] Ibid.

[102] Ibid., 263. See also J. Swetnam, *Jesus and Isaac: A Study of the Epistle to the Hebrews in the Light of the Aqedah*, AnBib 94 (Rome: Biblical Institute, 1981), 32–33, who makes the same point. Anderson, "Who are the Heirs," 263–66, suggests the justification element is absent from Hebrews (the verb δικαιόω is not found) and that the author of Hebrews does not view righteousness as a gift from God. This leads Anderson to conclude erroneously that the author of Hebrews and Paul "hold different views" on this issue. Actually they do not; it is simply a matter of a different focus.

[103] Of course it could be argued that Paul was writing to Gentiles in Romans and Galatians, and to Jewish Christians or Jews in Hebrews; hence the shift in focus could be explained. But in Romans Paul does not address only Gentiles; at the very least he speaks to a mixed audience of Jews and Gentiles. The same could be said of Galatians. Furthermore, the way in which the author of Hebrews fails to use the "gentile promise" portion of Gen 22 raises doubts about his supposed Gentile orientation, as Anderson noted ("Who are the Heirs," 262).

[104] J. Barclay and J. Sweet, eds., "Hebrews," in *Early Christian Thought in its Jewish Context* (Cambridge: Cambridge University Press, 1996), 157.

The majority of New Testament scholars still accept that there are more theological differences than similarities between Hebrews and the Pauline Letters, and that makes the Pauline hypothesis less probable.

Leonard devotes more than 110 pages to a study of the vocabulary and style of Hebrews compared with the Pauline Letters. Ironically, we find the best argument for the Pauline hypothesis in this study, as well as the most devastating argument against it. He observes that Hebrews possesses a broader vocabulary than any of the Pauline Letters, and that it shows "a sense of nicety that is very rare in other books of the N. T. outside of the Lucan writings."[105] Nevertheless, Leonard charts 56 words that are unique to Paul and Hebrews.[106] This is the largest number of unique words for Paul and Hebrews, a fact that in my opinion furnishes the greatest evidence for Pauline authorship.

The remainder of Leonard's discussion on the literary form of Hebrews offers evidence that the Pauline Letters share some stylistic features with this epistle. He observes, for example, that

> τε [te] is coupled with γὰρ [gar] at the beginning of a sentence only in Hebrews, Romans and second Corinthians; that such an unusual triple particle as τοιγαροῦν [toigaroun] presents itself only in Hebrews and first Thessalonians; that the exclusively Pauline νυνὶ δέ [nuni de] (occurring eighteen times in six epistles) turns up twice [sic] in Hebrews as a typically Pauline opening for a conclusion.[107]

He points out that the imagery and metaphorical usage of Hebrews also share a certain similarity to Paul (although this correlation is not always limited to Paul and Hebrews in the New Testament).[108]

Yet Leonard also presents an overwhelming argument against Pauline authorship: stylistic dissimilarity. So forceful is the evidence (the use of particles, the definite article, the use of *para* as a comparative preposition, the absence of the preposition *sun*, the use of the perfect in an aorist sense, the use of *hyperbaton*, rhetorical elegance, the placid calmness of expression, the flowing sentences, and rhythmic characteristics), that he is forced to admit that this material probably did not originate with Paul.[109] He opts for the likelihood of an

---

[105] Leonard, *Authorship*, 111.
[106] Ibid., 119.
[107] Ibid., 122.
[108] Ibid., 138–45.
[109] Ibid., 107, 216.

amanuensis who, with greater freedom than is usually granted, gave the epistle its stylistic color. Interestingly enough, Leonard considers Luke the most likely choice.[110]

Over the next three chapters of his book, Leonard examines the range of biblical quotations and the way they are cited in Hebrews compared with Paul's Letters (I will deal with this in chap. 3). Black notes that the author of Hebrews cites the Old Testament with some form of the verb "to say" (cf. 1 Cor 6:16; 15:27; 2 Cor 6:2; Gal 3:16; Eph 4:8; 5:14).[111] However, Black fails to mention that Paul's preferred method of quotation, "it is written," never occurs in Hebrews. He suggests Paul uses "to say" in Hebrews since he is writing to Hebrew Christians and thus uses the more rabbinical formula. So while Hebrews is somewhat distinctive in the way it cites other biblical texts, it does show some similarity to both Luke and Paul, and would seem to be more like Luke than Paul (see chap. 3).

Leonard's final chapter surveys the exegetical methods of Hebrews in its use of scriptural material in comparison with the Pauline Letters. His conclusion is in the main correct: there is nothing in Hebrews (with respect to quoting and interpreting Old Testament passages) that precludes Pauline authorship. But since all the New Testament writers treated the Old Testament with a certain homogeneity, this evidence cannot be given special status in favor of Pauline authorship.

Leonard provides many examples of Pauline thought and influence in Hebrews. The reference to "our brother Timothy" in Heb 13:23 reminds one of Paul since Timothy was so closely associated with the Pauline circle. And as Westcott observed, Paul always places the name "Timothy" first when he uses his name with *adelphon* (a total of ten times in the Pauline Letters), yet the writer of Hebrews places the adjective before the name in 13:23.[112] The benediction of 13:24–25 is reminiscent of Pauline Letters: "Salute all them that have the rule over you, and all the saints. They of Italy salute you. Grace be with you all, Amen."

An overall evaluation of Leonard's arguments for Pauline authorship of Hebrews leads to the following conclusions. First, without a doubt this is the most comprehensive compilation of evidence for

---

[110] Ibid., 218.
[111] Black, "Who Wrote Hebrews?" 5.
[112] Westcott, *Hebrews*, 451.

the view. When one couples Leonard's work of with that of Stuart and Forster a century earlier (who devoted almost 800 pages between them to the defense of Pauline authorship[113]), it becomes clear that the Pauline hypothesis cannot be as easily dismissed as modern scholars suppose. Paul's name must remain near the top of the list of possible candidates for authorship.

Second, Leonard gives too much weight to the testimony of the church fathers in favor of Paul's authorship.[114] Third, some of his evidence suffers from non-exclusivity (i.e., lexical, stylistic, or conceptual evidence that is not unique to the Pauline Letters and Hebrews, but is found in other New Testament writers). I am not suggesting that this evidence is inadmissible, only that it cannot be given as much weight as Leonard seems to give it.

Fourth, Leonard includes Paul's speeches in Acts in his comparative analysis of Hebrews. While I consider these speeches to be genuinely Pauline, I believe Leonard underestimates (or ignores) Luke's role in assembling and editing this material. One could argue (in comparing Paul's speeches with Hebrews) that they confirm Lukan, rather than Pauline, authorship of Hebrews. New Testament scholars would consider Leonard's methodology here to be somewhat flawed.[115]

Fifth, Leonard's argument for Paul is often that there is no essential contradiction between Paul and Hebrews, rather than a positive argument based on evidence. This is usually his *modus operandi* when there is little or no evidence with which to make a positive comparison. While it is at times necessary to show that two works do not contradict one another in vocabulary, style, or content, this hardly

---

[113] M. Stuart, *A Commentary on the Epistle to the Hebrews*, 4th ed., ed. and rev. R. D. C. Robbins (Andover: Warren F. Draper, 1876), esp. 117–56; and C. Forster, *The Apostolical Authority of the Epistle to the Hebrews* (London: James Duncan, 1838). Stuart's work was the leading 19th century argument for Pauline authorship. Yet, as J. Conder noted, in Stuart's zeal he labors to prove, "in opposition to every critic ancient and modern, that Hebrews abounds in Hebraisms" (*The Literary History of the New Testament* [London: Seeley, Burnside & Seeley, 1845], 448). Yet Stuart notes that Luke's style is nearer to Hebrews than the style of Barnabas (in the pseudo-epistle) to which Tertullian ascribes authorship. Forster's work is the most complete tabulation of vocabulary similarities between Paul and Hebrews and includes a harmony of the parallel passages comparing vocabulary, style, and content. Linnemann drew heavily upon Forster's work for her recent articles cited above.

[114] This is also a problem with Black's argument for Paul in "Who Wrote Hebrews?" 3–26.

[115] Forster, *The Apostolical Authority*, 61–63, makes the same mistake when he notes Paul's use of τιμωρέω in Acts 22:5 and 26:11 compared with Heb 10:29. He sees this as evidence of Paul's authorship, but it could just as easily be evidence for Lukan authorship.

constitutes positive evidence for a particular author. Leonard tends to minimize the differences between the Pauline Letters and Hebrews.

In summary, the following problems provide the greatest evidence against the Pauline hypothesis. First, Paul's name does not appear in the prologue as it does in his other writings. There are 13 letters of Paul in the New Testament canon, and each one contains a salutation which identifies the writer as the great apostle. In fact, the first word in the text in each letter is Paul's name. In Hebrews, however, Paul's name does not occur, the readers clearly knowing who the author was.

Second, Hebrews lacks the characteristic salutation that begins each of the Pauline Letters. After identifying himself, it was Paul's custom to state the location of the recipients of his letter, as for example Rom 1:7: "to all that be in Rome. . . ." Then a typical Pauline greeting would follow: "Grace and peace be to you from God our father and from the Lord Jesus Christ." Significantly, Hebrews lacks all three of these salutary characteristics that mark the Pauline Epistles. This fact has caused many scholars to deny Pauline authorship to Hebrews.

Third, from a stylistic perspective, Hebrews is certainly divergent in many ways from the other letters of Paul. This fact has been noted from earliest times in the history of the church. As noted above, Clement of Alexandria, Origen, and Eusebius all mentioned the difference in style between the known writings of Paul and the epistle to the Hebrews. Godet writes,

> It is strange indeed that [Paul] should have written in polished Greek to the Hebrews, while all his life he had been writing to the Hellenes in a style abounding with rugged and barbarous Hebraisms.[116]

There is a certain similarity between chap. 13 and the writings of Paul. This has led some scholars to make the unlikely suggestion that Paul may have added this chapter to the letter.[117] Others have suggested that it is a fragment from an otherwise unknown Pauline Epistle. However, chap. 13 gives no hint of having been added to Hebrews by

---

[116] F. L. Godet, *A Commentary on the Gospel of Luke*, 4th ed., trans. E. W. Shalders and M. D. Cusin, (New York: Funk & Wagnalls, 1887), 320.

[117] Conder, *Literary History*, 466, speculates that Silas and Luke are the same individual, who wrote Hebrews but perhaps died and then Paul appended the exhortations to chap. 13. He states that if Hebrews were not written by Paul, "both internal and external evidence would lead us to refer its composition to Silas or Luke."

Paul or anyone else. Floyd Filson has conclusively shown it to be an integral part of the text.[118]

It must be stated at this point that stylistic comparisons cannot in and of themselves prove or disprove Pauline authorship of Hebrews conclusively. The key word here is "conclusively." It can be demonstrated that an author may change his style deliberately to accommodate his subject matter. Furthermore, over the period of an author's life, his style can change to such a degree that one can speak of an author's "early" writings and his "later" writings not only in terms of thought patterns and content, but also in terms of style. Therefore, it would be overstating the case to suggest on the basis of stylistic comparisons that Paul *could not* have written Hebrews.

However, literary studies have shown that stylistic comparisons can furnish rather strong evidence for or against a particular author if we remember that we are dealing within the realm of probability. The Pauline Letters exhibit certain stylistic features that one the one hand tend to corroborate the supposition that Paul is the author of Hebrews; but that on the other hand the epistle is stylistically so unlike the Pauline Letters that we can say that Paul probably did not write it.[119] Narborough stated, "1 Peter is more Pauline than Hebrews, and yet no one would dream of assigning 1 Peter to St. Paul."[120] DeSilva pointedly remarked: "To suggest that Paul was simply writing in a different style, as if preaching in a synagogue, is a desperate attempt to hold on to Pauline authorship."[121]

---

[118] F. Filson, "*Yesterday: A Study of Hebrews in the Light of Chapter 13,*" SBT, vol. 4 (London: SCM, 1967), 15–16. F. Overbeck made an elaborate case for seeing the ending of Hebrews as a part of the church's effort to canonize the letter by attributing it to Paul (see B. Childs, *The New Testament as Canon: An Introduction* [London: SCM, 1984], 405). All such efforts, in light of the unity of the text itself, lack necessity and are exercises in futility. Some possibility exists for Schnelle's thesis that perhaps the author of Hebrews took a speech not originally intended for further distribution and provided an epistolary conclusion himself in order to send it as a real letter. Thus, Heb 13:22–25 can be understood as a supplement or cover letter (see U. Schnelle, *The History and Theology of the New Testament Writings*, trans. E. Boring [Minneapolis: Fortress, 1998], 374). However, in light of the unity of the epistle as evidenced by its argument and flow and noted by W. G. Übelacker, *Der Hebräerbrief als Appell, Untersuchungen zu exordium, narratio und postscriptum (Hebr 1-2 und 13,22–25)*, ConBNT 21 (Lund: Almzvist & Wiksell International, 1989), 197–201; and W. L. Lane, *Hebrews 9–13*, WBC (Dallas: Word, 1991), 405, the conclusion appears to be a part of the literary composition of the original author and not appended later.

[119] R. Brown noted that the Greek style of Hebrews is "very different from Paul's" and that when parallels in phrasing and theology are cited, differences exist in most of them" (*New Testament Introduction* [New York: Doubleday, 1997], 694).

[120] Narborough, *Hebrews*, 9.

[121] DeSilva, *Perseverance in Gratitude*, 24.

Recent work by Malherbe, Betz, and Kennedy on the New Testament and rhetoric demonstrate that Paul was aware of and made use of rhetorical methods in his writings.[122] These studies can be used to argue that Paul was capable of writing Hebrews and that it reflects his rhetorical style. However, Dean Anderson's *Ancient Rhetorical Theory and Paul* is a serious blow to many of the conclusions of this triumvirate, especially Kennedy.[123] In addition, Stanley Porter has raised a number of cautions concerning the use of rhetorical theory in interpreting Pauline literature.[124]

Fourth, the theological focus of Hebrews is different from Paul's writings.[125] As has been noted by many, there is a marked absence of characteristic Pauline thought, themes, and motifs. Delitzsch noted: "It is, and must remain, surprising that as we dissect the Epistle we nowhere meet with those ideas which are, so to speak, the very arteries of Paul's spiritual system."[126]

Hebrews has a different theological focus than Paul. The two authors are not contradictory, but there is clearly a different "feel" to Hebrews when compared to the Pauline Letters. For example, Paul never refers to Jesus as priest, though he did use concepts from the milieu of the cultus such as Passover, the mercy seat, and Jesus as an offering to God. Paul places more emphasis on the method of Christ's sacrifice; the author of Hebrews focuses more on the result.[127] Some find it difficult to conceive of Paul writing Heb 2:17 since his theology

---

[122] A. Malherbe, *Paul and the Popular Philosophers* (Minneapolis: Fortress, 1989); H. Betz, *Galatians: A Commentary on Paul's Letter to the Churches in Galatia*, Her (Philadelphia: Fortress, 1979); G. A. Kennedy, *New Testament Interpretation Through Rhetorical Criticism* (Chapel Hill: The University of North Carolina Press, 1984).

[123] See especially R. D. Anderson Jr., *Ancient Rhetorical Theory and Paul* (Louvain: Kok Pharos, 1996), 26–27, 249–57, where he summarizes his critique. On the use of Greek rhetoric as a tool of New Testament interpretation, see the bibliographic information in Daniel Buck, "The Rhetorical Arrangement and Function of OT Citations in the Book of Hebrews: Uncovering Their Role in the Paraenetic Discourse of Access," (Ph.D. diss., Dallas Theological Seminary, 2002), 81. R. D. Anderson, "The Theoretical Justification for Application of Rhetorical Categories to Pauline Epistolary Literature," in *Rhetoric and the New Testament*, ed. S. Porter and T. Olbricht, (Sheffield: Sheffield Academic Press, 1993), 100–22.

[124] Anderson, *Theoretical Justification*, 100–22.

[125] For theological differences see Guthrie, *New Testament Introduction*, 672–73; Westcott, *Hebrews*, lxxvii–lxxviii; J. Moulton and G. Milligan, *The Vocabulary of the Greek New Testament* (Grand Rapids: Eerdmans, 1952), 24–26; and Lindars, *The Theology of the Letter to the Hebrews*. This should not be interpreted to mean that Hebrews and Paul are "at odds" doctrinally. In fact, they are similar in many of their underlying concepts.

[126] Delitzsch, *Hebrews*, 2:412.

[127] J. E. Reynolds, "A Comparative Study of the Exodus Motif in the Epistle to the Hebrews" (Th.D. dissertation, Southwestern Baptist Theological Seminary, 1976), 207–8.

of the cross eliminated the need for a High Priest, the temple, and the Day of Atonement.[128] There is a distinct difference in the way Paul speaks of "the seed of Abraham" in his letters and the approach taken by Hebrews and Luke in Luke-Acts.[129] This should not be used to argue that Paul could not have written Hebrews, only that it makes it less likely that he did.

Fifth, the writer of Hebrews seems to place himself with second generation Christians in Heb 2:3, something that Paul would probably never do: "How will we escape if we neglect such a great salvation? It was first spoken by the Lord and was confirmed to us by those who heard Him." Paul elsewhere in his epistles identified himself as an "apostle," someone who had been an eyewitness of the resurrected Christ. In Acts 9, Luke recounts Paul's experience on the road to Damascus when he met Jesus Christ and became a Christian. Paul referred later to this experience in the context of his apostleship when he said that he was "one born out of due time" (KJV). Nowhere in the 13 epistles does Paul ever refer to himself as the writer of Hebrews does in 2:3. Thus, it is unlikely that Paul would have written such a statement.

Sixth, the unusual statement of Heb 13:22 ("Brothers, I urge you to receive this message of exhortation, for I have written to you briefly") does not fit well with the acknowledged length of Paul's other letters. As a matter of fact, Hebrews is longer than 11 of the 13 Pauline Epistles and more than twice as long as their average length. Unless Paul had addressed other epistles of considerably greater length to this same readership, it does not seem likely he would have written such a statement.

However, if Trudinger's interpretation of this statement is correct, then this verse could not be used against Pauline authorship. He suggested that Hebrews 13 contains statements of "authoritative advice" and "injunctional appeal" which fall within the lexical domain of

---

[128] As, for example, R. Anderson, "The Cross and Atonement from Luke to Hebrews," EvQ 71, no. 2 (1999): 141.

[129] See the discussion in J. B. Chance, "The Seed of Abraham and the People of God: A Study of Two Pauls," SBLSP, no. 32, ed. E. Lovering (Atlanta: Scholars Press, 1993), 384–411. Chance notes that in Luke-Acts, unlike Paul in Galatians and Romans, no character, including the narrator, refers to Gentiles as "children, seed, descendents, sons, daughters, or any other similar term of Abraham or any of the other ancestors of Israel. The seed of Abraham is the Jewish people. The gentiles are simply not in view" (p. 406). He later notes that Luke-Acts operates within a traditional Jewish social context. Of course, Hebrews takes a similar approach as Luke-Acts here.

paraklēsis, "exhortation," and for which the writer would have requested a patient hearing.[130] If *epistellō* can mean "enjoin" or "instruct" as Moulton and Milligan suggest in this instance,[131] then the proper translation would be something like "bear with my words of instruction and admonition, for my commands have been but brief!"[132]

Four problems scuttle this novel interpretation. First, it is indeed odd that no translator or commentator follows this line of interpretation. Second, it is doubtful that *paraklēsis* will bear such a restricted meaning in this context. This may explain why no translators or commentators have followed it. Third, it is also doubtful that *epesteila* can bear the restrictive meaning "to instruct" in this context. Fourth, Trudinger's translation, "words of instruction," fails to accurately translate the singular *logos*, "word," thus weakening the suggestion. It would seem then that this passage opposes the Pauline hypothesis.[133]

A number of authors since Spanheim and John Owen have proposed the possible connection between Peter's statement in 2 Pet 3:15–16 and Hebrews as evidence for Pauline authorship.[134] "Even as our beloved brother Paul also, according to the wisdom given unto him, wrote unto you; as also in all his epistles, speaking in them of these things; wherein are some things hard to be understood . . . ." Since Peter is writing to Jewish Christians of the Diaspora, the question arises which Pauline epistle is referred to here? Many have suggested that it is Hebrews. Peter's statement that some of Paul's writings are "hard to understand" parallels what the author of Hebrews says to his readers in 5:11: "We have a great deal to say about this, and it's difficult to explain, since you have become too lazy to understand."

Forster thought 2 Pet 3:15–16 alluded to Heb 5:11, 6:12, 9:26,28 and 10:39. He concluded that Peter unconsciously or consciously "imitated" Paul and this proves that Peter had studied all the Pauline

---

[130] P. Trudinger, "καὶ γὰρ διὰ βραχέων ἐπέστειλα ὑμῖν: A Note on Hebrews 13:22," *JTS*, New Series 23 (1972): 128–30.

[131] Moulton and Milligan, *The Vocabulary of the Greek Testament*, 245–46.

[132] Trudinger, "A Note on Hebrews 13:22," 130.

[133] R. Hoppin, *Priscilla's Letter: Finding the Author of the Epistle to the Hebrews* (Fort Bragg, CA: Lost Coast Press, 1997), 20, picks up on Trudinger's interpretation and uses it to defend Priscilla as the author of Hebrews. " . . . who would end the treatise with an outright apology? Who would apologize for giving orders—only a little? Was the author a woman?"

[134] Owen, *Hebrews*, 1:83–87, has the best discussion of this suggestion, but one can only smile when he concludes "I have insisted the longer upon this testimony, because, in my judgment, it is sufficient of itself to determine this controversy."

Epistles, including Hebrews.[135] F. F. Bruce countered this suggestion by pointing out that 2 Peter was not written specifically to Hebrew Christians and the reference in 2 Pet 3:15 is, in his words, "surely to Rom. 2:4."[136] It is doubtful to say the least that 2 Pet 3:15–16 applies to Hebrews at all. As Mclintock and Strong rightly noted, if the "you" whom Peter addresses refers to all Christians (2 Pet 1:1), the reference could not be limited to Hebrews. If it includes only the Jews named in 1 Pet 1:1, the author may be making special reference to the Galatians (Gal 6:7–9) and Ephesians (Eph 2:3–5), but not to the Hebrews.[137]

While there is some historical and internal evidence that Paul could have written Hebrews, the many examples of dissimilarity, coupled with the historical testimony that does not strongly support Pauline authorship, leads us to conclude that Paul probably did not write Hebrews.[138] New Testament scholarship has been reluctant to divorce the epistle to the Hebrews from Pauline influence,[139] yet it has also been reluctant to identify the epistle as Paul's. It would seem that the best solution to the evidence of the epistle itself would be to deny Pauline authorship, but to acknowledge that the writer was considerably influenced by Paul and may have been associated with him. All the names suggested for authorship by the church fathers possessed the distinction of having at one time or another been a part of the Pauline circle.[140]

---

[135] Forster, *Apostolical Authority*, 38–39. See also his full discussion on pp. 625–44.

[136] F. F. Bruce, *The Epistle to the Hebrews*, NICNT, rev. ed. (Grand Rapids: Eerdmans, 1990), 20.

[137] J. Mclintock and J. Strong, "Epistle to the Hebrews," *Cyclopedia of Biblical, Theological and Ecclesiastical Literature* (Grand Rapids: Baker, 1969), 4:146.

[138] R. Brown, *An Introduction to the New Testament* (New York: Doubleday, 1997), 694, states that the evidence against Paul writing Hebrews is "overwhelming."

[139] Windisch considers the author of Hebrews to be nearer to Pauline thought and themes than any other New Testament writer, but he rejected Pauline authorship (*Der Hebräerbrief*, 2nd ed., HNT 14 [Tübingen: Mohr, 1931], 128–29).

[140] In recent years, the discussion has continued as to whether or not the author belonged to the Pauline circle. Primitive Christian tradition furnished Schröger "Der Hebräerbriefópaulinisch?" in *Kontinuität und Einheit*, ed. F. S. F. Mussner, P. G. Müller and W. Stenger (Freiburg/Basel/Vienna: Herder, 1981), 211–22 with the basis for any similarity between Paul and Hebrews. A. Strobel, *Der Brief an die Hebräer*, 13th ed. (Göttingen: Vandenhoeck & Ruprecht, 1991), 13–15, suggested that the author might have belonged to the circle of people involved in later Pauline missionary work. Some have suggested that the epistolary conclusion (Heb 13:22–25), while similar to the Pauline form, could have been added to the letter by someone other than the author, perhaps by the editor of a collection of Pauline Letters, as in, for example, Schnelle, *The History and Theology of the New Testament Writings*, 376–81. Schnelle also pointed out that if the conclusion is original, "the only positive indication that could be based on it is that the author of Hebrews wants his writing to be understood within the context of Pauline theology." A more positive comparison of Hebrews with the Pauline school of thought was suggested by Ruager,

Collins evaluated Hebrews against the Pauline Epistles and like-wise concluded that Paul was not the author.[141] Hurst, after briefly evaluating the history of discussion regarding Pauline influence upon the author of Hebrews, drew the following three conclusions: (1) The differences rule out Hebrews as "deutero-Pauline" in the sense of literary borrowing by a Pauline disciple. (2) The similarities indicate an interaction with the same ideas normally identified with Paul himself, and rule out the view of Menegoz and others that the author could not at some point have been a disciple of Paul. (3) If it is recognized that there is a sense in which the apostolic tradition grew in a way in which Paul and his associates may have had a significant part, there may be a basis for claiming Pauline influence in the epistle without recourse to the literary solution [that Paul wrote it].[142]

Likewise, Windisch listed a number of similarities between Paul and Hebrews, concluding that a disciple of Paul or someone else with the same theological approach reproduced similar elements in the tradition.[143] Based on his comparison of Galatians with Hebrews, Witherington denies Pauline authorship, but suggests that it is "likely" the author of Hebrews reflects Pauline influence (particularly from Galatians) at key points in the argument. He also considers it likely that the author of Hebrews was a part of the larger Pauline circle.[144]

Brevard Childs pointed out there is an important indirect link between Paul and Hebrews that the early church recognized but misinterpreted when it sought to solve the issue historically. Since the writer was a co-worker with Timothy, Hebrews should not be assigned to a later stage in the development of the post-apostolic church. It functions canonically as distinct yet complementary to the Pauline corpus. Childs

---

Hebräerbrief, Bibelkoommentar, Band 22 (Neuhausen -Stuttgart: Hanssler, 1987), who argued that the author worked with Timothy and was a member of the Pauline circle, and by K. Backhaus, *Der Hebräerbrief und die Paulus-Schule,* BZ 37 (1993): 183–208, who argued that the conclusion of Hebrews indicates contacts between the author and the Pauline school in Rome. (See p. 187 for a succinct listing of Christological and soteriological parallels between the Pauline Epistles and Hebrews.) The opposite conclusion has been drawn by James Thompson, who concluded the recipients of Hebrews were probably located at Rome and acquainted with Timothy, but "the relationship between Hebrews and the Pauline tradition is minimal" (J. Thompson, "The Epistle to the Hebrews and the Pauline Legacy," *ResQ* 47, no.4 [2005]: 206).

[141] R. F. Collins, *Letters Paul Did Not Write: The Epistle to the Hebrews and the Pauline Pseudepigrapha,* GNS 28 (Wilmington: Glazier, 1988), 39–55.

[142] L. D. Hurst, *The Epistle to the Hebrews: Its Background and Thought* (Cambridge: Cambridge University Press, 1990), 124.

[143] Windisch, *Der Hebräerbrief,* 128–29.

[144] B. Witherington III, "The Influence of Galatians on Hebrews," *NTS* 37 (1991): 146–52.

goes on to note that historically, Manson may be right in connecting the letter with Stephen, but canonically the letter's major relationship is with the Pauline corpus.[145] This connection with Paul actually aids the arguments for Luke, Barnabas, and Apollos, since they were all part of the Pauline circle. But, of course, no one was as consistently associated with Paul as Luke. Furthermore, the connection with Stephen would be further evidence for Luke, as will be shown below. For Schnelle, the whole issue comes down to the relationship of Hebrews to the Pauline school, with two possibilities. Either the author belonged to the Pauline circle, or Hebrews was composed from the beginning as an anonymous writing with no intent of being linked to Paul.[146]

We conclude, then, that the best reading of the evidence suggests that Paul is not the author of Hebrews. Dogmatic conclusions like that of Spicq that Pauline authorship is "impossible" are not called for.[147] Forster's comment concerning Michaelis's point that the Greek style of Hebrews is significantly different from Paul (and thus excludes him from authorship) is particularly pungent: Michaelis's treatment "is as conveniently superficial as the conclusion which he here draws is presumptuously dogmatic."[148] It is better to reach a more judicious conclusion like Davidson's: "It is the diversity amid the similarity [with Paul's writings] which makes a different writer probable."[149] Present attitudes on the subject of Pauline authorship can best be summed up by MacNeill and Guthrie, one writing in the early twentieth century, the other in the latter half of the twentieth century. MacNeill wrote:

> In the course of this study numerous instances of contact with Pauline thought have appeared. But in every case the similarity has been somewhat superficial. The point of view and the method of presentation have been quite different. It would be exaggerating to say that the writer of this epistle was not influenced by Paul and his letters. But it is clear that this influence has been greatly exaggerated.[150]

---

[145] B. Childs, *The New Testament as Canon: An Introduction* (London: SCM, 1984), 416.

[146] Schnelle, *The History and Theology of the New Testament Writings*, 380–81. Schnelle opts for the latter: " . . . the author cannot be seen as a member of the Pauline school. It is rather the case that Hebrews represents an independent theology" (p. 376).

[147] Spicq, *Hébreux*, 1:154.

[148] Forster, *Apostolical Authority*, 24.

[149] S. Davidson, *Introduction to the Study of the New Testament*, 2nd ed. (London: Longmans, Green & Co., 1882), 1:215. Davidson has an excellent presentation of the external (patristic) evidence for and against Pauline authorship on pages 220–35.

[150] H. L. MacNeill, *The Christology of the Epistle to the Hebrews: Including Its Relation to the Developing Christology of the Primitive Church* (Chicago: Chicago University Press, 1914), 143.

Guthrie said:

It should be noted that differences from Paul do not amount to disagreements with Paul. . . Nor must it be supposed that these doctrinal differences necessarily exclude Pauline authorship. Yet, if they do not require its rejection, it must be admitted that they appear to suggest it.[151]

---

[151] Guthrie, *New Testament Introduction*, 673.

Chapter 3

THE LINGUISTIC ARGUMENT: LEXICAL, STYLISTIC, AND TEXTLINGUISTIC EVIDENCE

The work of the theologian is always preceded by and predicated on the work of the philologian. The obvious point of departure in any study of authorship is the language of the text itself. Barring clear external, historical testimony regarding authorship, comparisons of the unattributed work with a suspected author must begin at the linguistic level. Until we look at the linguistic phenomena, we cannot continue the discussion of authorship. We begin by studying the lexical and stylistic data at the lower discourse level of words, phrases, clauses, and sentences; we then move to the higher levels of paragraphs, sections, and ultimately the entire discourse. The linguistic data provides the strongest evidence to support or deny theories of authorship.

Hebrews and the New Testament

Before we begin a specific linguistic comparison of Hebrews with Luke-Acts and the Pauline Letters, we need to examine how it compares with other New Testament documents. Outside the Pauline Letters and Luke-Acts, Hebrews has been compared to Mark, the Johannine Gospel and Letters, and the Petrine Letters.

Hebrews and Mark

Graham compares three points in Mark with Hebrews: (1) the vocabulary of awe used to describe God and His work, (2) the picture of Jesus as leader and pioneer, and (3) the emphasis on Jesus' complete involvement in human misery. From these points Graham drew two conclusions. First, there is evidence here of a reaction to persecution somewhat different from other New Testament writings. Second, this reaction comes not from the church at large, but from the church at Rome. The climax of Mark is the rending of the veil, which is alluded to in Heb 10:19–21.Thus, perhaps Mark and Hebrews emanate from the same church.[1]

---

[1] A. A. K. Graham, "Mark and Hebrews," *SE* 4 (1968): 411–16.

Hebrews and John

Spicq's commentary cites 16 parallels between Hebrews and the Johannine Letters, mostly conceptual or theological similarities such as a high Christology (Jesus as Son and Word, revelation of God), soteriology, the prologues (Heb 1:1–3; John 1:1–18), and Christ functioning as priest (Heb 4:14–16) and our advocate (1 John 2:1–2). He concludes that the author of Hebrews was most likely dependent on an early catechesis behind the Johannine writings, which later found its way into John's Gospel and letters, and furthermore, that the author of Hebrews had some direct contact with John when he wrote his Gospel.[2] Hickling likewise detects a parallel between John and Heb 2:10–18, suggesting that a common tradition and way of viewing and teaching Christianity undergirded both.[3] Raymond Brown places Hebrews and John in the fourth of his four typological categories of various groups in early Christianity based on their shared stance toward the law.[4] Yet none of these authors posit any direct dependence, literary or otherwise.

Hebrews and the Petrine Letters

The similarities between these letters have long been recognized by scholars.[5] Lester Reddin conjectures that Peter was the author of Hebrews based on his comparisons.[6] The author should be sought from among those whose work was mainly with Jews or Jewish Christians. Peter holds the place of primacy here. From a study of the discourses of Peter in Acts it is obvious that he was "versed" and "mighty" in the Scriptures. Peter was martyred in Rome in AD 64, according

---

[2] C. Spicq, L'Épître aux Hébreux (Paris: Librairie Lecoffre, 1952–53), 1:109–38.

[3] C. J. A. Hickling, "John and Hebrews: The Background of Hebrews 2:10–18," NTS 29 (1983): 112–16. "It is reasonable to conjecture that a somewhat erudite Christianity of this kind was to be found among those closely in touch with educated Greek-speaking Judaism . . . " (115).

[4] R. Brown, "Not Jewish Christianity and Gentile Christianity but Types of Jewish/Gentile Christianity," CBQ 45 (1983): 74–79. Cf. R. Brown and J. Meier, Antioch and Rome (New York: Paulist, 1983), 1–9.

[5] See, for example, T. E. S. Ferris, "A Comparison of I Peter & Hebrews," CQR 111 (1930): 123–27, who argued that Hebrews depends on 1 Peter; H. Attridge, The Epistle to the Hebrews, Her (Philadelphia: Fortress, 1989), 30–31; W. L. Lane, Hebrews 1–8, WBC 47a (Dallas: Word, 1991), cx–cxii. L. D. Hurst provides a good discussion of the differences in The Epistle to the Hebrews: Its Background and Thought, SNTSMS 65 (Cambridge: Cambridge University, 1990), 125–30.

[6] L. Reddin, "Hebrews a Petrine Document," BSac 68 (1911): 684–92.

to tradition. The starting point in determining the date of Hebrews should be 10:32, a reference to the "earlier days" when the reader had faced much suffering. Is this suffering to be identified with the persecution under Claudius about AD 52, or with that under Nero in AD 64? Reddin opts for the Claudian persecution.[7]

Reddin identifies four lines of evidence to support his theory. First, a similarity in Old Testament quotations, which are taken uniformly from the LXX (Paul uses both the LXX and Hebrew original). Second, both were written to Hebrew Christians in the Diaspora, and during times of persecution.

Third, vocabulary affinities are noted. The following words are common to 1 Peter and Hebrews :

1. *parepidēmos*—(Heb 11:13; 1 Pet 1:1; 2:11). It is used nowhere else in the New Testament.
2. *rhantismos*—(Heb 12:24; 1 Pet 1:2). This word is found nowhere else in the New Testament. In both passages it is used in connection with blood.
3. *antitupos*—(Heb 9:24; 1 Pet 3:21). It is used only here in the New Testament, and in both instances it is an explicit Old Testament reference.
4. *ennoia*—(Heb 4:12; 1 Pet 4:1). It appears only here in the New Testament.
5. *poimēn*—With reference to Christ (Heb 13:20; 1 Pet 2:25). These are the only instances in the New Testament outside the teaching of Jesus.
6. *episkopeō*—(Heb 12:15; 1 Pet 5:2). This verb is found nowhere else in the New Testament.
7. *geuomai*—(Heb 6:4–5; 1 Pet 2:3). This is used only here in the New Testament.

Fourth, conceptual parallels are noted:

1. Jesus is exalted above the angels (Heb 1:3–4; 1 Pet 3:22).
2. Christ's sacrifice is final (Heb 9:26; 1 Pet 3:18).
3. Christians are described as a building (Heb 3:6; 1 Pet 2:5).
4. Christian service is like the offering of sacrifices (Heb 13:15; 1 Pet 2:5). The language of Paul in Rom 12:1–2 is not analo-

---

[7] Ibid., 685–87.

gous here. Although Paul uses *thusia* in a similar way, he uses the verb *paristemi*, which is never used of a priestly act.[8]

Reddin observes that the rhetorical structure and style of Hebrews differ from Peter, but his response is weak. He admits the difference, but says this is "inevitable" because Hebrews is argumentative while 1 Peter is "exhortative."[9] But it is not clear what he means by this. Also, the statement in Heb 2:3 would seem to exclude Peter. Reddin says the answer lies in the way the first person plural personal pronoun is used. In 2:3 the author is simply identifying himself with his readers and not denying that he had not seen nor heard the Lord.[10]

Nevertheless, there is some similarity between Hebrews and the Petrine Letters, especially 1 Peter.[11] Earle Ellis dates 1 Peter c. AD 63–64. He says it was probably used by 1 Clement, which was written from Rome in AD 69–70 (following Edmundson). Perhaps the similarities can be explained partly by the fact that both were written from Rome and at about the same time. L. D. Hurst notes that Hebrews and 1 Peter belong together, both written to bolster the faith of Christians facing persecution.[12] I think a better explanation is that Peter had some relationship with Luke, and this had some influence on his writing. It was occasionally suggested in the past that Silas (Silvanus) and Luke were the same individual,[13] and that Silvanus was at least the courier of the letter, if not an amanuensis for Peter. O. D. Foster notes similarities between Hebrews and 1 Peter as well as between Acts and 1 Peter. With respect to the latter, he suggests the possibility that Luke borrowed from 1 Peter.[14]

---

[8] Ibid., 688–89.

[9] Ibid., 691.

[10] Ibid., 691–92.

[11] See the many examples cited in E. C. Selwyn, *The Christian Prophets and the Prophetic Apocalypse* (London: Macmillan & Co., 1900), 160–63. Selwyn thinks Luke was Peter's amanuensis (see chapter 6). Narborough also noted the similarities between Hebrews and 1 Peter, suggesting they are extensive enough to suggest a literary connection. F. D. V. Narborough, *The Epistle to the Hebrews* (Oxford: Clarendon Press, 1930), 12–15. He accepts the Petrine authorship of 1 Peter and believes Peter died in the Neronian persecution. He thus believes 1 Peter influenced Hebrews, not vice versa.

[12] Hurst, *Epistle to the Hebrews*, 130.

[13] Argued by E. C. Selwyn, in *Saint Luke the Prophet* (London: Macmillan & Co., 1901), following Schwanbeck. See especially 75–178. See also J. Conder, *A Literary History of the New Testament* (London: Seeley, Burnside & Seeley, 1845), 466. See the discussion of this point in chap. 6 below.

[14] O. D. Foster, "The Literary Relations of the 'First Epistle of Peter' with Their Bearing on the

The following is my list of similarities between 1 and 2 Peter and Hebrews.

1 Peter		Hebrews
3:15	account	13:17
3:16	clear conscience	10:22
3:18	Christ died for sins once that he may bring us to God	9:1–28
3:20	Noah	11:7
3:21	clear conscience	10:22
3:22	Jesus gone into heaven, at the right hand of God, with angels subject to him	1:4; 2:8
4:1	Christ suffered in the flesh	2:9–10,17–18; 5:7–8
4:5	they will give an account to him ready to judge the living and dead	4:13
4:8	love for one another	10:14; 13:1
4:9	hospitality	13:2
4:13	share Christ's sufferings	2:10–18; 13:12–13
4:17	judgment to begin with household of God	2:1–4; 6:4–6; 10:26–31; 12:25–29
5:2	flock of God	13:7,17
5:4	chief shepherd	13:20
5:5	subject to elders	13:7,17
5:9	same experience of suffering required of your brothers	2:10–18
5:12	I have written briefly	13:22
5:13	she who is at Babylon, sends you greetings	13:24
2 Peter		**Hebrews**
1:3	godliness	12:28
1:4	great promises	6:13–20
1:7	godliness, brotherly love, love	12:28; 13:1
1:8–9	keep you from being ineffective and unfruitful, for whoever lacks these things is blind and shortsighted and has forgotten that he was cleansed from his old sins	5:11–6:6
1:11	entrance	10:19
1:16	eyewitnesses	2:1–4

Date and Place of Authorship," *Transactions of the Connecticut Academy of the Arts and Sciences* 17 (New Haven: Yale University Press, 1913), 491, 508.

2 Peter		Hebrews
1:19	we have the prophetic word more sure	2:1–4
1:19	you will do well to pay attention	2:1
2:21	way of righteousness, to turn back from the holy commandment	6:6; 10:26
3:2	remember predictions of prophets and the commandment of the Lord through your apostles	2:1–4
3:4	the fathers	1:1
3:5	by the Word of God heavens existed long ago	1:2–3
3:7	by the same Word the heavens and earth	1:2–3
3:9	Lord is not slow about his promise	10:37
3:15	our beloved brother Paul	13:23

Lexical similarity of Luke-Acts, Paul, and Hebrews

The large number of words unique to Hebrews and Luke-Acts is striking. Of course lexical similarity is not the *sine qua non* of authorship and must be considered in proper perspective. Nevertheless, as Westcott pointed out, "No impartial student can fail to be struck by the frequent use [in Hebrews] of words characteristic of St. Luke among writers of the New Testament."[15] C. P. M. Jones examined the lexical similarity between Luke-Acts and Hebrews, and with balanced judgment notes the following:

> Luke-Acts and Hebrews are both writings of considerable length, in which there would be plenty of scope for casual overlapping, as may well be the case with many words . . . which are used in different senses and contexts in the two writings; some words only occur in quotations from the Septuagint, and many of the words are compound verbs whose coining seems to be a common feature among later New Testament writers. Moreover, one can compile lists of words peculiar to Hebrews and the pastoral epistles, to Hebrews and I Peter and James, even to Hebrews and St. Paul, as well as those peculiar to Luke-Acts and the later non-Pauline epistles in general, which should be taken into account. But when all deductions have been made, the verbal correspondences are so numerous [between Luke-Acts and Hebrews] that a substantial area of common phraseology remains . . . which may well be indicative of a closer kinship in the presence of other corroborating factors.[16]

---

[15] B. F. Westcott, *The Epistle to the Hebrews* (London: Macmillan, 1892; repr., Grand Rapids: Eerdmans, 1955), xlviii.

[16] C. P. M. Jones, "The Epistle to the Hebrews and the Lucan Writings," in *Studies in the Gospels: Essays in Memory of R. H. Lightfoot*, ed. D. E. Nineham (Oxford: Basil Blackwell, 1955), 117–18.

Long ago, Frederick Gardiner counted 34 words unique to Luke-Acts and Hebrews.[17] Hawkins in his *Horae Synopticae* counted 38 words unique to these two works.[18] Plummer charts 40 unique words.[19] However, there are actually no fewer than 53 words found in Hebrews that occur nowhere else but in Luke-Acts.

I arrived at this number by working through Moulton and Geden's *Concordance to the Greek New Testament* and the lexical lists in Morgenthaler's *Statistik Des Neutestamentlichen Wortschatzes*. Table 1 below catalogs the lexical items unique to Luke-Acts and Hebrews. Each Greek word is listed, followed by its English translation and its scriptural reference. An "H" stands for Hebrews while "L" and "A" represent Luke and Acts respectively.

The significance of this overlap of vocabulary may be better appreciated by comparing these findings with the number of words peculiar to Luke and Acts in the New Testament. This total, exclusive of proper names, is 58.[20] In other words, Luke and Acts share 58 words that occur nowhere else in the New Testament, and this is only a few more than the 53 words shared by Luke-Acts and Hebrews. Given that Hebrews is considerably shorter than Luke and Acts, this lexical evidence argues strongly for common authorship.

Table 1: Vocabulary unique to the writings of Luke and Hebrews in the New Testament

Greek Word	English Translation	Scripture Reference
metochos	"partakers"	H. 1:9; 3:1,14; 6:4; 12:8; L. 5:7
palaioō	"to become old"	H. 1:11; 8:13; L. 12:33
eklepō	"to cease, fail"	H. 1:12; L. 16:9; 22:32; 23:45
archēgos	"author"	H. 2:10; 12:2; A. 3:15; 5:31
apallassō	"to release"	H. 2:15; L. 12:58; A. 19:12
hilaskomai	"to propitiate"	H. 2:17; L. 18:13

---

[17] F. Gardiner, "The Language of the Epistle to the Hebrews as Bearing upon its Authorship," *JBL* 7 (1887):1–27.

[18] J. C. Hawkins, *Horae Synopticae: Contributions to the Study of the Synoptic Problem*, 2nd ed. (Oxford: Clarendon, 1909), 192.

[19] A. Plummer, *Luke, A Critical and Exegetical Commentary on the Gospel According to Saint Luke*, ICC, 5th ed. (New York: Scribner, 1922), lix.

[20] Hawkins, *Horae Synopticae*, 175. My own list does include four proper names, so excluding proper names the unique words in Luke-Acts and Hebrews would be 49.

Greek Word	English Translation	Scripture Reference
katapausis	"rest"	H. 3:11,18; 4:1,3,5,10,11; A. 7:49
kaitoi	"and yet"	H. 4:3; A. 14:17
katapauō	"to cease"	H. 4:4,8,10; A. 14:18
boētheia	"help"	H. 4:16; A. 27:17
Aarōn	"Aaron"	H. 5:4; 7:11; 9:4; L. 1:5; A. 7:40
eulab(eia/ēs/eo-mai) (cognates of the root *eulab*	"piousness, pious, to act piously"	H. 5:7; 11:7, 12:28; L. 2:25; A. 2:5; 8:2; 22:12
aitios	"cause"	H. 5:9; L. 23:4,14,22; A. 19:40
euthetos	"fit"	H. 6:7; L. 9:62; 14:35
katapheugō	"to flee"	H. 6:18; A. 14:6
agkura	"anchor"	H. 6:19; A. 27:29,30,40
esōteros	"inner"	H. 6:19; A. 16:24
sunantaō	"to meet"	H. 7:1,10; L. 9:18,37; 22:10; A. 10:25; 20:22
patriarchēs	"patriarch"	H. 7:4; A. 2:29; 7:8,9
hierateia	"office of priesthood"	H. 7:5; L. 1:9
teleiōsis	"perfection"	H. 7:11; L. 1:45
pantote	"complete, perfect"	H. 7:25; L. 13:11
kephalaion	"main thing"	H. 8:1; A. 22:28
diatithēmi	"make a covenant"	H. 8:10; 9:16,17; 10:16; L. 22:29; A. 3:25
politēs	"citizen"	H. 8:11; L. 15:15; 19:14; A. 21:39
eiseimi	"go into"	H. 9:6; A. 3:3; 21:18,26
lutrōsis	"redemption"	H. 9:12; L. 1:68; 2:38
schedon	"almost"	H. 9:22; A. 13:44; 19:26
anōteron	"above, higher"	H. 10:8; L. 14:10
paroxusmos	"provoke"	H. 10:24; A. 15:39
huparxis	"possession"	H. 10:34; A. 2:45
paroikeō	"sojourn"	H. 11:9; L. 24:18
astron	"star"	H. 11:12; L. 21:25; A. 7:43; 27:20
porrōthen	"afar off"	H. 11:13; L. 17:12
anadechomai	"to receive"	H. 11:17; A. 28:7
asteios	"well-pleasing"	H. 11:23; A. 7:20

Greek Word	English Translation	Scripture Reference
diabainō	"pass through"	H. 11:29; L. 16:26; A. 16:9
eruthros	"red"	H. 11:29; A. 7:36
Aiguptoi	"Egypt"	H. 11:29; A. 7:22,24,28; 21:38
Samouēl	"Samuel"	H. 11:32; A. 3:24; 13:20
paraluō	"to be disabled"	H. 12:12; L. 5:18,24; A. 8:7; 9:33
anorthoō	"to restore"	H. 12:12; L. 13:13; A. 15:16
orthos	"upright, straight"	H. 12:13; A. 14:10
phuō	"grow"	H. 12:15; L. 8:6,8
enochleō	"trouble, annoy"	H. 12:15; L. 16:18
ēchos	"report, sound"	H. 12:19; L. 4:37; 21:25; A. 2:2
entromos	"trembling"	H. 12:21; A. 7:32; 16:29
apographō	"to enroll"	H. 12:23; L. 2:1,3,5
asaleutos	"unmoved"	H. 12:28; A. 27:41
anatheōreō	"to examine"	H. 13:7; A. 17:23
lusiteleō/ alusitelēs	"profitable"/"unprofitable"	H. 13:17; L. 17:2,17
epistellō	"to write"	H. 13:22; A. 15:20; 21:25
Italia	"Italy"	H. 13:24; A. 18:2; 27:1,6

Hebrews contains 169 *hapax legomena* and 168 other words not found in Luke or Acts. It is interesting that Hebrews and Luke-Acts have the highest ratio of *hapax legomena* to total vocabulary in the entire New Testament. Both are noted for rich vocabulary. Hebrews has a total word count of 4,942, comprising a total vocabulary of 1,038 words, distributed as follows:

- 354 nouns   34.1% of vocabulary
- 361 verbs   34.8%
- 36 names   3.5%
- 133 adjectives   12.8%
- 66 adverbs   6.4%
- 88 other   8.4%[21]

---

[21] R. Morgenthaler, *Statistik des neutestamentlichen Wortschatzes* (Zürich: Gotthelf, 1958), 162–64, and D. Young, "A Grammatical Approach to Hebrews," (Ph.D. diss., Dallas Theological Seminary, 1973), 10–12.

There are 337 words found in Hebrews but not in Luke or Acts. Of these, 16.2% are *hapax legomena*, while another 16.2% of the vocabulary does not occur in Luke-Acts. Thus two-thirds of the vocabulary of Hebrews (67.6%) occurs in Luke-Acts. This represents a significant level of recurrence and strongly links Hebrews with Luke-Acts.

The Relationship of Luke-Acts, Paul, and Hebrews

Among New Testament writers there is a close similarity of vocabulary between Paul, Luke, and Hebrews. This similarity is so pronounced that in a little-known work over a century ago, H. H. Evans argued strongly for the Pauline authorship of Acts.[22] Although his argument is flawed, his evidence is weighty and must have some significance. He notes that there are 1,000 words in Acts that are also found in the (13) Pauline Letters. There are 250 words (including more than 30 proper names) that are unique to Acts and Paul. There are also 200 particles that the three share, with 50 unique to Paul and Acts. Some 500 phrases in Acts are also used by Paul, the majority of which are unique to Acts and Paul. There are 35 figures of speech common to Paul and Acts, and 50 examples of absolute identity of language in Acts and the letters regarding Paul's personal history. Evans concludes that the author of Acts "not only sees everything eye to eye with St. Paul, but he sees everything *with the eyes* of St. Paul."[23] Much has been discovered in Pauline and Lukan studies since Evans made that statement; such an assertion would not be made today. Yet the fact remains, substantiated by clear linguistic parallels, that a close lexical kinship exists between Paul and Luke compared to the other New Testament writers. Scholars recognize that this similarity can be demonstrated lexically, and to some extent stylistically. Luke Johnson notes, "It is important to recognize that Luke accurately represents not only a number of distinctively Pauline themes, but does so in language which is specifically and verifiably Paul's."[24] This similarity is especially pronounced when comparing the Pastoral Letters with

---

[22] H. H. Evans, *Saint Paul, the Author of the Acts of the Apostles and of the Third Gospel*, 2 vols. (London: Wyman, 1884–86 [1904]). Linguistic dissimilarities between Luke and Acts have been noted by S. Levinsohn, *Textual Connections in Acts*, SBLMS 31 (Atlanta: Scholars Press, 1987). There is, of course, a very early tradition affirming Lukan authorship of both Luke and Acts. Eusebius wrote in *Ecclesiastical History* 3.4, " . . . and the Acts of the Apostles, which he [Luke] composed, receiving his information with his own eyes, no longer by hearsay" (19).

[23] Ibid., 209.

[24] L. T. Johnson, *The Acts of the Apostles*, SP 5 (Collegeville, MN: Liturgical, 1992), 367.

Luke and Hebrews. Hawkins provides the following comparisons of
the vocabularies of the Gospels and the Pauline corpus:

- 32 words are found only in Matthew (or Matthew and Acts)
  and in Paul.
- 22 words are found only in Mark (or Mark and Acts) and in
  Paul.
- 103 words are found only in Luke (or Luke and Acts) and in
  Paul.
- 21 words are found only in John (or John and Acts) and in
  Paul.

He points out that there are approximately 78 words found only
in Acts and Paul in addition to the 44 of the 103 that are found also
in Luke. A comparison of the characteristic words and phrases of the
Synoptic Gospels with the Pauline corpus reveals that slightly more
than half of those in Matthew are found in Paul, slightly less than half
of those in Mark are found in Paul, while two-thirds of those in Luke
also occur in the Pauline Letters.[25]

The usual assumption from this data is that Luke has been influenced by Paul. Certainly that explains some (or perhaps most) of the
linguistic data. However, I would suggest that given the explosion
of Lukan research over the past 50 years, and the status of Luke as a
writer and theologian, the possibility of Lukan influence on Pauline
style should not be ruled out, especially in the Pastorals.

Hawkins has also pointed out the close connection in vocabulary
among Luke-Acts, Paul, and Hebrews when compared with the other
Gospel writers.[26] Indeed the same is true when the other New Testament writers are included in the analysis. The vocabulary evidence
clearly reveals Luke-Acts, Paul, and Hebrews to be in closer proximity
to one another than to the rest of the New Testament writers.

Stuart[27] and Leonard[28] count 56 words that are unique to the Pauline Letters and Hebrews. Those who have supported Pauline authorship have appealed to this lexical similarity as evidence.[29] In my view,

---

[25] Hawkins, *Horae Synopticae*, 189–90.

[26] Ibid., 192–93.

[27] M. Stuart, *A Commentary on the Epistle to the Hebrews*, 4th ed., ed. and rev. R. D. C. Robbins
(Andover: Warren F. Draper, 1860), 149–52.

[28] W. Leonard, *Authorship of the Epistle to the Hebrews* (Rome: Vatican Polyglot Press,
1939), 119.

[29] Both Stuart and Leonard are dependent on the outstanding research done on the linguistic

this single point is the most effective argument for the Pauline authorship of Hebrews. If Paul is not the author, how are we to account for
this high degree of similarity? In matters relative to theological outlook, there is a recognized dissimilarity between Paul and Hebrews in
many areas. I do not consider this to be an insurmountable argument
against Pauline authorship for the simple reason that an author can
vary his theological vocabulary in addressing different themes and
readers. Such may have been the case with Paul if he wrote Hebrews.
However, I will demonstrate that Hebrews is much closer to Luke-
Acts in theological outlook than to Paul.

Furthermore, the most forceful argument against the Pauline authorship theory (according to most scholars) is the stylistic dissimilarity between Hebrews and the Pauline corpus. I intend to demonstrate
that Hebrews is stylistically much closer to Luke-Acts than to the Pauline corpus, a fact affirmed by both ancient and modern scholars.

Given these arguments against Pauline authorship, coupled with
the greater lexical correlation of Luke, Paul, and Hebrews (compared
with the other New Testament writers), plus the fact that there are
32 words unique to Luke, Paul, and Hebrews (in addition to the 53
words unique to Luke-Acts and Hebrews), the theory that makes the
most sense is to posit Lukan authorship for Hebrews.

The lexical as well as historical evidence supports the contention
that Luke was a contemporary of Paul and part of the Pauline circle.[30]
If Luke were indeed Paul's traveling companion and a close associate for many years, the lexical similarity between Luke and Paul is
not surprising. In fact, we might be surprised if their vocabulary did
not greatly overlap, considering they shared the same experiences of

---

relationship between the Pauline Letters and Hebrews by C. Forster in *The Apostolical Authority
of the Epistle to the Hebrews: an inquiry, in which the received title of the Greek epistle is vindicated,
against the cavils of objectors, ancient and modern, from Origen to Sir J. D. Michaelis, chiefly upon
grounds of internal evidence hitherto unnoticed: comprising a comparative analysis of the style and
structure of this epistle, and of the undisputed epistles of St. Paul, tending to throw light upon their
interpretation* (London: J. Duncan, 1838). Without the aid of a computer or many other tools
available today, Forster managed to tabulate lexical and phrase similarities between Hebrews
and the Paul only, Hebrews, the Paul, and other New Testament occurrences, and other parallel
or semi-parallel material appearing in Paul and Hebrews, with a discussion totaling more than
600 pages. The evidence, especially lexical, that Forster, and then Stuart and Leonard presented,
makes it abundantly clear that the tacit dismissal of the Pauline hypothesis is not warranted.

[30] D. Buckwalter has noted that the "undefined Pauline summary statements" found in Paul's
address to the Ephesian elders in Acts 20 indicate the possibility that Luke's audience had some
kind of personal contact or association with Paul. D. Buckwalter, *The Character and Purpose of
Luke's Christology* (Cambridge: Cambridge University Press, 1996), 73.

travel, imprisonment, difficulties, and triumphs over a period of years. If Luke wrote Hebrews, then the vocabulary connection of Luke, Paul, and Hebrews is easily explained.

Thus, the 56 words unique to Paul's Letters and Hebrews are not as strong an argument against Luke in the face of the total linguistic evidence regarding shared vocabulary between Paul and Luke. These 56 words are actually evidence for Luke, because they illustrate that the author of Hebrews, if not Paul, was certainly close to him or heavily influenced by him.

Therefore, in light of Luke's close association with Paul, especially during the latter years of Paul's life, and in light of the many lexical similarities between Luke and Paul that can probably be accounted for on this basis, it does not seem unwarranted to suggest that Luke is more likely to be the author of Hebrews than Paul.[31] This suggestion is strengthened by the fact that the Pauline Letters are theologically and stylistically distinct from Hebrews, while Luke-Acts can be shown to be very similar in these respects. Pauline and Lukan vocabulary converge, but Pauline and Lukan style diverge. Some of the arguments in favor of Pauline authorship are simultaneously arguments in favor of Luke. However, most arguments against Pauline authorship are generally not applicable to Luke.

Luke-Acts, Hebrews, and the Apocryphal Books

Other interesting lexical information arises from a comparison of the vocabulary of Luke, Acts, and Hebrews with some of the Apocryphal books, specifically the Maccabean writings. Clarke compiled the following statistics:

- 37% of vocabulary in 2 Maccabees recurs in Acts.
- 35% of vocabulary in 2 Maccabees recurs in Luke.
- 30% of vocabulary in 2 Maccabees recurs in Matthew.
- 22% of vocabulary in 2 Maccabees recurs in Hebrews.
- 44% of vocabulary in 3 Maccabees recurs in Acts.

---

[31] For example, the high correlation of shared vocabulary between the Pastoral letters and Luke-Acts has led S. Wilson, *Luke and the Pastoral Epistles* (London: SPCK, 1979), to argue erroneously for Lukan authorship of the Pastorals. But even in the closing personal remarks of Heb 13:17–19 (stylistically similar to a Pauline letter) there are three words or phrases that are never used by Paul—ἀλυσιτελές (Heb 13:17; cf. λυσιτελεῖ in Luke 17:2), λόγον ἀποδώσοντες (Heb 13:17; cf. Luke 16:2), ἀποκατασταθῶ (Heb 13:19; cf. Acts 1:6; 3x in Mark)—while all three occur in Luke, and two are unique to him and the author of Hebrews.

- 43% of vocabulary in 3 Maccabees recurs in Luke.
- 34% of vocabulary in 3 Maccabees recurs in Matthew.
- 28% of vocabulary in 3 Maccabees recurs in Hebrews.
- 2 words occur only in 2 and 3 Maccabees and Matthew.
- 0 words occur only in 2 and 3 Maccabees and Mark.
- 9 words occur only in 2 and 3 Maccabees and Luke.
- 27 words occur only in 2 and 3 Maccabees and Acts.

His conclusions are illuminating:

> When allowance has been made on the one hand for the smaller extent of Hebrews, and on the other for the number of common words which must inevitably be found in every book, the degree of affinity evinced by Lk.-Acts and Hebrews towards 2 and 3 Maccabees seems substantially the same. . . . These figures suggest that Luke may have read 2 and 3 Maccabees before writing Acts. . . . It was no doubt known to the author of Hebrews who belonged to the same literary circles as Luke.[32]

Gregory Sterling argues that Luke-Acts, along with Josephus, are examples of Hellenistic apologetic historiography.[33] He points out that Robert Doran (in his *Temple Propaganda: The Purpose and Character of 2 Maccabees*) has emphasized the apologetic element in 2 Maccabees, although Sterling does not place 2 Maccabees in the category of apologetic historiography because of its narrow scope. He suggests that 2 Maccabees "might prove to be an important work to compare with Luke-Acts."[34] Likewise Martin Hengel affirms this comparison with 2 Maccabees.[35]

Ancient evidence seems to point to Antioch as the center of religious interest in the Maccabees.[36] We know from both Scripture and tradition that Luke was associated with the church in Antioch. If the recipients of Hebrews were located in Antioch, as I shall argue,

---

[32] W. K. L. Clarke, "The Use of the Septuagint in Acts," *The Beginnings of Christianity, Part I: The Acts of the Apostles*, ed. F. J. Foakes-Jackson and K. Lake (London: Macmillan, 1920; repr., Grand Rapids: Baker, 1979), 2:74–75. See J. Fitzmyer, *The Gospel According to Luke X-XXIV: Introduction, Translation, and Notes*, AB 28a (Garden City: Doubleday, 1985), 1307, who finds an allusion to 4 Macc. 7:19 in Luke 20:37–38.

[33] G. Sterling, *Historiography and Self-Definition: Josephus, Luke-Acts and Apologetic Historiography*, NovTSup 64 (Leiden: Brill, 1992), 387.

[34] Ibid.

[35] M. Hengel, "The Geography of Palestine in Acts," in *The Book of Acts in its Palestinian Setting*, The Book of Acts in its First Century Setting, ed. R. Bauckham (Grand Rapids: Eerdmans, 1995), 4:44.

[36] V. Burch, *The Epistle to the Hebrews, its Sources and Message* (London: Williams & Norgate, 1936), 130.

and if they were former Jewish priests who had some interest in the Maccabean writings, then this correlation of shared vocabulary between Luke-Acts and Hebrews can be seen as further evidence of Lukan authorship.

Medical Terminology and Imagery in Hebrews

Early church tradition identified Luke as a medical doctor,[37] and this tradition continues to be accepted by many today.[38] A quarter-century before Hobart's *Medical Language of Saint Luke* (1882),[39] Delitzsch suggested (in an appendix to his commentary on Hebrews) that the medical terminology found therein might be evidence for Lukan authorship. Believing that Luke was the independent author (although writing at Paul's behest and composing Hebrews from Pauline statements), Delitzsch argued that Luke's vocation as a physician harmonized well with the content of Hebrews with its anatomical (4:12–13), dietary (5:12–14), and therapeutic (12:12–13) passages.[40] Hobart's work soon followed. In it he cites evidence that Luke's writings show a certain medical coloring as illustrated from Galen, Hippocrates, and others, thus concluding Luke-Acts was written by a physician (Col 4:14). In the third edition of *Leading Ideas of the Gospels*, Alexander provided a rather full listing of medical words appearing in Hebrews that had been furnished him by Hobart.[41] He viewed this as evidence

---

[37] See, for example, Irenaeus, *Haer.* III.1.1.

[38] L. Alexander, *Preface to Luke's Gospel: Literary Convention and Social Context in Luke 1:1–4,* SNTSMS 78 (Cambridge: Cambridge University Press, 1993), attempted to show clear parallels between the prefaces of Luke-Acts and prefaces of other technical treatises, especially medical writings. M. Hengel and A. M Schwemer, *Paulus zwischen Damaskus und Antiochien: Die unabekannten Jahre des Apostels,* WUNT 108 (Tübingen: Mohr-Siebeck, 1998), 18–22, likewise affirmed the tradition that Luke was a physician. See also A. Weissenrieder, *Images of Illness in the Gospel of Luke: Insights of Ancient Medical Texts,* WUNT 164, 2 Reihe (Tübingen: Mohr-Siebeck, 2003), 365–66, who concluded with respect to how Luke speaks of illness in his Gospel: "The author of Luke-Acts had a particular interest in images of illness and healing, which were plausible within the ancient medical context, and far exceed word analogies" (365). Weissenrieder confirmed Luke's use of medical terminology along with his penchant for expressing images of illness along the lines of medical theories current in his day. She likewise concluded that whether or not Luke was a physician "remains uncertain" (366).

[39] W. K. Hobart, *The Medical Language of St. Luke: A Proof from Internal Evidence that "The Gospel According to St. Luke" and "The Acts of the Apostles" Were Written by the Same Person, and that the Writer Was a Medical Man* (Dublin: Hodges, Figgis, 1882 repr., Grand Rapids: Baker, 1954).

[40] F. Delitzsch, *Commentary on the Epistle to the Hebrews,* trans. T. L. Kingsbury (Edinburgh: T&T Clark, 1871–72), 2:415.

[41] W. Alexander, *Leading Ideas of the Gospels,* 3rd ed. (London: Macmillan, 1892), 317–19.

for the Lukan authorship of Hebrews. In 1909, Harnack's *Luke the Physician* appeared in which he accepted Hobart's evidence as supporting the biblical notion that Luke was a physician.[42]

However, in 1912 Cadbury's *The Style and Literary Method of Luke* challenged Hobart's evidence and conclusion. Comparing Luke's medical language with the LXX and other Hellenistic nonmedical writers, Cadbury concluded that the style of Luke bore no more evidence of medical training than did the language of nonmedical writers.[43] He argued that the unitary authorship of Luke-Acts could not be predicated on the so-called medical language of Luke. But a secondary result was that the medical background for Luke could not be appealed to solely based on the use of medical terminology.

Today most New Testament scholars accept Cadbury's critique and conclusion. For example, both Fitzmyer and Ellis think that Cadbury has made the better case.[44] But A. T. Robertson argues otherwise. He concedes that Hobart overstated his case and made claims the evidence could not bear. But after careful study of Hobart and Cadbury, he argues that the weight of evidence favored Hobart.

> Most impressive of all is it to read Mark's reports of the miracles and then Luke's modifications. And then the reading of the Gospel and the Acts straight through leaves the same conviction that we are following the lead of a cultivated physician whose professional habits of thought have colored the whole in many subtle ways. This positive impression refuses to be dissipated. . . .[45]

Robertson critiqued Cadbury's assessment of Hobart and Harnack, but his criticism has been left largely unanswered. He pointed out that matters of medical interest appear in incidental ways in the writings of Luke-Acts.[46] With his use of medical language and imagery, Luke was doing more than revealing the linguistic capabilities of an educated man; he was also exposing the professional interest of a physician.[47]

---

[42] A. von Harnack, *Luke the Physician: The Author of the Third Gospel and the Acts of the Apostles*, ed. W. D. Morrison, trans. J. R. Wilkinson (New York: J. P. Putnam's Sons, 1907), 175–98.

[43] H. J. Cadbury, "The Style and Literary Method of Luke," HTS 6 (Cambridge: Harvard University Press, 1920), 50–51.

[44] J. Fitzmyer, *Luke I–IX*, 51–53; E. E. Ellis, *The Gospel of Luke*, NCBC (Grand Rapids: Eerdmans, 1974; repr., London: Oliphants, 1977), 43.

[45] A. T. Robertson, *Luke the Historian in Light of Research* (Edinburgh: T&T Clark, 1920), 12.

[46] Ibid., 91.

[47] Ibid., 95. For Robertson's entire discussion see 90–102.

Creed, Geldenhuys, and Hendriksen have written commentaries on Luke's Gospel that agree with Robertson's assessment.[48]

Since there is ample reason to accept the testimony of Scripture and the internal evidence of Luke's writings regarding his medical vocation,[49] it follows that any significant occurrences of medical terminology in Hebrews may be used as evidence of Lukan authorship. We have seen that Delitzsch, a careful scholar, came to this conclusion even before Hobart's work appeared. When a Greek scholar like A. T. Robertson asserts that Luke's language makes it likely he was a physician, it persuades me that the medical terminology in Hebrews supports Lukan authorship.

What is significant about such terminology in Hebrews is that it occurs in three primary passages: 4:12–14; 5:12–14; and 12:12–13. The first thing that strikes us about 4:12–14 is that only in Luke and here in Hebrews do we find the exact phrase "double-edged sword." Second, the phrase "sharper than," where *huper* is the comparative preposition, is compared by Westcott to Luke 16:8.[50] Third, the phrase "joints and marrow" uses technical physiological terms that occur nowhere else in the New Testament. Fourth, Eagar notes that the preposition *enōpion*, "before, in the sight of" followed by *autou* "him" in the phrase "from him" as a synonym for Christ are "essentially Lucan."[51]

Finally, the term here translated "sword," *machaira*, sometimes has the technical meaning of a surgeon's knife. Michaelis argues that the context forbids the translation of "sword," and instead the image is

---

[48] J. M. Creed, *The Gospel According to St. Luke* (London: Macmillan, 1942), xix–xxi; N. Geldenhuys, *Commentary on the Gospel of Luke*, NICNT (Grand Rapids: Baker, 1951); W. Hendriksen, *Exposition of the Gospel According to Luke*, NTC (Grand Rapids: Baker, 1978), 4–5. C. Hemer, *The Book of Acts in the Setting of Hellenistic History*, ed. C. Gempf (Tübingen: J. C. B. Mohr [Paul Siebeck], 1989), 310–12, argued that Cadbury's critique of Hobart "does not amount to disproof of its essential contention."

[49] G. H. R. Horsley, *New Documents Illustrating Early Christianity: A Review of the Greek Inscriptions and Papyri Published in 1977* (Sydney, Australia: Macquarie University Ancient History Documentary Research Center, 1982), 19–21, and Hengel and Schwemer, *Paulus zwischen Damaskus und Antiochien*, 18–22, have shown that ancient medical doctors often traveled as itinerants. See also W. Marx, "Luke, the Physician, Re-examined," *ExpTim* 91 (1980): 168–72, and B. Witherington III, *Conflict and Community in Corinth* (Grand Rapids: Eerdmans, 1995), 459–64, who aligns himself with the traditional position that Luke was Paul's personal doctor. Fitzmyer offers an excellent defense of the tradition that Luke was a doctor as well as an uncircumcised Semite and occasional companion of Paul. *Luke I–IX*, 35–59, and *Luke the Theologian: Aspects of His Teaching* (New York: Paulist Press, 1989), 1–26).

[50] Westcott, *Hebrews*, 102.

[51] A. Eagar, "The Authorship of the Epistle to the Hebrews," 120.

a knife used by a priest or butcher, or possibly a surgeon. He points out that surgeons' knives were sometimes two-edged while ordinary knives were not usually so.[52] How fitting if such imagery came from the pen of Luke the physician.[53]

If the usual translation of "sword" is retained, then the simile is mixed at best, but if it is a reference to the surgeon's knife, then the thought of the passage has greater coherence. The possibility that this word should refer to the surgeon's knife, coupled with the other evidences of Lukan color in these verses, furnishes an argument in favor of Luke's authorship.

Eagar notes that 5:12–14 shows a certain medical influence that may be indicative of Lukan authorship. This passage is replete with medical and physiological terms: *nēpios*, *sterea*, *trophē*, *exis*, *aisthetērion*, and *diakrisis*, all fall under this heading, and *teleiōtēs* has a double medical meaning. *Astheneia* (a favorite Lukan word) and its companion term *asthenēs* are the regular Greek medical names for "sickness" and "sick"; and *teleios*, with its derivatives, is used by Hippocrates to signify "healthy."[54]

The third passage, Heb 12:12–13, has six words that are primarily Lukan: *paralelumena*, *gonata*, *anorthōsate*, *orthos*, *chōlon*, and *iathē*. Three of these six (*paralelumena*, *anorthōsate*, and *orthos*) are unique to Luke and Hebrews in the New Testament. The use of *anorthoō*, "strengthen," in Heb 12:12 is found in a quote from Isa 35:3, although *anorthoō* is not found in the LXX of Isaiah but was added to Heb 12:12 by the writer. Similarly, when Luke quotes Amos 9:11 in Acts 15:16, he uses *anorthoō*, which does not appear in the LXX of Amos 9:11.

How much can we make of this evidence? If we say that such passages would be unlikely from Paul, then we are overstepping the evidence. Certainly Paul (or someone else) could have written such statements. But given the scriptural description of Luke as a physician, the evidence that his vocabulary reflects medical interests, and the fact that some of the vocabulary in these three sections is unique to Luke-Acts and Hebrews, it does not seem unwarranted to interpret this evidence in favor of Lukan authorship for Hebrews.

---

[52] W. Michaelis, "μάχαιρα," *TDNT*, 4:524–27.
[53] See A. Eagar, "The Authorship of the Epistle to the Hebrews," 119–20.
[54] Ibid., 119.

Other Lexical Similarities between Luke-Acts and Hebrews

Gardiner concluded from his lexical comparison that the letter to the Hebrews was linguistically most comparable with the writings of Luke and Paul.[55] I will link some of his findings to those of other sources[56] and to some of my own to illustrate further the similarity between the Lukan corpus and Hebrews.[57]

The Greek word for "star" has two forms in the New Testament, *astron* and *astēr*, which are both common in the LXX. However, the former is used exclusively by Luke and Hebrews, while the latter is used by all other New Testament writers (three times in Paul, twenty-one times elsewhere).

The verb *erchomai*, "to come," which (along with its many compound forms) is more common in narrative than in other discourse types, is found frequently in Luke's writings and in Hebrews, but is relatively rare in Paul. This is important in that Luke and Acts are primarily narrative, but Hebrews is not.

The occurrences of the first person singular verbal endings and the personal pronoun *egō,* "I," are markedly limited in both the Lukan corpus and Hebrews, reflecting a reluctance to personalize the message. On the contrary, Paul is quite fond of the first person singular personal pronoun. The use of the third person personal pronoun *autos*, the demonstrative pronoun *ekeinos*, and the reflexive pronoun *heautou* in Hebrews and Luke is about the same, whereas Paul and the other New Testament writers use them much less frequently.

Adverbs of space such as *ekei*, *hopou, pou*, and *hode* are used about equally in Luke and Hebrews, while they are very infrequently used by Paul. The adverb *hōsei* and the conjunction *hoste* are used in about the same proportion in Luke and Hebrews. Both are much more rare in Paul and the rest of the New Testament. Luke prefers *heteros* to *allos* in his writings. Pauline usage is about equal, whereas Hebrews uses *heteros* four times and *allos* twice.

---

[55] Gardiner, "The Language of the Epistle to the Hebrews as Bearing upon its Authorship," 1–27.

[56] Delitzsch, *Hebrews*; A. Eagar, "The Authorship of the Epistle to the Hebrews," *Expositor* 10 (1904): 74–80, 110–23.

[57] I have not footnoted every time I draw material from Gardiner, Delitzsch, Lünemann, or Alexander in this section or in the section on stylistic similarities. The reader should consult their works listed in the bibliography.

The lexical group *agapaō*, "to love," and *agapētos* is very common in Paul's writings, but rare in both the Lukan corpus and Hebrews. The lexical group comprising *alētheia, alēthēs*, etc., is less frequent in Luke and Hebrews than in the rest of the New Testament, the proportions in their writings being about the same.

The noun *hiereus*, "temple," occurs 14 times in Hebrews, nine times in the Lukan corpus, but not at all in Paul, and nine times in the rest of the New Testament. The noun *archiereus*, "high priest," occurs 70 times in Hebrews, 37 times in Luke, and not once in Paul. Of course, the subject matter of Hebrews requires the use of these lexical terms. Yet as it will be shown below, the priests, the high priests, and the temple are prominent in Luke's writings, and Hebrews presents the greatest exposition of the high priesthood of Christ in the New Testament. Compared with the other Gospel writers and the rest of the New Testament, Luke and Hebrews have a common interest in the priesthood, as is reflected by the lexical counts.

Hebrews uses *skēnē*, "tabernacle," 10 times; it occurs five times in Luke, never in Paul, and only five times in the rest of the New Testament. Another lexical similarity is in Luke 2:26 and Heb 11:5 where the exact phrase, *me idein thanaton*, "not to see death," is found. The only other place in the New Testament where a similar phrase occurs is John 8:51, where John employs a different Greek word for "see" and a stronger negative.

Other lexical links in the three books include use of *oikoumenē*, "inhabited world," and *polis*, "city." "Inhabited world" occurs once in Matthew, once in Paul, three times in Revelation, three times in Luke, five times in Acts, and twice in Hebrews.

The words *metanoia*, "repentance," and *aphesis*, "forgiveness," occur rarely outside the writings of Luke and Hebrews. The term *metanoia* occurs once in Mark, twice in Matthew, four times in Paul, and once in 2 Peter. It is used five times in Luke, six times in Acts, and three times in Hebrews. The word *aphesis* is used twice in Mark, once in Matthew, twice in Paul, but five times in Luke, five times in Acts, and twice in Hebrews.[58] Normally the genitive *hamartiōn* (or as in Eph 1:7, the genitive *paraptōmatōn*) follows the noun *aphesis* in the New Testament, or *hamartiōn* is contextually present (as in Mark

---

[58] Cf. Jones, "The Epistle to the Hebrews and the Lucan Writings," 119–20, and see the discussion on forgiveness in the jubilary theology of Luke in chap. 6. Luke's Gospel lays particular emphasis on forgiveness of sins as an essential constituent of salvation.

3:28 where it precedes *aphesis* in v. 29). Of the 18 occurrences of this noun in the New Testament, it appears alone only in Heb 9:22 and Luke 4:18 (twice). The concept of repentance is a dominant motif in Luke and Hebrews.

The verb for "cleansing," *katharizō*, is used six times in Matthew, four times in Mark, three times in Paul, once in James, and twice in 1 John. It occurs seven times in Luke, three times in Acts, and four times in Hebrews. It is used of the cleansing of the heart and con-science only in Acts 15:9 and Heb 9:14; 10:2. The word *hēgoumenoi*, "leaders" or "chief leaders," occurs 10 times in the New Testament: once in Matthew, once in Paul, and once in 2 Peter, but four times in Luke-Acts and three times in Hebrews. Only in Acts and Hebrews is the word used to refer to the leaders of the church.

A similar phrase in Luke 10:20 and Heb 12:23 is a compounded form of the verb *graphō*, "to write," plus *ouranois*, "in heaven." In the Lukan passage, Jesus tells the disciples to rejoice that "their names are written in heaven," while the Hebrews passage refers to the church of the firstborn, which is "written" or "enrolled in heaven." A simi-lar concept is found in both the Pauline and Johannine writings: the names of believers inscribed in "the book of life." But the precise phrase "written in heaven" occurs only in Luke and Hebrews.

A comparison of Luke 16:2 with Heb 13:17 reveals another paral-lel occurring nowhere else in the New Testament. In the parable of the unjust steward in Luke 16, the owner commands the steward to "give an account," *apodos ton logon*. In Heb 13:17 the readers are exhorted to obey their leaders since the leaders must one day *logon apodōsontes*, "give an account." This concept of giving an account also occurs in Rom 14:12, but a different verb for "give" is conjoined with *logon*, "account."

Zechariah praises God in Luke 1:68–69 because He has "visited" (*epeskepsato*) His people. Twice in this hymn we find a reference to this divine "visitation." The verb *episkeptomai* is common in the LXX, where it pictures God's care for His people. It is used in this Hebraic sense in the New Testament only in Luke-Acts (Luke 1:68,78; 7:16; Acts 15:14) and Heb 2:6, where it appears in a quotation from Psalm 8. The christological nuance of Luke's use of this verb[59] fits well with

---

[59] See the excellent discussion in G. Hotze, *Jesus als Gast: Studien zu einem christologischen Leitmotiv im Lukasevangelium*, in Forschung zur Bibel 111 (Würzburg: Echter Verlag, 2007), 301–7.

the christological perspective of Hebrews in its choice of an Old Testament quotation in Heb 2:6 that uses this verb.

In the next few pages, I list further examples of lexical similarity that may help identify the author of Hebrews. Since these examples have varying evidential weight, I will divide them in two groups. Division one consists of examples that carry stronger weight because they illustrate lexical similarity unique to Luke-Acts and Hebrews, in contrast with the rest of the New Testament. Division two consists of examples that carry lesser weight because they illustrate lexical similarity prominent for the most part in Luke-Acts and Hebrews, but which also occur somewhere else in the New Testament. The 53 words unique to Luke, Acts, and Hebrews listed in Table 1 are not repeated here unless appearing with other words unique to Luke-Acts and Hebrews.

Division One

Peipastheis, "suffering" (Heb 2:18), is used to describe the suffering of Christ as in Luke 22:28.

The use of *schedon*, "almost," with *pas*, "all," occurs only in Heb 9:22; Acts 13:34; 19:26. This adverb occurs nowhere else in the New Testament.

The use of *pan*, "all," with the phrase *ex henos*, "from one," occurs only in Acts 17:26 and Heb 2:11. The phrase "from one" occurs only five times in the New Testament.

The phrase *eis ton kairon*, "in time," occurs only in Luke 1:20 and Heb 9:9.

The phrase *houtoi pantes*, "these all," occurs twice in Acts and twice in Hebrews, but nowhere else in the New Testament.

The adverb *eti*, "still, yet," occurs 93 times in the New Testament, but only three times with the infinitive (twice in Luke and once in Hebrews). Furthermore, the adverb *eti* followed by the conjunction *de* occurs three times in Luke, once in Acts, and twice in Hebrews, but nowhere else in the New Testament.

The noun *dakroun*, "tears," occurs 10 times in the New Testament (twice in Luke, twice in Acts, twice in Paul, twice in

John, and twice in Hebrews). The genitive *dakroun* preceded by the preposition *meta*, "with tears," occurs in Acts 20:19,31 and Heb 5:7; 12:17. The conjunction *kai*, "and," preceding the genitive *dakroun* occurs only in Acts 20:19 and Heb 5:7.

Acts 15:33 and Heb 11:31 are the only places in the New Testament where the phrase *met eirēnēs*, "with peace," occurs.

The phrase *eis to panteles*, "to the uttermost," occurs in Luke 13:11 and Heb 7:25. These are the only occurrences of the noun *panteles* in the New Testament. In both instances the noun is preceded by *eis to*. Notice that in each clause the verb *dunamai*, "to be able," is used. This is a rather remarkable similarity of not only vocabulary but style as well.

The use of the passive infinitive *legesthai*, "it was said," occurs only four times in the New Testament: three times in Hebrews and once in Luke.

The use of the aorist passive *elalēthē*, "it had been said," occurs only in Luke 2:20 and Heb 11:18.

The nominative feminine singular present passive participle *legomena* occurs twice in the New Testament: Luke and Hebrews. Likewise, the dative neuter plural present passive participle *legomenois* occurs only four times in the New Testament: three in Acts and once in Hebrews.

The phrase *ton kurion hēmōn Iēsoun*, "our Lord Jesus," occurs only in Acts 20:21 and Heb 13:20.

The phrase *apo mikrou heōs megalou*, "from the least to the greatest," occurs only twice in the New Testament: Acts 8:10 and Heb 8:11.

The phrase *meta tas hēmeras*, "after the days," occurs just three times in the New Testament: twice in Acts and once in Hebrews.

In the New Testament the phrase *stomata machairēs*, "edge of the sword," appears twice: Luke 21:24 and Heb 11:34. In addition, the phrase *machairan distomon,* "two-edged sword," occurs in Heb 4:12.

The use of the preposition *kata* followed by *ton tupon*, "according to the pattern," occurs only in Acts 7:44 and Heb 8:5. In both cases it refers to God giving the pattern for the tabernacle to Moses.

The use of the verb *heuren*, "to find," with the accusative *charin*, "grace," occurs only three times in the New Testament: Luke 1:30, Acts 7:46, and Heb 4:16. In all three cases the usage occurs with reference to God.

The use of *pragmatōn* to mean "facts" or "actions" occurs in the New Testament only in Heb 6:18, Luke 1:1, and Acts 5:4.

The use of *osphuos* meaning "the ideal aspect of human generation" occurs only in Heb 7:5,10 and Acts 2:20.

The use of the noun *ergazomai* followed by the accusative *dikaiosunēn* occurs only in Heb 11:33 and Acts 10:35.

The use of the verb *tuchōsin* with the noun *anastaseōs* occurs only in Heb 11:35 and Luke 20:35.

The use of *metanoias gar topon* in Heb 12:17 and *topon te apologias* in Acts 25:16 are semantically parallel, and this usage occurs nowhere else in the New Testament.

The *hapax legomenon metriopathein* occurs in Heb 5:2 and compares with the only other occurrence of *metrios* in the New Testament, in Acts 20:12. The word *metrios* does not occur in the LXX.

The use of *pleiones* in Heb 7:23 compares to its use in Acts without genitive or comparative marks, in the sense of "a large number." This usage is exclusively Lukan.

The noun *timōrias* and the verb *timōria* occur in the New Testament only in Heb 10:29 (the former) and Acts 22:5 and 26:11 (the latter). Note that in Acts 22:5 and in Heb 10:29, the usages are preceded by *axon* and *axiothēsetai* respectively.

• The use of *apodidomi* in the middle voice meaning "sell" is found only in Heb 12:16; Acts 5:8; and 7:9.

The use of the third inflectional form (dative case) *panti*, "all," followed by *tō laō*, "the people," and the fourth inflectional form (accusative case) followed by *ton laon*, "all the people," is unique to Luke-Acts and Hebrews in the New Testament. The former occurs six times: five in Luke-Acts and once in Hebrews. The latter occurs twice, once each in Luke and Hebrews.

Ekdochē (only in Heb 10:27) and *prosdokia* (twice in the New Testament: Luke 21:26 and Acts 12:11) share the same root and are used of fearful, apprehensive anticipation only in Heb 10:17 and Luke 21:26.

Division Two

Both Luke and the writer of Hebrews avoid the use of *euaggelion* for the gospel and employ a variety of paraphrases. Luke uses it only twice, and Hebrews never uses it. It is frequent in Paul's Letters.

The phrase *zōn gar ho logos tou theou* in Heb 4:12 may be compared to its only counterparts, 1 Pet 1:23 and Acts 7:38, where the phrase is *logia zōnta*, "living words."

The verb *emphanizō*, "to appear, to make known," occurs 10 times in the New Testament, once in Matthew, twice in John, five times in Acts, and twice in Hebrews. In Heb 11:14 and five places in Acts it has the sense "to make known."

The verb *diamarturomai*, "to testify," occurs only four times in the New Testament: Acts 2:40; 23:11; 1 Thess 4:6; and Heb 2:6.

Eispherō, "to go into, to bring into," occurs eight times in the New Testament, once in Matthew, once in Paul, once in Hebrews, five times in Luke-Acts.

The pronominal adjective *brachus*, "short, small, little," occurs once in John, four times in Luke-Acts, three times in Hebrews, but nowhere else in the New Testament.

The verb *dialegomai*, "to converse, argue, or discuss," occurs 13 times in the New Testament: once in Mark, once in Jude, 10 times in Acts, and once in Hebrews.

The verb *diegeomai*, "to recount," occurs twice in Mark, seven times in Luke-Acts, and once in Hebrews. It is followed by the preposition *peri*, "concerning, about," only in Luke 1:1 and Heb 11:32.

The noun *ethos*, "custom," occurs once in John, once in Hebrews, and 10 times in Luke-Acts.

The adverb *pantothen*, "from all sides," occurs just three times in the New Testament: Mark 1:45; Luke 19:43; and Heb 9:4.

The proper noun *Aiguptos*, "Egypt," occurs four times in Matthew, once in Jude, once in Revelation, 19 times in Acts (16 in chap. 5), and five times in Hebrews (three in chap. 11 alone).

The noun *parembolē*, "encampment," occurs once in Revelation, six times in Acts, and three times in Hebrews.

The noun *plēthos* occurs two times in Mark, two times in John, once each in James and Peter, eight times in Luke, 17 times in Acts, and once in Hebrews.

The noun *akron* occurs six times in the New Testament: twice in Matthew, twice in Mark, once in Luke, and once in Hebrews. The usages in Matthew and Mark occur in Synoptic parallels. Luke uses the accusative case articular singular form of the noun as does Hebrews, while Matthew and Mark use the second inflected form in an anarthrous construction.

The verb *hupostrephō* is a Lukan word that occurs only once in Mark, Paul, and 2 Peter, but 21 times in Luke, 12 in Acts, and once in Hebrews.

The noun *chronos* occurs three times in Matthew, twice in Mark, nine times in Paul, seven times in Luke, 17 times in Acts, and three times in Hebrews.

The noun *boulē* occurs twice in Luke, eight times in Acts, twice in Paul, and once in Hebrews.

The phrase *apo katabolēs kosmou*, "from the foundation of the world," occurs once in Matthew, twice in Revelation, once in Luke, and twice in Hebrews.

The use of *kai* with the feminine personal pronoun *autē*, translated "and she," occurs once in Paul, once in Revelation, five times in Luke, and once in Hebrews.

Rhēma, "word," occurs 33 times in Luke-Acts, five times in Matthew, twice in Mark, 12 times in John, eight times in Paul, three times in Peter, once in Jude, and four times in Hebrews. It is used with the genitive *theou* seven times and is translated "Word of God" twice in Luke, twice in John, twice in Hebrews, and once in Paul. In only two of these seven occurrences of this phrase is the genitive noun *theou* placed before *rhēma*: Luke 1:37 and Heb 6:5.

The phrase *oikos Israēl* or *oikos Iakōb*, outside of two occurrences in Matthew, is found once in Luke, three times in Acts, and twice in Hebrews (see discussion in chap. 5 below).

The phrase *kata panta* occurs three times in Paul, twice in Acts, and twice in Hebrews.

The use of *kaloumenos* with names or appellations is a Lukan usage and occurs outside Luke-Acts only in Hebrews and Revelation.

The phrase *tis ex humōn*, "which of you," occurs three times in Matthew, once in John, once in James, five times in Luke, and twice in Hebrews. In eight of the 12 occurrences, the indefinite pronoun *tis* is separated from the preposition by an intervening noun, verb, pronoun, or conjunction. Only Luke 11:5; John 8:46; Heb 3:13; and 4:1 use the phrase without any intervening words.

The use of the phrase *kath hēmeran*, "daily," occurs once in Matthew, once in Mark, five times in Luke, six times in Acts, twice in Paul, and twice in Hebrews. It is infrequent in Matthew, Mark, and Paul, but not in Luke-Acts. This is quite important for our discussion because the comparison of the Synoptic Gospels supports the suggestion that this phrase is characteristically Lukan. The fact that it occurs twice in Hebrews is notable in that Hebrews is only about one-fourth the length of Luke-Acts or the Pauline Letters. The phrase also occurs in Heb 3:8 and 3:13 (with one intervening word between the preposition and the noun).

The use of the present infinitive *legein*, "to say or speak," occurs five times in Matthew, eight times in Mark, once in John, 18 times in Luke-Acts, four times in Paul, four times in Hebrews, and once in James. Again, considering the relative lengths of these books, there is a correlation between Luke-Acts and Hebrews. Furthermore, only in Luke 11:27 and Heb 8:13 is the infinitive preceded by both the preposition *en* and the article *tō*. This example along with the preceding two all involve the New Testament author's use of a form of the verb *legō*. The fact that in all three cases Luke and Hebrews can be correlated against the rest of the New Testament writers lends support to the argument for Lukan authorship of Hebrews.

The lexical item *laos*, "people," occurs twice in Mark, four times in Peter, 12 times in the Johannine epistles, 12 times in Paul, 84 times in Luke-Acts, and 13 times in Hebrews. Again, Luke-Acts and Hebrews show a comparable proportion in terms of usage. Note further that the use of this noun with the adjective *pas*, "all," occurs once in Matthew, once in Paul, twice in Hebrews, and 16 times in Luke-Acts.

The adjective "most high," *hupsistos*, occurs once in Matthew, twice in Mark, nine times in Luke-Acts, and once in Hebrews, for a total of 13 occurrences in the New Testament. In four of these (Mark 5:7; Luke 8:28; Acts 16:17; and Heb 7:1) the adjective qualifies the noun *theou* in the genitive case, and the phrase is translated "of the most high God."

A rather striking lexical example of the agreement of Luke-Acts with Hebrews (against Pauline usage) is found with the verb *eiserchomai*, "to go into." It occurs 36 times in Matthew, 30 times in Mark, 20 times in the Johannine epistles, three times in James, but only four times in the entire Pauline corpus. Yet it is used 82 times in Luke-Acts and 17 times in Hebrews. The contrast with Paul's usage is evident. Furthermore, this is a compound verb formed by the preposition *eis* and the regular verb *erchomai*. Such compound verbs are found with greatest frequency in Luke-Acts, Paul, and Hebrews, but especially in

Luke-Acts and Hebrews. Four more examples of compound verbs and their frequencies are listed below.

Ekpherō, "to go out," occurs once in Mark, once in Paul, but five times in Luke-Acts and once in Hebrews.

eisakouō, a strengthened form of *akouō*, "to hear," occurs once in Matthew, once in Paul, twice in Luke-Acts, and once in Hebrews.

The lexical item *ekzēteō*, "to seek out," occurs once in 1 Peter, twice in Paul, three times in Luke-Acts, and twice in Hebrews (11:6; 12:17).

The verb *eisagō*, "to bring in," occurs only nine times in the New Testament: once in John, seven times in Luke-Acts, and once in Heb 1:6.

The compound verb *metalambanō*, "to partake," occurs seven times in the New Testament: four in Acts, once in Paul, and twice in Hebrews (6:7; 12:10).

The compound verb *epilambanomai*, "to take," occurs 19 times in the New Testament: once in Matthew, once in Mark, 12 times in Luke-Acts, twice in Paul, and three times in Hebrews. In addition, the phrase *tēs cheiros autou* (*autōn*) follows the verb only in Acts 23:19 and Heb 8:9.

The use of the nominative form *heteroi*, "others," occurs once in Matthew, four times in Luke-Acts, and once in Hebrews. In Luke 11:16; Acts 2:13; and Heb 11:36, it is followed by *de* and a participle.

The combination of *megas . . . mikros* does not occur in Paul nor in the Gospels, but appears three times in Acts, once in Hebrews (Heb 8:11), once in James, and five times in Revelation. The frequency in Revelation is probably due to the subject and theme.

The use of the aorist active indicative third person singular form of *laleō*, "to say or speak," is found outside the five narrative books in the New Testament (Matthew-Acts) only in Hebrews and Revelation. The aorist active indicative third person plural form of this verb occurs three times in Revelation, once in Jude, once in Peter, once in James, four times in Luke-Acts, and once in Hebrews. There is a parallel between Acts 16:32 and Heb 13:7 in that the aorist active indicative third person plural form is followed by a dative personal pronoun, the articular accusative *ton logon*, and the genitive *theou* (*kuriou* in the Acts passage): "They spoke to him (us) the word of the Lord (God)." Neither of the two forms occurs in Paul.

Simcox noted that three times in Hebrews divine revelation is described by the use of the verb *laleō* with the subject *theos*, and that this same phrase occurs twice in Luke, four times in Acts, once in John, and nowhere else in the New Testament.[60]

The present active indicative third person singular *marturei*, "to bear witness," occurs six times in John, once in Acts, and once in Hebrews. The structure of the clauses in Acts and Hebrews are quite similar in that each verb is followed by the dative personal pronoun, the conjunction *kai*, "and," and an articular proper noun. The clause in Acts 22:5 reads "all the elders bear witness to me" while the clause in Heb 10:15 reads "the Holy Spirit bears witness to us." The lexical item *martus* and its cognates are found most frequently in the Johannine Epistles, somewhat frequently in the writings of Luke-Acts and Hebrews, and relatively infrequently in Paul. The present passive participle nominative masculine singular *marturoumenos*, for example, is found only three times in the New Testament, twice in Acts and once in Hebrews (7:8).

The noun *anamnesis*, "remembrance," appears just three times in the New Testament: Luke 22:19 (the Lord 's Supper pericope), 1 Cor 11:24–25 (a passage parallel to Luke 22:19), and Heb 10:3. This comparison is given further weight in that neither Matthew nor Mark (in their accounts of the Lord's Supper) includes this word, yet both Luke and Paul do. This is a further example of the close connection between the writings of Luke and Paul, and between Luke, Paul, and Hebrews.

The nominative, genitive, dative, accusative and vocative plural forms of *patēr*, "father," occur 53 times in the New

---

[60] W. H. Simcox, *The Writers of the New Testament* (London: Hodder & Stoughton, 1902), 50.

Testament: 31 in Luke-Acts, seven in Paul, five in Hebrews, seven in the Johannine writings, and three in the rest of the New Testament. In addition, the use of *patris*, "fatherland," occurs eight times in the New Testament: seven in the Gospels (two in Luke) and once in Heb 11:14. This indicates that Luke and Hebrews show considerable interest in the patriarchs.

The subordinating conjunction *mēpote* occurs 25 times in the New Testament: eight in Matthew, twice in Mark, nine in Luke-Acts, once in John, once in Paul, and four times in Hebrews (2:1; 3:12; 4:1; 9:17).

The verb *saleuō*, "to be shaken," occurs 15 times in the New Testament: twice in Matthew, once in Mark, eight times in Luke-Acts, once in Paul, and three times in Hebrews (12:26–27 [twice]).

The verb *mellō*, "to be about to do anything," occurs nine times in Matthew, twice in Mark, 20 times in the Johannine corpus, once in James, three times in the Petrine corpus, 39 times in Luke-Acts, 14 times in Paul, and eight times in Hebrews.

The phrase *toutōn tōn hēmerōn* occurs twice in Acts and once in Hebrews. The preposition *en* followed by the dative *tais hēmerais* "in the days," occurs twice in Matthew, three times in the Johannine corpus (all in Revelation), 18 times in Luke-Acts, and once in Hebrews.

The phrase *en tō orei*, "in the mountain," occurs twice in John, twice in Luke-Acts, and once in Heb 8:5, but nowhere else in the New Testament.

The phrase *dia pantos*, "always," occurs once in Matt 18:10, once in Mark 5:5, four times in Luke-Acts, twice in Paul, and three times in Hebrews (2:15; 9:6; 13:15).

The phrase *eis peripoiēsin psuchēs*, which occurs in Heb 10:39, corresponds semantically with Luke 21:19.

The adjective *monogenēs* occurs three times in Luke (7:12; 8:42; 9:38), four times in John (1:14,18; 3:16,18), once in 1 John 4:9, and once in Heb 11:17. John uses it only to refer to the everlasting Son, whereas Luke and Hebrews use it only to refer to men.

The construction *tou pneumatos tou hagiou* (referring to the Holy Spirit) occurs twice in Mark, once in Luke, once in John, 13 times in Acts, once in Paul, and once in Hebrews. This is predominantly a Lukan construction, and with one exception in Ephesians is never used by Paul.

The noun *technitēs* occurs four times in the New Testament: Acts 19:24, 38; Heb 11:10; Rev 18:22.

The verb *psēlaphaō* occurs four times in the New Testament: Luke 24:39; Acts 17:27; Heb 12:18; and 1 John 1:1.

The verb *anakampto* occurs four times in the New Testament: Matt 2:12; Luke 10:6; Acts 18:21; Heb 11:15.

The use of *agiazomenoi* to refer to Christians is predominantly found in Luke's writings and Hebrews.

There are 43 words (apart from the 53 that are unique to Luke-Acts and Hebrews) in Hebrews of which half or more of their other occurrences in the New Testament are in Luke-Acts.[61]

Conclusion of Lexical Similarity

I have not tried to discuss vocabulary differences between the Lukan corpus and Hebrews. We should keep in mind two things in this regard. First, theme and subject matter determine lexical choice to a great extent. Some vocabulary differences can undoubtedly be accounted for in this fashion. Second, there are some lexical differences between Luke and Acts, but similarities outweigh the differences.[62] My purpose has been to illustrate the remarkable lexical similarities that characterize the three works and suggest that these are best explained by common authorship.

Simcox, after carefully sifting through the evidence, concludes that Luke's language, both lexically and stylistically, has more in common

[61] A. Eagar, "The Authorship of the Epistle to the Hebrews," 122.
[62] Hawkins, *Horae Synopticae*, 182.

with Hebrews than is true of other New Testament writer.[63] Agreement with this assessment continues to the present time.

Stylistic Similarity

Greek scholars have pointed out that while there is a common substratum of ideas, expressions, and religious terminology that undergirds all New Testament writers, it is nevertheless possible to examine the linguistic features that distinguish the work of one author from another.[64] Stylistic studies can furnish evidence that, when tempered with other matters of external and internal evidence, can be used as a discriminating factor in questions of authorship.

Within literary stylistics, there are two basic types and purposes of stylistic analyses: (1) Descriptive stylistics, where the purpose is simply to describe style in a given writing, and (2) Explanatory stylistics, where the purpose is to use the stylistic data to explain something. Two additional categories may be subsumed under Explanatory stylistics: (1) Extrinsic, where the goal is author identification or determination of chronology for a set of writings, and (2) Intrinsic, where the goal is hermeneutical and the goal is to establish meaning.[65]

The Importance of Style in Questions of Authorship Identification

As Botha has pointed out, "style" is notoriously difficult to define.[66] We may generally define an author's style of writing, following an Aristotelian line, as more about the manner of writing than about the matter of content. "Style has to do with the *choice* available to users of language, and since these choices are determined by specific needs and circumstances, style is a *contextually determined* phenomenon."[67] Yet we must make clear at the outset that a rigid distinction between form and content cannot be maintained. Different genres of literature

---

[63] W. H. Simcox, *The Writers of the New Testament,* 52–53.

[64] Robertson, *Luke the Historian,* 116–37; N. Turner, *Syntax,* in J. H. Moulton, *A Grammar of the Greek New Testament,* 4 vols.; 3rd and 4th vols. by N. Turner (Edinburgh: T&T Clark, 1906), 3:1–4.

[65] G. Leech, "Stylistics," in *Discourse and Literature,* ed. T. A. van Dijk (Amsterdam: John Benjamins, 1985), 39.

[66] E. Botha, "Style in the New Testament: The Need for Serious Reconsideration," *JSNT* 43 (1991): 71.

[67] Ibid., 78–79.

demand different styles; that is, different contents demand different forms.[68]

Sometimes stylistic differences between texts written by different authors are viewed as trivial in that they are more or less expected results based on the subject matter of the texts.[69] Examples would include the use of tense forms, the use of personal pronouns, and the proportion of verbs to nouns. Clauses in scientific texts are considerably longer than those in popular writings, primarily because of the genre.

Even textual features of a more abstract nature (such as the frequency of articles and the use of prepositions) are not necessarily indicators of individual linguistic style; sometimes they are based on the nature of the text being considered. Yet any study that attempts to evaluate an author's style of writing has a generally agreed-upon notion that the variability of some stylistic features within the writings of a single author is small when compared with the variability among different authors, especially in the same genre.[70]

I am working under the assumption that an author's use of non-content words is less variable than his use of content words, and hence a more helpful indicator in questions of authorship identification. However, an author's use of content words must never be excluded in attempts at author identification. Ellegard's explanation for this is worth noting:

> Even if the subject-matter very largely determines the vocabulary used in a text, we must not forget that the author's choice of subject-matter, in its turn, is in quite a high degree due to his more or less permanent interest, or even to his temperament. Most writers have their pet subjects. And even when writing on a different subject, an author's main interest may break through in metaphors and illustrations.[71]

Stylistic studies are important in questions of authorship for at least two reasons. First, through comparative studies, attempts are made to find an author who could have written the text based on his acknowledged style in other writings. Second, through comparative

---

[68] A. Ellegard, "Genre Styles, Individual Styles, and Authorship Identification," in *Text Processing, Proceedings of Nobel Symposium* 51, ed. S. Allen (Stockholm: Almqvist & Wiksell International, 1982), 519.

[69] Ibid., 521.

[70] Ibid., 528.

[71] A. Ellegard, *Who was Junius?* (Stockholm: Almqvist & Wiksell, 1962), 101–2.

studies, attempts are made to exclude most others within the circle of suspected authors that could have written the text.[72]

These considerations are important for the theory of Lukan authorship of Hebrews. If we arbitrarily narrow the field of candidates to those who are New Testament authors (something that cannot be done with certainty), Luke and Paul are the most obvious candidates because of vocabulary, stylistic, and conceptual similarities. It has been shown based on lexical comparison alone that Luke is more likely to be the author than Paul. In this section on stylistic comparison, it will be shown again that such is the case.

In 1986, Anthony Kenny's *A Stylometric Study of the New Testament* was published. It was the first attempt to make use of a full grammatical database (provided by Timothy and Barbara Friberg) as the foundation of a stylometric study of the New Testament. Stylometry is the study of quantifiable features of style that appear in a text (whether spoken or written). The operative word here is "quantifiable." Kenny's work provides statistical data that one may use to compare and contrast the writings of one author with another.[73] While stylometry may be used for different purposes, Kenny's interest is the problem of authorship attribution in the New Testament. He makes use of 99 textual features (such as the number of occurrences of *kai* and the number of neuter articles) as a basis of comparison for the major sections of the New Testament.[74]

Kenny applies the statistical data to the following questions: Was Acts written by Luke? Was the Apocalypse was written by John? Can the 13 letters traditionally credited to Paul be attributed to him stylistically? Should Hebrews be attributed to Paul? Kenny's work is thorough, and his conclusions are judiciously offered. He is quite clear that statistical studies alone, apart from other methods of analysis, cannot definitely settle questions of authorship. However, he states that "it is possible to see which parts of the New Testament resemble

---

[72] Many linguists believe that 100,000 words of an author are needed to prove authorship, and that the disputed work should contain 10,000 words. Since the entire New Testament contains approximately 180,000 words, questions of authorship cannot be settled by stylistic considerations alone. See F. Andersen, "Style and Authorship," *The Tyndale Lecture*, vol. 21, no. 2. (Parkland, Australia: Tyndale Fellowship for Biblical Studies, 1976), and N. Enkvist, *Linguistic Stylistics* (The Hague: Mouton, 1973).

[73] Statistical evidence has only a limited use in stylistics. See the discussion in S. Ullmann, *Language and Style* (Oxford: Basil Blackwell, 1964), 118–19.

[74] See A. Kenny, *A Stylometric Study of the New Testament* (Oxford: Clarendon Press, 1986), 123–24, for a complete listing of these features.

other parts more or less closely, and on the basis of this to make reasonable conjectures about authorship."[75]

Based on his data, Kenny concludes Acts was written by Luke the Evangelist. Interestingly, he offers no opinion on whether Hebrews is Pauline, but states that he was interested to note "the surpassing number of features in which it resembles the Pauline corpus."[76] He made no comment about the similarity or dissimilarity of Luke-Acts to Hebrews. However, when one compares the data from studying the 99 stylistic features, it appears that Hebrews is closer to Luke-Acts (especially to Acts and the Pauline Letters) than to the other New Testament writers.

In 2002 George Barr published a fascinating article on the impact of scalometric studies on the New Testament letters. Scalometry is "the measurement of scale-related patterns in texts."[77] Statistical studies of textual differences that ignore scale variability in a text often wrongly attribute such variations to differences in authorship. For example, Barr notes all the Pauline Letters "show a contrast between an opening section with comparatively long sentences, and a following section with comparatively short sentences (a high-scale section followed by a low-scale section)."[78] Sometimes these are related to genre, as when a doctrinal section is followed by a practical section. At other times, there is no significant change in genre, but a change in scale occurs. This change does not necessarily indicate a different author. The Pauline Letters exhibit certain "prime patterns" that "invariably occur at the beginning of an epistle." This pattern is "more complex than a simple contrast between longer and shorter sentences." Another pattern is discernible: a certain cyclical use of longer and shorter sentences at the beginning of each letter. When these

---

[75] Ibid., 1.

[76] Ibid., 121.

[77] G. Barr, "The Impact of Scalometry on New Testament Letters," *ExpTim* 114 (2002): 3. Barr's 1994 Ph.D. diss. at the University of Edinburgh was titled "Scale in Literature—with reference to the New Testament and other texts in English and Greek." Six additional articles dealing with this subject have appeared in the journal *IBS*: "Scale and the Pauline Epistles," *IBS* 17 (1995): 22–41; "Contrasts in Scale and Genre in the Letters of Paul and Seneca," *IBS* 18 (1996): 16–25; "The Structure of Hebrews and of 1st and 2nd Peter," *IBS* 19 (1997): 17–31; "The Preaching of Paul and Silvanus," *IBS* 21 (1999): 102–18; "Scalometry and the Dating of New Testament Epistles," *IBS* 22 (2000): 71–90; and "The Written and the Spoken Word," *IBS* 23 (2001): 167–81. Barr's evidence adds weight to the acknowledged stylistic differences between Hebrews and the Pauline Epistles, and provides further evidence against Pauline authorship.

[78] Ibid.

patterns are fed into a computer, a mathematical model is generated "that shows the 'shape' of the typical structure of these texts."[79] The result is that common characteristics found in the Pauline corpus (Romans through Philemon) can be identified. Every Pauline letter exhibits a common prime pattern, but the question is, How is one to evaluate this data? Assessment of the evidence requires comparison with a broad survey of other texts, both ancient and modern. In addition to all New Testament texts, Barr surveys a host of other texts, including the complete works of Isocrates, Cicero's *Ad Verrem*, most of the works of the church fathers, works by John Ruskin and Thomas Carlyle, the Federalist Papers, and sermons by James Stewart. Barr concludes: "Nowhere in that wide survey have patterns been discovered that are associated with discourse units and that might be confused with the Pauline patterns."[80] Galatians and 1 and 2 Corinthians exhibit the same structural characteristics as Ephesians, Colossians, and Philippians. Furthermore, Barr discovered the Pastoral Letters exhibit this same structural pattern. This has obvious implications for the question of Pauline authorship of the Pastoral Letters and other disputed Pauline Letters. It is also clear from Barr's study that Hebrews is stylistically distinct from them. Since Luke and Acts are not letters, Barr did not attempt to compare Hebrews with them.

Although there are other stylistic features in the New Testament that could be studied using stylometric methodology, I do not examine them in this work. Kenny cautions that there are no sure-fire "stylistic fingerprints," since such features can be varied intentionally by an author, and impressively copied by a forger.[81]

Kenny's data reveal that *statistically* the argument for Lukan authorship cannot be confirmed or denied. It cannot be confirmed because Hebrews is not so much like Luke-Acts (and so unlike the rest of the New Testament) that we can make a dogmatic statement as to common authorship. It cannot be denied because there is reasonable similarity that could be interpreted in favor of common authorship (given the fact that Hebrews is of a different genre than Luke-Acts and given the other corroborating factors—not only stylistically but lexically, theologically, and historically—that are presented in this

---

[79] Ibid., 4.
[80] Ibid., 5.
[81] Kenny, *Stylometric Study*, 120–21.

study). Nevertheless, stylistic considerations in addition to statistical data are important to us for the question at hand.

Evidence of Stylistic Similarity between Luke-Acts and Hebrews

Since the early church, scholars who studied the Letter to the Hebrews have commented on its remarkable stylistic parallels with Luke-Acts. The church fathers established an early tradition favoring Lukan involvement in the authorship of Hebrews. Clement of Alexandria, for example, is quoted by Eusebius:

> . . . the Epistle to the Hebrews is the work of Paul. . . . It was written to the Hebrews in the Hebrew language; but . . . Luke translated it carefully and published it for the Greeks, and hence the same style of expression is found in this epistle and in the Acts.[82]

An examination of New Testament literature, all of which is Koine Greek, reveals that only the writings of Luke and Hebrews approach the standard of Classical Greek. Wallace places Hebrews and Luke-Acts at the top of the list of biblical books for their range of levels of literary koine.[83] Examples of a near-Classical style observable in both Luke and Hebrews—frequent use of the genitive absolute, frequent insertion of material between adjective and noun and article and noun, the use of lengthy and balanced sentences, and relatively few Hebraisms—are more typical of Luke and Hebrews than of any other New Testament writer.[84]

Yet in spite of clear evidence of near-Classical style, both Luke and Hebrews, along with several other New Testament books, show evidence of Semitic style. This is particularly confusing in regard to Luke because he has long been considered to be Greek, a supposition I will challenge below. Luke, when compared with Matthew, is at times even more Semitic. For example, Luke is quite fond of beginning paragraphs and episodes with the Hebraistic *kai egeneto* and *en*

---

[82] Eusebius, *Ecclesiastical History*, 6.14.

[83] D. Wallace, *Greek Grammar Beyond the Basics* (Grand Rapids: Zondervan, 1996), 30.

[84] Cf. N. Turner, *Style*, in J. H. Moulton, *A Grammar of New Testament Greek* (Edinburgh: T&T Clark, 1976), 4:106–13. Davidson noted: "We do not maintain that the language of Hebrews is free from Hebraisms, but that the diction is purer than Paul's. In respect to purity, it stands on a level with the latter half of the Acts, where many of the expressions quoted by Stuart from Hebrews as Hebraisms are also found." S. Davidson, *An Introduction to the Study of the New Testament*, 2nd rev. ed. (London: Longmans, Green & Co., 1882), 1:209.

tais hēmerais ekeinais, a somewhat odd stylistic device for a Greek author supposedly writing to a Greek audience.

Franz Delitzsch notices the stylistic similarities between the Lukan corpus and Hebrews, and while he does not catalog them, he notes them frequently.[85] Lünemann, on the other hand, has collated the stylistic similarities noted by Delitzsch. His list fills seven pages of text.[86] Lünemann criticizes Delitzsch's interpretation of the stylistic data as uncritical. Several points arose after carefully sifting through both Delitzsch's evidence and Lünemann's critique of it. First, Lünemann is correct that some of the stylistic data noted by Delitzsch are not unique to Luke-Acts and Hebrews, but may have occurred elsewhere in the New Testament. Second, when they are found elsewhere, it is usually in the Pauline Letters, which further confirms the unique kinship among the writings of Luke, Paul, and Hebrews. Third, even considering stylistic data that occur elsewhere in the New Testament, the sheer bulk of the similarity between Luke-Acts and Hebrews cannot be ignored. Fourth, Lünemann grants that there is an amazing amount of similarity between Luke-Acts and Hebrews, but he rejects Lukan authorship based on the presupposition that Luke was a Gentile and the author of Hebrews was Jewish.

I shall list and in some cases briefly discuss the stylistic similarities between the Lukan corpus and Hebrews. Some of these examples were noted by Delitzsch and cataloged by Lünemann (in these cases, the reader should consult the sources). Others I have discovered through comparative research in the biblical texts using linguistic tools.[87] As in the discussion on lexical similarity, I shall divide these examples into two sections. Division One includes examples that are unique to Luke-Acts and Hebrews in the New Testament. Division Two lists examples that, while not unique to Luke-Acts and Hebrews, serve to illustrate the similarity of the three books.

---

[85] See Delitzsch, *Hebrews*, 2 vols., passim.

[86] G. Lünemann, *The Epistle to the Hebrews*, trans. M. Evans, *Critical and Exegetical Handbook to the New Testament*, ed. H. A. W. Meyer (New York: Funk & Wagnalls, 1885), 356–62.

[87] In addition to standard resources such as Hawkins, *Horae Synopticae*; R. Morgenthaler, *Statistik des Neutestamentlichen Wortschatzes* (Frankfurt am Main/Zurich: Gotthelf-Verlag, 1958); and W. F. Moulton and A. S. Geden, *A Concordance to the Greek New Testament* (Edinburgh: T&T Clark, 1897). I used Collison's unpublished dissertation "Linguistic Usages in the Gospel of Luke" (Ph.D. diss., Southern Methodist University, 1977); *The Computer Bible* (1988); the grammatical tags developed by T. and B. Friberg; and the LOGOS and BibleWorks software.

Division One

The use of the particle *kaitoi* (Heb 4:3) is found elsewhere only in Acts 14:17.

The preposition *dia* with the genitive is used of time that someone passes through, in Luke 5:5, Heb 2:15, and Acts 1:3.

The preposition *para* with the comparative (Heb 1:4) corresponds to Luke 3:13.

The infinitive *prosechein* followed by the dative is found only in Heb 2:1 and Acts 16:14.

The word *hōs* with the infinitive is found only in Luke 9:52, Acts 20:24, and Heb 7:9.

The future infinitive occurs only in Acts and Hebrews.

The use of the accusative participle with the dative pronoun is an example of Classical Greek, and occurs in Heb 2:10; Luke 1:74; Acts 11:12; 15:22; and 25:29.

The use of the future participle to express purpose is found only in Acts 8:27 and Heb 13:17.

The present passive participle *euēggelismenoi*, "to evangelize" (Heb 4:2), is used of people to whom the gospel is proclaimed in Luke 7:22.

The word *homoiōthēnai*, "to be made like" (Heb 2:17), is used in the same fashion as in Acts 14:11.

The comparative adjective followed by *huper* (Heb 4:12, "sharper than") has its counterpart in Luke 16:8 (where the phrase "wiser than" is used).

The infinitival *perikeitai* occurs only in Heb 5:2 and Acts 28:20.

The preposition *apo* in Heb 5:7 occurs in the same unusual construction in Luke 19:3; 24:41; Acts 12:14; 20:9; 22:11.

The use of *echein*, "to have," with a following infinitive (Heb 6:13) is near-Classical style and occurs four times in Luke-Acts.

The phrase *tou idiou haimatos*, "his own blood," occurs only in Heb 9:12; 13:12; Acts 20:28. There are many occurrences of the phrase *haima autou* "his blood" throughout the New Testament, but only in Acts and Hebrews is the other construction used.

The use of the preposition *dia* with *pneumatos* occurs only in Heb 9:14; Acts 1:2; 11:28; 21:4.

The use of *kai autos*, "and this," with a proper name occurs in Heb 11:11 and is found in only three other places in the New Testament, all in Luke-Acts (Luke 20:42 [variant reading]; 24:15; Acts 8:13).

The use of the preposition *dia*, "because," followed by *to mēdemian*, "not one," occurs only in Acts 28:18 and Heb 10:2.

The juxtaposition of the indefinite relative *ti*, "some, something," with the preposition *para* occurs only in Acts 3:5, Heb 2:7,9.

The use of the article *ho* followed by the untranslated *te* and a noun or substantivized participle occurs once in Luke, seven times in Acts, once in Hebrews, and nowhere else in the New Testament.

The use of the present participle of the verb "to be," *ōn*, followed by the negative *ouk*, occurs only twice in Luke, twice in Acts, and twice in Hebrews.

The conjunction *kai* followed by the preposition *pros* and a verb of speaking occurs only in Luke and Hebrews.

Simcox noted that there is a "real resemblance" to Luke in the way Hebrews uses *paschein*, "to suffer," without an object for the passion of Christ (cf. Luke 22:15; 24:46; Acts 1:3; 17:3; Heb 2:18; 9:26; 13:12).[88] This is distinct from the Pauline usage of *paschō*, where it appears in an absolute sense three times, but never in reference to Christ.

The use of the preposition *meta*, "with," preceding *parrēsias*, "boldness," occurs only in Luke-Acts and Hebrews.

[88] W. H. Simcox, *The Writers of the New Testament*, 49–50.

The use of the dative plural personal pronoun *hemin*, "to us," immediately before *ho logos* occurs only three times in the New Testament: once in Acts and twice in Hebrews.

The use of the present infinitive *pathein*, "to suffer," following the imperfect verb *edei*, "to be necessary," occurs only four times in the New Testament: twice in Luke, once in Acts, and once in Hebrews. In two of these four examples (Luke 17:25; Heb 9:26), the pronominal adjective *polus*, "much, many," occurs between the verb and the infinitive.

The use of *kai touto*, "and this," preceding *poieō*, "make, do," occurs only in Luke 5:6 and Heb 6:3. There are 23 total occurrences of *kai touto* in the New Testament.

The relative pronoun *hos* followed by the preposition *en* and an articular plural noun occurs only in Acts 14:16 and Heb 5:7.

The particle *ei* followed by *men oun* occurs only four times in the New Testament: twice in Acts (19:38; 25:11) and twice in Hebrews (7:11; 8:4).

The subordinating conjunction *hoti* followed by the nominative masculine plural relative pronoun *autoi* occurs six times in Matthew, twice in Luke, and once in Hebrews. The six instances in Matthew are all in the Sermon on the Mount, where the standard phrase, "Blessed for they . . . " occurs. It is significant that we encounter this phrase only in Luke and Hebrews outside of its use in Matthew.

The nominative plural participle *ōn*, "being," followed by *huios*, "son," occurs only in Luke 3:23 and Heb 5:8.

The preposition *kata* followed by the accusative *nomon*, "according to the law," occurs twice in John, twice in Luke, three times in Acts, and twice in Hebrews. In Luke 2:22 and Heb 9:22 the concept of "cleansing" is adjoined to this prepositional phrase. This phrase is connected with the proper name "Moses" where agency is affirmed ("law of Moses" or "given by Moses") only in Luke 2:22 and Heb 9:19.

The conjunction *kai* followed by the adverb *hōde*, "and here," occurs four times in the New Testament: Luke 4:23; Acts 9:14,21; Heb 7:8.

The conjunction *kai* followed by the nominative plural article *hoi* and the untranslated *men* is unique to Acts and Hebrews in the New Testament (two occurrences each).

The phrase *epi ton oikon* occurs twice in Luke, four times in Hebrews (3:6; 8:8 [twice]; 10:21), but nowhere else in the New Testament.

The phrase *tou patros* followed by the relative *hēn* occurs only twice in the New Testament: Acts 1:4 and Heb 7:10.

Ho laos followed by *gar* occurs twice in the New Testament: Luke 19:48 and Heb 7:11.

The use of *eti* followed by *de* in a climactic sense occurs only in Heb 11:36, Luke 14:26, and Acts 2:26.

The verb *sunantaō* occurs only in Luke, Acts, and Hebrews. It is followed by *autō* in Luke 9:37 and Heb 7:10.

Division Two

The conjunction *te* (Heb 1:3) is rarely found in the New Testament except in Luke, Paul, and Hebrews, but is used most frequently in Luke and Hebrews (three times in John, 25 times in Paul, 159 times in Luke-Acts, and 20 times in Hebrews). The proportions are especially striking when we remember that the Lukan and Pauline corpora are each approximately four times longer than Hebrews.

The juxtaposition of the untranslated particle *te* with the conjunction *kai* occurs once in Matthew, once in the Johannine corpus, twice in James, 31 times in Luke-Acts, nine times in Paul, and 10 times in Hebrews.

The conjunction *de* is found in the third position only in Heb 1:13; Luke 15:17; Acts 27:14; Gal 3:23.

hothen occurs six times in Hebrews, never in Paul, four times in Matthew, once in 1 John, and four times in Luke-Acts. It is used in the logical sense in Acts and Hebrews, but never in Paul.

The adverb *exō* with the genitive case does not occur in Paul or John but, in addition to the Synoptics, appears 10 times in Luke-Acts and three times in Hebrews.

The use of *dunatai* with the aorist infinitive is most frequent in Luke and Hebrews.

The phrase *posō mallon*, "how much more," is common to Luke and Hebrews.

The phrase *touto to haima*, "This is the blood . . . ," occurs five times in the New Testament, all in the context of the Last Supper and all with the noun *diathēkē*, "covenant":

Matt 26:28	*touto gar estin to haima mou tēs diathēkēs*
Mark 14:24	*touto estin to haima mou tēs diathēkēs*
Luke 22:20	*touto to potērion hē kainē diathēkē en tō haimati mou*
1 Cor 11:25	*touto to potērion hē kainē diathēkē estin en tō emō haimati*
Heb 9:20	*touto to haima tēs diathēkēs*

In the examples above only Luke and Hebrews omit the equative verb while the others employ it.

In Heb 9:22, the use of *haimatekchusia*, "shedding of blood," has the same root (*ekcheō*) as *ekchunnomai*, "poured out," which is used by the Synoptics in the account of the Last Supper (Matt 26:28; Mark 14:24; Luke 22:20; and nowhere else in the New Testament).

In the New Testament, the use of the preposition *meta* followed by an articular infinitive occurs twice in Mark, once in Paul, once in Hebrews, and seven times in Luke-Acts.

The use of the preposition *apō*, "from," with the feminine relative pronoun *hēs*, "which," occurs once in Peter, twice in Paul, five times in Luke-Acts, and twice in Hebrews (7:13; 11:15).

The use of the conjunction *oun*, "therefore," followed by the untranslated *men* occurs once in Mark, twice in John, four times in Paul, but 28 times in Luke-Acts and three times in Hebrews.

The preposition *pros* followed by the accusative relative pronoun *hon*, translated "to whom," occurs once in Peter, twice in Luke, and twice in Hebrews (4:13; 11:18), but nowhere else in the New Testament.

The use of the preposition *meta* followed immediately by *de* occurs three times in Matthew, three times in Mark, twice in John, three times in Luke, eight times in Acts, and twice in Hebrews (9:3,27), but nowhere else in the New Testament.

The use of the adverb *heōs*, "until," followed by the untranslated *an*, occurs once in Matthew, once in Mark, twice in Luke-Acts, and once in Heb 1:13, but nowhere else in the New Testament.

The preposition *peri* followed by the genitive relative pronoun *hou*, "concerning whom," occurs 11 times in the New Testament: once each in Matthew, John, and Paul, and twice in Luke, five times in Acts, and once in Heb 5:11.

The conjunction *kai* followed by the adverb *hos*, "and as," pronoun *hou*, "concerning whom," occurs 11 times in the New Testament: once each in Matthew, John, and Paul, twice in Luke, five times in Acts, and once in Hebrews.

The preposition *epi* (contracted form *ep'* before a word beginning with a vowel), followed by the accusative relative pronoun *hon*, "upon whom," occurs only in Hebrews outside of the narrative books of the New Testament: once in Matthew, once in Mark, twice in Luke, once in John, once in Acts, and once in Hebrews.

The use of *dia to* + infinitive is a characteristically Lukan construction: it occurs three times in Matthew, three times in Mark, once in John, once in Paul, but 13 times in Luke-Acts, and five times in Hebrews.

The verb *prostithēmi* occurs 19 times in the New Testament: twice in Matthew, once in Mark, eight times in Luke, six times in Acts, once in Paul, and once in Heb 12:19. The infinitival form occurs only in Matthew, Luke, and Hebrews.

The verb *huparchō* is a Lukan favorite that occurs in Luke-Acts 40 times out of its 60 occurrences. It is found in Hebrews once, but the usage in Hebrews is unique in that it is followed by the pronoun *humōn* (as in Luke 12:33) and that the participial form *huparchontōn* occurs only in Luke, Acts, and Heb 10:34.

The use of the articular infinitive with the preposition *en* is also a linguistic usage of Luke. It appears three times in Matthew, twice in Mark, four times in Paul, but 40 times in Luke-Acts, and four times in Hebrews.

The use of the article *tou* before infinitives is predominantly Lukan but also occurs in Hebrews.

The phrase *hē genea hautē*, "this generation," occurs five times in Matthew, three times in Mark, eight times in Luke, once in Acts, and once in Hebrews.

The genitive *heautou* followed by *kai* occurs five times in the New Testament: once in Matthew, three times in Luke, and once in Heb 9:7.

The cumulative effect of these stylistic similarities provides a forceful argument in favor of Lukan authorship of Hebrews. When we consider that Luke-Acts is primarily narrative discourse while Hebrews is hortatory discourse, these parallels are the more convincing, because the difference in discourse genres would (to some extent) govern the style expressed in the writing. Furthermore, some of the parallels above occur only in the Gospels and Acts. Since the Gospels are narrative discourse (and the Synoptic Gospels share a significant amount of common material among themselves), the fact that a certain lexical item or stylistic feature occurs only in them and Hebrews would further bolster the argument for Lukan authorship.

In addition to the stylistic features listed, other examples link Luke-Acts with Hebrews. Both Luke and Hebrews show a marked stylistic similarity in their frequent employment of the participle.

The ratio of participles to total verbs and verbals is nearly identical in Hebrews and the last half of Acts. Han's *Parsing Guide* lists over 16 pages of verbs and verbals from Hebrews. There are 297 participles in Hebrews, an average of 18 per page in Han's guide. The last 16 and a half pages in the guide for Acts (a string of text equivalent in length to Hebrews) show 308 participles, an average of 18.5 per page.[89] This is a larger average than in the Pauline corpus or the rest of the New Testament.

Another interesting stylistic parallel among the three writings concerns the position of participial and adjectival phrases qualifying an articular noun. In nonbiblical Greek, the participial and adjectival phrases normally occur between an article and its noun. Jewish Greek (i.e., Greek heavily influenced by Hebrew or Aramaic) has a tendency to place the adjectival phrase after the noun as is done in Semitic languages, with the article repeated. Turner notes the immediate parallel between Hebrews and the "we" sections of Acts (see Table 3).[90]

Table 3: Positions of participial and adjectival phrases qualifying an articular noun in Hebrews and the "we" sections of Acts

	Between-position	**Post-position**
Hebrews	6:4,7; 7:27; 9:6,11,12, 15; 10:1; 11:10,29; 12:1, 2; 13:12	2:5; 6:4,7; 8:2; 9:2,4,8, 9; 10:15; 13:20
"We" Sections	16:13; 27:34; 28:2,16	16:17; 21:11; 28:2,9

A final stylistic parallel between the Lukan corpus and Hebrews is found in the use of the first person plural personal pronouns "we" and "us." In the so-called "we" sections of Acts, Luke employs "we" to show that he was present with Paul at the time of the events described.[91] It has been suggested that Luke's "we" may have been a literary form employed for effect as well as to suggest the author's personal involvement in the events narrated.[92] In studying the book

---

[89] N. Han, *Parsing Guide to the Greek New Testament* (Scottsdale: Herald Press, 1971), 282–97.

[90] N. Turner, *Style*, 110.

[91] Irenaeus furnished early evidence in favor of the traditional view that Luke was a traveling companion of Paul in *Adv. Haer.* 3.14.1: "this Luke was inseparable from Paul." Fitzmyer modified the view of Irenaeus by identifying Luke as the "sometime" companion of Paul, since he believed Luke was not in Paul's company during the period from AD 50–58. J. Fitzmyer, *Luke the Theologian*, 4–5.

[92] For a comprehensive analysis of the "we" passages, including the history of research, see

of Hebrews, one is immediately impressed by the frequent use of "we" and "us." Indeed, the first person plural personal pronoun or the corresponding verb ending appears 61 times in Hebrews and 50 times in Acts 16–28. When we consider that Paul characteristically uses the first person personal pronoun "I," and that of all the New Testament writers, only Luke and the author of Hebrews make such extensive use of "we," the parallel becomes even more striking.

There is beyond question an impressive array of evidence to link Luke with Hebrews. The fact that this association has been recognized since the days of the church fathers further supports the proposal that Luke was the independent author.

Köhler suggested that Luke had a hand in the writing of Hebrews,[93] while at the same time K. Stein noted that the style of Hebrews was closer to Luke's two volumes than to any other New Testament writer.[94] Eight years later, in his commentary on Hebrews, Stein accepted

---

J. Wehnert, *Die Wir-Passagen der Apostelgeschichte, Ein lukanisches Stilmittel aus jüdischer Tradition*, GTA 40 (Göttingen: Vandenhoeck & Ruprecht, 1989). Wehnert evaluates the tradition-historical background of the "we" passages, comparing them especially to Ezra and Daniel. He suggests that the "we" passages function as a stylistic device taken over from Jewish tradition. If this is the case, then we have further evidence for the Jewish background of Luke himself. If one takes the view that the "we" passages do not indicate the author's presence with Paul in Acts and are purely stylistic, the favorable comparison with Hebrews is still valid. W. S. Kurz, *Reading Luke-Acts: Dynamics of Biblical Narrative* (Louisville: WJK, 1993), 111–24, appears to accept the historical accuracy of the narrator in the "we" sections, but focuses on the narrative importance of the "we" sections (rather than their historical import) as it reflects the presence of the narrator at the time of the events. H. Riley, *Preface to Luke* (Macon: Mercer University Press, 1993), 111–16, has an excellent discussion on the historicity of the "we" sections from the perspective of one who has done significant work on the Synoptic problem. See also P. Walker, *Jesus and the Holy City: New Testament Perspectives on Jerusalem* (Grand Rapids: Eerdmans, 1996), 107n195. Porter argues that the "we" sections were a source document that the author of Acts used, preserving its first-person form. S. Porter, "The 'We' Passages," in *The Book of Acts in its Greco-Roman Setting*, ed. D. W. J. Gill and C. H. Gemph (Grand Rapids: Eerdmans, 1994), 545–74. Although Porter's argument is certainly possible, it is not sufficient in my view to overturn the traditional view that the author of the "we" passages was Luke himself. Schmidt concluded from his study of the style of the "we" sections that no basis exists for isolating this material from the rest of Acts. He found insufficient evidence to suggest that the "we" sections were either added to a source or retained from a source, even a source from the same author. D. Schmidt, "Syntactical Style in the 'We'-Sections of Acts: How Lukan is it?" *SBLSP*, ed. D. Lull (Atlanta: Scholars Press, 1989), 300–8. Edmundson's point is well-taken: "There are few passages in ancient historical literature more clearly the work not merely of a contemporary writer but of an observant eye-witness than is the narrative contained in the last seven chapters of Acts" (*The Church in Rome in the First Century* [London: Longmans, 1913], 87).

[93] J. F. Köhler, *Versuch über die Abfassungszeit: der epistolischen Schriften im Neuen Testament und der Apokalypse* (Leipzig: J. A. Barth, 1830), 206–9.

[94] K. Stein, *Kommentar zu dem Evangelium des Lucas: nebst einem Anhange über den Brief an die Laodiceer* (Halle: Schwetschke & Sohn, 1830), 293–95.

the possibility that Luke was the independent author based on the stylistic similarities noticed by Grotius, Köhler, and others.[95]

Henry Alford made this interesting admission with respect to Lukan authorship of Hebrews and the supposition of Luke's Gentile background:

> Could we explain away the inference apparently unavoidable from Col. iv. 14, such a supposition [Luke's authorship of Hebrews] would seem to have some support from the epistle itself. The students of the following commentary will very frequently be struck by the verbal and idiomatic coincidences with the style of St. Luke. The argument, as resting on them, has been continually taken up and pushed forward by Delitzsch, and comes on his reader frequently with a force which at the time it is not easy to withstand.[96]

No less an authority than B. F. Westcott had this to say concerning the stylistic resemblance between the Lukan corpus and Hebrews:

> It has been already seen that the earliest scholars who speak of the Epistle notice its likeness in style to the writings of St. Luke; and when every allowance has been made for coincidences which consist in forms of expression which are found also in the LXX or in other writers of the N.T., or in late Greek generally, the likeness is unquestionably remarkable.[97]

On the authorship of Hebrews, Nigel Turner remarked:

> Were he [the author] Luke, and were Luke a Gentile proselyte, the secularisms in Hebrews may be due, as in the "diary" (the We sections), to its being written in the early days of Luke's Christian life before he had acquired much Jewish Greek. Kümmel is unwarrantably dogmatic. "Hebrews . . . diverges so strikingly from Acts in style . . . that the author of Acts is not to be considered as the author of Hebrews."[98]

Turner regarded Luke as a candidate for the authorship of Hebrews. But his comment about the dogmatism of Kümmel is especially pertinent. A cursory reading of commentaries on Hebrews reveals that Luke is often dismissed based on Kümmel's statement. The evidence demonstrates that Luke does not diverge "strikingly" from Acts stylistically. F. F. Bruce left no room for doubt on the issue: "Stylistically

---

[95] K. Stein, *Der Brief an die Hebräer: theoretisch-practisch erklärt und in seinem grossartigen Zusammenhange dargestellt* (Leipzig: Carl Heinrich Reclam, 1838), 5.

[96] H. Alford, *Alford's Greek Testament: An Exegetical and Critical Commentary*, vol. 4, part 1, *Prolegomena and Hebrews*, 5th ed. (Cambridge: Deighton, Bell, & Co., 1875; repr., Grand Rapids: Guardian Press, 1976), 53.

[97] Westcott, *Hebrews*, lxxvi.

[98] N. Turner, *Style*, 112. W. Kümmel, *Introduction to the New Testament* (Nashville: Abingdon, 1975), 281.

Hebrews is closer to the writings of Luke than to anything else in the New Testament."[99] In a similar vein, Samuel Davidson remarked:

> We do not maintain that the language of Hebrews is free from Hebraisms, but that the diction is purer than Paul's. In respect to purity, it stands on a level with the latter half of the Acts, where many of the expressions quoted by Stuart from Hebrews as Hebraisms are also found.[100]

Iutisone Salevao argued against Lukan authorship in that "differences of style . . . outweigh the points of affinity between Hebrews and Luke-Acts," and then a few pages later quotes approvingly F. F. Bruce, who said that Hebrews is stylistically closer to Luke-Acts than any of the New Testament writers.[101] Salevao does not offer evidence concerning the differences but, like so many before him, appears simply to take Kümmel's position as final. Here we stand on perhaps the firmest evidence for Lukan authorship: the evidence of vocabulary and style.

Use of Old Testament Quotation Formulae in Luke-Acts, Hebrews, and Paul[102]

Before comparing quotation formulae in Luke-Acts with Hebrews and Paul, it might be helpful to hear Fitzmyer's assessment of the Lukan use of quotation formulae:

> The Lucan formulas are not in every instance an exact equivalent, but they resemble the Palestinian Jewish formulas enough to reveal how close the mode of citation actually is. In using such formulas, Luke thus shows his dependence on a genuine Palestinian Jewish custom of quoting Scripture in other writings. This is to be noted, because Luke is the evangelist who has been most influenced by his Hellenistic ambiance. Despite it, his interpretation of OT passages reveals his dependence on such a Palestinian Jewish exegetical tradition.[103]

---

[99] F. F. Bruce, *The Epistle to the Hebrews*, NICNT, rev. ed. (Grand Rapids: Eerdmans, 1990), 19.

[100] S. Davidson, *An Introduction to the Study of the New Testament, Critical, Exegetical, and Theological* (London: Longmans, Green, 1868), 209.

[101] I. Salevao, *Legitimation in the Letter to the Hebrews: The Construction and Maintenance of a Symbolic Universe*, JSNTSup 219, ed. S. Porter (New York: Sheffield Academic Press, 2002), 98, 107.

[102] A more complete analysis of Luke's use of the Old Testament is presented in chap. 6.

[103] J. Fitzmyer, "The Use of the Old Testament in Luke-Acts," *SBLSP*, ed. E. Lovering (Atlanta: Scholars Press, 1992), 529.

This quote establishes that Luke was well within the Jewish world of Scripture use. This point will be important later when we evaluate the evidence for Luke's Jewish background.

Perhaps one of the most graphic illustrations of stylistic similarity may be found in the employment of quotation formulae by an author. Both Luke and the writer of Hebrews have a marked preference for the use of *legei* ("to say") in Scripture citations. This can be contrasted with the Pauline writings, where Paul alternately employs *legei* and *gegraptai* ("it is written"). The following tables illustrate the quotation formulae as they appear in Luke, Acts, and Hebrews.

Table 4 — Old Testament Quotation Formulae in Luke-Acts

Citation Formulae	Reference
gegraptai	L. 2:23
gegraptai . . . prophētou	L. 3:4
gegraptai	L. 4:4,8,10,17
gegraptai	L. 7:27
eipen	L. 10:27
gegraptai	L. 20:17
legei	L. 20:37
gar Dauid legei en biblō psalmōn	L. 20:42
gegraptai	A. 1:20
legei ho theos	A. 2:17
Dauid gar legei	A. 2:25
Dauid . . . legei de autos	A. 2:34
Mōusēs men eipen	A. 3:22
ho theos . . . legōn pros Abraam	A. 3:25
ho tou patros hēmōn dia pneumatos hagiou stomatos Dauid paidos sou eipōn	A. 4:25
eipen pros auton	A. 7:3
elalēsen de houtōs ho theos	A. 7:6
ho theos eipen	A. 7:7
eipōn	A. 7:27
eipen de autō ho kurios	A. 7:33
eipontes	A. 7:35
ho Mōusēs ho eipas	A. 7:37

Citation Formulae	Reference
eipontes tō Aarōn	A. 7:40
gegraptai en biblō tōn prophētōn	A. 7:42
ho prophētēs legei	A. 7:48
eipen marturēsas	A. 13:22
en tō psalmō gegraptai tō deuterō	A. 13:33
eirēken	A. 13:34
en heterō legei	A. 13:35
to eirēmenon en tois prophētais	A. 13:40
entetaltai hēmin ho kurios	A. 13:47
sumphlonousin hoi logoi tōn prophētōn kathōs gegraptai	A. 15:15
gegraptai	A. 23:5
to pneuma to hagion elalēsen dia Esaiou tou prophētou pros tous pateras humōn legōn	A. 28:25,26

Table 5 — Old Testament Quotation Formulae in Hebrews

Citation Formulae	Reference
eipen	1:5
kai palin	1:5
legei	1:6
legei	1:7
pros de ton theoni	1:8
kai	1:10
eirēken	1:13
diemarturato de pou tis legōn	2:6
legōn	2:12
kai palin	2:13
legei to pneuma to hagion	3:7
en tō legesthai	3:15
eirēken	4:3
eirēken gar pou	4:4
kai en toutō palin	4:5
en Dauid legōn . . . proeirētai	4:7
ho lalēsas pros Auton . . . en heterō legei	5:5–6

Citation Formulae	Reference
ho theos . . . legōn	6:13–14
martureitai	7:17
dia tou legontos pros auton	7:21
legei	8:8
legōn	9:20
legei	10:5
anōteron legōn	10:8
marturei de ēmin kai to pneuma to hagion	10:15
ton eiponta	10:30
pros hon elalēthē	11:18
Mōusēs eipen	12:21
legōn	12:26
eirēken	13:5
legein	13:6

For comparative purposes, I have listed in the following table all the quotation formulae that occur in Paul's Letter to the Romans. In the discussion below, quotation formulae from the entire Pauline corpus will be considered.[104]

Table 6 — Old Testament Quotation Formulae in Romans

Citation Formulae	Reference
gegraptai	1:17
gegraptai	2:24
gegraptai	3:4
gegraptai	3:10
ti gar hē graphē legei	4:3
Dauid legei	4:6
legomen gar	4:9
gegraptai	4:17
kata to eirēmenon	4:18
ho nomos elegen	7:7
gegraptai	8:36

---

[104] See R. Longenecker, *Studies in Paul, Exegetical and Theological* (Sheffield: Phoenix Press, 2006), 67–93, for an excellent analysis of Paul's use of Scripture in Romans.

Citation Formulae	Reference
[ ]*	9:7
epaggelias gar ho logos houtos	9:9
errethē autē	9:12
gegraptai	9:13
tō Mōusei gar legei	9:15
legei gar hē graphē	9:17
hōs kai en tō Hōsēe legei	9:25
Ēsaias de krazei	9:27
kai kathōs proeirēken Ēsaias	9:29
gegraptai	9:33
alla ti legei	10:8
legei gar hē graphē	10:11
[ ]*	10:13
gegraptai	10:15
Ēsaias gar legei	10:16
[ ]*	10:18
Mōusēs legei	10:19
Ēsaias . . . legei	10:20
pros de ton Israēl legei	10:21
en ēlia ti legei hē graphē	11:2
gegraptai	11:8
kai Dauid legei	11:9
gegraptai	11:26
[ ]*	11:34
gegraptai	12:19
[ ]*	13:9
gegraptai	14:11
gegraptai	15:3
gegraptai	15:9
kai palin legei	15:10
kai palin	15:11
kai palin Ēsaias legei	15:12
gegraptai	15:21
*The brackets indicate OT quotations without citation formulae.	

A preliminary examination of quotation formulae in Luke-Acts, Romans, and Hebrews provides for some tentative conclusions. First, Luke seems to shift from using *gegraptai*, "it is written," in his Gospel to a form of *legei*, "he/it says," in Acts. Second, the writer of Hebrews never uses *gegraptai* but is very fond of *legei*.

Third, the unusual form *en heterō legei*, "one somewhere says" or "in another place he says," is found only in Acts 13:35 and Heb 5:6. Fourth, Luke seldom makes use of the MT and the author of Hebrews never uses it. Both quote from the Septuagint or from a text different from either the MT or the Septuagint.[105] Paul, on the other hand, quotes sometimes from the MT and sometimes from the Septuagint.

Luke uses *gegraptai* 14 times, nine in the Gospel and five in Acts. He uses *legei*, *eipen*, or some other form of "to say" or "to speak," 27 times. There are 41 Old Testament quotations in Luke-Acts, excluding allusions or paraphrases. Furthermore, 14 of the Old Testament quotations occur in the Gospel while 27 occur in Acts. This means that nearly two-thirds of the uses of *gegraptai* occur in the Gospel, which contains only one-third of all the quotations. Thus, with two-thirds of the quotations occurring in Acts (a total of 27), *gegraptai* is used only five times (less than 20%). It would thus seem that Luke is determined to use *gegraptai* less frequently in Acts.

Excluding allusions or paraphrases, Hebrews contains at least 28 Old Testament quotations.[106] The most striking thing about citation formulae in Hebrews is the absence of *gegraptai*. A second feature that is conspicuous in Hebrews is the preference for the present tense in citation formulae (18 out of 25 examples), usually some form of the verb *legō*. Third, most of the quotations in Hebrews are from the Pentateuch and the Psalter.

In Romans, there are 44 Old Testament quotations excluding allusions or paraphrases. *Gegraptai* occurs 16 times, while some form of *legei* (or any verb of speaking) occurs 20 times. On five occasions, it would seem that a citation is made with no citation formula. I have used the closed brackets [ ] in Table 6 to mark these occurrences.

---

[105] Specifying the *Vorlage* used in Hebrews has been difficult. The consensus is that the author used some form of the Greek Old Testament.

[106] It is difficult to count the quotations exactly because one man's explicit quotation is another man's implicit quotation or allusion. The count of actual quotations usually ranges from 28 to 42. See D. Buck, "The Rhetorical Arrangement and Function of OT Citations in the Book of Hebrews: Uncovering Their Role in the Paraenetic Discourse of Access" (Ph.D. diss., Dallas Theological Seminary, 2002), 15, for a representative listing.

What conclusions can be drawn from this data regarding author-ship? First, Hebrews is in some ways unlike both Paul and Luke in its choice of citation formulae. For example, the absence of *gegrap-tai* in Hebrews is inexplicable. It cannot be explained on the sup-position that the audience included only Jews (Matthew's Gospel, long considered to have been written to a Jewish audience, often uses *gegraptai* as a quotation formula). For whatever reason, the author of Hebrews chose not to use *gegraptai*. Is it possible the explanation lies in the author's own theological understanding of the Old Testament, coupled with his desire to focus on the old and new covenants? Perhaps he desired to point out that Christianity was the logical outcome of Judaism, and that any return to Judaism constituted a lack of understanding of the radically new nature of Christianity. Yet at the same time, the author in no way wished to suggest that the Old Testament Scriptures were not binding on the people of God. Indeed, the point of the prologue to Hebrews is that the same God who spoke in the past through prophets continues to speak today in His Son Jesus Christ. Furthermore, the Scriptures are still speaking to the people of God. To emphasize this point he avoids *gegraptai*, "it stands written," and employs a form of the verb "to speak," usually in the present tense. If Luke is the author of Hebrews, and if all three works were written in the decade of the 60s, it is unlikely the move away from *gegraptai* can be explained as a stylistic shift.

A second characteristic of Hebrews that is markedly different from Luke or Paul is the absence of the name of the human author of Scrip-ture. Both Luke and Paul employ "David says" and "Moses says" in their citation formulae, but these are never found in Hebrews.

Yet for all this, there are striking similarities between Luke and Hebrews over against Paul in the choice of citation formulae. First, both Luke and Hebrews employ the noun *theos* with some form of the verb "to say," while this construction is never found in Romans or the rest of the Pauline corpus.[107] Second, both Luke and Hebrews employ the participle *eipontes* in quotation formulae, and this construction is never found in the Pauline corpus. Third, the form *eirēken* occurs three times in Hebrews and once in Luke-Acts (Acts 13:34), but is

---

[107] Lane notes that of the 35 Old Testament quotations in Hebrews, God is the grammatical subject of 20 (*Hebrews 1–8*, cxvii).

never used by Paul. Fourth, in Heb 2:6 the form *diemarturato*, "to tes-
tify," is used as a quotation formula; although it does not appear as an
Old Testament citation formula in Luke-Acts, it is found in Acts 2:40.
This is the only other occurrence of this form in the New Testament.
Fifth, the participle *legōn*, "saying," never occurs in the Pauline cor-
pus as a citation formula, but it does occur in both Hebrews and Acts.
Sixth, the phrase "the Holy Spirit says" as a quotation formula occurs
twice in Hebrews and twice in Acts, but never in the Pauline corpus.

It would seem on the evidence from Acts that Luke regards Scripture more as a spoken word than a written word. The difference between Luke's use of *gegraptai* in his Gospel and Acts, according to
Jervell, is a result of Luke's dependence on tradition.[108] This emphasis
on the "spoken" aspect of Scripture is paralleled in only one other
New Testament book: Hebrews. It is decisive that God speaks in
Scripture for the author of Hebrews, and this concept is "determina-
tive for Luke in Acts."[109]

Three conclusions follow from this evidence. First, Hebrews is
unique in its choice of quotation formulae in the ways just listed.
Second, Hebrews shares some similarities with both Luke and Paul
in the choice of quotation formulae. Third, in at least six ways listed
above, Hebrews and Luke agree in their choice of quotation formulae.
We may conclude that Hebrews, while not identical to either Luke
or Paul in choice of quotation formulae, is much more akin to Luke-
Acts than to the Pauline corpus.[110] Based on this evidence, the Pauline
hypothesis is weakened and the similarities between Luke-Acts and
Hebrews furnish an additional link for the three works.[111]

Arnold points out: "Along with Luke's view of the past in general, his quotations establish continuity and cohesion between past

---

[108] J. Jervell, *The Unknown Paul: Essays on Luke-Acts and Early Christian History* (Minneapolis: Augsburg, 1984), 124.

[109] Ibid.

[110] The foregoing evidence makes it difficult to see why Hanson would not compare Hebrews
with Luke-Acts as he does with John and Paul, and furthermore, why he would state that in
Scripture use, "the nearest to the author of this epistle is Paul." A. Hanson, "Hebrews," in *It is
Written: Scripture Citing Scripture. Essays in Honour of Barnabas Lindars S. S. F.*, ed. D. A. Carson
and H. G. M. Williamson (Cambridge: Cambridge University Press, 1988), 299.

[111] W. Leonard, *Authorship,* devoted a considerable amount of space to examining how
Hebrews uses the Old Testament, in an effort to show the possibility of Pauline authorship.
See especially 265–87 where he dealt with citation formulae. He argued for Paul on the basis
that Hebrews is not totally unlike the Pauline Letters in method of Scripture citation. I have
attempted to show that it is Luke rather than Paul who is closer to Hebrews in this area, and
that he is the more likely author.

and present. As a hermeneutical technique, he finds testimony in the Old Testament to the significance and meaning of the events he describes."[112] This "continuity and cohesion" between past and present is precisely what we find in the author's use of the Old Testament.

Luke, Hebrews, and the Septuagint

Many excellent works are available that deal with the use of the Old Testament in Hebrews,[113] so only a brief word is needed here. Eleven quotations in Hebrews are from the Pentateuch, one is from the historical books, seven from the prophets, one from Proverbs, and 18 from the Psalms. Of the 38 quotations, 29 are taken from the Pentateuch and the Psalms. Twenty-one of the 38 are unique to Hebrews.

Most of these quotations are taken from the LXX. The author never employs the MT. The way in which the author of Hebrews has interwoven the quotations from the Old Testament into his argument shows how much he revered the Old Testament and appealed to it to reinforce his case.

The major point is that while Paul makes use of both the MT (Hebrew) and the Septuagint for his quotations, Luke seldom quotes from the MT, and the author of Hebrews never quotes from it. Both quote from the Septuagint or from a nonextant text not equivalent to either the MT or the Septuagint.[114] Other New Testament writers use of the Septuagint, but no one uses it with such near-exclusivity as do Luke and the author of Hebrews. Thus, Luke and Hebrews stand closer

---

[112] B. Arnold, "Luke's Use of the Old Testament in Acts," in *History, Literature and Society in the Book of Acts*, ed. B. Witherington III (Cambridge: Cambridge University Press, 1996), 321.

[113] See, for example, M. Karrer, "The Epistle to the Hebrews and the Septuagint," in *Septuagint Research: Issues and Challenges in the Study of the Greek Jewish Scriptures*, ed. W. Kraus and R. G. Wooden, SBLSCS 53 (Atlanta: Society of Biblical Literature, 2006), 335–53; R.Gheorghita, *The Role of the Septuagint in Hebrews*, WUNT 2, Reihe 160 (Tübingen: Mohr Siebeck, 2003); Westcott, *Hebrews,* 469–95; Clarke, "The Use of the Septuagint in Acts," 2:66–105; H. F. D. Sparks, "The Semitisms of St. Luke's Gospel," *JTS* 44 (1943): 129–38; S. J. Kistemaker, *The Psalm Citations in the Epistle to the Hebrews* (Amsterdam: Wed. G. Van Soest, 1961); G. Howard "Hebrews and the Old Testament Quotations," *NovT* 10 (1968): 208–16; F. L. Horton, "Reflections on the Semitisms of Luke-Acts," in *Perspectives on Luke-Acts*, ed. C. Talbert (Danville, Va.: Association of Baptist Professors of Religion, 1978), 1–23; and J. Fitzmyer, "The Use of the Old Testament in Luke-Acts," 524–38.

[114] A. Hanson, *The Living Utterances of God: The New Testament Exegesis of the Old Testament* (London: Darton, Longman & Todd, 1983), 105.

together in their use of the LXX for Old Testament quotations in that they use it "with the same leisurely and learned thoroughness."[115]

Luke's use of Septuagintal Greek led F. L. Horton to posit a possible synagogue background for Luke, his audience, or both.[116] References to Scripture occur 26 times in Luke: 16 when Jesus speaks, and three times by the narrator.[117] Esler likewise argues for a synagogue background for Luke-Acts on the basis that Luke's readers would be familiar with his Septuagintal Greek from their previous association with the synagogue.[118]

Dawsey has noted that the narrational formulas used by Luke are all common to the Septuagint and that many of them are not attested translations of contemporary Semitic speech. They are archaic Hebrew idioms which survived only in the language of the Septuagint.[119] How many of these formulas Luke may have taken over from his sources is a debated issue. Dawsey finds three things noteworthy about Luke as narrator. First, the style of the third person narrator is different from the first person seen in the prologue and from other characters who speak in the Gospel. This was Luke's design, according to Dawsey. Second, "proper sound, harmony, and rhythm were considered by the author to be important aspects of the narration." Luke intended his work to be heard rather than read silently. Third, the narrator assumes in the story that the Christian community is "the proper context for hearing the gospel."[120] The point remains that Luke, traditionally seen as a Gentile writing to a Gentile audience, has used a non-Greek narrational style.

With respect to Luke's use of the LXX, Nigel Turner has suggested that the Hebraisms, which are often found in Luke's writings,[121] are mediated by the LXX. "It is of high significance that the most literary and most Greek of the writers of the New Testament is the writer to show most strongly the influence of the Hebraistic LXX."[122] W. F.

---

[115] J. Drury, *Tradition and Design in Luke's Gospel: A Study in Early Christian Historiography* (Atlanta: John Knox, 1976), 21.

[116] Horton, "Reflections on the Semitisms of Luke-Acts," 1–23.

[117] See J. Dawsey, *The Lukan Voice: Confusion and Irony in the Gospel of Luke* (Macon, Ga.: Mercer University Press, 1986), 29, for the complete listing.

[118] P. Esler, *Community and Gospel in Luke-Acts: The Social and Political Motivations of Lucan Theology*, SNTSMS 57 (Cambridge: Cambridge University Press, 1987), 36–45.

[119] J. Dawsey, *The Lukan Voice*, 25.

[120] Ibid., 32.

[121] See the list in J. M. Creed, *Gospel According to Luke*, lxxix–lxxxiv.

[122] N. Turner, "The Quality of the Greek of Luke-Acts," in *Studies in New Testament Language*

Albright points out the surprising fact that "Luke's Greek is relatively literary, yet Hebrew-Aramaic influence is in some ways clearer in his Gospel than elsewhere."[123] Robert Lindsey found, while translating the Gospels into modern Hebrew, that Luke was "almost easier to translate into idiomatic Hebrew than was Mark."[124]

Finally, in a sociolinguistic study of Luke-Acts, Jonathan Watt has produced evidence indicating Luke's bilingual "capacity for language choices in the face of multiple social determiners, and to highlight the feasibility of an ancient writer doing just what many modern speakers are known to do: vary their register to reflect social circumstances."[125] The linguistic term for this is "code-switching," and Watt suggests that Luke's "modulation of Semitic features" is an example. Luke's purpose would be to enhance his narrative literarily.[126]

What are we to make of all this? John Wenham's comments sum up the options.

> It is conceivable that Luke was a Gentile and that his source material came to him in Hebraic Greek and that, despite his command of literary Greek, he resisted the temptation to polish it up, thus acting the part of editor, rather than author. But it would be easier to believe that the author of this masterpiece was entirely at home with his material and that the gospel was truly his. In other words, he had known the scriptures in Hebrew and Greek from childhood.[127]

The Argument from Textlinguistic Considerations

Textlinguistics, otherwise known as discourse analysis, studies meaning in larger units of discourse above the sentence level.[128] In this section, we will evaluate (1) the prologues to Luke, Acts, and

---

and Text, ed. J. K. Elliott (Leiden: Brill, 1976), 400.

[123] W. F. Albright, *History, Archeology and Christian Humanism* (London: Black, 1965), 37.

[124] R. Lindsey, *Hebrew Translation of the Gospel of Mark* (Jerusalem: Dugith, 1970), 12.

[125] J. Watt, *Code-Switching in Luke-Acts*, Berkeley Insights in Linguistics and Semiotics 31, gen. ed. I. Rauch (New York: Peter Lang, 1997), 94–95.

[126] Ibid.

[127] J. Wenham, "The Identification of Luke," *EvQ* 63 (1991): 9–10. This article, along with Wenham's *Redating Matthew, Mark and Luke* (Downers Grove: InterVarsity, 1992), which argues that all three Synoptic Gospels were in existence by AD 55, presents a good case for Luke's Jewish background as well. See chap. 6 below.

[128] See D. Allen, "The Discourse Structure of Philemon: A Study in Textlinguistics," in *Scribes and Scriptures: New Testament Essays in Honor of J. Harold Greenlee*, ed. D. A. Black (Winona Lake, Ind.: Eisenbrauns, 1992), 77–78.

Hebrews, (2) the similarity between Acts 7 and Hebrews 11, and (3) macrostructure and superstructure in Luke-Acts and Hebrews.[129]

The Prologues to
Luke, Acts, and Hebrews[130]

A study of the prologues of Luke-Acts and Hebrews is important for several reasons. First, as Schuyler Brown reminds us, "any hypothesis concerning the purpose that the author of Luke-Acts may have had in writing must, if it is to lay serious claim to acceptance, be based on the work as a whole."[131] The textual starting point for the search of an author's purpose should be the prologue, if there is one. Second, a prologue furnishes the reader with clues as to the inclination, direction, interest, or point of view of the author. Third, a prologue is most likely to illustrate an author's style since no source materials are involved.

---

[129] See especially the commentaries by Lane and Ellingworth; also W. G. Übelacker, *Der Hebräerbrief als Appell: Untersuchungen zu exordium, narratio und postscriptum (Hebr 1–2 und 13, 22–25)*, ConBNT 21 (Lund: Almqvist & Wiksell International, 1989); G. Guthrie, *The Structure of Hebrews: A Text-Linguistic Analysis* (Leiden: Brill, 1994); and C. Westfall, *A Discourse Analysis of the Letter to the Hebrews: The Relationship Between Form and Meaning*, Library of New Testament Studies 297, ed. M. Goodacre (London: T&T Clark, 2006), 1–87, 297–301.

[130] Alexander, *The Preface to Luke's Gospel*, surveyed prefaces in ancient Greek literature and concluded that Greek scientific writing of the Hellenistic and Roman periods furnished the closest parallel to the Lukan prologue. She thus rejected attempts to read Luke-Acts as Greek history. Whereas Lukan scholars often had not given enough attention to the preface in the search for genre and purpose, Alexander goes to the opposite extreme and fails to note that once one gets past the preface, there is nothing in the text of Luke-Acts resembling the scientific treatises that follow such prefaces. Mount has offered a salient critique of Alexander, noting that she has too narrowly conceived the similarities and differences between Greek scientific writings and Greek historical writings, and has confused the question of whether Luke-Acts is Greek historiography with the issue of whether Luke uses the conventions of Hellenistic historiography in his work. Christopher Mount, *Pauline Christianity: Luke-Acts and the Legacy of Paul*, NovTSup 104 (Leiden: Brill, 2002), 64–65, 73, 77. See also David Aune's critique of Alexander's work on the Lukan prologue in "Luke 1:1–4: Historical or Scientific Prooimion?" in *Paul, Luke and the Graeco-Roman World: Essays in Honour of Alexander J. M. Wedderburn*, ed. A. Christophersen, C. Claussen, J. Frey, and B. Longenecker, JSNTSup 217 (London: Sheffield Academic Press, 2002), 138–48; and J. Green, *The Theology of the Gospel of Luke*, New Testament Theology Series, gen. ed. J. Dunn (Cambridge: Cambridge University Press, 1995), 16–21.

[131] S. Brown, *Perspectives on Luke-Acts*, Talbert Perspectives in Religious Studies, ed. C. H. Talbert (Danville, VA: Association of Baptist Professors of Religion, 1978), 99.

Table 7 — The Prologues of Luke, Acts, and Hebrews

Luke 1:1–4
Many have undertaken to compile a narrative about the events that have been fulfilled among us, just as the original eyewitnesses and servants of the word handed them down to us. It also seemed good to me, since I have carefully investigated everything from the very first, to write to you in orderly sequence, most honorable Theophilus, so that you may know the certainty of the things about which you have been instructed.

Acts 1:1–5
I wrote the first narrative, Theophilus, about all that Jesus began to do and teach until the day He was taken up, after He had given orders through the Holy Spirit to the apostles whom He had chosen. After He had suffered, He also presented Himself alive to them by many convincing proofs, appearing to them during 40 days and speaking about the kingdom of God. While He was together with them, He commanded them not to leave Jerusalem, but to wait for the Father's promise. "This," [He said, "is what] you heard from Me; for John baptized with water, but you will be baptized with the Holy Spirit not many days from now."

Hebrews 1:1–4
Long ago God spoke to the fathers by the prophets at different times and in different ways. In these last days, He has spoken to us by [His] Son, whom He has appointed heir of all things and through whom He made the universe. He is the radiance of His glory, the exact expression of His nature, and He sustains all things by His powerful word. After making purification for sins, He sat down at the right hand of the Majesty on high. So He became higher in rank than the angels, just as the name He inherited is superior to theirs.

The following comparative features among the prologues may be observed. First, they share a relatively similar length. Second, they represent a literary skill that is unequaled in the rest of the New Testament. Blass describes the prologue of Luke's Gospel as "a remarkable specimen of fine and well-balanced structure, and at the same time of well-chosen vocabulary."[132] Luke's prologue is a single sentence of six balanced and symmetrical clauses. Both the protasis and the apodosis are evenly balanced. Without a doubt, the prologue of Luke stands in the tradition of Classical Greek. The same could be said for the prologue to Hebrews. Both Luke and the author of Hebrews are described by most New Testament scholars as the most literary writers of the New Testament.[133]

Third, all three prologues are retrospective and prospective. In Luke 1:1–4, Luke informs us that many have written and that he now intends to write an account as well. In Acts 1:1–5, reference is made to the former treatise (Gospel of Luke) and the things Jesus began to

---

[132] F. Blass, *Philology of the Gospels* (London: Macmillan, 1898), 7.
[133] W. H. Simcox, *The Writers of the New Testament*, 16.

do and to teach. This is followed by a reference to future events (e.g., the disciples are told to wait in Jerusalem for the promise of the Holy Spirit). Acts is a rehearsal of events from the coming of the Spirit in Jerusalem at Pentecost to the arrest of Paul in Rome, a period of approximately 30 years. The prologue in Hebrews looks back to the fact that God "spoke" in times past, and forward to the fact that God continues to speak in His Son. The statement that God spoke "long ago," "to the fathers," and "by the prophets" in Heb 1:1 is semantically paralleled in Acts 3:21 (where God spoke "by the mouth of His holy prophets from the beginning") and in Acts 7:3,37 (where we learn that God spoke "to the sons of Israel"). In all three prologues there is a retrospective and prospective feature on the semantic level.

Fourth, there seems to be a propensity to alliterate with the Greek letter "p" in all three prologues. Five times each in Luke and Hebrews, words beginning with the letter "p" occur; in both cases, all come before the main verb in the sentence. This alliteration seems to be used for stylistic effect.[134]

Fifth, there is an absence of *de* or *kai* in the prologue of Luke and Hebrews, which illustrates the high Classical Greek style characteristic of these flowing sentences. Sixth, a considerable length of text is sandwiched between the subject and verb of each prologue, and each sentence nucleus contains an overt subject, verb, and indirect object, but no direct object.

Seventh, a number of words or phrases in the prologue to Hebrews are either unique to or primarily characteristic of Luke's writings. For example, the use of *polus* as a prefix (*polumerōs*, "many times"; *polutropōs*, "in many ways") to add to the rhetorical effect is evidence of stylistic design. The use of the third inflectional form *tois patrasin*, "to the fathers," is found only in Heb 1:1; 8:9; and Acts 7:44. The phrase "by the prophets," *en tois prophētais*, occurs only in John 6:45; Acts 13:40; 24:14; and Heb 1:1. The aorist active verb *elalēsen*, "has spoken," occurs 31 times in the New Testament: 13 in Luke-Acts, twice in Hebrews, 14 times in the other Gospels, twice in Revelation, but never in Paul. This verb, which is characteristic of narrative

---

[134] A. Eagar, "Authorship," 114. After listing other places where π-alliteration occurs in comparison to Luke's prologue, Alexander fails to note its occurrence in the prologue to Hebrews. Rather inexplicably (with the exception of a comment about the use of πολύς in the prologue), she mentioned none of the seven comparisons I have made between the Lukan prologues and Hebrews. Alexander, *The Preface to Luke's Gospel*.

discourse in the New Testament, occurs only four times outside the Gospels and Acts. The aorist active indicative third singular verb *ethēken* (from *tithēmi*) occurs 11 times in the New Testament with examples in Luke, Acts, and Heb 1:2, but never in Paul. The aorist middle participle *poiēsamenos* occurs only in Heb 1:3 and Acts 25:17 throughout the New Testament. The phrase *tōn hēmerōn toutōn* (Heb 1:2) occurs only in Acts 5:36 and 21:38.

These seven factors suggest a high degree of similarity among the three prologues. It is not likely that all these factors can be considered a coincidence. They could be interpreted as evidence for common authorship.

The style of Luke's prologue can be compared to Josephus in his *Against Apion*, a two-volume work like Luke-Acts.[135] Josephus wrote in the latter quarter of the first century (approximately 25 years after Luke-Acts), and thus is roughly a contemporary of Luke. The English translation of the first sentence of each volume is given below for comparison with the style of the prologues in Luke-Acts.[136]

> In my history of Antiquities most excellent Epaphroditus, I have, I think, made sufficiently clear to any who may peruse that work the extreme antiquity of our Jewish race.

> In the first volume of this work, my most esteemed Epaphroditus, I demonstrated the antiquity of our race. . . . I shall now proceed to refute the rest of the authors who have attacked us.

The relevance of comparing the Lukan prologue to that of Josephus illustrates that a use of near-Classical style need not be an argument against Luke's Jewishness. Josephus was a Jew of priestly descent who employed a style similar to Luke's prologue. Since the Jewish Josephus could write in this fashion, then (the Jewish?) Luke could as well. Once Luke concludes the Hellenistic prologue, he immediately shifts and writes more in the vein of Old Testament biblical history (see chap. 5 below). As Alexander noted:

> There is a family resemblance between Luke and the hellenistic Jewish writers, and this should warn us to be wary of certain well-worn assumptions of Lucan scholarship, such as the assumption that a writer who adopts a Greek

---

[135] See the discussion by G. Sterling, *Historiography and Self-Definition*, 365–69, who also has compared the prologues of Luke-Acts to the prologue in Josephus' *Against Apion*.

[136] Josephus, *Against Apion*, 163–65, 293–95.

preface-style must be making a direct appeal to the wider cultural world of the Greeks, whether apologetic or polemical.[137]

Second, this comparison reveals that Luke has introduced his two-volume work in the same manner as other authors of his day. Third, the prologue names Theophilus as the recipient or intended reader. The language of the prologue makes it likely that Theophilus is more than just the one to whom Luke is dedicating his work. Theophilus is a historical individual to whom Luke addressed the work in the same way that Epaphroditus was the intended reader of Josephus' *Against Apion*.[138] Fourth, Luke's prologue informs us that he intended his work to be considered as a historical account in the same way that Josephus wrote of the history of the Jewish people. As Sterling says: "The apex of Hellenistic Jewish historiography reached in the *Antiquitates Judaicae* of Josephus is complemented by Luke-Acts . . . ."[139]

The similarity between the Lukan prologue and Heb 2:1–4 has often been noted. For example, Conder said Heb 2:1–4 "strikingly corresponds" to the Lukan prologue. "It would be strictly appropriate as proceeding from the companion of St. Paul. It is, indeed, remarkable, how everything seems to favour the idea, that the Evangelist had some hand in its composition."[140] The judgment of ancient and modern scholarship is unanimous that the style of Hebrews is discernibly different from Paul.

[137] Alexander, *The Preface to Luke's Gospel,* 167.

[138] Mount commented on the works of Josephus: "In none of his extant works is there any evidence that he writes as a representative of a specific Jewish community seeking a self-understanding in the aftermath of the Roman defeat of the Jewish rebellion. Josephus writes as an individual to other educated individuals and intends his works to be taken seriously in the context of Hellenistic literature." C. Mount, *Pauline Christianity,* 74–75. The application of this to the author of Luke-Acts is significant. It is usually argued that Luke is writing as a representative of the Pauline community, or to a larger community, Gentile, Jewish, or mixed. I propose that Luke wrote to an individual named Theophilus as the preface states. Theophilus is more than Luke's patron; he is the intended reader. See the full discussion of this in C. Mount, *Pauline Christianity,* 60–83, and chap. 7 below.

[139] G. Sterling, *Historiography and Self-definition,* 393. See also C. Mount, *Pauline Christianity,* 70–71; and S. Mason, "Chief Priests, Sadducees, Pharisees and Sanhedrin in Acts," in *The Book of Acts in its Palestinian Setting,* vol. 4, in The Book of Acts in its First Century Setting, ed. R. Bauckham (Grand Rapids: Eerdmans, 1995), 175: "The basic divergence of religious perspective between Luke and Josephus makes their agreement in basic assumptions remarkable." See also Mason, "Chief Priests, Sadducees, Pharisees and Sanhedrin in Acts," 158–77; and H. Schreckenberg and K. Schubert, *Jewish Historiography and Iconography in Early and Medieval Christianity* (Minneapolis: Fortress, 1992), 42–49, for a contrast and comparison of Luke-Acts and Josephus. Schreckenberg has an excellent bibliographic summary of the history of research on the relationship of Luke-Acts and Josephus, 51n117.

[140] J. Conder, *Literary History of the New Testament,* 454.

The significance of the Lukan prologue for the theory of Lukan authorship of Hebrews lies not only in how closely it can be compared to the prologue of Hebrews, but also in what it tells us about the mind-set of Luke. Luke has placed the historical events of the gospel in the context of the LXX, which he views as having been fulfilled in the gospel (Luke 24:44–47). In this way he asserts the certainty of the *logōn* of Luke 1:4. As Joel Green so aptly put it: "For Luke, narrative is proclamation. Luke has in mind the use of history to preach."[141] His approach is consistent with that of the author of Hebrews.

Comparison of Acts 7 and Hebrews 11

The two longest summaries of Old Testament history occur in Acts 7 and Hebrews 11. Although Hebrews 11 is an example list, it is couched in a historical framework. The number of parallels between the two has led many scholars to posit a common tradition underlying both.[142] A careful study of these parallels both in vocabulary and thought leads me to take this "common tradition" idea a step further and argue that the same author could be responsible for both. First, I will make a comparison of Acts 7 to the book of Hebrews and then compare Acts 7 and Hebrews 11 specifically.

Stephen's defense in Acts 7 totals 1,022 words in Greek according to the Westcott and Hort text. Nearly 90 percent of the vocabulary there recurs in Hebrews. Acts 7 has 301 vocabulary words, and nearly 70 percent of these are in Hebrews. Brown commented:

---

[141] J. Green, *The Theology of the Gospel of Luke*, 19.

[142] Many view the author of Hebrews as Stephen's theological successor. See F. D. V. Narborough, *The Epistle to the Hebrews*; C. Spicq, "Alexandrismes dans L'Épître aux Hébreux," *RB* 58 (1951): 481–502; W. Manson, *The Epistle to the Hebrews: an Historical and Theological Reconsideration* (London: Hodder & Stoughton, 1951); N. Dahl, "The Purpose of Luke-Acts," in *Jesus in the Memory of the Early Church: Essays* (Minneapolis: Augsburg, 1976), 87–98; R. W. Thurston, "Midrash and 'Magnet' Words in the New Testament," *EvQ* 51 (1979): 22–39; and Hurst, *Epistle to the Hebrews*. They have each argued for some correlation between Acts 7 and Heb 11. Thurston argued that a common body of Midrash underlies these sections (24). His article contains the most complete listing of parallels. See more recently P. E. Hughes, "The Epistle to the Hebrews," *The New Testament and its Modern Interpreters*, ed. E. Epp and G. MacRae (Philadelphia: Fortress, 1989), 356. For opposing views, see H. Montefiore, *A Commentary on the Epistle to the Hebrews*, BNTC (London: Adam and Charles Black, 1964), 137; M. H. Scharlemann, *Stephen: A Singular Saint*, AnBib 34 (Rome: Pontifical Biblical Institute, 1968), 165–75; M. Isaacs, *Sacred Space: An Approach to the Theology of the Epistle to the Hebrews*, JSNTSup 73 (Sheffield: Sheffield Academic Press, 1992), 65–66; and Koester, who says, "Stephen's speech . . . emphasizes the abiding quality of the Jewish law in a manner so different from Hebrews that it seems unlikely that both writings stem from the same Christian circle." C. R. Koester, "The Epistle to the Hebrews in Recent Study," *CR* 2 (1994): 130.

These proportions seem the more remarkable if we count the Seventh of Acts a transcript from the Aramaic, but Hebrews the best of Testament Greek; if we note that of the hundred (103) words lacking in the latter, some fifty (54) are found in Stephen's O. T. quotations; that of his three hundred, twenty-six are used by him alone in the N.T.: that fourteen are found elsewhere in Testament solely with Luke, his reporter; also that twenty-eight of his three hundred are proper names; and that perhaps a dozen of the earlier words might have been deliberately avoided by a later writer for reasons of tact in addressing the Christians of Hebrews.[143]

Both Acts 7 and Hebrews cite the Old Testament with very similar quotation formulae. Both employ the phrase "God says," and 39 times out of 50 some form of the verb "say" is used.

Abraham appears prominently in both Acts 7 and Hebrews. The phrase "congregation in the desert" occurs in Acts 7 and may be directly compared to Heb 13:11–13. Acts 7:38 speaks of "living oracles," as does Heb 4:12. Exodus 25:40 is quoted in the New Testament only in Acts 7:44 and Heb 8:5. In both Acts 7:53 and Heb 2:2, the law is described as being mediated by angels.

Nils Dahl notes that Acts 7:44–50 and Heb 4:1–11 are parallel in thought and argument form. Hebrews 4:8–9 states: "For if Joshua had given them rest, He would not have spoken later about another day. A Sabbath rest remains, therefore, for God's people." Dahl paraphrases Acts 7:47–50:

> Solomon built a house for him. But had Solomon's temple been the fulfillment of David's prayer for a dwelling-place, and its cult the worship of which God spoke to Abraham, the prophet would not have said: Heaven is my throne and earth my footstool. What house will you build for me, says the Lord, or what is the place of my rest? Did not my hands make all these things?[144]

The Jews rejected Jesus in favor of their hopes that centered on the temple, thus imputing permanence to it. Stephen attacked the idea of temple permanence in Acts 7:48 when he used the term "made with hands." Hebrews 9:11,24 express the same theological concept using the same term. The immutability of Christ and the passing nature of the temple are subjects of interest for both Luke and the author of Hebrews.

---

[143] J. V. Brown, "The Authorship and Circumstances of Hebrews," *BSac* 80 (1923): 514.

[144] N. Dahl, "The Story of Abraham in Luke-Acts," in *Studies in Luke-Acts*, ed. L. E. Keck and J. Louis Martyn (New York: Abingdon Press, 1976), 75. See also the discussion of Acts 7:46–47 in the section on Luke's use of Scripture in chap. 5 below.

Stephen argues in Acts 7:53 that to abide within a rigid legalism is tantamount to failing to interpret properly the law's own intention. This is precisely what the writer of Hebrews argues.[145] W. Manson has sought to find the key to Hebrews by examining the history of the world mission of Christianity from its inception in the work of Stephen. He found numerous similarities between Stephen's apologia and Hebrews:[146]

(a) the attitude of Stephen to the cultus and law of Judaism;
(b) his declaration that Jesus means to change and supersede these things;
(c) his sense of the divine call to the people of God as a call to go out;
(d) his stress on the ever-shifting nature of Israel's life and the ongoing homelessness of the faithful;
(e) his thought of God's Word as living;
(f) his incidental allusion to Joshua in connection with the promise of God's "rest";
(g) his idea of the angels as the ordainers of God's law;
(h) his directing of his eyes to heaven and to Jesus.

Manson's thesis is that the author of Hebrews was a Hellenist like Stephen. Schenck suggests it is "more likely that the author of Acts had Christians like the author of Hebrews in mind *as he portrayed Stephen.*"[147] For Schenck, the most interesting parallel between Hebrews and Stephen is the latter's attitude toward the Jerusalem temple in contrast to the wilderness tabernacle. Stephen is favorable toward the tabernacle, but his "tone changes notably" toward the temple in Acts 7:47–48. According to Schenck, the Jewish leadership should have known that "Heaven is my throne . . . . what is My [place of] *katapausis* ["rest"] (7:49)."[148] Schenck goes on to suggest "that the author of Acts might have known the book of Hebrews and intentionally echoed its rhetoric in Acts 7."[149] Yet Schenck mentions how the

---

[145] C. F. B. Moule, "Sanctuary and Sacrifice in the Church of the New Testament," *JTS* 1 NS (1950): 30.

[146] W. Manson, *The Epistle to the Hebrews*, 23–37.

[147] K. Schenck, *Cosmology and Eschatology in Hebrews: the Settings of the Sacrifice*, SNTSMS 143, gen. ed. J. Court (Cambridge: Cambridge University Press, 2007), 192. Emphasis original.

[148] Ibid.

[149] Ibid.

author of Acts records Paul's offering in the temple in Acts 21:23–26, "an act that the author of Hebrews indicates is definitively unnecessary in the light of Christ's sacrifice."[150] Schenck's suggests difference between the author of Acts and Hebrews is unwarranted, however, when one considers the fact that Paul's offering had nothing to do with a sacrifice for sin (nor does Luke imply such) but rather was the fulfillment of Paul's vow, something any Jewish Christian might be expected to do. Like Luke, the author of Hebrews is not so critical of the temple when it comes to matters beyond atonement.

J. Bowman offers additional similarities between Acts 7 and Hebrews.[151] In Acts 7 there is emphasis on the notion that God's revelation transcends national boundaries (Acts 7:2,9,30,31,36,38). In Heb 2:5–18, Jesus is the universal savior who came in order that he might taste death for everyone. In Acts 7:17–29, God's revelation is independent of culture, while in Heb 7:4–10 the non-Jewish Melchizedek blesses Abraham and his descendents. In Acts 7:44–50, God's revelation is not bound to the temple, the temple cultus, or the tabernacle. In Hebrews, faith is said to be independent of the city of Jerusalem and the temple is apparently never mentioned (Heb 11:10,14–16,23–31; 13:12–14). The rejection of God's prophets is prominent in Acts 7:25,26,35,36,51–53; in Heb 3:17–19, and portions of the eleventh chapter, where national Israel persecuted God's prophets and rejected his message.

Nixon's comment about the Exodus motif in Acts and Hebrews links the two works: "The most striking piece of Exodus typology in the whole book [Acts] is the way in which the word *ekklēsia* was taken over from the Jewish "congregation in the desert."[152]

A specific comparison of Acts 7 and Hebrews 11 yields further parallels between the two pericopes. Luke sees Israel's history as woven together with individuals like Abraham, Moses, and David, who constitute the backbone of the nation's history. Acts 7:2–8 and Heb 11:8–19 speak of Abraham, stressing his faith in God, which enabled him to leave his native land for an unknown destination. Stephen and the author of Hebrews set forth, more than any other New Testament writers, the true nature of Israel and the church as the wandering

---

[150] Ibid., 193.

[151] J. Bowman, *Hebrews, James, I and II Peter*, Layman's Bible Commentary 24 (Atlanta: John Knox, 1962), 11.

[152] R. E. Nixon, *The Exodus in the New Testament* (London: Tyndale, 1963), 23.

people of God. For Luke, Abraham remains the "father of the Jews" and is never said to be the father of Christians. Only when Jews are addressed in Luke-Acts are Abraham and his descendents called "our fathers."[153]

While God's promise to Abraham is discussed in Luke, the Pauline Letters, and Hebrews, Luke and Hebrews are most alike in their perspectives. Both Luke and Hebrews stress God's oath and promise to Abraham, and both stress Abraham's sojourn as a foreigner in the land of promise (cf. Heb 11:11–12; Acts 7:5–8). Both emphasize the fact that Abraham had neither land nor children when God made the covenant with him to give him both (Heb 11:9–13; Acts 7:5). In Heb 10:19–23, the central hortatory section of the letter, the exhortation to "hold on to the confession of our hope" refers to the Abrahamic promise. If the phrase "he who promised is faithful" is taken as an allusion to the argument in 6:13, then the readers were in danger of disregarding the Abrahamic promise by failing to recognize the priestly office of Christ. The notion of Christians as heirs of the Abrahamic promise was an emphasis of Jewish Christianity in the early years of the church (cf. Acts 3:25–26).

Acts 7 speaks of the 120 years of Moses' life in three spans of 40 years each, something that was also of interest to the writer of Hebrews, as can be deduced from his quotation of Psalm 95 in Heb 3:7–4:13. Both Acts 7 and Hebrews 11 speak of Abraham, Isaac, Jacob, and Joseph in succession. Both speak of Moses as hidden three months by his parents and describe his life in similar detail. Both avoid the word "temple," making the rare substitution of the term "house." Both share the same concept of the tabernacle.

The most recent treatment of this subject can be found in L. D. Hurst who, after examining Manson's thesis and the response to it, concludes that "the parallels are impressive and numerous enough to suggest that some form of Manson's case is plausible."[154] Hurst did not, however, posit any direct literary dependence of Hebrews on Acts 7. Likewise, Edvin Larsson concluded: "the entire pattern of promise

---

[153] Dahl, *The Purpose of Luke-Acts*, 48.

[154] L. D. Hurst, *The Epistle to the Hebrews: Its Background and Thought* (New York: Cambridge University Press, 1990), 106. B. Childs comments, "In my judgment, his [Manson's] ability to bring the letter of Hebrews out of its position of isolation within the NT and show important lines of theological connection with Acts is more significant than his detailed historical reconstruction which remains quite hypothetical." B. Childs, *New Testament as Canon: An Introduction* (London: SCM, 1984), 412.

and fulfillment in Hebrews forms a mighty illustration to this line of thought in the speech of Stephen."[155]

The following table presents the linguistic parallels from the Greek texts of Acts 7 and Hebrews 11.

Table 8 — Linguistic Comparison of Acts 7 and Hebrews 11

Acts 7	Hebrews 11
paroikon (v. 6)	*parōkēsen* (v. 9)
en gē allotria (v. 6)	*eis gēn tēs epaggelias hōs allotrian* (v. 9)
exelthe (v. 3)	*exelthein, exelthein* (v. 8)
kai deuro eis tēn tēn	*kai exēlthen mē epistamenos pou*
hēn an soi deixō (v. 3)	*erchetai* (v. 8)
(semantic equivalents)	
klēronomian (v. 5)	*sugklēronomōn* (v. 9)
epleggeilato (v. 5)	*epaggelias* (v. 9)
Isaak ton Iakōb (v. 8)	*Isaak kai Iakōb* (v. 9)
spermati (v. 5)	*spermatos* (v. 11)
to sperma auto (v. 6)	*soi sperma* (v. 18)
elalēsen de houtōs ho theos (v. 6)	*pros hon elalēthē* (v. 18)
Iōsēph (v. 9)	*Iōsēph* (vv. 21, 23)
Death of Jacob and Joseph, burial in the promised land after departure from Egypt	Death of Joseph, mention of departure from Egypt and instructions about burying his bones in the promised land
(semantic equivalents)	
kai ouch hēuriskon (v. 11)	*kai ouch hērisketo* (v. 5)
eteleutēsen (v. 15)	*teleutōn* (v. 22)
eplēthunthē (v. 17)	*plēthei* (v. 12)
Aiguptō (v. 17)	*Aigupto, Aigupton, Aiguptioi* (vv. 26, 27, 29)
laos (v. 17)	*laō* (v. 25)
basileus (v. 18)	*basileōs* (v. 23, 27)
He dealt deceitfully with our race and oppressed our forefathers by making them leave their infants outside so they wouldn't survive. (v. 19)	By faith Moses, after he was born, was hidden by his parents for three months, because they saw that the child was beautiful, and they didn't fear the king's edict. (v. 23)
(semantic paraphrase equivalents)	
egennēthē Mōusēs (v. 20)	*Mōusēs gennētheis* (v. 23)

---

[155] E. Larsson, "Temple Criticism and the Jewish Heritage," *NTS* 39 (1993): 394.

Acts 7	Hebrews 11
asteios (v. 20)	*asteion* (v. 23)
thugatēr Pharaō (v. 21)	*thugatros Pharaō* (v. 24)
eis huion (v. 21)	*huios* (v. 24)
Moses, powerful in speech and actions (v. 22) (Semantic parallel)	Moses, [having become great] (v. 24) (Semantic parallel)
ephugen (v. 29)	*ephugon* (v. 34)
eruthra thalassē (v. 36)	*eruthran thalassan* (v. 29)
prophētōn (vv. 37, 42)	*prophētōn* (v. 32)
proskunein (v. 43)	*prosekunēsen* (v. 21)

The writer of Hebrews may have used Acts 7 as his source for chap. 11. But the many linguistic and semantic parallels in Acts 7 and Hebrews, especially in chap. 11, suggest that these two sections may have been written by the same person.[156] The evidence can be interpreted in favor of Luke as the author of Hebrews.

Luke's portrait of Paul in Acts as someone faithful to the Lord, a "hero" in the Hellenistic Jewish culture, is similar to the presentation of the "heroes of the faith" in Hebrews 11. Actually, there are many "heroes" in the narrative of Acts, some of whom receive only minor attention but, like the list of Hebrews 11, are all distinguished by their faith and faithfulness.

Taking his lead from Stephen's comment about Solomon in Acts 7:47, Peter Doble examines the possibility that Luke's use of Scripture "substructure" in the birth narratives and Stephen's speech might clarify the question of whether the speech is a polemic against the temple. Doble accepts the view (with Dodd and others) that what often appear to be scriptural citations or allusions in the text are in fact markers that "call into play" a larger context of Scripture and

---

[156] Filson argued that the parallels to Heb 11 found in Acts 7 cannot be because of Luke's own style since they appear only in this one speech in Acts. F. V. Filson, *"Yesterday." A Study of Hebrews in the Light of Chapter 13*, SBT 4, ed. C. F. D. Moule, P. Ackroyd, F. V. Filson, et. al. (London: SCM, 1954), 24. He suggests that they must come from Luke's use of a source. Whether or not a source was involved, Luke chose to use Stephen's speech at a crucial juncture in his narrative, and his theology was greatly influenced by it. Given the other lexical and stylistic parallels between Luke-Acts and Hebrews, it seems warranted to explain the similarities by a common author. Jelonek, "Chrystologia listu do Hebrajezykow," *Analecta Cracoviensia 17* (1985): 253–57, argued that Luke wrote Hebrews as a continuation of Stephen's speech. See also Thurston, "Midrash and 'Magnet' Words," 22–39.

invite the reader to consider the whole without quoting the whole.[157] Modulating the scriptural "harmonics" of the scene of the boy Jesus in the temple (occurring at the end of the birth narrative) with the genealogy given in Luke 3 (where Solomon is omitted, unlike Matthew's genealogy which includes him), Doble concludes that Luke depicts Jesus as David's proper descendent, like the young Solomon.[158] With respect to Luke's use of Scripture, Doble notes that twice in Luke 24, Jesus transmits his "scriptural self-understanding" to the apostles, and this is programmatic for the sermons and speeches in Acts. With the exception of Paul's Areopagus sermon, all the speeches in Acts make extensive use of Scripture. We are told repeatedly that Scripture was quoted to prove Jesus was the Messiah. From this clear Christological focus and the centrality of Scripture, why should any other aim be posited for Stephen's speech? Doble concludes that the speech is not a polemic against the temple, but rather an attempt to present Jesus as the enthroned Christ in the Davidic line.[159]

We find a similar exegetical approach in Hebrews, especially in chap. 1. The author of Hebrews is interested in far more than simply "proving" that Christ is superior to the angels. This was not, as will be argued, an issue for the readers. The view that Heb 1:5–14 was a polemic against angel worship fails to consider the entire context of the paragraph and the whole book. The real issue in Heb 1:5–14 is the relationship of the Son to the Father, not to the angels.

Also note the connection of angels mediating the law of Moses in Acts 7:53 with the same statement in Heb 2:1–4. Stephen accused the Jewish leaders of not keeping the law, just as the author of Hebrews accuses his readers of failing to obey the Word spoken "through angels" in 2:2.

Doble concluded from the use of scriptural allusion that Theophilus would understand Stephen's vision of the enthroned Savior to mean that Jesus now sits on David's throne. God's promise to David of an everlasting kingdom has been fulfilled in the exaltation of Jesus in Acts 7:55.[160]

---

[157] P. Doble, "Something Greater Than Solomon: An Approach to Stephen's Speech," in *The Old Testament in the New Testament: Essays in Honour of J. L. North*, ed. S. Moyise, JSNTSup 189 (Sheffield: Sheffield Academic Press, 2000), 190–91.
[158] Ibid., 188–89.
[159] Ibid., 189–206.
[160] Ibid., 204.

Macrostructure and Superstructure in Luke-Acts and Hebrews

Teun A. van Dijk has done extensive work on macrostructures and superstructures in discourse,[161] and has shown that the notion of discourse topic can be made explicit in semantic terms.[162] Distinguishing between sentential topics and discourse topics, he points out that the former determine the distribution of information along sequences of sentences (which van Dijk understands as paragraphs), while the latter reduce, organize, and categorize semantic information of sequences as wholes.[163] Simply put, the macrostructure of a discourse is the semantic notion of global meaning such as topic, theme, or gist. It is the abstract or summary that captures the topic of the discourse.

A second term, "superstructure," is used by van Dijk to describe structures that have a global notion at the "syntactic" level.[164] Whereas macrostructures are semantic, superstructures are schematic or structural. Hence macrostructures describe overall structure at the notional (semantic) level, while superstructures describe the information organization at the surface structure level. Van Dijk uses a third term, "microstructures," to describe the structure of information at the "local" semantic level, such as the meaning of words, phrases, and clauses.[165] Van Dijk points out that without the notion of microstructure, we cannot distinguish what macrostructures are.

Macrostructures are global semantic information only relative to the microstructures of discourse, cognition, and interaction. In other words, for different discourses or interaction sequences, the same type of information may function either as microstructure or as macrostructure, depending on its semantic role in the whole.[166]

These three levels are not independent of one another in a text, but are systematically related in that macrostructures are derived from microstructures. Thus, the primary function of the macrostructure

---

[161] T. A. van Dijk, *Text and Context: Explorations in the Semantics and Pragmatics of Discourse,* Longman Linguistics Library 21 (London: Longman, 1977); id., *Macrostructures: An Interdisciplinary Study of Global Structures in Discourse Interaction and Cognition* (Hillsdale, NJ: Erlbaum, 1980).

[162] van Dijk, *Text and Context,* 131.

[163] Ibid., 132.

[164] Ibid., 11.

[165] Ibid., 13.

[166] Ibid.

of a text is twofold: the organization and reduction of complex information.[167]

Analyzing the macrostructures and superstructures of Luke-Acts and Hebrews may provide some insight into the argument for common authorship. I shall examine the structure of Luke-Acts first and then consider Hebrews. Finally, I will make a comparison of the three texts with a view to testing the theory of Lukan authorship for Hebrews.

Macrostructure and Superstructure in Luke-Acts

The structure of Luke and Acts has been probed recently in great detail. Luke's Gospel is now generally viewed as the most literary and structurally artistic Gospel in the New Testament canon. Henry Cadbury has shown Luke's fondness for parallelism.[168] Praeder surveys the cataloging and analysis of suggested Lukan parallels from the nineteenth century to 1984.[169] Building on the work of C. F. Evans, M. Goulder has shown the Lukan travel narrative (Luke 9:51–19:46) is chiastic.[170] A chiasm (from the Greek *chiasmos*, "a placing crosswise") comes from the Greek letter "chi" (χ), and refers to an inverted order of words, clauses, sentences, and paragraphs, which forms the pattern ABBA.[171]

The A and B elements correspond lexically or semantically to produce a chiasm. The Lukan travel narrative is a rather large section of embedded material in the overall discourse framework. The chiastic

---

[167] Ibid., 14.

[168] H. J. Cadbury, *The Making of Luke-Acts* (New York: Macmillan, 1927). I shall continue Cadbury's custom of referring to Luke's two volumes as "Luke-Acts" throughout the discussion, Parsons and Pervo notwithstanding! J. Verheyden, "The Unity of Luke-Acts: What Are We Up To," in *The Unity of Luke-Acts*, ed. J. Verheyden (Leuven: Leuven University Press, 1999), 3–56, provides the best recent survey on the unity of Luke-Acts.

[169] S. M. Praeder, "Jesus-Paul, Peter-Paul, and Jesus-Peter Parallelisms in Luke-Acts: A History of Reader Response," *SBLSP*, ed. K. H. Richards (Atlanta: Chico, 1984), 23–39.

[170] M. D. Goulder, "The Chiastic Structure of the Lucan Journey," in *SE* II, ed. F. L. Cross (Berlin: Akademie Verlag, 1964), 195–202.

[171] Other chiastic patterns can be noted. N. W. Lund, *Chiasmus in the New Testament* (Chapel Hill, N.C.: University of North Carolina Press, 1942), was one of the first to make an in-depth study of the phenomenon of chiasmus in the New Testament. More recently, I. Thomson, *Chiasmus in the Pauline Letters*, JSNTSup 111 (Sheffield: Sheffield Academic Press, 1995), 13–45; and J. Harvey, *Listening to the Text: Oral Patterning in Paul's Letters*, ETS Studies 1, ed. D. Baker (Grand Rapids: Baker, 1998), 97–118, offer good discussions of the background, methodology, function, and use of chiasmus.

superstructure of this section (as presented by Goulder) is reproduced in Table 9.

Table 9 —The Chiastic Framework of Luke's Travel Narrative According to Goulder

Luke 10:31–13:30	Luke 14:1–18:30
10:21–24: The kingdom is revealed to babes. Blessed are the disciples for they see.	18:15–17: The kingdom is to be received as a child.
10:25–37: Jesus is confronted with the question: What shall I do to inherit eternal life? The answer elicits teaching by Jesus.	18:18–30: Jesus is confronted with the question: What shall I do to inherit eternal life? The response elicits more teaching from him.
10:38–42: The story of Mary and Martha de-emphasizes the importance of good works.	18:9–14: The parable of the Pharisee and the publican de-emphasizes the importance of good works.
11:1–13: God's willingness to answer prayer is seen.	18:1–8: God's willingness to answer prayer is seen.
11:14–36: A healing is followed by a discussion of the signs of the kingdom of God and a warning about the last judgment.	17:11–37: A healing is followed by a discussion of the signs of the kingdom of God and a warning about the last judgment.
11:37–54: At a meal, Jesus rebukes the Pharisees and lawyers for their sins.	17:1–10: An exhortation to rebuke one's brother when he sins is followed by a parable about a meal.
12:1–48: Three themes are treated in this order: (1) hell, (2) riches, (3) faithful stewardship.	Luke 16: Three themes are treated in this order: (1) unfaithful stewardship, (2) riches, (3) hell.
12:49–13:9: Four themes are present in this order: (1) transcendence of family loyalty, (2) prudent action taken ahead of time, (3) repentance, (4) the fruitless tree being cut down.	14:25–15:32: Four themes are present in this order: (1) transcendence of family loyalty, (2) prudent action taken ahead of time, (3) tasteless salt thrown away, (4) repentance.
13:10–17: A woman is healed on the Sabbath. Jesus says the Jews treat an ox and ass better than a person.	14:1–6: A man is healed on the Sabbath. Jesus says the Jews treat an ox and ass better than a person.
13:18–30: Parables of the kingdom of God are concluded by the exclusion of privileged ones from the Messianic banquet and the inclusion of the disadvantaged.	14:7–24: Parables relating to the kingdom are concluded by the exclusion from the Messianic banquet of certain privileged people and the inclusion of the disadvantaged.
13:31–33: A prophet cannot perish outside Jerusalem.	13:34–35: Jerusalem is the city that kills the prophets and stones those who are sent to her.

Talbert suggests that Paul's journey to Jerusalem in Acts 15:1–21:26 mirrors the Lukan travel narrative and that Luke's literary design at this point is revealed by the chiastic framework of this section as well.[172] Table 10 illustrates the chiastic structure.

Table 10 —The Chiastic Structure of Acts 15:1–21:26

Acts 15:1–18:11	Acts 18:12–21:26
15:1–29: Paul and others go to Jerusalem, and on the way report on the Gentile mission. The report is well received and they are welcomed on their arrival in Jerusalem. Jewish Christians raise the issue of the law and circumcision. There is a meeting involving Paul and James over the matter. The decision of James is sent in a letter to other churches.	18:12–21:26: Paul and others go to Jerusalem and are received gladly. Their report on the Gentile mission is well received. Jewish Christian concern over the law and circumcision is raised. There is a meeting involving Paul and James over the matter. The earlier decision by James that was sent in a letter is upheld.
15:30–16:15: Paul returns to the cities where he had earlier preached the gospel. He is forbidden by the Holy Spirit to speak in Asia. A vision calls him to Macedonia.	20:13–21:14: The Ephesian elders sorrow because they will not see Paul again. The Holy Spirit warns against going to Jerusalem. Bondage and suffering await Paul there.
16:16–40: An exorcism by Paul, followed by a riot. The Philippian jailer is converted.	19:11–20:12: Certain Jews try to imitate Paul's exorcisms. A riot ensues, and Paul saves Eutychus' life.
17:1–15: Synagogue debates.	19:8–10: Synagogue debates.
17:16–34: The Athenians who are already religious are taught accurately about true religion by Paul.	18:24–19:7: Apollos and 12 disciples who are already on the way to being Christians are taught accurately about true religion by Paul and his helpers.
18:1–11: Paul argues in the synagogue, and reference is made to the ruler of the synagogue. God promises Paul that no harm will befall him in the city.	18:12–23: Paul argues in the synagogue, and reference is made to the ruler of the synagogue. God's promise to Paul that no harm will befall him in Corinth is fulfilled.

David and Doris Blood have suggested a chiastic framework for the first major section of Acts.[173] They analyze the entire book of Acts as follows:

---

[172] C. Talbert, *Literary Patterns, Theological Themes and the Genre of Luke-Acts*, SBLMS 20 (Atlanta: Scholars Press, 1974), 56–58.

[173] D. and D. Blood, "Overview of Acts," *NOT* 74 (1979): 2. They understand Acts 1:1–11 as an "introductory tie" to Luke's Gospel.

Introductory Tie	1:1–11
Part I	1:12–19:20
Division 1	1:12–6:7
Division 2	6:8–9:31
Division 3	12:25–16:5
Division 4	13:25–16:5
Division 5	16:6–19:20
Part II	19:21–28:31
Introduction	19:21–22
Division 1	19:23–21:16
Division 2	21:17–23:11
Division 3	23:12–26:32
Division 4	27:1–28:16
Division 5	28:17–31

These divisions are all justified linguistically by Blood and Blood, and there is no need to cover the same ground here. The chiasmus in the first major section is formed by five summary statements given at the end of each embedded section (see Table 11).[174]

Table 11 — Chiastic Structure of the Five Summary Statements in Part 1 of Acts

A *ho logos* (6:7)
  B *hē ekklēsia* (9:31)
    C *ho logos* (12:24)
  B´ *hai ekklēsiai* (16:5)
A´ *ho logos* (19:20)

Blood and Blood note that this feature of the first section of Acts gives prominence and provides unity as the topics of each of the five summary statements are brought to the forefront and chiastically arranged.[175]

They suggest the following as a theme statement or macrostructure for Acts: "Against adversity, the Spirit-empowered witness about Jesus expands, through the disciples, from Jerusalem to the Aegean area and then extends, through Paul's trial, to Rome."[176] Acts 1:8 would appear

---

[174] Ibid., 11.
[175] Ibid.
[176] Ibid., 4.

to be the programmatic verse for the entire book in that it describes the geographical expansion of the apostles' witness. Thus, Luke begins his Gospel in Jerusalem and concludes it in Jerusalem with the ascension. He begins Acts with the ascension in Jerusalem, and concludes it with the gospel reaching Rome and with Paul's imprisonment there. All this is artistically brought together in the superstructure of the text by the use of a chiastic framework.[177] Not only are there large sections of Luke-Acts that bear the earmarks of chiastic arrangement, but some scholars see the entire two-volume work as one large chiasm.

Robert Morgenthaler was one of the first to study the linguistic parallelism that pervades Luke-Acts. He notes that such parallelism and chiasm is not restricted to the lower levels of the Lukan text, but the entire discourse follows this structure. He analyzes the Gospel of Luke with the following chiasm:[178]

Scene 1:	Jerusalem narratives	1:5–4:13
Scene 2:	On the road (in Galilee)	4:14–9:50
Scene 3:	On the road (in Samaria)	9:51–19:44 to Jerusalem
Scene 4:	Jerusalem narratives	19:45–24:52

His analysis of Luke-Acts reveals parallelism of the A B A´, A B A´ B´ type:[179]

I. Scenes in Jerusalem	Luke 1:5–4:13
I. Travel narrative	4:14–19:44
II. Scenes in Jerusalem	19:45–24:53
III. Scenes in Jerusalem	Acts 1:4–7:60
II. Travel narrative	8:1–21:17
IV. Scenes in Jerusalem	21:18–26:33
III. Travel narrative	27:1–28:31

In a similar vein, Goulder has suggested that Luke-Acts is structured as one overarching chiasm with the following sections: Galilee-

---

[177] D. Wiens, *Stephen's Sermon and the Structure of Luke-Acts* (North Richland Hills, Tex.: BIBAL Press, 1995) argues that Stephen's speech is actually the basic outline that Luke uses for his Gospel. He suggests that the literary structure of the speech is paralleled by the overall structure of Luke-Acts. The chiastic outlines are presented on pp. 241–66. Some of these chiastic structures appear forced, but Wiens has presented enough to confirm that Luke is fond of chiastic structure.

[178] R. Morgenthaler, *Die lukanische Geschichts-schreibungals Zeugnis: Gestalt und Gehalt der Kunst des Lukas* (Zurich: Zwingli, 1949), 1:172.

[179] Ibid., 163.

Samaria-Judea-Jerusalem-Resurrection-Jerusalem-Judea-Samaria-the uttermost parts of the earth.[180] The resurrection is the central panel in Goulder's chiasm.

Kenneth Wolfe argues that Goulder's analysis is essentially correct, but needs modification at one point. Rather than the resurrection being the central panel, Wolfe suggests that the ascension should be considered the central point.

> Luke clearly places the resurrection in the Jerusalem panel. The statement at the beginning of the journey section (Luke 9:51) makes the ascension (*analempsis*) the end of his journey to Jerusalem. At the end of the Gospel Luke has Jesus leave the city and ascend (Luke 24:50–51). In the summary of the contents of his first volume Luke indicates that he had written about what Jesus had done until the day when he ascended (*anelemphthe* [sic] Acts 1:2). The summary ends with a second narration of the ascension and a promise of the return (Acts 1:9–11).[181]

Thus Wolfe argues for the structure of Luke-Acts as follows:

A Galilee, Luke 4:14–9:50
　　B "Journey to Jerusalem" (through Samaria and Judea), Luke 9:51–19:40
　　　　C Jerusalem, Luke 19:41–24:49
　　　　　　D Ascension, Luke 24:50–51
　　　　　　D´ Ascension, Acts 1:1–11
　　　　C´ Jerusalem, Acts 1:12–8:1a
　　B´ Judea and Samaria, Acts 8:1b–11:18.
A´ To the end of the earth, Acts 11:19–28:31[182]

Ethel Wallis also identifies Luke-Acts as chiastic. According to her, the discourse structure yields the following statement of the "germinal idea" or three-point summary:

> The Jewish prophet Jesus was persecuted and condemned for his teaching: he was killed but rose from the dead according to his own prediction; he commissioned the surrogate prophets (apostles) Peter and Paul to complete his mission.[183]

---

[180] M. D. Goulder, "The Chiastic Structure of the Lucan Journey," 138; Morgenthaler, *Die lukanische Geschichts-schreibungals Zeugnis: Gestalt und Gehalt der Kunst des Lukas*, 195–96.

[181] K. Wolfe, "The Chiastic Structure of Luke-Acts and Some Implications for Worship," *SwJT* 22 (1980): 67.

[182] Ibid.

[183] E. E. Wallis, "The First and Second Epistles of Luke to Theophilus," *JOTT* 5.3 (1992): 229.

Her view of Luke's chiastic structure is pictured as a pyramid with
Luke and Acts forming the two sides and Jesus' resurrection and ascension serving as what she calls the "macropeak" of the Luke-Acts
narrative:[184]

Prologue
Stage
Inciting moment in Lk 4:28
A   Rising Action (conflict) 4:28–13:35
      B   Suspense (no conflict) 14:1–19:44)
            C   Peak (climax and resolution) 19:45–24:53
            C´   Peak (resolution-denouement) Acts 1:3–6:7
      B´   Denouement 1 (the church in Judea) Acts 6:8–12:25
A´   Denouement 2 (the church beyond Judea) Acts 13:1–22:22
Inciting final moment in Acts 22:22
Finale
Epilogue

Wallis's analysis of the text provides further linguistic confirmation
that Luke has chosen to use chiasm as a special stylistic device to
convey his message.

The chiastic framework discussed above for the whole of Luke-Acts
is superimposed over the constituent structure of the Gospel. It does
not always correspond exactly with the constituent structure, yet it
overlies it as a separate principle of cohesion and functions to achieve
an overall sense of unity to the two-volume work.

As a leading Lukan scholar, Talbert has published numerous works
on the subject. He suggests the following outline for Luke's Gospel
and offers substantial linguistic evidence to support it.[185]

Prologue — 1:1–4
Life of Jesus prior to his public ministry — 1:5–4:15
Galilean ministry of Jesus — 4:16–9:50
Journey to Jerusalem — 9:51–19:44
Last days in Jerusalem; Jesus' death, resurrection, and ascension
      — 19:45–24:53

---

[184] Ibid., 230–31.
[185] C. Talbert, *Reading Luke: A Literary and Theological Commentary on the Third Gospel* (New
York: Crossroads, 1982), vii–viii.

These major units correspond closely to the structure suggested by both Goulder and Wolfe.

Fearghus Fearghail has also demonstrated the parallelism between the structures of Luke-Acts. He formulated a corresponding literary structure for both volumes. Each has a *proemium*, an introductory narrative section preparing the reader for the full narrative to follow, and a narrative proper arranged in tripartite structure according to geographical considerations.[186]

Luke 1:1–4	Acts 1:1–26
Luke 1:5–4:44	Acts 1:15–26
Luke 5:1–9:50	Acts 2:1–8:3
Luke 9:51–19:48	Acts 8:4–21:17
Luke 20:1–24:53	Acts 21:18–28:31

According to Fearghail, Luke makes use of this geographical arrangement to give his two-volume work a "strong sense of movement and continuity in keeping with the programme set out in the proemium."[187] This narrative continuity of movement underlines the theological continuity between Israel and the church as the people of God.

Significant works appearing in the last several years that deal with this subject include Andrew Clark, *Parallel Lives,* and Douglas Mc-Comiskey, *Lukan Theology in the Light of the Gospel's Literary Structure.*[188] Clark notes the importance of identifying criteria for assessing valid parallels in Luke-Acts such as similarity not only in content, but also in language, literary form, sequence, structure, and theme.[189] Clark illustrates and discusses several parallels in Luke-Acts, including parallels between John the Baptist and Jesus found in Luke 1–4,[190] Peter and Paul preaching parallels in Acts,[191] Stephen in relation to

---

[186] F. Fearghail, "The Introduction to Luke-Acts: A Study of the Role of Luke 1:1–4:44 in the Composition of Luke's Two-Volume Work," AnBib, *Investigationes Scientificae in Res Biblicas,* vol. 126 (Rome: Edtrice Pontificio Istituto Biblico, 1991), 84, 181.

[187] Ibid., 181.

[188] A. Clark, *Parallel Lives: The Relation of Paul to the Apostles in the Lucan Perspective,* Paternoster Biblical and Theological Monographs (Carlisle, Cumbria, U.K./Waynesboro, Ga.: Paternoster, 2001); D. McComiskey, *Lukan Theology in the Light of the Gospel's Literary Structure,* Paternoster Biblical Monographs (Milton Keynes, U.K.: Paternoster, 2004).

[189] Clark, *Parallel Lives,* 75–77.

[190] Ibid., 101–10.

[191] Ibid., 230–60.

Jesus and the apostles,[192] and parallels between Peter and Paul's commission and miracles.[193]

Although we are not interested at this point in delving into Luke's theological reasons for his extensive use of parallelism, Clark's thesis is that Luke is demonstrating continuity and unity in at least three ways: (1) God's dealing with His people in the Old Testament and in the church; (2) the work of Jesus and His disciples; and (3) the Jewish mission based in Jerusalem and the Gentile mission based in Antioch.[194] Clark's work reveals Luke's extensive use of synkrisis, a rhetorical device which the author of Hebrews makes significant use of as well.[195]

McComiskey interacts primarily with the work of Tannehill and Talbert on the subject of parallelism in Luke-Acts, and followed with an evaluation of Old Testament texts and Greco-Roman literature bearing similar structure to Luke. He then proposes and defends a fourfold cyclical narrative structure for Luke 4:14–24:53.[196] Since enough has been shown here to illustrate Luke's extensive use of parallelism, and since this feature of Luke's style is now well-recognized in New Testament studies, we need not go into further detailed examples.[197]

The many Jesus-Peter and Jesus-Paul parallels one finds in Luke-Acts exemplify Luke's overall scheme of continuity in salvation history. Zwiep captures the cruciality of the 40-day interval between the resurrection and ascension in Luke's theology: "The function of the forty days leading up to the ascension is to ensure the continuation of Jesus' preaching. They are a 'last rehearsal' before the Church is launched into the mission of the world on the day of Pentecost, ten days later."[198]

---

[192] Ibid., 261–80.

[193] Ibid., 331–35.

[194] Ibid., 337.

[195] Ibid., 320–21. Synkrisis involves describing two lives for purposes of comparison.

[196] D. McComiskey, *Lukan Theology in the Light of the Gospel's Literary Structure*, Paternoster Biblical Monographs (Milton Keynes, U.K.: Paternoster, 2004), 204–84.

[197] Among other examples that could be given, see the parallels in Acts 10 between the Cornelius episode and Jonah (R. Wall, "Peter, 'Son' of Jonah: The Conversion of Cornelius in the Context of Canon," in R. Wall and E. Lemcio, *The New Testament as Canon: A Reader in Canonical Criticism*, JSNTSup 76 [Sheffield: Sheffield Academic Press, 1992], 129–40); and the parallels between the Zechariah narrative in Luke 1 and the Cornelius narrative in Acts 10 (J. Green, "Internal Repetition in Luke-Acts: Contemporary Narratology and Lucan Historiography," in *History, Literature, and Society in the Book of Acts*, ed. B. Witherington [Cambridge: Cambridge University Press, 1996], 294).

[198] A. W. Zwiep, *The Ascension of the Messiah in Lukan Christology* (Leiden: Koln, 1997), 171. The way Luke writes Acts indicates that, for Zwiep, the preaching of Christ as proclaimed by Paul "goes back to and has the full support of the Jerusalem community" (p. 174).

Using the foregoing structural evidence, the foundation is laid for extracting a possible macrostructure for Luke-Acts. Luke has addressed his two-volume work to an individual named Theophilus (Luke 1:1–4), with the intent of confirming his faith in the Gospel account he has heard. Whether or not Theophilus was a Christian at the time of Luke's composition cannot be known with certainty. If he were not, then Luke's purpose would have been to elicit faith in his reader. However, it seems the most plausible reading of the prologue suggests that Luke's purpose was to confirm Theophilus' faith. Wallis notes that it is as if Luke were saying: "Theophilus, consider the words and deeds of Jesus, the great and final Prophet. . . . Be reassured—here is proof of his authenticity."[199]

As shown above, Luke centers his two-volume work on Christ's ascension. Furthermore, he presents Jesus as God's final prophet to the people. In the denouement of the Gospel, the postresurrection episode on the road to Emmaus, Wallis notes that Jesus functions in the role of prophet, and that this fact is the focal point.

> The bereft disciples declared that he [Jesus] was a prophet, powerful in word and deed (24:19). Perhaps, they had been mistaken. To them Jesus said, How foolish and slow of heart to believe all that the prophets have spoken! (24:25).[200]

The prologue to Acts (1:1–5) provides a summary of the Gospel, especially in the first two verses. The following is my translation from the Greek text:

> The former book I have made, O Theophilus, concerning all things which Jesus began to do and to teach, until the day in which, after he had given commandment by the Holy Spirit to the apostles whom he had chosen, he was taken up.

I have deliberately placed the words "he was taken up" at the end of the sentence because Luke has placed the Greek verb at the end of the clause for special focus. This is further linguistic evidence that the ascension serves as the focal point of Luke's Gospel. Thus, according to Acts 1:1–2, there are three overarching categories found in the Gospel: (1) the things Jesus did, (2) the things Jesus taught, and (3) the ascension of Jesus.

---

[199] Wallis, "Thematic Parallelism and Prominence in Luke-Acts," 9.
[200] Ibid., 10.

Orchard and Riley have suggested that Acts 1:1–2 provides a good summary of Luke's Gospel. They point out that after the introduction and infancy narratives in Luke 1:1–3:38, Luke concentrates on the things Jesus began to do (4:1–9:50), then on what Jesus began to teach (9:51–18:30). Finally, Luke centers on the events of the passion and resurrection, concluding his Gospel with the ascension.[201]

From the above analysis, taking into account Luke's prologues in both the Gospel and Acts, the thematic statements offered by Wallis and Blood and Blood, and the structural analysis of Talbert, Goulder, Wolfe, and Wallis, the macrostructure for Luke-Acts could be presented as follows:

> Writing to Theophilus, Luke intends to inform him about the life, death, resurrection, and ascension of Jesus Christ, God's final prophet. Jesus' life prior to His public ministry includes the infancy narrative (Luke 1–2) and His pre-public ministry culminating in the statement about the beginning of His Galilean ministry (4:14–15). Jesus' deeds are recounted in 4:16–9:50 with special emphasis on His healing activity. The journey to Jerusalem is a section primarily devoted to Jesus' teaching, culminating in His arrival at Jerusalem. The final section (19:45–24:53) narrates His conflict with the religious leaders, His arrest, trial, death, resurrection and ascension. The prologue to Acts announces the theme that what Jesus began to do on earth, he now continues to do in heaven. Beginning at Jerusalem, the spread of the gospel continues to Judea and Samaria, and finally to the uttermost part of the earth, when Paul arrives in Rome. The growth of the gospel is accompanied by persecution, yet the word of God and the number of disciples continues to multiply.

Luke has told the Christian story with great literary expertise. His ability to interweave narratives in parallel structures is clear. His knowledge and use of Greek literary methods is also evident, and will be further demonstrated in the chapters below.

Macrostructure and Superstructure in Hebrews

We turn now to a consideration of the Letter to the Hebrews and its structure. The traditional way of looking at the structure of Hebrews was summed up well by John Brown almost 150 years ago:

---

[201] B. Orchard and H. Riley, *The Order of the Synoptics: Why Three Gospels?* (Macon, Ga.: Mercer University Press, 1987).

> The Epistle divides itself into two parts—the first Doctrinal, and the second Practical—though the division is not so accurately observed that there are no duties enjoined or urged in the first part, and no doctrines stated in the second.[202]

According to this analysis, Hebrews consists of two main divisions: 1:5–10:18 and 10:19–13:17. A thematic introduction (1:1–4) precedes Part One, and a conclusion (13:18–21) and postscript (13:22–25) follow Part Two. Part One is described as "doctrinal," "dogmatic," or "kerygmatic" while Part Two is labeled "practical," "parenetic," or "ethical."[203]

Although a few scholars still accept this traditional bipartite structure, it is increasingly clear that this thesis must be modified. For example, O. Michel concludes that the most salient sections of Hebrews are the hortatory passages.[204] Kümmel concurs and says the hortatory passages (2:1–4; 3:7–4:11; 5:11–6:12; 10:19–25; 12:1–2) function as the goal and purpose of the entire discourse.[205] F. F. Bruce agrees with this assessment and argues that the climax of Hebrews is found in 10:19–25. "The preceding argument leads up, stage by stage, to this exhortation, and what comes after reinforces it.[206]

The text bears out this analysis, for in 13:22 the author speaks of his text as "a word of exhortation." Thus, of the four major discourse types (narrative, procedural, expository, and hortatory), Hebrews is best described by the last category. The imperatives and hortatory subjunctives in the letter will be ranked at the highest thematic level.

The detailed analysis of the structure of Hebrews by A. Vanhoye launched the modern quest for the structure of Hebrews.[207] He posits the following chiastic structure for Hebrews:

---

[202] J. Brown, *An Exposition of the Epistle of the Apostle Paul to the Hebrews*, ed. D. Smith, The Geneva Series of Commentaries (Edinburgh: William Oliphant & Co., 1862; repr., Edinburgh: Banner of Truth Trust, 1961), 10.

[203] Ibid.

[204] O. Michel, *Der Brief an die Hebräer*, KEK, ed. H. Meyer (Göttingen: Vandenhoeck & Ruprecht, 1975), 27.

[205] W. Kümmel, *Introduction to the New Testament*, rev. ed., trans. H. C. Kee (Nashville: Abingdon, 1975), 390.

[206] F. F. Bruce, "The Structure and Argument of Hebrews," *SwJT* 28 (1985): 6.

[207] A. Vanhoye, *La Structure Litteraire de l`epitre aux Hebreux*, 2nd ed (Paris: Desclee De Brouwer, 1963); id., "Discussions sur la Structure de l`epitre aux Hebreux," *Bib* 55 (1974): 349–80; id., "Literarische Struktur und theologische Botschaft des Hebräerbriefs," *SNTSU* 4 (1979): 119–47. This is just a small sampling of Vanhoye's many writings on the subject. L. Vaganay, "Le Plan de L'Épître aux Hébreux," in *Mémorial Lagrange* (Paris: Gabalda, 1940), 269–77, argued that Hebrews was symmetrically structured into five major sections. Building upon this, Vanhoye, *La Structure*, analyzed the literary devices used in Hebrews and posited a chiastic framework for the epistle. He also critiqued Vaganay as well as other suggested literary structures. J. Bligh, "The Structure of Hebrews," *HeyJ* 5 (1964): 170–77, and J. Swetnam, "Form and Content in Hebrews

1:1–4
Introduction
          1:5–2:18
          Eschatology
               3:1–5:10
               Ecclesiology
                    5:11–10:39
                    Sacrifice
               11:1–12:13
               Ecclesiology
          12:14–13:19
          Eschatology
13:20–21208
Conclusion

One of the most significant studies on the structure of Hebrews is Linda Lloyd Neeley's "A Discourse Analysis of Hebrews."[209] She interacts with Vanhoye's conclusions, and while she feels his structural breaks must be modified, she fully concurs that Hebrews was structured in an overall chiastic framework. Accepting Hebrews as an example of hortatory discourse with large sections of embedded exposition, she presents the following outline of its discourse structure:[210]

Thematic Introduction —	1:1–4
Point 1 —	1:1–4:13
Point 2 —	4:14–10:18
Peak (Point 3) —	10:19–13:21
Conclusion —	13:20–21
Finis —	13:22–25

Neeley takes the theme statements from the three embedded discourses and produces the following macrostructure for Hebrews:

7–13," *Bib* 55 (1974): 333–48, offered critiques of Vanhoye's work. Swetnam believed that greater attention must be paid to content and not literary devices. J. Bligh, *Chiastic Analysis of the Epistle to the Hebrews* (Heythrop: Athenaeum, 1966), also argued for the chiastic structure of Hebrews. L. Dussaut, *Synopse structurelle de L'Épître aux Hébreux: Approche d'analyse structurelle* (Paris: Desclée, 1981), 18–151, argued for a symmetric structure to Hebrews involving chiasm. See also Guthrie, *Structure*, 3–41, and Westfall, *Discourse Structure*, 1–21, for a survey of scholarship on the structure of Hebrews.

[208] Vanhoye does not include 13:22–25 since vv, 20–21 are the actual benediction.

[209] Her thesis, completed in 1976, was published in *OPTAT* (1987): 1–146.

[210] Ibid., 41.

ED1   God has spoken to us in his Son

ED2   who as our high priest has offered a complete sacrifice for sins and by this obtained salvation for us.

ED3   Therefore let us draw near to God with a true heart in full assurance of faith in Jesus and the sufficiency of his finished sacrifice; let us hold fast the confession of the hope in him without wavering, and let us consider each other to stir up to love and good works.[211]

The fact that both Vanhoye and Neeley have proposed an overall chiastic structure for the book is of interest to us in our investigation of authorship. We have already shown that Luke chose this literary approach to convey the superstructure of his two-volume work.

While Vanhoye's chiastic analysis has merits, Neeley's analysis of the chiastic structure is more linguistically thorough and compelling since she pays attention to features of both surface and semantic structure. Hebrews, like Luke-Acts, is shown to have low-level examples of chiasm (paragraphs, sections, etc.) as well as chiasm at the highest structural level. With reference to this phenomenon of chiasm in Hebrews she remarks:

> A special feature of the lexico-semantic unity of Hebrews is a chiastic ordering of major semantic divisions in the discourse as a whole. These divisions, not corresponding exactly with the organization of Hebrews into embedded discourses on different levels of embedding, form another system of organization which is superimposed on the constituent structure and is also distinct from the backbone of the book.[212]

This is precisely what we have discovered to be the case with Luke's two-volume work. Luke-Acts is primarily narrative discourse with large sections of embedded exposition, while Hebrews is primarily hortatory discourse with large sections of embedded exposition. If Luke is the author of all three works, he would appear to be quite comfortable with the cohesive literary device of chiasm.

---

[211] Ibid., 61. "ED" stands for "Embedded Discourse."

[212] Ibid., 61–62. This phenomenon is not unusual in ancient authors, as Talbert, *Literary Patterns*, 13–14n68; and 64n10, has said.

Neeley's chiasm may be displayed as follows:[213]

A 1:1–4:13
   B   4:14–6:20
       C   7:1–28
       C´   8:1–10:18
   B´   10:19–10:39
 A´   11:1–13:25

Table 12 illustrates the parallels between sections A and A´ of the chiasm.[214] The parallels between B and B´ are given by Neeley in Tables 14, 15, and 16. These tables show parallel introductions, parallel warnings, and parallel reminders, respectively. I have shown these parallels in the three tables below using the English translation of each section.

Table 12 — Parallels between Heb 1:1–4:13 and Heb 11:1–13:21

chaps. 1–2	chap. 11
expository embedded discourse	expository embedded discourse
3:1	12:2–3
the apostle and high priest of our confession, Jesus . . .	completer of faith, Jesus . . . for consider him who endured such slander . . .
3:6–8	12:5
Therefore, as the Holy Spirit says, Today if you hear his voice, do not harden your hearts . . .	exhortation that speaks to you as a son, My son, do not despise the chastening of the Lord . . .
4:1	12:15
Let us therefore fear lest . . . any of you should seem to fall short (*husterēkenai*).	. . . watching lest anyone lack (*husterōn*) the grace of God . . .
4:11–13	12:25,28–29
Let us be diligent to enter that rest, lest anyone fall into the same example of unbelief, for the word of God is living and powerful before him, but all things are naked and opened before the eyes of him to whom we must give account.	See that you refuse not him that speaks. . . . let us have grace whereby we may serve . . . for our God is a consuming fire.

---

[213] Ibid., 62.
[214] Ibid., 63.

Table 13 — Parallel Introductions — 10:19–25; 4:14–16[215]

10:19–25	4:14–16
Having therefore, brothers, boldness to enter the holy place by the blood of Jesus and having a great high priest over the house of God, let us draw near with a true heart in full assurance of faith; let us hold firm the confession of hope without wavering, for faithful is the one who promises.	Having therefore a great high priest who has passed into heavens, Jesus the son of God, let us hold firm our confession. For we have not a high priest who is not able to sympathize with our weaknesses, but having been tempted in everything similarly, yet without sin. Let us draw near therefore with boldness to the throne of grace that we may receive mercy and find grace for well-timed help.

Table 14 — Parallel warnings — 10:26–31; 6:4–8[216]

10:26–31	6:4–8
For if we sin willfully after receiving the knowledge of the truth, there no longer remains any sacrifice for sins, but a fearful expectation of judgment and jealousy of fire which shall consume the enemies. He who disregarded the law of Moses died without mercy on the testimony of two or three witnesses; of how much greater punishment shall he be thought worthy who has trampled the Son of God underfoot and considered common the blood of the covenant by which he was sanctified and insulted the Spirit of Grace? For we know the one who said, Vengeance is mine; I will repay, and again, The Lord shall judge his people. It is a fearful thing to fall into the hands of the living God.	For it is impossible to renew again to repentance those who have been once enlightened and become sharers in the Holy Spirit and tasted the good word of God and the powers of the coming age, and fall away since they are recrucifying to themselves the Son of God and exposing Him to contempt. For the ground that drinks in the rain that often falls on it and brings forth useful vegetation for those for whom it is cultivated receives blessing from God, but that which bears thorns and thistles is worthless and close to being cursed, whose end is to be burned.

---

[215] Ibid., 52–53.
[216] Ibid., 54.

Table 15 — Parallel reminders — 6:9–20; 10:32–39[217]

10:32–33	6:9–10
But recall the former days, in which when you had been enlightened, you endured a great struggle of sufferings sometimes being exposed publically to reproach and affliction, and sometimes being sharers with those so treated. For you sympathized with those in bonds, and accepted the seizing of your goods with joy, knowing that you have a better and more lasting possession.	But we are persuaded better things about you, beloved, and things accompanying salvation, though we speak thus. For God is not unrighteous that he would forget your work and the love which you have shown to his name, in having ministered to the saints as you do now also.
10:35–39	**6:11–20**
Do not throw away therefore your confidence, which has great reward. For you have need of patience that when you have done the will of God you may receive the promise. For yet a little while and he that is coming will come and not delay, but my righteous one shall live by faith, and if he shrinks back, my soul will have no pleasure in him. But we are not of those who shrink back and are lost but of those who believe to the keeping of their souls.	But we desire that each one of you show the same diligence toward the full assurance of hope to the end, that you be not sluggish, but imitators of those who through faith and patience inherit the promises. For when God promised Abraham, since he had no greater to swear by, he swore by himself, saying Surely blessing I will bless you and multiplying I will multiply you, and thus through patience he obtained the promise. . . . This hope we have as an anchor for the soul—secure and firm . . . .

The parallels between the Cs of the chiasm are listed below in Table 16. The verbal parallels as well as the extensive semantic parallels between these two sections contrast differing aspects of the old and new covenants.

Table 16 — Parallels between 7:1–28; 8:1–10:18[218]

7:11–12	8:7–8
If therefore perfection were through the Levitical priesthood, for under it the people received the law, what further need was there for another priest to arise after the order of Melchizedek and not called after the order of Aaron? For when there is a change of priesthood, there is of necessity also a change of the law.	For if that first had been faultless then there would have been no occasion for a second. For finding fault with them he says, Behold, the days come, says the Lord, when I will make a new covenant with the house of Judah . . .

---

[217] Ibid., 54–55.
[218] Ibid., 64–65.

7:18–19	8:6
For there is a setting aside of the former commandment because of its weakness and uselessness, for the law made nothing perfect, but the bringing in of a better hope did, through which we draw nigh to God.	But now he has obtained a more excellent ministry to the degree that he is mediator of a better covenant which is established upon better promises.
7:20–22	**9:15**
And inasmuch as not without an oath—for those on the one hand were made priests without oaths, but he with an oath through the one who said to him, the Lord swears and will not repent, You are a priest forever—to the same degree Jesus has become the pledge of a better covenant.	And because of this he is the mediator of a new covenant, that by means of death to redeem from the transgressions that were under the first covenant, they which are called might receive the promise of eternal inheritance.
7:25–28	**9:24–28**
So then, he is able to save to the fullest those who come through him to God, living always to make intercession for them. For such a high priest was fitting for us—holy, guileless, undefiled, separated from sinners, and made higher than the heavens, who had no need every day, as those high	For Christ entered not the holy place made with hands, the representation of the true, but into heaven itself, now to appear in the presence of God for us, not that he might offer himself often, as those high priests every year entered the holy place with the blood of others, since it would then have been necessary for him to have suffered
priests, first to offer sacrifices for his own sins, then for those of the people, for this he did once for all when he offered up himself. For the law appointed men high priests who have weakness; but the word of the oath which came after the law, the Son, who is perfected forever.	often from the foundation of the world, but now once at the end of the ages has he appeared to put away sin through the sacrifice of himself. And just as it is appointed to men once to die, but after this the judgment, so also Christ, having been offered once to bear the sins of many, the second time without sins shall appear for salvation to those who eagerly await him.
	10:11–14
	And every priest stands daily ministering and offering often the same sacrifices which can never take away sins, but this one, when he had offered one sacrifice for sins forever sat down at the right hand of God, then waiting until his enemies be made a footstool for his feet. For by one offering he has perfected forever those who are sanctified.

The preceding tables reveal the extensive parallelism and resulting chiastic organization that pervades Hebrews. The author has carefully constructed his text into one overarching chiasm.

The question we must ask relative to this study is, Does the use of parallelism, chiasm, and *inclusio* we have seen in Luke-Acts and Hebrews provide evidence for common authorship? In recent times, the New Testament writings have undergone extensive study from a literary/linguistic perspective. In addition to Luke-Acts and Hebrews, chiastic frameworks have been suggested at the discourse level for Matthew, Mark, Romans, 1 and 2 Corinthians, Galatians, Philippians, Philemon, and Revelation. With regard to the Pauline Letters, both Ian Thomson and John Harvey have concluded (rightly, in my judgment) that Paul's use of chiasmus, while at times spanning several paragraphs or chapters, is usually limited to the lower levels of discourse.[219]

Paul apparently never used chiasm as an overarching literary device for any of his letters. He uses chiasm frequently, however, on the lower discourse levels, but it has not been demonstrated that he uses it at the highest level, that of an entire discourse. This serves as additional linguistic evidence against Pauline authorship of Hebrews.

Yet it must be admitted that Luke-Acts and Hebrews are not unique compared with the other New Testament authors in the use of chiasm as an overarching framework—if the chiastic structures posited for Matthew, Mark, and Revelation turn out to be valid. Blomberg believes that the chiasms posited for Matthew "inevitably prove vague and break down at crucial points."[220] Wendland acknowledges low-level chiasms in Revelation (7:13–14), but says it is "of a very loose, thematic variety (which may often be interpreted simply as inclusion). . . . " He found no overarching chiastic structure for Revelation.[221] On the other hand, M. Lee has posited a chiastic structure for Revelation that appears to have some linguistic merit.[222]

The excesses to which some have gone to find an overarching chiastic structure (e.g., in some of the Pauline Letters) have been

---

[219] I. Thomson, *Chiasmus in the Pauline Letters*, 213–32; J. Harvey, *Listening to the Text*, 283–86.

[220] C. Blomberg, *Matthew*, NAC (Nashville: B&H, 1992), 23.

[221] E. R. Wendland, "7 x 7 (x 7): A Structural and Thematic Outline of John's Apocalypse," *OPTAT* 4 (1990): 376–78.

[222] M. Lee, "A Call to Martyrdom: Function as Method and Message in Revelation," *NovT* XL (1998): 174–90.

criticized by Harvey.[223] Often an outline is superimposed on the text that has only slight semantic justification and little or no linguistic parallelism.

What are we to make of all this? It would seem we have to admit that Luke-Acts and Hebrews may not be unique among the New Testament writings in terms of chiastic frameworks. Yet it also seems that the evidential basis for (and acceptance of) a chiastic structure for Luke-Acts and Hebrews can be demonstrated more readily than most of the New Testament, where chiasm has been posited as an overarching framework).

Thus, a further similarity is found between Luke and Hebrews in the use of parallelism and chiasm, whereas Paul did not use these literary devices at the discourse level. The evidence merits a positive comparison between Luke-Acts and Hebrews, and this provides a further argument for Lukan authorship of Hebrews since both Luke and the author of Hebrews apply this literary technique at the macro level of the discourse.

The Use of Rhetorical Features in Luke-Acts and Hebrews

The preceding evidence confirms what has been suggested in recent years in Lukan studies: Luke is quite a skilled literary artist. Since the rhetorical artistry of Hebrews is well known, Luke can reasonably be compared to the author of Hebrews in this area. We should remember, however, that Luke-Acts is narrative discourse with sections of embedded exposition. Hebrews is hortatory discourse with sections of embedded exposition. Recognizing their different discourse genres is vital. What is noteworthy here is that even though the two works represent discourse genres that to some extent govern their structure, there is still much similarity.

First, many of the rhetorical conventions in Hebrews can also be found in Luke and Paul. As demonstrated above, Luke makes prominent use of alliteration and assonance in his prologue, as does Hebrews. But in addition to these lower discourse-level rhetorical devices, Luke is quite capable of rhetorical features such as chiasmus at the highest level of discourse.

Kota Yamada argues that the historiography of Acts is rhetorical, particularly along Ciceronian lines. He identifies the two major trends

---

[223] J. Harvey, *Listening to the Text*, 140, 176–79, 204, 223–24, 245–48, 282.

of historiography in Greco-Roman antiquity: political and rhetorical. The latter has several types of schools (Isocratean, Peripatetic, and the mixed type). The rhetoric of Cicero falls into the category of mixed type. He made six comparisons between Luke-Acts and Ciceronian rhetoric, concluding that the literary genre of Acts is a Ciceronian type of rhetorical history where Luke uses rhetorical principles from Greco-Roman rhetorical historiography.[224]

The speech is a significant feature of rhetorical historiography. The role of the speeches in Luke-Acts is well recognized. Almost a third of Acts contains speeches. Yamada notes that although the content of the speeches given to Gentile and Jewish audiences differs, the structure is similar. The speeches in Acts consist of (1) introduction (*exordium*), (2) kerygmatic words of the cross and resurrection (*narratio*), (3) Old Testament quotations (*probation*), and (4) admonitions (*peroratio*). The mission speeches follow the pattern of deliberative rhetoric. The defense speeches of Paul follow the structure of forensic oratory: (1) introduction (*exordium*), (2) charges and description of the defendant (*narratio*), (3) body of the apology (*probation*), (4) claims of innocence (*refutatio*), and (5) conclusion (*peroratio*).[225]

Conclusion

The foregoing lexical, stylistic, and textlinguistic evidence supports Lukan authorship. Based on lexical comparison, Hebrews has more in common with Luke-Acts than any other New Testament work. Luke or Paul could be the author in view of the large, unique vocabulary they have in common with Hebrews (Luke shares 53 lexical items with Hebrews, and Paul shares 56). On this basis alone, one can draw no certain conclusions in favor of Luke over Paul. However, when other lexical data are considered, Luke's writings tend to be more closely aligned with Hebrews than do the Pauline Letters. Thus, the 53 words unique to Luke and Hebrews become a significant argument for Lukan authorship.

Stylistically, Hebrews is closer to Luke-Acts than to the Pauline corpus; therefore, on this basis, Luke is a more probable candidate. The method of Scripture citation as well as the use of the Septuagint

---

[224] K. Yamada, "A Rhetorical History: the Literary Genre of the Acts of the Apostles," in *Rhetoric, Scripture and Theology: Essays from the 1994 Pretoria Conference*, JSNTSup 131, ed. S. Porter and T. Olbricht (Sheffield: Sheffield Academic Press, 1996), 230–50.

[225] Ibid., 247.

in Hebrews links the book more closely with Luke-Acts. The judgment of ancient and modern scholarship is unanimous in concluding that the style of Hebrews is discernibly different from Paul.[226] This fact furnishes the most significant evidence against Pauline authorship. Recently, as noted above, a few have attempted to revive the theory of Pauline authorship. As far as I can tell, no new evidence has been presented for this case that Stuart and Leonard did not introduce in the eighteenth and nineteenth centuries.

> Whether in terms of grammar, vocabulary, and style, of rhetorical strategy, use of literary conventions, or creative skill, Luke is given a high rating. Among New Testament writers, this author ranks among those who have the best command of the Greek language and is one of its most versatile and literarily accomplished.[227]

Luke-Acts and Hebrews exhibit similar tendencies in their prologues, despite Luke and Hebrews being different discourse genres. This difference makes the comparison of prologues all the more significant. Luke's prologue reads like a narrative prologue while Hebrews does not. Yet the similarities are there and can be interpreted as evidence for common authorship.

A comparison of the macrostructures and superstructures of Luke-Acts and Hebrews reveals a tendency to superimpose a chiastic framework over the entire discourse. While chiasm is not rare in the New Testament at the lower discourse levels, it is somewhat rarer at the highest discourse level, and hence a positive comparison for our thesis has been made.

Before we close our discussion on style, perhaps it would not be too cumbersome to introduce a lengthy but comprehensive quotation on this subject from Samuel Davidson's *New Testament Introduction*:

> What is the conclusion to be drawn from style? If the tone of the writer be elevated, rhetorical, polished, is it not unlike Paul's? Let it be admitted that the apostle's style varies in his epistles; the dissimilarity here observable is not explained by that; because the diversity which appears in his writings is

---

[226] S. Davidson, *An Introduction*, 212, has put it as well as anyone: "Every reader feels the style is unlike Paul's. The periods are regular and rounded; the rhythm oratorical and smooth. The structure of sentences is more exact than the Pauline; with less abruptness and vigour. Full-toned expressions, words of a poetical complexion, are abundant. Instead of the apostle's dialectic method, his fiery energy and impassioned style, we have the stately and polished eloquence of one who built up rhythmical periods."

[227] E. Richard, "Luke: Author and Thinker," in *New Views on Luke and Acts*, ed. E. Richard (Collegeville, MN: Liturgical, 1990), 15.

compatible with substantial unity. Let it also be admitted that Paul's relation
to the Palestinian Christians differed from his relation to other believers,
because he was not one of their teachers. Yet he did not found the Roman
church; and the style of the epistle addressed to it is very different from
that of the present. The object he had in view and the subject discussed will
not explain the elevated tone; these did not need a loftier diction than the
subjects of some Pauline epistles. The contents of the letter to the Romans
demanded an equally oratorical style. If it be thought that because the epistle
resembles a treatise on a great subject it should be dignified, calm, and sol-
emn; yet Paul's fire does not burst forth even in the hortatory part, where
no trace of his characteristic manner appears. And is it not strange that the
apostle should adopt a purer Greek and higher style of writing in an epistle
addressed to Jewish Christians—to readers who were the worst judges of
good Greek?[228]

> Had they been cultivated Gentiles, an elegant tone would have been appropri-
> ate; why polish the diction and round the periods for the use of Jewish believ-
> ers? We are therefore brought to the conclusion, that the apostle Paul did not
> write the letter. . . . It is the diversity amid similarity [with Paul's writings]
> which makes a different writer probable.[229]

One nagging question remains: How are we to account for the lexical similarities that clearly exist among Luke, Paul, and Hebrews; the
stylistic similarity between Luke and Hebrews; and the stylistic dissimilarity between Paul and Hebrews? The best reading of the evidence is that these factors point to Luke as the author of Hebrews—or
at the very least as coauthor with Paul. The same evidence that dis-
tances Paul from Hebrews actually links Luke with it.

Having studied the linguistic data, what evidence might we find regarding the Lukan authorship theory from a comparison of the theme
and purpose of Luke-Acts and Hebrews? A comparison of these elements reveals that the works are substantially the same in some respects. To this analysis we now turn.

---

[228] This last statement illustrates the problem I discuss in the excursus at the end of chap. 6.
See, for example, Borgen's comment, "Scholars no longer regard the distinction between Pales-
tinian and Hellenistic Judaism as a basic category for our understanding of Judaism." P. Borgen,
The New Testament and Hellenistic Judaism, ed. P. Borgen and S. Giversen (Aarhus, Denmark:
Aarhus University Press, 1995; repr. Peabody, MA: Hendrickson, 1997), 11.

[229] S. Davidson, *Introduction*, 214–15.

Chapter 4

THE PURPOSES OF LUKE-ACTS AND HEBREWS COMPARED[1]

T he purpose of this chapter is to present evidence for the Lukan authorship of Hebrews based on a comparison of the purpose(s) of Luke-Acts and Hebrews. Of course, two authors may write to different audiences (or even to the same audience) with the same purpose in mind. Identity of purpose between two works does not by itself point to identity of authorship. However, if there is lexical and semantic evidence in the prologues of Luke-Acts and Hebrews and in the hortatory sections of the works, such evidence would link the works more closely and should be considered in the question of authorship attribution.

The Purpose of Luke-Acts

Determining the purpose or purposes of Luke-Acts has been a challenge for Lukan scholars. The history of research on this question has yielded diverse results.[2] Morgenthaler demonstrated the many ways

---

[1] Much of this chapter appeared in my article, "The Purposes of Luke-Acts and Hebrews Compared: An Argument for the Lukan Authorship of Hebrews," in *The Church at the Dawn of the 21st Century* (Dallas: Criswell Publications, 1989), 223–35.

[2] See F. Bovon, *Luke the Theologian: Fifty-five Years of Research (1950–2005)*, 2nd rev. ed. (Waco: Baylor University Press, 2006), which is the most comprehensive survey of research on all Lukan questions, including purpose. See also R. Maddox, *The Purpose of Luke-Acts* (Edinburgh: T&T Clark, 1982); E. Richard, "Luke—Writer, Theologian, Historian: Research and Orientation of the 1970's," *BTB* 13 (1983): 3–15; R. Brawley, "The Pharisees in Luke-Acts: Luke's Address to Jews and His Irenic Purpose," (Ph.D. Diss., Princeton Theological Seminary, 1978); R. Brawley, *Luke-Acts and the Jews: Conflict, Apology, and Conciliation* (Atlanta: Scholars Press, 1987); P. Esler, *Community and Gospel in Luke-Acts: The Social and Political Motivations of Lucan Theology*, SNTSMS 57 (Cambridge: Cambridge University Press, 1987); and J. Jervell, *The Theology of the Acts of the Apostles* (Cambridge: Cambridge University Press, 1996). In addition to Bovon's volume, a plethora of monographs addressing the historical, social, and literary background of Luke-Acts has appeared. A helpful summary of some of these can be found in F. Downing's article, "Theophilus's First Reading of Luke-Acts," in *Luke's Literary Achievement: Collected Essays*, JSNTSup 116, ed. C. M. Tuckett (Sheffield: Sheffield Academic Press, 1995), 91–109. See also S. Spencer, "Acts and Modern Literary Approaches," in *The Book of Acts in Its Ancient Literary Setting*, ed. B. Winter and A. Clarke (Grand Rapids: Eerdmans, 1993), 381–414. D. Peterson's article in the same volume, "The Motif of Fulfillment and the Purpose of Luke-Acts," is a helpful study (83–104). More recently, see Peterson's "Luke's Theological Enterprise: Integration and Intent," 521–44, which is a good summary of these themes. D. Peterson, *Witness to the Gospel: The Theology of Acts* (Grand Rapids: Eerdmans, 1998), which he co-edited with I. H. Marshall. A short and accessible summary of the proposed Lukan purposes with helpful

in which Luke parallels scenes and events in his Gospel with similar scenes and events in Acts. The result is a pattern of twofoldness, not only in form but in content, with the twin themes of Jewish rejection and Gentile acceptance permeating the two-volume work.[3]

We must ask how Luke's purpose is achieved through this structure and content. But first we must determine whether Luke is writing to Jewish Christians or Gentile Christians. Morgenthaler's insight regarding whether Luke is addressing the Jewish or the Gentile question is that the answer depends on the direction in which one looks (in Luke-Acts).[4]

Given the state of Lukan studies today and Luke's obvious interest in Jewish matters, it seems the question is not really either/or but both/and. Luke does not attempt to answer either the Jewish or the Gentile question alone, but rather both at the same time. These two questions furnish the twin pillars upon which Luke constructs his primary purpose for writing: to confirm the faith of Theophilus and to motivate him to press on in the Christian life despite problems and temptations. God's great salvation plan, begun in the Old Testament, is now consummated in Christ and His church. Christianity is the fulfillment of the Old Testament hope of Israel. Bock summed up the matter: "If there is some movement toward a general consensus on Luke, it is that his two volumes are an explanation of the origins of the new community now known as the church—an exercise in what today would be called sociological legitimization."[5]

Recent Lukan studies have produced many articles and books dealing with the Jewishness of Luke-Acts. The idea that Luke was writing to Jewish Christians is not new. In 1841, Schneckenburger discussed the purpose of Acts and concluded that it was written to Jewish Christians.[6] In 1970, A. J. Mattill, building on Schneckenburger, argued that Luke's purpose in Acts was to defend Paul against the charges of

bibliography can be found in W. Liefeld, *Interpreting the Book of Acts*, in Guides to New Testament Exegesis (Grand Rapids: Baker, 1995), 30–33.

[3] R. Morgenthaler, *Die lukanische Geschichts-schreibungals Zeugnis: Gestalt und Gehalt der Kunst des Lukas* (Zurich: Zwingli, 1949), 1:190. See also C. K. Barrett, *Luke the Historian in Recent Study* (London: Epworth, 1961), 37–41.

[4] Ibid.

[5] D. Bock, "Luke," *The Face of New Testament Studies: A Survey of Recent Research*, ed. S. McKnight and G. Osborne (Grand Rapids: Baker, 2004), 350.

[6] M. Schneckenburger, *Über den Zweck der Apostelgeschichte* (Berne: C. Fischer, 1841), 127–51.

Jewish Christians.[7] Building on Schneckenburger, Jervell argued that the main purpose of Acts was to solve the problem of the relationship of Christians to the Jewish law.[8] In a similar vein, D. Juel and R. O'Toole both suggested a Jewish audience for Luke-Acts.[9]

It is now acknowledged that Luke-Acts may have been written to a Jewish Christian audience, which represents a major paradigm shift. However, I do not think Schneckenburger, Mattill, and Jervell have captured Luke's main purpose. A defense of Paul's apostolic authority or his Jewishness (both of which may be legitimate thematic notions in Acts) does not adequately reflect the Lukan purpose nor take into account the unity of Luke-Acts. Whatever purpose Luke envisaged, it must have embraced both volumes, and this is not adequately treated by Schneckenburger, Mattill, and Jervell.[10]

Houlden argued that Luke's purpose was motivated by the resentment of Jewish Christians toward the growing number of Gentile Christians in the church.[11] The late date (late first or early second century) that he assigns to Luke-Acts is partly why he views the purpose in this way. But the evidence does not support such a late date.[12]

Certainly the data in Luke-Acts reflects a tension between unregenerate Israel and the new people of God. Houlden granted this tension and rightly concluded that one cannot choose between a pro- or anti-Jewish stance in Luke. He erred by assuming a late date for Luke-Acts

---

[7] A. J. Mattill, "The Purpose of Acts: Schneckenburger Reconsidered," in *Apostolic History and the Gospel: Biblical and Historical Essays Presented to F. F. Bruce on His 60th Birthday*, ed. W. W. Gasque and R. P. Martin (Grand Rapids: Eerdmans, 1970), 117.

[8] J. Jervell, *Luke and the People of God: A New Look at Luke-Acts* (Minneapolis: Augsburg, 1972).

[9] D. Juel, *Luke-Acts: the Promise of History* (Atlanta: John Knox, 1983); R. O'Toole, "Acts 2:30 and the Davidic Covenant of Pentecost," *JBL* 102 (1984): 245–58. Regarding the supposed Roman apologetic purpose for Luke-Acts, it seems difficult to overcome the salient critique offered by Barrett: "No Roman official would ever have filtered out so much of what to him would be theological and ecclesiastical rubbish in order to reach so tiny a grain of relevant apology" (C. K. Barrett, *Luke the Historian*, 63).

[10] D. Buckwalter noted many scholars view Luke's purpose as a negative response to a particular situation. He felt this needs to be nuanced with the idea that Luke addressed some need or deficiency in the reader's understanding, much the way Priscilla and Aquila did with Apollos. In addition, Buckwalter suggests that Luke is "reemphasizing" certain Christian teachings already familiar to readers "in order to encourage them to persevere in their Christian walk." D. Buckwalter, *The Character and Purpose of Luke's Christology* (Cambridge: Cambridge University Press, 1996), 72. Buckwalter's approach has merit.

[11] J. Houlden, "The Purpose of Luke," *JSNT* 21 (1984): 53–65.

[12] See chap. 7.

and then suggesting Luke's Christians were not directly involved in Jewish relations, but were concerned with a conflict in the church.

The problem that motivated Luke to write may have been internal, but it was not a conflict between Jewish and Gentile Christians. Houlden's thesis does not fully consider Luke's prologue in determining the Lukan purpose. As Bock stated, "Luke argues that the Christianity was a natural extension of Judaism."[13]

Before we offer an interpretation of Luke's purpose, identifying certain presuppositions is in order. Some may dispute one or more of these, but the evidence of Luke-Acts can be interpreted in this way. First, Luke-Acts should be treated as a unity both in structure and purpose.[14] Focusing on the purpose of Luke or of Acts alone will lead to a skewed perspective and truncate Luke's overall purpose.[15]

Second, Luke is writing to Jewish Christians, and not to a purely non-Christian Jewish audience or a purely Gentile audience. Third, any description of the Lukan purpose must examine the prologues of both Luke and Acts. Here Luke comes close to giving us his overt statement of purpose. Fourth, issues of continuity or discontinuity must be granted in Luke's writing. These are twin foci that emphasize continuity more than discontinuity.[16] Here the Jewish question and the Gentile question are both reflected. Houlden is right: "If the choice is merely between Luke's being pro-Jewish and anti-Jewish, then incongruity is inescapable."[17]

My approach to the Lukan purpose involves a synthesis of the valuable insights of Morgenthaler, Van Unnik, Maddox, Juel, and O'Toole. Morgenthaler's careful study of the Lukan structure reveals

---

[13] D. Bock, "Luke," 351.

[14] J. Dawsey, "The Literary Unity of Luke-Acts: Questions of Style—A Task for Literary Critics," NTS 35 (1989): 48–66.

[15] The literature on this subject is substantial, but the majority of scholars still consider Luke-Acts as a literary unity. J. Verheyden, "The Unity of Luke-Acts: What Are We Up To," in The Unity of Luke-Acts, ed. J. Verheyden (Leuven: Leuven University Press, 1999), 3–56, provides one of the best surveys of the unity of Luke-Acts. C. Rowe, "History, Hermeneutics and the Unity of Luke-Acts," JSNT 28 (2005): 131–57, is also helpful and accessible. The most recent work arguing against literary unity is P. Walters, The Assumed Authorial Unity of Luke and Acts: A Reassessment of the Evidence, SNTMS 145 (Cambridge: Cambridge University Press, 2009), esp. pp. 190–94.

[16] In discussing the implications of his work on the Isaianic New Exodus for the study of the theology and narrative of Luke and Acts, David Pao remarked that "both the continuity and the discontinuity with the past have to be recognized." D. Pao, Acts and the Isaianic New Exodus (Tübingen: Mohr Siebeck, 2000), 252. See especially chap. 2 (37–69) on this subject.

[17] J. Houlden, "The Purpose of Luke," 60.

the necessity of viewing Luke-Acts as a unity when it comes to the question of purpose. His statement that Luke-Acts is both pro-Jewish and pro-Gentile should provide the necessary corrective to anyone who would lean on the evidence too hard in either direction.

Some may wish to shoot me with my own gun here in light of chap. 6, where I will emphasize the Jewish aspects of Luke-Acts. (I emphasize these factors not to determine purpose, but to argue the probability that Luke was Jewish.) The factors that have caused scholars to suggest Luke was a Gentile or wrote to Gentiles are well known and are not presented here.[18]

R. O'Toole's suggestion that Luke has one dominant theme to which all others are subordinate seems correct. That theme, he argued, is "that God who brought salvation to his people in the Old Testament continues to do this, especially through Jesus Christ."[19] This may be Luke's dominant theological theme, but it is not the dominant purpose. Theme and purpose, though intertwined in a given work, must be differentiated here. Luke's overall purpose is hortatory, not expository. His exposition (theme) undergirds his attempt to exhort his reader/readers to a course of action (purpose). O'Toole does not deny this; he simply does not bring out the hortatory purpose of Luke's theme clearly enough.

The importance of Luke's prologue to establish his purpose is now widely recognized. Juel concluded from Luke 1:4 that Luke had a hortatory intent of persuasion. The primary motivation for Luke-Acts arose from within the believing community rather than outside it.[20] But his second-century date for Luke-Acts is too late. Juel cannot adequately account for the need of Luke's readers to cope with their separation from the Jewish community. He simply assumed that such a separation had already taken place.

These Jewish Christians, according to Juel, needed clarification of their identity in a second-century church. But was it clarification they needed, or motivation to continue as the people of God (in continuity with the Old Testament) in spite of Jewish opposition? Juel's description of Luke's purpose is essentially correct if we understand

---

[18] For the evidence that Luke was a Gentile or wrote to a Gentile audience, see J. Fitzmyer, *The Gospel According to Luke (I-IX): Introduction, Translation, and Notes*, AB 28 (Garden City: Doubleday, 1981), 35–62. Cf. also the collation of the evidence by P. Esler, *Community and Gospel in Luke-Acts*, 30–45.

[19] R. O'Toole, *The Unity of Luke's Theology*, GNS 9 (Wilmington: Michael Glazier, 1984), 17.

[20] Juel, *Luke-Acts: the Promise of History*, 119.

"clarification" to entail motivation, but placing the readers in the second-century is too late. Why not allow for a date during the 60s just prior to the Jewish War? Jewish Christians of this period needed to know that their identity as the people of God was secure, and their flagging confidence needed bolstering in the face of stiff opposition and persecution.

Likewise, Maddox concluded from Luke 1:4 that Luke wrote "to assure the Christians of his day that their faith in Jesus is no aberration, but the authentic goal towards which God's ancient dealings with Israel were driving."[21] Luke has two great doctrinal emphases, according to Maddox. One is ecclesiology, where Luke addresses the question, "Who are the people of God?" His second emphasis is eschatology, but not in the sense argued by Conzelmann and Käsemann. The early church lives in a time of fulfillment, when salvation is available. Yet there remains the ultimate fulfillment that the church awaits with confidence and hope.[22] With such a message of assurance, Luke wrote to motivate his readers to follow Jesus with unwavering loyalty. Is this not the tenor of Hebrews as well? Its emphasis on eschatology in a pastoral context of exhortation and encouragement are well known.

Bock has acknowledged the significant Jewish influence in Luke's Gospel along with an emphasis on perseverance: "The emphasis on themes such as perseverance seems to suggest an audience that needs to endure with the community in light of Jewish rejection rather than an audience to whom is directed a strictly evangelistic appeal to enter into salvation."[23] He concluded that Luke's purpose is not so much evangelistic "as it is an invitation to embrace and persevere in the faith, to experience that salvation to the full, recognizing that God has designed both Jew and Gentile to be a part of the new community."[24] "The issue of Jewish rejection explains the pastoral concern to reassure Theophilus about the integrity of the movement and to call for perseverance."[25]

Van Unnik argued in 1960 that Acts must be seen as the "confirmation" of the Gospel of Luke.[26] His article has often been neglected in

---

[21] Maddox, *The Purpose of Luke-Acts*, 187.

[22] Ibid., 185–86.

[23] Bock, "Luke," 371.

[24] Ibid. See also D. Bock, *Luke 1:1–9:50*, BECNT (Grand Rapids: Baker, 1994), 14–15.

[25] Bock, "Luke," 351.

[26] W. C. van Unnik, "The Book of Acts,' the Confirmation of the Gospel," NTS 4 (1960): 26–59.

the discussion concerning the purpose of Luke-Acts. Maddox was one of the few who made reference to it, in the first chapter of *The Purpose of Luke-Acts*, and he promised that it would surface again. Indeed it did, in Maddox's last chapter, where he presents his views of Luke's purpose. Clearly Maddox viewed Van Unnik's thesis as the most valid description of Luke's overarching purpose.

Van Unnik considers the overall purpose of Luke-Acts as presenting God's plan of salvation through Jesus, and to show how it was brought to those who did not see Jesus incarnate.[27] Van Unnik believes Heb 2:3–4 describes what Luke accomplished with his two-volume work.[28] He implied that Luke may have written to give "certainty" to one who was about to embrace Christianity.[29] But Van Unnik's next statement is nearer to the truth: "It may be that Luke compiled his book for people like those in Hebrews who were wavering in their faith."[30] Luke's prologue would make such a purpose likely.

Here we are placed on the most fruitful trail of Luke's overall purpose, a trail followed by Maddox and, to a certain extent, O'Toole. Morgenthaler blazed this trail when he suggested that Luke's structure was a crucial key to understanding his purpose, which was to testify with the mouths of two witnesses (hence the parallelism in Luke-Acts). Having followed all the other trails, Maddox found they kept leading him back to the pastoral purpose that Van Unnik originally suggested: do not waver in your faith, be reassured, press on to the goal.

Van Unnik explored a number of parallels between the prologues of Luke-Acts and Heb 2:3–4 and concluded that the Hebrews passage furnishes the clue to understanding the Lukan purpose (at least for Acts):

> These words in the second half of this passage of the Epistle to the Hebrews may fittingly be used as a heading of Luke's second volume. I am firmly convinced that here we have found the scope of Acts, the angle under which we must see it to find the right perspective, or you may say: the hidden thread holding together the string of pearls.[31]

---

[27] Ibid., 49, 58; cf. also O'Toole, *The Unity of Luke's Theology*.
[28] Van Unnik, "The Book of Acts," 46–47.
[29] Ibid., 59.
[30] Ibid.
[31] Ibid., 49.

The following comparisons were made by Van Unnik. First, the phrase in Heb 2:3, *hētis archēn labousa laleisthai dia tou kuriou,* is parallel to Acts 1:1—*peri pantōn, ō Theophile, hōn ērxato ho Iēsous poiein te kai didaskein.* Second, a number of elements that are motifs in Acts are found in Heb 2:3–4: salvation, the idea of "bearing witness," signs and wonders, and distributions of the Holy Spirit. Third, the activity of God described in Heb 2:3–4 recalls Acts 14:3—Paul and Barnabas relied on the Lord, *tō marturounti [epi] tō logō tēs charitos autou, didonti sēmeia kai terata ginesthai dia tōn cheirōn autōn* ("who testified to the message of His grace by granting that signs and wonders be performed through them"). Fourth, the *sun* in the compound verb of Heb 2:4 calls attention to the fact that there are other witnesses too. Van Unnik refers this to the preceding verb *ebebaiōthē.* The phrase "those who heard him" in Heb 2:3 indicates witnesses, which corresponds to Acts 1:8: "and you will be my witnesses." Fifth, Jesus is the *archēgon tēs sōtērias* in Heb 2:10, and this designation of Him is found only in Acts 3:15 and 5:31 in the rest of the New Testament.[32]

The meaning of Heb 2:3–4 is that there is a solid bridge between the saving activity of Jesus and those who have had no personal contact with Him. This salvation is confirmed and sanctioned by God; His miraculous gifts solidify the bridge between Jesus and His followers. But it is possible to reject the outcome of this salvation (Christian maturity) through unbelief and disobedience. The purpose of Hebrews is to exhort the readers to firmness in their faith.[33]

Hebrews 2:3–4 thus becomes an excellent explanation for the link between the Gospel of Luke and Acts. The remainder of Van Unnik's article summarizes how this comes about through a discussion of the concept of "salvation" in Acts, the concept of "witness," the fact that this witness is brought by God Himself, and the Lukan concept of receiving this salvation message.[34] Van Unnik concluded that it was possible for the Lukan purpose to be similar to that of Hebrews: to challenge believers to mature and not to waver in their faith.[35]

---

[32] Ibid., 47–48.

[33] Ibid., 48.

[34] Ibid., 50–58.

[35] Buckwalter noted that the circumstances that prompted Luke to write may have been his readers' fears over the imminent threat of Paul's death or its recent occurrence. Buckwalter finds Van Unnik's proposal "intriguing," but unlikely. He concluded that since the warnings in Hebrews are not found in Luke-Acts, the recipients of Hebrews, contrary to Luke-Acts, are already adrift. Buckwalter, *Character and Purpose of Luke's Christology,* 74. I do not see the force

Van Unnik's conclusions about the notion of "witness" found in Luke-Acts and Hebrews were confirmed by Trites, who said, "The idea of witness appears a number of times in the Epistle to the Hebrews, a fact suggested by the use of words drawn from the vocabulary of witness . . . and the idea of witness is very similar to that which is unfolded in greater detail in the Book of Acts."[36] "For the writer of Hebrews, as for Luke, the truth of one kind of testimony required confirmation by another, in this case, by the testimony of the scriptures."[37] After pointing out that Hebrews speaks of the Jewish law of evidence, signs and wonders functioning as confirmatory testimony, and the testimony of God Himself through the Scriptures, Trites notes that "in all these ways it [Hebrews] deserves to be compared to the Book of Acts, where the same themes are developed and expanded."[38] Luke parallels key characters in the infancy narrative with the disciples in Luke 24 and in Acts. This suggests that the meaning of "eyewitnesses" in Luke 1:2 should be expanded to include more than the disciples of Jesus. Zechariah, Elizabeth, Mary, Simeon, Anna, the women at the tomb, and characters in Acts such as Barnabas and Stephen were probably also intended.[39]

The parallels between the purposes of Luke-Acts and Hebrews begin to emerge when one considers the following facts. First, the stated purpose in the prologue of Luke is to give his readers "certainty." Second, the connection of the Acts prologue and the book as a whole to

---

of this reasoning since Luke-Acts is narrative genre and thus would not have the overt "hortatory" nature of Hebrews. Furthermore, by the choice and arrangement of his material, Luke has shown how an author can have a hortatory intent using narrative genre. Michael Goulder discerned a "difference of motive" in the parabolic material of Matthew and Luke; whereas Matthew's parables are virtually all "indicative," Luke's are more often "imperative in intention." According to Goulder, most of the Lukan parables are "plainly hortatory." M. Goulder, *Luke: A New Paradigm* (Sheffield: JSOT Press, 1994), 101. The serious tone of Hebrews may also reflect the turbulent times of the Jewish War that began in AD 66. Or, much less likely, Luke's Gospel could be dated c. AD 40, as E. Selwyn suggested. E. Selwyn, *Saint Luke the Prophet*, (London; New York: Macmillan, 1901). This would put perhaps 25 or more years between Luke and Hebrews. Buckwalter thought Luke probably wrote "under ordinary circumstances" rather than a crisis situation. D. Buckwalter, *Character and Purpose of Luke's Christology*, 72. I find little evidence of what could be called "ordinary circumstances" for the church between AD 30 and AD 70.

[36] A. Trites, *The New Testament Concept of Witness*, SNTSMS 31 (Cambridge: Cambridge University Press, 1977), 217.

[37] Ibid., 218.

[38] Ibid., 221.

[39] See K. Kuhn, "Beginning the Witness: The αὐτόπται καὶ ὑπηρέρται of Luke's Infancy Narrative," *NTS* 49.2 (2003): 237–55.

Heb 2:3–4, and the similarity between the theme of how God brings salvation in Luke-Acts and the prologue of Hebrews links the three books. Third, both Luke and the author of Hebrews pay careful attention to the reception of the message of salvation.

The Purpose of Hebrews[40]

The question of the purpose of Hebrews likewise has generated considerable disagreement. O. Michel, W. Kümmel, and others have rightly suggested that the purpose of Hebrews must be extracted primarily from the hortatory sections.[41] Unlike Luke-Acts, which is an example of narrative discourse in terms of surface structure, Hebrews is hortatory discourse. As a result, imperatives and hortatory subjunctives are ranked at the highest thematic level and are most diagnostic of purpose. The large expositional sections dealing with the nature of the high priesthood of Christ and the atonement are structurally subordinate to the hortatory sections, which convey the author's purpose in writing.[42]

The readers of Hebrews were suffering from a state of "arrested development" in their Christian life. Overlooking the fact that salvation included redemption plus growth and progress toward maturity, these readers needed to be challenged to fulfill their part of God's redemptive purpose.[43]

The traditional view that Hebrews was written to Jewish Christians in danger of relapsing into Judaism has fallen into disrepute. The internal evidence of the book indicates a congregation under stress of growing persecution from without and spiritual lethargy

---

[40] For an overview, consult D. Guthrie, *New Testament Introduction*, 4th rev. ed. (Downers Grove: InterVarsity, 1990), 688–95; A. Lincoln, *Hebrews: A Guide* (London: T&T Clark, 2006), 52–68; R. E. Glaze, *No Easy Salvation: A Careful Examination of the Question of Apostasy in Hebrews* (New Orleans: Insight Press, 1966), 13–18; Ellingworth, *The Epistle to the Hebrews: A Commentary on the Greek Text*, NIGTC (Grand Rapids: Eerdmans, 1993), 78–80; and C. Koester, *Hebrews: A New Translation with Introduction and Commentary*, AB 36 (New York: Doubleday, 2001), 64–79. Whatever the purpose[s] may be, the letter makes no contrast between Jews and Gentiles.

[41] O. Michel, *Der Brief an die Hebräer*, KEK, ed. Heinrich Meyer (Göttingen: Vandenhoeck & Ruprecht, 1975), 27; W. Kümmel, *Introduction to the New Testament* (Nashville: Abingdon, 1975), 390; and G. Guthrie, *The Structure of Hebrews: A Text-Linguistic Analysis* (Leiden: Brill, 1994), 143.

[42] See G. Guthrie, *The Structure of Hebrews*, 143, and G. Hughes, *Hebrews and Hermeneutics*, SNTSMS 36 (Cambridge: Cambridge University Press, 1979), *passim*.

[43] Ibid.

within. Readers faced the danger of failing to pursue Christian maturity through obedience and faithfulness to Christ and His word.[44] A healthy by-product of viewing Hebrews in this way is that the problem of the so-called apostasy passages is greatly lessened. The harsh language of 6:1–6 and 10:26–39 does not describe the possibility of apostasy, but the results of God's judgment on a Christian who disobeys God's Word and fails to pursue Christian maturity.[45]

The preceding chapter has shown the linguistic similarity between the prologues of Luke-Acts and Hebrews. This similarity was both structural and semantic. We have also seen Van Unnik's comparison of Heb 2:3–4 with the book of Acts and his conclusion that Luke-Acts and Hebrews have similar purposes. I would like to extend this thesis a bit by examining additional parallels between the hortatory passages in Hebrews with certain sections of Luke-Acts.

In Hebrews, considerable emphasis is placed on the concept of the *logos* as it is spoken by the prophets and heard by the people. Hebrews never uses the quote formula *gegraptai* but regularly uses some form of *legei*. This use of *logos* is found prominently in several hortatory passages, which is important to our thesis. For example, in Heb 1:1–4 the emphasis is on the fact that God who spoke in times past has in these last days spoken in His Son. This thematic statement in the prologue functions programmatically for the entire letter.[46] In 2:1–4, the first hortatory paragraph in the letter, we have a reference to what the readers had "heard," the "word" spoken by angels, the salvation that was first "spoken" by the Lord, and finally the confirmation of it to the readers of Hebrews by those who "heard" it first. The things spoken and the hearing of the Word semantically dominate this paragraph.

In the second major hortatory section (3:7–4:12) we once again find references to the Word spoken by the Holy Spirit in the quote formula *legei* and then a statement about the importance of "hearing" His voice (3:7,15,16; 4:7). Hebrews 4:2 refers to the Israelites in the wilderness who had "heard" the "word" but failed to act on it.

---

[44] H. Hobbs, *Hebrews: Challenges to Bold Discipleship* (Nashville: B&H, 1971). I have argued this position at length in *Hebrews*, NAC (Nashville: B&H, 2010), forthcoming.

[45] See T. K. Oberholtzer, "The Warning Passages in Hebrews, Part 1 (of 5 parts): The Eschatological Salvation of Hebrews 1:5–2:4," *BSac* 145 (1988): 83–97. See also R. Gleason, "A Moderate Reformed View," in *Four Views of the Warning Passages in Hebrews*, ed. H. Bateman (Grand Rapids: Kregel, 2007), 336–77.

[46] Hughes, *Hebrews and Hermeneutics*, 5–24.

Again in 4:8 Joshua "spoke" about a future day. In 4:11–12 Christians are to be diligent and not disobey because the "word of God" judges them. The word *logos* in the sense of "account" occurs at the end of v. 13. Indeed this entire section (3:7–4:13) is bracketed by references to the "word" that the Spirit spoke (3:7) and to the "word of God" that brings judgment (4:12–13).[47]

In the third hortatory section of Hebrews (5:11–6:12) once again hearing the Word is semantically dominant. The writer has much to "speak" (5:11) and his "word" (i.e., discourse) to the readers is difficult for them to understand because they are "dull of hearing." Although the readers should be teachers, they need to be taught the beginning of the *logois*, "oracles," of God (5:12). They are unskilled in the "word" of righteousness (5:13). They are to proceed from the elementary teachings of the "word" of Christ to maturity (6:1). They have tasted the good *rhēma*, "word," of God (6:5). The emphasis here is on hearing the Word and obeying it, resulting in spiritual growth.

The sixth major hortatory section (12:12–29) refers to Israel in the wilderness. God spoke from the mountain in a "voice of words" so that those who "heard" excused themselves for fear, asking that the "word" not be addressed to them (12:19). In 12:24 the new covenant "speaks" better things than the covenant with Abel. Then follows the imperative: "take heed" that you refuse not Him who "speaks" (12:25), whose "voice" shook the earth (12:26).

Finally, in Hebrews 13, the readers are exhorted to remember their leaders who "have spoken God's word" to them (13:7). The last use of *logos* in Hebrews occurs in 13:22 where the entire letter is called a "message of exhortation" and the readers are exhorted to obey it.

This brief survey of the use of "word" in Hebrews confirms that the prologue functions in a programmatic way for the entire letter. The author never loses sight of the fact that God spoke in times past but now speaks through His Son to the readers of the letter.

Turning to Luke-Acts, we find a similar emphasis on the Word of God spoken through Jesus and the apostles, and the importance of God's people receiving it. In the Lukan prologue (1:1–4) *logos* occurs twice; the second is in the *hina* clause of v. 4, where the Lukan purpose is stated. In the prologue to Acts (1:1–5) there is likewise a dual

---

[47] H. Hauser, *Strukturen der Abschlusserzählung der Apostelgeschichte: Apg. 28,16–31*, AnBib 86 (Rome: Biblical Institute Press, 1979), 218, noted the concept of the Word of God found in Heb 4:12 serves as a good definition of the Lukan presentation of the "word" in Acts.

use of *logos*: in v. 1 (referring to a former written "account") and in v. 4 (the verbal form *legōn*). The interesting use of *akouō*, "to hear," is found in v. 5 where Luke shifts from indirect to direct discourse (with Jesus as the speaker) without any quotation formula. Thus the idea of that which is heard is again placed in emphasis.[48]

The most thorough analysis of the Lukan conception of "word" is O'Reilly's *Word and Sign in the Acts of the Apostles*.[49] His assessment of Lukan theology at this point is confirmed by the lexical data above. In Acts, Luke uses the phrase *ho logos tou Theou* (4:31; 6:2,7; 8:14; 11:1; 13:5,7,44,46; 16:32; 17:13; 18:11). It also appears in Luke 5:1; 8:11,21; 11:28. In Acts, the phrase *ho logos tou kuriou* occurs many times as well (8:25; 12:24; 13:48,49; 15:35,36; 19:10,20). *Ho logos* appears in Acts in the following places: 4:4; 6:4; 8.4; 10:36, 44; 11:19; 14:25; 16:6; 17:11; 18:5; 20:7; and in Luke 1:2; 8:12, 13,15. The word *rhēma* can also describe the Christian message in Acts but always in the plural. Although the Spirit is the source of the Word in Acts, the Word still holds pride of place in the narrative.[50]

O'Reilly demonstrated Luke's chiastic literary structure for both the opening five chapters of Acts as well as the Stephen story in 6:1–8:1.[51] Acts 1–8 covers the preaching of the Word in Jerusalem with the twin foci of the prophet preaching a Word that commands obedience, and the concomitant signs and wonders that authenticate the Word.[52]

The Word of Jesus brings the definitive fulfillment of God's promises. Jesus brings the eschatological Word of God's salvation, and the preaching of the apostles is a "witness" to the fulfillment of that Word, not a new promise (Word). The Lukan community had not

---

[48] The verb ἀκούω occurs 90 times in Acts (60 in Luke), five times in Acts 28:22–28. The reception of the Word is a critical concept for Luke. For a good discussion of the concept of revelation and the language of seeing and hearing in Luke-Acts, consult D. Crump, *Jesus the Intercessor: Prayer and Christology in Luke-Acts*, Biblical Studies Library (Grand Rapids: Baker, 1992), 34–41.

[49] L. O'Reilly, *Word and Sign in the Acts of the Apostles: A Study in Lukan Theology*, Analecta Gregoriana 243 (Rome: Editrice Pontificia Universita Gregoriana, 1987). See also S. A. Panimolle, *Il discorso di Pietro all'assemblea apostolica* (Bologna: EDB, 1976–78), 2:75–126; Claus-Peter März, *Das Wort Gottes bei Lukas* (Leipzig: St. Benno-Verlag, 1974).

[50] O'Reilly, *Word and Sign*, 11. By situating the birth of the church on the day of Pentecost, Luke portrays the church as the eschatological realization of the assembly of Israel at Sinai. The Sinai typology contributes to Luke's understanding of the Word. See also E. Haenchen, *Acts*, 14th ed. trans. Noble and Shinn; rev. and updated by R. Wilson (Philadelphia: Westminster, 1971), 174.

[51] See Appendix I and II.

[52] O'Reilly, *Word and Sign*, 213.

encountered Jesus in the flesh. Luke's purpose is to show continuity: "the continuity of the present preachers of the word with the apostles, the continuity of the apostles' preaching with that of Jesus, and finally, the continuity of Jesus with the Old Testament revelation through the prophets."[53]

O'Reilly noted that the *logos tēs sōtērias,* "message of this salvation," in Acts 13:26 is the literary and theological center of Acts.[54] This phrase occurs in Paul's discourse at Pisidian Antioch. Paul's discourse is referred to as a "message of encouragement" here in Luke's narrative. The only other place we find this phrase is Heb 13:22.

The chiastic structure of Peter's sermon at Pentecost (Acts 2:14–40) confirms that the real theme of the speech is the Word:

> A　*statheis* (v. 14)
> 　B　*epēren tēn phōnēn autou kai apephthegxato*
> 　　C　*ta rhēmata mou*
> 　　　D　*epi pasan sarka* (v. 17)
> 　　　　E　*hoi hioui humōn kai hai thugateres humōn*
> 　　　　　F　*ekcheō apo tou pneumatos mou* (v. 18)
> 　　　　　　G　*terata en tō ouranō anō kai sēmeia* (v. 19)
> 　　　　　　　H　*to onoma kuriou* (v. 21)
> 　　　　　　　　I　***sōthēsetai . . . akouate tous logous toutous*** (vv. 21–22)
> 　　　　　　　H´　*Iēsoun ton Nazōraion* (v. 22)
> 　　　　　　G´　*terasi kai sēmeiois*
> 　　　　　F´　*tou pneumatos . . . execheen* (v. 33)
> 　　　　E´　*tous teknois humōn* (v. 39)
> 　　　D´　*kai pasin tois eis makran*
> 　　C´　*heterois te logois* (v. 40)
> 　B´　*diemarturato kai parekalei*
> A´　*legōn*

---

[53] Ibid., 214–15. Compare also P. Bolt, "Mission and Witness," in *Witness to the Gospel,* 191–214. See his survey of the uses of *logos* in Acts on p. 214.

[54] Ibid., 218. B. Witherington also notes that Luke uses the term σωτηρία for salvation only at the beginning and end of Luke-Acts. B. Witherington, "Salvation and Health in Christian Antiquity: the Soteriology of Luke-Acts in its First Century Setting," in *Witness to the Gospel,* 157.

O'Reilly explained:

The central element of the whole symmetry is clearly ἀκούσατε τοὺς λόγους τούτους [*akousate tous logous toutous*] and it is perfectly balanced by a – a′ and c – c′ (speaking the word) at the two extremities. More specifically it is the word of apostolic preaching that consists in witnessing (b′) and prophetic utterance (b). It is a word which must be listened to (ἀκούσατε [*akousate*], v. 22; ἐνωτίσασθε [*enōtisasthe*], v. 14). It is a word of salvation, as the position of *sothesetai* in the structure indicates. This is confirmed at the end of the speech by the chiasm of vv. 40 and 41 which has the imperative σώθητε [*sōthēte*] sandwiched in between. The word being preached is the λόγος τῆς σωτηρίας [*logos tēs sōtērias*] (Acts 13:26) which is the theme not only of this speech but of Acts as a whole and indeed of the entire Lucan writings.[55]

O'Reilly concluded his final chapter regarding the Word of the Lord in Acts in a way all too reminiscent of Hebrews:

The ultimate fulfillment of the prophetic word is the personal word. God spoke his word in the past by the prophets, now he speaks by a Son. . . . As glorified Lord he is the final word of God to Israel and the world. He is both the Saviour and the word of this salvation.[56]

This emphasis on the Word as God's Word is a result of Lukan redaction, as can be seen in the interpretation given to the parable of the Sower and the saying about Jesus' true relatives (Luke 8:21).[57] The connection of Acts 2:4 with Luke 1:67 and Acts 4:31 is often missed. Note that in all three places the issue of being filled with the Spirit and speaking is paramount.

Luke 1:67: *kai Zacharias . . . eplēsthē pneumatos hagiou kai eprophēteusen*

Acts 2:4: *kai (pantes) . . . eplēsthēsan pneumatos hagiou kai ērxanto lalein heterais glōssais.*

Acts 4:31: *kai (hapantes) tou hagiou pneumatos kai elaloun ton logon tou Theou.*

In Acts 4:31 the verb *lalein* is used in a phrase that corresponds exactly with the two previous ones. However, here for the first time in Acts the object of *lalein* is explicitly the Word of God. *Lalein* has become a technical term for preaching the Christian gospel, and it

---

[55] O'Reilly, *Word and Sign*, 71.

[56] Ibid., 221.

[57] See H. Schürmann, "Lukanische Reflexionen über die Wortverkundigung in Lk 8, 4–21," *Wahrheit und Verkundgung* 44 (1967): 213–28; O'Reilly, *Word and Sign*, 41.

appears repeatedly in Acts (4:29; 8:25; 10:44; 11:19; 13:42,46; 14:25; 16:6,32). The verb is also used in this sense without the object (Acts 4:1,17,20,40; 6:10; 11:15,20; 13:45; 14:1,9; 16:13,14; 18:9,25). From this, O'Reilly rightly concluded that the parallel texts above suggest the "Word" has not lost its prophetic or pneumatic overtones in the process (as the use of *lalein* elsewhere in Acts shows—Acts 3:21,22,24; 28:25; also Luke 1:55,70). "It still refers to prophetic utterance under the influence of the Spirit and its object is now more clearly than ever what might be called the proper object of all prophetic utterance, the word of God."[58]

Luke's characterization of Jesus' teaching as the Word of God (5:1; 8:11,21; 11:28) furnishes a clue to the way he understood that Word as it was preached in the early church.[59] The word of salvation in Acts is a saving word only because it is the *logos tou kuriou*. This phrase means the word about Jesus and the Word of Jesus. The coming of Jesus was heralded by all the prophetic figures of the infancy narrative (Luke 1:43,47,68; 2:29,36) whose utterance is described by the verb *lalein* (1:45,46; 2:17,33,38). He is the Savior without whom there could not be a word of salvation.[60]

O'Reilly noted that Luke's view of preaching in Acts is a prophetic activity:

> The word of the preacher was truly the word of the now glorified Jesus who spoke through him. The Pentecost preaching of the word is clearly rooted in the immediately preceding gift of the Spirit and, as the use of the verb λαλεῖν [*lalein*] in particular shows, so is every other utterance of the word in Acts. And since the proclamation denoted by λαλεῖν [*lalein*] means prophetic utterance, we conclude that the preaching of the gospel in Acts is understood by Luke as an essentially prophetic activity. As preachers of the word, the disciples of Jesus are prophets whose ministry is in strict continuity with that of the prophets of the past, but above all with that of Jesus, the eschatological prophet.[61]

---

[58] O'Reilly, *Word and Sign*, 59–60.

[59] In the Gospels, the phrase "Word of God" is used for the teachings of Jesus only in Luke (5:21; 8:11, 21; 11:28). See "Word of God," in *Dictionary of Judaism in the Biblical Period*, ed. J. Neusner and W. S. Green (Peabody, MA: Hendrickson, 1996), 676.

[60] O'Reilly, *Word and Sign*, 60–61.

[61] Ibid., 89–90. "The word/sign duality which is so strongly emphasized in the Lucan theology of the word can now be seen to be due to Luke's wider theological outlook, in particular to his emphasis on prophecy and fulfillment in the unfolding of salvation history. Luke understands the word of God in the New Testament very much along Old Testament lines, and the duality to which we have been referring is a strong feature of the Old Testament word of God, especially of the prophetic word." O'Reilly, *Word and Sign*, 215. In Acts 26:23, the risen Christ

Peter's sermon in the precincts of the temple (3:19–26) is chiastic in structure:

A   to him (the prophet whom God will raise up) (v. 22)
   B   you shall *listen* (*akousesthe*)
      C   In whatever he tells (*lalēsē*) you
   B´   every soul that does not *listen* (v. 23)
A´   to that prophet

The words of the prophet that command attention are central (C); the command to hear and the dire consequences of not hearing form an *inclusio*.[62]

Luke's compositional design is reflected at the beginning of Peter's Pentecost sermon (Acts 2:16–21) and at the conclusion of his temple sermon (Acts 3:22–26), where an Old Testament quotation frames the content of both. In Acts 2:18, Luke adds to the Joel quote the words *kai prophēteusousin*, expressing his own special focus. The point is that the preaching of the apostles represents the eschatological renewal of prophecy. Luke presents the resurrected and ascended Jesus as the climax of the prophetic line beginning with Moses. Through the testimony of Christ's witnesses, the voice of the risen Jesus continues to be heard. Note the words added by Luke to the quotation in Acts 2:16–21: *legei ho theos* (17); *kai prophēteusousin* (18); *anō, sēmeia*, and *katō* (19). Note also Luke's alteration, *en tais eschatais hēmerais* in Acts 2:17, and its usage by the author of Hebrews in 1:1–2. In Acts 3:22–26, the risen Jesus preaches through the apostles the eschatological message of repentance. Acts 26:24 explicitly makes the risen Jesus the speaker of Paul's prophetic message.[63] In this fashion, Luke has rhetorically "bookended" Acts to make his point to Theophilus.[64]

Luke's focus on the importance of accurately hearing God's Word can be seen in a comparison of his comments after the parable of the Sower with Mark, who writes, "Pay attention to *what* you hear" (Mark 4:24); Luke writes, "Take care *how* you listen" (Luke 8:18). All this dovetails nicely with what we find in Hebrews. A common theological

---

is the speaker of Paul's prophetic message to the nations. R. F. O'Toole, "Some Observations on *Anistemi*, 'I raise,' in Acts 3:22,26," *Science et Esprit* 31 (1979): 90.

[62] Ibid., 108.

[63] O'Toole, "Some Observations . . . ," 85–92; and R. Dillon, "The Prophecy of Christ and His Witnesses According to the Discourses of Acts," *NTS* 32 (1986): 549.

[64] See Dillon, "The Prophecy of Christ and His Witnesses," 544–48.

pattern with respect to hearing the Word begins to emerge in Luke-Acts and Hebrews.

In addition to these parallels, other lexical evidence occurs in the Lukan prologue and in strategic places in the hortatory sections of Hebrews, and lends further weight to the theory of Lukan authorship. In Luke 1:2, those who delivered to the readers the account of God's salvation in Christ were eyewitnesses from the *archē*, "beginning." This same semantic concept occurs in the prologue to Acts (1:1) in the verbal form *archō*. It appears again in Heb 2:3 in the clause "first [*archēn*] spoken by the Lord," as noted by Van Unnik. What he did not state is that the noun occurs again in Heb 3:14 in the clause, "if we hold firmly until the end the reality that we had at the start [*archēn*]." It occurs twice again in Heb 5:12; 6:1: "the basic principles of God's revelation" and "the elementary message about the Messiah" respectively. All three of these occurrences are in the hortatory sections, and two of the three are semantically similar to the Lukan prologues.

There is a degree of similarity between Luke-Acts and Hebrews in words or concepts that appear in the same lexical domain of certainty or proof. In Luke 1:4, the purpose of writing was that Theophilus might know the "certainty," *asphaleian*, of the things in which he had been instructed. In Acts 1:3, Jesus presented Himself alive to the apostles with many "convincing proofs," *tekmēriois*. In Heb 2:2, that which was spoken by angels was "legally binding," *bebaios*. Likewise in 2:3 those who heard the Lord "confirmed," *ebebaiōthē*, the great salvation to the readers. In Heb 3:14 we have the phrase "if we hold firmly [*bebaian*] until the end the reality [*hupostaseōs*] that we had at the start." Again, in Heb 6:19, we have an anchor for the soul, both "sure," *agkuran*, and "firm," *bebaian*. In Luke 1:1 the verb *plērophoreō*, "have been fulfilled," carries the idea of certainty that its cognate noun *plērophoria* expresses. This noun appears twice in Hebrews (6:11 and 10:22), both in hortatory sections. This concept of certainty, assurance, and confirmation is prominent in Luke-Acts and Hebrews.

Finally, Luke 1:4 refers to Luke's purpose that Theophilus may "know," *epiginōskō*, the certainty of the things concerning which he was instructed. The cognate noun form of this verb, *epignōsis*, occurs in Heb 10:26 (again in a hortatory passage).

What we find in the Lukan prologues lexically and semantically is also in numerous places throughout the hortatory sections of Hebrews. The Lukan emphasis on the "Word of God" and the importance of "hearing" that word appears in Hebrews as well. The parallels between Heb 2:3–4 and the purpose of Luke-Acts, as noted by Van Unnik, are enhanced and fortified by the additional lexical and semantic parallels drawn from the lexical domain of "certainty" that pervades the three works. Finally, the hortatory sections of Hebrews convey the most information and hence are the most important for discerning purpose. When they are compared with the prologues of Luke-Acts, the ground is laid for showing that the three works focus on a similar purpose. This fact, coupled with additional evidence of similarity, suggests that Luke may have been the author of Hebrews.

Some have conjectured because of the use of "former" in Acts 1:1 that Luke intended to write a third volume.[65] Although I think this is unlikely, if it were true, Hebrews would fit in the trilogy quite nicely. Luke shows in his narrative how Christianity has fulfilled Judaism, the law, and the prophets. His great interest in Jewish matters has become better known and appreciated by Lukan scholars. Hebrews approaches these subjects more from an expository/hortatory angle than the narrative of Luke-Acts, but the theme and purpose are much the same.

If Theophilus needed reasons why his catechesis was true, Luke provides them through the narrative framework of Luke-Acts. God's great work of salvation through Jesus is presented in Luke and confirmed in Acts. If the recipients of Hebrews needed to leave the elemental truths of Christianity and go on to maturity, then the author has fulfilled his purpose of exhorting them to do so by showing the theological superiority of Christianity to Judaism. This is accomplished by alternatively showing matters of continuity and discontinuity between the old and new covenants, a theme prominent in Luke-Acts as well. Luke's purpose is to write the story of Jesus followed by the narrative of the founding and growth of the early church. Luke does this, to be sure, but his real purpose is to write the overall narrative of salvation history including the continuity and fulfillment of God's grand narrative.[66]

---

[65] As, for example, E. Selwyn in *Saint Luke the Prophet*, 41.

[66] J. Green, *Theology of the Gospel of Luke*, New Testament Theology Series, gen. ed. J. Dunn (Cambridge: Cambridge University Press, 1995), 47.

The traditional view that the readers of Hebrews were "wavering" between Christianity and Judaism can find support from the Lukan prologue in that Theophilus needs to be assured of the certainty of what he has been taught. However, a better explanation for the purpose of Hebrews would be that the readers needed to pursue spiritual maturity. The Lukan prologue can also be interpreted in this way as suggesting that what Theophilus needed was assurance that Christianity is true, and that Christ has fulfilled the old by bringing in the new.[67] Although it is not overtly stated in Luke's prologue, we may infer that when Theophilus gains "certainty," he will be encouraged to mature in his knowledge and practice of Christianity. According to Maddox, Luke writes

> to reassure the Christians of his day that their faith in Jesus is no aberration, but the authentic goal towards which God's ancient dealings with Israel were driving. . . . With such a message of reassurance, Luke summons his fellow-Christians to worship God with whole-hearted joy, to follow Jesus with unwavering loyalty, and to carry on with zeal, through the power of the Spirit, the charge to be his witnesses to the end of the earth.[68]

Is not this precisely what the author of Hebrews emphasizes in 4:14–16 and 10:19–25? These two paragraphs are semantically related and chiastically arranged, and both function in the overall macrostructure of the discourse as the introduction to each of the last two major sections of Hebrews.

Peterson's closing paragraph in his concluding chapter in *Witness to the Gospel: the Theology of Acts* illustrates the similarity between Luke-Acts and Hebrews:

> The prominence of Jesus' suffering in the Gospel and the extension of that suffering to his representatives in Acts provides a profound link between the two volumes of Luke's work. Readers are encouraged to follow the example of the earliest believers, and Paul in particular, by holding fast to the same gospel and continuing to be active in its dissemination, even in the face of persecution from without and conflict from within the churches.[69]

---

[67] Witherington says the Lukan prologue "suggests that the person to whom this document was written was already a Christian . . . but needed assurance and clarification about a variety of matters." B. Witherington, "Salvation and Health in Christian Antiquity," 165.

[68] Maddox, *The Purpose of Luke-Acts*, 187.

[69] Peterson, "Luke's Theological Enterprise," 544.

Change the references from Luke and Acts to Hebrews, and this paragraph would aptly describe what is expressed in that letter as well.

Conclusion

A comparison of the Lukan prologues with the prologue and hortatory sections of Hebrews reveals a number of lexical and semantic parallels that link these three works to a common purpose. The fact that Luke-Acts differs from Hebrews in discourse genre makes these lexical and semantic parallels all the more remarkable. Given further corroborating factors, as I have argued elsewhere, this evidence can be interpreted as supporting Lukan authorship of Hebrews.

One of the main arguments against Lukan authorship has been theological. In recent years, Luke has come to be viewed as a theologian of significant stature. Are there areas of theological similarity between Luke-Acts and Hebrews? The evidence to answer this question will now be considered.

Chapter 5

THE THEOLOGY OF LUKE-ACTS AND HEBREWS COMPARED

Chapters 5 and 6 are closely linked. Much of the material in chap. 6 that illustrates Luke's Jewishness is also theological in nature. In this chapter, I present *comparative* evidence that illustrates the close theological similarity of Hebrews and Luke-Acts.[1] The best way I can describe these two chapters is that it's like being a photographer in the darkroom watching the pictures develop. As the image gradually appears and the features become more distinct, one begins to see Luke the Jew rather than Luke the Gentile, and the shadowy *auctor* of Hebrews resembles more and more the author of Luke-Acts.

In 1955, C. Jones wrote "The Epistle to the Hebrews and the Lukan Writings," in which he argued cogently that there is a certain "family likeness" between Hebrews and the Lukan corpus, especially with regard to Christology and eschatology. This relationship, he says, has not so much been unobserved by modern scholars, but rather "unlooked for."[2] He suggested this is true for two reasons. First, until rather recently in New Testament scholarship, Luke was often regarded as a historian who collected and arranged his sources with little or no theological interest or purpose. On the other hand, scholars have regarded Hebrews as the work of a theologian par excellence. But Lukan studies have shifted and Luke is now viewed as a theologian of some stature. This shift is perhaps no more clearly reflected than in the title of Marshall's work on Luke-Acts, *Luke: Historian and Theologian* (1970).[3] Jones pointed out that this shift in thinking provides the

---

[1] Among good summary treatments of the theology of Luke-Acts, cf. J. Green, *The Theology of the Gospel of Luke*, New Testament Theology Series, ed. James Dunn (Cambridge: Cambridge University Press, 1995); J. Jervell, *Luke and the People of God: A New Look at Luke-Acts* (Minneapolis: Augsburg, 1972); id., *The Unknown Paul: Essays on Luke-Acts and Early Christian History* (Minneapolis: Augsburg, 1984); id., *The Theology of the Acts of the Apostles* (Cambridge: Cambridge University Press, 1996); E. Franklin, *Christ the Lord: A Study in the Purpose and Theology of Luke-Acts* (London: SPCK, 1975); and D. Bock, "A Theology of Luke-Acts," in *A Biblical Theology of the New Testament*, ed. Roy Zuck and D. Bock (Chicago: Moody, 1994), 87–166.

[2] C. Jones, "The Epistle to the Hebrews and the Lukan Writings," in *Studies in the Gospels: Essays in Memory of R. H. Lightfoot*, ed. D. E. Nineham (Oxford: Basil Blackwell, 1955), 113.

[3] I. H. Marshall, *Luke: Historian and Theologian* (Exeter: Paternoster, 1970).

impetus to scale the barrier that has separated Luke and his writings from Hebrews.[4]

A second reason scholars have not pursued a connection between the two is the widespread tendency to regard Luke-Acts as a work of Gentile provenance with perhaps even an anti-Jewish bias,[5] while regarding Hebrews as the work of an author whose knowledge of and reverence for the Jewish institutions is so apparent. Again, however, the Gentile provenance of Luke-Acts has been questioned in recent years and alternative hypotheses have been offered.[6] Indeed, it is my contention that a Jewish provenance for Luke-Acts better fits the data (see chap. 6). Jones presents some of this data in such a way that the reader begins to feel the Jewish interests of Luke.

> St. Luke does indeed depict God's salvation in Christ as a light to lighten the gentiles [*sic*], but it is equally the glory of thy people Israel (Lk. 2:32). The latter St. Luke tries to make clear in many ways: by his description of the ideal law-loving piety from which the Lord arose in his opening chapters (1:5 to end of 2), which are deeply influenced by the language and associations of the Septuagint, . . . by the thrice-repeated mourning of the Lord over Jerusalem (13:34, 35, 19:41–44, 23:28–31); by his desire to mitigate as far as possible the guilt of the Jews for the crucifixion (eg., 23:27,28, 23:31, Acts 3:17);

---

[4] C. Jones, "The Epistle to the Hebrews and the Lukan Writings," 114.

[5] The most outspoken proponent of the (minority) view that Luke is anti-Judaic is Jack Sanders, especially in *The Jews in Luke-Acts* (London: SCM, 1987). More balanced treatments can be found in R. C. Tannehill, "Israel in Luke-Acts: A Tragic Story," *JBL* 104 (1985): 69–85; id., *The Narrative Unity of Luke-Acts: A Literary Interpretation*, 2 vols. (Philadelphia: Fortress, 1986, 1990); R. L. Brawley, *Luke-Acts and the Jews: Conflict, Apology, and Conciliation*, SBLMS 33 (Atlanta: Scholars Press, 1987); J. B. Tyson, *Images of Judaism in Luke-Acts* (Columbia, SC: University of South Carolina Press, 1992); C. A. Evans, "Prophecy and Polemic: Jews in Luke's Scriptural Apologetic," in *Luke and Scripture: The Function of Sacred Tradition in Luke-Acts* (Minneapolis: Fortress, 1993); and the six articles appearing in Part III of *Literary Studies in Luke-Acts: Essays in Honor of Joseph B. Tyson*, ed. R. Thompson and T. Phillips (Macon: Mercer University Press, 1998), excepting Sanders's article. Stenschke perceptively noted that Luke's portrayal of Gentiles prior to conversion would imply an anti-Gentile stance. "Luke's unflattering portrait of the Gentiles also contains many elements indirectly commending Jews. His portrait of Gentile God-fearers is a strong recommendation of Judaism . . . . Luke equally or even to a greater extent condemns non-Christian Gentiles." C. Stenschke, *Luke's Portrait of Gentiles Prior to Their Coming to Faith*, in WUNT, reihe 2; 108 (Tübingen: J. C. B. Mohr [Paul Siebeck], 1999), 392. J. Weatherly, *Jewish Responsibility for the Death of Jesus in Luke-Acts*, JSNTSup 106 (Sheffield: Sheffield Academic Press, 1994), 50–90, argues that one must distinguish between Jewish leaders and the people of Israel in Luke's approach, because Luke avoids condemning the entire nation for the sins of their leadership. For a full bibliography on this subject, see G. Harvey, *The True Israel: Uses of the Names Jew, Hebrew, and Israel in Ancient Jewish and Early Christian Literature* (Leiden/New York: Brill, 1996), 189n12.

[6] Cf. Jervell, *Luke and the People of God*; id., "The Acts of the Apostles and the History of Early Christianity," *ST* 37 (1983): 17–32; id., *The Unknown Paul*; id., *Theology of the Acts of the Apostles*; and E. Franklin, *Christ the Lord*.

by his placing the Lord's resurrection and ascension in or near Jerusalem, so that the holy city becomes not only the scene of the end of the Lord's work on earth but also the center from which the new Church radiates (Acts 1:4, 8); by emphasizing the temple as the place of the disciples' praise at the end of the gospel (Lk. 24:53) and as one of the focal points of the Christian fellowship after Pentecost (Acts 2:46, 3:1, 5:12, 6:7); and by two passages (Lk. 24:25–27, 44–47) which teach more explicitly than any other gospel passage the complete fulfillment of the Jewish Scriptures in the crucifixion and resurrection of the Christ, a theme illustrated in extensio in the speeches in Acts.[7]

Christology in Luke-Acts and Hebrews[8]

In the past, much of the discussion of Lukan Christology occurred against the backdrop of the history-of-religions school. Today this is no longer the case. In addition, much of the discussion in the past assumed that Luke and his readers were Gentiles. Although some believe Luke and/or his readers were Gentile, this assumption no longer hinders investigation into Lukan Christology.[9]

Since Christological considerations are the bedrock of Hebrews, I will begin by drawing a comparison between the Christologies of Hebrews and Luke-Acts. The prologue to Hebrews (1:1–4) is a magnificent description of Jesus as the glorified, enthroned Son of God. Hebrews not only implies a resurrected Christ, but emphasizes His ascension and exaltation as well. Jesus is said to have seated Himself at the right hand of the majesty on high (Heb 1:3), and the author never loses sight of this throughout the letter (Heb 8:1; 10:12; 12:2).

This enthronement Christology (or exaltation Christology as it is sometimes called) is exactly what we find in Luke-Acts.[10] Luke's narrative is constructed so as to bring Jesus not only to Jerusalem and the cross, but beyond to the resurrection (and especially the ascension

---

[7] C. Jones, "The Epistle to the Hebrews and the Lukan Writings," 114–15.

[8] The literature on this subject for both Luke-Acts and Hebrews is immense. For helpful bibliography relative to Luke-Acts, consult C. M. Tuckett, "The Christology of Luke-Acts," in J. Verheyden, *The Unity of Luke-Acts* (Leuven, Belgium: Leuven University Press, 1999), 133 and *passim*, along with P. Pokorný, *Theologie der lukanischen Schriften*, Forschungen zur Religion und Literatur des Alten und Neuen Testaments 174 (Göttingen: Vandenhoeck und Ruprecht, 1998), 110–72. For Hebrews, consult the recent bibliographies in commentaries by H. Attridge, W. Lane, P. Ellingworth, and H. Köester. For both, see A. Hultgren, *New Testament Christology: A Critical Assessment and Annotated Bibliography*, in *Bibliographies and Indexes in Religious Studies*, 12 (New York: Greenwood, 1988).

[9] C. Fletcher-Louis, *Luke-Acts: Angels, Christology and Soteriology*, WUNT 94 (Tübingen: Mohr Siebeck, 1997), 26.

[10] Tuckett, "The Christology of Luke-Acts," 164.

and exaltation). In the lengthy episode of the two disciples on the road to Emmaus, the resurrected Christ says: "Didn't the Messiah have to suffer these things and enter into His glory?" (Luke 24:26). After this, Jesus appears to His disciples in the upper room. Then Luke concludes his Gospel with the account of the ascension (Luke 24:49–53).

Again, in the introduction to Acts (1:1–11), Luke recounts Christ's ascension, in essence revisiting the narrative ground he covered in the conclusion of his Gospel. Luke 9:51 is a major structural division in the narrative, and it is precisely at this juncture that the narrator looks ahead to the conclusion of his work and speaks of "the days . . . for Him to be taken up," *analēmpsis*, the same Greek word used in Acts 1:2,11, and 22 to speak of the ascension. Stephen, in Acts 7:55, saw Jesus standing on the right hand of God. Among the Gospel writers, Luke places the greatest emphasis on the ascension of Christ (Matthew and John do not record it).

Jürgen Roloff saw in Peter's identification of Jesus with God in Acts 2:21 a reflection of Luke's belief in a Christology similar to Phil 2:5–11 and Heb 1:3–4.[11] Likewise, Buckwalter concluded that Luke's Christology viewed Jesus as God's "co-equal."[12]

Gerhard Lohfink argues that whereas Paul and the rest of the New Testament writers viewed the resurrection of Jesus as His exaltation to the throne in fulfillment of the Davidic promise, Luke "altered" this pattern. Luke differentiated between the resurrection and the exaltation, with the ascension culminating in His exaltation via His being seated on the throne.[13] Yet from a functional standpoint, as Chance has rightly pointed out, Luke did not sharply differentiate between the resurrection and the ascension, as evidenced by Acts 2:30–31.[14] Luke's focus is on the ascension and resultant exaltation, as is true for the author of Hebrews.

---

[11] J. Roloff, *Die Apostelgeschichte* (Göttingen and Berlin: Vandenhoeck & Ruprecht and Evangelische Verlagsanstalt, 1988), 54–55.

[12] H. D. Buckwalter, "The Divine Savior," in I. H. Marshall and D. Peterson, *Witness to the Gospel: The Theology of Acts* (Grand Rapids: Eerdmans, 1998), 107–23.

[13] G. Lohfink, *Die Himmelfahrt Jesu: Untersuchungen zu den Himmelfahrts—und Erhohungstexten bei Lukas*, SANT 26 (München: Kosel, 1971), 242–50.

[14] J. B. Chance, *Jerusalem, the Temple, and the New Age in Luke-Acts* (Macon: Mercer University Press, 1988), 64–65.

R. H. Fuller has argued that in the early church, three Christologies circulated: two-foci, exaltation, and epiphany.[15] Talbert describes the nature of the Christology of Luke-Acts, noting that whereas John employs an epiphany Christology,

> Luke-Acts employs an exaltation Christology: Jesus in his earthly life is the descendent of David and heir to the promises of the Jewish scriptures. By virtue of his resurrection he is raised to the exalted status of God's son with power. In the present he rules from heaven as Lord overall, intervening on behalf of his people to deliver and protect them. . . . Exaltation Christology functioned to express the church's experience of Jesus Christ in a two-fold way: as the present Lord who rules from heaven, and as the historical figure whose story is normative for us.[16]

It is also interesting to compare the theological posture of the prologue to Hebrews with Luke 1–2. The author of Hebrews makes a great effort to emphasize that Jesus is God's final revelation to the Jewish nation. God has spoken (aorist participle) in times past, but in these last days he has spoken (aorist indicative) decisively in His Son. This is precisely what Luke's Gospel conveys in the lengthy prelude to Jesus' ministry. The coming of Jesus fulfills the Old Testament Scriptures and the hopes of a longing Israel. This fact is confirmed by numerous personalities, including Zechariah the priest, Mary, Elizabeth, Simeon, and Anna. It might be said that Heb 1:1–4 is a good theological synopsis of what is stated in narrative fashion in Luke 1–2.

Hebrews brings to the fore, perhaps more than any other New Testament book, the concept of the perfection of Christ.[17] The verb *teleioō*, "to perfect," and its cognates occur most often in Luke-Acts and Hebrews. Of further interest is that outside of Hebrews, the only place in the New Testament where Jesus is described by *teleioō* is Luke 13:32. Here the sense of "perfection" is identical to that found in Hebrews, namely, the attainment of heavenly perfection through suffering and death.[18]

Although Peterson does not think that *teleioō* as it is used in Luke and Hebrews carries with it the cultic significance it has in certain

---

[15] R. H. Fuller, *The Foundations of New Testament Christology* (New York: Scribner's, 1965), 5.

[16] C. Talbert, *Reading Luke* (New York: Crossroads, 1983), 20–21.

[17] The classic work on this subject is D. Peterson, *Hebrews and Perfection: An Examination of the Concept of Perfection in the Epistle to the Hebrews*, SNTSMS 47 (Cambridge: Cambridge University Press, 1982).

[18] Ibid., 33, 45.

LXX passages,[19] Ellis believes that *teleioō* in Luke 13:32 points to the goal of Christ's consecration and enthronement into the messianic office based on the Old Testament cultic background of the term.[20] Peterson's view (that we cannot assume *teleioō* had cultic significance for the author of Hebrews because we cannot expect his readers to have understood the connection[21]) would itself be invalid if the readership consisted of former priests as we argue below. The same could be said for Luke's understanding and use of the term in Luke 13:32 if his reader were Theophilus, a former high priest.

Peterson acknowledges that the cultic application of *teleioō* for "initiation" or "consecration" of a priest occurs "well into the Christian era," but he does not specify how long after Christ's death and resurrection this phrase, "well into the Christian era," indicates. He argues that, based on the LXX usage of *teleioō* alone, it cannot be suggested that in Hebrews the term carries the sense of priestly consecration.[22]

Derrett has skillfully pointed out that the Lukan use of *teleioumai* in Luke 13:32 is consistently mistranslated, and that behind this word stands the Hebrew original *ʾĕšālēm*, meaning, in effect, "I shall die." The saying in v. 32 is "an extremely artful punning epigram," arising in an environment of Hebrew speakers.[23] Behind the Hebrew word, according to Derrett, we find "a hint of *ʾšullam*, 'I shall be offered as a peace-offering (*šelem*)' . . . an entirely suitable fate for the Servant of the Lord (Isa 42:19 *mešullām*), for all vows must be paid at Jerusalem (Ps 65:2 *yᵉšullam neder*)."[24] Derrett believes Deut 16:16–17:7 stands behind Luke 13:31–35, yet he suggests that "the idea of Jesus presenting the people as an offering, or of Jesus being Himself an offering, which a preacher could certainly develop with the aid of this Deuteronomy passage, has been ignored by Luke in his composition of our pericope."[25] Ignored by Luke? Could it be that Luke (the Jew), writing to a former Jewish high priest, has made this play on words deliberately? Likewise, does not the Lukan employment of *teleioumai*,

---

[19] Ibid., 28–30.

[20] E. E. Ellis, *The Gospel of Luke*, NCBC (Grand Rapids: Eerdmans, 1974; repr., London: Oliphants, 1977), 189.

[21] Peterson, *Hebrews and Perfection*, 29.

[22] Ibid., 47.

[23] J. D. M. Derrett, "The Lucan Christ and Jerusalem: τελειοῦμαι (Luke 13:32)," ZNW 75 (1984): 36–37.

[24] Ibid., 39. Derrett points to the popular etymology of Hb. "Jerusalem" as "possession of peace."

[25] Ibid., 43.

a word whose concept plays such an important role in the Christology and soteriology of Hebrews, furnish another link among the three works?

Swetnam has observed the link between Luke's theological concept of the "testing" of Jesus (e.g., Luke 22:28) and the posture of the writer to Hebrews with respect to the same concept.[26] Heb 2:18 and 4:15 emphasize Jesus' testing through suffering and His resultant perfection. On the concept of the testing and perfection of Christ, Luke and Hebrews are in close agreement. Luke emphasizes Jesus' faithfulness to God via temptations and His acceptance of death as God's will.[27]

The concept of Jesus as the ruler over Israel in the latter days, in fulfillment of the Davidic prophecies in 2 Sam 7:14 and the Christological designation of Jesus as the Son in Ps 2:7, is prominent in Heb 1:5–13 and 5:5; it is also found in many places throughout Luke's writings (e.g., Luke 1:32–33; Acts 2:30; 13:33).[28] Although Luke never directly quotes 2 Sam 7:14, it is a key Old Testament passage, along with Ps 2:7, undergirding His infancy narratives (Luke 1–2), Peter's sermon at Pentecost (Acts 2), and Paul's speech in the synagogue in Pisidian Antioch (Acts 13).[29] There is a conceptual allusion to 2 Sam 7:14 behind the Christological discussions of much of Luke-Acts and Hebrews; yet, with the exception of a non-Christological allusion in 2 Cor 6:18 (where it applies to Christians instead of Christ), this passage is nowhere quoted or alluded to in the rest of the New Testament.

---

[26] J. Swetnam, *Jesus and Isaac* (Rome: Biblical Institute, 1981), 175.

[27] See J. Neyrey, *The Passion According to Luke: A Redaction Study of Luke's Soteriology*, Theological Inquiries: Studies in Contemporary Biblical and Theological Problems, gen. ed., L. Boadt (New York: Paulist Press, 1985), 179–82.

[28] R. Brawley traces Luke's view of Christ's fulfillment of the Davidic and Abrahamic covenants in Luke 1–4. He shows how Luke resolves the ambivalence between the two covenants when Zechariah echoes Gabriel's allusion to the Davidic covenant to Mary by speaking of a horn of salvation in the house of God's servant David (Luke 1:69). This salvation is then grounded in God's fidelity to a promise to Abraham in Luke 1:72–73. "The Davidic covenant is a particular way God's promise to Abraham comes to fulfillment." R. Brawley, "The Blessing of All the Families of the Earth: Jesus and Covenant Traditions in Luke-Acts," *SBLSP* 33, ed. E. Lovering (Atlanta: Scholars Press, 1994), 252–68, specifically 256. Luke was not creating a new thing with this correlation; Abrahamic and Davidic covenant traditions were already united in some of Israel's traditions according to R. Clements, *Abraham and David: Genesis XV and its Meaning for Israelite Tradition* (Naperville, IL: Alec Allenson, 1967), 47–60, 81–82.

[29] See D. Bock, *Proclamation from Prophecy and Pattern*, JSNTSup 12, ed. D. Hill (Sheffield: JSOT Press, 1987), 60–89, 240–49; R. F. O'Toole, "Acts 2:30 and the Davidic Covenant of Pentecost," *JBL* 102 (1983): 245–58; D. Goldsmith, "Acts 13:33–37: A Pesher on II Samuel 7," *JBL* 87 (1968): 321–24; and F. F. Bruce, "To the Hebrews or to the Essenes?" *NTS* 9 (1962–63): 217–32. Both O'Toole and Goldsmith suggest that Acts 13:32–37 may be a pesher on 2 Samuel 7:12–16.

Likewise, Ps 2:7 is quoted only by Luke and Hebrews (Acts 13:33; Heb 1:5; 5:5).

It is not just significant that Ps 2:7 appears only in Acts and Hebrews, but that it is used in a similar way in both books. In the context of Heb 1:5, where the significance of Christ's enthronement is thematic, the *sēmeron gegennēka* of Ps 2:7 refers to the manifestation of Christ's Sonship at His placement at the right hand of God by means of His resurrection and ascension. This is paralleled in Acts 13:33, where Paul's use of Ps 2:7 is applied to the resurrection of Christ.[30] The motif of Jesus as the Davidic ruler in fulfillment of 2 Sam 7:14 and Ps 2:7 holds greater significance for Luke and Hebrews than for any other New Testament writer.

The description in Heb 5:7 of Jesus praying in the garden on the eve of His crucifixion is nearly identical to the account of that event in Luke 22:44. Heb 5:7 describes Jesus as praying with "loud cries and tears." All three Synoptics mention the prayer in the garden of Gethsemane, but only Luke describes Jesus thus: "being in anguish, He prayed more fervently, and His sweat became like drops of blood . . ." (Luke 22:44).[31] Only Luke records the visit of the strengthening angel, an example of the purpose of angels as recorded in Heb 1:14. Luke is the Gospel writer known for his interest in and emphasis on the humanity of Christ; Hebrews, more than any other New Testament letter, emphasizes the humanity of Christ and His ability as our great high priest to identify with those who are His. It is only in Heb 5:8 and Luke 2:52 that we have a statement regarding Jesus' inner human development. Along this line, Barnabas Lindars speaks of the creative theology of the author of Hebrews, noting that the author's metaphorical use of the priesthood concept for Jesus is derived from the Gethsemane tradition.[32]

---

[30] Peterson, *Hebrews and Perfection*, 85. See W. Pannenberg, *Systematic Theology*, trans. G. Bromiley (Grand Rapids: Eerdmans, 1991), 1:306, where he remarked that Luke, by quoting Ps 2:7 (and not Isa 42:1) in Luke 3:22, "perhaps has in view the installation of Jesus as high priest, like Heb 1:5 and 5:5."

[31] For a detailed discussion of the similarities between the Gethsemane prayer and Heb 5:7–8, consult T. Lescow, "Jesus in Gethsemane bei Lukas und im Hebräerbrief," *ZNW* 58 (1967): 215–39. See also the bibliography in R. Brown, *The Death of the Messiah: From Gethsemane to the Grave, A Commentary on the Passion Narratives in the Four Gospels* (New York: Doubleday, 1994), 1:111–16.

[32] B. Lindars, *The Theology of the Letter to the Hebrews* (Cambridge: Cambridge University Press, 1991), 126.

W. R. Paton suggested that the Greek word *agōnia* was often used to describe the kind of agony that a runner experienced in an athletic contest prior to the start of the race, and that this meaning best fits Luke 22:44.[33] He has since been supported in this theory by Neyrey[34] and Brown.[35] Brown points out that in 4 Macc the martyr Eleazar is compared to a noble athlete, and in 2 Macc 3:16–17 the high priest experiences *agōnia* of soul that leads to physical trembling.[36] The relationship of Luke-Acts to the Maccabean writings has already been established.

The parallel to Heb 5:7–10; 6:20 (where Jesus is said to be the "forerunner") and also to 12:1–2 (where the same Greek word *agōnia* occurs) is unmistakable. In Heb 12:1, the race is said to be *ton prokeimenon hēmin agōna*, "the race that lies before us." This same participle is used again in v. 2 in reference to the "joy" that "lay before Him." The implication is that God set the joy before Jesus and thus set the race before us. The Lukan description of Jesus in the garden of Gethsemane complements these passages in Hebrews in a remarkable way.

High Priesthood of Jesus in Luke-Acts?

Beyond question, the high priesthood of Christ plays an important role in the Christology of Hebrews.[37] However, Luke-Acts does not appear at first to describe Jesus as a high priest.[38] This may seem to weaken the possibility of Lukan authorship for Hebrews. If Luke wrote Hebrews, why is such emphasis placed on Christ's high priesthood there, but little or no reference is made to it in his two-volume narrative? Luke's lexical choice, revealing his keen interest in the

---

[33] W. Paton, "ΑΓΩΝΙΑ (Agony)," *Classical Review* 27 (1913): 194. See also discussions on the meaning of this term in W. Grundmann, *Das Evangelium nach Lukas* (Berlin: Evangelische Verlagsanstalt, 1971), 412; T. Lescow, "Jesus in Gethsemane," 223; J. W. Holleran, *The Synoptic Gethsemane* (Rome: Gregorian University Press, 1973), 97–99; E. Stauffer, "*agōn*," *TDNT* 1:135–40; and V. C. Pfitzner, *Paul and the Agon Motif* (Leiden: Brill, 1967).

[34] J. Neyrey, "The Absence of Jesus' Emotion—The Lucan Redaction of Lk 22, 39–46," *Bib* 61 (1980): 153–71; also see his *The Passion According to Luke*, 58–62.

[35] Brown, *The Death of the Messiah*, 1:189–90.

[36] Ibid.

[37] See the important discussion on this subject by O. Cullmann in *The Christology of the New Testament*, trans. S. Guthrie and C. Hall, rev. ed. (Philadelphia: Westminster Press, 1963), 83–107.

[38] G. Friedrich, "Beobachtungen zur messianischen Hohepriestererwartung in den Synoptikern," in *ZTK* 53 (1956): 265–311, points out traces of a high priest Christology in the Synoptic Gospels.

priests and matters pertaining to them, has already been discussed (see above and chap. 6). He may have addressed his two-volume work to a former Jewish high priest, and Hebrews may have been written to converted priests; both views are argued below. I have already shown the Christological similarities among the three works, and this provides a conceptual base for suggesting Lukan authorship.

Yet the question of Luke's apparent silence on the priestly or high-priestly ministry of Jesus must be addressed. While Luke may not overtly describe the priestly ministry of Jesus in Luke-Acts, he alludes to and illustrates it in a most dramatic fashion, especially at the beginning of his Gospel and at the conclusion. Furthermore, it is Luke (more than any other New Testament writer outside Hebrews) who in his Christology, his use of the Old Testament, and his nuanced references to the temple cultus, actually sketches for us Jesus' priestly ministry.

In the Old Testament, prophets, kings, and priests were anointed with oil, which was symbolic of their God-ordained calling and their being set apart to lead and serve the people. Of the four Gospel writers, Luke alone speaks of the anointing of Jesus (Luke 17:10–19). Luke unmistakably links the descent of the Spirit on Jesus at His baptism with the Spirit-anointing described by Jesus in Luke 4:18 (when He quoted Isa 61:1 in the Nazareth synagogue).[39] Anointing is significant in Acts as well (4:25–27; 10:36–42). The author of Hebrews is the only other New Testament writer to refer to the anointing of Jesus (1:9 in an Old Testament quotation).

Jesus' sermon in Nazareth (Luke 4:16–30) is now viewed by Lukan scholars as clearly programmatic for Luke.[40] There is, however, a significant debate over exactly how Luke portrays Jesus. Five suggestions vie for attention here. (1) Jesus is viewed as a prophet.[41] (2) Jesus is viewed as the prophet like Moses.[42] (3) Jesus is viewed as the Davidic Messiah.[43] (4) Jesus is viewed as the servant of Yahweh.[44]

---

[39] M. Strauss, *The Davidic Messiah in Luke-Acts: The Promise and its Fulfillment in Lukan Christology*, JSNTSup (Sheffield: Sheffield Academic Press, 1995), 202–3.

[40] Cf. A. Falcetta, *The Call of Nazareth: Form and Exegesis of Luke 4:16–30*, Cahiers De La Revue Biblique 53 (Paris: J. Gabalda, 2003).

[41] See J. Fitzmyer, *The Gospel According to Luke (I–IX): Introduction, Translation, and Notes*, AB 28 (Garden City: Doubleday, 1981), 530; J. Nolland, *Luke 1:1–9:20*, WBC 35A (Dallas: Word, 1989), 196.

[42] I. H. Marshall, *Commentary on Luke*, NIGTC (Grand Rapids: Eerdmans, 1978), 178.

[43] As, for example, R. Stein, *Luke*. NAC 24 (Nashville: B&H, 1992), 156.

[44] As, for example, Ellis, *Luke*, 98.

(5) Jesus is viewed as a priestly messiah.[45] This last option is what we need to explore in light of the present study. I think it likely that several—perhaps even all—of the options above were true for Luke. The first two options are essentially the same, identifying Jesus as prophet. The next two are also essentially identical, presenting Jesus as the Messiah/Servant of Yahweh. So we have only three real options here. There is no doubt that Luke portrays Jesus as an eschatological prophet and as the kingly Messiah. What is not so readily accepted is that Luke also presents Him as God's High Priest.

Luke's view of Jesus as High Priest is shown in at least three ways. First, Jesus prays for Peter that his "faith may not fail" (Luke 22:31–32). Here the intercessory ministry of Jesus, also highlighted in Hebrews, is tangibly expressed in Jesus' earthly life. In Luke's account of the return of the 70 (Luke 10:17–20), Jesus tells them not to rejoice in the subjugation of demons, but rather to rejoice "that your names are written in heaven" (v. 20). This is probably an allusion to Dan 12:1. On the Day of Atonement, the high priest would pray that the names of the people would be written in the Book of Life.

Second, Luke records that at the crucifixion Jesus prayed, "Father, forgive them, because they do not know what they are doing" (Luke 23:34). Daube argues that this prayer has a thoroughly Jewish background and was for the Jews primarily, not the Romans (although they may have been included).[46] What is of interest here is the connection that Daube makes between Num 15:25–26 (a reference to the liturgy on the Day of Atonement, where an unwitting offense by the community is forgiven) and Luke 23:24, and then with Heb 5:2 (where the Jewish high priest, to whom Jesus is compared, has "compassion on the ignorant and on them that are out of the way").[47] Could it be that Heb 5:2 serves as a commentary on Jesus' prayer according to Luke, and that this is further evidence of Luke's depicting Jesus as High Priest interceding for His people?[48] Throughout Luke's Gospel, Jesus is characterized by the priestly attributes of sympathy, compassion, and mercy.

---

[45] As, for example, W. H. Brownlee, "Messianic Motifs of Qumran and the New Testament," *NTS* 3 (1956–57): 206.

[46] D. Daube, "For They Know Not What They Do: Luke 23:24," *StPatr* 4 (TU 79) (Berlin: Akademie, 1961), 58–70.

[47] Ibid., 65–67.

[48] Cf. also J. L. Houlden, "The Purpose of Luke," *JSNT* 21 (1984): 56–59.

Finally, in the account of Jesus' ascension (Luke 24:50–51), Jesus lifts up His hands and blesses the disciples. While he is engaged in this act, He is "carried up into heaven." Talbert's words express the meaning of this act:

> This act of blessing is like that of the high priest, Simon, in *Sir* 50:19–20. With a priestly act the risen Jesus puts his disciples under the protection of God before he leaves them. . . . Just as the gospel began with the ministry of the priest Zechariah, so it ends with Jesus acting as priest for his flock (cf. Heb 2:17; 3:1; 6:19–20).[49]

Note especially the references to Hebrews that describe this act theologically and the position of the ascended Lord in heaven. Of the four Gospel writers, only Luke recounts the ascension of Jesus. It is the focal point of his two volumes, as we have observed.

Luke has often been viewed as having little or no interest in the priesthood of Jesus.[50] But, as Andrews Mekkattukunnel has demonstrated, Luke's apparent lack of interest in Jesus' priesthood vanishes in light of a closer reading of Luke.[51] Many are reluctant to see any

---

[49] Talbert, *Reading Luke*, 233. Cf. Ellis, *Luke*, 279; Marshall, *Luke*, 908–9; and W. Hendriksen, *Exposition of the Gospel According to Luke*, NTC (Grand Rapids: Baker, 1978), 43. See D. D. Sylva, "The Temple Curtain and Jesus' Death in the Gospel of Luke," *JBL* 105 (1986): 239–50. Note especially 247n22, which lists those who see a priestly blessing in Luke 24:50–53: Schlatter, Daube, Ellis, Tinsley, Arndt, Schmithals. Those who see it specifically as a high-priestly blessing include Van Stempvoort, "The Interpretation of the Ascension in Luke and Acts," *NTS* 5 (1957–58): 30–42; Marshall, *Luke*, 908–9; N. Geldenhuys, *Commentary on the Gospel of Luke*, NICNT (Grand Rapids: Eerdmans, 1951); Grundmann, *Das Evangelium nach Lukas*, 3:453–54; G. Schneider, *Das Evangelium nach Lukas*, 2 vols, ÖTK (Gütersloh: Gutersloher Verlagshaus; Würzburg: Echter Verlag, 1977); C. Stuhlmueller, "The Gospel According to Luke," in *The Jerome Bible Commentary* (London: Chapman, 1968), 115–64; and R. Karris, "Luke 23:47 and the Lucan View of Jesus' Death," *JBL* 105 (1986): 65–74. Recently, this has been argued beyond a reasonable doubt by A. Mekkattukunnel, *The Priestly Blessing of the Risen Christ: An Exegetico–Theological Analysis of Luke 24, 50–53*, in *European University Studies*, Series 23, Theology 714 (Bern: Peter Lang, 2001). For the opposing view, see C. Westermann, *Blessing in the Bible and in the Life of the Church* (Philadelphia: Fortress, 1978).

[50] As, for example, Marshall, *Luke*, 909; R. Dillon, *From Eye-Witness to Ministers of the Word: Tradition and Composition in Luke 24*, AnBib 82 (Rome: Biblical Institute Press, 1978), 176; J. Nolland, *Luke 18:35–24:53*, WBC 35 (Dallas: Word, 1993), 1227–28; followed by D. Bock, *Luke 9:51–24:53*, BECNT 3b (Grand Rapids: Baker, 1996), 1945, all deny that Luke has any interest in a priestly Christology although most also pointed out that Luke's account of the ascension in 24:50–51 parallels *Sir*. 50:20–23. I agree with D. Farrow, *Ascension and Ecclesia* (Grand Rapids: Eerdmans, 1999), 25, who also sees in Luke's account of the ascension "weighty evidence" for a priestly Christology. "Are we not invited throughout (another uniquely Lukan story, about the boy Jesus in his Father's house, deserves mention here) to see in Jesus something of Samuel as well as David, and of the priestly as well as the kingly?" I might add, do we not see the same priestly and kingly roles combined in Hebrews?

[51] Mekkattukunnel, *The Priestly Blessing*, 176–77.

priestly Christology in Luke because of the assumption that he has no theology of the cross. However, Luke has his own way of highlighting the sacrificial aspect of Jesus' death. Mekkattukunnel made the point that "Luke omits not only Jesus' saying in Mark 10:45, but the whole Marcan pericope (Mark 10:35–45) in which it occurs. However, Luke takes up much of this Marcan material in the Last Supper context (cf. 22:24–27)."[52] He further said that Luke sets Jesus' death within the Passover time frame, and this points to the sacrificial character of His death (Luke 22:1,7,8,11,13,15; Exod 12:14,25,27).[53]

As Carpinelli has demonstrated, Jesus' words over the bread and cup at the Last Supper clearly express the sacrificial nature of His death.[54] (Observe the allusion to Jer 31:31–34, and the new covenant only in the Lukan account of the Last Supper.[55]) This new covenant allusion is "unmistakable," according to Rata,[56] and renders inexplicable the negative judgment of Ravens that "Luke did not speak of the new covenant."[57]

Mekkattukunnel argues that Luke views Jesus' death on the cross as fulfilling and surpassing the Old Testament temple and priesthood. For Luke, Jesus is the supreme high priest and perfect mediator between God and humanity.[58] Carpinelli comes to the same conclusion:

> As Jesus ascends, Luke depicts him giving Aaron's blessing as the high priest would after sacrifice on the Feast of Atonement. The sacrificial nd expiatory interpretation of the cup connects with the Lucan running allusion to Sirach 50, where the glory and function of the high priest in the liturgy of the Day of Atonement are magnified. . . . In Luke 22:14–23 and 24:50–53 Jesus is thus depicted functioning as a priest. The bread as memorial and the cup as the token of the covenant in Jesus' blood lay the narrative base for depicting the ascending Jesus completing the liturgy of the Day of Atonement. Jesus' giving

---

[52] Ibid., 177.

[53] Ibid. "The emphatic way in which Luke presents Jesus as the 'firstborn' (2:7, 23) reminds us of the Passover lamb which was the ranson [sic] for the deliverance of the Israelites first-born children."

[54] F. G. Carpinelli, "'Do This as My Memorial' (Luke 22:19): Lucan Soteriology of Atonement," *CBQ* 61 (1999): 74–91.

[55] But which is a foundational Old Testament passage for Hebrews 8 and 9.

[56] T. Rata, "The Covenant Motif in Jeremiah's Book of Comfort: Textual and Intertextual Studies of Jeremiah 30–33" (Ph.D. diss., Trinity Evangelical Divinity School, 2003), 194.

[57] D. Ravens, *Luke and the Restoration of Israel* (London: Sheffield Academic Press, 1995), 202.

[58] Mekkattukunnel, *The Priestly Blessing*, 180–81.

the cup as new covenant in his blood and imparting Aaron's blessing bring narratively to full view Luke's image of Jesus' relation to the temple.[59]

Stempvoort, along with others, has cited the *inclusio* formed by the failed priestly blessing of Zechariah in the birth narratives with the completed blessing given by the new High Priest in the final scene of Luke's Gospel. This blessing was an essential element at the conclusion of every temple service, including that of the incense offering that Zechariah was officiating, according to Luke 1:5–25. Zechariah's service was an unfinished *leitourgia*, but at the conclusion of Luke's Gospel there is the finished *leitourgia* given by the priest Jesus.[60] Stempvoort makes the comment in a footnote: "It may have been possible that Luke chose *anaph. [anapherein]* because of its being in the LXX the technical term for offering."[61]

Kapic notes Luke's extensive use of the idea of blessing/benediction (Luke 1:42,64,68–69; 2:28–32; 9:28–36 [the transfiguration account]; concluding with Jesus' blessing the disciples at His ascension in Luke 24:50–53). Luke uses the concept mostly at the beginning and end of his Gospel. Following Kleinig, Kapic argues that Luke's portrayal of the transfiguration parallels in many ways Aaron's liturgical blessing in the Old Testament. This blessing/benediction was given by the priest to the people, and could *only* be given by the priest.[62]

---

[59] Carpinelli, "'Do This as My Memorial,'" 90.

[60] P. A. Stempvoort, "The Interpretation of the Ascension in Luke and Acts," 35, 39. See also M. Parsons, *The Departure of Jesus in Luke-Acts: The Ascension Narratives in Context* (London: Sheffield Academic Press, 1987), 69–111; A. W. Zwiep, *The Ascension of the Messiah in Lukan Christology* (Leiden: Koln, 1997), 88. Both R. Brown, *Birth of the Messiah*, ABRL (New York: Doubleday, 1993), 281–82, and E. Schweizer, *Das Evangelium nach Lukas*, Das Neue Testament Deutsch, Teilband 3 (Göttingen: Vandenhoeck und Ruprecht, 1982) 251, argue that this priestly blessing counteracts Zechariah's inability to bless the congregation at the beginning of the Gospel (Luke 1:21–22). This *inclusio* (sandwich structure) highlights this event and indicates Jesus' priestly activity.

[61] Ibid., 36.

[62] K. Kapic, "Receiving Christ's Priestly Benediction: A Biblical, Historical, and Theological Exploration of Luke 24:50–53," *WTJ* 67 (2005): 248. See also V. Kleinig, "Providence and Worship: The Aaronic Blessing: Numbers 6:22–27," *Lutheran Theological Journal* 19 (Dec. 1985): 120–24. E. Schürer, *A History of the Jewish People in the Time of Jesus Christ*, trans. S. Taylor and P. Christie, second division (Peabody, MA: Hendrickson, 1994 repr.), 2:82, noted that only priests could perform the final blessing to conclude the synagogue liturgy, and if no priest was present, the blessing was not pronounced but made into a prayer (pp. 82–83; see 82n143 concerning the lifting of hands only as high as the shoulders in the country, but above the head in the temple). Giving blessings and being blessed are constant motifs in Luke-Acts. R. Strelan, *Luke the Priest: The Authority of the Author of the Third Gospel* (London: Ashgate, 2008), 137, considered the possibility that the aged Simeon, who blessed the baby Jesus in the temple, may have been a priest because he blesses God and pronounces a blessing on Joseph

The use of *eulogein,* "blessing," occurs three times in Luke 24:50–53. Kapic, following Nolland, notes the close resemblance of this to Lev 9:22–23: "Aaron lifted up his hands toward the people and blessed them. He came down after sacrificing the sin offering, the burnt offering, and the fellowship offering. Moses and Aaron then entered the tent of meeting. When they came out, they blessed the people, and the glory of the LORD appeared to all the people."[63]

Since the priestly blessing in the Old Testament (and other Jewish literature) commonly occurred only after the completion of sacrifice(s), Kapic concludes that the priestly blessing confirmed for the people that the sacrifice was accepted and their sins were forgiven. The benediction was more than an option in the Jewish liturgy; it functioned as "a necessary conclusion to the priestly atoning activity."[64] Kapic's read on Luke's pastoral intention at this point is accurate in my view: "The people of God were consistently reminded, through this blessing, of *God's presence and faithfulness* despite their sins, and it was this blessing that would become such a comfort to those weary and exiled believers who questioned if their God had forgotten them."[65]

Kapic points out that the motif of blessing continues in Acts and plays a vital role at the conclusion of Peter's second sermon after Pentecost: "You are the sons of the prophets and of the covenant that God made with your forefathers, saying to Abraham, *And in your seed all the families of the earth will be blessed.* God raised up His Servant and sent Him first to you to bless you by turning each of you from your evil ways" (Acts 3:25–26). With respect to Luke's understanding, "Blessing has reached a climax with the incarnation, and now preaching points specifically to the personified Benediction for salvation."[66]

Kapic connects Luke's portrait of Jesus' ascension with passages in Hebrews: "Jesus departs and blesses his disciples at the same time; he had made the perfect and final sacrifice, securing the forgiveness of sins for his people (Heb 7:26–27; 10:12)."[67] Recall the author's

and Mary (Luke 2:34). Anna, also in the temple, is not a priest and so does not pronounce a blessing (Luke 2:37).

[63] Kapic, "Receiving Christ's Priestly Benediction," 251. See also Nolland, *Luke 18:35–24:53,* 1227.
[64] Nolland, *Luke 18:35–24:53,* 259.
[65] Kapic, "Receiving Christ's Priestly Benediction," 252.
[66] Ibid., 253.
[67] Ibid., 252.

benediction in Heb 13:20–21, connecting atonement with blessing (which Luke does in his Gospel and Acts).

Hamm has argued that there are seven places in Luke-Acts with allusions to the Jewish Tamid service: (1) Zechariah in the temple, Luke 1:5–25; (2) Peter and John at the temple at the ninth hour, Acts 3:1; (3) Cornelius praying at the ninth hour, Acts 10; (4) the Pharisee and the tax collector in the temple, Luke 18:9–14; (5) Jesus' death at the sixth hour and the Centurion's response, Luke 23:44–47; (6) Jesus' statement, "Do this as my memorial," Luke 22:19b; and (7) Jesus' benediction before His ascension, Luke 24:50–53.[68] Hamm correctly concludes that Zechariah's priestly work in the temple (as recorded in Luke 1:5–22) was the incense portion of the afternoon Tamid service.[69] For Hamm, Zechariah's temple activity and Jesus' benediction in Luke 24 "frame the Third Gospel and suggest that the Tamid service functions as an important symbolic background in Luke's narrative theology."[70]

The significance of all this for the Lukan authorship of Hebrews is well summarized by Mekkattukunnel, although he is not arguing for it:

> The priestly blessing fits in well at the finale of the Gospel narrative. For it is here that the risen Christ, after his one-for-all sacrifice on the cross, appears in glory to his disciples. Luke is thus alluding to the fact which the author of the Letter to the Hebrews states explicitly in 8–9. The then existing cultic system was intrinsically incapable of effecting the mediation between God and humankind. For the Jewish high priest did not enter God's dwelling on the Day of Atonement but entered a material human building (Heb 9:1,8,24) in which the Most High does not dwell (Acts 7:48; 17:24). Christ's sacrifice changes the situation completely, surpassing the old system of sacrifice. Christ's sacrificial offering in his own blood through "the greater and more perfect tent" (Heb 9:11; Luke 23:45) made him "mediator of the new covenant" (Heb 9:11–15; Luke 22:20; Jer. 31:31–34). So Luke is all the more justified in depicting Christ after his passion and resurrection in a priestly manner.[71]

Luke says Jesus was "carried up" (*analambanomai*) in Luke 24:51. This verb's usage in the context of being "carried up" to heaven carries

---

[68] D. Hamm, "The Tamid Service in Luke-Acts: The Cultic Background behind Luke's Theology of Worship (Luke 1:5–25; 18:9–14; Acts 3:1; 10:3,30)," *CBQ* 65 (2003): 215–31.

[69] Ibid., 221.

[70] Ibid., 231.

[71] Mekkattukunnel, *The Priestly Blessing*, 207–8.

a range of connotations, and all of them are, according to Zwiep, "from a (Hellenistic) Jewish or Jewish Christian milieu. In the period relevant to the present investigation I have not been able to find a rapture text with *analēmpsis* or *analambanomai* outside the Jewish or Christian realm. If Luke's wording rings a bell, it is a Jewish or biblical one. . . ."[72] Zwiep compares Sir 50:20–23 to Luke 24:50–53 and notes no fewer than six verbal parallels and one semantic parallel.[73] Luke's entire ascension scene is not informed by Hellenism, according to Zwiep, but rather by biblical Judaism.[74] Zwiep correctly notes there is something of an *inclusio* in Luke 24:53 and Luke 2:37. Luke's final picture in his Gospel is of the disciples regularly worshiping God in the temple. Compare this with Luke 2:37, where Anna is presented in the same fashion as a worshiper in the temple precincts. "Luke's emphasis is on the continuity of the new found Christian community with Israel."[75]

Green believes Luke "demonstrates no interest" in portraying Jesus as a priest, but said if he were doing so, "it is certainly of interest that Jesus would thus function as a priest *outside* [emphasis his] of Jerusalem."[76] Of course, Hebrews 13 concludes with this very point! What Luke narrates at the close of his Gospel, the author of Hebrews emphasizes at the close of his letter. In the final few chapters of Luke's Gospel, Jesus operates within the temple confines and then retreats, only to return in the next episode. After the resurrection, however, Jesus no longer appears within the temple confines, and ascends to heaven from outside Jerusalem rather than from the temple or its precincts. Luke's narrative of the ascension and Jesus' relationship to the temple could not be closer to what we find in Hebrews (specifically in Hebrews 13). Thus, the theme of Jesus as high priest can be illustrated from Luke's Gospel, and becomes a significant argument for the Lukan authorship of Hebrews.

Chance wrongly states that Luke's approach separates him from the dominant pattern in non-Lukan Christianity, which was "to associate

---

[72] Zwiep, *Ascension of the Messiah in Lukan Christology*, 82. Zwiep compares the Lukan account with Old Testament and intertestamental Jewish rapture traditions such as the Elijah tradition, the rapture stories of 4 Ezra, 2 Baruch, and 2 Enoch.

[73] Ibid., 88.

[74] Ibid., 93–94.

[75] Ibid., 94.

[76] J. Green, *The Theology of the Gospel of Luke*, New Testament Theology Series, gen. ed. J. Dunn (Cambridge: Cambridge University Press, 1995), 860–61.

Jesus with the literal cult only in a *negative* sense, portraying Jesus as replacing the cult with himself or his church." To suggest that Luke gives Jesus "a distinctively cultic character which does not nullify the temple cult," and that the action of Jesus in Luke 24:50 "offers an affirmation of the cult," is to misread the evidence.[77] What Luke is affirming is the fulfillment of the cult in Jesus.

Luke's emphasis on Jesus' radical holiness in terms of His sinlessness, innocence, and nearness to God may allude to the Old Testament's emphasis on cultic holiness. Neyrey provides numerous examples from each of these three categories in Luke-Acts to illustrate this point.[78] Perhaps this is another way Luke presents Jesus as the High Priest, as one who is qualified for His position as well as His sacrifice for sins because of His radical holiness.

Luke alone records the healing of the ten lepers, (Luke 17:11–19). He tells them to "go and show yourselves to the priests." Why would Jesus say that? According to Luke, Jesus did not heal them and then tell them to go to the priests. When a person was cleansed from leprosy, he had to appear before the priest and be declared ceremonial clean before he could re-enter society. But when Jesus told them to show themselves to the priests, they still had leprosy! In desperation, they obeyed, and Luke 17:14 indicates "while they were going," they were healed. Of course, nine went their way, but one came back to Jesus and thanked Him. The tenth leper came back and "showed himself" to Jesus to express gratitude for being healed. The symbolism here is difficult to miss: the cleansed leper showed himself to Jesus, who in Luke's view is God's High Priest.

Further evidence for Luke's emphasis on the priesthood of Jesus may be adduced from Irenaeus (c. AD 120–202), Jerome (c. AD 347–420), and Augustine (AD 354–430) in their discussions on the interrelationship of the Synoptic Gospels. Irenaeus was among the earliest to link the four living creatures in Rev 4:6–8 to the four Gospels. He linked the ox with Luke's Gospel because it pictured Jesus' "sacrificial and sacerdotal order."[79] Irenaeus also observed that Luke's Gospel

---

[77] J. B. Chance, *Jerusalem, the Temple, and the New Age in Luke-Acts* (Macon: Mercer University Press, 1988), 63. Note the use of ἀναβαίνω in Peter's sermon in Acts 2:34, the cultic significance of which is pointed out by T. F. Torrance, *Space, Time and Resurrection* (London: Oxford Univ. Press, 1976), 108–9. D. Farrow's work, *Ascension and Ecclesia*, discusses the role of the ascension in the New Testament and supports Luke's priestly Christology.

[78] Neyrey, *The Passion According to Luke*, 163–65.

[79] Irenaeus, *Against Heresies*, 3.14.1.

begins with Zechariah the priest in the temple offering a sacrifice. Jerome applied the ox to Luke for the same reasons. While Matthew seems to emphasize Christ's kingship, Luke, according to Augustine, emphasizes His priesthood. He derives this distinction primarily from a study of the differing genealogies found in Matthew and Luke. Matthew carries the line of Jesus from David through Solomon, thus emphasizing the kingly aspect of the descent. Luke differs from Matthew at this point, tracing Jesus' descent through David's son Nathan, who was never a king. Thus, Augustine appends the symbol of the lion in Revelation 4 (kingship) to Matthew's Gospel and the symbol of the bull (priestly sacrifice) to Luke's Gospel.[80]

Christological Titles in Luke-Acts

The lexical pair *archēgos* and *sōtēr* as titles for Jesus occur together in the New Testament only in Acts 5:31 and Heb 2:10. This is significant in and of itself, but the parallels do not stop there. *Archēgos* appears in the New Testament only four times: Acts 3:15; 5:31; Heb 2:10; and 12:2. Johnston observes that there are other verbal agreements concomitant with the use of *archēgos*, namely "six common to Luke and Hebrews; two found in Luke, Acts and Hebrews; and five (besides ἀρχηγός [*archēgos*]) in Hebrews and Acts. . . ."[81] Jones points out the additional similarity between the phrase *archēgon tēs sōtērias* in Heb 2:10 and *archēgon tēs zōēs* in Acts 3:15, "since in Aramaic the same term, *hayye*, means both 'life' and 'salvation.'"[82]

This concept of "pioneer" or "leader" can also be compared to *aitios*, "source," in Heb 5:9 where we have the phrase "source of eternal salvation." The word *aitios* occurs only five times in the New Testament: three times in Luke, once in Acts, and once in Hebrews.

In Heb 2:10 and 12:2 where *archēgos* occurs, Jesus is said to have been made "perfect" (*teleiōsai*) and to be the "perfecter" (*teleiōtēn*) of our faith. The noun *teleiōsis* occurs only twice in the New Testament: once in Luke and once in Hebrews. Hebrews 2:10 compares very closely to the words of Jesus in Luke 13:32, when he said: "I'm driving out demons and performing healings today and tomorrow, and on the third day I will complete My work" (*teleioumai*). Such linguistic

---

[80] See also M. Parsons, "Who Wrote the Gospel of Luke?" *BR* 17 (2001): 12–21, 54–55.

[81] G. Johnston, "Christ as ARCHEGOS," *NTS* 27 (1981): 381–85.

[82] D. L. Jones, "The Title 'Author of Life (Leader)' in the Acts of the Apostles," *SBLSP* 33 (1994): 627–36.

usages, unique to Luke-Acts and Hebrews, attributed to Jesus and invested with the same (or very similar) meanings between the two works, appear more than coincidental.

The Lukan use of *kurios*, "Lord,"[83] as a reference to God is found frequently in Hebrews, but infrequently in the Pauline Letters. In Luke, it occurs at least 18 times in the birth narratives alone. The significant study of this subject by Rowe begins with the birth narratives in Luke and shows how Luke's use of *kurios* there "shapes fundamentally both the construction of the identity of God and Jesus in the Gospel narrative and our perception of it."[84] Luke introduces Jesus as "Lord" in Luke 1:43 and again in Luke 2:11. The next two chapters reveal Luke's intentional ambiguity in his use of the term "Lord." For Rowe, to ask about the identity of the "Lord" is to answer "God" and "Jesus." He states:

> Yet within the ambiguity the structure and movement of the story shift the focus from *kurios ho theos* to the *kurios Christos*. The narrative itself is the theology: the coming of the *kurios Christos* is the coming of the *kurios ho theos*. The opening of the Gospel thus narrates, in the move from promise to active fulfillment, the presence of the God of Israel in the life of Jesus.[85]

This ambiguity occurs throughout Luke and Acts, as can be seen in the sermon at Nazareth in Luke 4, the healing of the paralytic in Luke 5:17–26, the sending of the 70 in Luke 10:1–24, the quotation of Ps 110:1 in Luke 20:41–44, and Peter's sermon at Pentecost in Acts 2. Guthrie remarks that the use of *kurios* for God is so frequent in Acts "that it is all the more remarkable when the title is undoubtedly used of Jesus."[86] Peter, citing Joel 2:32, applies the title to Jesus. Fletcher-Louis speaks of an "established scholarly tradition which sees in the use of this title, and the interest in his name an identification of Jesus with Yahweh."[87] Although it is not unknown in the Pauline Letters, "Lord" is used there primarily as a title for Jesus and not as a reference to God.[88] "Through narrative development, Luke uses *kurios* to

---

[83] For a survey of literature on this subject, consult C. Rowe, *Early Narrative Christology: The Lord in the Gospel of Luke*, BZNW 139 (Berlin: Walter de Gruyter, 2006), 1–9.

[84] Ibid., 199–200.

[85] Ibid., 200.

[86] D. Guthrie, *New Testament Theology* (Downers Grove: InterVarsity, 1981), 294.

[87] Fletcher-Louis, *Luke-Acts: Angels, Christology and Soteriology*, 21. Fletcher-Louis adds: "Given the recent work of Fossum, and others on the Jewish speculation on God's Name, this Lukan material begs further consideration in the context of a very specific Jewish tradition."

[88] For the usage in Paul, see Rowe, *Early Narrative Christology*, 221–26.

make an essential claim about the relation between Jesus and the God of Israel: Jesus of Nazareth is the movement of God in one human life so much so that it is possible to speak of God and Jesus together as *kurios*."[89] Rowe observes that Luke stresses "the totality of the life of Jesus *kurios* as the embodied revelation of *kurios ho theos*."[90] This is of course a precise description of Heb 1:1–2.

In Luke 20:41–44, Jesus quotes Ps 110:1. The Christological use of "Lord" in Ps 110:1 ("The Lord declared to my Lord") and the use of the Greek possessive pronoun *mou*, "my," are often linked by commentators to the first use of "Lord" in Luke 1:43 where Elizabeth in her song exclaims ". . . that the mother of my Lord should come to me?" As Rowe notes, "Luke's *kurios* Christology is wrought in intimate connection to the Jewish Scriptures. . . . Psalm 110:1 is, hence, the scriptural *Ausgangspunkt* [starting point] for the construction of the identity of the *kurios* in the larger story, as Luke develops narratively the potential theological and Christological significance inherent in the word-play."[91] The theological significance of Ps 110:1 for the author of Hebrews is well known.

The use of the title "Son of God" for Jesus in Luke-Acts and Hebrews merits continued study. Lukan studies confirm that this title bears significant weight in Luke-Acts.[92] It also carries important theological weight in Hebrews, as Jesus is described as "Son" in the prologue before any other title is used. The theological development of Jesus as both "Son" and "High Priest" is fundamental to the argument of Hebrews. In fact, the sonship motif is as significant in Hebrews as the high priesthood.

Further study on the use of Christological titles in Luke-Acts and Hebrews is needed, but enough similarity can be shown to merit a positive comparison for our purposes of authorship identification, and the evidence above supports our contention of Lukan authorship of Hebrews.

---

[89] Ibid., 217–18.

[90] Ibid., 218.

[91] Ibid., 175–76.

[92] E.g., see the discussion in Green, *The Theology of the Gospel of Luke,* 26–27, 55–67; and Neyrey, *The Passion According to Luke,* 166–79.

Summary of Christological Comparison in Luke-Acts and Hebrews

In summary, there is a common Christological substratum undergirding Luke-Acts and Hebrews. In both we find an emphasis on Christ's humanity, His completed work, and His present glorified state. The concept of Jesus as the great High Priest, which is so prominent in Hebrews, is more prominent in Luke-Acts than in any other New Testament book. Along this line, Jervell remarks, "the Messiah of Luke-Acts is the most Jewish Messiah within the New Testament."[93]

Eschatology in Luke-Acts and Hebrews

From the standpoint of eschatology, Luke-Acts and Hebrews also share common ground. Comparison between the eschatological outlooks of Luke-Acts and Hebrews is made difficult by the debated issues relative to the three books. Fitzmyer states that Lukan eschatology is the most difficult and most controversial aspect of Lukan theology today.[94] The primary question revolves around whether Conzelmann's assertion is correct that Luke did not expect an imminent eschaton, and instead presents a "modified" version of the other synoptic writers (i.e., a delayed parousia). Conzelmann assumes that the early Christian church lived with the hope of an imminent return of Christ, but when this was not realized, a crisis arose. Luke wrote to ease this theological crisis by issuing a thoroughgoing reinterpretation of the early church's view.

While it is beyond the scope of this work to present a thorough discussion of these matters, Conzelmann's thesis has been taken to task and must be substantially modified.[95] Fitzmyer accurately portrays the Lukan eschatological outlook as (1) in line with the other synoptic writers in his belief in an imminent return of Christ, (2) reflective of the already/not yet tension where the present is a time

---

[93] Jervell, *The Theology of the Acts of the Apostles*, 13, 121.

[94] Fitzmyer, *The Gospel According to Luke (I–IX)*, 1:231.

[95] See, for example, Fitzmyer, *Luke I–IX*, 1:231–34; Franklin, *Christ the Lord*, 9–47; and E. E. Ellis, *Eschatology in Luke*, FBBS 30 (Philadelphia: Fortress, 1972). Gaventa notes the failure of Conzelmann's thesis because he sought Luke's theology only in his redactional changes to his sources, "a methodological blooper of the first rank." B. Gaventa, "Towards a Theology of Acts: Reading and ReReading," *Int* 42 (1988): 146–57. See also Marshall, *Luke: Historian and Theologian*, 19–20; and J. T. Carroll, *Response to the End of History: Eschatology and Situation in Luke-Acts*, SBLDS 92 (Atlanta: Scholars Press, 1988).

of eschatological fulfillment (realized eschatology) and yet there is a consummation at the Second Coming of Christ, and (3) a desire on Luke's part to shift the emphasis from the eschaton to the *sēmeron* "today" to show that present Christian conduct is informed by eschatological themes.[96] These factors should be kept in mind when comparing Lukan eschatology with that of Hebrews.

Eschatology is as difficult a subject in Hebrews as in Luke-Acts because of the debate over a supposed platonic dualism at the heart of the book. There is without a doubt a dualism that pervades Hebrews. The crucial question is whether this dualism is to be accounted for as platonic thought mediated through Philo of Alexandria, or whether it is better accounted for under the rubric of apocalyptic Judaism mediated through the Old Testament Scriptures and cultus. Again, numerous books and articles have been written on this subject, and it is beyond our scope to delve into the question extensively. Suffice it to say that the supposed dependence of Hebrews on Philo has been severely shaken in recent years, and it seems best to accept the Old Testament apocalyptic background as the most adequate explanation.[97]

To what extent are Luke-Acts and Hebrews similar with regard to eschatology? Jones states that to

> prove the existence of what we may call a family likeness, shared by Luke and Hebrews, it is not sufficient to point to general and specific correspondences alone: it is also necessary to show, as far as may be possible, that the two writings stand together in contrast to the other families of writings in the New Testament.[98]

Jones devotes half of his article to discussing the eschatological similarities between Luke-Acts and Hebrews and how they differ from the other books of the New Testament, especially Mark, the Pauline corpus, and the Johannine writings. The argument is involved and need not be rehearsed here. The key difference is that there is less

---

[96] J. Fitzmyer, *The Acts of the Apostles: A New Translation with Introduction and Commentary*, AB (New York: Doubleday, 1998), 231. See also Ellis, *Eschatology in Luke*.

[97] Crucial literature includes R. Williamson, *Philo and the Epistle to the Hebrews* (Leiden: Brill, 1970); C. K. Barrett, "Eschatology of the Epistle to the Hebrews," in *The Background of the New Testament and its Eschatology: C. H. Dodd Festschrift*, ed. W. D. Davies and D. Daube (Cambridge: Cambridge University Press, 1956), 363–93; L. D. Hurst, "Eschatology and 'Platonism' in the Epistle to the Hebrews," *SBLSP* (Chico, CA: Scholars Press, 1984); L. D. Hurst, *The Epistle to the Hebrews: Its Background of Thought* (New York: Cambridge University Press, 1990). M. Isaacs, *Sacred Space: An Approach to the Theology of the Epistle to the Hebrews*, JSNTSup 73 (Sheffield: Sheffield Academic Press, 1992), 55, supported Williamson's conclusion.

[98] Jones, "The Epistle to the Hebrews and the Lucan Writings," 129.

emphasis on the parousia in Luke-Acts and Hebrews than in Mark, Paul, or John. This does not constitute a contradiction between the New Testament writers; rather, it merely illustrates the different emphases in their writings.

This change of emphasis is evident in Luke 22:69 when compared with the parallel account in Mark 14:62. Mark concludes his version with a reference to the parousia. However, Luke omits any reference to the parousia and concludes with, "But from now on the Son of man shall be seated at the right hand of the power of God." Thus Luke places the emphasis on the exaltation of Christ at the right hand of God. As Franklin points out, Luke's emphasis here is controlled not by a desire to express a delay in the parousia, but by the desire to emphasize present belief along with future hope.[99]

Jones's thesis that there is a "family likeness" in eschatological matters between Luke-Acts and Hebrews in comparison with the rest of the New Testament writers has been confirmed by other New Testament scholars. For example, John Drury writes,

> . . . Luke and Hebrews are fundamentally at one. Prophecy and fulfillment make sense of the relation between the Christian "now" and the Jewish "then" in both their schemes. In Hebrews the old cultic regulations are fulfilled in Christ's eternal and heavenly priesthood, the earnest looking forward of the old historical characters in the perfection of Christian existence. The earthly life of Jesus is the middle of time, the "little while" which links these separate epochs by his coming as both fulfillment and forerunning pioneer. The faithful Christian is set between this centre and the end. In Hebrews as in Luke the fires of earlier eschatological expectation have cooled . . . because the Church has found plenty to get on with in the present.[100]

Likewise, Goppelt places his treatment of Luke and Hebrews in the same chapter because of their similar theological emphases when compared with the rest of the New Testament. In every respect Hebrews offers an interpretation of the gospel that is not dependent on Paul and John. It was written for the community on a long journey; they were growing tired under the pressure of a hostile society. In this way Hebrews exhibits the greatest affinity with Luke-Acts in the New Testament.[101]

---

[99] Franklin, *Christ the Lord*, 28.

[100] J. Drury, *Tradition and Design in Luke's Gospel: a Study in Early Christian Historiography* (Atlanta: John Knox, 1976), 21.

[101] L. Goppelt, *Theology of the New Testament*, ed. J. Roloff, trans. J. Alsup, (Grand Rapids: Eerdmans, 1982), 2:265–66.

Goppelt points out that Luke and Hebrews have less emphasis on the parousia than other New Testament writings. They focus more on individual eschatology, in keeping with their emphasis on Christ's exaltation more than His parousia. In Goppelt's words, "That meant: the expectation became permeable to an individual eschatology."[102]

Franklin summarizes Luke's eschatological focus on the exaltation of Christ:

> He writes to meet the ambiguities in the lives of his readers caused by doubts, persecutions, and disappointments. In this situation he summons them to make an act of faith in the present lordship of Jesus, in the present transcendent reality of the kingdom. Their hopes are removed from this world; they rest on faith in the unseen.[103]

A comparison of this statement with Goppelt's analysis of Hebrews reveals the close proximity with which Luke-Acts and Hebrews stand:

> The community to which the author addressed himself was comparable to the people of Israel during the wilderness wanderings. Like Israel back then, so now the community too was in danger of succumbing to fatigue (3:12f.); it became disappointed that the path to the promised land had become so long and arduous. Without the imagery that meant: the community had become dismayed over the fact that the revelation of glory promised it had not come about visibly and instead it experienced one new affliction after another (3:7ff.; 6:12; 10:36ff.; 12:4–11). This sense of dismay produced a result typical for the second generation. Christians began to flag in their striving to lead a life by faith (2:13; 12:4) and conformed themselves once again to a life of worldly standards (13:13f.).[104]

One might also examine Luke's alteration of the wording of his quotation from Joel 2:28 in Acts 2:17. Where the LXX reads *meta tauta* (lit. "after these things"), Luke has inserted *en tais eschatais hēmerais* ("in the last days"). The only other place where this phrase occurs is in the LXX of Isa 2:1–3 (note that the phrase does not occur in the parallel to the Isaiah passage, Mic 4:1–3), and the Isaiah passage is significant for Luke's interpretation of Pentecost. The author of Hebrews makes use of a similar phrase in the Greek text of Heb 1:2.

The eschatological perspectives of Luke and Hebrews are quite similar, and the texts seem to reveal a similar background and need on the part of the readership. This theological similarity, particularly

---

[102] Ibid., 288.

[103] Franklin, *Christ the Lord,* 47.

[104] Goppelt, *Theology,* 2:242.

as it stands over against the other New Testament writers, furnishes another argument for the Lukan authorship of Hebrews.

Prophecy/Promise and Fulfillment in Luke-Acts and Hebrews

It is generally recognized that the theme of prophecy and fulfillment plays a major role in Lukan theology.[105] Against Conzelmann, Luke distinguishes two salvation-historical eras: the time of prophecy and the time of fulfillment. The time of fulfillment is divided into the time of Jesus and the time of His witnesses, and the latter can be differentiated into the time of the eyewitnesses and the time after that, including the Lukan generation (Luke 1:1–4).[106] Luke presents Jesus as God's final prophet who stands in the long line of prophets as the culmination of God's address to His people. However, he presents the tradition in a way that stresses the role of Jesus as prophet by characterizing His teaching as the "Word," or "Word of God," even where it is not so designated in his sources.[107] This theological motif, which pervades Luke-Acts, is also characteristic of the letter to the Hebrews.

In an excursus on the fulfillment of prophecy in Luke-Acts at the end of his commentary, Talbert argues that in Luke, fulfilled prophecy comes from three types of sources: (1) the Jewish scriptures, (2)

---

[105] See, for example, T. R. Carruth, "The Jesus-as-Prophet Motif in Luke-Acts," (Ph.D. diss., Baylor University, 1973); Talbert, *Reading Luke*, 234–40; id., *Acts* (Atlanta: John Knox, 1984), 91–103; Fitzmyer, *Acts*, 287–301; R. Karris, *What Are They Saying about Luke and Acts? A Theology of the Faithful God* (New York: Paulist, 1979). More recent efforts synthesize and evaluate the state of scholarship on this subject: Bock, *Proclamation from Prophecy and Pattern;* M. Strauss, *The Davidic Messiah in Luke-Acts: The Promise and its Fulfillment in Lukan Christology,* JSNTSup 110 (Sheffield: Sheffield Academic Press, 1995); A. Hastings, *Prophet and Witness in Jerusalem: A Study in the Teaching of St. Luke* (Baltimore: Helicon, 1958); P. G. Voss, *Die Christologie der lukanischen Schriften in Grundzügen* (Paris/Brugge: Brouwer, 1965), 155–70; G. R. Greene, "The Portrayal of Jesus as Prophet in Luke-Acts" (Ph.D. diss., Southern Baptist Theological Seminary, 1975); P. S. Minear, *To Heal and to Reveal: The Prophetic Vocation According to Luke* (New York: Seabury, 1976); A. George, *Études sur l'oeuvre de Luc* (Paris: Gabalda, 1978), 79–84; D. Hill, *New Testament Prophecy* (London: Marshall, Morgan & Scott, 1979), 48–49. Cf. D. Moessner, *Lord of the Banquet: The Literary and Theological Significance of the Lukan Travel Narrative* (Minneapolis: Fortress, 1989), for this theme as it is played out in the Lukan travel narrative. See also S. van den Eynde, "Children of the Promise: On the *diathēkē* Promise to Abraham in Luke 1:72 and Acts 3:25," in *The Unity of Luke-Acts* (Leuven: Leuven University Press, 1999), 469–82.

[106] F. Bovon, *Luke 1: A Commentary on the Gospel of Luke 1:1–9:50*, trans. C. Thomas, Her (Minneapolis: Fortress, 2002), 11.

[107] See L. O'Reilly, *Word and Sign in the Acts of the Apostles: A Study in Lukan Theology*, Analecta Gregoriana 243 (Rome: Editrice Pontificia Universita Gregoriana, 1987), 36.

a living prophet (Zachariah, Simeon, etc.), and (3) heavenly beings (angels and the resurrected Jesus).[108] In his prologue, Luke refers to the "events" he is about to narrate as having been "fulfilled." Fitzmyer recognizes that these events "belong to a past and a present which are not unrelated to what God has promised in the Old Testament."[109]

The infancy narratives (Luke 1–2) function in Luke's overall general plan to show the continuity of salvation history. The ministry of Jesus is firmly rooted in and emerges from the Old Testament Scripture and history of Israel. The temptation narrative in Luke 4 is presented by Luke so as to parallel Jesus with the Old Testament prophet Moses.[110] The preaching of Jesus at Nazareth in Luke 4 functions as the commencement of His prophetic role.[111] Jesus assumed the role of the long-awaited eschatological prophet with His statement, "Today as you listen, this Scripture has been fulfilled" (Luke 4:21). The public ministry of Jesus inaugurated here is cast by Luke alone in the mold of the calling and fate of the eschatological prophet.

The arrival of Jesus in Jerusalem (and the events leading up to His arrest and crucifixion) are narrated by Luke in such a way as to emphasize the following themes:

1. The rejection and death of Jesus is described in terms of the martyrdom of the prophets in the Old Testament.
2. The catalyst that prompted the plot to kill Jesus was that He had assumed a prophet's role and overstepped the boundaries of the interpretation of the Torah by official Jewry.
3. Jesus is portrayed not merely as a prophet, but as the final prophet.
4. Jesus was rejected like all of God's prophets.
5. In Luke 24, the prophetic role of Jesus is stressed in that He is seen not only as the object of prophecy, but as a prophet in His own right who brings to completion the Word of God.[112]

---

[108] Talbert, *Reading Luke*, 234–40.

[109] Fitzmyer, *Luke I–IX*, 289.

[110] Ibid., 136.

[111] Crump notes, "It is clear that Luke presents Jesus as looking upon himself as *the* final prophet, from the very beginning of his earthly ministry." He adds: "Consequently, this also indicates that *Luke* presents Jesus as the final Prophet from the beginning of his ministry." D. Crump, *Jesus the Intercessor: Prayer and Christology in Luke-Acts*, Biblical Studies Library (Grand Rapids: Baker, 1992), 139. Of course this is precisely the point of the author of Hebrews in 1:1–2.

[112] Carruth, "The Jesus-as-Prophet Motif in Luke-Acts," 254–55.

The scheme of prophecy and fulfillment continues in Acts with the emphasis on the Abrahamic promise in Stephen's speech in Acts 7.[113] Furthermore, in Acts, Luke has identified Jesus with three figures of Jewish eschatological expectations, who are described in prophetic categories: the Servant-Messiah, the Prophet like Moses (Acts 3:22; 7:37), and the returning Elijah (prominent in the language and details of the ascension narrative).[114] From this it becomes quite evident that the motif of prophecy and fulfillment plays a crucial role for Luke.

More recently, David Moessner has dealt thoroughly with the connection of Jesus as the Prophet like Moses in the framework and theology of the Lukan travel narrative.[115] He suggests that in this narrative Jesus' speech parallels that of Moses, and that the journey of Jesus toward Jerusalem recapitulates Israel's journey in the wilderness as presented in Deuteronomy. Like Carruth, Moessner believes that Luke casts Jesus in His public ministry as an eschatological prophet in Luke 4:16–30. He argues based on Luke 9:1–50 that Jesus emerges from the Galilean ministry bound for Jerusalem as the Prophet like Moses.[116] In Luke 10:1, the sending out of the 70 compares to Num 11:16, where Moses appoints the 70 elders. Jesus conceived of His death as another exodus in Luke 12:50.

Jesus' journey to Jerusalem is immediately preceded by the transfiguration on the mountain (Luke 9:28–36). He is portrayed by Luke here as the Prophet like Moses (Deut 18:15–19). Of the three Synoptics, Luke's version of the heavenly declaration (v. 35) is the only one that matches the vocabulary and word order of the LXX of Deut 18:15b. Moessner writes:

> Thus, like all Israel, who on the mountain hundreds of years earlier witnessed the authoritative revelation of the divine voice through Moses, so now on the mountain the three disciples, representing the Twelve and hence the twelve tribes of all Israel, witness the definitive revelation of the divine voice

[113] N. Dahl, "The Story of Abraham in Luke-Acts," *Studies in Luke-Acts*, ed. L. E. Keck and J. L. Martyn (New York: Abingdon, 1966), 139–58.

[114] Carruth, "The Jesus-as-Prophet Motif in Luke-Acts," 293.

[115] Moessner, *Lord of the Banquet*. The purpose of the travel narrative in Luke has been variously understood. For a summary listing of proposals with bibliography, see D. Pao, *Acts and the Isaianic New Exodus* (Grand Rapids: Baker, 2002), 2–5. Previously published in 2000 by Mohr (Paul Siebeck) as volume 130 in WUNT, Series 2.

[116] Moessner, *Lord of the Banquet*, 56. The prophetic parallels of Moses in Deuteronomy to Jesus in Luke 9:1–50 are set forth on pp. 60–70.

through Jesus, God's Chosen Son. Like Moses, Jesus is called to mediate the voice of God.[117]

The notion of Jesus as God's final prophet is highlighted in the Lukan travel narrative, which is "the story of the journeying salvation of the New Exodus prophesied by Moses to the people of the Horeb covenant as the fulfillment of the promises to Abraham and his descendants."[118] Moses' words in the LXX of Deut 1:1 are remarkably similar to Jesus' words in Luke 24:44.

In Acts, Luke continues the story by narrating the "journeying of the people of God whose leaders imitate their Prophet Messiah in proclaiming the glad tidings of the kingdom of God." The longest journey section of Acts (19:21–28:31) has many similarities to the Lukan travel narrative.[119]

David Pao's significant study of the Isaianic New Exodus motif in Acts illustrates the crucial role that Isaiah plays in the narrative framework of Luke-Acts.[120] Pao demonstrates that the extended quotation of Isa 40:3–5 at the beginning of Jesus' ministry is programmatic for the rest of the Lukan narrative. He finds that an allusion or explicit quotation of Isaiah can be found in all five of the programmatic statements in the narrative of Luke-Acts: Luke 4:16–30; Luke 24:44–49; Acts 1:8; 13:46–47; and 28:25–28.[121] The references in Acts to Christianity as the "way" also illustrate the role of the Isaianic New Exodus for Luke's narrative theology. Pao's book illuminates this concept and use of Scripture, as well as the importance of the "exodus" theme for Luke.

It is clear that Luke-Acts is deliberately cast in a journey motif beginning with Jesus as God's eschatological prophet and continuing with the people of God who expand the salvation journey (via Paul) to the ends of the earth, Rome. Luke's view of Moses (as seen from his portrait of Jesus as the Prophet-like-Moses in Luke 9:1–50 and Acts 7) confirms that the prophecy in Deut 18:15–16 is "clearly one of the dominant themes in Luke's Christology."[122] Indeed, the appearance of

---

[117] Ibid., 61.

[118] Ibid., 290.

[119] Ibid., 296–97.

[120] See Pao, *Acts and the Isaianic New Exodus*.

[121] Ibid., 109.

[122] M. R. D'Angelo, *Moses in the Letter to the Hebrews*, SBLDS 42 (Missoula, MT: Scholars Press, 1979), 3. Dodd notes that explicit reference to Deut 18:15 occurs only in Acts, C. H. Dodd, *According to the Scriptures: The Substructure of New Testament Theology* (London: Nisbet & Co.,

the exodus theme in strategic places in Luke reveals his theological attempt to parallel Moses' work of redemption for Israel with Jesus' work of redemption in Jerusalem.[123]

Turning to Hebrews, does the prophecy-fulfillment motif play a leading role in the author's conceptual framework? Can the theological construct of the letter be described in any way as a "journey" similar to what we find in Luke-Acts? Finally, does the author of Hebrews approach the Prophet like Moses motif in a similar fashion to Luke-Acts? We shall find that all of these questions can be answered in the affirmative.

The prophecy-fulfillment motif plays a crucial role in Hebrews from the very outset of the book. The prologue (1:1–4) states that God has spoken in former days by the prophets, but now He has spoken by His Son. Jesus is here presented as God's final revelation, His final prophet through whom God has decisively spoken. This may be compared to the prologue in Luke where the events to be narrated are described as having been fulfilled.[124]

The prologue to Hebrews reveals the author's conception of the history of revelation as longitudinal: earlier and piecemeal forms of God's address have been replaced by Jesus as God's final address. For the writer of Hebrews, both continuity and discontinuity are factors to be recognized in the process of revelation history. Thus, Heb 1:1–4 states theologically what Luke narrates historically in his Gospel.

Hughes has shown through a careful literary analysis of the text how the prologue in Hebrews functions in a programmatic way. The writer draws a contrast between Jesus and the angels (1:5–2:4), Jesus and Moses (3:1–6), and Jesus and the Aaronic priesthood (4:14–5:10; 7:1–28); it is the motif of God's new revelation that serves as the guiding paradigm for the development of the argument.[125]

1957), 55. See also R. Nixon, *The Exodus in the New Testament* (London: Tyndale, 1963); and J. Reynolds, "A Comparative Study of the Exodus Motif in the Epistle to the Hebrews," (Ph.D. diss., Southwestern Baptist Theological Seminary, 1976), 243, who notes Acts is more similar to Hebrews on this issue than any other New Testament book. Recently, the work of K. Schiffner, *Lukas liest Exodus: Eine Untersuchung zur Aufnahme ersttestamentlicher Befreiungsgeschichte im lukanischen Werk als Schrift-Lektüre*, BWA(N)T (Stuttgart: W. Kihlhammer, 2008), addresses this subject in great depth. See esp. 217–414.

[123] As stated by P. Walker, *Jesus and the Holy City: New Testament Perspectives* (Grand Rapids: Eerdmans, 1996), 79–80.

[124] Fitzmyer, *Luke I–IX*, 293.

[125] G. Hughes, *Hebrews and Hermeneutics*, SNTSMS 36 (Cambridge: Cambridge University Press, 1979), 6.

The relationship of the old to the new serves as a key theme in Hebrews, which is also true with Luke-Acts. Franklin has noted that Luke views the institutions and revelatory events of the past as having been superseded by the new act of God in Christ. This invalidates for Luke any attempt to cling to the old.[126] In Luke, Jesus is set over against the old Israel; in Acts it is the church as the new people of God who exhibit both elements of continuity and discontinuity with the people of God in the old order, and the entire plot is set in the "journey" motif.

This theme, which is certainly not alien to the rest of the New Testament, finds its greatest focus in Luke-Acts and Hebrews, and thus a further conceptual similarity among the three books is adduced.

To illustrate the "journey" motif of Hebrews, one need only recall the title of Käsemann's *The Wandering People of God*, which for our investigation could be changed to *The* Journeying *People of God*. The motif is clearly seen in Heb 3:7–4:13 and 10:19–13:21. In the latter section Käsemann examines the verbs of motion that illustrate the journey motif.[127] The culmination of this journey is presented in Heb 13:13–14, where the readers are exhorted to "go to Him outside the camp, bearing His disgrace. For here we do not have an enduring city; instead, we seek the one to come." Whereas Acts portrays in a narrative framework the people (Christians) of the "Prophet like Moses" journeying in the midst of persecution, the author of Hebrews portrays in a hortatory framework the same Christians on that same journey as being challenged to "go to" the end of their journey. The journey motif dovetails nicely in Luke-Acts and Hebrews.[128]

Furthermore, the notion of suffering along the way is paramount in Luke-Acts as, for example, Acts 14:22b: "It is necessary to pass through many troubles on our way into the kingdom of God." The same motif is prominent in Hebrews with such statements as "you have not yet resisted to the point of shedding your blood" (Heb 12:4), and, "Let us then go to Him outside the camp, bearing His disgrace" (Heb 13:13).

---

[126] Franklin, *Christ the Lord*, 44.

[127] E. Käsemann, *The Wandering People of God: an Investigation of the Letter to the Hebrews*, trans. from the 2nd German edition by R. Harrisville and I. Sandberg (Minneapolis: Augsburg, 1984), 23.

[128] "Hebrews is the classic Christian restatement of the Old Testament journey motif." D. Farrow, *Ascension and Ecclesia on the Significance of the Doctrine of the Ascension for Ecclesiology and Christian Cosmology* (Grand Rapids: Eerdmans, 1999), 33.

Finally, the role of Moses in Hebrews can be compared to Luke-Acts. Moses is an important figure in the explication of Christology in Luke, John, Paul, and Hebrews. D'Angelo has argued that the Pauline and Johannine pictures of Moses in the framework of their Christologies stand over against that of Luke, whose approach is somewhat different.[129] Based on Hebrews' use of Exod 25:40 as a foundational text for its argument, and that Luke likewise cites this text at a pivotal point (Acts 7:44), we can see that the role of Moses in Luke-Acts and Hebrews is quite similar.

The importance of Exod 25:40 for the exegetical principle of Hebrews 8–9 is well known. The use of *tupos*, "type," in this section as well as its function in the overall theological argument is likewise crucial. Exod 25:40 and "type" are linked by Luke in Acts 7:44 and illustrate their theological kinship.[130]

There are numerous similarities between Acts 7 and Hebrews 11 regarding the career of Moses, which have already been mentioned and which further illustrate the conceptual similarity between Luke-Acts and Hebrews. Both Exod 2:11–15 and Exod 25:40 are alluded to in Acts 7 and Hebrews 11. For Luke and the author of Hebrews, Jesus is the prophet like Moses as well as the architect of a better tabernacle than the one made according to the *tupos* given to Moses on the mountain. Edvin Larsson concludes a study of temple criticism and Acts 6–7 with the statement: "The entire pattern of promise and fulfillment in Hebrews forms a mighty illustration to this line of thought in the speech of Stephen."[131]

The concept of "promise" in Hebrews is apparent in the frequent use of the *epaggelia* word group[132] (14 times), and is related to the discussion above. The word *epaggelia* does not occur in Matthew or Mark. It occurs once in Luke, eight times in Acts, and 24 times in Paul. Karris points out that Luke's writings reveal his keen interest in the faithfulness of God who both makes and keeps promises.[133] Luke

---

[129] D'Angelo, *Moses in the Letter to the Hebrews*, 3–10.

[130] J. Héring, *The Epistle to the Hebrews* (London: Epworth, 1979), 66–70. Cf. D'Angelo, *Moses in the Letter to the Hebrews*, 257, for the opposite view that the function and role of "type" and the tabernacle are different in Hebrews and Luke-Acts.

[131] E. Larsson, "Temple Criticism and the Jewish Heritage," *NTS* 39 (1993): 394.

[132] For a discussion of the use of ἐπαγγελία in Hebrews, see P. Ellingworth, *Commentary on Hebrews*, NIGTC (Grand Rapids: Eerdmans, 1993), 238–39; and W. Kurz, "Promise and Fulfillment in Hellenistic Jewish Narratives and in Luke and Acts," in *Unity of Luke-Acts*, 147–70.

[133] Karris, *What Are They Saying about Luke and Acts?*

seems interested in answering the question, "Has God been faithful to the promises He has made to Israel?" Luke's answer is an unqualified "yes," and he uses the proof from prophecy schema to drive the point home. This is, of course, precisely what we find in Hebrews.

Hebrews and Paul appear to differ on the interpretation of "promise." Paul cites Gen 15:6 as the key reference for the promise of descendents to Abraham, whereas Hebrews looks to Genesis 22. Abraham's faith was counted to him as righteousness prior to his circumcision (Genesis 17). When he became the father of all Jews who believe, he also became the father of all Gentiles who believe without being circumcised. This is Paul's focus in Romans 4, especially vv. 10–11, and Galatians 3; hence his appeal to Genesis 15 rather than Genesis 22.

Paul gives a Gentile focus to the promise made to Abraham in Romans 4. However, in Hebrews, one does not find any Gentile interpretation given to an Abrahamic promise. In fact, Gentiles are never mentioned in Hebrews. Paul shows scant interest in the "promised land" of Israel. Texts regarding Abraham's descendents are spiritualized by Paul to refer to Gentiles as well as Jews. Hebrews does virtually the opposite. The author spiritualizes the passages about the land, and never includes Gentiles as referents to passages about Abraham's descendents.[134]

After surveying all the passages in Luke-Acts referring to Abraham, Brawley concludes that these passages furnish a key in understanding Luke's characterization of God.[135] Luke begins with the infancy narratives where both Gabriel's announcement (1:32–33) and answer to Mary (1:37) echo Gen 18:14, which proclaims the power of God to keep His promises. Genesis 22:18, perhaps the *sine qua non* promise of God to Abraham, is quoted in Acts 3:25; 13:28–29; 16:19–31; and 19:1–10.[136] This concept is likewise key for both Paul and Hebrews.

---

[134] These and other related points showing the different foci of Paul and Hebrews are brilliantly discussed in C. P. Anderson, "Who Are the Heirs of the New Age in the Epistle to the Hebrews?" in *Apocalyptic and the New Testament: Essays in Honor of J. Louis Martyn*, JSNTSup 24, ed. J. Marcus and M. Soards (Sheffield: Sheffield Academic Press, 1989), 255–77.

[135] R. Brawley, "Abrahamic Covenant Traditions and the Characterization of God in Luke-Acts," in *The Unity of Luke-Acts*, 109–32.

[136] See the excellent article by S. van den Eynde, "Children of the Promise: on the *diathekē*-promise to Abraham in Luke 1:72 and Acts 3:25," in *The Unity of Luke-Acts*, 469–82.

Additional Arguments

Luke-Acts, Hebrews, and Qumran

Prior to the discovery of the Qumran Scrolls, the body of Jewish writings closest chronologically to the New Testament was the Rabbinic literature ranging from the third to the sixth centuries AD. Years ago, Bruce Metzger studied the formulae used to introduce Old Testament quotations in both the Mishnah (the earliest of the Rabbinic corpus) and the New Testament. Later, Fitzmyer studied the formulae used to introduce quotations of the Old Testament in the Dead Sea Scrolls and compared them with Metzger's findings and the New Testament. Surprisingly, not a single formula found in Metzger's list corresponded to any formula in Fitzmyer's list. The New Testament usage was closer to that of the Dead Sea Scrolls than the Mishnah.[137]

An interesting area of comparison is the similarity of ideas among Luke-Acts, Hebrews, and the Qumran writings.[138] In an addendum to Munck's commentary on Acts, Albright and Mann illustrate the convergence of ideas in certain sections of Acts and Qumran.[139] M. de Jonge and A. S. van der Woude point out that 11Q Melchizedek connects the expressions [*hmbsr*] and [*hmsyh*] in the context of Isa 52:7 and Isa 61:1–2, and that Luke 4:18–30 and Acts 10:36–38 both represent possible parallel connections.[140] Furthermore, chaps. 1, 2 and 3 of Hebrews may have a Qumran background when compared with 11Q Melchizedek. J. de Waard concludes that the resemblance between Acts, Hebrews, and Qumran was so great that some connection must have existed among these writings.[141]

Hebrews emphasizes Christ as a member of the tribe of Judah, instead of portraying Him as a priestly messiah from the Levitical line. Perhaps a plausible explanation for this is that the recipients of Hebrews were being influenced by the Qumranian sect, and the writer

---

[137] J. Fitzmyer, "The Usage of Explicit Old Testament Quotations in Qumran Literature and in the New Testament," in *Essays on the Semitic Background of the New Testament* (Missoula, MT: Scholars Press,1974), 3–58; also see id., *Responses to 101 Questions on the Dead Sea Scrolls* (New York: Paulist, 1992), 105–6.

[138] The Dead Sea Scrolls date from the middle of the second century BC to AD 68.

[139] J. Munck, *The Acts of the Apostles*, AB 31 (New York: Doubleday, 1967), 264–67.

[140] M. de Jonge and A. S. van der Woude, "11Q Melchizedek and the New Testament," *NTS* 12 (1966): 301–26. See also C. A. Evans and J. Sanders, *Luke and Scripture: the Function of Sacred Tradition in Luke-Acts* (Minneapolis: Fortress, 1993), 61–63.

[141] J. de Waard, *A Comparative Study of the Old Testament Text in the Dead Sea Scrolls and in the New Testament* (Leiden: Brill, 1965), 82.

was compelled to counter the Qumranian notion that the Aaronic (Levitical) messiah was more important than the messiah of Israel.[142] To argue the high priesthood of Christ after the order of Melchizedek rather than from Aaron makes little sense if one does not understand the argument to be a polemic against someone claiming superiority for the Levitical line. However, if the major focus of the author of Hebrews was on the Sonship of Christ and His relation to the Father (the high priest motif supporting this), then the need to interpret the discussion as polemical is significantly reduced.

Qumran emphasized such things as ritual baths, angels as saviors, two messiahs, and that the Aaronic line was superior to any other. Luke-Acts and Hebrews allude to many of these ideas. Recently, George Brooke offered a positive comparison of Luke-Acts with the halakhic text 4QMMT, which was officially published in 1994. He observed a number of similarities, including the emphasis that both place on Jerusalem and the temple.[143]

I am not positing any historical connection among Luke-Acts, Hebrews, and the Qumran community. Although there are some similarities, they are outweighed by the differences.[144] The recipients of Hebrews were not members of the Qumran community, but may have been in some way influenced by some of their teachings, and thus the similarities can be accounted for.[145] Brevard Childs makes the salient point that the basic theological differences in perspective between a closed, ceremonially oriented community such as Qumran, and the call for an open, Christologically centered church of Hebrews, continues to be obvious even to the casual reader.[146] The same might be said for the church in Acts. Furthermore, Hebrews presents Melchizedek as exclusively a priestly figure, whereas in the Qumran community he functioned more as an eschatological figure of judgment to come,

---

[142] F. C. Fensham, "Hebrews and Qumran," *Neot* 5 (1971): 9–21.

[143] G. Brooke, "Luke-Acts and the Qumran Scrolls: The Case of MMT," in *Luke's Literary Achievement: Collected Essays*, ed. C. M. Tuckett, JSNTSup 116 (Sheffield: Sheffield Academic Press, 1995), 72–90.

[144] For examples, see Fitzmyer, *Responses to 101 Questions on the Dead Sea Scrolls*, 102–4.

[145] F. F. Bruce, "To the Hebrews or to the Essenes?" *NTS* 9 (1962–63): 217–32. Ellis notes that a connection between Hebrews and Qumran is "not improbable," but Hebrews' traditions find their closest parallel in other New Testament documents. E. Ellis, *The Making of the New Testament Documents*, Biblical Interpretation Series 39, ed. R. A. Culpepper and R. Rendtorff (Leiden: Brill, 1999), 286–87.

[146] B. Childs, *The New Testament as Canon: An Introduction* (London: SCM, 1984), 411.

according to 11QMelchizedek.[147] Although there are similarities, the Qumran community viewed Melchizedek overall in a different way than did the author of Hebrews.

Isaacs explains the difference between the argument used by the author of Hebrews and that of the Qumran community relative to the temple and the priests. Hebrews demonstrates the superiority of Jesus' priesthood to Aaron's. She then states:

> This argument is far more subversive than Qumran's allegation that the Temple's present high-priestly incumbents, by disregarding the rule of primogeniture, had forfeited their claim to be true heirs of Zadok, or, for that matter, any Pharisaic criticisms of their performance of the pre-scribed rituals. Ultimately, for Hebrews it is not only the Levitical priesthood which is inadequate; even Melchizedek does not provide the definitive model for Jesus, since he resembles Jesus, the son of God (7:3) rather than vice versa. The logic of our author's argument is that there is no longer any role for an on-going priesthood, Aaronic or otherwise![148]

Charles Anderson's cogent assessment is worth noting. Hebrews "readily fits into the Jewish sectarian pattern," which Shaye Cohen describes as a common feature of Jewish sectarianism: polemic against the temple, and particularly its impurity and priestly illegitimacy. However, Anderson observes the difference between Hebrews and Jewish sectarianism: "While Hebrews speaks of ineffectiveness rather than impurity, the temple, the priesthood and the temple ritual legitimated under the former covenant constitute the antithesis of the new and 'true' temple, priesthood and cultic activity."[149] This distinction between ineffectiveness (Hebrews) and impurity (Jewish sectarianism) is worth making.

Angelology

Luke records more instances of angelic activity than any other New Testament writer, and Hebrews is the New Testament book most interested in their theological status.[150] Notice the discussion of angels

---

[147] See the discussion in M. Isaacs, "Hebrews," in *Early Christian Thought in its Jewish Context*, ed. J. Barclay and J. Sweet (Cambridge: Cambridge University Press, 1996), 153.

[148] Isaacs, "Hebrews," 154.

[149] Anderson, "Who are the Heirs of the New Age in the Epistle to the Hebrews," 277. See also S. J. D. Cohen, "The Significance of Yavneh: Pharisees, Rabbis, and the End of Jewish Sectarianism," *HUCA* 55 (1984): 27–53.

[150] J. Green, for example, comments: "Luke's narrative is not itself concerned with an angelology per se, but represents angels only in their subordinate role as those who serve the divine project" (*The Theology of the Gospel of Luke*, 40). This is something of an understatement of

in Heb 1:5–14, where they are described as having worshiped at the nativity. Luke alone among the Gospel writers records this event. Luke has no fewer than 23 clear references to angels in his Gospel and 21 references in Acts. In Luke's Gospel, angelic activity is mentioned throughout the first two chapters (in 14 verses), 9:26; 12:8–9; 15:10; 20:36; 22:43; and 24:4–7. In Acts, note 5:19; 6:15; 7:30,35,38,53; 8:26; 10:3,7,22; 11:13; 12:7–11,15,23; 23:8–9; and 27:23. Angelic activity is referred to in Hebrews in 1:5–14; 2:2,5–9,16; 12:22, 23; and 13:2.

Fletcher-Louis has demonstrated Luke's interaction with Jewish tradition on the subject of angelomorphic humanity. In Luke 24, Luke made use of "a Jewish angelomorphic category as a dialogue partner, insisting that Jesus is more fully human than an angel. . . . The full humanity of the risen Jesus would have been more problematic for a Jewish readership, than his full Divinity."[151] Of course, the author of Hebrews has a keen interest in comparing Jesus to the angels in Hebrews 1, and this comparison is clearly theologically motivated. Our purpose here is not to delve into the intricate question of whether or not the New Testament authors make use of angelomorphic categories in their Christological formulations, but rather to show the Jewish background of Luke's writings in this area. Fletcher-Louis could speak of Luke-Acts as being "consciously constructed, both Christologically and soteriologically, in conscious interaction with Jewish traditions of human angelomorphism."[152] He also states that his work "provided substantial evidence to support a Jewish Luke-Acts," and that "various passages dealing with the angelic can only make sense in a specifically Jewish context (Son of Man *passim*; Lk 20:27–40; 24:36ff; Acts 23:8–9)."[153] Fletcher-Louis concludes: "From the point of view of Luke's interest in angels it is worth noting that here we have one small but important piece of corroboratory evidence for a Jewish Luke-Acts."[154]

The Lukan Temptation Narrative (Luke 4:1–13) and Hebrews

Luke places his account of Jesus' temptation within the Old Testament context of Israel's testing in the wilderness. The parallels and

---

Luke's theological interest in angels, but essentially correct in what it affirms. This is identical to the theological perspective of the author of Hebrews.

[151] Fletcher-Louis, *Luke-Acts: Angels, Christology and Soteriology*, 249.

[152] Ibid., 32.

[153] Ibid., 253.

[154] Ibid., 19.

contrasts Luke draws between Jesus' faithfulness through trials and Israel's failure are obvious. Examples include (1) the divine leading (Luke 4:1; Deut 8:2), (2) the correlation of 40 days in Luke's narrative with the 40 years of Israel's wanderings, (3) the statement that Jesus is God's son (Luke 4:3,9) parallels Israel as God's son (Exod 40:22, 23), and (4) the biblical texts cited by Jesus during His testing clearly derive from Israel's testing in the wilderness.[155]

The significance of the faithfulness of Jesus in contrast with the unfaithfulness of Israel during the time of the wilderness wanderings is a prominent part of the argument of Hebrews. Jesus is called a "faithful" high priest in Heb 2:17, and in 3:2 the author says about Him, "He was faithful to the One who appointed Him, just as Moses was in all God's household." In 3:6 Jesus is said to be "faithful as a Son . . . ." Then follows the lengthy section on the wilderness wanderings and Israel's unfaithfulness (3:7–4:13).

Hebrews and the Pisidian Discourse of Acts 13

A comparison of Paul's speech at the synagogue of Antioch in Pisidia in Acts 13:14–41[156] with Hebrews reveals a number of parallels. First, the phrase "word of exhortation" (Acts 13:15) is used in Heb 13:22 to describe the literary genre of the letter. Swetnam points out that this word was used to describe a "homily" or sermon in Jewish synagogue worship.[157] These are the only two occurrences of this phrase in the New Testament.

Second, the emphasis on the forgiveness of sins in Acts 13:38–39 is also in Hebrews (e.g., 9:13–14). I have already shown the lexical similarity between Luke-Acts and Hebrews in the use of *aphesis,* "forgiveness," and that this word is used a majority of the times in Luke-Acts and Hebrews.

Third, the reference to Israel spending 40 years in the wilderness (Acts 13:18) also occurs in Heb 3:17 and in Stephen's speech in Acts 7:36. Fourth, the quotation of Ps 2:7 (Acts 13:33) occurs also in Heb 1:5 and 5:5, but nowhere else in the New Testament. There is a greater connection here than just the fact of quotation. The correlation of

---

[155] See the discussion in Green, *The Theology of the Gospel of Luke,* 26–28.

[156] See E. Lovestam, *Son and Saviour: A Study of Acts 13:32–37,* Coniectanea Neotestamentica 18.5–87 (Lund: C. W. K. Gleerup, 1961), and Bock, *Proclamation from Prophecy and Pattern,* for a complete discussion of Acts 13:14–41.

[157] J. Swetnam, "On the Literary Genre of the 'Epistle' to the Hebrews," *NovT* 11 (1969): 268.

2 Sam 7:11–14 and Ps 2:7 finds clear expression in Luke-Acts and Hebrews in the New Testament.[158] Lovestam states that the quotations of Ps 2:7 in Acts 13:32–33 and Heb 1:5; 5:5 are "of special interest in the present investigation, especially as Luke's writings and Hebrews have various clear points of contact with one another."[159]

Lovestam's work highlights the fact that the Davidic covenant is important to Luke, and is the covenant that has been fulfilled. But he misses Luke's integration of the same Christological categories in dealing with the Gentiles (Acts 13) as he did earlier with a Jewish audience (Acts 2).[160]

Fifth, the unusual citation formula *en heterō legei*, "also said in another passage," occurs in Heb 5:6 and nowhere else in the New Testament.

These similarities are heightened by the fact that the writer to Hebrews chose to describe his work as a "word of exhortation," a phrase possibly used in the sense of a synagogue homily, and that Luke describes Paul's address to the synagogue at Antioch with this same phrase.

In this vein, the remarks of J. Swetnam may serve to further the case for Lukan authorship of Hebrews:

> L. Zunz, in his classic study (Die gottesdienstlichen Vortrage der Juden, historisch entwickelt), says that some homilies were called *brkwt wnhmwt*. Now *nht* is a root whose forms are translated by *paraklesis* in the Septuagint. Is this coincidence casual or is there some intrinsic interconnection? P. Billerbeck says that the homily in the synagogue was properly styled a kerugma. This statement would seem to be borne out in the case of Luke's account of Jesus' preaching in the synagogue, for it is the word used at Lk. iv 44 to describe this activity. The term is also used of Paul's preaching in the synagogue at Acts ix 20. The apparent conflict in terminology between *paraklesis* and *kerugma* might be explicable on the basis of a distinction between types of homilies: the term *kerugma* might be used for a homily which formally proclaims; the term *paraklesis* might be used for a homily which formally consoles. It is worth noting that both Hebrews and the homily delivered at

---

[158] Lovestam, *Son and Saviour*, 12–14, 26–27, 39–40.

[159] Ibid., 26–27.

[160] A fact noted by G. Herrick, "Isaiah 55:3 in Acts 13:34: Luke's Polemic for Equality of Gentile Participation in Davidic Promise," (Ph.D. Diss., Dallas Theological Seminary, 1999), 55–56. Herrick agrees with Goldsmith ("Acts 13:33–37: a Pesher on II Samuel 7") that Luke understood and consciously used Isa 55:3 in Acts 13 (p. 57). He also rightly notes a crucial difference between Luke-Acts and the Old Testament and Intertestamental period's view of the Davidic hope: It is offered to both Jews and Gentiles. He cogently notes that there are many texts in the Old Testament that universalize the Gentile blessing, but there is only one Davidic text that does so—Isa 55:3 (p. 317).

Pisidian Antioch stress the forgiveness of sins, and that the word *kerugma* (*kerussein*) is not found in Hebrews.[161]

If Luke were the author of Hebrews and if his readers were Jewish Christians (former priests), then he has addressed them with a "word of exhortation" in the same way Paul addressed the synagogue in Pisidian Antioch. As a traveling companion with Paul for many years, Luke must have heard Paul preach in synagogues on numerous occasions. Perhaps he was influenced by this method of address and felt that his readers would respond better to it than any other method. Robinson has pointed out that the theme of holding fast to the Lord found in Acts (and specifically in Paul's sermon in 13:14–41) is "very much the tenor of Hebrews."[162]

Hebrews 6:1–2 and Acts

In Heb 6:1–2, there is a remarkable correspondence of thought and language to the entire book of Acts. The following parallels can be observed.[163]

repentance from dead works	–	Heb. 9:14; Acts 2:3; 3:19; 14:15–17; 17:30
faith in God	–	Acts 14:15–17; 15:9
baptism	–	Acts passim
laying on of hands	–	Acts 8:14–17
resurrection of the dead	–	Acts 17:18,31
eternal judgment	–	Acts 17:31; 24:25

Only in Hebrews and Acts are baptism and the laying on of hands mentioned as being part of the rite of Christian initiation (Acts 2:38; Heb 6:2). Notice how repentance and faith are very carefully distinguished in Heb 6:1–4. This corresponds to Acts 20:21, where Paul is recorded to have distinguished the two very carefully.

---

[161] Swetnam, "On the Literary Genre of the 'Epistle' to the Hebrews," 267–68.
[162] J. A. T. Robinson, *Redating the New Testament* (London: SCM, 1976), 218.
[163] Jones, "The Epistle to the Hebrews and the Lucan Writings," 125.

The Theological Significance of 'the House of Israel'
in Luke-Acts and Hebrews

In the New Testament, the people of God are frequently designated God's "house." The church is sometimes described as the "house of God" or the "temple of God" (as in 1 Cor 3:16; 6:19; Eph 2:19–22; 1 Tim 3:15; 1 Peter 2:4–10; 4:17; and probably Heb 10:21).[164]

A second use of "house" with the meaning of "family" or "race" is also found in the New Testament. This usage is restricted to the writings of Matthew, Luke, and Hebrews (Matt 10:6; 15:24; Luke 1:27,33,69; 2:4; Acts 2:36; 7:42,46; Heb 3:1–6; 8:8,10; 10:21 [where it carries a meaning similar to the people of God being the church above]).[165] The use of *epi* with *ton oikon* "over the house" followed by the possessive genitive occurs only five times in the New Testament, once in Luke and four times in Hebrews.

One clear observation from this data is that Luke and Hebrews stand over against Paul in their employment of this concept of "God's house" as family or race. Second, Luke and the writer of Hebrews are quite interested in such phraseology as can be established by consulting a concordance on the Greek term *oikos*, "house," as used with "God, Jacob, David, and Israel." Third, with the exception of Matthew, the phrase "house of Israel" is confined in the entire New Testament to the writings of Luke and Hebrews.

The Theological Concept of sēmeron, "Today,"
in Luke-Acts and Hebrews

The word *sēmeron*, "today," occurs 41 times in the New Testament: eight times in Matthew, once in Mark, 20 times in Luke-Acts, three times in Paul, once in James, and eight times in Hebrews. As with "house," most of the occurrences are restricted to the writings of Matthew, Luke, and Hebrews. This term has both a non-theological as well as a theological use in the New Testament. Most of the occurrences of *sēmeron* fall under the former category, with the meaning of "today" (as opposed to yesterday or tomorrow). However, in Luke 4:21; Acts 13:33; Heb 1:5; 4:7; and 5:5, the term "today" carries with it both Christological and eschatological implications.[166] Psalm 2:7 is

---

[164] O. Michel, "*Oikos*," TDNT Abridged, 674–75.

[165] Ibid.

[166] E. Fuchs, "σήμερον," TDNT Abridged, 102–25. On Luke's use of the concept of "today," see also E. Richard, ed., *New Views on Luke and Acts* (Collegeville, MN: Liturgical, 1990), 57.

quoted in three of these passages (Acts 13:33; Heb 1:5; 5:5), and the use of this verse is exclusive to Luke and Hebrews.

The usage in Luke 4:21 is important for our consideration in that Luke uses this statement to show that the "today" was not only for the audience in Jesus' presence at the event itself, but that it extends to his audience (the readers of his Gospel after the events of Luke 4).[167] The seven occurrences of this word "today" from Heb 1:5–5:5 are used by the author of Hebrews in exactly the same way as in Luke 4:21 and Acts 13:35. God's "today" of salvation is available (even up to the present time) with the result that three times (3:7–8,15; 4:7) Hebrews quotes Ps 95:7–8: "Today, if you hear His voice, do not harden your hearts." Note it is "today" that sins are forgiven (Luke 5:26) and "today" that demons are cast out (Luke 13:32). Zacchaeus is told "today" salvation has come to his house (Luke 19:9). Jesus said to the thief on the cross: "Today you will be with me in paradise" (Luke 23:43).[168]

Schürmann correctly states that it is inaccurate to say Luke understood the *sēmeron* in Luke 4:21 only historically. Luke knows the *peplērōtai* that the *sēmeron* fulfills is—here and now—actualized in the Word.[169] This conceptual similarity, especially with the quotation of Ps 2:7 on three occasions (all in the writings of Luke and Hebrews) lends further weight to the theory.

Apostasy and Perseverance in Luke-Acts and Hebrews

Moffatt points out that Hebrews' emphasis on apostasy (and drawing back in fear of suffering) is aptly illustrated in the words of Jesus in Luke 12:5: "I will show you whom to fear—fear Him who after he has killed has power to cast you into Gehenna. Yes, I tell you, fear Him." Moffatt suggests that this illustrates the spirit and situation of Hebrews, where the writer warns his readers by reminding them of "the living God" and of the judgment.[170]

---

[167] Cf. E. Schweizer, *Jesus*, trans. D. Green (Richmond: John Knox, 1971), 140; E. Franklin, *Christ the Lord*, 71; Marshall, *Commentary on Luke*, 185; D. Tiede, *Prophecy and History in Luke-Acts* (Philadelphia: Fortress, 1980); and J. Kodell, "Luke's Gospel in a Nutshell," *BTB* 13 (1983): 16–18. Green in *The Theology of the Gospel of Luke*, 94, says that "the Lukan emphasis falls above all on salvation in the present." See also D. Sweetland, "Luke the Christian," in *New Views on Luke and Acts*, ed. E. Richard (Collegeville, MN: Liturgical, 1990), 56–57.

[168] Cf. Sweetland, "Luke the Christian," 57.

[169] H. Schürmann, *Das Lukasevangelium*, HTKNT 3/1–2 (Freiburg im Breisgau: Herder, 1984), 233. See also on this subject O'Reilly, *Word and Sign*, 223.

[170] J. Moffatt, *A Critical and Exegetical Commentary on the Epistle to the Hebrews*, ICC (Edinburgh: T&T Clark, 1924; repr., Edinburgh: T&T Clark, 1963), xxxvi.

Stenschke's study of the concept of an "evil generation" in Luke-Acts also reveals parallels to Hebrews. Following His transfiguration, Jesus meets a man whose son has an unclean spirit. The man implores Jesus to cast the spirit out of his son, noting that the disciples were not able to cast him out. Jesus addresses those present, including the disciples, as an "unbelieving and rebellious generation" (Luke 9:41, alluding to Deut 32:5). Stenschke documents that the disciples are included in this verdict. Now this chapter of Deuteronomy is quoted and alluded to many times in the New Testament, especially by Paul in Romans and Hebrews. As Stenschke notes, the occasion for this rebuke by Jesus is not rejection of Him, but failure on the part of the disciples "to continually believe and act according to the instruction and authority received earlier and successfully practiced previously (Luke 9:2,6)."[171] It is not uncommon in Acts for speeches to conclude with grave warnings (as in Acts 7:51–53; 13:40–41; and 28:25–27). What Luke records was preached, and the way it was preached (exposition, exhortation, warning) is found as well in Hebrews.[172]

The concepts of apostasy and perseverance are clearly significant in the theology of Luke.[173] For example, Schuyler Brown observes that the word *peirasmos* occurs in four places after the temptation narrative of Luke 4, and it is "always associated with sin, especially that of apostasy." [174] In addition, the connection of *peirasmos* with divine discipline (*paideia*) and with struggle (*agōn*), so clearly seen in Hebrews, is also found in a number of places in Luke-Acts, as stated by Brown.[175]

The Concept of the "Way"

Luke is the New Testament writer who refers to the Christian faith as the "way" (Acts 9:2; 18:25–26; 19:9,23; 22:4; 24:14,22).[176] This

---

[171] C. Stenschke, "The Need for Salvation," in *Witness to the Gospel*, ed. I. H. Marshall and D. Peterson (Grand Rapids: Eerdmans, 1998), 137–39. This has crucial bearing on the interpretation of the warning passages in Hebrews, since it is possible for believers to hear a harsh statement like this from Jesus.

[172] See also D. Seccombe, "The New People of God," in *Witness to the Gospel*, 369.

[173] See, for example, S. Brown, *Apostasy and Perseverance in the Theology of Luke*, AnBib 36 (Rome: Pontifical Biblical Institute, 1969).

[174] Ibid., 17.

[175] Ibid., 31–33. Of course these notions are not absent in Paul or other New Testament writers.

[176] See Green, *The Theology of the Gospel of Luke*, 102. Brown provides a good discussion of this theme in Luke-Acts in *Apostasy and Perseverance*, 131–45.

terminology is foreign to the Pauline Letters and the other New Testament texts, with the exception of Hebrews. Swetnam suggests that the theme of the "way" in reference to Christianity appears in Heb 10:20.[177] It also appears in Heb 3:10 and 9:8.

The Lukan Theology of the Cross

Ever since Conzelmann's conclusion that there is no direct soteriological significance in the suffering or death of Jesus, according to Luke,[178] many Lukan scholars have been reluctant to view Lukan soteriology otherwise.[179] Were Conzelmann's thesis accurate, it would be difficult, although not impossible, to envision Luke as the author of Hebrews. In recent years, however, this issue has been re-evaluated, resulting in a growing dismissal of Conzelmann's opinion.[180]

We begin by noting the conclusion reached by Joel Green with respect to the passion narratives in all the Gospels: there is no "prominent or pervasive emphasis on the soteriological implications of the cross."[181] The point is important. Green argues that the passion narratives had their *sitz im leben* in the context of the Lord's Supper

---

[177] Swetnam, *Jesus and Isaac,* 265.

[178] H. Conzelmann, *The Theology of Saint Luke* (New York: Harper & Brothers, 1960), 201.

[179] See W. Kümmel, "Current Theological Accusations Against Luke," *ANQ* 16 (1975): 134. Cadbury maintains that the account of Jesus' death is "told" rather than explained. H. Cadbury, *The Making of Luke-Acts* (New York: Macmillan, 1927), 280. There are two primary passages in Luke-Acts that explicate a view of the atonement: Luke 22:19–20 and Acts 20:28. Though these verses suggest a vicarious atonement to the death of Christ, many scholars remain unconvinced on two grounds: (1) There are textual questions related to each of these verses that cause some to doubt their authenticity, and (2) the issue of Luke's use of sources causes some to view the theology of these two texts as non-Lukan. Recent studies have shown that both of these objections rest on shaky ground. For example, B. Billings, *Do This in Remembrance of Me: The Disputed Words in the Lukan Institution Narrative (Luke 22.19b–20): An Historical-Exegetical, Theological and Sociological Analysis* (London: T&T Clark, 2006), 177, has shown that the longer textual reading of Luke 22:19–20 is "almost certainly genuine" and reflects Luke's own construction without the use of sources. On the authenticity of Luke 22:19b–20, see B. Metzger, *Textual Commentary,* 148–50; J. Green, *The Death of Jesus: Tradition and Interpretation in the Passion Narrative,* WUNT 2/33 (Tübingen: Mohr, 1988), 35–41; Jeremias, *Eucharistic Words,* 139–59; and Marshall, *Gospel of Luke,* 799–807.

[180] See, for example, C. K. Barrett, "Theologia Crucis—in Acts?" in *Theologia Crucis, Signum Crucis: Festschrift für Erich Dinkler zum 70. Geburtstag,* ed. C. Andersen and G. Klein (Tübingen: Mohr [Paul Siebeck], 1979), 73–84; Gaventa, "Towards a Theology of Acts: Reading and ReReading"; Neyrey, *The Passion According to Luke*; and Moessner, *Lord of the Banquet.* Neyrey says, for example: "No, it is wrong to say that Luke has no soteriology at all, no *theologia crucis*" (p. 190). Sweetland remarks that "the scholarly consensus . . . has moved away from Conzelmann's position on both Lukan soteriology and Lukan eschatology" (D. Sweetland, "Luke the Christian," 57). For a helpful collection of essays addressing this issue see D. D. Sylva, ed., *Reimaging the Death of the Lukan Jesus,* in BBB 73, (Frankfurt am Main: Hain, 1990).

[181] Green, *The Death of Jesus,* 321.

celebration in the early church. The testimony of the eucharistic words clearly emphasized Jesus' death as redemptive; additional explicit testimony to its atoning significance was unnecessary in the passion narrative. "Simply put, the passion narrative assumes the eucharistic emphasis on the soteriological effects of the death of Jesus."[182] Green thus suggests that the Gospel writers all viewed the cross as having atoning significance, but their narrative focus did not make it explicit since it was already in the church's eucharistic practice. My point here is that none of the four Gospel writers presents a "prominent emphasis" on the soteriological implications of the cross, and Luke should not be singled out (as Conzelmann did) as having little or no emphasis in comparison with the others.

Fuller has pointed out that Luke had as many references to the atoning work of Jesus on the cross as Mark (two each). He calls it unfair to suggest that Luke had no theology of the cross.[183] Likewise, Fitzmyer concludes Luke did indeed have a theology of the cross, based on his exegesis of Luke 23:43,[184] but he does not see any expiatory significance to the cross in Luke's Gospel. This appears to be the case with Karris and Neyrey, both of whom affirm a Lukan theology of the cross, but seem to think that Luke posits salvation without expiation.

Joel Green wisely notes that although Luke did not emphasize a *theologia crucis*, neither did he oppose it. He points out that

> The sheer frequency of times we read in Acts of the divine necessity (δεῖ) [*dei*] of the suffering of Jesus is warning enough that salvation has not come *in spite of* the crucifixion of Jesus. What is more, the specifically covenantal language employed in 20:28 (περιποιέομαι) [*peripoieomai*], "to acquire . . . and 20:32; 26:18 (ἁγιάζω) [*hagiazō*], "to sanctify". . . reminds us of Luke's record of Jesus' last meal with his disciples wherein he grounds the "new covenant" in his own death (Luke 22:19–20).[185]

Witherington adds his voice to the growing number of scholars who see a theology of the cross in Luke-Acts: "It is not accurate to

---

[182] Ibid., 322.

[183] R. H. Fuller, "Luke and the Theologica Crucis," in *Sin, Salvation, and the Spirit*, ed. D. Durken (Collegeville: MN.: Liturgical, 1979), 214–20.

[184] Fitzmyer, *Luke the Theologian*, 203–33. See also Fitzmyer, *The Gospel According to Luke X– XXIV*, 1395, where he compares the Lukan theology of *paschein* exhibited in the Last Supper account with what one finds in Hebrews and 1 Peter.

[185] J. Green, "'Salvation to the End of the Earth' (Acts 13:47): God as Savior in the Acts of the Apostles," in *Witness to the Gospel*, 99.

say that Luke has no or at least no adequate theology of the cross, and that he does not connect it with salvation."[186] Later in the same article he says, "It turns out to be incorrect to say either that Luke fails to affirm or has no clear concept of what salvation in the future amounts to, or to say that Luke has no clear theology of the cross or understanding of its connection with salvation."[187]

The Lukan travel narrative concludes with the significant statement that Jesus must go to Jerusalem and die there to effect salvation ("release" or "forgiveness," *aphesis*) as the Prophet like Moses of Deuteronomy.[188] Furthermore, in the Lukan passion narrative, "it would appear that sacrificial language, especially that of a covenant sacrifice, is uppermost, though not necessarily so."[189] That Jesus quoted Isa 53:12 (in Luke 22:37) should not be overlooked. The only overt citation of Isaiah 53 in the Synoptic Gospels occurs in Luke's Last Supper discourse. Also, its strategic location in the overall Lukan discourse is quite significant. Luke's audience could not help but make the connection between the Suffering Servant of Isaiah 53 and Jesus' death. How can Luke record this and not have a theology of the cross?[190] To conclude, as does Hultgren, that for Luke "the cross is not regarded as the decisive moment at which sin or sins and their consequences were borne once for all for the benefit of others" seems less than compelling.[191]

In Acts, the call to suffering that the Prophet like Moses fulfilled is now extended to the apostles and people of God. Specifically, the careers of both Stephen and Paul are patterned after the suffering journey of Jesus. Such an identification of the people of God with their eschatological Prophet's suffering lies behind the statement in Acts 14:22b: "It is necessary to pass through many troubles on our way

---

[186] B. Witherington, "Salvation and Health," in *Witness to the Gospel*, 159.

[187] Ibid., 161.

[188] Moessner, *Lord of the Banquet*, 323–25. See also his "'The Christ Must Suffer,' The Church Must Suffer: Rethinking the Theology of the Cross in Luke-Acts," *SBLSP*, ed. D. Lull (Atlanta: Scholars Press, 1990), 165–95. "Though Luke does not articulate the effects of Jesus' death in the atonement terminology of a Mark or Paul, nevertheless, it will be seen that 'the release/forgiveness of sins' is Luke's characteristic expression of the saving, atoning action of God, and that this formulation is peculiarly forged to the suffering or death of Christ" (p. 167).

[189] Ibid., 323.

[190] Ibid., 165–95. For the significance of Isaiah 53 in Luke, consult U. Mittmann-Richert, *Der Sühnetod des Gottesknechts: Jesaja 53 im Lukasevangelium*, WUNT 220 (Tübingen: Mohr Siebeck, 2008). On Luke 22:14–38 at the Last Supper, see pp. 110–61, esp. pp. 313–15.

[191] Hultgren, *New Testament Christology*, 86.

into the kingdom of God." But it is not only the people's identification with the suffering of Jesus that Luke explicates. He is at pains to underscore (in events such as Jesus' baptism and His eating and drinking with sinners) the solidarity of Jesus with the sinful people of God.[192] This is, of course, a theological theme found throughout Hebrews.

Furthermore, the logic of Peter's sermon in Acts 3 depends on the atoning death of Jesus for its force. That Peter does not develop the death of Jesus in a Pauline fashion in no way suggests that he (or Luke) did not have a theology of the cross.[193]

Scott Cunningham has shown how Luke uses the theme of persecution as a vehicle in pursuit of his theological agenda. He summarizes his results in six statements:

1. Persecution is part of the plan of God.
2. Persecution is the rejection of God's agents by those who are supposedly God's people.
3. The persecuted people of God stand in continuity with God's prophets.
   The link between Israel's prophets, Jesus, and the disciples is present in Acts, but "firmly established" in the Gospel. The rejected prophet motif "legitimizes Jesus as a commissioned messenger sent by God, which means that his message must be taken seriously."
4. Persecution is an integral consequence of following Jesus.
5. Persecution is the occasion of the Christian's perseverance.
6. Persecution is the occasion of divine triumph.

Cunningham believes Luke has a theology of the cross in that he attaches positive significance to suffering itself. Luke sees forgiveness as grounded in Jesus' death, according to Luke 22:19–20.[194]

From this point it is only a small step to such passages in Hebrews as "you have not yet resisted to the point of shedding your blood" (Heb 12:4) and "Let us then go to Him outside the camp . . . " (Heb 13:13). What the author of Hebrews exhorts, the author of Luke-Acts

---

[192] Ibid., 324.

[193] See the discussion in D. Moessner, "Jesus and the 'Wilderness Generation': The Death of the Prophet Like Moses According to Luke," in *SBLSP*, 1982, ed. K. H. Richards (Chico, Calif.: Scholars Press, 1982), 338–40.

[194] S. S. Cunningham, *Through Many Tribulations: The Theology of Persecution in Luke-Acts*, JSNTSup 142, ed. S. Porter (Sheffield: Sheffield Academic Press, 1997), 337–39. See also Green, "'Salvation to the End of the Earth' (Acts 13:47)," 100.

narrates regarding the history of the people of God from Pentecost to the arrival of Paul in Rome in Acts 28.

Howard Marshall has argued that a theology of the cross is present in Luke-Acts, although with a different emphasis from that found elsewhere in the New Testament.[195] Dormandy notices Luke's substitution of *traumatizō* for *apokteinō,* which occurs in Matthew and Mark, as demonstrative of Luke's keenness to underline Jesus' death as unique, and this view is "shared emphatically by the writer to the Hebrews."[196] Buckwalter observes that Luke assumes a great deal of knowledge from his readers; otherwise the expression "the church of God, which he purchased with his own blood" (Acts 20:28) would be dangerously confusing—as it would suggest almost a patripassionistic point of view—based on the contents of Luke-Acts alone. "Luke's readers were in all probability able to unpack this compressed theological statement in Acts 20:28."[197] On this basis, it is arguable that Jesus' death as vicarious represented not only the thinking of Paul and Luke, but that of Luke's readers as well.[198]

Neyrey has shown that the obedience (Luke 22:42) and faith (Luke 23:46) of Jesus are pivotal events in the Lukan perspective of soteriology. After comparing both Paul and Hebrews with the Lukan perspective, Neyrey concludes that "the profiles of Jesus in Romans and Hebrews and Luke-Acts are remarkably similar."[199]

Richard Anderson, in an article comparing the atonement in Luke and Hebrews, finds a number of similarities, especially concerning a theology of the cross. Anderson believes that Theophilus is the former high priest, as I do. This identification furnishes the basic clue to Luke's theology. Luke does not develop an atoning significance to the death of Jesus because he believes, like all Jews, that the action

---

[195] I. H. Marshall, "The Christology of Luke-Acts and the Pastoral Epistles," in *Crossing the Boundaries: Essays in Biblical Interpretation in Honour of Michael D. Goulder,* ed. S. Porter, P. Joyce, and D. Orton (Leiden: Brill, 1994), 181.

[196] R. Dormandy, "Heb. 1:1–2 and the Parable of the Wicked Husbandmen," *ExpTim* 100 (1989): 373.

[197] D. Buckwalter, *The Character and Purpose of Luke's Christology* (Cambridge: Cambridge University Press, 1996), 73.

[198] Ibid.

[199] Neyrey, *The Passion According to Luke,* 189–90. Ravens's negative appraisal of Luke and Hebrews with respect to a theology of the atonement is uncalled for. His statement, "On every point Luke stands opposed to the writer of Hebrews," misses or misunderstands the evidence linking the two. D. Ravens, *Luke and the Restoration of Israel,* JSNTSup 119 (Sheffield: Sheffield Academic Press, 1995), 167.

of the high priest on the Day of Atonement brings forgiveness for the sins of a nation. Luke did not want to equate Jesus with the high priest because he did not want to offend Theophilus. Jews believed that the death of the high priest had atoning significance as well. The atonement procured by the cross replaced both the high priest and the Day of Atonement.[200]

Two significant works recently surfaced that speak to Luke's *theologia crucis*: Peter Doble's *The Paradox of Salvation: Luke's Theology of the Cross*, and Francis Carpinelli's article, "'Do This as My Memorial' (Luke 22:19): Lucan Soteriology of Atonement." Both affirm that Luke indeed has a theology of the cross. Doble asks the salient question: "If, according to Luke, salvation is not to be found in the cross *per se* where may it be found?" Since Luke emphasizes Jesus' approaching death more than the other Synoptists, "why should an evangelist with no *theologia crucis* make so much of the passion?"[201] These questions have nagged scholars since Conzelmann.

The central point for those who see no theology of the cross in Luke is the absence of Mark 10:45 in Luke's account. Doble says this assumes Markan priority. If Luke did not use Mark, the point is severely weakened (its absence cannot be said to be an exclusion). Doble makes his case not from the assumption of Markan priority, but from the character and development of Luke's own composition.[202]

The focus of Doble's study is Luke 23:46–47, where the centurion at the cross refers to Jesus as *dikaios* rather than as "Son of God" (as do the other two Synoptists). Upon examination of *dikaios* in Luke-Acts, Doble concludes that Luke's use of this word "belongs to a specific realm of discourse—the piety and theology of first-century Judaism." The usual translation of "innocent" ignores the Lukan usage and obscures Luke's theology of the cross.[203] Doble thinks the *Wisdom of Solomon* is the background for Luke's use of *dikaios*. The paradox of salvation in Luke is that Jesus died according to the Scriptures and yet was vindicated by the resurrection and exaltation.

Doble points out Luke's portrayal of Jesus as *archēgos* (Acts 3:15; 5:31) is an essential element in his *theologia crucis*.[204] Those who

[200] R. Anderson, "The Cross and Atonement from Luke to Hebrews," *EvQ* 71 (1999): 128–29.
[201] P. Doble, *The Paradox of Salvation: Luke's Theology of the Cross*, SNTSMS 87 (Cambridge: Cambridge University Press, 1996), 5–6.
[202] Ibid., 12.
[203] Ibid., 158–60.
[204] Ibid., 231.

follow Jesus as "leader" must suffer with Him. It is of course significant for our purposes that *archēgos* occurs only four times in the New Testament: twice in Acts and twice in Hebrews. The theme of Jesus' solidarity with His people as their *archēgos* is as important in Hebrews as it is in Acts.

Doble concludes his work by noting, "Luke is not Paul, nor is he John, but his substantial, two-volume work offers a narrative theology of the cross, firmly rooted in Israel's scripture."[205] The key word here is "narrative." Luke does not offer an exposition of Jesus' death like Paul because that was not his purpose. Neither do the other gospel writers explain the death of Jesus methodologically as does Paul. The complaint lodged against Luke (that he has not affirmed a Pauline doctrine of the atonement) cannot be sustained in light of the above. Luke has not explained the atonement as Paul has, but he certainly has, by virtue of the way he has structured his Gospel and by the speeches in Acts, a theology of the atonement.

Francis Carpinelli offers an incisive argument for a Lukan theology of the cross in his study of Luke 22:19.[206] He argues that a theology of the cross in Luke-Acts is hindered by three factors: overinterpreting Luke's omission of Mark 10:45, collapsing the notion of expiation into redemption, and misreading Luke 22:19.[207] The LXX provided Luke a rich theological source of expiation. The memorial established at the Last Supper has its roots in the cultic theology of the LXX and is used by Luke to give soteriological meaning to the cross.[208]

Carpinelli's research improves upon Jeremias's selection and analysis of data in two ways. First, aided by the computer, Carpinelli was able to search the terms *eis mnēmosunon* and *eis anamnēsin* in the *Thesaurus Linguae Graecae*[209] and thus cover a broader range of data than Jeremias. Second, Jeremias[210] does not pursue the extent of the interchangeability of *eis mnēmosunon* with *eis anamnēsin* in the LXX's use of them to render the MT's expression of Judaic cultic practice. After careful linguistic analysis, Carpinelli concludes that Luke 22:19 depicts Jesus as ordaining a cultic memorial after the manner of Jewish piety where a divinely-elected mediator provides a cultic memorial

---

[205] Ibid., 243.
[206] Carpinelli, "'Do This as My Memorial,'" 74–91.
[207] Ibid., 74.
[208] Ibid., 75.
[209] CD ROM D; Irvine: University of California Irvine, TLG Project, 1992.
[210] J. Jeremias, *The Eucharistic Words of Jesus*, 3rd ed. (London: SCM, 1966), 237–55.

so that others may have their sins expiated. This is, for Luke, an interpretive principle for Jesus' relationship to God.[211] Carpinelli translates Luke 22:19 then as "Do this as *my* memorial," namely, "as a permanent cultic means of access to God's regard which I set up for you." He concludes:

> If Luke's εἰς μνημόσυνον [*eis mnēmosunon*] (Acts 10:4) and εἰς ἀνάμνησιν [*eis anamnēsin*] (Luke 22:19) are functionally synonymous and are continuous with septuagintal cultic terminology, the door is opened to recovery of Luke's theology of atonement. His profound knowledge of septuagintal Greek allows one to assume his awareness of their equivalence in the LXX. Furthermore, he never explains them to his reader.[212]

Carpinelli observes Luke's allusion to Sirach 50 in portraying Jesus' act of blessing at His ascension (Luke 24:50–51), a gesture that the high priest performed after he completed the sacrifice on the Day of Atonement. The force of this allusion, according to Carpinelli, suggests that Luke has an expiatory theology of Jesus' blood.[213]

Carpinelli compares Lev 24:5–9, the bread memorial, with Luke 22:19. In Lev 24:5–9, bread, memorial, and covenant are associated in the cultic soteriology of the LXX. In Exod 12:14, the Passover is appointed by God as a memorial for Israel. Luke clearly views the Last Supper as a Passover meal. "Hence, bread and memorial bring to the Lucan scene of the Last Supper the soteriology of cultic covenant. The words concerning the cup make association with covenant explicit by introducing the primary expiatory symbol. God gives blood for atonement."[214]

Carpinelli views Luke's eucharistic words as infusing sacrificial and expiatory meaning to the cross. Furthermore, Luke's omission of Mark 10:45 does not downplay the atoning nature of Jesus' death.[215] He concludes:

> By choosing the tradition that has εἰ˝ ἀνάμνησιν [*eis anamnēsin*] with the eucharistic words, our evangelist makes the memorial piety surrounding the cross explicit and, therefore, forcefully channels his implied reader's understanding. Alms, bread, cup, blood, memorial, sacrifice, atonement,

---

[211] Carpinelli, "'Do This as My Memorial,'" 75–79.
[212] Ibid., 80.
[213] Ibid., 83.
[214] Ibid., 87.
[215] Ibid., 88.

priesthood, and covenant are threads of one cultic cloth in the LXX and, quite possibly, in Luke-Acts.[216]

In conclusion, the works of Barrett, Fuller, Neyrey, Moessner, Witherington, Doble, and Carpinelli make it impossible to argue Luke has no *theologia crucis*. Clearly one reason many have inferred this is Luke's omission of Mark 10:45. But this argument assumes Markan priority, an assumption many have called into question, especially in recent years. In light of the current state of synoptic and Lukan studies, it can no longer be dogmatically asserted that Luke has no theology of the cross. Hence, a significant theological barrier against the Lukan authorship of Hebrews is removed. Of course, the fact that Luke does have a theology of the cross does not furnish direct evidence for Lukan authorship of Hebrews, any more than Paul and Hebrews having a similar view of the atonement proves that Paul wrote it. It does suggest, however, that Luke's theology of the atonement is not so dissimilar to that of Hebrews as to discredit him from being the author. Indeed, in the ways noted above, Luke shares a number of similarities with Hebrews, especially Christologically. Furthermore, Carpinelli's points are well taken in that the memorial scene in Luke's Gospel can be interpreted as uniting "threads of one cultic cloth."[217]

Finally, Scaer has argued Luke probably made use of the Jewish martyrological tradition in his presentation of Jesus' suffering and death. Scaer does not argue for Luke's dependence on this tradition, merely that he has most likely borrowed some of its themes in his own presentation.[218] This again is evidence of Luke's Jewish orientation.

The Concept of Salvation in Luke-Acts and Hebrews

One of Luke's main themes, if not his chief theme, is the centrality of God's purpose to bring salvation to both Jews and Gentiles. The concept of salvation is seen as the unifying factor within the Lukan discourse.[219]

Hebrews is concerned with showing how God has brought salvation through His Son, the High Priest who makes eternal atonement

---

[216] Ibid.

[217] Ibid.

[218] P. Scaer, *The Lukan Passion and the Praiseworthy Death*, New Testament Monographs 10, ed. S. Porter (Sheffield: Sheffield Phoenix Press, 2005), 79–89.

[219] For example, J. Green, *The Gospel of Luke*, NICNT (Grand Rapids: Eerdmans, 1997), 21–25. See also his *Theology of the Gospel of Luke*.

for sins.[220] In Heb 2:3 the author uses *tēlikautēs sōtērias* with the noun *sōtērias* "so great salvation." Compare this to *ho logos tēs sōtērias tautēs* in Acts 13:26. The Lukan idea of the gospel is often expressed as salvation, as can be seen from Luke 1:69,71,77; Acts 2:47; 4:12. The same form of expression occurs in Hebrews: 1:14; 2:10; 5:9; 6:9; 19:28.

Priestly Terminology in Luke-Acts and Hebrews

Luke begins his Gospel in the temple with the experience of Zechariah the priest. Zechariah's prophecy identifies the purpose of messianic redemption as enabling the people of God to worship and serve Him (Luke 1:74). The Greek word *latreuein*, "to serve," appears more frequently in the LXX than in secular Greek. It occurs approximately 90 times in the LXX, but only once in the Prophets. It is often associated with worship or service to God, which is rendered in the tabernacle and temple by the priests. It is very similar in meaning to *leitourgeō*, which is used in the LXX almost exclusively for the service of the priests and Levites in the temple.[221] It is interesting that only Paul, Luke, and Hebrews use this word group in the New Testament. Paul, unlike Luke and Hebrews, uses *leitourgeō* in a non-cultic way in all but two instances. Luke, however, uses it to define Zechariah's priestly service in Luke 1:23, and he uses it of the church with a cultic background in Acts 13:2. Both these uses correlate with Hebrews.

The significance of its use in Acts 13:2 is what it communicates about Luke's outlook and theology. Since this word was used uniquely in the LXX in a technical sense to describe the priestly service, and since it was not used to describe the worship/service of the nation as a whole, it would seem Luke's use indicates his understanding of the church to be much the same as that of the author of Hebrews.[222]

The Intercessory Ministry of Jesus in Luke-Acts and Hebrews

One of the finest studies on this subject is David Crump's *Jesus the Intercessor: Prayer and Christology in Luke-Acts*.[223] After surveying the

---

[220] See, for example, Ellingworth, *Hebrews*, 73–74.

[221] K. Hess, "λατρεύω" and "λειτουργέω" in *NIDNTT*, 3:549–53.

[222] Cf. Peterson's discussion of Luke's usage in "The Worship of the New Community," in *Witness to the Gospel*, 387–88. Peterson does not make the connection with Hebrews as I do, but the connection is evident based on the lexical similarity.

[223] D. Crump, *Jesus the Intercessor: Prayer and Christology in Luke-Acts*, WUNT 49 (Tübingen: Mohr/Siebeck, 1992; Grand Rapids: Baker, 1999). Other works on this subject include

New Testament data concerning Christ's intercessory prayer ministry, Crump makes the significant observation that Hebrews' presentation of Jesus' earthly prayer life is distinctive. He then comments, "Jesus' earthly devotion to prayer is shown to be one of the factors contributing to his ability to offer intercession in heaven. This relationship between earthly piety and heavenly intercession is an important element in Luke's description of Jesus as well."[224]

Other connections between Acts and Hebrews can be discerned from Crump's discussion of Jesus' heavenly intercession in Acts, particularly as it relates to Stephen's speech (where Jesus is said to be "standing" at the right hand of God).[225] We must note the significance of the connection between Acts 7:55–56, Ps 110:1, and Hebrews.[226] Crump states that when the author of Hebrews refers to Christ's "sitting," he always does so to underscore the finality of Christ's work.[227] But in reference to Christ's ongoing mediatorial work in Heb 7:25, no mention is made of Ps 110:1. Although both the author of Hebrews and the author of Ps 110:1 express a theology of intercession, there was "an inherent difficulty," according to Crump, in expressing such theology in the language of the Psalm. His next statement is important for our discussion: "In this regard, Hebrews is really not very different from Luke-Acts. For Luke clearly knew of the traditional use of Ps 110:1 (Acts 2:34), but he too found it inadequate for the expression of his theology of intercession."[228]

According to Crump, the author of Hebrews integrates the theme of intercession within the broader presentation of Jesus' high priesthood, whereas Luke presents Jesus as the intercessory, eschatological prophet. Jesus stands as God's final prophet, he says, not as priest, in Acts 7.[229] Crump's view that there are no grounds in either Luke or

---

S. Balentine, *Prayer in the Hebrew Bible: The Drama of Divine-Human Dialogue* (Minneapolis: Fortress, 1993); O. Cullmann, *Das Gebet im Neuen Testament* (Tübingen: Mohr, 1994); and P. Miller, *They Cried to the Lord: The Form and Theology of Biblical Prayer* (Minneapolis: Fortress, 1994).

[224] Ibid., 18.

[225] Ibid., 176–203. Crump lists and evaluates the various interpretations of Jesus "standing" in Stephen's vision. He argues convincingly for a judicial significance. See his summary on this point on p. 193.

[226] See D. M. Hay, *Glory at the Right Hand: Psalm 110 in Early Christianity*, SBLMS 18 (Nashville/New York: Abingdon Press), 132., who sees in Acts 7:55–56 a possible allusion to Ps 110:1 with intercessory connotations.

[227] Crump, *Jesus the Intercessor*, 197.

[228] Ibid.

[229] Ibid., 197–98.

Acts for proposing a heavenly high priest theology as in Hebrews[230] cannot be sustained in light of the evidence presented above. Jesus intercedes in His earthly and heavenly ministry as the Prophet like Moses in Luke-Acts; yet this does not preclude Him from doing so in priestly terms as well. Crump also overlooks the programmatic prologue to Hebrews which, prior to unpacking the high priestly theology that comes later in the letter, actually focuses on the *prophetic* role of the Son: "Long ago God spoke to the fathers by the prophets at different times and in different ways. In these last days, He has spoken to us by [His] Son." Hebrews may focus on the priestly aspects of Jesus' ministry, but it does so within the broader context of the prologue and His prophetic ministry. Luke and Hebrews are not as dissimilar as Crump believes.

In the conclusion to his chapter on the intercessory ministry of Jesus in Luke's Gospel, Crump's helpful insights have the effect of linking Luke with Hebrews, although he does not flesh this out:

> Luke demonstrates that the prayers of Jesus, both in whom he does and does not pray for, are crucial to deciding the question of a disciple's apostasy. This was true not only during Jesus' earthly ministry, but also in the subsequent period of the church. . . . his intercessions not only mediate the Father's revelation, and thus his calling, but they also are fundamental to the disciple's perseverance in that call. Judas illustrates the fate of those who are not included within the intercessory prayers of Christ. The prayers of the ascended Savior are a wall standing between the Christian professor and the satanic attacker, protecting the believer in the midst of temptation. . . . Luke maintains that disciples are still to resist temptation through prayer, but he also teaches that the formation, composition and preservation of the church continues to be a product of the prayers of the ascended Jesus.[231]

Much of this correlates with Hebrews, not least the issue of apostasy (which is beyond the scope of our investigation). The role of the ascended, interceding High Priest in Hebrews is the doctrinal foundation for the warnings against apostasy in Hebrews, however that apostasy is to be interpreted. It would seem that Luke and the author of Hebrews are operating on the same wavelength with respect to the concept of priestly terminology and heavenly intercession.

---

[230] Ibid., 199, 232.
[231] Ibid., 175.

Money and Possessions in Luke-Acts and Hebrews

Luke devotes more material to the theme of possessions than the other Gospel writers. This theme is continued in Acts, especially in the early chapters. The past 25 years of Lukan research has examined this theme more than any other social issue.[232]

Yet Luke's treatment of this topic reveals that, although important, it is more of a secondary—or even tertiary—matter in his overall purpose. Throughout Luke-Acts, in fact, there is no endorsement of any social or political agenda.

References in Hebrews to the past and present generosity of the recipients (6:10) and to their acceptance of the plundering of their possessions—"knowing that you have a better and an enduring possession for yourselves in heaven" (10:34)—means they were people of means. The use of economic metaphors (such as in 10:35; 11:6,26) reveals the author's interest in this aspect of the Christian life. In Hebrews 13, where the author makes a number of brief exhortations, we find two statements regarding the use of possessions and money: "Your life should be free from the love of money. Be satisfied with what you have" (13:5), and "Don't neglect to do good and to share, for God is pleased with such sacrifices" (13:16). Finally, as Robinson has pointed out, the author's main metaphor for salvation is drawn "from the world of property: coming into, or getting possession of, an inheritance (1:2,4,14; 6:12, 17; 9:15; 11:7–8; 12:17)."[233] I have already pointed out the linguistic similarity between Heb 13:17 and Luke 16:2 above.

Fletcher-Louis's study of Luke 14:25–35 led him to conclude that Luke's inclusion of this parable reveals a priestly ecclesiology.[234] In the parable, Jesus introduces renunciation of wealth as a criterion for discipleship. Fletcher-Louis observes a strong Levitical subtext here, in that the priests and Levites were not to own land, but to minister to

---

[232] See, for example, L. T. Johnson, *The Literary Function of Possessions in Luke-Acts*, SBLDS 39 (Missoula, MT: Scholars Press, 1977); R. Karris, "Poor and Rich: The Lukan *Sitz im Leben*," in *Perspectives on Luke-Acts*, ed. C. Talbert (Danville, VA.: Association of Baptist Professors of Religion, 1978); W. Pilgrim, *Good News to the Poor: Wealth and Poverty in Luke-Acts* (Minneapolis: Augsburg, 1981); D. Seccombe, *Possessions and the Poor in Luke-Acts*, SNTSU B/6 (Linz: SNTSU, 1982).

[233] J. A. T. Robinson, *Redating the New Testament* (London: SCM, 1976), 212.

[234] C. Fletcher-Louis, "Jesus Inspects His Priestly War Party (Luke 24:25–35)," in *The Old Testament in the New Testament: Essays in Honor of J. L. North*, ed. S. Moyise, JSNTSup 189 (Sheffield: Sheffield Academic Press, 2000), 126–43.

the Lord and be supported by the tithes of the rest of the nation.[235] If the recipients of Hebrews were former priests as I argue below, then Luke's focus might point in that direction.

It would appear that the author of Hebrews shared a social concern with Luke. Just as this concern is a secondary issue in Luke-Acts, it is likewise not a part of the central argument of Hebrews, but its presence is sufficiently felt throughout. Luke and Hebrews are once again very similar in outlook on the matter of money and possessions.

Hebrews and the Sermons of Acts

L. O. Bristol studied the elements of early Christian preaching identified in Dodd's *Apostolic Preaching and its Developments* and found them reflected in the sermons of Peter in Acts and in the book of Hebrews, which is probably a written sermon.[236] The author of Hebrews shared the same conceptual approach as Luke with regard to early Christian preaching, which furnishes additional evidence for Lukan authorship of Hebrews.

Bristol notes differences, however, in the use of the Old Testament in Peter's sermons in Acts and in Hebrews. Hebrews quotes a number of passages that play a crucial role in his developing argument. When these are compared with Peter's use of the Old Testament, there is a twofold development, according to Bristol. First, Hebrews uses a wider array of passages. Second, unlike Peter's preaching, Hebrews distinguishes between Old Testament passages referring to the first coming of the Messiah and those referring to His second coming.

In spite of this, there is remarkable continuity between what we find in Hebrews and Acts in terms of use of the Old Testament in preaching. First, the Jewish concept of "this age" versus "the age to come," with the advent of the Messiah as the dividing line, is clearly articulated in the sermons of Peter as well as in Hebrews, particularly in the first two chapters. Second, the earthly life of Jesus receives scant mention in Acts, where the focus is rather on the resurrection and ascension. The same is true of Hebrews. Third, after discussing three purposes for the death of Jesus according to Hebrews, Bristol compares this with early Christian preaching in Acts and concludes

---

[235] Ibid., 140.

[236] L. O. Bristol, "Primitive Christian Preaching and the Epistle to the Hebrews," *JBL* 68 (1949): 89–97.

that "the idea of Jesus as Pioneer of salvation is common to both."[237] He does, however, record some disparity. In Hebrews, Jesus becomes the Pioneer through the discipline of His suffering and death. In Acts this is accomplished through by the resurrection. Bristol observes that the concept of Jesus as High Priest in a heavenly sanctuary "is completely foreign to the preaching in Acts."[238]

Is it? Bristol fails to give due consideration to the end of Luke and the beginning of Acts, where the ascension is pivotal. He also fails to see in Stephen's vision of Jesus standing (Acts 7) the same emphasis that is in Hebrews. While the concept of the high priestly role of Jesus is not as defined in Luke-Acts as it is in Hebrews, it is, as I have demonstrated, not absent.

Fourth, the forgiveness of sins is highly prominent in both Luke-Acts and Hebrews, as can be demonstrated lexically. Bristol misses this crucial connection when he notes that in Acts, forgiveness of sins comes by faith in Jesus, whereas in Hebrews it comes because Jesus died "to prepare himself for the high priestly position and as High Priest can minister unto that forgiveness."[239] The Lukan emphasis on forgiveness of sins comes by faith in Jesus precisely *because* Luke believes such forgiveness is available based on the death of Jesus.

Fifth, Bristol claims that Acts does not describe Christianity as a new covenant as does Hebrews. Yet, though the terminology is not used, everything in Acts semantically identifies Christianity as a new covenant. Also, in the synoptic accounts of the Last Supper, only in Luke does Jesus say the cup is the "new covenant" in His blood.

Sixth, Bristol correctly recognizes that both Acts and Hebrews consider the resurrection and exaltation as one act, with the emphasis on the exaltation. Furthermore, the purpose of the exaltation according to Acts and Hebrews is the same—to show God's approval of Christ at the end of His earthly life. Bristol stumbles again over the evidence when he states, "In Acts no account is taken of the pre-existence of Christ." But again, it is now recognized that Luke's Christology clearly includes Christ's preexistence.

Seventh, little is said about the parousia in Peter's sermons in Acts. But the subject is not missing (see Acts 2:34–35; 3:20–21). Likewise

---

[237] Ibid., 95.
[238] Ibid.
[239] Ibid.

in Hebrews, references to the parousia are incidental rather than explicit.[240]

Bristol concludes, "We do well to see the summary of basic Christian teachings in Hebrews 6:1–2. Here we find repentance and faith in the sense of trust in God, baptism and the gift of the Holy Spirit, resurrection and judgment. All these find a place in the primitive Christian preaching in Acts."[241]

When one compares Peter's quotation of Joel 2:28–32 (in Acts 2:16–21) with the quotation of Deut 18:19 (in Acts 3:22–26), it would seem that apostolic preaching represents a renewal of prophecy. As Dillon points out, in this renewal "the voice of the risen Christ is heard, through the testimony of his witnesses, as the awaited voice of the 'prophet like Moses.'"[242] Dillon carefully lists and analyzes the words Luke added to the LXX of the Joel passage in Acts 2:17–19, and the altered words *en tais eschatais hēmerais* in Acts 2:17 from the Joel passage, showing Luke's effort to depict this renewal of prophecy through the preaching of the apostles. He concludes, "The risen Lord (Acts 3:22–26) is depicted as the exponent of the eschatological message of repentance, as in Acts 26:23. Acts 26:23 explicitly makes the risen Christ the *speaker* of Paul's prophetic message to the nations."[243] For Luke, "Preaching in Acts is really the personal prophecy of the risen Christ. This, and not some absentee Christology, is authentic Lucan theory of salvation."[244]

When we compare Luke's use of Scripture and sermons in Acts to that of Hebrews, we find a similar theological treatment. The author of Hebrews makes almost constant use of forms of the Greek *legei*, "to say or speak," and his use of the present tense in quotation formulae indicates his view that Scripture is the voice of God speaking to the church in the present time. Significantly, on two occasions (Heb 2:12–13; 10:5–7) the author of Hebrews places Old Testament Scripture on the lips of Jesus, indicating his theological understanding that all the Old Testament is the voice of Jesus speaking to the church. This is consistent with the author's programmatic assertion in Heb 1:1–2 that God is now, "in these last days," speaking to us in His Son.

---

[240] Ibid., 96.

[241] Ibid., 97.

[242] R. Dillon, "The Prophecy of Christ and His Witnesses According to the Discourses of Acts," NTS 32.4 (October, 1986), 544.

[243] Ibid., 546.

[244] Ibid., 549.

The Melchizedek Tradition in Luke-Acts and Hebrews

The Melchizedek tradition found in late Judaism "provides an interesting parallel to what is found in Luke-Acts regarding Jesus," says Joel Green.[245] Of course, the prominence of Melchizedek in Hebrews is well known. According to the fragmentary text from Qumran Cave 11, a mysterious and heavenly, mediatorial figure named Melchizedek is God's eschatological agent in bringing salvation and judgment. To what extent this figure in late Judaism is related to the Melchizedek of Genesis 14 is debated. The point is that in this Melchizedek tradition "we have parallels to the idea prevalent in Lukan thought of the soteriological functions of an exalted human being."[246] Luke, like the author of Hebrews, is concerned with more than the historicity of the cross. He probes its theological significance as well.

New Covenant Theology in Luke-Acts and Hebrews

The first reference in Luke's Gospel to "covenant" occurs in Zechariah's song (1:72), where he declares that God has "remembered His holy covenant." From this point forward, Luke "presses relentlessly toward the final traumatic events of Jesus' life in which it becomes progressively clearer that in Jesus' ministry, death and resurrected life the covenant has its fulfillment."[247]

The phrase "the new covenant" (*hē kainē diathēkē*) in Luke 22:20 is a direct allusion to the only occurrence of the precise Hebrew phrase (*běrît ḥǎdāšâ*) found only in Jer 31:31 (LXX 38:31, where the noun precedes the adjective). Zechariah's *Benedictus* contains a host of Old Testament quotations and allusions, which are helpfully charted verse by verse in Raymond Brown's *The Birth of the Messiah*.[248] The Greek term *diathēkē*, "covenant," occurs only four times in the Gospels, twice in Luke (Zechariah's Song at 1:72 and Jesus at the Lord's Supper at 22:20). Luke alone preserves the words of Jer 31:31–34 in Luke 22:20 with reference to the new covenant, indicating his interest in the concept. Luke makes use of "covenant" in Zechariah's prophecy

[245] J. Green, "The Death of Jesus, God's Servant," in *Reimaging the Death of the Lukan Jesus*, BBB 73 (Frankfurt am Main: Anton Hain, 1990), 13.

[246] Ibid., 17.

[247] P. E. Leonard, "Luke's Account of the Lord's Supper Against the Background of Meals in the Ancient Semitic World and More Particularly Meals in the Gospel of Luke," (Ph.D. diss., University of Manchester, 1976), 288.

[248] R. Brown, *The Birth of the Messiah*, ABRL (New York: Doubleday, 1993), 386–89.

(Luke 1:72) at the naming and circumcision of John the Baptist, who was to "go before the Lord to prepare His ways, to give His people knowledge of salvation through the forgiveness of their sins (Luke 1:76–77). Two words occur here that may echo Jer 31:31–34: "knowledge" and "forgiveness." We have already seen the significance that "forgiveness of sins" has for Luke, a theological notion that is for him a summary of Jesus' main purpose in coming to earth to die on the cross.[249] Luke's Gospel concludes with Jesus commissioning the disciples to preach "repentance for forgiveness of sins" (Luke 24:45–49). Wilson's conclusion is significant:

> The absence of direct quotations of Jeremiah 31:31–34 from Luke's Gospel does not require that we conclude that there is an absence of New Covenant theology. The one reasonable clear allusion to Jeremiah's prophecy which is found in Luke 22:20 suggests that Luke may have been more influenced by this strand of theology than first appearances suggest. The prophecy of Zechariah demonstrates a concern on Luke's part to incorporate material into his Gospel that signals a new era in God's dealings with his people.[250]

Recent Studies on the Theology of Hebrews

In the past few years, three works have appeared on the theology of Hebrews. Rissi finds in Hebrews an approach not unlike that of some of the Dead Sea Scrolls. The recipients of Hebrews are approaching God directly in a mystical, spiritual sense, which obviated any need for atonement. Hence the author emphasizes Christ's atonement along with the High Priest and Melchizedek themes, which were focal in the writings of the Qumran sect.[251]

Recent scholarship stands firm, however, in its refusal to see any real connection between Hebrews and the Qumran writings. In addition, Lindars critiques Rissi's thesis for failing to observe the structural emphasis of pastoral concern that is so prominent in significant sections of Hebrews, where the writer reassures his readers of Jesus'

---

[249] For example, Fitzmyer, *Luke I –IX*, 223, and Strelan, *Luke the Priest*, 134, make it clear that repentance and forgiveness are at the heart of the gospel in Luke-Acts.

[250] A. Wilson, "Luke and the New Covenant: Zechariah's Prophecy as a Test Case," *The God of Covenant: Biblical, Theological and Contemporary Perspectives*, ed. J. Grant and A. Wilson (Leicester: Apollos, 2005), 177.

[251] M. Rissi, *Die Theologie des Hebräerbriefes: ihre Verankerung in der Situation des Verfassers und seiner Leser* (Tübingen: Mohr, 1987), 3–25.

concern as their High Priest. Such passages suggest that the readers are deeply troubled by their sense of sin.[252]

This apparent self-consciousness of sin is a key factor in Lindars's assessment of the theology and purpose of Hebrews.[253] The key to the crisis that precipitated the writing can be found in 13:7–16:

> The next words warn against "strange teachings" and unprofitable "foods" (verse 9). What is meant has to be deduced from the substance of the whole of the letter. We are helped by the contrast in verse 10, where Hebrews claims that "we have an altar from which those who serve the tent have no right to eat." Those who serve the tent are clearly the Levitical priests, as described in chapter 9. This suggests that the strange teachings are the details of atonement sacrifice which were there set out. If so, the whole point at issue is a felt need on the part of the readers to resort to Jewish customs in order to come to terms with their sense of sin against God and need for atonement. Thus the central argument of the letter is precisely a compelling case for the complete and abiding efficacy of Jesus' death as an atoning sacrifice.[254]

The readers were neglecting to meet with the church (Heb 10:25) and were reverting to synagogue worship in order "to feel the benefit of the sacrificial system." The reason for this was their own consciousness of sin (Heb 9:9,14; 10:2). Since atonement is "constantly attended to" in the Jewish sacrificial system, their return to the Jewish community offered a practical way of coping with their need. The purpose of Hebrews is to explain to the readers how Christ's sacrifice not only dealt with their past life, but also their present (and future) sins. Reversion to the Jewish sacrificial system as a means of dealing with their present sin is not the answer, according to Hebrews.[255]

Lindars's theory founders on his suggestion that early Christian teaching did not make plain that post-baptismal sins are covered by Christ's death. The preaching of Peter and Paul in Acts as well as the Pauline Letters contradicts this aspect of Lindars's theory. If his assessment of the recipients' need is accurate, the problem lay in their spiritual immaturity and their failure to receive spiritual truth according to Heb 5:11–6:3; it did not lie in the early church's lack of theological clarity regarding the application of the atonement to sin in the life of a Christian. Yet if the recipients were converted priests, what Lindars suggests may have led to this need. If any group within the

---

[252] Lindars, *The Theology of the Letter to the Hebrews*, 25.
[253] Ibid., 8–15.
[254] Ibid., 10.
[255] Ibid., 12–14.

early church would have been in danger of what Lindars suggests, converted priests would be at the top of the list. Lindars's theory has the advantage of merging into a unified whole the doctrinal heart of the letter, the hortatory sections, and the practical exhortations of Hebrews 13.

Marie Isaacs adopts a post-AD 70 date for Hebrews and conjectures that the letter was written to Jewish Christians who were distraught over the destruction of the temple. Hebrews was written to point out that the permanent place of worship with a permanent high priest is heaven, where the Melchizedekian High Priest Jesus has entered forever and gained access for all who follow Him. Hebrews furnishes the readers with a reinterpretation of the Old Testament Scriptures dealing with sacred space.[256]

Like Lindars's proposal above, there is nothing in Isaacs' reconstruction of the theology and purpose of Hebrews that would preclude Lukan authorship (or, for that matter, the recipients from being Christian former priests). If there were any people overly loyal to the "sacred space" of the cultus after becoming Christians, it would be former priests.

Lindars briefly critiques the proposed reconstructions of Spicq, Montefiore, and Schmithals as speculative, since they base their reconstructions on supposed links with other parts of the New Testament (Spicq with Stephen; Montefiore with Apollos and the Jewish converts at Corinth; Schmithals with the estrangement between church and synagogue after AD 70).[257] Montefiore and Schmithals have both been faulted for the speculative nature of their reconstructions. However, the case is somewhat different with Spicq. For some time now, scholars have identified the connection between Acts 7 and Hebrews even when they have no interest in making some connection with the identity of the recipients, as Spicq does.

Conclusion

In the areas of Christology, eschatology, and prophecy and fulfillment, there is clear conceptual similarity between Luke-Acts and Hebrews. Many additional areas of similarity have been explored, including (but not limited to) the concept of salvation, theology of the

---

[256] Isaacs, *Sacred Space*, 15–67.
[257] Lindars, *The Theology of the Letter to the Hebrews*, 4–6.

cross, priestly terminology, and new covenant theology. The theological similarity that can be identified in Luke-Acts and Hebrews reinforces their overall conceptual approach to Christianity and provides an additional linchpin in the case for Lukan authorship.

The evidence of similarity between Luke-Acts and Hebrews can no longer be summarily dismissed by comments like Kendrick's: "In regard to Luke, noble as are the two undoubted productions of his pen, they furnish no indications of that depth of thought, and that profound knowledge of the Old Testament, which would have enabled him to write the Epistle to the Hebrews."[258] A. B. Bruce's remark, made over a hundred years ago, is strikingly presumptuous today: "He [Luke] certainly could not have been the author. The striking contrast between his account of the agony in the garden and that given in the Epistle is sufficient to settle the question."[259] Moffatt was no doubt aware of some of the parallels cited in this chapter, but argued that a common theological milieu is all that can be postulated.[260] I find it difficult to conceive of two theological communities so similar and yet unconnected in the early days of the church.

Godet was willing to go a step further than Moffatt, and argued that the writings of Luke are temporally and ideologically related to Hebrews:.

> For internal analogies compare the following . . . In Luke, the transformation of the Mosaic system into spiritual obedience. In the Epistle to the Hebrews, the transformation of the Levitical cultus into a spiritual cultus. In both, the idea of the human development of Jesus forming the foundation of the Christology.[261]

Eagar notes that Hebrews comes naturally as a third volume in the series following Luke-Acts:

> In word and thought the author treads in S. Stephen's footsteps. He follows, logically, the work and teaching of S. Paul. In this only book of the New Testament are unfolded in theory the relation between Judaism and Christianity, the doctrine of Christ's Priesthood and Sacrifice, the necessary merging of

---

[258] See C. Moll, "Hebrews," *Lange's Commentary on the Holy Scriptures, Critical, Doctrinal and Homiletical*, trans. and ed. A. C. Kendrick (Grand Rapids: Zondervan, n.d.), 10.

[259] A. B. Bruce, "Hebrews, Epistle to," *A Dictionary of the Bible Dealing with its Language, Literature, and Contents Including the Biblical Theology*, ed. J. Hastings (New York: Charles Scribner's Sons, 1902), 338.

[260] Moffatt, *Hebrews*, lxiv.

[261] F. L. Godet, *A Commentary on the Gospel of Luke*, 4th ed., trans. E. W. Shalders and M. D. Cusin (New York: Funk & Wagnalls, 1887), 548.

Judaism in a universal Church. The texts already cited from the Gospel canticles might fully form its all-sufficient motto.[262]

Goppelt concludes that Hebrews' interpretation of the gospel is "fully independent alongside Paul and John." The Christians addressed in Hebrews were growing weary and weak from the pressure of a hostile society. In this fact, Hebrews shares an affinity with Luke more than any other New Testament document. Goppelt saw a "whole series of particulars" of agreement between Luke and Hebrews as well. He cites the "linguistic proximity" of the books, including "characteristic technical terms of community parlance," such as Christ as *archēgos*, church leaders as *hēgoumenoi,* and Jesus having been perfected (*teteleiōtai*).[263] In addition, both Luke and Hebrews address a church situation "in a similar direction." The farewell address of Paul to the Ephesian elders (Acts 20) and the farewell discourse of Jesus (Luke 22) remind one of Heb 13:7–8. Goppelt concludes that the above points of contact "suggest that the theology of Hebrews and that of Luke should be considered together."[264]

Luke was a theologian in his own right and was quite capable of writing a work such as Hebrews. The greatest argument against Lukan authorship has always been his supposed Gentile background. There is actually a great deal of evidence from Luke-Acts to support the thesis that Luke was Jewish. We turn now to this issue.

---

[262] Eagar, "The Authorship of the Epistle to the Hebrews," 112.

[263] Goppelt, *Theology,* 2:265–66.

[264] Ibid., 266.

Chapter 6

THE IDENTITY OF LUKE AND THE JEWISH BACKGROUND OF LUKE-ACTS

The greatest objection to the Lukan authorship of Hebrews has always been the dual supposition that Luke was a Gentile whereas the author of Hebrews was Jewish. Neither of these suppositions is certain, and it is possible be that Luke was both a Gentile and the author of Hebrews. I think it highly probable that the author of Hebrews was Jewish, and this has kept most scholars from considering Luke as a candidate for authorship. On what basis have scholars assumed Luke's Gentile background? Is there any external or internal evidence that would support a Jewish background for Luke?

The Identity of Luke[1]

The name "Luke" occurs three times in the Pauline Epistles: Phlm 24; Col 4:14; and 2 Tim 4:9–11. He is called a "physician" in Col 4:14. There is a long-standing church tradition beginning with the Muratorian Canon (c. AD 170–80) that identifies the author of Luke-Acts as Luke the physician. Lines 2–8 of that canon read:

> The third book of the Gospel: According to Luke. This Luke was a physician. After the ascension of Christ, when Paul had taken him along with him as one devoted to letters, he wrote it under his own name from hearsay. For he himself had not seen the Lord in person, but, insofar as he was able to follow (at all), he thus began his account with the birth of John.[2]

Further evidence for Lukan authorship of Luke-Acts is found at the end of the second century in Irenaeus's *Adversus Haereses*: "Luke, too, the companion of Paul, set forth in a book the gospel as preached by him."[3] The extrabiblical *Prologue to the Gospels*, dated at the end of the second century AD, describes Luke as "a Syrian of Antioch, by profession a physician, the disciple of the apostles, and later a follower of Paul until his martyrdom. He served the Lord without distraction,

---

[1] A thorough review of the history of research on this issue can be found in J. Fitzmyer, *The Gospel According to Luke (I–IX): Introduction, Translation, and Notes*, AB 28 (Garden City: Doubleday, 1981), 35–62.

[2] K. Aland, *Synopsis Quattuor Evangeliorum Locus Parallelis Evangeliorum Apocryphorum et Patrum Adhibitis* (Stuttgart: Wurttembergische Bibelanstalt, 1964), 538.

[3] Irenaeus, *Adversus Haereses*, 3.4.1.

without a wife, and without children. He died at the age of eighty-four in Boeotia, full of the holy Spirit."[4] The title *Euangellion kata Lukan*, "the Gospel According to Luke," appears at the end of the oldest extant manuscript of Luke, dating c. AD 175–225. Eusebius summarized the tradition concerning Luke in the early fourth century:

> Luke, who was of Antiochian parentage and a physical by profession, and who was especially intimate with Paul and well acquainted with the rest of the apostles, has left us, in two inspired books, proofs of that spiritual healing art which he learned from them. One of these books is the Gospel, which he testifies that he wrote as those who were from the beginning eye-witnesses and ministers of the word delivered unto him, all of whom, as he says, he followed accurately from the first. The other book is the Acts of the Apostles which he composed not from the accounts of others, but from what he had seen himself. And they say that Paul meant to refer to Luke's Gospel wherever, as if speaking of some gospel of his own, he used the words, "according to my Gospel."[5]

These references show a solid tradition confirming Luke as the author of the Gospel and Acts.[6] He is said to be a doctor by profession.[7] There is no reference in these statements regarding Luke's ethnic background. Some have assumed that if Luke were from Antioch, he must have been a Gentile. However, Josephus suggests that a Jew from Antioch could have been called an "Antiochene."[8] Parsons concluded

---

[4] Aland, *Synopsis Quattuor*, 533.

[5] Eusebius, *Church History*, 3.4. *A Select Library of Nicene and Post–Nicene Fathers of the Christian Church*, 2nd Series, ed. P. Schaff and H. Wace, trans. A. McGiffert (Oxford: Parker & Co., 1890; repr., Edinburgh: T&T Clark, 1997), 1:136–37.

[6] See I. H. Marshall, "Acts and the 'Former Treatise,'" in *The Book of Acts in Its Ancient Literary Setting*, ed. B. W. Winter and A. D. Clarke (Grand Rapids: Eerdmans, 1993), 4:163–82.

[7] The medical language of Luke was discussed by W. Hobart, *The Medical Language of St. Luke* (Dublin: Hodges, Figgis, & Co., 1882), and H. Cadbury, "Lexical Notes on Luke-Acts: II. Recent Arguments for Medical Language," *JBL* 45 (1926): 190–209. More recently, G. H. R. Horsley, *New Documents Illustrating Early Christianity: A Review of the Greek Inscriptions and Papyri Published in 1977* (Sydney: Macquarie University Ancient History Documentary Research Center, 1982), 19–21, and M. Hengel and A. Schwemer, *Paulus zwischen Damaskus und Antiochien*, WUNT 108 (Tübingen: Mohr-Siebeck, 1998), 18–22, have shown that ancient medical doctors often traveled as itinerants. See also W. Marx, "Luke, the Physician, Re–examined," *ExpTim* 91 (1980): 168–72. B. Witherington III, *Conflict and Community in Corinth* (Grand Rapids: Eerdmans, 1995), 459–64, aligns himself with the traditional suggestion that Luke may have been Paul's personal doctor. Fitzmyer offers an excellent defense of the tradition that Luke was a doctor as well as an uncircumcised Semite and sometime companion of Paul. See J. Fitzmyer, *The Gospel According to Luke (I–IX)*, 35–59, and id., *Luke the Theologian: Aspects of His Teaching* (New York: Paulist Press, 1989), 1–26.

[8] Josephus, *Against Apion*, 2:39.

that "even the tradition that Luke was from Antioch . . . does not preclude his being Jewish."⁹

Not one of the church fathers identified Luke as a Gentile. Lardner's knowledge of the church fathers, reflected in his *The Credibility of the Gospel History* published in the eighteenth century, is undisputed. He commented on Luke's ethnic background from the perspective of the fathers:

> None of the writers . . . call him a Gentile. Some in Jerom's [*sic*] time, whose names we do not know, said, Luke had been a Jewish proselyte . . . none that I remember, expressly say that he was converted from Gentilism to Christianity. . . . All our writers who speak of Luke as a companion and disciple of apostles, must have supposed him to be a Jew.¹⁰

Lardner himself held this view, and considered the matter so clear-cut that he was quite surprised that the subject was even debated.¹¹ Plummer, writing late in the nineteenth century, mentioned Hoffmann, Tiele, and Wittichen as scholars who held the same view.¹² A host of scholars have advocated Luke's Jewish background, including A. C. Clarke, A. Schlatter, B. S. Easton, E. Ellis, J. Drury, D. Juel, R. Denova, and J. Jervell, while others admit the possibility.¹³

The tradition mentioned in Eusebius that Luke was a Godfearer has often been accepted since Godfearers are mentioned in Acts.¹⁴ Jerome said Luke may have been a proselyte to Judaism, but A. T.

---

⁹ M. Parsons, "Who Wrote the Gospel of Luke?" *BRev* 17 (2001): 19. Parsons also noted: "The narrative of Acts can also be read as supporting the view that Luke was a Jew or at least deeply interested in Judaism." M. Parsons, *Luke: Storyteller, Interpreter, Evangelist* (Peabody, MA: Hendrickson, 2007), 7.

¹⁰ N. Lardner, *The Works of Nathaniel Lardner* (London: William Bell, 1838), 5:362–63.

¹¹ Ibid., 5:364; and 6:137.

¹² A. Plummer, *Gospel According to St. Luke*, 4th ed., ICC (Edinburgh: T&T Clark, 1901), xix. Tiele sought to show that the Hebraisms in Luke's writings were an indication of Luke's Jewish background (J. N. Tiele, *Theologische Studien und Kritiken* [1858]: 4:753–55). See also A. Deissmann, *Light from the Ancient East* (London: Hodder, 1927), 438; E. C. Selwyn, *St. Luke the Prophet* (London/ New York: Macmillan, 1901), 37.

¹³ See E. Ellis, *Gospel of Luke*, NCBC (Nashville: Thomas Nelson & Sons, 1966; repr., London: Oliphants, 1977); the remainder of this chapter and the bibliography below. W. F. Albright argued that Luke was a Jewish Christian in his *New Horizons in Biblical Research* (London: Oxford University Press, 1966), 49. He argued on the basis of the Aramaic form of his name in Greek and the Hebrew idioms in the three poems in Luke 2–3.

¹⁴ Eusebius, *Church History*, 3.4.6. J. Nolland, *Luke 1–9:20*, WBC 35A (Dallas: Word, 1989), xxii–xxiii, says Luke's primary reader may well be a Godfearer. Cf. P. J. Tomson, "Gamaliel's Counsel and the Apologetic Strategy of Luke-Acts," in *The Unity of Luke-Acts*, ed. J. Verheyden, BETL 142 (Leuven/Louvain, Belgium: Leuven University Press, 1999), 603.

Robertson concluded that in all probability this was not the case.[15] Most scholars up to the mid-twentieth century believed that Luke was a Gentile, and a Greek rather than a Roman. Some have suggested that Luke may have been a freed slave. D. A. Hayes conjectured that Luke was born a slave in the household of Theophilus, a wealthy official at Antioch. After educating Luke as a physician, Theophilus set him free, and later came to Christianity through Luke.[16]

Robertson allowed for the possibility that Origen and Chrysostom were correct in identifying the reference in 2 Cor 8:18; 12:18 to Luke. This would make him the companion of Titus in bearing the Corinthian letter to its readers. Some have argued that Luke was Titus's brother based on 2 Cor 12:18, but this is just conjecture.[17]

There is an old tradition, from at least the fourth century, that Luke was one of the 70 sent out by Jesus.[18] Wenham argued for this based on Luke's use of this pericope, its length, and the "intimate details" that imply an eyewitness.[19] Wenham also argued for the validity of another tradition, dating to the tenth century or (probably) before, which identified Luke as the unnamed disciple on the road to Emmaus (Luke 24).[20] Both theories are interesting and certainly possible, although most scholars don't find either to be plausible. Such theories, however, especially that Luke was one of the 70, clearly consider Luke to be Jewish.

On the question of Luke's birthplace, Antioch in Syria has the greatest evidence.[21] The Codex Bezae (a "Western" text) on Acts 11:28 has the first "we" verse in Acts as occurring in Antioch: "And there

---

[15] A. T. Robertson, *Luke the Historian* (Nashville: B&H, 1920), 18.

[16] D. A. Hayes, *The Synoptic Gospels and the Book of Acts* (New York: The Methodist Book Concern, 1919), 179–82, 197.

[17] Robertson, *Luke the Historian*, 20–21; see, e.g., F. Badcock, *The Pauline Epistles and the Epistle to the Hebrews in Their Historical Setting* (New York: Macmillan, 1937), 217.

[18] Epiphanius of Cyprus, *Panarion*, 51.110.

[19] J. Wenham, "The Identification of Luke," *EvQ* 63 (1991): 5–7.

[20] Ibid., 29–32. See Lardner, *Works*, 2:87.

[21] Church tradition suggested Antioch in Syria as Luke's home. Cf. Eusebius, *Ecclesiastical History*, 3.4.6; A. Strobel, "Lukas der Antiochener (Bemerkungen zu Act 11:28D)," *ZNW* 49 (1958): 131–34; R. Glover, "'Luke the Antiochene' and Acts," *NTS* 11 (1964–65): 97–106. In favor of Antioch of Pisidia and Philippi see R. Rackham, *The Acts of the Apostles* (London: Metheun & Co., 1904; repr., Grand Rapids: Baker, 1978); W. Ramsay, *Luke the Physician and other Studies in the History of Religion* (London: Hodder & Stoughton, 1908; repr., Grand Rapids: Baker, 1956); and W. T. Whiteley, "Luke of Antioch in Pisidia," *ExpTim* 21 (1909–10): 164–66. W. Ramsay, *Saint Paul the Traveler and Roman Citizen* (New York: G. P. Putnam's Sons, 1904), 162–63, 302–4, argued Luke was a Macedonian and that Eusebius's words mean Luke "belonged to a family that had a connection with Antioch." S. Carpenter synthesized the views by suggest-

was great rejoicing; and when we were gathered together one of them stood up and said . . . ." This early tradition associates Luke with Barnabas and Paul at Antioch. Blass argued that this reading was to be accepted, and clearly showed that Luke was a member of the church at Antioch.[22] We have already seen that Eusebius (and others) spoke of Luke as an Antiochian by birth. This early tradition is confirmed by Acts. Clearly Luke displays a special interest in, even preference for, the church at Antioch.[23] This makes sense if he was a native of Antioch or had lived there for some time, or if Theophilus was from Antioch (or both).[24]

We know practically nothing Luke's education and time of conversion. The only thing we can say is that if the Western reading of Acts 11:28 is correct, then Luke was a Christian and member of the Antiochian church by c. AD 42.

The majority of New Testament scholars tend to view Luke as a Gentile Christian, and the only Gentile writer of the New Testament.[25] The evidential basis for such a conclusion consists in Luke's command of the Greek language, his occasional avoidance of Semitic words (when compared with the other Synoptics), the omission of Jesus' controversies with the Pharisaic understanding of the law, the transformation of local Palestinian customs and certain details into Hellenistic counterparts, and an inference drawn from Col 4:10–14.[26] This evidence, though admittedly skimpy and capable of differing

---

ing Luke was an Antiochian who had a medical practice at Philippi (S. Carpenter, *Christianity According to St. Luke* [New York: MacMillan Co., 1919], 20).

[22] F. Blass, *Philology of the Gospels* (London: Macmillan, 1898), 131.

[23] See A. Plummer, *A Critical and Exegetical Commentary on the Gospel According to Saint Luke*, ICC, 5th ed. (New York: Scribner, 1922), xxi; Robertson, *Luke the Historian*, 22; and J. Fitzmyer, *The Acts of the Apostles: A New Translation with Introduction and Commentary*, AB (New York: Doubleday, 1998), 46–47.

[24] G. Sterling, *Historiography and Self–definition: Josephus, Luke-Acts and Apologetic Historiography*, NovTSup 64 (Leiden: Brill, 1992), 327, suggests that the Lukan interest in Antioch is the *basis* of the tradition rather than evidence for it (emphasis mine).

[25] E.g., F. Bovon, *Luke 1: A Commentary on the Gospel of Luke 1:1–9:50*, trans. C. Thomas, Her (Minneapolis: Augsburg, 2002), 8, states: "Luke was most likely a Greek by birth, who turned to Judaism early in life; he belongs to that circle of sympathizers whom one designates 'God-fearers'."

[26] Fitzmyer, *Luke I–IX*, 41–42. From the fact that Luke points out the Sadducean unbelief in the resurrection in Acts 22, P. J. Tomson inferred that Luke did not grasp Paul's midrash on the high priest, thus confirming the tradition that Luke was a Gentile. P. J. Tomson, "Gamaliel's Counsel and the Apologetic Strategy of Luke-Acts," in Verheyden, *The Unity of Luke-Acts*. Given the evidence of Luke's grasp of the Old Testament and his own use of Jewish interpretive techniques, I find this inference hardly justified.

interpretations, has been enough to convince most scholars of Luke's Gentile origin. However, each of these has been brought into question in more recent years.

But the evidence may just as readily yield to another interpretation. We have seen numerous examples from Luke-Acts that could suggest Luke was writing from a Jewish perspective and primarily for a Jewish audience. Does the textual and historical evidence found in Luke-Acts best support a Gentile or a Jewish background for Luke? If a Gentile background is assumed, then is Luke a Roman or a Greek? If a Jewish background is assumed, then is he a Palestinian or Hellenistic Jew? It is my contention that Luke was a Hellenistic Jew with cosmopolitan training and interests.[27]

What does the historical and textual evidence reveal about Luke's name? Ramsay discovered in the papyri of Pisidian Antioch that "Luke" and "Lucius" were used interchangeably for the same individual.[28] The phenomenon is similar to our use of pet names and shortened forms of longer, more formal names, such as "Robert" and "Bob." "Luke" is found three times in the Pauline corpus: Col 4:14: 2 Tim 4:11; and Phlm 24. "Lucius" occurs twice in the New Testament: Acts 13:1 and Rom 16:21. In the latter passage, Lucius is coupled with Jason of Thessalonica and Sosipater of Berea. Paul refers to them all as "kinsmen," that is, Jews (cf. Rom 9:3; 16:7,11).

It has been suggested that Luke and the Lucius of Acts 13:1 may be the same individual. Others have said that perhaps the Lucius of Acts 13:1 and Rom 16:21 is Luke. It may be that the Lucius of Acts 13:1 and Rom 16:21 are the same individual.[29] There are good reasons for suggesting the Lucius of Rom 16:21 and Luke are identical.[30]

---

[27] The old argument that Luke's "universalism" is evidence for his Gentile ethnicity has been shown to be fallacious. Gaston rightly said, "That this so called 'universalism' of Luke's gospel is an unexamined myth handed down from one generation to the next is argued persuasively by N. Q. King." L. Gaston, *No Stone on Another: Studies in the Significance of the Fall of Jerusalem in the Synoptic Gospels*, NovTSup 23 (Leiden: Brill, 1970), 320n2.

[28] W. Ramsay, *The Bearing of Recent Discovery on the Trustworthiness of the New Testament,* 4th ed. (London: Hodder & Stoughton, 1920), 370–84; cf. also Robertson, *Luke the Historian,* 16–17, and W. M. Calder, "Christians and Pagans in the Graeco-Roman Levant," *Classical Review* 36 (1924): 29–31.

[29] E. C. Selwyn attests to this possibility (*St. Luke the Prophet,* 19). H. Grotius, cited in Lardner, *Works,* 5:369.

[30] Origen knew of people who identified the Lucius of Rom 16:21 with Luke, thus giving an early tradition in favor of this interpretation. See his *Commentary on the Epistle to the Romans: Books 6–10,* in *Fathers of the Church,* trans. T. Scheck, vol. 103 (Washington, D.C.: Catholic University of America Press, 2001), §39. Ephrem of Syria (fourth century) attests to this

The names of the men who gathered around Paul in Corinth, where he wrote Romans, are found in two places in the New Testament: Rom 16:21 and Acts 20:4–5. A comparison reveals two names common to both lists: Timothy and Sopater. But in Acts 20:5–6, Luke was present, as indicated by his use of "us" and "we." Interestingly enough, a "Lucius" is mentioned in the Roman list. Thus, there were simultaneously in Paul's company a "Luke" and a "Lucius." It seems probable that these two names refer to the same individual. If so, the question may be asked, Why does Paul refer to Luke on three occasions as "Luke" and as "Lucius" only in Rom 16:21? Paul may have chosen to use Luke's more formal name since Paul was personally unknown to the Christians at Rome. Similarly in the Romans list, "Sosipater" is used, the more formal spelling of "Sopater," which occurs in Acts 20:4. There is no mention of a "Lucius" in the Acts list, which is what we should expect if Luke is Lucius, and there is no "Luke" in the Romans list, only a Lucius. On all other occasions when Paul uses the name "Luke," it is in writing to churches or groups he had previously visited with Luke; thus Luke's familiar name is used. Origen attests to this identity of Luke and Lucius, giving us a rather early tradition in its favor. Reicke, who also identifies Luke and Lucius, concludes,

> If this hypothesis is accepted, the New Testament indicates that Luke the Evangelist was Jewish in origin. This is the simplest explanation of interest shown by the Gospel of Luke and the Acts of the Apostles in the redemptive history of the Old Testament, in preaching among the Jews, and in Jewish Christian traditions.[31]

Calder observed that Ramsay's evidence, although not conclusive, makes it "highly probable" that Luke's formal name was "Lucius" and not "Lucanus" because of "the frequency of the former and the rarity of the later name in the Greek East at this period."[32]

The chief objection to this identification is found in some scholars' interpretation of Col 4:10–14. Some have inferred from the listing of Luke's name separately from those "of the circumcision" that Luke was a Gentile. An examination of the textual evidence places this

---

connection. B. Reicke made the connection in his commentary on Luke: *The Gospel of Luke*, trans. R. Mackenzie (Richmond: John Knox, 1964), 24. E. E. Ellis thinks it probable (*History and Interpretation in New Testament Perspective*, Biblical Interpretation Series, 54 [Leiden: Brill, 2001], 92). For a recent argument identifying Luke with Lucius of Cyrene (Acts 13:1), see Wenham, "The Identification of Luke," 32–41.

[31] Reicke, *Luke*, 24.

[32] Calder, "Christians and Pagans in the Graeco-Roman Levant," 30.

inference on less stable ground. In vv. 10 and 11, three men are said to be "of the circumcision." In vv. 12 and 13, Epaphras is mentioned as being from Colossae. Then Luke is mentioned in v. 14. This is usually understood to mean that Luke is contrasted with those Jews and is therefore a Gentile. However, this interpretation has been contested for the following reasons: If Luke were a Gentile, why is there no clear mention of that fact, as there is with Titus in Galatians 2 and Timothy in Acts 16? Luke was a close associate of Paul, as were Titus and Timothy. Second, the train of thought has been broken in Col 4:10–14 by the intervening two verses dedicated to Epaphras. Third, perhaps Luke is mentioned last as being especially close to Paul. Fourth, Paul is not complaining that only three of his countrymen labored with him. Rather, he is commending three men who, though Jews, stood by him in some critical situation in the past (note the aorist verb "became" in v. 11). Finally, the assumption from these verses that Luke was a Gentile was never made by the church fathers.[33]

Albright has argued that one should not infer from Col 4:10–14 that Luke was uncircumcised.[34] His argument turns on the meaning of *hoi ontes ek peritomēs*. The phrase is usually translated "they of the circumcision" and interpreted to mean Jews. He suggests that the phrase be translated "they of the circumcision party" as in Gal 2:12, and thus refers to the Judaizers who insisted that circumcision was necessary for salvation.

Fitzmyer disputed Albright's interpretation on two counts. First, it makes no sense to say that the three men named were the only ones of the circumcision party who had been a comfort to Paul. Second, the phrase "one of yourselves" in v. 12 calls for the more general meaning of "converts from Judaism" for the phrase "they of the circumcision."[35] Even if the phrase does not mean "they of the circumcision," Wenham

---

[33] See the excellent discussions by Lardner, *Works*, 5:363; Reicke, *The Gospel of Luke*, 10–24; and Wenham, "The Identification of Luke," 10–16. Wenham's evaluation of the evidence is the most thorough. He argues cogently that we cannot infer a Gentile background for Luke from Col 4:11–14. Ellis argues the same point, noting what is now acknowledged by all, that first-century Judaism was in no way homogenous; various groups existed with different approaches to Judaism. The same complexities were brought into the church. Hence, he suggests that Aristarchus, Mark, and Jesus Justus (mentioned in Colossians 4) were Jewish Christians of the stricter type, whereas Luke was a more moderate Hellenistic Jew. E. Ellis, "'Those of the Circumcision' and the Early Christian Mission," *SE IV* (1968): 390–99.

[34] J. Munck, *The Acts of the Apostles*, rev. W. F. Albright and C. S. Mann, AB 31 (New York: Doubleday, 1967), 266.

[35] Fitzmyer, *Luke I–IX*, 44.

has conclusively shown, based on its usage elsewhere, that it cannot be assumed to refer to Christians of Jewish birth. It could apply to Christian Jews of a stricter mind-set concerning the law.[36] Strelan also argued against the common interpretation of Colossians 4 that Luke was a Gentile. He noted Selwyn's argument that Paul would not call himself "of the circumcision," yet no one would deny that Paul was a circumcised Jew; neither would Paul place Luke in that category. Strelan suggested the phrase "of the circumcision" more than likely referred to Jewish believers who were ritually strict.[37]

It is not at all obvious, as Wenham cogently argued, that Epaphras is a Gentile. There is no reason to think the church at Colossae lacked the usual nucleus of Jewish converts. The Colossian heresy was basically a Jewish and/or pre-gnostic heresy of some sort. Would the first missionary to Colossae, Epaphras (Col 1:5–7), have been a Gentile? Since it was Paul's philosophy to go to the Jews first, is it likely he would have chosen a Gentile for this role?[38] Wenham further stated how this applied to Luke at Jerusalem as well. When Luke accompanied Paul to Jerusalem, it was the presence of the uncircumcised Gentile Trophimus that nearly got Paul killed. Yet there is no hint of any trouble over Luke. "It is easier to see him acting as Paul's aide if he was a Jew by birth or a circumcised proselyte, than if he were a mere Gentile convert."[39]

It would seem precarious to dogmatically propose a Gentile background for Luke based on Colossians 4 alone. If Luke and Lucius were the same individual in the New Testament, then the statement about Lucius in Rom 16:21 makes it certain that Luke was a Jew.[40] We should at least heed the caution of Ralph Martin who doubted we should conclude from Colossians 4 that Luke was a Gentile. He said, "There is considerable evidence to argue the case that he was a

---

[36] Wenham, "The Identification of Luke," 13.

[37] R. Strelan, *Luke the Priest: the Authority of the Author of the Third Gospel* (Burlington, VT: Ashegate, 2009), 105.

[38] Ibid., 15.

[39] Ibid., 16.

[40] Some argue that the association of Luke with Antioch in Syria supports the notion that he was a Gentile. Two factors weaken such an argument. First, although Luke is, according to ancient tradition, said to be a native of Antioch, he is never said to be Greek. Second, Josephus's statement (*Against Apion*, 2:1 §39) that "our Jewish inhabitants of Antioch are called Antiochenes" could be used to support the argument that Luke was a Jew from Antioch. See Fitzmyer, *Luke I–IX*, 45.

Hellenistic Jew."[41] David Pao's recent extensive study of Luke's use of Isaiah in Luke-Acts led him to conclude, "Luke is most likely a god-fearer if not himself a Jew."[42]

At the very least, Eric Franklin is right:

> Whether Luke was himself a Jew must remain an open question. At any rate, however, he must have been one who was influenced supremely by the Jewish faith, one who loved our nation, who was moved by its law and captivated by its Scriptures, one who was led to see in Jesus a fulfillment of its hopes and a widening of its promises.[43]

Clarke, in reference to Plummer's comment about Luke being the "versatile Gentile," strongly supported the opposite idea that Luke must have been a Jew if he is to be considered the author of Luke-Acts:

> I find this theory of the versatile Gentile very unconvincing. Greek was the literary language of the East and known to all Jews with any claim to culture. It is easy to see that a Jew when writing Greek would from time to time use native idioms and constructions. It is difficult to conceive the case of a Greek who became so saturated with Hebraic idioms as to use them when writing in his own tongue. If, therefore, the meaning of Col. iv. 10–14 is that Loukas was a Greek, it is hard to suppose that he wrote either of the works attributed to him.[44]

Jervell came to a similar conclusion.

> That Luke was able to write Greek in a good style does not show that he was a Gentile—many Jews did so. In spite of his ability to write decent Greek, he does so only seldom and sporadically. Most of his work he presents in what may be called biblical Greek, clearly influenced by the Septuagint, a Jewish book, written for Jews and not for Gentiles. Luke's stylistic home was the synagogue. He was a Jewish Christian.[45]

---

[41] R. Martin, *Colossians: The Church's Lord and the Christian's Liberty* (Exeter: Paternoster, 1972), 146.

[42] D. Pao, *Acts and the Isaianic New Exodus* (Tübingen: Mohr Siebeck, 2000), 25.

[43] E. Franklin, *Christ the Lord: A Study in the Purpose and Theology of Luke-Acts* (Philadelphia: Westminster, 1975), 79. Cf. G. Harvey, *The True Israel: Uses of the Names of Jew, Hebrew and Israel in Ancient Jewish and Early Christian Literature,* AGJU 35 (Leiden: Brill, 1996), 194; and Jervell, who patently says Luke is Jewish. Also J. Jervell, *The Theology of the Acts of the Apostles* (Cambridge: Cambridge Univ. Press, 1996), 5.

[44] A. C. Clarke, *Acts of the Apostles* (Oxford: Clarendon, 1933), 393.

[45] Jervell, *Theology of Acts,* 5. Selwyn (*St. Luke the Prophet,* xxi), commented: "Luke was a Jew and there is no ground for the other supposition." Many argue, like M. Goulder, that the Semitisms in Luke 1–2 are not because of a Hebrew or Aramaic source, but are Luke's own Septuagintal style. M Goulder, *Luke: A New Paradigm* (Sheffield: JSOT Press, 1994), 115.

Strelan argued recently for Luke's Jewishness on two grounds: (1) Luke's knowledge and use of the Old Testament Scriptures, and (2) his authority to write as he did. Strelan reasoned that the authority of a writer in a small community of Christians in the first century was a crucial issue, and a Jewish teacher would be more easily accepted than a Gentile one.[46] He argued that Luke was a priest, "largely on the basis of the question of his authority."[47] Among other evidence cited by Strelan is Luke's focus on repentance and forgiveness. "It seems reasonable to suggest that a priest, involved as he was in the Temple cult and its sin offerings, in purity laws, in teaching the people to live according to the laws and commandments of God, would be attracted to—and therefore would highlight—the aspect of repentance and forgiveness as understood in the gospel."[48]

Ellis made the somewhat startling suggestion that Paul's "kinsmen" referred to in Rom 16:7,11,21 were his relatives. If the Lucius of Rom 16:21 is identified with Luke, as Ellis thought probable, then Paul reveals something about his familial relationship with Luke as well as his strategy for doing mission work:

> He utilized contacts with his relatives in charting the evangelization of Thessalonica and Berea and, upon their conversion, accepted them as fellow workers in the mission and used their homes as house-churches for his congregations. If Luke was also a kinsmen, it would not only put to rest the traditional but mistaken view that Luke was a Gentile but would also explain Paul's mission route to Troas. He traveled there with the intention of adding a confidant to his team who was familiar with the area and was apparently already ministering in Troas (Acts 16:10, "we").[49]

Another issue to consider is the occasional suggestion that Luke and Silas are the same person.[50] Before exploring this possibility, we need to examine what we know of Silas (Silvanus) in the New Testament. Peter informs his readers that Silvanus is the courier of the letter (1 Pet 5:12). Most scholars believe he is the same individual named in 1 Thess 1:1 and 2 Thess 1:1 as a joint author of these letters

---

[46] Strelan, *Luke the Priest*, 106.

[47] Ibid., 113. This suggestion goes well beyond the bounds of evidence.

[48] Ibid., 135. Strelan suggested that Luke also demonstrates strong interest in teaching and in biblical interpretation, two common roles of priests. Also, the issues and concerns discussed at the Jerusalem Council (Acts 15) all had to do with matters of purity, which would have been the concern of priests (pp. 132–33).

[49] Ellis, *History and Interpretation in New Testament Perspective*, 92–93.

[50] E.g., see Selwyn, *St. Luke the Prophet*, 75.

with Paul and Timothy. He is likewise considered by most to be the same as the Silas of Acts 15:40, whom Paul chose as a partner for his second missionary journey.[51] He is present at the Jerusalem Council (Acts 15) and one of the "leading men among the brethren." Paul speaks of himself and Silas in 1 Thess 2:6 as "apostles of Christ." E. G. Selwyn said of him: "He may well have been one of those 'eyewitnesses and ministers of the word' on whom St. Luke drew for his Gospel (Lk. 1:2); and the affinities observable between 1 Peter and St. Peter's speeches in Acts, as well as other parts of the narrative in Acts 1–15, are perhaps to be traced to information which he supplied; all the more as Luke and Silas were for some time fellow–travelers."[52] It is clear that his responsibilities and position were significant.

One of the critical interpretive issues in 1 Peter is the meaning of 5:12. Was Silvanus the amanuensis for Peter or was he the courier of Peter's letter?[53] The bulk of scholarship today opts for the latter. Whether or not one accepts traditional Petrine authorship, or views Silvanus as the amanuensis or the courier, 1 Peter shows a remarkable similarity to both the writings of Luke (especially Acts) and Hebrews, as can be demonstrated from a cursory look at the commentaries.[54]

Selwyn is representative of those who have argued Silvanus was more than an amanuensis. He considered it unlikely that Peter was indebted to Silas only for the style of 1 Peter, and thinks that one who had been a joint author with Paul would not have been relegated by Peter to a "merely literary office" as amanuensis. He would have made his own contribution to the content as well as the language of the letter. In other words, "he drafted, or helped to draft, it."[55]

Though not the first, Selwyn argued in 1901 that Silas and Luke were the same individual. This is seldom advocated today, but his

---

[51] E.g., see discussions in J. B. Lightfoot, *Notes on the Epistles of St. Paul* (Peabody, MA: Hendrickson, 1993); and E. G. Selwyn, *The First Epistle of St. Peter: The Greek Text with Introduction, Notes, and Essays*, 2nd ed. (London: MacMillan & Co., 1947; repr., Grand Rapids: Baker, 1981) 9–17.

[52] Selwyn, *First Peter*, 11–12.

[53] See the discussion of this matter in the commentaries, especially J. Elliott, *First Peter*, ed. W. F. Albright and D. N. Freedman, AB 37b (New York: Doubleday, 2000), 123–24. The best overall treatment of this issue is E. R. Richards, "Silvanus Was Not Peter's Secretary: Theological Bias in Interpreting διὰ Σιλουανοῦ . . . ἔγραψα," *JETS* 43.3 (2000): 417–32. The bulk of scholarship also denies Petrine authorship.

[54] See, for example, C. Bigg, *A Critical and Exegetical Commentary on the Epistles of St. Peter and St. Jude*, 2nd ed., ICC (Edinburgh: T&T Clark, 1902), 21–22; P. Achtemeier, *1 Peter*, Her (Minneapolis: Fortress, 1996), 14–15; 20–21.

[55] Selwyn, *First Peter*, 11–12.

evidence is not without some merit. Selwyn claimed that Silas's movements in Acts, when compared with the "we" sections, result in a rather startling fact: "Whenever the We-document is present Silas is unmentioned; as soon as he is mentioned again, the We-document ceases."[56] One never finds the two (Silas and Luke) in the same place together. This appears to be true in both the Pauline Letters and in Acts.

Selwyn supposed that the "we" source documents in Acts were from Silas, a companion of Paul and thus an eyewitness, and that Luke used them in Acts. But Luke made a somewhat "fragmentary" use of the document, i.e., using it sometimes without the "we," even though for long periods of time, beginning with Acts 15:40, Silas was with Paul. The first "we" section occurs after Silas joins Paul, and it is usually surmised that Luke begins the "we" section here because he joined Paul in Macedonia (or just before arriving there). Thus, the absence of Silas in the "we" sections of Acts coupled with his presence when the "we" sections are not found, led Selwyn to propose that Luke is Silas, also called Silvanus by Paul and Peter.[57]

Selwyn also concluded that 2 Peter was written at Rome under the immediate direction of Peter, in his infirmity and old age, and that the amanuensis was Luke. He arrived at this view prior to deciding that Luke and Silas were the same individual.[58] Of course, Selwyn interpreted 1 Pet 5:12 to mean that Peter wrote by the agency of Silvanus, (rather than that he sent the letter by Silvanus). Virtually all scholars consider Silvanus to be a form of "Silas" and thus to refer to Paul's missionary companion. Furthermore, the linguistic similarities between 2 Peter and Luke-Acts are more easily explained by this theory.

Comparing the Old Testament quotations in 1 Peter with those in 2 Peter reveals a remarkable contrast in terms of their number. First Peter contains no fewer than 36 quotations; 2 Peter contains only six. While 2 Peter quotes from only three Old Testament books, the

---

[56] E. C. Selwyn, *St. Luke the Prophet*, 84. In the mid-nineteenth century, J. Conder conjectured that Silas and Luke are the same individual, that Silas (Luke) wrote Hebrews, but perhaps then died and Paul appended the exhortations to chapter 13. He states that if Hebrews were not written by Paul, "both internal and external evidence would lead us to refer its composition to Silas or Luke." J. Conder, *The Literary History of the New Testament* (London: Seeley, Burnside & Seeley, 1845), 466.

[57] Ibid., 41.

[58] Ibid., 111.

predominant quotations in 1 Peter are from those books, namely, Isaiah (11), Psalms (8), and Proverbs (5).

Selwyn compared the conceptual similarity between the Petrine writings and Luke. In 2 Pet 2:15, *misthon adikias* compares with Acts 1:18, *ek misthou tēs adikias*, in reference to Judas. He observed Blass's correlation of Acts 20:3 with 2 Pet 1:20 (*ginesthai gnōmēs*) "to become part of a decision," a Classical phrase occurring nowhere else in the New Testament.[59] He found other more tenuous connections, such as *muōpazōn* added to the *tuphlos* in 2 Pet 1:9 as a possible indication of a medical diagnosis.[60] Selwyn compared the parable of the Wicked Husbandmen in the Synoptics and found "unexpected light" to support the theory that Luke was the amanuensis for the Petrine Letters. I shall quote his entire argument:

> Mark and Matthew have given a clue to the identity of "the builders" with "the husbandmen," which is conspicuous by its absence in Luke. They have quoted just one more expression from the introductory passage in Isaiah than Luke has: "and built a tower." Obviously the owner employed his own labourers to build; thus the builders can be readily identified with the husbandmen in the midst of Mark and Matthew. Not so does Luke understand the bearing of "the builders." To him the husbandmen have been husbandmen for ages past throughout the history of the Jewish Church; the builders, on the other hand, are those of the days of Christ, who having the materials and the power to build the house of God with Jesus as the chief corner-stone, reject Him, but at their peril. He expressed this peril of stumbling, and possibly worse; in words which clearly enough recall the very same passage of Is viii 14 which we have seen was familiar with him in this connexion in I Pet ii 7 and in I Pet iv 17, and to which he also referred in 2 Pet i 10, "make your calling and election sure: for while ye do this ye surely shall never stumble; for thus shall richly be provided for you the entrance into the eternal kingdom of our Lord." Only when the thread of thought is supplied by the connexion of Is viii 14, Is xxviii 15, and Ps cxviii 22, which are all illustrated by the light of Enoch xci 13 . . . , do we gain the clue to the understanding of passages so remote as Luke xx 18 and 2 Pet i 10f. The very expression "ye shall not surely" (οὐ μὴ [*ou mē*] with aorist subjunctive) in the latter place takes us back to the same construction in Is xxviii 16. These facts are most conclusive evidence that none but Luke, the author of Luke, can be the author of I Peter and of 2 Peter. They are not explained by the simple supposition that before writing his Gospel Luke had studied the two Epistles carefully. No mere reader could have so deeply imbibed their inward meaning as to reproduce, in connexion with the wicked husbandmen, the thought

---

[59] Ibid., 160.
[60] Ibid., 150.

of the spiritual stone of stumbling where St Mark had before him only that of the chief corner-stone.[61]

Selwyn pointed out that apart from 1 and 2 Peter, Peter's teaching is not found anywhere but in Acts,[62] and concluded: "Thus the hand of Silvanus, of which St. Peter so candidly avows in his conclusion that he has availed himself, is abundantly attested in the style, structure and contents of 1 Peter. The only view which takes account of all the phenomena is that Luke is Silas, just as Silas is Silvanus."[63]

If this theory is correct (and one readily admits its conjectural nature), then the connection between Luke and Hebrews becomes stronger for obvious reasons. Both Bigg and E. G. Selwyn cited the affinities between Hebrews and 1 Peter. Selwyn said they are "striking."[64] He found the similarities between Hebrews 13 and 1 Peter to be strong enough that some relationship beyond common tradition and circumstances must be posited.[65] Selwyn concluded that it is possible Silas was with the author of Hebrews when he wrote, thus explaining the similarities. The many other lexical and conceptual similarities between the Petrine Letters and Hebrews would be more easily understood (much the same way as the parallels between the Pastoral Epistles with Luke would be) if Silas functioned as Peter's amanuensis.

If Luke and Silas are not the same individual, as most scholars believe, their close relationship in the Pauline circle as revealed in Acts and their proximity to Peter in Acts could shed light on the similarities among the writings of Luke, Hebrews, and the Petrine Letters. Narborough found the similarities extensive enough to suggest that the author of Hebrews was influenced by 1 Peter. He opted for Petrine authorship of 1 Peter and suggests 1 Peter was written before Hebrews since Peter died during the Neronian persecution.[66] When all the similarities are tabulated and evaluated, they reveal that 1 and 2 Peter have more affinities with Luke and Hebrews than with any

---

[61] Ibid., 196–97.

[62] Ibid., 166.

[63] Ibid., 160–61.

[64] C. Bigg, *A Critical and Exegetical Commentary on the Epistles of St. Peter and St. Jude*, ICC, 2nd ed. (Edinburgh: T&T Clark, 1902); Selwyn, *First Peter*, 463. Statements such as "you are a King's house . . . a body of priests" in 1 Peter would parallel the thought of Hebrews.

[65] See the chart in Selwyn, *First Peter*, 465, for the similarities of Heb 13:20–21 with both Hebrews and the Thessalonian letters.

[66] F. D. V. Narborough, *The Epistle to the Hebrews* (Oxford: Clarendon, 1930), 12.

other document. This is of some interest for our theory of the Lukan authorship of Hebrews.[67]

Jewish Aspects of Luke-Acts

In recent years, the increasing awareness of the intensely Jewish aspects of Luke's writings has prompted a reevaluation of their theology and readership. However, many have mentioned "the familiarity with Jewish affairs" that Luke "assumes on the part of his readers."[68] The prevailing paradigm of Luke's supposed Gentile orientation began to be seriously challenged in the early 1970s by Jacob Jervell's *Luke and the People of God* (1972), and Eric Franklin's *Christ the Lord: A Study in the Purpose and Theology of Luke-Acts* (1975), both of whom argued that the traditional understanding of Luke's background and purpose was wrong.[69] Lukan scholars have probed this subject for several decades, and both Luke's Gospel and Acts are viewed by many today against a Jewish background.[70]

---

[67] Sometimes it is suggested that the author of 1 Peter used Hebrews, or that a common milieu explains the similarities. Wohlenberg made a thorough examination of the similarities between 1 Peter and Hebrews and concluded that the best solution was to posit common authorship (G. Wohlenberg, "Wer hat den Hebräerbrief verfasst?" *NKZ* 24 [1913]: 742–62). While I think Peter is the author of both letters attributed to him, these studies exemplify the strong connection between Hebrews and the Petrine Letters. Whether or not Silas is Luke (and this is very doubtful), somehow the high degree of similarity for Luke-Acts, Hebrews, and the Petrine Letters must be explained. I find it doubtful that the similarities can be explained simply by appeal to a common milieu.

[68] E. D. Burton, "The Purpose and Plan of the Gospel of Luke," *Biblical World* 16 (1900): 258.

[69] See also J. Jervell, *The Unknown Paul: Essays on Luke-Acts and Early Christian History* (Minneapolis: Augsburg, 1984), and his *Theology of the Acts of the Apostles*.

[70] For additional material dealing with the Jewishness of Luke-Acts not specifically discussed here, see G. Lohfink, *Die Sammlung Israels: Eine Untersuchung zur lukanischen Ekklesiologie* (Munich: Kosel, 1975); and J. C. O'Neill, *The Theology of Acts in its Historical Setting* (London: SPCK, 1961), 146–65. O'Neill discusses Luke's debt to Hellenistic Judaism. See also Goulder, *Luke: A New Paradigm*, 116–19. The question of Luke's attitude toward the Jews has received intense scrutiny in recent years. The collection of essays dealing with this topic in Tyson 1988, where eight scholars present their views pro and con on the issue, is very helpful on this subject. See also J. Tyson, *Images of Judaism in Luke-Acts* (Columbia: University of South Carolina Press, 1992), and S. Mason, "Chief Priests, Sadducees, Pharisees and Sanhedrin in Acts," in *The Book of Acts in Its Palestinian Setting*, ed. R. Bauckham (Grand Rapids: Eerdmans, 1995), 115–78. J. Sanders in *The Jews in Luke-Acts* (Philadelphia: Fortress, 1987) defends the view that Luke had a strongly anti–Jewish bias. A balanced presentation appears in Part III, the last six chapters of *Literary Studies in Luke-Acts: Essays in Honor of Joseph B. Tyson*, ed. R. Thompson and T. Phillips (Macon: Mercer University Press, 1998), 235–344, where Susannah Heschel, Robert Tannehill, Robert Brawley, Jack Sanders, Thomas Phillips, and Richard Thompson all address this subject.

For example, Joseph Tyson's *Images of Judaism in Luke-Acts* is a significant study on this subject. He notes a "remarkable imbalance" in that Luke displays keen interest in the Jews who accepted Jesus and those who did not, but there is no such interest in Gentiles, especially those who reject the gospel. He further states,

> Story after story in both the gospel and Acts tells of Jewish acceptance or rejection of the message of Jesus, the apostles, and Paul. In addition, verbal images of Jewish people, institutions, piety, and religious practices add color to the narratives. The interest in Jewish religious life is remarkable, especially in Acts, and, despite the author's sympathy with the mission to the Gentiles, there is no corresponding interest in Gentile religious life. What little there is pales into insignificance when compared with the rich detail about Jewish traditions.[71]

Tyson points out that many of the activities, experiences, and conflicts of the lead characters of Acts involve questions of Jewish religious observance. Furthermore, internal conflict in the early church has implications for the wider Jewish community. "These relationships are among the fundamental concerns revealed in Luke-Acts."[72]

Luke skillfully integrated both Hellenistic and Jewish components in his two-volume work.[73] While not denying the Hellenistic outlook of Luke-Acts, or Luke's obvious interest in the Gentile mission, Jervell and others have shown that it is possible to interpret them as having been written from a Jewish perspective and for a Jewish audience. Maddox, against Jervell, denies that Luke attempts to associate the Gentiles in the church with Israel. Houlden wonders whether Maddox's description of the issue does justice to the positive aspects of Luke's portrayal of Judaism. He concludes that it does not, and for several reasons. First, Luke emphasizes the large-scale success of the Christian mission in and around Jerusalem. "This material sits uneasily with the blanket condemnations of Israel elsewhere; and if Luke's dominant attitude towards Judaism is to emphasize God's well-merited judgment upon it, then it is hard to understand his deliberate introduction of episodes that point the mind in another direction."[74]

---

[71] Tyson, *Images of Judaism in Luke-Acts*, 3.

[72] Ibid., 4. Strelan notes that in addition to Luke's allusions to the Old Testament throughout Luke-Acts, "Luke's choice of vocabulary in his narrative to describe people's reactions is so typically 'Jewish'." Strelan, *Luke the Priest*, 112.

[73] E. Richard, "Luke: Author and Thinker," in *New Views on Luke and Acts*, ed. E. Richard (Collegeville, MN: Liturgical, 1990), 15–32.

[74] Houlden, "Purpose of Luke," 55.

The fact is, Luke does not view judgment on Judaism and Jewish support for Jesus and the new church as incompatible. Second, Luke depicts the expansion of Jesus' ministry and the church as being built on a Jewish foundation in a way that is unparalleled in the New Testament. Third, Jesus and the early church "lean in a Jewish direction." Examples include their temple attendance and Paul's Nazarite vow.[75]

I will argue for the probability that Luke was a Jew and wrote primarily for a Jewish audience. This is based on evidence brought to light by recent research and on the number of textual features that indicate a Jewish background for both writer and audience. Hebrews is adjudged by most scholars to have been written by a Jew. Since the possibility of Luke's Jewish background must now be acknowledged, a major obstacle for Lukan authorship has been removed.

Birth Narratives of Luke 1–2[76]

Luke begins his two-volume work with a very stately Hellenistic prologue, then plunges the reader into two chapters of distinctly and sometimes minutely-detailed Jewish events and terminology. It is not only Luke's knowledge of these details, much of which one could obtain from the LXX, but that in many cases his knowledge extends beyond the LXX. For example, Luke 1:5 reflects knowledge of the recommended marriage of priests to the "daughters of Aaron." This is not found in the LXX and goes beyond anything in the Pentateuch concerning priests. It is, however, part and parcel of first-century practice within Judaism.[77] Likewise, the use of lots to determine which priest should offer incense (Luke 1:9) is not found in canonical Scripture but is implied in extrabiblical Jewish literature.[78]

The Greek of the Lukan infancy narrative is heavily Semitic when compared with the rest of the Gospel. This has been explained

---

[75] Ibid., 53–58. Houlden believes Maddox has not placed Luke's attitude toward the Jews in proper focus.

[76] I do not concur with New Testament scholars who suggest that the infancy narratives were not originally part of the Third Gospel. See the critique of this position in Tyson, *Images of Judaism*, 43–45. Tyson's discussion of the infancy narratives occurs on pp. 42–55. Furthermore, the programmatic nature of these chapters is now generally recognized. See, for example, D. Tiede, *Luke*, ACNT (Minneapolis: Augsburg, 1988), 39.

[77] See Str-B 2:68–71, as noted by Goulder, *Luke: A New Paradigm*, 116.

[78] Goulder, *Luke: A New Paradigm*, 116. See E. Schürer, *History of the Jewish People in the Time of Jesus Christ*, trans. S. Taylor and P. Christie (Edinburgh: T&T Clark, 1885), 2:287, who identifies this implication from *Mishna Shekalim*, 5.1. See also M. Hengel, "The Geography of Palestine in Acts," in *The Book of Acts in its Palestinian Setting*, 42.

primarily in two ways. The "translation theory" suggests that Luke has translated one or more Hebrew or Aramaic sources. A variant of the translation theory suggests that the author of Luke's Gospel had access only to the Greek translation of an original Hebrew source. The more widely held "imitation theory" suggests that Luke imitated Septuagint Greek.[79] Either way, it is generally agreed that the Greek of Luke's infancy narrative reflects Septuagintal influence and that the narrative is characteristic of Luke's own style. Why would Luke write in this fashion? Theological considerations may provide a partial answer to this question. It is also possible that Luke was not a Gentile.

It is not only the style but the content of these two chapters that is Septuagintal. C. K. Barrett argued that Luke was a historian in the Greek tradition, but Drury proposes that Luke was more of a historian in the storytelling tradition of the Old Testament, the Apocrypha, and Josephus.[80] Gärtner evaluates the Greek and Jewish methods of historiography and concludes that Luke followed the course of events from a Jewish perspective, both in his narrative sections as well as his use of speeches.[81]

The sudden shift from the stately Hellenistic prologue to details of Jewish life, including features of the temple and its practices, is noteworthy to say the least. The entire birth narrative (with its distinct Jewish flavor) is odd if Luke wrote for a Gentile audience, but natural if he wrote for a Jewish audience. Both the *Magnificat* (Luke 1:46–55) and the *Benedictus* (Luke 2:28–32) are filled with statements

---

[79] The best treatment of this subject is C. Jung, *The Original Language of the Lukan Infancy Narrative* (London: T&T Clark, 2004), esp. 210–15. See also S. Farris, *The Hymns of Luke's Infancy Narrative: Their Origin, Meaning, and Significance*, JSNTSup 9 (Sheffield: JSOT Press, 1985), 31–50.

[80] C. K. Barrett, *Luke the Historian in Recent Study* (London: Epworth, 1961), 7–15; J. Drury, *Tradition and Design in Luke's Gospel* (Atlanta: John Knox, 1976), 8. The literature on this subject has expanded significantly in recent years. See especially related articles and bibliography in *The Book of Acts in its Ancient Literary Setting*, ed. B. Winter and A. Clarke, vol. 1 (Grand Rapids: Eerdmans, 1993), and *The Book of Acts in its Palestinian Setting* in the six-volume series *The Book of Acts in its First Century Setting*, ed. B. Winter (1995). L. Johnson, *A Commentary on the Gospel of Luke*, SP 3 (Minneapolis: Liturgical, 1991), 5–8, argues that Luke fits better into the category of Hellenistic historiography. See also G. Sterling, *Historiography and Self-definition: Josephus, Luke-Acts and Apologetic Historiography*, NovTSup 64 (Leiden: Brill, 1992). Schreckenberg calls Luke and Josephus "theological historians," and notes the similar ways in which Luke and Josephus arrange and edit their material according to similar viewpoints. H. Schreckenberg and K. Schubert, *Jewish Historiography and Iconography in Early and Medieval Christianity, Jewish Traditions in Early Christian Literature* 2 (Assen/Maastricht: Van Gorcum; Minneapolis: Fortress, 1992), 45–47.

[81] B. Gärtner, *The Areopagus Speech and Natural Revelation*, trans. C. H. King, ASNU 21 (Uppsala: Gleerup, 1995), 26–28.

and references that would make little sense to a Gentile reader unfamiliar with Jewish customs. Emphasis is placed on Jesus' circumcision, a point omitted by the other Gospel writers. Luke alone records the presentation of the child Jesus in the temple, and His subsequent teaching activity there as a child of twelve.

Jerusalem and especially the temple command the reader's attention in Luke 1–2. The geographical center is Jerusalem, with the temple at the center of that (Luke 1:5–23; 2:22–39,41–51). Temple activity is prominent as Luke recounts the burning of incense, the circumcision and naming of the child Jesus, the purification rite with its accompanying sacrifice, and the celebration of the Passover. Focus on spiritual piety is evidenced by references to obedience to the law, prayer, and fasting. Theologically, Luke is at pains to demonstrate first-century Israel as God's people in continuity with the Israel of the Old Testament law, prophets, and promises. Take note of the references to Aaron (1:5), Elijah (1:17), Nazarites (1:15), David (1:27,32,69; 2:4,11), Abraham (1:55,73), the prophets (1:70), the fathers (1:72), Moses (2:22), scribes (2:46), and not least the many references to the Jewish messianic hope that pervades the two chapters (1:32–33; 2:11,25–26,29–32,38).[82]

Eagar points out that the content of these two chapters reveals not only Luke's Jewish perspective, but also the similarity in conception and purpose to the Book of Hebrews. Eagar says that Luke's Gospel of the childhood "rings with the same music that sounds through the whole letter to the Hebrews."

> Behind this great group of pictures, the poet and artist of the Evangelists shows dying Judaism, shorn of it's prophetic power, widowed and forlorn; he tells us how, at the Advent of Him whose coming was told "aforetime to the Fathers by the forth-tellers," the dumb religion broke out into its Te Deum of joy; he, and he alone, has saved for us the story of how the surroundings of Christ at His birth summed up the meaning of all Revelation that had been and foretold all Revelation that was to be.[83]

Luke has placed his message of eschatological salvation in the setting of Jerusalem and the temple in the infancy narratives.[84] Chance

---

[82] See, among many who have pointed out this intensely Jewish coloring, W. B. Tatum, "The Epoch of Israel: Luke I–II and the Theological Plan of Luke-Acts," *NTS* 13 (1966–67): 184–95.

[83] A. Eagar, "The Authorship of the Epistle to the Hebrews," *Expositor* 6 (1904): 111.

[84] Tyson says the infancy narratives "display a form of Judaism that is temple-centered" (*Images of Judaism*, 49).

suggests this might be evidence that Luke was familiar with contemporary Jewish thinking on this point and that he imitated it.[85]

Priests in Luke-Acts

It can easily be established from Luke's writings that he had a definite interest in priestly matters. His Gospel begins with the story of Zechariah the priest performing his temple duty. Besides informing us that Zechariah was chosen by lot (see above), Luke tells us he was a priest "of the division of Abijah" (1:5), but gives no explanation as to what this means. Details of his service "according to the customs of the priesthood" (1:9) are given. Even when Luke describes Elizabeth, he indicates that she is from a priestly family, being "of the daughters of Aaron" (1:5). Such statements assume a great deal of Jewish knowledge on the part of Luke's his readers.[86]

According to Luke 22:54, Jesus is led to the house of the high priest during His trial. He is then led into the council chamber (Luke 22:66). This chamber is the *sunedrion*, a place distinguished by the members of the high council also called by this name. The other Gospel writers do not add this detail. Mason suggests that Luke knew trials were conducted in a special chamber and not in the home of the high priest.[87] One may at least say that if Luke was a Gentile, he was thoroughly conversant with Jewish priestly practices and took valuable space to record a number of details that might otherwise have been of little interest to a Gentile reader.

Turning to Acts, we find Luke referring to many priests who had become obedient to the faith (6:7). In 19:14, he mentions the seven sons of the Jewish high priest Sceva and their escapades. Why include such material if Luke is writing to Gentiles only? Of particular interest is that in Acts 23:3–5 Paul rebukes the high priest, then apologizes when he learns that it was indeed the high priest he had addressed. The book of Acts speaks of priests or high priests many times: 4:1,5,6, 3,36; 5:17; 6:7; 7:1; 9:1; 19:14; 22:5,30; 23:2,3,4,5,14; 24:1; 25:2,15.

---

[85] J. Chance, *Jerusalem, the Temple, and the New Age in Luke-Acts* (Macon: Mercer University Press, 1988), 56.

[86] See the interpretive aside on the incense offering in the temple in J. Green, *Luke*, NICNT (Grand Rapids: Eerdmans, 1997), 68–69.

[87] Mason, "Chief Priests, Sadducees, Pharisees and Sanhedrin in Acts," 146.

Jerusalem and the Temple in Luke-Acts[88]

Luke says more about the temple than any other writer in the New Testament. His Gospel begins and ends in the temple, displaying much about Luke's purpose and theology.[89] The word "temple" occurs in Luke 1:9 and again in Luke 24:53, the last verse of the last chapter. It occurs 14 times in Luke and 24 times in Acts. The Gospel of Luke can be divided into three principle parts based on Luke's use of the construct "Temple/Jerusalem": (1) Luke 1–2, (2) Luke 3:1–19:27, and (3) Luke 19:28–24:52.[90] Luke uses a chiastic arrangement at the beginning and end of his Gospel relative to the temple:[91]

"Temple"
(Luke 1:5)

    "Descent"
    (Gabriel to Zechariah and Mary)
    Luke 1:9,26–27
        "Blessing"
        (Luke 1:67)
        "Blessing"
        (Luke 24:50)
    "Ascent"
    (Luke 24:51)

"Temple"
(Luke 24:53)

---

[88] Among the many works on this subject, two of the more significant are M. Bachmann's *Jerusalem und der Tempel: Die geographisch–theologischen Elemente in der lukanischen Sicht des jüdischen Kultzentrums* (Stuttgart: W. Kohlhammer, 1980), and H. Ganser-Kerperin, *Das Zeugnis des Tempels: Studien zur Bedeutung des Tempelmotivs im lukanischen Doppelwerk*, Neutestamentliche Abhandlungen 36 (Münster: Aschendorffsche Verlagsbuchhandlung, 2000). See also Chance, *Jerusalem, the Temple, and the New Age in Luke-Acts*; F. Weinert, "The Meaning of the Temple in Luke-Acts," *BTB* 11 (1981): 85–89; Taylor, "Luke-Acts and the Temple," in *The Unity of Luke-Acts*, 709–21; and C. R. Hutcheon, "'God Is With Us': The Temple in Luke-Acts," *SVTQ* (2000): 3–33.

[89] Although all agree that the temple is highly significant in Luke-Acts, there is less agreement about how Luke himself views the temple and its cultus. Most think Luke views the temple in a positive to ambivalent light. Others, like J. H. Elliott, "Temple versus Household in Luke-Acts: a Contrast in Social Institutions," *Hervormde Teologiese Studies* 47 (1991): 88–90, believe Luke's attitude toward the temple was negative.

[90] So Elliott, "Temple versus Household in Luke-Acts," 88–90, and Weinert, "The Meaning of the Temple in Luke-Acts," 85–86.

[91] So Hutcheon, "'God is With Us'," 3–33.

For Luke, the temple is the place where the gospel is first announced. He records that Jesus visited the temple four times. The first visit was as an infant when He was brought there by his parents in fulfillment of the Jewish law (Luke 1–2). The second visit came when Jesus was a boy of 12 and talked with the teachers in the temple precincts. The third visit occurred at the climax of the temptation of Christ, where Luke followed a different order than in Matthew and Mark, with Satan bringing Jesus to the temple in the third temptation (Luke 4:9). On His final visit to the temple, Jesus entered Jerusalem on Palm Sunday, moved immediately to the temple area and cleansed it, then confronted the leaders of Israel with the choice to accept or reject Him.

Shuler notes the literary double *inclusio* surrounding the temple locale in Luke 1–2. Luke opens with Zechariah in the temple and closes with Jesus' family in the temple (2:22–40). Luke 2:37–38 is the closure of the family scene in the temple with the child Jesus, and this is paralleled by the scene of Jesus in the temple at age 12, set exclusively in the temple (Luke 2:41–51).[92] Luke alone records the visit of Jesus to the temple at age 12. The time of this visit, at the Passover, is also significant for Luke. Farmer conjectures that Luke includes this account "as a foreshadowing of the end of his ministry in Jerusalem during the festival."[93] Hutcheon views the fact that the 12-year-old Jesus was missing for three days after the family's Passover visit as a "resurrection cipher."[94] He also observes that Luke creates an *inclusio* by bringing together two elderly couples, Zechariah and Elizabeth, and Simeon and Anna, at the beginning and end of the infancy narrative, all within the confines of the temple.[95]

Acts begins with the church meeting daily "in the temple complex" (Acts 2:46). Luke has a "precise knowledge of Jewish customs" when he mentions the time of prayer "at three in the afternoon" (Acts 3).

---

[92] P. Shuler, "The Rhetorical Character of Luke 1–2," in *Literary Studies in Luke-Acts: Essays in Honor of Joseph B. Tyson*, 187, 189. Likewise, F. Fearghail notes the significance of the temple in Luke-Acts. The infancy narratives foreshadow its passing. P. Shuler, *The Introduction to Luke-Acts: A Study of the Role of Luke 1, 1–4, 44 in the Composition of Luke's Two-volume Work*, AnBib 126 (Rome: Edtrice Pontificio Istituto Biblico, 1991), 152.

[93] W. R. Farmer, *Maccabees, Zealots, and Josephus: An Inquiry into Jewish Nationalism in the Greco-Roman Period* (New York: Columbia University Press, 1956), 140.

[94] Hutcheon, "God With Us," 14.

[95] Ibid., 13.

This was the time of the afternoon sacrifice, which concluded with an incense offering and the priestly blessing.[96]

Paul continually preaches in the Jewish synagogues until he reaches Rome. If Paul's quotation of Isaiah 6 at the end of Acts 28 is meant by Luke to suggest Isaiah's "temple vision," then Acts too forms an *inclusio* with the use of the temple concept at the beginning and end.[97] Why does Luke feel compelled to give so much attention to the temple? No doubt it played an important part in the early history of the church. But if Luke's audience consisted of Gentiles, or if he were a Gentile, as is traditionally believed, why is such emphasis placed on the Jewish relationship to the early church—especially their relationship to the temple? As Taylor observes, Luke is deeply interested in the validity of the temple, yet he posits a path to salvation for the Jewish people apart from it and its sacrificial system. Taylor's conclusions would place Luke in the same milieu as the author of Hebrews.[98] Ellis recognizes that of the New Testament documents, Acts and Hebrews alone "accentuate the role of the Jerusalem temple."[99] Likewise, Craig Evans claims, "Luke believes that true worship not only can take place apart from the physical temple but that it can take place only in relationship to the temple not made with hands."[100] This could be interpreted as evidence that Luke was Jewish or writing to a Jewish audience, or both.

Baltzer argues that Luke presents a Christological interpretation of the temple. In Ezekiel, the "glory of Jahweh" in the temple is a significant motif. During the intertestamental period a connection developed between the divine presence of the Lord in the temple and the presence of salvation. This divine presence was equated with

---

[96] So Hengel, "The Geography of Palestine in Acts," 42.

[97] So K. Baltzer, "The Meaning of the Temple in the Lukan Writings," *HTR* 58 (1965): 277; E. Larsson, "Temple Criticism and the Jewish Heritage," *NTS* 39 (1993): 394; and Hutcheon, "'God With Us,'" 4.

[98] Taylor, "Luke-Acts and the Temple," 709–21. Taylor assumes that Luke-Acts was written after AD 70 and places Luke's presentation of the temple in this context. I date Luke-Acts along with Hebrews prior to AD 70, but within the decade of the 60s. According to Taylor, Luke implies the temple had lost its significance even before it was destroyed. Jewish Christians should not seek the restoration of Jerusalem, but should "embrace the diffusion of divine presence in the life and mission of the church" (p. 721). Taylor is correct, but Luke made his point prior to the destruction of the temple.

[99] E. Ellis, *Making of the New Testament Documents*, in Biblical Interpretation Series 39 (Leiden: Brill, 1999), 318.

[100] C. A. Evans and J. Sanders, *Luke and Scripture: The Function of Sacred Tradition in Luke-Acts* (Minneapolis: Fortress, 1993), 199.

"glory" in rabbinic literature. The Targumim of Ezekiel mentions the divine presence leaving the temple and moving to the Mount of Olives to stir the people to repentance. Baltzer then relates this to Luke's constant association of the concept of "glory" with Jesus (as in Luke 2:32; 19:38; 24:26). He further observes that each of these references appears in material unique to Luke. For Luke, Jesus represents the presence of God's salvation (Luke 2:30). Unlike Mark, Luke adds the detail of Jesus' descent from the Mount of Olives (Luke 19:37). For Baltzer, Jesus is the new "divine presence" and "glory," which in Jewish thought was associated with the temple. The meaning and significance of the temple for Luke is to be found Christologically.[101]

From Jesus' use of this parable in Luke 14:24–35 Fletcher-Louis concludes that "Luke articulates a priestly ecclesiology."[102] Fletcher-Louis presents three examples under the heading "Levitical Discipleship." First, Jesus' words in Luke 14:26, as commentators often note, allude to Moses' blessing of Levi in the LXX version of Deut 33:9. Fletcher-Louis finds this parable "replete with language and imagery which means Jesus' followers are being gathered into a specifically Levitical or priestly community."[103] This is significant not least because the church-as-temple theme, while found clearly in Paul and Peter, is usually assumed to be absent from Lukan theology. Second, Luke 14:33 resumes the thought of the preceding passage by introducing another requirement for discipleship: willingness to renounce one's wealth. This theme is also clearly Lukan.[104] Fletcher-Louis cites the "strongly Levitical subtext" because the Pentateuch required priests and Levites to be landless and dependent on tithes from the people. Luke mentions the Levite Barnabas (Acts 4:36–37), who sold a piece of his property and brought the proceeds to the disciples. Luke 14:33 and Acts 4:37 are even more closely connected linguistically by the repetition of *huparchō,* "possess, belong." This not only indicates Luke's knowledge of the Torah's Levitical requirement, but provides "sound proof that Luke understood such surrender of property as a priestly calling."[105] (We saw in the previous chapter how the author of

---

[101] Baltzer, "The Meaning of the Temple in the Lukan Writings," 263–77.

[102] C. Fletcher-Louis, "Jesus Inspects His Priestly War Party (Luke 24:25–35)," in *The Old Testament in the New Testament: Essays in Honor of J. L. North,* ed. S. Moyise, JSNTSup 189 (Sheffield: Sheffield Academic Press, 2000), 134.

[103] Ibid., 139.

[104] See, for example, Luke 12:33 and 18:22.

[105] Fletcher-Louis, "Jesus Inspects His Priestly War Party," 140–41.

Hebrews shares with Luke a view of money and possessions.) Third, Luke 14:34–35 ends the pericope with the analogy of salt that is common to all three Synoptic Gospels. Among the suggested conceptual backgrounds for this saying is the use of salt, which was added to sacrifices, an extrabiblical point made in *Jubilees* and elsewhere. Fletcher-Louis suggests the possibility that Luke is using "salt" as a metonym for the whole sacrificial institution. If so, this saying would fit "into the flow of thought within the Gospel as well as the early Christian attitude towards the Jerusalem temple as the place of its sacrificial cult within the dispensations of salvation history: if the sacrificial cult has ceased to fulfill its intended soteriological function then it is destined to destruction."[106] Fletcher-Louis concludes that the whole of Luke 14:25–35 "is dominated by priestly concerns."[107]

Chance cites Luke 20:17–18 as a possible indication that Luke viewed Jesus as the true temple, or at least the foundation stone of the true temple, the church. Stone imagery is common in association with the temple in the New Testament. But more significant, the saying appears in a temple setting between two other passages dealing with the destruction of the temple or the city. Chance doubts this connection, however, noting that stone imagery was also used in the New Testament as a picture of judgment against those who reject the gospel.[108]

Jesus' prophecy concerning the destruction of Jerusalem and the temple is of special interest to Luke. All explicit references are in Luke's so-called "special material." Of course, those most naturally interested in the fate of Jerusalem would not be Gentile Christians but Palestinian Jews and Jewish Christians before AD 70, further evidence of Luke's Jewish interest. Gaston argues that the Lukan predictions of the destruction of Jerusalem and the temple have their *sitz im Leben* in the missionary preaching of the early church to Jewish believers in Jerusalem.[109] Gaston further argues that the centurion episode (Luke 7:6–9) and the Cornelius episode (Acts 10:28) function not primarily as the genesis of the Gentile mission, but "to shame an all too particularistic Israel. . . ." These two events are signs of the eschatological

---

[106] Ibid., 141–42.

[107] Ibid., 143.

[108] Chance, *Jerusalem, the Temple, and the New Age in Luke-Acts*, 44–45.

[109] Gaston, *No Stone on Another*, 244.

appearance of salvation to the Gentiles. Luke, according to Gaston, uses these events in his narrative to shame Israel.[110]

In Luke 19:47–48 and 21:37–38, Luke summarizes Jesus' confrontation with Israel for the last time. It is "not unimportant" that the location of these encounters was the temple, according to Chance.[111] Luke has consciously focused on the temple in a way different from Mark. Unlike Mark, where Jesus comes and goes from the temple area, Luke omits all indications that Jesus left the temple area. "In Luke, once Jesus enters the temple, he never leaves its precincts until he finally departs." Luke 19:47–49 and 21:37–38 serve as summaries that bracket the temple scenes, thus giving Jesus' temple ministry a definite beginning and end.[112]

Carpinelli believes the description of Lukan theology as salvation history is not sufficient to integrate the many cultic narrative themes and motifs found in Luke-Acts. A theory of "cultic evolution" explains more with fewer assumptions. Carpinelli notes that Luke begins and ends his Gospel with worship in the temple. Mary is a cousin to a daughter of Aaron. Zechariah, a priest, defines the goal of God's saving action in Christ in cultic terms (Luke 1:74–75). Luke uses cultic language to interpret God's will in saving the Gentiles (Acts 15:14; *laos* in Acts 18:10 designates Israel as the elect cultic community). Jesus is found at the temple in every phase of His life, from birth to exaltation. Jerusalem is central to Luke as the place of departure and continual return. He portrays Paul as a devotee of the temple. The conflict in Acts is predominantly with the chief priests and not the Romans. Luke never rejects the Mosaic law. Prayers are often connected with worship in the temple. Many priests became Christians (Acts 6:7).[113]

> Cultic motifs in Luke-Acts are symbolic, recurrent, and redactional (thus avoidable), and they are focused in the narrative's high points; these are attributes of purposeful, thematic communication.[114]

---

[110] Ibid., 314. Gaston argues that Acts 1–15 was not written for Gentiles, but for Jewish Christians. When Gentiles are discussed, it is "exclusively from the standpoint of Israel" (p. 310). For Gaston, the Gentiles are brought into Luke-Acts not so much for their own sake as for what their example can teach Israel (p. 320).

[111] Chance, *Jerusalem, the Temple, and the New Age in Luke-Acts*, 61–62.

[112] Ibid., 62.

[113] F. Carpinelli, "'Do This as My Memorial' (Luke 22:19): Lucan Soteriology of Atonement," *CBQ* 61 (1999): 89.

[114] Ibid.

Carpinelli interprets the death of Jesus in the Gospel as Luke's attempt to center "on the way Jesus relates to God, in order to evince in Jesus' dying a consummate act of hope, the essence of the temple's system of worship."[115] He even proposes that "Cultic categories subsume historical ones."[116]

Carpinelli also suggests that Luke carries on a "running allusion" to Sirach 50 in Luke 9:31–24:53. The expiatory interpretation that Luke attaches to the cup at the Last Supper shows this, along with the words Luke applies to Jesus throughout this section. In Luke 22:14–23 and 24:53, Luke presents Jesus as a priest. "The bread as memorial and the cup as the token of the covenant in Jesus' blood lay the narrative base for depicting the ascending Jesus completing the liturgy of the Day of Atonement."[117] From Carpinelli's perspective, nothing could be less "Gentile" or more "Jewish." Hengel raises the tantalizing point that in contrast with Luke 1:8 (where Luke mentions Zechariah's service at the time of the sacrifice in the temple), in Acts Luke speaks only of the fixed hour of prayer. Might it be, Hengel queries, that Luke knew the temple was no longer a place of sacrifice but a place of prayer for the early church?[118]

Luke thus both affirms and denies the temple. He affirms its past status, but denies that it has a future because of Jesus' advent. Luke's attitude appears to be derived from Jesus, who similarly affirmed it yet pronounced its destruction.[119] Barrett summarizes Luke's attitude toward the temple as it is found in Acts:

> Luke . . . means to say to Judaism both Yes and No. Neither his Yes nor his No is as sharp and clear as Paul's Yes and No, but they are not unrelated to them. . . . The Old Testament is right, of course; but it must be rightly understood. Judaism is the heir of the Old Testament; but to fulfill itself it must become Christian, and if it fails to accept the invitation to do so it disinherits itself. The Old Testament could and must be understood as a Christian book, but the Temple could only be destroyed because it could not be taken over as a Christian institution.[120]

---

[115] Ibid.

[116] Ibid., 90.

[117] Ibid.

[118] Hengel, "The Geography of Palestine in Acts," 42.

[119] This point is well made by P. W. L. Walker, *Jesus and the Holy City* (Grand Rapids: Eerdmans, 1996), 68.

[120] C. K. Barrett, "Attitudes to the Temple in the Acts of the Apostles," in *Templum Amicitae: Essays on the Second Temple Presented to Ernst Bammel*, ed. W. Horbury, JSNTSup 48 (Sheffield: JSOT Press, 1991), 366–67.

This is precisely the perspective we find in the Book of Hebrews.

Moving from a discussion of the temple to the city of Jerusalem itself, one discovers Luke attaches both a geographical and a theological significance to the city (cf. Acts 1:8, where it is the site from which the worldwide Christian mission began).[121] Luke records the preaching of Paul in the synagogues, and when Paul comes to Rome, Luke stresses in Acts 28 that he came as a prisoner from Jerusalem. When Paul arrives in Rome, Luke records that he called for the Jewish leaders and not the leaders of the Christian church. After some of the Jews believe (but others do not), Paul quotes Isaiah 6 in Acts 28:26–27 and emphasizes that the Jews have brought God's judgment on Jerusalem and the temple because of their obduracy. The whole of Paul's controversy in Rome is seen to be within the framework of Judaism.

Lampe outlines the obvious interest that Luke places on the centrality of Jerusalem in his Gospel and Acts. For example, he writes: "The Gentile Gospel ends with the Lord commanding the eleven to stay in the city of Jerusalem, and the last words of the story are that they were continually in the Temple blessing God. Nothing could be less Gentile."[122]

Lampe further observes:

> But the Gentile gospel opens in the heart of Jerusalem where a Jewish priest is carrying out his ritual duties in the Temple. The central episode in Luke's infancy narrative is the Presentation: the coming of the Lord's Messiah to the Temple, the revelation to Simeon of God's salvation, and the testimony to this given by Anna to all those who were awaiting the redemption of Jerusalem. . . . An intense interest in Jerusalem is characteristic of the early part, not of Matthew but of Luke the Gentile.[123]

Luke has arranged more than one-third of his Gospel in the framework of a journey on which Jesus has "set his face to go to Jerusalem" (Luke 9:51). Three times during this travel narrative the reader is informed of the journey and that Jerusalem is the destination (Luke 9:51; 13:22; 17:11). In addition, Luke often locates Judean towns with reference to Jerusalem. Bechard observes that Luke uses the term "Judea" not only in a topographical sense, but also with a broader

---

[121] See Walker, *Jesus and the Holy City*, 57–112, for an excellent treatment of this subject. Also D. Bechard, "The Theological Significance of Judaea in Luke-Acts," in *The Unity of Luke-Acts*, 675–91, notes Luke's effective use of geography in the service of his theology.

[122] G. Lampe, *St. Luke and the Church of Jerusalem* (University of London: The Athlone Press, 1969), 3.

[123] Ibid., 3–4.

theological sense. This usage is reflected in both the Gospel and Acts. Prior to the Cornelius episode in Acts, Luke uses "Judea" to denote the region surrounding Jerusalem. With the advent of the new stage in the apostolic mission following Cornelius, Luke reverts to his custom of using the term in a less-restricted theological sense.[124]

Both the temple and the city of Jerusalem are clearly emphasized in the early part of Luke's Gospel (1:5–4:13) and in the concluding section (19:45–24:53). This prominence of the temple and the city in both Luke and Acts is one of the distinguishing features of his writings.

Why does Luke make Jerusalem central? Its historical importance for early Christianity is part of the answer. But, as Johnson pointed out, more than historical recollection is involved. The city and the temple stand as symbols of the people Israel. "Jerusalem, in short, is the place of pivot in Luke's story of the Prophet and the people."[125] Perhaps this is because Luke was Jewish.

In Acts 1:8, Luke distinguishes Jerusalem as a district separate from the rest of Judea (cf. Luke 5:17; Acts 10:39). The Mishnah divided Judea into three parts: mountain, Shephelah, and valley, with Jerusalem viewed as a separate district. This is evidence of Luke's intimate acquaintance with the rabbinical phraseology.[126] Bechard, in an article on the theological significance of Judea in Luke-Acts, demonstrates how Luke makes effective use of geography in the service of his theology.[127] Hebrews does this also, as Walker who points out.[128]

The significance of Jerusalem and the temple for Luke has been recognized for some time. Rosner says that "Luke has a preoccupation with Jerusalem."[129] According to O'Neill, "In the whole of Luke-Acts it is Jerusalem that controls the history."[130] And Walker points out that one-sixth of the narrative of Luke-Acts is either located in the temple or concerned with its fate.[131]

---

[124] Bechard, "The Theological Significance of Judaea in Luke-Acts," 681–91.

[125] Johnson, Luke, 15.

[126] A. Edersheim, Sketches of Jewish Social Life in the Days of Christ (New York: James Pott & Co., 1881; repr., Grand Rapids: Eerdmans, 1990), 73.

[127] Bechard, "The Theological Significance of Judaea in Luke-Acts," 691. For bibliography on the importance of Jerusalem for Luke's Gospel, see 675n1.

[128] Walker, Jesus and the Holy City, 213–22.

[129] B. Rosner, "Acts and Biblical History," in The Book of Acts in its Ancient Literary Setting, ed. B. W. Winter and A. D. Clarke (Grand Rapids: Eerdmans, 1993), 1:80.

[130] J. C. O'Neill, The Theology of Acts in its Historical Setting (London: SPCK, 1961), 72.

[131] Walker, Jesus and the Holy City, 60.

The presence of the exodus theme at strategic places in Luke's Gospel reveals his attempt to parallel Moses' work of redemption for Israel with Jesus' work of redemption. The words of Moses in the LXX of Deut 1:1 are remarkably similar to Jesus' words in Luke 24:44.[132] The disciples are "led" from Jerusalem to the Mount of Olives, where the ascension occurs. The action is viewed as a "proleptic sign" that the time will come when Christians will need to go out from Jerusalem.[133] Filson observes the conceptual similarity between Jesus' statement in Luke 21:21 in the Apocalyptic Discourse, "Then those in Judea must flee to the mountains! Those inside the city must leave it," and Heb 13:13–14.[134] Here the readers are exhorted to go forth "outside the camp" as Jesus did "bearing His disgrace." Both Luke and Hebrews emphasize this connection.

Walker argues that Luke draws a subtle but real distinction between the "people" of Jerusalem and the "city" of Jerusalem. Although Jesus passed judgment on the "city," He continued to be concerned for the "people" as demonstrated in Luke 13 and 19. Walker then notes, "The author of Hebrews shares Luke's perception that Jesus, despite his critique of Jerusalem, continued to be concerned for its inhabitants."[135] Walker's point about the centrality of Jerusalem gives some insight into Luke's approach:

> In Acts Luke draws attention to Jerusalem's centrality for the early church and its integral involvement in the gospel's going out to "all nations" not primarily in order to make a point about Jerusalem, but rather to make a point about the Christian message which first started there. It is not that Jerusalem must be seen as forever central in Christian understanding; it is rather that the Christian gospel must not be dismissed as marginal. The Christian message is authentically Jewish, and the Church a legitimate heir of Judaism. Luke emphasizes Jerusalem, not for its ongoing theological significance in the present, but for its capacity to offer validation in the past.[136]

---

[132] Ibid., 79–80.

[133] See J. Manek, "The New Exodus in the Book of Luke," *NovT* 2 (1957): 14; and P. W. L. Walker, *Jesus and the Holy City*, 80.

[134] F. Filson, *'Yesterday,' A Study of Hebrews in the Light of Chapter 13*, SBT 4 (London: SCM, 1967), 64.

[135] Walker, *Jesus and the Holy City*, 219; cf. also Chance, *Jerusalem, the Temple, and the New Age in Luke-Acts*, 61.

[136] Walker, *Jesus and the Holy City*, 87.

The Lukan Conception of the Relationship
of Judaism to the Church

Further supporting Luke's Jewish background is the way he understood the Jewish nation and its relationship to the church.[137] According to Vine, there is a Jewish emphasis in Acts that indicates a situation and readership with a strongly Jewish background and where an answer is urgently needed to the question of who has the truth, Christians or Jews?[138]

The interpretation of Luke's theology of mission most widely held today is that only after the Jewish people rejected the gospel offer was the door opened for the Gentiles to be saved. However, in light of the text of Acts, this thesis must be modified. Luke does not describe a Jewish people who rejected the gospel *en masse* save for a small minority of believers. Rather, Israel consists of two groups: the repentant and the obdurate. The former group, those Jews who believed in the Messiah, Luke considered to be the true Israel. Consequently "Israel," as the term is used by Luke,[139] refers to God's people consisting not of Jews and Gentiles, but of the repentant portion of national Israel. According to him, the church did not separate itself from Israel; rather, the unrepentant portion of national Israel forfeited its elect position as God's people, and the Church (both Jew and Gentile) continued as the true people of God.[140] This is not to deny that God still has an eschatological plan for national Israel (see Romans 9–11), nor is it to suggest an amillennial interpretation of the Church as the new Israel. What I am suggesting is that it is not true that the rejection of the kingdom by Israel is what opened the door of the gospel to the Gentiles.

Acts is usually understood to portray Gentiles as willing to accept the gospel promptly, but Jews as generally rejecting it. But a careful reading of Acts shows both Jews and Gentiles accepting the gospel, with the impression left by Luke that the Jews are in the majority.[141] According to Scripture, the Gentiles have a share in salvation through the promises to Israel. The mission to the Jews was a necessary

---

[137] I am heavily indebted in this section to J. Jervell, *Luke and the People of God* (Minneapolis: Augsburg, 1972); id., *The Unknown Paul*; and Franklin, *Christ the Lord.*

[138] V. Vine, "The Purpose and Date of Acts," *ExpTim* 96 (1985): 45–48.

[139] See Harvey, *The True Israel.*

[140] Jervell, *Luke and the People of God,* 19.

[141] Ibid., 22.

precursor before salvation was extended to the Gentiles. It is remarkable that in Acts, Luke records the great success of the mission to the Jews, not its failure. Again and again he reports mass conversions: 2:41,47; 4:4; 5:14; 6:1,7; 9:42; 12:24; 13:43; 14:1; 17:10–12; 19:20; 21:20. These accounts belie any contention that Israel rejected Christ *en bloc*. Most of the references to Gentiles are to "God-fearing" Gentiles, already related to Israel and Judaism via the synagogue (e.g., 13:43; 14:1; 17:4,12). In Acts 10, the Jewish piety of Cornelius is emphasized. Throughout, Luke reports a widespread acceptance of the gospel by the Jewish people despite strong opposition, and he describes conversion of Jews and Gentiles as occurring simultaneously, rather than consecutively. The last picture of the Jews in Acts reveals an Israel divided over the Messiah (28:24–29).[142]

It seems important to Luke to show that the Jewish Christian church is a part of the reconstituted people of God. Observe his use of the phrase "men, brethren," and that this form of address is not restricted to members of the Jewish Christian community. He characteristically uses this form throughout Acts as a Jewish address, while the term "brothers" for Gentiles is consistently avoided (2:29, 37; 7:2; 13:26,38; 15:7,13; 22:1; and 28:17).[143]

Of further interest is the significance that Luke ascribes to the election of Matthias (Acts 1:15–26) to fill the vacancy created in the apostles by Judas's apostasy and death. Luke carefully states there was a company of 120 brethren, the minimum number of men who could establish a community with its own council, by Jewish law.[144] The exegesis of this passage and its explanation in relation to the rest of the book is most difficult, and most commentators discuss it only in vague generalities. The question must be asked why the apostles found it necessary to elect a twelfth man to fill the vacancy created by the loss of Judas, but did not recognize a similar need after the martyrdom of James. Since Jesus called the 12 disciples to perform a particular function, and since that function was not to be a self-perpetuating body, the importance of the 12 must be seen primarily in their number and not in their persons. Luke viewed the 12 as having eschatological significance. Their presence challenges Israel to accept her renewal and join the reconstituted people of God. In some sense

---

[142] Ibid., 44.
[143] Ibid., 50.
[144] I. H. Marshall, *Acts*, TNTC (London: Leicester, 1960), 62.

the 12 must be understood as the foundation of the remade Israel as well as the foundation of the Church.[145]

In Peter's speech recorded in Acts 3, v. 26 implies that the missionary message has a further objective beyond the Jews.[146] Thus, before God instituted the Gentile mission and before the Jewish nation had the chance to reject the gospel offer, Peter was aware of God's acceptance of the Gentiles. The addition of the Gentiles is a part of the restoration of Israel. Peter says that God sent the Messiah to Jews first with the intention of reaching Gentiles through them, and that Gentiles are added to complete the restoration of Israel.

As a result of Peter's sermon, many Jews and proselytes were converted; others rejected the gospel. This is usually understood to mean that after the gospel was rejected by the Jews, it was preached to Gentiles, thus making the Gentile mission the result of Jewish obduracy. However, the partial rejection by the Jews was not prerequisite to the Gentile mission because the mission to Gentiles was already contained in the command of God. Moreover, it seems odd that the apostles should continue to preach in Jewish synagogues after Paul's declaration that they would turn to the Gentiles (Acts 13:46). In Acts 18:6, Paul says for the second time, "From now on I will go to the Gentiles." Why would Luke continue throughout Acts to report mass conversions of Jews, while making only passing reference to Gentile converts? The answer seems to be that Luke portrayed the church not as a totally new institution, created in response to the Jewish rejection of the gospel, but rather was newly opened to Gentiles through the fulfillment of God's promises to Israel. Everywhere Paul preaches, Jews repent and are portrayed as members of God's true people.[147] As Jervel explains,

---

[145] Cf. S. Brown, *Apostasy and Perseverance in the Theology of Luke*, AnBib 36 (Rome: Pontifical Biblical Institute, 1969), 94–97; Jervell, *Luke and the People of God*, 65; Franklin, *Christ the Lord*, 95–99; K. Giles, "Apostles Before and After Paul," *Churchman* 99 (1985): 241–56; and more recently Evans and Sanders, *Luke and Scripture*, 154–70; A. Clark, "The Role of the Apostles," in *Witness to the Gospel*, ed. I. H. Marshall and D. Peterson (Grand Rapids: Eerdmans, 1998), 169–90.

[146] Jervell, *Luke and the People of God*, 54–55. I am heavily indebted to Jervell for the next several paragraphs.

[147] See the full discussion in Jervell, *Luke and the People of God*, 41–59. Moessner, differing from Jervell, argues that both believing and non-believing Jews constitute the one people of God. Believing Jews and believing Gentiles together constitute the Church and continually call unbelieving Israel to repentance. When Paul arrived in Rome, some Jews did respond, proving that repentance and inclusion in God's people was still a possibility (D. Moessner, "Paul in Acts: Preacher of Eschatological Repentance to Israel," *NTS* 34 [1988]: 102–3).

The reason for the preaching in the synagogues is a simple one: Christianity is for Luke the religion of Israel. The Synagogue scenes do not signal the transition from mission among Jews to Gentile mission. This is not the case even in 13,46 and 18,6. But the rejection of the gospel in one synagogue leads to preaching in other synagogues . . . . And there is not one, single, definite transition from mission among Jews to mission among Gentiles. But the preaching is delivered in a way which shows that mission among Gentiles is connected with the mission among Jews, and that Acts contains no mission solely for Gentiles.[148]

Consider Luke's presentation of the events surrounding the Jerusalem conference in Acts 15. James quoted from the Book of Amos in reference to the recent conversion of certain Gentiles.

After these things I will return and will rebuild David's tent, which has fallen down. I will rebuild its ruins and will set it up again, so that those who are left of mankind may seek the Lord—even all the Gentiles who are called by My name, says the Lord who does these things, which have been known from long ago.

The Cornelius story is cited as proof that the restoration of the fallen house of David has already occurred, and that the Gentiles are seeking the Lord.[149] The point here is that James considered the Amos passage to be fulfilled (although such an interpretation does not preclude its being fulfilled eschatologically, i.e., during the millennium). James stated that the Gentile conversion was the fulfillment of God's promises to Israel. This should not be understood to mean the promises to Israel had been transferred to the Gentiles—thus excluding Israel—but rather that the Gentiles had gained a share in what had been given to Israel. This fits well with Paul's theology of Israel in Romans 9–11.

Paul's parable of the olive tree in Rom 11:16–24 illustrates the relationship between Israel and the Church. The olive tree is a reference to Israel, but nowhere does Paul state that Israel as a whole has been set aside. Rather, he points out that "some of the branches" have been "broken off." Those branches represent the unbelieving portion of Israel as God's people.

The wild olive represents the Gentile world. Gentile Christians are grafted into the good olive tree, which represents God's people.

---

[148] J. Jervell, "The Acts of the Apostles and the History of Early Christianity," *Studia Theologica* 37 (1983): 20.

[149] Jervell, *Luke and the People of God*, 51.

Gentile Christians are grafted into that tree and are not designated as a new tree. We may infer from this that there is continuity from God's people under the old covenant to God's people under the new covenant. The fact that some branches were broken off does not imply that all of them were. The Gentiles are told that they have no ground for boasting because they have not displaced Israel; rather, they have been grafted onto Israel and are now members of the "people of God." The point of this parable is that the root of Israel is never uprooted to make way for a new "tree," but rather it continues to give nourishment to God's people.

Therefore, it is incorrect, according to Jervell, to say that only after the Jews have rejected the gospel is the way opened to the Gentiles. It would be more accurate to say that only after Israel has accepted the gospel can the way to the Gentiles be opened. Throughout Acts, both Peter and Paul emphasize in their speeches to Jews the sharing of the Gentiles in salvation, while they mention their commission to Israel in their speeches to Gentiles.

It is interesting how Luke portrays the influence of the Jerusalem church on the Gentile mission in Acts 21:15–25. Reports are made in v. 19 to the Jerusalem church on the mission to the Gentiles. Verse 21 mentions that Jerusalem is informed about Paul's preaching among Jews in the Diaspora. The Jerusalem church can even impose ritual acts on Paul as recorded in Acts 21:23–24. They makes decisions regarding how Gentiles should live, because they maintain the apostolic decree (21:25).[150]

Farris observes how well Luke's infancy narratives fit with Jervell's theological framework. Luke inserted these narratives at the beginning of his Gospel to "anticipate the motif of the restoration of Israel accomplished by the apostolic preaching of the gospel."[151] Maddox summarizes Jervell's assessment of the general ideas found in Acts:

> In chapters 1–8 a renewed Israel is established, on the basis of repentance, piety according to the Law, and faith in Jesus. Luke repeatedly mentions the enormous numerical success of the mission among the Jews, a success which is to be understood as continuing while the diaspora–mission is going on, for by the time we come to 21:20 a high proportion of the population of Judaea must be Christian, if we are to take the figures seriously. Ch. 9–15 deal with

---

[150] Jervell, *Theology of Acts*, 22.

[151] S. Farris, *The Hymns of Luke's Infancy Narratives*, JSNTSup 9 (Sheffield: JSOT Press, 1985), 158.

the question of Gentiles, and show how they are allowed, both in principle and in practice, to be associated with Israel.[152]

Marilyn Salmon asks the crucial question: was Luke an insider or outsider in his relationship to Judaism? Her conclusion is that Luke was Jewish, and she offers four primary reasons. First, Luke makes certain distinctions among groups of Jews. Noting that such distinctions do not prove a Jewish writer, she wonders why an outsider (Gentile) would be interested in narrating the success of the mission to Jews in Acts as extensively as Luke has done.

A second argument for Luke's Jewish background is how Jesus (in the Gospel) and Paul (in Acts) are careful to give attention to Torah observance. Jesus acts in accordance with the law throughout the Gospel, and Paul is presented in Acts as a "model Pharisee."

Third, the prominence given to the Gentile mission in Acts is usually taken to imply a Gentile writer and audience. But "Gentile" means "not Jewish" and therefore reflects, according to Salmon, a Jewish perspective of the world.

Fourth, Luke's reference to Christianity as a *hairesis,* "sect," in Acts 24:5 and 28:22 implies that he was an insider. "If Luke is merely recording historical fact, this textual clue may not be relevant here, but if in relating the past he is revealing something of his own situation . . . then his use of αἵρεσις [*hairesis*] suggests that he considers himself an insider."[153]

The significance of the Lukan conception of the relationship of Israel and the church coupled with the irenic position toward the Jews as a whole throughout his writings support the case for Luke's Jewish background. I find myself in agreement with Brawley's assessment: "The standard for understanding Luke's view of the relation between Christianity and Judaism should pivot 180 degrees. That is, rather than setting Gentile Christianity free, Luke ties it to Judaism. And rather than rejecting the Jews, Luke appeals to them."[154]

Norman Peterson has identified six pericopes in Luke-Acts that have a common pattern and theme of confrontation and rejection.

---

[152] R. Maddox, *The Purpose of Luke-Acts* (Edinburgh: T&T Clark, 1982), 34.

[153] M. Salmon, "Insider or Outsider? Luke's Relationship with Judaism," in *Luke-Acts and the Jewish People,* ed. J. Tyson (Minneapolis: Augsburg, 1988), 79–80.

[154] R. Brawley, *Luke-Acts and the Jews: Conflict, Apology, and Conciliation,* SBLMS 33 (Atlanta: Scholars Press, 1987), 159. See also his "The God of Promises and the Jews in Luke-Acts," in *Literary Studies in Luke-Acts: Essays in Honor of Joseph B. Tyson,* 279–96.

Luke uses them as a literary device to show that Christianity both emerged from and was the legitimate successor of Judaism.[155]

According to Donaldson, Luke exhibits a more positive attitude toward the Jewish origins of the church than is found in any other second-century Gentile Christian writer.[156] Although a Gentile writer could certainly have produced a work like Luke-Acts, it is more probable that the data confirms the author was Jewish.

The Use of Scripture in Luke-Acts

One area that has received widespread attention in recent years is Luke's understanding and use of Scripture. While this aspect of Lukan studies is clearly ongoing, it has become evident that Luke has an amazingly broad and deep understanding of the Old Testament.[157] This can be seen in a host of articles and monographs dealing with this subject, such as Darrell Bock in *Proclamation from Prophecy and Pattern: Lucan Old Testament Christology*.[158] We can only touch on the highlights of this immense field of study, but by doing so we will be

---

[155] N. Peterson, *Literary Criticism for New Testament Critics* (Philadelphia: Fortress, 1978), 88–91. J. Kolasny develops this concept with a focus on Luke 4:16–30 in "An Example of Rhetorical Criticism: Luke 4:16–30," in *New Views on Luke-Acts* (Collegeville, MN: Liturgical, 1990).

[156] T. L. Donaldson, "Moses Typology and the Sectarian Nature of Early Christian Anti-Judaism: A Study in Acts 7," *JSNT* 12 (1981): 44.

[157] Ellis noted, for example, that the pre-formed tradition that appears in Luke 1–2 and Acts appears at times to be more assimilated into Luke's style than traditions in the Pauline Letters. Ellis, *The Making of the New Testament Documents*, 141. Dupont remarks regarding Luke's sources in Acts: "The information is not only reported in his own style, in its very substance it generally reflects his personality. Everything is done as if Luke were at the origin not only of the edited versions, but even the sources on which that version is based." J. Dupont, *The Sources of Acts: The Present Position* (London: Darton, Longman and Todd, 1964), 166. This has some bearing on our investigation of Luke's use of the Old Testament as compared with Hebrews.

[158] D. Bock's work demonstrates that Schubert's umbrella approach to the Lukan use of Scripture as "proof from prophecy" is inadequate to cover the Lukan methodology. D. Bock, *Proclamation from Prophecy and Pattern*, JSNTSup 12 (Sheffield: JSOT Press, 1987). Other works that cover this ground are summarized well by D. Pao, *Acts and the Isaianic New Exodus*, 8–10. See also D. Moessner, *Lord of the Banquet: The Literary and Theological Significance of the Lukan Travel Narrative* (Minneapolis: Fortress, 1989); C. A. Evans and J. Sanders, *Luke and Scripture*, 171n2, for other major studies through 1987; the bibliography in C. Kimball, *Jesus' Exposition of the Old Testament in Luke's Gospel*, JSNTSup 94 (Sheffield: JSOT Press, 1994), 216–39 and 14n5; and J. R. Wagner, "Psalm 118 in Luke-Acts: Tracing a Narrative Thread," in *Early Christian Interpretation of the Scriptures of Israel: Investigations and Proposals*, JSNTSup 148; *Studies in Scripture in Early Judaism and Christianity*, ed. C. A. Evans and J. Sanders, vol. 5 (Sheffield: Sheffield Academic Press, 1997), 155 [bibliography in 155n2].

in a position to assess Luke's use of Scripture and compare it with that of Hebrews.

Luke makes extensive use of the Old Testament in both of his volumes. Unlike Paul, all of his quotations are from the LXX.[159] There are no fewer than 20 specific quotations of Scripture in Acts.[160] It is also evident that Luke's two volumes are replete with scriptural allusions and echoes. The story of Jesus is presented in Luke-Acts as part of God's overall plan, and Luke's use of Scripture weaves that story into the very fabric of God's salvation history.[161] Luke presents Jesus as an expositor of Scripture with his programmatic positioning of the Nazareth Sermon in Luke 4 and his concluding Emmaus episode in Luke 24. While Matthew and Mark record the fact of Jesus' teaching in the synagogues, only Luke specifically mentions the text of Isaiah in Luke 4.

Luke's treatment of Scripture is systematic, well thought out, organized, and coherent. The careful accuracy he announces in his prologue extends to his use of Scripture. Both exegetical terms as well as techniques reminiscent of rabbinical and other Jewish literature occur in Luke-Acts. His record of Jesus' use of the Old Testament resembles the Jewish exegetical technique *gezerah shavah* in Luke 4:18–19, where two texts from Isaiah are combined.[162] Ellis points out that Acts includes summaries of sermons, some of which exhibit patterns of explicit midrash.[163] As Bock has cogently noted, it is not the fact of Luke's use of this technique but rather the *extent* of it that is significant.[164]

---

[159] On Luke's use of citation formulae and his dependency on the LXX, see "Use of Old Testament Quotation Formulae in Luke-Acts, Hebrews, and Paul" in chap. 3.

[160] For locations, see Pao, *Acts and the Isaianic New Exodus*, 4.

[161] See J. Green, *Theology of the Gospel of Luke*, New Testament Theology Series (Cambridge: Cambridge University Press, 1995), 24–26. Also note Evans and Sanders: Luke's presentation of the story of Jesus "was greatly influenced by the language and themes of Scripture and the way Scripture was interpreted in Jewish and Christian circles of his time." Evans comments a few pages later: "Luke does not borrow slavishly but freely modifies and adapts the LXX in creative ways." Evans and Sanders, *Luke and Scripture*, 83. The latter comment is especially significant in comparing Luke's use of Scripture with Hebrews.

[162] B. J. Koet, *Five Studies on Interpretation of Scripture in Luke-Acts*, Studiorum Novi Testamenti Auxilia XIV (Leuven-Louvain, Belgium: Leuven University Press, 1989), 141–42. Luke has made use of Isaianic texts as a framework for his two-volume work (p. 143). See also Pao, *Acts and the Isaianic New Exodus*, for a complete exploration of this subject.

[163] Ellis, *The Making of the New Testament Documents*, 140. See also his "Midrashic Features in the Speeches of Acts," in *Melanges Bibliques En Hommage Au B. Rigaux* (Gembloux: Duculot, 1970), 303–12. "There are in Acts a number of affinities with the *pesher* technique, which is usually defined in terms of its use in certain Qumran writings" (p. 306).

[164] Bock, *Proclamation from Prophecy and Pattern*, 271–72.

The significance of Luke 4:18–19 (Jesus reads the text of Isa 61:1–2 in the Nazareth synagogue) is crucial for understanding Luke's Gospel. Porter contends that this passage "is a clear instance of prophetic fulfillment of the Old Testament as seen both by Luke and by Jesus, and that the passage itself provides guidance to both the major themes of the Gospel and Jesus' ministry. In other words, this passage uses the Old Testament to outline Jesus' mission and, hence, to describe the purpose of the Gospel itself."[165] According to Porter, Luke 4:18–19 indicates in summary fashion: (1) Jesus is the Messiah proclaiming salvation; (2) Jesus identifies with His people in their suffering; (3) Jesus comes as God's final eschatological prophet; (4) Jesus comes as King, bringing the message of the coming of God's kingdom; (5) Jesus comes as God Himself, proclaiming and accomplishing His purposes; (6) God's purpose is salvation for His people and judgment for those not His people; and (7) The message of salvation extends beyond the Jews to the Gentiles as well.[166] Porter correctly concludes that these themes "are introduced, explicated, and/or developed within Luke and Acts through Scripture. . . . the notion of fulfillment of scriptural texts seen as prophetically uttered is a fundamental hermeneutical principle in Luke-Acts."[167] This is precisely the case with the author of Hebrews.

T. L. Brodie produces decisive evidence that Luke made use of the Elijah/Elisha narratives (1 Kings 17–2 Kings 9) in composing Luke-Acts.[168] Moessner and Blomberg show the significance and influence of Deuteronomy for Luke.[169]

David Pao's study of the Isaianic New Exodus theme from Isaiah 40–55 in Luke-Acts reveals Luke's perspective of the church as the true heir of Israel's traditions. The intricate knowledge and interweaving of quotations and concepts from this portion of Isaiah in Luke-Acts illustrates Luke's profound scriptural knowledge and insight. Pao states in his conclusion:

---

[165] S. Porter, "Scripture Justifies Mission: The Use of the Old Testament in Luke-Acts," *Hearing the Old Testament in the New Testament*, ed. S. Porter (Grand Rapids: Eerdmans, 2006), 117.

[166] Ibid., 117–19.

[167] Ibid., 126.

[168] T. L. Brodie, *Luke the Literary Interpreter: Luke-Acts as a Systematic Rewriting and Updating of the Elijah-Elisha Narrative* (Rome: Pontifical University of St. Thomas Aquinas, 1987). See also Evans and Sanders, *Luke and Scripture*, 70–83.

[169] Moessner, *Lord of the Banquet*; C. Blomberg, "Midrash, Chiasmus, and the Outline of Luke's Central Section," in *Gospel Perspectives III: Studies in Midrash and Historiography*, ed. R. T. France and D. Wenham (Sheffield: JSOT Press, 1983), 217–61.

The influence of the Isaianic vision cannot be limited to isolated quotations and allusions. The entire Isaianic New Exodus program provides the structural framework for the narrative of Acts as well as the various emphases developed within this framework.[170]

Kurz and Evans have analyzed Luke 22:14–38, but from different angles. Kurz compares it to both Greco-Roman and biblical (including apocryphal) farewell addresses, concluding that Luke stands closer to the biblical models.[171] Evans develops the theological significance of Luke combining two sources (Mark and Q) and notes that it is even more striking that Daniel 7 and Psalm 122 are combined in at least one Jewish midrash as well.[172] Luke 22:30 is based on Daniel 7 and Psalm 122, and Evans believes the Lukan use "reflects the essential aspects of their interpretation in early Judaism. Luke's combination of dominical material suggests that he understood and agreed with this interpretation."[173]

The significance of the Emmaus episode in Luke 24 for Luke's view of Scripture is well known. In Luke 24:45, Jesus includes the Psalms as the third part of the Old Testament Scriptures, following the Law and the Prophets. It is interesting that he does not say "the writings," the normal designation for the third part of the Jewish Scriptures, but rather he says "the Psalms." Of course he is using the Psalms as nomenclature inclusive of that section of Scripture. What is interesting is the role this episode plays as an introduction to the first few chapters of Acts, where we find 13 different Psalms cited a total of 15 times in Acts 1–5.[174]

The Emmaus episode illustrates how important Scripture was to Jesus and the early church, and Luke emphasizes Jesus' transmission of His own scriptural hermeneutic concerning Himself to the disciples (Luke 24:27,32,45–46). Again, in Jesus' last appearance to the disciples in Jerusalem before His ascension, Luke mentions the transmission to the apostles of Jesus' scriptural self-understanding. These

---

[170] Pao, *Acts and the Isaianic New Exodus*, 250.

[171] W. S. Kurz, "Luke 22:14–38 and Greco–Roman and Biblical Farewell Addresses," *JBL* 104 (1985): 251–68. Likewise J. Neyrey, *The Passion According to Luke: A Redaction Study of Luke's Soteriology* (New York/Mahway: Paulist, 1985).

[172] Evans and Sanders, *Luke and Scripture*, 168–70.

[173] Ibid., 170.

[174] Citations with references are listed by D. Moessner, "Two Lords 'at the Right Hand'?: The Psalms and an Intertextual Reading of Peter's Pentecost Speech (Acts 2:14–36)," in *Literary Studies in Luke-Acts, Essays in Honor of Joseph B. Tyson*, 215.

two scenes serve to elucidate the central role Scripture plays not only for Jesus but also in the church's life.[175]

Luke's use of Scripture in Acts is no less intricate than in his Gospel. As Arnold points out: "Besides his use of *imitation* in which he consciously shapes his narrative in Old Testament garb and uses many direct quotations of Old Testament texts in the speeches of Acts, there are also numerous subtle quotations used in characterizing his speakers."[176] Luke sometimes references the Old Testament without an explicit quotation formula. According to Arnold, Luke uses such subtle quotation to express his own ideological point of view.[177]

Mark Strauss's analysis of Luke's use of Isa 55:3 in Acts 13:34 further highlights Luke's knowledge of and use of the Old Testament. He argues that the citation of Isa 55:3 serves a dual function in Acts: as a demonstration of the eternal nature of the Davidic covenant and its application to Luke's hearers because of the covenant's fulfillment in Christ.[178] Strauss states this would require a measure of theological pre-understanding on the part of Luke's audience regarding his use of Isa 55:3. My point is to illustrate Luke's insight in his use of the Old Testament and what this might imply regarding his audience (Jewish or Gentile).

In Acts 15:15–17, Luke paraphrases Amos 9:11–12 from the LXX, as Evans says, "enriched by a few words from Jer 12:15 and Isa 45:21 . . . (Luke is probably aware of these contributions, hence the plural reference to 'the words of the prophets.')"[179] This illustrates again Luke's intricate knowledge of the Old Testament Scriptures and his ability to interweave them into his overall narrative.

At the conclusion of Acts, Paul cites Isa 6:9–10. This citation was used by Jesus in His explanation of the purpose of parables (Luke 8:10). As Bovon suggests, Luke is saying: "Scripture belongs to us Christians. The last word in my work goes to Paul and the Christian understanding of Scripture: Scripture gives definitive testimony

---

[175] P. Doble, "Something Greater than Solomon: An Approach to Stephen's Speech," in *The Old Testament in the New Testament: Essays in Honour of J. L. North*, ed. S. Moyise, JSNTSup 189 (Sheffield: Sheffield Academic Press, 2000), 189.

[176] B. Arnold, "Luke's Characterizing Use of the Old Testament in the Book of Acts," in *History, Literature, and Society in the Book of Acts*, ed. B. Witherington (Cambridge: Cambridge University Press, 1996), 302.

[177] Ibid., 308.

[178] M. Strauss, *The Davidic Messiah in Luke-Acts: The Promise and its Fulfillment in Lukan Christology*, JSNTSup 110 (Sheffield: Sheffield Academic Press, 1995), 166–74.

[179] Evans and Sanders, *Luke and Scripture*, 170.

regarding Israel's hardening of heart."[180] Because Luke cites only the
Old Testament prophets in Acts (with the exception of Acts 17:28),
Bovon concludes, "Thus Luke unambiguously aligns himself with the
Jewish tradition."[181] Of significant interest in our comparison with the
author of Hebrews, Bovon observes how Luke viewed the written text
of the Old Testament as the very voice of the Spirit of God: "According to Luke, the Spirit has not written but spoken."[182]

Evans concludes that Scripture "has a systematic function in the
Lukan narrative—its presence is neither superficial nor secondary."[183]
This comment indicates the seriousness and significance that Luke
attaches to the Old Testament. He has made profound use of Israel's
Scripture in his narrative and in no way comes up short when compared with other New Testament writers. Luke's theological capacity
to integrate the Old Testament with apostolic preaching and teaching
is as intricate as any New Testament writer, including the author of
Hebrews.

Larkin suggests that Luke's uses of quotations and allusions are
"context pointers" in that they reflect a development grounded in the
larger literary context of the original Old Testament citations. It is
Luke's style in his allusions and citations of the Old Testament to
use only the material that is part of the narrative account, rather than
cite texts as fulfilled by inserting them into the story as proofs the
way Matthew does. By doing this, Luke sets the stage for the reader
to relive the events through carefully constructed narratives integrat-
ing Old Testament material rather than using block quotations in an
apologetic fashion (again as in Matthew.[184]

Stephen's speech is often read (erroneously in my view) as an an-
ti-temple polemic. Peter Doble presents evidence that counters this
reading of the speech and illustrates Luke's use of the Old Testament.
Doble attempts to answer the questions of why no reference to Solomon is found in Jesus' genealogy (but is found at the conclusion of

---

[180] F. Bovon, "'Well Has the Holy Spirit Spoken to Your Fathers Through the Prophet Isaiah'
(Acts 28:25)," in *Studies in Early Christianity* (Tübingen: Mohr Siebeck, 2003), 116.

[181] Ibid., 117. Bovon notes that Luke's method of Scripture citation can be related to Jewish
tradition in the Qumran *Community Rule* and to 1 and 2 Maccabees.

[182] Ibid., 118.

[183] Ibid., 218.

[184] W. J. Larkin, "Luke's Use of the Old Testament in Luke 22–23," (Ph.D. thesis, University
of Durham, 1974), 641–44. See also Bock's summary discussion of Larkin's work in *Proclamation from Prophecy and Pattern*, 43–46.

Stephen's speech), and what we might learn about Luke's use of Scripture based on the Solomonic reference in Acts 7:47.[185] Doble suggests that Luke's reader(s) "upon hearing the scriptural harmonics of the prologue's closing scene, and of the genealogy which followed, would have recognized that Luke pictured the boy Jesus as David's 'proper' descendent, no less admirable than the young Solomon. . . . "[186]

After noting the significance that Scripture plays in Luke-Acts, particularly in the sermons recorded in Acts, Doble identifies one of Luke's characteristics as

> his exploring of scripture as the major interpreter of the Jesus–event. Luke's writing presupposes that his readership was attuned to the same kind of sensitivity, and that at least that community for which he was writing was already convinced that in *Torah*, psalms and prophets (Lk. 24.44) they would find clues to God's plan of salvation, given by Jesus himself, to help them grasp what was really "going on" in Jesus' life, death and exaltation. So Luke's earlier, cryptic signals to Theophilus concerning the 12-year-old Jesus' visit to the Temple, should lead later readers to expect similar stylistic tautness in other notes of scripture.[187]

Doble accepts the view that sometimes citations or allusions to the Old Testament are markers or signals that invite the reader to consider the whole context of the citation or allusion. The reader is invited to make "substantial inter-textual links." He suggests a similar inter-textuality is in play at Acts 7:46–47.[188]

Doble thinks that Stephen's reference to Solomon illustrates Luke's interest in David and the Davidic throne. Most of Luke's use of Scripture in the speeches in Acts is Christological. The reference to Solomon in Acts 7:46–47 occurs between two Scripture references: an allusion to Ps 132:5 and a citation of Isa 66:1–2a. Psalm 132 has as its theme the temple and God's promise to David that his kingdom would continue. Verse 12 speaks of the conditional nature of God's promise: "If your sons keep my covenant and my decrees . . . their sons also . . . shall sit on your throne." The final two verses of the psalm affirm what God would do for David in terms of the temple: "There will I cause a horn to sprout up for David; I have prepared a

---

[185] Doble, "Something Greater," 181–207.
[186] Ibid., 188.
[187] Ibid., 190–91.
[188] Ibid., 191.

lamp for my *christen* (anointed one). His enemies will I clothe with disgrace, but on him, his crown will glean" (Ps 132:17–18 LXX).[189]

Immediately before Luke's reference to Solomon is an allusion to a psalm linking the temple, David, and the Messiah. Remembering that an important element in Luke's plan was that Jesus would occupy the throne of David (Luke 1:32), the likelihood of a connection is increased. Additionally, Doble notes the similarity of Ps 132:17–18 with the LXX ending of Solomon's prayer at the dedication of the temple (2 Chr 6:41–42). The semantic equivalents of the beginning of Psalm 132, "O Lord, remember in David's favor . . . ," and the ending of Solomon's prayer, "O Lord God, remember your steadfast love for your servant David . . . ," would probably not be lost on the reader.[190] There are strong verbal links between Isa 66:1–2a and Psalm 132.

Doble suggests from this analysis that readers of Acts 7:46–47 should explore Solomon's prayer and see it as the "middle term" between Psalm 132 and Isaiah 66. Luke's concern would thus be more with Solomon and his successors than with the temple. Stephen (and Luke) would not be engaged in a temple polemic. Doble believes that the unexpressed remainder of the Isaiah text

> is essentially concerned with the outworking of the christological conditional. "Isaiah" knew, as Luke and Theophilus knew, that David's succession broke up under Solomon. . . . Readers enter this stage of Luke's "outworking" through a substructure comprising a Song of Ascents (Psalm 132), the Chronicler's report of Solomon's prayer and then the extended Isaiah reflection on that prayer.[191]

One of the points of Stephen's speech is that the Jewish religious leaders were like Solomon in that they had not kept Torah (Acts 7:53). Like Ps 132:18 and Isa 66:5–6, Stephen speaks of God's retribution on enemies. Thus, according to Doble, Isaiah's oracle has provided a context for a deeper understanding of Stephen's vision of the opened heaven and the enthroned Son. The verbal links between Acts 7:55–56 and Isaiah are "heaven" and "glory."[192]

> Given Luke's programmatic commitment to Jesus' reception of David's throne (Lk. 1:32), his references to the cloud in Acts 1:9, to Jesus' passage to heaven (1:10), to Stephen's seeing God's *doxa* ("glory") (7:55) and to his clear

---

[189] Ibid., 192–93.
[190] Ibid., 193–94.
[191] Ibid., 198–99.
[192] Ibid., 202–3.

identification of Jesus with the Son of man (7:56), it is not difficult to deduce that Theophilus would naturally "hear" Luke's report of Stephen's vision as that of the enthronement of the Son of man, not, of course, on God's throne, but on David's.[193]

If Doble's reading is correct, then Stephen's real point is that God's promise to David has been fulfilled in the exaltation of Jesus.

The significance of this is threefold. First, we see the insight with which Luke uses Scripture in his narrative. Second, if Doble's inferences are correct, then Luke exhibits profound knowledge of the Scriptures and assumes the same in his readers. Third, the connection with the theological focus of Hebrews cannot be missed.

As an example of the intricacy of Luke's knowledge and use of the Old Testament, consider the puzzling reference to the "finger of God" in Luke 11:20. The expression is clearly Old Testament, having no parallels in Graeco-Roman literature. The phrase occurs in Exod 8:19 and Deut 9:10. The best analysis of this expression in Luke is by Edward Woods. He argues that both Old Testament texts above are brought together by Luke in 11:20 as a pesher argument "in order to make the further equation of Exodus deliverance *leading* to a new Sinai. . . . " This was important for Luke's Jewish audience; he asserted continuity between Israel's Exodus tradition and Jesus. The context of the transfiguration preceding the "finger of God" reference further highlights Jesus as the Prophet like Moses who is mighty in word and deed. Jesus acts by the "finger of God" (Exod 8:19) at Luke 11:20.[194]

> Luke can assure his *Jewish* audience in particular that the God who is currently at work in and through Jesus, is none other than the God of the ancient Exodus. The "finger of God" expression makes this point well. It is a *pesher* argument. . . . For this reason, there is both *continuity* with the past and *discontinuity*, because Jesus is the promised Messiah who will now bring about a new and greater Exodus (Lk. 9:31) through his own death on the cross. This gives the most satisfactory interpretation of the "finger of God" (Lk. 11:20) at the wider narrative level of Luke-Acts.[195]

Clearly the above evidence, coupled with numerous other recent studies on Luke's use of Scripture, has shown that Luke handles the Old Testament like a Jew. He possesses an intricate knowledge of the

---

[193] Ibid., 203.
[194] E. Woods, *The 'Finger of God' and Pneumatology in Luke-Acts*, JSNTSup 205, ed. S. Porter (Sheffield: Sheffield Academic Press, 2001), 60, 99–100, 243.
[195] Ibid., 253–54. Emphasis original.

LXX and uses it with deftness in his overall narrative. James Sanders contrasts Luke's use of Scripture with Matthew's: "One must often rummage around in the Targums, midrashim, and Jewish commentaries to learn how a passage of Scripture functioned for Matthew."[196] On the contrary, Luke's knowledge of Scripture derived from careful reading. "Whether before conversion Luke had been a Gentile or a Reform Jew, he knew certain parts of Scripture in such depth that unless the modern interpreter also knows the Septuagint or Greek Old Testament very well indeed he or she will miss major points Luke wanted to score."[197]

With respect to Luke's use of Scripture in his overall hermeneutics and what that tells us about Luke's audience, Rebecca Denova's salient point is worth noting: "When a particular interpretation from Scripture is offered as an argument, Luke anticipates a response by other Jews, not Gentiles."[198] Denova notes further that the point of view expressed by Luke is consistently that of the Jewish Scriptures:

> In my view, this type of argument strongly suggests that the ethnic background of the author of Luke-Acts is Jewish, and that he presented arguments that were of some importance to Jews. . . . [I]n the case of Luke-Acts we have an example of an author who was able to relate the books of Isaiah, Psalms, and the books of the Minor Prophets and produce a story that demonstrated the harmony of the rest of Scripture and contemporary events. In other words, when Luke combines portions of Isaiah with Psalms, or Amos with Jeremiah and the Pentateuch, he never understands them to be "out of context" in relation to his understanding that "all the scriptures" are fulfilled in the events concerning Jesus of Nazareth and his followers. At other times, he could create an association with Scripture without citation, relying upon a nuanced understanding of narrative type. This suggests that Luke knew precisely where to look for the elements of his story. Far from being a "recent" Gentile convert, such knowledge surely marks our author as someone steeped in the biblical traditions of Israel. Luke-Acts, we may conclude on the basis of a narrative-critical reading, was written by a Jew to persuade other Jews that Jesus of Nazareth was the messiah of Scripture and that the words of the prophets concerning "restoration" have been "fulfilled."[199]

---

[196] Evans and Sanders, *Luke and Scripture*, 16.

[197] Ibid., 18. Sanders also notes that among the Gospel writers, Luke is the most explicit in insisting that knowledge of what God is doing in Christ is dependent on knowledge of the Scriptures.

[198] R. Denova, *The Things Accomplished Among Us: Prophetic Tradition in the Structural Pattern of Luke-Acts*. JSNTSup 141 (Sheffield: Sheffield Academic Press, 1977), 226.

[199] Ibid., 230–31. It is interesting to note in Acts 13:1–21:14 how Scripture quotations are confined to narratives involving Jews and to speeches in which Jews are addressed. Scripture is employed only allusively in speeches to Gentiles.

Koet comes to the same conclusion regarding Luke's audience: "I have to conclude that this high esteem for the Scriptures and their interpretation is most plausibly explained as an issue for the community for whom Luke wrote. Such an understanding is especially to be expected within Jewish circles. . . . there was a significant Jewish Christian presence among Luke's audience."[200] He further identifies Luke as Jewish, based on his use of Scripture and his interest in Jewish practices.[201] Likewise Bovon comments, "The author had a good education encompassing Greek rhetoric as well as Jewish methods of exegesis."[202]

Finally, how does Luke's attitude toward and use of Scripture compare with the author of Hebrews? It can no longer be claimed that Luke is a mere historian operating from a somewhat limited theological ability.[203] Second, Luke has been shown to possess knowledge of the Old Testament commensurate with the author of Hebrews. Third, Luke's method of using Scripture (direct citation, allusion, "echoes," etc.) is not unlike what is found in Hebrews. David Moessner recently demonstrated the theological and hermeneutical uses that Peter makes of Psalm 16 and Psalm 110 in his sermon at Pentecost.[204] Psalm 110 plays a similar role in Hebrews, which argues the theological significance of the Son's seat at the "right hand" of God (cf. the use in Acts 2, as well as Acts 7).

Portions of Psalm 118 are quoted in the Synoptic Gospels (both double and triple tradition), John, Acts, 1 Peter, and Heb 13:6. Several allusions are found in these writings with only two possible allusions in Paul (Rom 8:31 and 2 Cor 6:9). In Luke's usage, the LXX *ho erchomenos* (Ps 117:26) is Messianic in force and has become a formal title for Luke. It is used as a designation of the Messiah outside the four Gospels only in Acts 19:4 and Heb 10:37.[205] This psalm figures

---

[200] Koet, *Five Studies*, 157.

[201] Ibid., 160n46. C. Kimball likewise asserts Luke's Jewishness in his *Jesus' Exposition*, 45.

[202] Bovon, *Luke 1: A Commentary on the Gospel of Luke 1:1–9:50*, 8. He thinks it likely that Luke was a Greek by birth, but turned to Judaism early in life.

[203] Against the surprising statement made by Black that "Luke does not appear in Scripture as an expert doctrinal teacher, but rather mainly as historian" (D. A. Black, "Who Wrote Hebrews?" *Faith and Mission* 18 [2001]: 21). This comment fails to take into account the past 40 years of Lukan studies that have clearly shown Luke's profound theological ability and the possibility, even likelihood, that he was Jewish.

[204] Ibid., 215–32.

[205] See Bock, *Proclamation from Prophecy and Pattern*, 112; Wagner, "Psalm 118 in Luke-Acts," 161.

heavily in Luke's theology and is found in quotation outside the Gospels only in Acts, Hebrews, and 1 Peter.[206]

Fourth, it has been shown above that Luke's quotation formulae come closest to Hebrews in comparison with the rest of the New Testament writers. The Lukan notion of the validity of the Word as the speech of God, while similar to all New Testament writers, is more like the emphasis we find in Hebrews than anywhere else. Fifth, the Old Testament "double context" (historical and present) is prominent in Luke's use of Scripture, but his focus is clearly on the latter,[207] as it is in Hebrews with its emphasis on "today." Sixth, Bock's choice of the word "pattern" for the title of his book illustrates Luke's narrative writing as fulfillment of Old Testament patterns that point to the presence of God's saving work.[208] This is an emphasis of Hebrews. Finally, Bock has shown that Luke's Christology moves from the concept of Jesus as Messiah to Jesus as Lord. "The goal of Luke's Christology is the portrayal of Jesus' Messianic office ultimately in terms of Jesus' absolute position at the right hand of God as Lord of all."[209] Bock highlights Luke's emphasis on Jesus' exaltation at the right hand of God. This is also a foundational theological construct for the author of Hebrews. Kimball concludes his study of Luke's use of Scripture by noting, "The Lukan Christological exposition employed a pesher fulfillment motif and several midrashic techniques to show that the Old Testament found its typological and prophetic fulfillment in Jesus."[210]

Without diminishing the unique place Hebrews holds in the New Testament in terms of its rich theology, rhetorical style, and masterful use of the Old Testament, it seems appropriate to suggest that the Lukan approach to Scripture is more like what we find in Hebrews than anywhere else in the New Testament.

In the last paragraph of *Luke and Scripture*, Evans summarizes Peter's (and Luke's) use of Joel in Acts 2 with words that move beyond

---

[206] See the excellent article by Wagner, especially the conclusion and following table of quotations and allusions to Psalm 118 in Luke-Acts ("Psalm 118 in Luke-Acts," 174–78).

[207] Bock, *Proclamation from Prophecy and Pattern*, 272. Kimball notes the formula "God of Abraham, Isaac, and Jacob" was used to claim the same covenant benefits for the present generation, as in Acts 3:13 and Heb 11:16. Kimball, *Jesus' Exposition*, 172.

[208] Ibid., 274.

[209] Ibid., 270. Kimball says Luke's exposition of Psalm 110 and the *kurios* title in Luke 20:41–44 should be compared with Acts 2:34–35 and Heb 1:13. Kimball, *Jesus' Exposition*, 202.

[210] Kimball, *Jesus' Exposition*, 201.

the scope of that chapter and encompass the Lukan conception of Scripture in the unfolding plan of God's salvation:

> Long ago the fire was seen on Sinai and the voice of God was heard. . . . now once again God has spoken. The Lukan narrative illustrates and testifies how these prophetic traditions had come to be experienced in the Christian community . . . but the real issue is how Christian history and experience are understood from a scriptural point of view.[211]

It is not that the Christian story is written and the Old Testament is thus "updated" by the New Testament writers, least of all Luke. It is rather that the story of Jesus and the early church is told in light of the Old Testament Scriptures. One might say that for Luke, the Old Testament Scripture is necessary to interpret God's new work of salvation through Jesus. Luke does two primary things in Luke-Acts: he interprets Scripture, and he tells the story of the Christ event and the concomitant birth and growth of church. For Luke, God's action in history in the Christ event cannot be understood apart from the Old Testament. This is, of course, the approach of the author of Hebrews, who used the Old Testament to fashion his hortatory discourse. Considering how Luke used Scripture in his narrative, what might we expect of him were he to write a letter such as Hebrews? We would expect him to incorporate Scripture, much as has been done in Hebrews.

Additional Evidence

We have already considered some of the proposals of Jacob Jervell with respect to Luke's approach to Judaism. Two additional arguments from him support our thesis.

Jervell argues that some of Luke's omissions from Mark (he assumes Markan priority) betray his pro-Jewish point of view. For example, he suggests that Luke's omission of Mark 7:1–23 does not reveal an anti-Jewish or pro-Gentile orientation as is usually suggested, but just the opposite is the case. The passage deals with Jewish cleanliness and defilement, so it has been assumed that Luke regarded it as irrelevant for his Gentile audience. Jervell contends, however, that Luke omitted this section because he did not wish to cast Jesus as critical of rabbinic halakah. Luke's purpose is to present Jesus as a loyal Jew; hence

---

[211] Evans and Sanders, *Luke and Scripture*, 224.

his avoidance of the Markan section.[212] To my mind, Jervell's work succeeds at least in showing Luke's intent to cast Jesus and Paul in the most favorable light for Jewish readers.

Another hint concerning the Jewish provenance of Luke-Acts is found in Luke's treatment of the Samaritans. Nowhere does he explain who the Samaritans are as John does in John 4:9. The introduction to the "travel narrative" (Luke 9:51) is nearly unintelligible without previous knowledge of the Samaritans and the relationship between Gerazim and Jerusalem. Luke expects a great deal from his readers on this subject. If his audience comprised Jewish Christians, they would be aware of the Samaritan situation, and there would be no need for Luke to explain it.[213]

There is a linguistic feature of the Gospel of Luke that may reinforce the suggestion of Luke's Jewish background. In the *Magnificat* of Luke 1, there is an unusual combination of tenses in vv. 46–47, a phenomenon that has generated a number of unsatisfactory explanations. Randall Buth has proposed a solution that makes the most sense of the data.[214]

There is a feature of Hebrew poetry called "tense-shift" in which the tenses in adjacent clauses are switched purely for rhetorical effect. Nothing in the surface or semantic structure of the text requires such a change. Furthermore, such tense switching is not a property of either Greek or Semitic discourse. The LXX translation of the Psalms does not reflect tense-shifting. Therefore, Luke could not have used the LXX as a model for his composition of the *Magnificat*. Buth's suggestion is that the *Magnificat* is an original Hebrew poem, which either Luke or (more likely) someone else carefully translated into Greek.

Buth summarizes his study of Hebrew poetic tense-shifting with the following five points:

1. In Hebrew poetry the tense will sometimes shift from past-complete to present-future-past-habitual, or vice versa, without a change in the referential world.

2. This tense-shifting is both a cohesive device in Hebrew poetry and a way of enhancing the formal beauty or aesthetic quality of a poem.

---

[212] Jervell, *Luke and the People of God*, 133–47.

[213] See Jervell's discussion in *Luke and the People of God*, 113–27.

[214] R. Buth, "Hebrew Poetic Tenses and the Magnificat," *JSNT* 21 (1984): 67–83.

3. This phenomenon is attested in Hebrew poetry from about 1000 BC.
4. This does not seem to be a natural feature of either Greek or Aramaic.
5. The LXX, by avoiding this tense phenomenon, could not have served as a vehicle for teaching such a poetic device to Christian readers of Greek or to Luke.[215]

The unusual combination of the present and aorist tenses in Luke 1:46–47 can best be explained by the phenomenon of Hebrew tense-shifting. Luke was sensitive enough to this phenomenon to have used it in his Gospel. Yet it would be very unusual if Luke had been the Gentile writer scholars supposed him to be. The question must be asked: where did Luke learn such niceties of the Hebrew language? Some have argued that Luke composed the *Magnificat*. If so, where did he learn this subtlety of Hebrew poetry if he was a Gentile? Buth believes someone other than Luke translated the poem into Greek and preserved the Hebrew poetic tense-shift despite normal Greek usage and despite the usual translation practice of the Septuagint.[216]

Luke may have received this information from Mary the mother of Jesus through personal interview. She could have related the incident and her response in Hebrew, and Luke conveyed carefully the tense-shift of her poetic *Magnificat* in his Greek text. Either way one approaches the problem, Luke has used his source(s) and method of composition to preserve a textual feature that makes awkward Greek, yet reflects careful translation from a (possible) Hebrew original, a fact that further illustrates his knowledge of Jewish textual features as well as his possible Jewish background.

In summary fashion, Buth remarks:

> The results of this study legitimize the verbs in Luke 1.46–47 and give us a sense of appreciation for them. The Greek verbs, although based on a Hebrew poem, are not necessarily the result of ignorance on the part of a translator. A satisfactory explanation does not need a translator who could not understand Hebrew or Aramaic; someone who understood Hebrew verbs provides a better explanation.[217]

---

[215] Ibid., 73–74.
[216] Ibid., 74–75.
[217] Ibid., 75.

The linguistic evidence argues against someone of Greek background writing the song. Buth argues against Luke writing it because he assumes Luke was a Gentile. Luke could have been a Gentile who received information directly from Mary and preserved the unique phenomenon of Hebrew tense-shift in his Greek narrative. If so, why would he translate it into odd-sounding Greek? I think the better explanation is that Luke had a Jewish background.

Buth has also proposed a solution to the problem of the plural *kurioi,* "owners," found in Luke 19:33. Interpreters have sought to explain the strangeness of the plurality of owners as perhaps a reference to the owner and his wife. Buth suggests, however, that Luke employed a Hebraism by which a single owner of an animal would be referred to in the plural.

In the parallel account in Mark 11:5, the men are not referred to as "owners" but a plural noun phrase is used: "And some of those standing there said to them . . . . " Buth argues that if his suggestion is correct, Mark cannot be the source for Luke.

> The alternative would be to say that Luke accidentally produced a good Mishnaic Hebrew idiom from Mark's plural. Such is not probable since there is no reason or motivation for calling all of the men owners.[218]

Buth suggests that Luke acquired this Hebraism from a Hebrew source, but is it possible that no sources were involved and that the idiom came from Luke himself? If so, it would be further evidence of Luke's Jewish background and orientation.

Luke 14:26–27 may furnish another indication of Luke's knowledge of Hebrew:

> If anyone comes to Me and does not hate his own father and mother, wife and children, brothers and sisters—yes, and even his own life—he cannot be My disciple. Whoever does not bear his own cross and come after Me cannot be My disciple.

If these verses are translated from Greek into Hebrew, there is a wordplay on the verbs "hate" and "bear," which contain the same consonants in Hebrew (*ś-n-ʾ* "hate," *n-ś-ʾ* "bear"). If this wordplay was

---

[218] R. Buth, "Luke 19:31–34, Mishnaic Hebrew, and Bible Translation: is κύριοι τον πωλον Singular?" *JBL* 104 (1985): 683. Nolland, however, thinks Buth has not offered adequate justification. J. Nolland, *Luke 18:35–24:53*, WBC 35c (Dallas: Word, 1993), 925.

intended by Luke, Jewish readers would probably recognize it, where-as Gentile readers clearly would not.[219]

Another example bears mentioning. Turner points out that Luke shows a preference for the order noun-numeral rather than numeral-noun and that this usage of the adjective after the noun reflects the Semitic order.[220]

Robert Sloan made a penetrating analysis of the theology of Luke's Gospel in which he argued for the programmatic significance of Jesus' first sermon recorded in Luke 4:16–30. Jesus begins His sermon in the synagogue in Nazareth with a quotation from Isa 61:1–2a and 58:6. The prophet Isaiah had applied the Torah passages about the Sabbatical Year and the Year of Jubilee (Exod 21:2–6; 23:10–12; Lev 25; Deut 15:1–18; 31:9–13) to the Israelites returning from the Babylonian exile. Jesus, in turn, applies them to His Israelite audience, who then must be poor, bound, blind, and oppressed. "Jesus' own subsequent use . . . of this priestly terminology . . . was lost on neither Jesus' Nazareth audience nor the Jewish readers of the gospel of Luke."[221]

Sloan continues to present evidence that the theological concept of the Year of Jubilee undergirds several themes prominent in Luke's Gospel. He examines especially Luke 6:20–38, the first half of the Sermon on the Mount, and Luke 11:4, the so-called "fifth prayer" of the Lord's Prayer, and concludes:

> The influence of the jubilee/sabbath year legislation . . . upon the message and self-understanding of Jesus is attestable not only in the Nazareth pericope . . . but is manifested persistently, if not pervasively, throughout the gospel of Luke, and has in fact to some extent conditioned the theological shaping and presentation of the gospel materials by Luke.[222]

According to Sloan, the Year of Jubilee theologically serves to illustrate that God's salvation is both present and future. Christ inaugurated it

---

[219] S. Lachs, "Hebrew Elements in the Gospels and Acts," *JQR* 71 (1980): 40–41.

[220] N. Turner, *Syntax*, in *A Grammar of the Greek New Testament* (Edinburgh: T&T Clark, 1963), 3:349.

[221] R. Sloan, *The Favorable Year of the Lord* (Austin: Scholars Press, 1977), 1; cf. id., "The Favorable Year of the Lord: An Abbreviation and Addenda," in *Chronos, Kairos, Christos II*, ed. J. Vardaman (Macon, GA: Mercer Univ. Press, 1998). See also S. Ringe, "A Gospel of Liberation: An Explanation of Jubilee Motifs in the Gospel of Luke" (Ph.D. diss., Union Theological Seminary, New York City, 1980), and his *Jesus, Liberation, and the Biblical Jubilee*, OBT 19 (Philadelphia: Fortress, 1985)

[222] Sloan, *The Favorable Year of the Lord*, 111–12.

by His first coming and will consummated it at His second coming.[223] The term *aphesis*, commonly used in the New Testament for "forgiveness," occurs twice in Jesus' quotation of Isaiah in Luke 4:18, but with the meaning "freedom" or "[set] free." Luke apparently considered the term *aphesis* to convey considerable theological weight since of its 17 total occurrences in the New Testament, 10 are found in Luke-Acts. Sloan explains that Luke's use of it represents the primary theological and verbal connection with the Levitical proclamation of Jubilee.[224] The term occurs twice in Hebrews, and interestingly enough, it occurs without any qualifiers in Heb 9:22 as in Luke 4:18.

All other occurrences of this word in the New Testament typically add some qualifier to complete its meaning, usually the genitive *hamartiōn*, "of sins." Guthrie remarks that the absolute use of the word in Heb 9:22 should be understood as a reference not just to forgiveness from specific sins, but to general deliverance or release.[225] As such, the writer of Hebrews may have used this term for its jubilary background as in Luke 4:18. The word itself, the lack of qualifiers in Luke 4:18 and Heb 9:22, and the possible jubilary background in both references further link Luke and Hebrews.

If Luke was a Greek writing only for a Gentile audience, his emphasis on Old Testament jubilary themes would be considered somewhat unusual. However, if Luke was Jewish (or at least writing for a Jewish audience), then these factors are more easily accounted for. At the very least, it should be obvious that Luke is thoroughly familiar with Old Testament Judaism and discloses his knowledge of and interest in the Judaic Scriptures, traditions, and theological outlook.

Robert Brawley interprets the evidence from Luke-Acts to indicate that Luke, more than any other writer in the New Testament, presents the Pharisees favorably. He concludes that part of Luke's purpose in writing his two-volume work was to encourage Jews to embrace Christianity.[226] Luke treats the Pharisees as respected representatives of Judaism with whom an appreciable segment of his audience would

---

[223] Ibid., 166; see also Sanders, *Luke and Scripture*, 84–92.

[224] Ibid., 36–37.

[225] D. Guthrie, *Hebrews*, TNTC (Grand Rapids: Eerdmans, 1983), 195.

[226] R. Brawley, "The Pharisees in Luke-Acts: Luke's Address to Jews and His Irenic Purpose" (Ph.D. Diss., Princeton Theological Seminary, 1978); id., *Luke-Acts and the Jews: Conflict, Apology, and Conciliation*. For the opposing view, see R. Karris, "Luke 23:47 and the Lucan view of Jesus' Death," in *Reimaging the Death of the Lukan Jesus*, Athenäums Monografien Theologie Bonner biblische Beiträge 73 (Frankfurt am Main: Anton Hain, 1990), 68–78.

identify.[227] Brawley offers an exegesis of several relevant passages and concludes that Luke's material is rich in persuasive admonition, written to persuade a Jewish audience that was still outside the church. Even if Brawley's thesis about Luke's view of the Pharisees is correct, while his view of Luke's purpose is not, his evidence favors a Jewish audience.[228]

Palmer illustrates how Luke employed in Acts 1:1–14 a number of elements characteristic of a Jewish farewell scene. While the genre of farewell scenes and speeches is common in Greek, Roman, and Jewish writings, Palmer notes how the Jewish features are prominent in the prologue to Acts. Such a farewell scene includes a statement of the nearness of death (or departure) either in the narrative or on the lips of the departing figure. Second, a specific audience is assembled by the departing figure. Third, sometimes there is a review of history with paraenetic intention. Fourth, the departing person may appoint a successor or transfer authority to another individual or group. Fifth, the last words of the departing figure are narrated, usually with brevity. Palmer illustrates each of these tendencies from Acts 1:1–14 and concludes that Luke deliberately fashioned his narrative account along the lines of a Jewish farewell scene.[229]

Further examples of the Jewish nature of Luke-Acts can be cited. On three occasions Luke records that Jesus died "on a tree." This is a distinctly Jewish way of referring to the crucifixion and occurs only two other times in the New Testament: Gal 3:13 and 1 Pet 2:24.

Otto Betz has analyzed the use of Isa 28:16 ("Look, I have laid a stone in Zion, a tested stone, a precious cornerstone, a sure foundation; the one who believes will be unshakable") in the New Testament, especially in Hebrews.[230] He recognizes its use by Paul in Rom 9:33; 10:11; 1 Cor 3:10–14; Eph 2:20; and Col 1:23; 2:5. It is also behind Jesus' words of warning, encouragement, and instruction to Peter in Matt 16:18 and Luke 22:31–32.[231] In the Luke passage we find Jesus praying for Peter "that his faith not fail." Here the intercessory

---

[227] Brawley, "The Pharisees in Luke-Acts," 159.
[228] See also Mason, "Chief Priests, Sadducees, Pharisees and Sanhedrin in Acts," 115–77.
[229] D.W. Palmer, "The Literary Background of Acts 1:1–14," *NTS* 33 (1987): 427–38.
[230] O. Betz, "Firmness in Faith: Hebrews 11:1 and Isaiah 28:16," in *Scripture: Meaning and Method: Essays Presented to A. T. Hanson for His Seventieth Birthday*, ed. B. Thompson (North Yorkshire: Hull University Press, 1987), 92–113.
[231] Ibid., 98–100.

ministry of Jesus highlighted in Hebrews is given tangible example in the earthly life of Jesus.

Max Wilcox finds the possibility of rabbinic traditional material underlying Luke 24:21.[232] He observes the similarities between *Pirqe de Rab Eliezer* (PRE) 48:82–86 and Luke 24:21. This section of PRE tells how "the mystery of redemption" of Israel was passed down from Abraham to Joseph and his brothers. Asher is said to have passed it on to his daughter, Serah, who lived to the time of Moses. When she heard that Moses had said "God has surely visited you" (Exod 3:16) she identified Moses as the man who would free Israel from Egypt, for she had heard from her father *"pqd ypqd 'tkm"* ("God shall surely visit you"; Gen 50:24–25 and Exod 13:19).

There is a "striking parallel" between the words used by Serah to commend Moses as the redeemer of Israel and the words in Luke 24:21, where Cleopas explains what the disciples had thought about Jesus prior to His death:

Serah (of Moses)	Cleopas (of Jesus)
He is the man who is about to Redeem/free Israel from Egypt.	He is the one who is about to Redeem/free Israel.[233]

No doubt some would suggest Luke was simply unaware of this parallel and that it was simply a part of his source. Yet given what we know of Luke's keen awareness of and interest in Jewish matters, perhaps this is further evidence of that.

Other examples of Jewish influence include the following from the Book of Acts:

16:3	Timothy was circumcised by Paul at the request of the Jews.
18:18	Paul shaved his head, for he had made a Jewish vow.[234]
21:20	"You see, brother, how many thousands of Jews there are who have believed, and they are all zealous for the law."

---

[232] M. Wilcox, "The Bones of Joseph: Hebrews 11:22," in *Scripture: Meaning and Method*, 114–30.

[233] Ibid., 119–20.

[234] See the recent discussion of this and why Luke mentions it in Acts in R. Tomes, "Why did Paul get his Hair Cut? (Acts 18.18; 21.23–24)," in *Luke's Literary Achievement: Collected Essays*, JSNTSup 116 (Sheffield: Sheffield Academic Press, 1995), 188–97.

| 21:23,24 | Jewish leaders advised Paul to join with four men who had made a vow and were now ready to fulfill the purification rites. He should pay the expenses to show the people in Jerusalem "that you yourself are also careful about observing the law." |
| 28:17 | Arriving in Rome, Paul summoned "the leaders of the Jews." |

If Luke was a Gentile writing to a Gentile audience, it is at least odd that he should use a number of chronological references that are distinctly Jewish. An example is the double reference to time in Luke 24:29: "It's almost evening, and now the day is almost over." Denaux and Van Wiele argue persuasively that these two time references in the Greek text, as well as the Hebrew equivalents, are synonymous expressions and refer to the afternoon hours between noon and about 6 p.m., and they actually point to the middle of this period, about 3 p.m. "The meal at Emmaus is an early evening meal, taking place [*pros esperan*], that is, at the ninth hour (=3 p.m.), the hour of the evening sacrifice (Num 28,4.8; cp. 2 Esdras 3,3), with which the gospel also began (cf. Lk 1,8–23), and which is the hour of the [sic] Jesus' death three days before (Lk 23,44)."[235] This interpretation of the double time expression in Luke 24:29 is often misinterpreted, according to Denaux and Van Wiele, because Western scholars have read their own cultural understanding of the concept of "evening" (sunset) into Luke's text.[236]

The following Jewish chronological references are found in Acts with several that are unique to Luke:

1:12	a Sabbath day's journey
2:1	when the day of Pentecost had arrived
16:13	on the Sabbath day
20:6	days of unleavened bread
20:16	to be at Jerusalem by the day of Pentecost
27:9	the Fast was already over[237]

---

[235] A. Denaux and I. Van Wiele, "The Meaning of the Double Expression of Time in Luke 24,29," in *Miracles and Imagery in Luke and John: Festschrift Ulrich Busse*, ed. J. Verheyden, G. Van Belle, and J. G. Van der Watt, Bibliotheca Ephemeridum Theologicarum Lovaniensium 218 (Leuven/Paris/Dudley, MA: Uitgeverij Peeters, 2008), 87.

[236] Ibid.

[237] Selwyn, *St. Luke the Prophet*, 37, concludes from this statement in 27:9 that the author of the "We" section [Luke] was Jewish.

Goulder describes the geographical references in Luke-Acts as "astonishingly accurate."[238] Given absence of maps and the ease with which errors can creep into second-hand stories, this level of accuracy is "strikingly impressive."[239] Jesus withdraws to Bethsaida (Luke 9:9–10) after Luke's statement that Herod, having heard of Jesus, was trying to see Him. This fact is not mentioned in the Markan parallel, but later in Mark 6:45. Goulder infers from this that Luke knew Bethsaida was outside Herod's jurisdiction and in the jurisdiction of Phillip.[240] If the inference is valid, it serves as another indication of Luke's accurate knowledge of Palestinian geography and political milieu. "There can have been very few members of the early Church with so wide a traveling experience, and the companion of Paul in Acts is one of them."[241]

The cumulative effect of this linguistic and conceptual data in Luke-Acts has contributed to the reassessment of Luke's background. The theory that a Jewish background for Luke best explains the textual data in his writings has gained support in recent years. One of the most significant paths being pursued in New Testament studies is the value of understanding Luke-Acts within a Jewish milieu. Luke demonstrates in his two-volume work that the church has her roots in God's people, Israel.[242]

---

[238] Goulder, *Luke: A New Paradigm*, 117.

[239] Ibid., 119.

[240] Ibid., 105.

[241] Ibid., 119. See additional evidence from Goulder discussed above under "Birth Narratives in Luke 1–2."

[242] Bovon and Blomberg register their disagreement with the trend in Lukan studies that Luke stresses continuity over discontinuity with Judaism in Luke-Acts. Bovon attributes the shift of opinion to a post-holocaust desire not to offend Jews and a widespread disregard of the major studies in the 1960s and 1970s. F. Bovon, "Studies in Luke-Acts: Retrospect and Prospect," *HTR* 85 (1992): 175–96. Blomberg criticizes studies holding this viewpoint by saying "they lack consistent narrative-critical analysis." C. Blomberg, "The Christian and the Law of Moses," in *Witness to the Gospel*, 399. Blomberg seems unaware of Denova's work published in 1997, a first-class study of Luke-Acts from a narrative perspective (see above under "The Use of Scripture in Luke-Acts"). Finally, most of those suggesting a Jewish milieu for Luke-Acts are not unmindful of the discontinuity that Luke emphasizes as well. Moessner and Tiede edit a multivolume series titled *Luke the Interpreter of Israel*. The first volume's title shows how Luke's understanding of Judaism is now viewed among those concentrating on Lukan studies: D. Moessner, ed., *Jesus and the Heritage of Israel: Luke's Narrative Claim upon Israel's Heritage* (Harrisburg, PA: Trinity Press International, 1999), esp. 2–4, 49–51, 60, 66–67, 96–97, 168–70, 208, 217, 244–49, 322–24, 368. In this volume, 17 scholars present a sea change of opinion that Luke is the interpreter of Israel. There is now an international consensus that Luke claims Jesus as Israel's true heritage.

Luke and His Reader(s)

What implications can we draw from the evidence that has culled from Luke-Acts? The wide-ranging references to Jewish practices, people, institutions, and overall milieu, with little or no explanation given, strongly suggests Luke assumes this knowledge in his readers. On the other hand, the rarity of Gentile religious practices or institutions mentioned in Luke-Acts also suggests the audience might be Jewish. Luke's presentation of Jesus in relationship to Jewish messianic and eschatological expectations reflects similar ideas current in intertestamental Jewish writings, and as Shellard notes, "Their presence in Luke, popularly regarded as the most 'Gentile' of the Gospels, is somewhat surprising."[243] The function of Scripture in Luke-Acts implies a reader who has intimate knowledge of the Jewish Scriptures in Greek. Luke tends to "think" in Jewish terms.[244]

Even Bock, who maintains Luke's Gentile background, admits,

> Yet, the heavy use of the Old Testament, the time spent on Jewish-Gentile relations, and the issues of Jewish dispute in Luke's Gospel, including the detail given to Jewish rejection, all suggest that the issue of Jewish influence is significant in the account. The emphasis on themes such as perseverance seems to suggest an audience that needs to endure with the community in light of Jewish rejection rather than an audience to whom is directed a strictly evangelistic appeal to enter into salvation.[245]

Conclusion

Like salt sprinkled throughout food, these many examples provide a Jewish flavor to Luke-Acts that cannot be missed. Furthermore, as Juel says, they cannot be dismissed solely because the major participants in the narrative are Jewish. What is more significant is Luke's interest in their Jewishness.[246] If Luke were a Gentile or if he were writing solely for Gentiles, we would certainly expect to find fewer Jewish elements in the narrative than we do. Furthermore, if the assessment of Luke's theology of Israel and her relationship to the Church presented above is correct, then it is obvious that his orientation was

---

[243] B. Shellard, *New Light on Luke: Its Purpose, Sources and Literary Context*, JSNTSup 215, ed. S. Porter (London: Sheffield Academic Press, 2002), 187–88.

[244] See the summary of Denova's work above under "The Use of Scripture in Luke-Acts."

[245] D. Bock, "Luke," in *The Face of New Testament Studies: A Survey of Recent Research*, ed. S. McKnight and G. Osborne (Grand Rapids: Baker, 2004), 371.

[246] D. Juel, *Luke-Acts: The Promise of History* (Atlanta: John Knox, 1983), 103.

more Jewish than has been generally recognized. We can at least say that Luke may indeed have been a Jew, and that he was concerned with the history of salvation and the nation of Israel.[247] For Luke, Christianity is the fulfillment of Judaism, and rather than rejecting the Jews because of their rejection of Christianity, Luke reveals an irenic spirit and purpose in his two-volume work.

Although Martin Hengel favors Luke's Gentile background, he recognizes that Luke has by far the best knowledge of Judaism, the temple cultus, synagogues, customs, and sects, and that he reports them in an accurate way.[248] Schreckenberg, although he believes Luke to be a Gentile, likewise affirms "Luke shows a certain interest in, almost an inner connection with, the Jewish background to the New Testament events and certainly shows no plain anti-Judaism."[249]

We can now say there is a significant amount of evidence pointing to the Jewishness of Luke-Acts. If Luke was not Jewish, he produced a two-volume work that in terms of content, language, and emphasis manifests an amazing knowledge of and interest in Jewish matters. Given this, a significant barrier against Lukan authorship of Hebrews is removed.

Excursus: Judaism and Hellenism in the Early Church.

Wayne Meeks reminds us that the adjectives "Jewish" and "Hellenistic" are practically no help in sorting out the variety of Christian groups in the early church. While this is perhaps a bit of an overstatement, it is a cogent reminder that this situation is the result of many factors, not the least of which is that the boundaries between the varieties of Judaism in the first century were not impermeable. Paul was a "Hebrew born of Hebrews" (Phil 3:5), yet he wrote "only and fluently in Greek."[250] Peder Borgen put it bluntly: "Scholars no longer regard the distinction between Palestinian and Hellenistic Judaism as a basic category for our understanding of Judaism."[251]

---

[247] Parsons: "The narrative of Acts can also be read as supporting the view that Luke was a Jew or at least deeply interested in Judaism" ("Who Wrote the Gospel of Luke?" 20).

[248] M. Hengel, *Zur urchristlichen Geschichtsschreibung* 59 (ET), 64.

[249] H. Schreckenberg and K. Schubert, *Jewish Historiography and Iconography in Early and Medieval Christianity*, 47.

[250] W. Meeks, "Judaism, Hellenism, and the Birth of Christianity," in *Paul Beyond the Judaism/Hellenism Divide*, ed. T. Engberg-Pedersen (Louisville: John Knox, 2001), 26–27.

[251] P. Borgen, *The New Testament and Hellenistic Judaism*, ed. P. Borgen and S. Giversen (Peabody, MA: Hendrickson, 1997 [originally published by Aarhus University Press, 1995]), 11.

Recent work by Malherbe, Betz, Kennedy, and their students on the Graeco-Roman rhetoric of Paul's era claims that Paul made "recognizable, sophisticated, and original use of the strategies common to the orators." Dean Anderson offers a trenchant rebuttal of this position.[252] Whatever one's position on Paul's awareness of and use or non-use of rhetoric, he frequently employed interpretative strategies of Scripture like those found among early and later Jewish interpretation, both sectarian and rabbinic. Paul was "all these things at once."[253] I might add, so was Luke. The incredible amount of "diffusionism" (to use Meeks's word) in the first century compels us to be less rigid in our discussions and theories of "Jew," "Greek," "Roman," "Hellenistic," "Jewish," "sectarian," and a host of other ethnicities and communities. Nikalaus Walter demonstrates the internal diversity of Hellenistic Diaspora Judaism and offers clear evidence that Hellenistic Judaism of the Diaspora established "branches" in Jerusalem. At the time of the early church there were synagogues in Jerusalem where Greek was the most commonly spoken language. Acts 6:9 indicates there were at least two and as many as five synagogues of "foreigners" of the Diaspora, which means there were communities organized according to nationalities.[254] This is important for the discussion surrounding the location of the recipients of Hebrews and why Hebrews was written in Greek. This permeability should both inform and temper our discussions of matters such as the ethnic background of Luke, the background of his recipients, the background of the author and recipients of Hebrews, and other related matters.

Consider two examples. One of the key arguments against a Palestinian destination of Hebrews is that surely the writer would have written in Hebrew if writing to the Jerusalem church. But that argument can no longer be maintained. A second example is found in the comment by Greek grammarian J. H. Moulton that Hebrews was written by someone who knew no Hebrew.[255]

---

[252] R. D. Anderson, *Ancient Rhetorical Theory and Paul*, rev. ed. (Leuven: Peeters, 1999).

[253] W. Meeks, "Judaism, Hellenism, and the Birth of Christianity," 26–27.

[254] N. Walter, "Hellenistic Jews of the Diaspora at the Cradle of Primitive Christianity," in *The New Testament and Hellenistic Judaism*, ed. P. Borgen and S. Giversen (Aarhus, Denmark: Aarhus University Press, 1995), 11. See his full discussion on pp. 37–58.

[255] J. H. Moulton, "New Testament Greek in the Light of Modern Discovery," in *The Language of the New Testament: Classic Essays*, JSNTSup 60 (Sheffield: JSOT Press, 1991), 78–79. This is a reprint from an article written in 1909.

One of the axioms of Higher Criticism has been that Palestinian authors could not write Hellenistic ideas, but rather such concepts belonged to a "later stage" of development. This has now been shown to be a patently false assumption. In the library at Qumran, there is evidence that the LXX was used in first-century Palestine even among very strict Jews. Surprisingly, an inscription dedicating a Jewish synagogue was made in Greek.[256]

Skarsaune's recent work is important on this subject. A study of the languages used in Israel during the time of Christ reveals koine Greek was common in Israel and Jerusalem. Evidence for this includes the use of Greek by several Jewish authors, and inscriptions in catacombs dating from the first to the sixth century AD and on ossuaries dating from roughly 65 BC to AD 135.[257] "We cannot differentiate between the Judaism in Israel and that of the Diaspora by saying that the latter was Hellenistic and the former not."[258]

The next chapter is my attempt to negotiate cautiously this minefield. Although I believe the evidence for Lukan authorship of Hebrews to be substantial, I am on much thinner ice when it comes to my theories about the recipient of Luke-Acts and the recipients of Hebrews, and even the Jewish background for Luke (though with respect to the latter, I do consider the evidence to point strongly in this direction). Lukan authorship of Hebrews is not dependent on them, nor should it be denied based solely on the appeal to what we expect should have been the case in the first century relative to "Judaism" or "Hellenism." Although we have learned much in recent years about the cultural milieu of the first-century church, there is simply still so much that we do not know.

---

[256] Ellis, *History and Interpretation in New Testament Perspective*, 45.

[257] O. Skarsaune, *In the Shadow of the Temple: Jewish Influences on Early Christianity* (Downers Grove: InterVarsity, 2002), 40–42. He has demonstrated that "Palestine" can no longer be equated with that which is "non-Hellenistic" (pp. 75–79).

[258] Ibid., 75.

Chapter 7

HISTORICAL RECONSTRUCTION: LUKAN AUTHORSHIP OF HEBREWS

The earlier discussion regarding Luke's Jewish interest and outlook removes a significant argument against his authorship of Hebrews by showing that Luke was capable of writing a book of such Jewish Christian character. The greatest objection to Lukan authorship is the supposition that he was a Gentile and therefore not likely to have written a work such as Hebrews. If the writer was a Gentile, he was surprisingly conversant with Jewish Scripture, theology, tradition, and history. Based on chaps. 5 and 6 above, the Lukan authorship of Hebrews can no longer be dismissed solely on the assumption that he was a Gentile.

At this point I will offer a holistic theory of Lukan authorship for Hebrews. The proposal includes identification of Theophilus as Luke's recipient for his Gospel and Acts, dating Luke and Acts prior to AD 70, involvement of Luke as the amanuensis for the Pastoral Epistles, the Roman provenance of Hebrews, identification of the recipients of Hebrews as converted former priests, location of the recipients in Syrian Antioch, and a pre-AD 70 date of composition.

The Recipient of Luke-Acts: Theophilus

A great deal of debate has swirled around the subject of the recipients of Luke's two-volume work. The bulk of New Testament scholarship has clearly opted for a Gentile audience. More recently, however, a number of works have appeared that question the Gentile background theory for Luke, the Gentile audience theory, or both, and propose the likelihood of a Jewish audience.[1] Jervell, Franklin, and others have presented evidence to show the Jewishness of Luke's orientation.[2] No doubt Gentile Christians read Luke's Gospel, but I suspect that his primary audience was Jewish. Other questions abound

---

[1] Parsons states, "This century has also witnessed a sharp attack on the traditional identification of Luke as a gentile writing for a gentile audience." M. Parsons, "Who wrote the Gospel of Luke," *BBR* 17 (2001): 18.

[2] J. Jervell, *Luke and the People of God: A New Look at Luke-Acts* (Minneapolis: Augsburg, 1972); E. Franklin, *Christ the Lord: A Study in the Purpose and Theology of Luke-Acts* (London: SPCK, 1975).

regarding Luke's audience. Was Hebrews addressed to a church or group of churches, a specific locale or a general audience, or an individual? Richard Bauckham has proposed that all four Gospels were written in the latter half of the first century to a general audience in the Mediterranean world.[3] I am proposing this is not the case with the Gospel of Luke.

I propose that the primary recipient of Luke's Gospel was an individual named Theophilus. The prologues to both Luke and Acts refer to this individual, but without further identification. Theories of his identity may be considered in three groups. (1) Some consider the name to represent a nonexistent individual or a group (the name means "lover of God"). Cadbury was a chief proponent of this view, calling Theophilus an "imagined addressee."[4] Crehan criticizes Cadbury's choice of second-century examples to indicate that Luke was not writing with an individual in mind. He points out that Cadbury's presupposition of a late date for Acts (early second century) is not now generally accepted by scholars, and it seems "probable" that Luke's Theophilus was a real individual.[5] Also, Luke uses the descriptor "most excellent," an honorific title suggesting reference to an actual individual. In the Book of Acts this title refers to Roman officials, which may have been the case with Theophilus. This view has found strong support from scholars, who often see Luke-Acts as an apologetic for toleration of Christianity in the Roman Empire. However, the problems with viewing Luke's purpose in this way are difficult to overcome.[6] In addition, Theophilus is not a Roman name, but was commonly used by Hellenistic Jews.[7] Strelan correctly points out that

---

[3] R. Bauckham, "For Whom Were the Gospels Written?" in *The Gospel for All Christians: Rethinking the Gospel Audiences,* ed. R. Bauckham (Grand Rapids: Eerdmans, 1998), 9–48. The quest for the Lukan community, like that of Hebrews, has yielded many suggestions, but little consensus.

[4] H. Cadbury, *Making of Luke-Acts* (New York: Macmillan, 1927), 203.

[5] J. H. Crehan, "The Purpose of Luke in Acts," *SE II,* Part I: *The New Testament Scriptures,* ed. F. L. Cross (Berlin: Akademie-Verlag, 1964), 356–58. Creech assesses the significance of Theophilus in Luke-Acts from a literary-critical angle, but concludes that a close reading of the text suggests Theophilus was a historical figure. R. Creech, "The Most Excellent Narratee: The Significance of Theophilus in Luke-Acts," in *With Steadfast Purpose: Essays in Honor of Henry Jack Flanders,* ed. N. Keathley (Waco, TX: Baylor Univ. Press, 1990), 107–26.

[6] Cf. E. Ellis, *The Gospel of Luke,* NCBC (Grand Rapids: Eerdmans, 1974; repr., London: Oliphants, 1977), 60.

[7] H. Leon, *The Jews of Ancient Rome* (Philadelphia: JPSA, 1960), 104.

the use of the honorific "most excellent" "need not indicate that the one so-addressed is superior to the writer."[8]

(2) Second, Theophilus may be a pseudonym for someone the author (perhaps for protection) does not wish to name. Perhaps "Theophilus" was this person's baptismal name. This category of theories is more widely supported today. Suggested individuals for which Theophilus may have been a pseudonym include Sergius Paulus, Gallio, Titus, Philo, and Agrippa II.[9] The primary weakness of these suggestions is the uncertainty that baptismal names were given and widely used at this time. Opinions differ on the question of whether Theophilus was a Christian. Some, like Zahn, believe the use of an honorific title indicates a non-Christian since there is no evidence that Christians used secular titles in addressing other Christians.[10] Some propose that Luke's addressee was a Godfearer.[11] However, v. 4 in the prologue to Luke ("so that you may know the certainty of the things about which you have been instructed") seems to indicate Theophilus was already a Christian.[12]

(3) The final theory (or group of theories) is that Theophilus was actually the name of Luke's intended reader.[13] This theory is the most

---

[8] R. Strelan, *Luke the Priest: the Authority of the Author of the Third Gospel* (Burlington, VT.: Ashegate, 2009), 108.

[9] The suggestion of Agrippa II was made by W. Marx in an interesting article, "A New Theophilus," *EvQ* 52 (1980):17–26.

[10] T. Zahn, *Introduction to the New Testament*, trans. J. Trout et. al. (New York: Charles Scribner's Sons, 1917; repr., Minneapolis: Klock and Klock, 1953), 3:34.

[11] See A. T. Kraabel, "The Disappearance of the 'Godfearers,'" *Numen* 28 (1981): 113–26, and "Greeks, Jews and Lutherans in the Middle Half of Acts," *HTR* 79 (1986): 147–57; J. Jervell, "The Church of Jews and Godfearers," in *Luke-Acts and the Jewish People: Eight Critical Perspectives* (Minneapolis: Augsburg, 1988), 11–20; and J. Tyson, *Images of Judaism in Luke-Acts* (Columbia: University of South Carolina Press, 1992), 35–39.

[12] So D. Guthrie, *New Testament Introduction*, 4th rev. ed (Downers Grove: InterVarsity, 1990), 95–96. It is certainly possible that Luke is attempting to get reliable information to Theophilus about Christianity in order to convert him. The use of κατηχέω in the Lukan prologue is the key issue here. Creech overstates the case when he says: "Only presuppositions could lead to the conclusion that Theophilus is a Christian reader. The narratological evidence suggests otherwise," and "The portrait . . . reconstructed by narratological methods, however, is that of a God-fearing Gentile being asked to consider Christianity." R. Creech, "The Most Excellent Narratee," 121, 126.

[13] Some have suggested that Luke did not write to Theophilus, but rather he dedicated the work to him. Although this was not an unknown practice at the time, the structure of the prologue makes this unlikely. C. Giblin, *The Destruction of Jerusalem According to Luke's Gospel: A Historical-Typological Moral*, AnBib 107 (Rome: Biblical Institute Press, 1985), 8, correctly notes: "The change of persons from Luke 1,1–2 ('they to us') with the main clause and its development in 1,3–4 ('I to you [sg.]') substantiates this specification. The respectful form of address (κρατιστε) further shows that Luke is not directing his work 'to any man in the street' or even

likely. At least two names have been proposed to identify the recipient of Luke-Acts. Jerome suggested that a certain Theophilus (who was an official in Athens and convicted of perjury by the Areopagus) may have been Luke's recipient. Others have proposed that Theophilus of Antioch (who is mentioned in the *Clementine Recognitions* and is said to have donated his house as a meeting place for the church) may have been Luke's addressee. Neither of these individuals lived during the time frame necessary to be considered as Luke's recipient.

There was a third individual prominent during the first half of the first century who has rarely been defended as Luke's Theophilus, namely, the high priest who served from AD 37–41.[14] Given the emphasis on priestly matters in Luke-Acts, we must consider that Luke may have written his Gospel for a Jewish high priest—perhaps to confirm his knowledge of Jesus and the early church, or to convert him to Christianity.

Theophilus was one of five sons of Annas, the high priest mentioned in the New Testament along with Caiaphas, son-in-law to Annas. Annas ruled from AD 6–15, and Caiaphas ruled from AD 18–36. All five sons served as high priest in Jerusalem before AD 70. Their names and years of service are Eleazer (AD 16–17), Jonathan (AD 36–37), Theophilus (AD 37–41), Matthias (AD 42–44), and Ananos II (3 months in AD 62).

Even after his reign, Annas seems to have wielded great authority, for he is mentioned along with Caiaphas in the New Testament as high priest (although Caiaphas was ruling at the time). This is because the office of high priest was hereditary and tenable for life, at least in the eyes of the people. Even a deposed high priest had considerable authority over the people.

The name of one of Annas's five sons is interesting in that it is Greek rather than Jewish. "Theophilus" means "lover of God" and is a Hellenized Greco-Roman name. The appearance of Greek names among the later Hasmoneans and the priesthood is not uncommon. For example, Jason the high priest changed his name from "Jesus."[15] Several studies have shown the appearance of Greek names among

---

to just anyone in a Christian community, but to a person of assumed affluence, influence, and education."

[14] I argued the case for Theophilus in 1987 in my Ph.D. diss. and again in articles in 1989, 1996, and 2001. Also, the case has been argued by R. Anderson in two articles appearing in *EvQ* (1997, 1999).

[15] J. Jeremias, *Jerusalem in the Time of Jesus* (Philadelphia: Fortress, 1969), 377.

the later Hasmoneans and the priesthood. Because of their Hellenistic outlook, the Jewish aristocracy often followed the practice of having two names. The New Testament reveals this practice. If Theophilus is a Hellenized version of some Jewish name, what could that name be? Robert Eisler proposes that Theophilus was also known as "Johannan" (John) for the following reasons:[16]

First, Theophilus is the Greek translation equivalent for the Hebrew "Johannan." When a non-Jewish name was adopted in addition to a Jewish one, it often had some connection, either phonological or semantic, with the original. It is probable that Jewish names lie behind some of the Greek and Latin names in Acts.[17]

Second, in Acts 4:6, Codex Bezae has "Jonathan" instead of "John" in a reference to members of the high priest's family. Since Josephus mentions Jonathan son of Annas in six passages, this variant in Acts 4:6 has been explained as a correction, since no "John" of the high priest's family was known. But such a correction would be unnecessary since a "John" son of Annas and an Alexander are both mentioned by Josephus. This John is introduced as *Ananiou Iōannēs,* "John (son of) Annas," and Josephus describes him as a commander of the Jewish forces at Gophna (where many priests lived) and Acrabetta around AD 66. Could this John be the son of an otherwise unknown Annas? One answer may be that an unknown leader would probably not have been introduced as "John, son of Annas," but as "a certain John, son of Annas." Since Josephus tells us that all of Annas's sons served as high priests (Theophilus was deposed and did not lose the office through death), and if "John" was Theophilus's Hebrew name, it is conceivable that these references apply to the same individual.[18] Even if this identification is mistaken, it would not preclude that Luke was writing to Theophilus, the former Jewish high priest.

A third reason for this identification of "John" with "Theophilus" is also drawn from Josephus. In his *Jewish Wars,* the name Theophilus does not occur, whereas the name John does; in his *Jewish Antiquities* the name Theophilus occurs, but "John, son of Annas," does not. Perhaps Josephus uses his Greek name in one volume and his Hebrew

---

[16] R. Eisler, *The Enigma of the Fourth Gospel* (London: Methuen & Co., 1936), 39–45.

[17] See H. Cadbury, *The Book of Acts in History* (New York: Harper & Brothers, 1955), 90.

[18] F. F. Bruce attests to the possibility of this identification by Eisler, but thinks it is "more likely" that the text refers to Jonathan based on the delta text. F. F. Bruce, *The Acts of the Apostles, The Greek Text with Introduction and Commentary* (Grand Rapids: Eerdmans, 1951), 119.

name in the other. A similar situation is found in the New Testament, where the names "John Mark," "John," and "Mark" all refer to the same person.

A fourth argument, not mentioned by Eisler, can be marshaled in favor of the possibility that Theophilus's Jewish name was John. The names of the Hasmonean sons were Judas Maccabeus, Jonathan, Simon, John, and Eleazer. Two of these five names correspond to two of Annas's five sons, namely Eleazer and Jonathan. But in the Hasmonean dynasty both a Jonathan and a John are found. Theophilus may have been given the name John as suggested above, then three of the five sons of Annas had names equivalent to the sons of Hashmon. It is altogether probable that Annas named some of his sons after the great Hasmonean line of a century and a half earlier. We know that the Sadducean high priestly family of Annas looked upon the Hasmonean dynasty as heroes of the faith, and at least two of Annas's sons bore their names. Studies show a high incidence of Hasmonean names from first-century Palestinian Jewish *onomastikon* as well as in Acts. This probably is indicative of the broad sympathies of the Jewish people, as Margret Williams notes, proven by their willingness to risk everything in AD 66 "in a Maccabaean-style fight for freedom."[19]

It cannot be maintained that a "John" and a "Jonathan" would be names too similar to appear in the same family; the Hasmonean family had sons with both names, and Jer 40:8 mentions the sons of Kareah—Johannan (John) and Jonathan. Clearly Theophilus also had a Hebrew name, and Johannan is a plausible suggestion.

If John, son of Ananias (Annas), mentioned by Josephus as commander of the Jewish forces in AD 66 is the same as Theophilus, who formerly served as high priest, then we may suggest the possibility that Luke knew him and wrote either to convert him to Christianity or (more likely, based on the prologue to Luke's Gospel) to instruct him as a new Christian. Conservative scholarship tends to date Luke-Acts between AD 61 and 65. Furthermore, the honorific title "most excellent" was used not only for Roman officials but also for high priests, at least in the second and third centuries.[20] We learn from Josephus of the important role played by the priests as guardians of the

---

[19] M. Williams, "Palestinian Jewish Personal Names in Acts," in *The Book of Acts in its Palestinian Setting*, ed. R. Bauckham (Grand Rapids: Eerdmans, 1995), 4:109.

[20] F. Foakes-Jackson and K. Lake, *The Beginnings of Christianity* (New York: Macmillan, 1942; repr., Grand Rapids: Baker, 1979), 505–8.

genealogical heritage. The priests were responsible to ensure purity, and they are referred to as "the most excellent men" (*hoi aristoi*).[21] Jeremias notes that even after removal from office, the high priest kept his title and authority.[22] Former high priests could be addressed as "most excellent."

According to Josephus, Theophilus was deposed in AD 41 by Herod Agrippa I. It could be that Theophilus was not as antagonistic to the new Christian sect as Herod wanted him to be, so he removed him from office in favor of someone less charitable. After all, it was Herod Agrippa I who put James to death (Acts 12), and Luke may have preserved this piece of information along with his unique account of Herod's death primarily as information that would interest Theophilus.[23]

Another interesting piece of archaeological evidence may advance the case for Luke's Theophilus as a former high priest. Barag and Flusser have written about an ossuary bearing an engraved Aramaic inscription: "*Yehohanah/Yehohanah daughter of Yehohanan/son of Theophilus the high priest.*[24]

Yehohanan was a popular masculine name among Jews during the Second Temple period. The feminine form of the name in the inscription, Yehohanah (Johanna), refers to the granddaughter of Theophilus, who died shortly after her grandfather's nomination as high priest in the spring of AD 37. If the Codex Bezae reading "Jonathan" is to be accepted in Acts 4:6, then it is possible that Luke's list of those who opposed the disciples in Jerusalem all belonged to the high priestly family of Annas, the father of Theophilus.[25] Luke also mentions "Joanna the wife of Chuza, Herod's steward" twice in his Gospel (Luke

---

[21] Josephus, *Against Apion*, 1.30. See also S. Mason, "Chief Priests, Sadducees, Pharisees and Sanhedrin in Acts," in *The Book of Acts in Its Palestinian Setting*, 173.

[22] Jeremias, *Jerusalem in the Time of Jesus*, 157. The role of the high priest in obtaining atonement for the people was a fixed tenet of Jewish theology. Because of this, Josephus (*War* 4.318) called the high priest "the captain of their salvation" (cp. Heb 2:10).

[23] The account of Herod's death is somewhat out of sync with the narrative unfolding in Acts. Why did Luke include this tidbit of information unless it was of some interest to his reader? Furthermore, everything about the account in Acts 12:20–24 is thoroughly Jewish, another evidence for the Jewishness of Luke. W. Allen, *The Death of Herod: The Narrative and Theological Function of Retribution in Luke-Acts* (Atlanta: Scholars Press, 1997), points out that the account of Herod's death appears "almost out of place" in Luke's narrative, but it plays a key role in the discourse structure of Acts (see esp. pp. 130–47).

[24] D. Barag and D. Flusser, "The Ossuary of Yehohanaḥ Granddaughter of the High Priest Theophilus," *IEJ*, 36 (1986), 39.

[25] Ibid., 43.

8:3; 24:10). In both places Joanna occurs as the middle name in a listing of three women, and in both lists Mary Magdalene's name occurs first. Given Luke's penchant for chiastic structures and inclusio, the placement of Joanna's name at the middle of both lists may be significant. Of course, if the recipient of Luke's Gospel was Theophilus as is being proposed, then the connection is evident, even startling.

The political milieu during the decade just prior to the fall of Jerusalem in AD 70 is significant to our investigation. Ananus II, brother of Theophilus, served for three months as high priest in 62 and played a leading role during the early stages of the Jewish War. As an "ardently patriotic Sadducean priest,"[26] he took advantage of the political instability (resulting from the sudden death of the Roman procurator Festus) to arrest and stone James, the brother of the Lord and leader of the Jerusalem church. Agrippa, wanting to keep himself in the good graces of Rome, immediately deposed Ananus before the new procurator arrived.[27] Ananus was later executed by the populace.

Robinson references the death of James in AD 62 to highlight how Luke missed a golden opportunity to serve his apologetic purpose by pointing out that it was the Jews and not the Romans who were the enemies of the gospel.[28] Robinson uses this as an argument against a post-70 date for Acts, along with Luke's omission of other significant events such as the Jewish War. However, Luke probably wrote Acts *after* AD 62 (though not long after), and he would have known about the death of James the Lord's brother. A better reason for Luke's omission of the death of James in 62 while including the death of James the brother of John in Acts 12 is to be found in his recipient, Theophilus. Since Ananus II was the brother of Theophilus, and Theophilus was probably already a Christian (Luke 1:4), the omission was for obvious reasons.

Of further interest is that Theophilus's son Matthias also served as high priest from AD 65–67 and was in office at the outbreak of the Jewish War in AD 66. Theophilus, if he were still alive, would have been vitally involved in these events along with his family. If Theophilus was Josephus's John son of Annas (commander of the Jewish forces

---

[26] B. Reicke, *The New Testament Era: The World of the Bible from 500 B.C. to A.D. 100*, trans. D. Green (Philadelphia: Fortress, 1968), 209.

[27] Josephus, *Antiquities*, 20.200–3.

[28] J. A. T. Robinson, *Redating the New Testament* (London: SCM, 1976), 89.

at Gophna and Acrabetta), then Theophilus was heavily engaged in the political arena of the time—very near the date of composition for Luke-Acts. Did Luke write his Gospel and Acts to the ranking high priest during the years just preceding the Jewish War?

Alford identifies Theophilus as the high priest in Acts 9:2 who supplied Paul with the documents for persecuting Christians at Damascus.[29] Later, in Paul's speech to the Jerusalem mob (Acts 22:4–5), he referred again to the high priest:

> I persecuted this Way to the death, binding and putting both men and women in jail, as both the high priest and the whole council of elders can testify about me. After I received letters from them to the brothers, I traveled to Damascus to bring those who were prisoners there to be punished in Jerusalem.

Alford suggests that Paul is referring to the high priest "of that day [who supplied the documents], who is still living, i.e., Theophilus."[30] This speech in Jerusalem occurred in AD 58. It is not unreasonable for Alford to suggest this identification since Theophilus left the office in AD 41. If these correlations are correct, then Theophilus was alive at the time Luke and Acts were written.

Further evidence for Alford's identification of the high priest to whom Paul refers can be found in the incident that immediately follows. The day after Paul's address to the Jewish mob, he is brought before the Jewish council with the high priest present (Acts 23:1–10). Paul's opening statement that he had lived "before God in all good conscience until this day" is followed immediately by the high priest Ananias's command that those standing beside Paul should strike him on the mouth. Paul retorts in v. 3, "God is going to strike you, you whitewashed wall! You are sitting there judging me according to the law, and in violation of the law are you ordering me to be struck?" The bystanders respond to Paul, "Do you dare revile God's high priest?" Paul responds surprisingly with all submission and humility, "I did not know, brothers, that it was the high priest. . . . For it is written, You must not speak evil of a ruler of your people'" (Acts 23:4–5).

Comparing Paul's statements in Acts 22:4–5 with 23:5, it is obvious that Paul either did not know who the high priest was or at least did not recognize him as the high priest in 23:5; however, he *did* know

---

[29] H. Alford, "Hebrews," in *Alford's Greek Testament: An Exegetical and Critical Commentary*, 7th ed. (Cambridge: Rivingtons & Deighton, Bell & Co., 1877), 97.

[30] Ibid., 245–46.

the high priest about whom he was speaking in 22:5.[31] Paul's reference in 22:5 was not to the ruling high priest at the time, Ananias. The question then becomes, who was he? Alford's suggestion of Theophilus is as plausible as any other.

This whole episode of Paul before the council in Acts 23:1–10 is easily explained if Luke's intended reader was a former high priest. Furthermore, Luke's inclusion of this incident and Paul's submissive response to the high priest is even more remarkable when we consider who the high priest was at this time. Bruce describes this high priest, Ananias:

> [He was] a notoriously unscrupulous and rapacious politician, [who] had been appointed High Priest by Herod of Chalcis about AD 47. He was, like most of the High Priests, a Sadducee. About 52 he was sent to Rome by Quadratus, legate of Syria, as responsible for risings in Judea, but was acquitted and was now at the height of his power. Even after his supersession in 58–59 he wielded great authority. He was assassinated in 66 in revenge for his pro-Roman policy.[32]

The point of interest here is not only the account of Paul's response but Luke's inclusion of this incident in Acts. If Luke's intended reader was Theophilus, a former high priest, then Luke deliberately presents Paul not as antagonistic to the law but faithful to his Jewish heritage—although he was a Christian. This is more easily explained on the theory of a Jewish rather than a Gentile audience. Rather than being a defense of Paul and/or Christianity to the Roman authorities, his purpose is to offer a defense to the ranking Jewish authorities, specifically to a former high priest.

Further light may be shed on the background of Luke's intended reader when we consider how Paul extricated himself from the angry council. Recognizing the bipartisan nature of the council (Sadducees and Pharisees), Paul took advantage of the theological difference between these groups (Sadducees denied physical resurrection). His diversion worked perfectly, and we are told that a dissension arose between the Pharisees and the Sadducees that diverted attention from Paul.

---

[31] See Alford's discussion ("Hebrews," 253) of the various theories on the meaning of Paul's words in v. 5 ("I did not know, brothers, that it was the high priest"). He concludes that the only meaning consistent with his words and the facts of history was that Paul really did not know it was the high priest who had spoken to him, probably because of Paul's poor eyesight.

[32] Bruce, *The Acts of the Apostles*, 409.

If Theophilus was already a Christian at the time of writing, then this scene, coupled with the Lukan emphasis on the resurrection throughout Luke-Acts, can be viewed as Luke's attempt to verify what Theophilus has already been taught regarding the resurrection of Christ. Luke more than the other synoptic writers speaks of the resurrection appearances of Jesus; in Acts the apostles are consistently said to be witnesses of the resurrection, and Luke records not only Paul's witness to the resurrection but also his use of it to drive a wedge between the Pharisees and Sadducees in Jerusalem. Luke takes great pains to point out on numerous occasions in Acts that Paul is in chains because of the "hope of the resurrection" or the "hope of Israel" (cf. 23:6; 24:15; 25:19; 26:6–7; 26:22–23; and 28:20). Luke mentions this concept in five of the last six chapters of Acts. If he is writing to Gentiles, this is an odd emphasis; yet if he is writing to a Jewish audience (specifically a former Sadducean priest) for the purpose of further instruction in Christian doctrine, then emphasis on the resurrection is to be expected.

As a Sadducee, the resurrection would be difficult for Theophilus to accept. Furthermore, while Paul could retain certain aspects of the Pharisee belief system and still be a Christian, one could not remain a Sadducee (denying the existence of angels, the resurrection, and the sovereignty of God in the affairs of men) and at the same time be a Christian.[33]

Throughout Luke-Acts, Luke emphasizes the role of angels in the overall plan of salvation. Angels figure prominently in the birth narrative of the Gospel, and they are also present after the resurrection at the end of the Gospel. Acts begins with angels speaking to the disciples, and numerous references to angelic activity appear throughout. Theophilus was being indoctrinated into the reality of the supernatural via angelic activity.

Finally, immediately after the incident recorded in Acts 23:1–10, the Lord "stood by" Paul and assured him that as he had testified in Jerusalem, he must also bear witness in Rome (Acts 23:11). The

---

[33] Cf. Bruce's comment on Acts 23:6: "We cannot imagine a Sadducee becoming a Christian, unless he ceased to be a Sadducee" (Bruce, *The Acts of the Apostles*, 411). Two of the best studies available on the Sadducees are J. Le Moyne, *Les Sadducees* (Paris: Gabalda, 1972), and A. J. Saldarini, *Pharisees, Scribes and Sadducees in Palestinian Society: A Sociological Approach*, The Biblical Resource Series (Grand Rapids: Eerdmans, 2001). See also T. Hatina, "Jewish Religious Backgrounds of the New Testament: Pharisees and Sadducees as Case Studies," in *Approaches to New Testament Study*, JSNTSup 120 (Sheffield: Sheffield Academic Press, 1995), 46–76.

emphasis on God's sovereignty and His governance of human affairs, over against the Sadducean denial, is narrated in vivid fashion. This theme is prominent in Acts.[34]

My conclusion, then—that Luke's reader is a former Sadducee and high priest who had been converted but needed instruction and encouragement because his former belief system was bankrupt—can be textually confirmed by observing the Lukan emphasis on (1) the resurrection, (2) angelic activity, (3) God's sovereign activity in guiding His people, and (4) the person and role of the Holy Spirit in God's plan of salvation.

Richard Anderson has also argued that Luke's recipient, Theophilus, was a former high priest. He notes that Luke-Acts has been shaped by the style of the Old Testament historical books but also by such works as 1 Maccabees. Such a format would be familiar to a high priest. We have seen above the similarity of Luke-Acts to the Maccabean writings, but Anderson's theory regarding the Lukan purpose is more ambitious: "Luke believes that a word from the High Priest addressed to the Jews throughout the world can stop the opposition of the Jews of the Diaspora, remove divisions in Judaism and lead to the final restoration of the reunited House of Israel."[35]

Anderson has uncovered some interesting features of Luke-Acts that strengthen the overall case for Luke's Jewishness, the possibility

---

[34] Cf. M. Powell's summary of God's control of history as seen in Acts (*What are They Saying about Acts?* [New York: Paulist Press, 1991], 39–40). See also J. Squires, *The Plan of God in Luke-Acts*, SNTSMS 76 (Cambridge: Cambridge University Press, 1993), and D. Moessner, "The 'Script' of the Scriptures in Acts: Suffering as God's 'Plan' (*boulē*) for the World for the 'Release of Sins,'" in *History, Literature and Society in the Book of Acts*, ed. B. Witherington III (Cambridge: Cambridge University Press, 1996), 218–50. Moessner's thesis is that "Luke presents the proclamation of the risen Christ, his resurrection or exaltation, and especially his rejection/crucifixion as the three critical components of the fulfillment of God's saving 'plan' for the world which has been announced in advance in Israel's Scriptures" (p., 221). Powell also shows that the Holy Spirit is a prominent theme in Luke-Acts, much more so than in Matthew and Mark combined. Cf. *What Are They Saying about Luke?*, 108–11; id., *What Are They Saying about Acts?*, 50–57; J. Shelton, *Mighty in Word and Deed: The Role of the Holy Spirit in Luke-Acts* (Peabody, MA: Hendrickson, 1991).

[35] R. Anderson, "Theophilus: A Proposal," *EvQ* 69.3 (1997): 204. Anderson assumes Luke viewed Christianity as a part of Judaism. He also suggests that Luke was written around AD 40–41 (as did E. C. Selwyn), when Theophilus was still in office. Luke's interest in Herod Antipas as reflected in his Gospel is because he wrote during his reign (p. 205). Following G. Wenham, *Redating Matthew, Mark and Luke: A Fresh Assault on the Synoptic Problem* (Downers Grove: InterVarsity, 1992), 230–37, Anderson believes Paul's reference in 2 Cor 8:18 is to Luke and the fame that followed publication of his Gospel. Anderson believes Acts was written c. AD 65–67. Luke's purpose was to quell rumors about Paul that threatened to split Israel (Acts 28) by establishing Jesus as a prophet like Moses (p. 202).

he wrote to a former high priest, and the possibility he also authored Hebrews. But I am not convinced of the grandiose purpose Anderson posits for Luke-Acts (though I applaud his efforts); he may exaggerate the significance of some of the evidence. He believes Luke's Gospel is pre-Pauline and that a theology of the cross represents a later stage of theological development. But this collides with the facts that early Christian preaching, even in Acts, demonstrates a theology of the cross. It is also unlikely that Luke wrote his Gospel as early as Anderson believes. Luke and Paul were contemporaries and had much in common, though they had some differences in emphasis. A pre-Pauline milieu for Luke seems wide of the mark. Anderson also argues for the absence of a theology of the cross in Luke's Gospel since Theophilus, as a high priest, would have viewed the high priest's action on the Day of Atonement as having atoning significance for the people. As we have seen above, this too is wide of the mark.

Anderson and I view the data of Acts differently with respect to the Lukan emphasis on divine activity. He believes this theme is developed "cautiously," given the beliefs of the Sadduceean priests regarding immortality and the resurrection.[36] But just the opposite is true. Luke was not about to soft-pedal so critical an aspect of the gospel as the resurrection. As demonstrated above and widely recognized in Lukan studies, Luke-Acts develops few themes with more force than the resurrection of Jesus. Luke 24:20 places responsibility for the crucifixion of Jesus at the feet of "our chief priests and leaders." All these points would be a stumbling block to an unconverted Sadduceean priest or high priest.

Where Anderson advances the case for Lukan authorship of Hebrews is in his comparison of Luke's Gospel with Hebrews. Lukan theology focuses on repentance, the high priest, and the Day of Atonement, as does Hebrews.[37] Anderson thinks it unnecessary to identify Luke as the author of Hebrews, since in his view Luke is writing to a high priest, and this explains his theological focus.[38] Nevertheless, Luke has much in common with Hebrews.

---

[36] Ibid., 140.

[37] The story of the "good thief," unique to Luke (23:39–43), furnishes evidence of a Lukan theology of repentance. It would have meaning for the high priest, since he would believe that repentance was the key to salvation. Cf. R. Anderson, "The Cross and Atonement from Luke to Hebrews," *EvQ* 71.2 (1999), 131–32.

[38] Ibid., 148–49.

In conclusion, the textual evidence as well as the historical circumstances make it possible to posit Theophilus, a former high priest, as Luke's intended reader. Harnack observes that Luke's treatment of James, when compared with Stephen, Philip, Barnabas, and Apollos, presupposes "that the four others are unknown, while it is assumed that he is known. The readers evidently knew—though this is nowhere stated—that he was the Lord's brother, and that he had become the head of the Primitive Community."[39] This would suggest the reader(s) was of Palestinian origin, but not necessarily so. For the purposes of our theory, if Theophilus were the recipient, he would undoubtedly have had knowledge of James, leader of the Jewish Christian congregation in Jerusalem. Positing a recipient who has connections with the temple and priests accounts for the interest Luke displays in these subjects.[40] Spencer argues that the recipients of Luke-Acts likely possessed a certain degree of wealth, an inference he drew from the "rhetorical argument and narrative trajectories involving material benefaction" of the speeches in the Galilean ministry section of Luke's Gospel.[41] If this interpretation is valid, it would certainly fit Theophilus as a former high priest.

The Date of Luke-Acts

The above discussion indicates that Luke-Acts was written prior to the destruction of Jerusalem in AD 70. In my view, Luke was written before Acts and with no more than about two years separating them. There are generally four major views on the dating of Luke-Acts:[42] (1) second-century date;[43] (2) AD 90–100 (primarily on the theory that

---

[39] A. Harnack, *The Acts of the Apostles,* trans. J. R. Wilkinson (New York: Putnam's Sons, 1909), 122. See also J. Tyson, *Images of Judaism in Luke-Acts* (Columbia: University of South Carolina Press, 1992), 29, who follows Harnack making this point.

[40] Creech notes Theophilus's "extensive knowledge of the language of religious experience and of the religion of Judaism," although he believes Theophilus was a Greek-speaking God-fearer ("The Most Excellent Narratee," 117, 122).

[41] P. Spencer, *Rhetorical Texture and Narrative Trajectories of the Lukan Galilean Ministry Speeches: Hermeneutical Appropriation by Authorial Readers of Luke-Acts,* Library of New Testament Studies 341 (London: T&T Clark, 2007), 200.

[42] Cf. the introduction in J. Fitzmyer, *The Gospel According to Luke X-XXIV: Introduction, Translation, and Notes,* AB 28a (Garden City: Doubleday, 1985), 53–57; and Robinson, *Redating.*

[43] E.g., J. Tyson, *Marcion and Luke-Acts* (Columbia: Univ. of South Carolina Press, 2006), 1–22; R. Pervo, *Dating Acts* (Santa Rosa, CA: Polebridge Press, 2006).

Luke made use of Josephus);[44] (3) AD 70–80;[45] and (4) between AD 57–65, usually 60–63.

A crucial question for the dating of Acts is the way Luke closes the book.[46] There are really only three alternatives for how matters worked out: (1) Paul's trial was described in another book, a view with no evidence to support it; (2) it was so well known that it did not need telling; or (3) it had not yet taken place.[47] The third view is to my mind the most likely explanation. Even if the trial had already taken place, would Luke not have mentioned Paul's death (c. AD 66–67) if it had occurred? None of the crucial events that occurred after AD 63 are mentioned in Acts. Absent are the burning of Rome in AD 64, the martyrdom of Peter and Paul, and the destruction of Jerusalem in AD 70. Furthermore, Acts seems to suggest that Rome's attitude toward Christianity was as yet undecided. This was certainly not the case after AD 64 when the Roman government became openly hostile to Christianity.[48]

Harold Riley reasons that Paul arrived in Rome in or about AD 60 and preached unhindered for two years. Whatever happened after AD 62 occurred before the Neronian persecution began in AD 65. The completion of Acts lies between these two dates, and the Gospel would have been written "a little earlier."[49]

Many of the monographs in Lukan studies opt for a late date for Luke-Acts with little or no internal or external evidence provided. This occurs in spite of the work of Harnack and Rackham on this subject, the significant and well-researched *Redating the New Testament* by John A. T. Robinson,[50] and the erudite scholarship of Colin

---

[44] For arguments against this view cf. A. von Harnack, *Luke the Physician*, trans. J. R. Wilkinson (London: Williams & Norgate, 1907), 24; A. Plummer, *A Critical and Exegetical Commentary on the Gospel According to Saint Luke*, ICC, 5th ed. (New York: Scribner, 1922), xxix.

[45] Plummer, *Luke*, xxxi, has arguments in favor of this view.

[46] See the excellent discussion of the history of scholarship on this issue in C. Hemer, *The Book of Acts in the Setting of Hellenistic History*, ed. C. Gempf (Tübingen: Mohr [Paul Siebeck], 1989), 383–87.

[47] See the discussion in Crehan, "The Purpose of Luke in Acts," 361.

[48] Cf. A. T. Robertson, *Luke the Historian* (Nashville: Broadman, 1920), 34–37. Likewise, Ellis questions whether the relatively generous allusions to Roman authorities in Acts could have been written without some qualification after AD 64. E. Ellis, *History and Interpretation in New Testament Perspective*, Biblical Interpretation Series 54 (Leiden: Brill, 2001), 35.

[49] H. Riley, *Preface to Luke* (Macon: Mercer University Press, 1993), 25.

[50] Ellis praises J. A. T. Robinson's work, which dates all of the New Testament books before AD 70, noting his work has "for 25 years stood unrefuted." E. Ellis, *History and Interpretation*, 31.

Hemer.[51] A quote from each of the latter two will suffice to make the point.

> Indeed what one looks for in vain in much recent scholarship is any serious wrestling with the external or internal evidence for the dating of individual books (such as marked the writings of men like Lightfoot and Harnack and Zahn), rather than an *a priori* pattern of theological development into which they are then made to fit.[52]

> This defense of the early date may seem bold to the point of rashness in the present climate. But it is perhaps the climate rather than the evidence which is against it.[53]

A. J. Mattill, summarizing a point made by Rackham in his argument for an early date for Luke-Acts, says it would be inexplicable for Luke not to tell his readers about Paul's martyrdom if he knew about it. "If the later date be correct, Luke is guilty of nothing less than a literary crime: he excites all his readers' interest in the fate of Paul, and then leaves him without a word as to the conclusion. Surely it is not what we should expect from an artist like Luke."[54]

Finally, I believe Luke left us with a linguistic signature that informs us he did not end the book of Acts abruptly at all; the ending is exactly how Luke planned it. A comparison of the prologue (Acts 1:1–4) to the last paragraph in Acts 28:30–31 reveals a tripartite lexical chiasm:

Acts 1:1–7—

Iēsous

didaskein

tēs basileias tou theou

Acts 28:30–31—

tēn basileian tou theou

didaskōn

Iēsou Christou

The evidence of a designed ending further bolsters the view that Acts closes as it does because Luke had simply brought the history of the

---

[51] Hemer, *The Book of Acts in the Setting of Hellenistic History*, 365–410

[52] Robinson, *Redating*, 8.

[53] Hemer, *The Book of Acts in the Setting of Hellenistic History*, 409.

[54] A. J. Mattill, "The Date and Purpose of Luke-Acts: Rackham Reconsidered," *CBQ* 40 (1978): 337.

church up to date. The Gospel of Luke begins and ends with a sand-wich chiasm (inclusio) as well.

Seccombe has rightly pointed out the unsuitability of the period AD 70–90 against which "to try to make sense of the ecclesiology of Acts."

> The destruction of Jerusalem and its temple made it easy for anyone wishing to advance a case for Christianity as a new people of God. One wonders why the author of Acts would be bothered with the kind of arguments he marshals if he was writing with its memory. That his Peter or his Paul should never even warn of it in their speeches (which Luke is alleged to have invented) is extraordinary. He could have advanced no more powerful argument for God's displeasure with Judaism and the legitimacy of Stephen, Paul and the new people of God than by drawing attention to the destruction of Jerusalem. His silence on this is as perplexing as his silence on the end of Paul and Peter, unless he wrote before any of these things had eventuated.[55]

Seccombe offers two other salient points to support a pre-AD 70 date for Luke-Acts. The amount of space given in Acts to establish the freedom of Gentile believers from circumcision and Jewish law "bespeaks a time when circumcision has some kudos in the wider world."[56] Second, the way in which Luke has represented the church in continuity with God's salvation in Israel's history over against the priests, the Sanhedrin, the Sadducees, and Pharisees "presumes a situation in which church and synagogue are in deep rivalry with the synagogue in the ascendant. This is as it was pre-66, not post-70."[57]

Daniel Falk's comparison of the prayers of Jerusalem Christians in Acts with what is known of Jewish prayers from other sources led him to conclude that Luke's portrayal is consistent with the pre-AD 70 evidential silence with regard to daily prayers in the synagogue. Acts records that prayer assemblies were held in the Temple. Acts also corroborates the evidence that Jewish prayer in the Second Temple period followed two patterns: one based on the time of day (sunrise and sunset) and the other based on the temple sacrifices (morning and afternoon). What is said about Jewish and Christian worship in Acts conforms more to a pre-70 date.[58]

---

[55] D. Seccombe, "The New People of God," in *Witness to the Gospel* (Grand Rapids: Eerdmans, 1998), 367. Note that this could easily be said for the dating of Hebrews as well.

[56] Ibid., 368.

[57] Ibid.

[58] D. Falk, "Jewish Prayer Literature and the Jerusalem Church in Acts," in Bauckham, *The Book of Acts in Its Palestinian Setting*, 267–301.

Ellis dates the Synoptics no later than the mid-60s because they display no knowledge of the destruction of Jerusalem nor of the flight to Pella in AD 66.[59] In his commentary on Luke, Ellis dated Acts about 70 AD. However, he revised this date recently based on Luke's use of the phrase "the ends of the earth" in Acts 1:8. Ellis studied its use in Classical writings and discovered it refers most often to Spain, but never to Rome. "In view of the meaning of 'end of the earth' in the Greco-Roman literature, the phrase in Acts 1:8 almost certainly alludes to the extension of the gospel to Spain, and more specifically, to the city of Gades."[60] Ellis concludes that Luke knew of Paul's plans for a Spanish mission. If Luke wrote before the mission was begun or during it, the open-ended conclusion of Acts may be clarified. Luke did not mention the mission to Spain, "because as he finished his volume, it was still outstanding."[61] If Luke wrote after the Spanish mission but during the Neronian persecution, other reasons (perhaps his desire to protect Paul or the Roman magistrate who released him) may have caused him to conclude Acts without mentioning Paul's prison release or the subsequent Spanish mission. If Luke wrote after AD 68, it is more difficult to understand why he would "record a preview of the gospel going to Gades and then say nothing more about it."[62] Ellis has furnished another piece of evidence to date Acts prior to AD 70.[63]

Therefore, the dates that would seem to fit the most facts would be c. AD 61 for Luke, and c. AD 63 for Acts, with the latter having been written from Rome. Luke could have written his Gospel in Caesarea or begun it there and finished it in Rome.

Luke the Author of Hebrews

The evidence from the church fathers indicates that Luke was considered by some to have written Hebrews (see chap. 1). The reason was the similarity of style between Luke-Acts and Hebrews. The history of scholarship concerning possible Lukan involvement in the production of Hebrews offers three hypotheses: (1) Luke translated

---

[59] Ellis, *The Making of the New Testament Documents*, 285.

[60] Ibid., 60.

[61] Ibid., 61.

[62] Ibid.

[63] See his entire discussion on the date of Acts. Ellis, *The Making of the New Testament Documents*, 53–63.

into Greek a Hebrew or Aramaic original written by Paul,[64] (2) Luke was the coauthor of Hebrews with Paul (who was the mind behind the letter and Luke wrote down his thoughts, with varying views on how much freedom he possessed in the process),[65] and (3) Luke was the independent author of Hebrews.[66]

Few, if any, modern scholars would argue for a Greek translation of a Hebrew or Aramaic original. The view that Luke could have helped Paul write Hebrews was somewhat popular in the nineteenth century, but fell into disrepute in the twentieth century because of the increasing popularity of the anti-Pauline hypothesis and the combination of two converging positions: namely that Luke-Acts was written late in the first century and not necessarily by Luke, and that Hebrews is likewise to be dated post-AD 70.[67]

In Heb 13:23–24, there are at least six clues concerning the background of the letter. First, the author and readers are associated with Timothy since he is referred to as "our brother." Second, both the author and Timothy are away from the readers and plan to travel to the readers' location shortly. Third, Timothy had apparently been imprisoned or at least detained and then released. Fourth, the author was probably in the same locale as Timothy, but was himself apparently not imprisoned. Fifth, the recipients are exhorted to greet their leaders, implying a location of considerable population—enough to have a church with multiple leaders. This may indicate that the writer is not addressing an entire church, but rather a smaller group within the church. Sixth, whether the author is writing from Italy or not, he sends greetings from Italian Christians who are with him.

---

[64] Clement of Alexandria, quoted by Eusebius, from Clement's *Hypotyposes*, in *Ecclesiastical History*, 6.14.

[65] J. L. Hug, *Introduction to the New Testament*, trans. D. Fosdick (Andover: Gould & Newman, 1836); and J. H. A. Ebrard, *Exposition of the Epistle to the Hebrews*, trans. and rev. A. C. Kendrick, *Biblical Commentary on the New Testament*, ed. H. Olshausen, 6 vols. (New York: Sheldon, Blakeman & Co., 1858).

[66] F. Delitzsch, *Commentary on the Epistle to the Hebrews*, trans. T. L. Kingsbury, 2 vols. (Edinburgh: T&T Clark, 1872; repr., Grand Rapids: Eerdmans, 1952); and A. Eagar, "The Authorship of the Epistle to the Hebrews," *Expositor* 10 (1904): 74–80, 110–23.

[67] Examples of recent refusals to consider Lukan authorship: P. Ellingworth, *Commentary on Hebrews*, NIGTC (Grand Rapids: Eerdmans, 1993), 13–14. H. Attridge, *The Epistle to the Hebrews*, Her (Philadelphia: Fortress, 1989), xlix. P. O'Brien dismisses the possibility of Lukan authorship with a single sentence: "Luke has been proposed as a candidate, but the points of connection between him and Hebrews are too slight to support a theory that he wrote the latter" (*The Letter to the Hebrews*, PNTC [Grand Rapids: Eerdmans, 2010], 6).

Lindars infers from Heb 13:17 that there was a rift between the leaders of the church and the group to whom Hebrews is addressed. If the leaders have to give an account "with grief," then "the implication is that the situation is extremely serious, and the leaders are at their wits end [sic] to know how to cope with it."[68] Lindars suggests the reason the author of Hebrews was involved in the first place is that he was a loved and respected member of the church. Lindars speculates that the leaders had written to the author of Hebrews and urged him to intervene. Since the author could not come in person (although he hoped to later), he responded with the Letter to the Hebrews. This accounts for its rhetorical character: his intervention was the last resort.[69]

The groundwork is now laid for a historical reconstruction of the circumstances surrounding the writing of Hebrews. I propose that Luke wrote Hebrews from Rome after the death of Paul and before the destruction of Jerusalem in AD 70. Scriptural evidence for this thesis can be adduced from a correlation of statements in the Pastoral Epistles with the text of Hebrews. Imprisoned in Rome, Paul penned 2 Timothy around AD 66 or 67; there he hints at his coming execution. Addressing Timothy, he says, "Make every effort to come before winter." Either before Timothy arrived or shortly thereafter, Paul was beheaded, and Timothy was apprehended either in route to Rome, or more likely at Rome, and was probably imprisoned. Hebrews 13:23 says Timothy "has been released," implying an imprisonment. The description of Timothy as "our brother" in Heb 13:23 is reminiscent of Paul and links both Timothy and our author with the Pauline circle. In 2 Tim 4:11 Paul comments, "Only Luke is with me," thus placing Luke in Paul's company at or near the time of his death in Rome, c. AD 66.[70]

The probability for the Lukan amanuensis of the Pastoral Epistles has been adjudged to be quite strong by a number of scholars. This is interesting because while Hebrews diverges significantly from the

---

[68] B. Lindars, *The Theology of the Letter to the Hebrews* (Cambridge: Cambridge University Press, 1991), 8.

[69] Ibid.

[70] J. F. Bleek, *Introduction to the New Testament*, 2nd ed., trans. W. Urwick (Edinburgh: T&T Clark, 1869), 2:95–96, infers from Heb 13:23, in connection with Paul's silence on Timothy's imprisonment in the Pastorals, that Hebrews was written by a member of the Pauline circle after Paul's death.

Pauline Letters, especially in style, it nevertheless shares a certain similarity with the Pastorals. Simcox observes,

> This Ep. [Hebrews] has several words and phrases in common, not with St. Paul's writings generally, but with the isolated and peculiar group of the Pastoral Epistles. If this stood alone, it might at most serve so far to narrow speculation as to the authorship of our Ep., as to suggest that it is by a man whose intercourse with St. Paul had been chiefly towards the close of the latter's life.[71]

Simcox notes that we are led a step further in this matter when we observes,

> [A] number of words and phrases are common to the Pastoral Epp. and Hebrews with St. John, or to Heb. and St. Luke only. Our first thought might be, that Origen was right—that St. Luke was the author of Heb. with or without suggestions from St. Paul, and that he may have been (in view of 2 Tim.iv.11 no one else could be) the amanuensis, or something more, of the Pastoral Epp.[72]

Although Simcox rejects Lukan authorship of Hebrews, he has clearly noticed that Luke's vocabulary has more in common with Hebrews than any other canonical writer, and that the Pastoral Epistles come next in degree of similarity.[73] An example of this similarity can be found in the appearance of the phrase *di' hēn aitian* nowhere in the New Testament except Luke 8:47; 2 Tim 1:6,12; Titus 1:12; and Heb 2:11.

Consider these four facts. First, of all the Letters of Paul, the greatest debate concerning alleged non-Pauline material centers on the Pastorals. Second, it is precisely in these letters that the similarity to Hebrews is most pronounced (with Romans coming in a close second). Third, there is a recognized degree of stylistic similarity among

---

[71] W. Simcox, *The Writers of the New Testament* (London: Hodder & Stoughton, 1902), 47.

[72] Ibid.

[73] Ibid., 52–53. See especially his appendix on pp. 116–53, where he compares the vocabulary of Luke with the later Pauline and Catholic Epistles as well as Hebrews. The evidence of a greater kinship for Luke, the Pastorals, and Hebrews can be clearly seen. See also J. B. Feuillet, "La doctrine des Épitres Pastorales et leurs affinites avec l'oeuvre lucanienne," *RevThom* 78 (1978): 163–74, who made this comparison and discussed it at length, concluding that the Pastorals were redacted by Luke. Cf. also J. B. Feuillet, "Le dialogue avec le monde non-chretien dans les epitres pastorales et l'epitre aux Hebreux. Premiere partie: les epitres pastorals," *Esprit et Vie* 98 (1988): 125–28, and "Le dialogue avec le monde non-chretien dans les epitres pastorales et l'epitre aux Hebreux. Deuxieme partie: l'epitre aux Hebreux," *Esprit et Vie* 98 (1988): 152–59, where he continues the argument for Lukan redaction of the Pastorals as well as similar Hellenistic background for the Pastorals and Hebrews.

Luke-Acts, the Pastorals, and Hebrews. Fourth, the medical imagery, which appears in the Pastorals but is largely absent in the rest of the Pauline Letters, is striking.[74] For example, should 2 Tim 2:15 be interpreted in a medical sense since the medical metaphor is clearly used two verses later? Regarding Philo's use of the concept of reason as a sharp instrument that excises vice from the soul, Malherbe says the medical metaphor of the Word as a scalpel is behind Heb 4:12.[75] These facts converge as evidential support for the Lukan amanuensis of the Pastorals.

If Luke were the amanuensis for the Pastorals, and if he were given greater liberty in the production of the letters in Paul's name because of Paul's second imprisonment, then the similarity between Luke-Acts, the Pastorals, and Hebrews provides a further argument in favor of Lukan authorship of Hebrews.

Since 1880, several scholars have argued for the independent Lukan authorship of the Pastorals, including H. J. Holtzmann, J. D. James, Robert Scott, and Stephen Wilson. These scholars have pointed out the difference in vocabulary and style that has caused many to discount the Pastorals as genuinely Pauline. They have further noted the similarities between the Pastorals and Luke-Acts and have found them to be persuasive enough to argue for independent Lukan authorship.[76] Riesner presents undeniable evidence that links Luke-Acts with the Pastoral Epistles. His historical survey of scholarship on this issue is combined with recently discovered evidence.[77]

---

[74] See A. Malherbe, "Medical Imagery in the Pastoral Epistles," in *Texts and Testaments: Critical Essays on the Bible and Early Church Fathers* (San Antonio: Trinity University Press, 1980), 19–35. Though Malherbe does not draw any connection with Hebrews, the sheer weight of the lexical data warrants such a comparison. In addition, Malherbe discusses the terminology of health and disease in the Pastorals and what this says to us about the author, readers, and nature of the church's teaching. The theme of obtuseness runs throughout the Pastorals and can be compared with what the author of Hebrews has to say in the warning passages, especially 5:11–6:3.

[75] Malherbe, "Medical Imagery," 24, 33.

[76] H. J. Holtzmann, *Die Pastoralbriefe* (Leipzig: Engelmann, 1880); J. D. James, *The Genuineness and Authorship of the Pastoral Epistles* (London: Longman and Green, 1906); R. Scott, *The Pauline Epistles* (Edinburgh: T&T Clark, 1909); S. Wilson, *Luke and the Pastoral Epistles* (London: SPCK, 1979). See the critique of this position in I. H. Marshall, *The Pastoral Epistles*, ICC (London and New York: T&T Clark, 1999), 87–88.

[77] R. Riesner, "Once More: Luke-Acts and the Pastoral Epistles," in *History and Exegesis: New Testament Essays in Honor of Dr. E. Earle Ellis for his 80th Birthday*, ed. Sant-Won (Aaron) Son (New York: T&T Clark, 2006), 239–58. Riesner critiques Marshall's argument against common Lukan authorship.

It is not my purpose to launch into a thorough discussion of the problem of the Pastorals.[78] I am convinced that they are genuinely Pauline. However, one must account for the significant difference between these writings and the other acknowledged Letters of Paul. The often-suggested proposal that Luke was the amanuensis for Paul during the latter's second Roman imprisonment seems to be the most fruitful.[79] Paul records in 2 Tim 4:11 that "only Luke is with me," providing a crucial clue that if he did use an amanuensis, Luke would be the most likely (if not the only) candidate. It is possible that the severity of the second Roman imprisonment made the use of an amanuensis necessary.[80]

Jeremias accepts the plausibility of an amanuensis for the Pastorals, but felt that Tychicus was a better candidate than Luke based on 2 Tim 4:11.[81] If Luke were the amanuensis, then the use of the third person would not be unusual for two reasons: he was not writing in his own name, and he was the only one with Paul. Interestingly, Jeremias's student E. Earle Ellis thought Luke is "plausibly suggested" to be the amanuensis.[82]

The most significant argument for Lukan amanuensis of the Pastorals is offered by C. F. D. Moule. He states that "Luke wrote all three Pastoral epistles. But he wrote them during Paul's lifetime, at Paul's behest and, in part (but only in part), at Paul's dictation."[83] If so, then freedom would have been allowed Luke in the composition of the letters, and hence the similarity to Lukan writings could be

---

[78] Cf. Marshall, *Pastoral Epistles*, 57–108.

[79] H. Riley, *Preface to Luke* (Macon: Mercer University Press, 1993), 115–16, also argues for the Lukan amanuensis of the Pastorals. He suggests that this would shed light on 1 Tim 5:23, where Timothy is urged to "use a little wine because of your stomach and your frequent illnesses." It is often noted that this verse interrupts the flow from v. 22 to 24 and has either been misplaced or was a gloss. Riley suggests that it is Dr. Luke's prescription inserted amid Paul's message! Lukan amanuensis for the Pastorals, or its possibility, is affirmed by G. Fee, *1 and 2 Timothy, Titus* (Peabody, MA: Hendrickson, 1988), 26; G. A. Knight, *The Pastoral Epistles*, NIGTC (Grand Rapids: Eerdmans, 1992), 50–52; W. D. Mounce, *Pastoral Epistles*, WBC 46 (Nashville: Thomas Nelson, 2000), cxxvii–cxxix; L. T. Johnson, *The First and Second Letters to Timothy*, AB 35a (New York: Doubleday, 2001), 89; R. Fuchs, *Unerwartete Unterschiede: Müssen wir unsere Ansichten über 'die' Pastoralbriefe revidieren?* (Wuppertal: R. Brockhaus, 2003), 145–49; and H. W. Neudorfer, *Der erste Brief des Paulus an Timotheus*, HTA (Wuppertal: R. Brockhaus and Giessen: Brunnen, 2004), 19.

[80] O. Roller, *Das Formular der Paulinischen Briefe* (Stuttgart: W. Kohlhammer, 1933), 20–21.

[81] Jeremias, *Jerusalem in the Time of Jesus*, 7–8.

[82] Ellis, *Making of the New Testament Documents*, 420.

[83] C. F. D. Moule, "The Problem of the Pastoral Epistles: a Reappraisal," in *BJRL* 47 (1965): 434.

explained.[84] Strobel agrees with Moule's assessment and provides a detailed comparison of the language and style of the Pastorals with Luke-Acts.[85] However, it is unclear whether he believes Luke to be Paul's amanuensis or the independent author, a fact for which he is rightly chided by Wilson.[86]

Wilson's contribution is his analysis of the theological similarity between the Pastorals and Luke-Acts. However, his conclusion that a later Luke wrote the Pastorals to rebut the gnostic misinterpretation of Paul (the major threat to the Lukan communities) is untenable.[87]

Drury likewise observes the close proximity of Luke and the Pastorals with Hebrews in matters of theology as well as vocabulary and style. Of particular interest is Drury's observation of the similar ethical concerns expressed in Luke, the Pastorals, and Hebrews 13. Marriage, money, obedience to leaders, and hospitality are all present as ethical themes in Luke-Acts, the Pastorals, and Hebrews.[88]

The upshot of all this is that there is evidence lexically, stylistically, and theologically that the Pastoral Epistles are most like Luke-Acts and Hebrews in the New Testament. A possible correlation of this evidence would be to suggest that Luke is the independent author of Luke-Acts and Hebrews and that he was the amanuensis of the Pastorals as well.[89]

The subject of Paul's use of a secretary in his letters is most ably treated by E. Randolph Richards and Michael Prior.[90] This subject is of

---

[84] Secretaries had some influence on the style and vocabulary of a letter. Cf. O. Roller, *Das Formular der paulinischen Briefe* (Stuttgart: W. Kohlhammer, 1933); E. R. Richards, *The Secretary in the Letters of Paul* (Tübingen: Mohr [Paul Siebeck], 1991), 194–98.

[85] A. Strobel, "Schreiben des Lukas? zum Sprachlichen Problem der Pastoralbriefe," *NTS* 15 (1969): 191–210.

[86] Wilson, *Luke and the Pastorals*, 2.

[87] Ibid., 4. See J.-D. Kaestli's critique of Wilson in "Luke-Acts and the Pastoral Epistles: the Thesis of a Common Authorship," in *Luke's Literary Achievement*, JSNTSup 116 (Sheffield: Sheffield Academic Press, 1995), 110–26. He rejects Pauline authorship and also rejects Moule's solution of Lukan amanuensis (ibid., 114–16). He solves the problem by suggesting that a later writer used the book of Acts for the personal information that is found in 2 Timothy. Cf. also Marshall's critique of Wilson in "The Christology of Acts and the Pastoral Epistles," in *Crossing the Boundaries: Essays in Biblical Interpretation in Honour of Michael D. Goulder*, ed. S. Porter, P. Joyce, and D. Orton (Leiden/New York: Brill, 1994), 167–82.

[88] J. Drury, *Tradition and Design in Luke's Gospel: A Study in Early Christian Historiography* (Atlanta: John Knox, 1976), 18–21.

[89] Recall F. Delitzsch's evidence for Lukan authorship of Hebrews in the medical metaphors in three clusters in the epistle: 4:12–13; 5:11–14; and 12:11–13. F. Delitzsch, *Commentary on the Epistle to the Hebrews*, trans. T. L. Kingsbury, 2 vols. (Edinburgh: T&T Clark, 1872; repr., Grand Rapids: Eerdmans, 1952), 415.

[90] Richards, *The Secretary in the Letters of Paul*; M. Prior, *Paul the Letter Writer and the Second*

significance for the authorship of Hebrews, especially for those who, like Origen, want to suggest ultimate Pauline authorship but with mediatorial assistance. We have seen that from the days of the church fathers, those who suggest Pauline authorship often resort to the suggestion that Luke was translator, redactor, secretary, or coauthor.

Richards said it is quite unlikely that Paul's reference to others by name was intended to indicate anything less than his active role in the composition of the letter. The evidence does not support a practice of including others in the address as a "nicety." What constitutes an active role is more debatable. The coauthors are apparently not full contributors on an equal level with Paul. On the other hand, they must have had some role in the writing of the letter.[91] Richards notes that an analysis of the singular versus plural verbs in Second Corinthians reveals that the use of "we" is not merely a literary device. It may indicate the input of Timothy.[92]

On the role of the *sunergoi,* "coworkers," in the Pauline Letters, Josephus used the same term to describe the literary assistants who helped him write his *Jewish War.* These *sunergoi* were assistants who aided him in translating his work, and their assistance extended beyond mere translation. This raises the question whether Paul had the same connotations in mind when he describes some of his colleagues as *sunergoi.* Unfortunately, there is no evidence to suggest the term was often used for secretarial assistants.[93]

A related problem is the anti-Marcionite prologues. In the prologue to Luke's Gospel, the description of Luke is unclear. Regul argues that the prologue implies Luke was Paul's literary assistant, in which case the secretarial role of Luke must be considered.[94]

According to Richards, however, the significance of the testimony is questionable. With reference to 2 Tim 4:13, he suggests Paul kept

---

Letter to Timothy, JSNTSup 23 (Sheffield: JSOT Press, 1989).

[91] This is supported by E. Ellis, *Prophecy and Hermeneutic in Early Christianity* (Grand Rapids: Baker Books, 1993), C. K. Barrett, *A Commentary on the First Epistle to the Corinthians* (Peabody, MA: Hendrickson, 1968), and H. A. W. Meyer, *Critical and Exegetical Handbook to the Epistles to the Corinthians* (New York: Funk & Wagnalls, 1884), 154. See 154nn113, 114, 115.

[92] Richards, *The Secretary in the Letters of Paul,* 156. Note the discussion in Prior, *Paul the Letter Writer,* 45, since Timothy is named as coauthor with Paul in 2 Corinthians, Philippians, Colossians, and Philemon, and with Paul and Silas in 1 and 2 Thessalonians. His role in some of the Pauline letters was "quite significant."

[93] Ibid., 158.

[94] J. Regul, *Die Antimarcionitischen Evangelienprologue,* Vetus Latina, no. 6 (Freiburg im Breisgau: Herder, 1969), 198–202.

notebooks. Harry Gamble theorizes that the first collection of Paul's Letters was in codex form (based on the theory that a secretary usually kept copies of letters and these copies were often codices). If this was the case, Paul's first letters arose from his personal copies and not from having the letters returned by recipients. This collection might easily have fallen into Luke's hands at Paul's death (2 Tim 4:11).[95]

Paul never speaks directly of how his letters were written. Why is Tertius, who never appears as a member of the Pauline band, used as a secretary here? It may not be coincidence that he is used to write down Romans, Paul's longest letter, the one with the strongest oral features, and one which contains a high frequency of oratorical rhetoric.[96] If this is the case, then it would serve as further evidence against the Pauline authorship of Hebrews on literary grounds.

Richards concludes that the evidence indicates that Paul frequently used a secretary, though it is unclear what the secretary did.[97] Prior thinks the differences between the Pastorals and other Pauline Letters are caused by Paul writing the Pastorals with no secretarial assistance.[98] However, this possibility does not address the frequent evidence of Lukan style in the Pastorals.

Alan Eagar suggests that the arguments in favor of Pauline authorship of Hebrews are equally as strong in favor of Luke. Furthermore, the objections that make the Pauline hypothesis unlikely do not apply to the Lukan hypothesis (anonymity, stylistic considerations, etc.). He concludes,

> All such arguments for the Pauline authorship of an Epistle as may also be applied to S. Luke become arguments for the Lucan authorship, since they are not affected, in his case, by the objections that make it impossible to apply them to S. Paul.[99]

He argues that where Paul would be most likely influenced by Luke, he would show the strongest traces of Lukan peculiarities. Where Luke was not working with documents (or with documents that were not written in Greek), the individuality of his style would be most

---

[95] Richards, *The Secretary in the Letters of Paul*, 165n169. See also pp. 3–7. Ellis notes that it was the custom in antiquity to retain copies of letters, and that Paul retained copies of his epistles for subsequent reference and because of the possibility of loss or damage in transit. Ellis, *History and Interpretation in New Testament Perspective*, 69.

[96] Richards, *The Secretary in the Letters of Paul*, 169–71 and discussion.

[97] Ibid., 189.

[98] Prior, *Paul the Letter Writer*, 45, 50.

[99] A. Eagar, "The Authorship of the Epistle to the Hebrews," *Expositor* 10 (1904): 74–80, 110–23.

evident. From evidence in the New Testament, Eagar contends that Luke's presence had some stylistic influence on Paul when he wrote Colossians, 2 Corinthians, and the Pastorals. He notes that in sections of Luke-Acts where we might expect the individuality of his style to be the strongest, there are many active verbals. Likewise, when Paul is said to have had Luke in his company at the time of writing, in these Pauline Epistles there is a higher percentage of active verbals. He concludes that the use of active verbals in the Pauline Letters "was probably due to the influence of S. Luke; and, as words of this class are more numerous in Hebrews than in any Pauline document, this deduction is obviously of some value in determining the authorship of our Epistle."[100]

Scholars have traditionally focused on the influence of Paul on Luke. In light of the shift of opinion in recent years regarding Luke as an accomplished theologian, perhaps the time has come to consider Lukan influence on Paul (especially if Lukan authorship of Hebrews is correct).[101]

J. A. T. Robinson describes the author of Hebrews in this way:

> The mantle of the Apostle [Paul] has in part fallen upon the writer himself. He can address his readers with a pastoral authority superior to that of their own leaders and with a conscience clear of local involvement (Heb. 13:17f.), and yet with no personal claim to apostolic aegis. There cannot have been too many of such men around.[102]

Luke was one of the few men who could be accurately described by these words. Already the author of a Gospel and of the only history of the Christian church from its inception through Paul's confinement in Rome (Acts), Luke was known and loved by many of the churches he had visited with Paul. Also, it is probably a safe assumption that the author was to some extent acquainted with the Pauline Letters, given the lexical similarity noted above. Who more than Luke would have had such knowledge of them?

---

[100] Ibid., 78.

[101] D. Seccombe writes, "Luke and Paul do appear to be at one in seeing a connection between the turning of the nation Israel to Christ and the Parousia. (Acts 3:19f; Rom 11:12,15) Reading Acts and Romans 11 side by side, one is struck by many suggestive similarities. The interesting thing is that Acts appears the more primitive, setting out the grist from which Paul has milled his extraordinary theology of the destiny of Jew and Gentile" ("The New People of God," 370–71). Note the implications of this comment for dating Acts and the Pauline Letters.

[102] Robinson, *Redating*, 219–20.

The factors above can be assembled into a theory of Lukan authorship of Hebrews in the following way. Luke was still in Rome at the
time of Paul's death. Timothy arrived, was imprisoned, and later was
released. Both were known to the Christians at Antioch, the destination I propose for the letter. Finally, Heb 13:24 says, "Those who
are from Italy greet you." This verse is naturally understood to mean
that some Christians now in Italy send greetings to a group living
elsewhere. Although it is true that "those who are from Italy" could
mean Italian expatriates, it seems more natural to understand it otherwise. The phrase in Greek (*hoi apo tēs Italias*) may be translated in
any of three ways: "they who are in Italy," "they who are from Italy,"
or "they who are away from Italy." There is a similar phrase in Acts
17:13—*hoi apo tēs Thessalonikēs Ioudaioi*, which in context clearly
refers to people living in Thessalonica. Thus, we have good reason for
translating the Hebrews phrase as "those who are in Italy."

In a recent dissertation, Mosser analyzes this phrase and concludes,
based on first-century usage, that the meaning "those who are in Italy" is most likely. Mosser observes, with reference to the use of *apo* in
Heb 13:24 and Acts 18:2 ("Aquila, . . . who had recently come from Italy), that these are not *grammatically* parallel. In Acts 18:2, the prepositional phrase *apo tēs Italias* modifies a participle (*elēluthota*, "having
come"), whereas in Heb 13:24 it modifies a pronominal article. In Acts
the prepositional phrase functions adverbially; in Hebrews it functions adjectivally. The adverbial use in Acts 18:2 "requires the force
of separation because of the participle. . . . No such motion is implicit
in the pronoun of Hebrews 13:24b.[103] This fact mitigates the effort
to use Acts 18:2 as evidence for a particular reading of Heb 13:24. It
is interesting to note the church fathers uniformly interpreted this
phrase in Heb 13:24 to mean the author was writing *from* Italy to a
destination *outside* Italy,[104] and this was the predominant interpretation until the eighteenth century. Matthew 24:17; Luke 11:13; Acts
17:13; and Col 4:16 furnish parallels to this use of *apo*. When used
in this sense, the preposition *apo* is given the meaning of "domiciled
at."[105] Koester recognizes the use in John 11:1 where Lazarus is "from

---

[103] C. Mosser, "No Lasting City: Rome, Jerusalem and the Place of Hebrews in the History of
Earliest 'Christianity,'" (Ph.D. diss., St. Mary's College, University of St. Andrews, 2004), 147.

[104] Many manuscripts, as early as the fifth century, carry the subscription stating the letter
was written from Rome.

[105] So J. Moffatt, *A Critical and Exegetical Commentary on the Epistle to the Hebrews*, ICC

Bethany," and was still in Bethany, and Acts 10:23, where Christians "from Joppa" were still in Joppa.[106] Making use of *Thesaurus Linguae Graecae*, Mosser searched all uses of the Greek *hoi apo* "those from" through the seventh century AD. He discovered, with respect to letters, "the tendency is for authors who identify themselves as 'from' a place to be *in* that place at the time of composition."[107] This has significant ramifications for Heb 13:24 and the Roman destination theory. It appears that most modern commentators tend to favor the interpretation of Heb 13:24 that locates the author outside Rome and sends greetings from Italian Christians to recipients located in Italy, probably in Rome. This perspective is primarily because of the ascendancy of the Roman destination theory over the past century, rather than the wording of 13:24. However, the alternative interpretation appears to have the edge linguistically.[108]

Ruth Hoppin points out the problem that develops when we accept the translation "they who are away from Italy." Why should the author, in writing to Rome, send greetings only from expatriate Italian Christians, and not from all Christians in his company or in his city at the time of writing? One possible answer is that the reference is to Jewish Christians who were expelled from Rome under the Claudian persecution c. AD 49, but who have regrouped at the location of the author. However, many Jews returned to Rome upon the death of Claudius in AD 54. It seems odd for the author to bypass other Christians in his city and mention only this group if he were indeed writing to Rome from a different locale outside Italy.[109]

(Edinburgh: T&T Clark, 1924; repr., Edinburgh: T&T Clark, 1963), 246, who cites evidence from Oxyrhynchus Papyrus i.81 as an example.

[106] C. R. Koester, *Hebrews*, AB 36 (New York: Doubleday, 2001), 581.

[107] Mosser, "No Lasting City," 146.

[108] See the discussion in Delitzsch, *Hebrews*, 2:406–7, and more recently Mosser, "No Lasting City," 136–58, who demonstrated the Greek prepositional phrase is used similarly in other epistolary greetings that locate the people at the place named, not away from that place. He further demonstrated that manuscript subscriptions based on this phrase are consistently interpreted "to indicate the place *from which* the epistle was written. Here we see scribal intuitions about the "natural" way to understand the Greek idiom" (p. 157). H. Windisch, *Der Hebräerbrief*, 2nd ed., HNT 14 (Tübingen: Mohr, 1931), 127, interpreted Heb 13:24 to indicate an Italian provenance and thus furnished a sufficient reason against a Roman destination.

[109] R. Hoppin, *Priscilla: Author of the Epistle to the Hebrews* (New York: Exposition Press, 1969), 103. The church fathers uniformly interpreted Heb 13:24 to mean that the author was in Italy at the time of writing. A. Nairne translated this verse, "Those who are in Italy and send their greetings with mine from Italy." Those who argue for Rome as the place of composition include H. Braun, *An die Hebräer*, HNT 14 (Tübingen: Mohr/Siebeck, 1984), 2; F. F. Bruce, *The Epistle to the Hebrews*, NICNT, rev. ed. (Grand Rapids: Eerdmans, 1990), 14; E. Gräßer, "Der

Luke informs us in his prologue to the Gospel that he was not an eyewitness to the events in the life of Christ, but that he has carefully verified the account and presented it in logical order. Thus, Luke appears to be a "second generation" Christian if we are permitted to use this term in a rather loose fashion. The interesting personal reference in Heb 2:3 is reminiscent of Luke's prologue, "How will we escape if we neglect such a great salvation? It was first spoken by the Lord and was confirmed to us by those who heard Him." This characterization of the author of Hebrews is semantically equivalent to Luke's prologue. In both places, the authors do not claim eyewitness status of the events of Jesus' life or death.[110] The phrase "it was first spoken" is reminiscent of Acts 1:1, where Luke introduces his second volume with "I wrote the first narrative, Theophilus, about all that Jesus began to do and teach." Furthermore, use of the word "first," *archēn*, in Heb 2:3 parallels the thought stated in Luke's prologue, "just as the original (*archēs*) eyewitnesses and servants of the word handed them down to us."

Drury has noted that Luke and Hebrews share "an underlying and clearly articulated view of history."[111] Hebrews 2:3 makes it clear that the writer of Hebrews (and Luke as well) recognized that a temporal gap separated them from the origin of Christianity. Drury continues, "The life of the Church is linked to its Lord's by the apostolic eyewitnesses and the providence of the Holy Spirit with God over all; Luke and Hebrews are fundamentally at one."[112]

Hebrews 2:2–4 reflects what we read in Acts relative to the early church: the signs, wonders, various miracles, and gifts of the Spirit

---

Hebräerbrief 1938–1963," *TRu* 30 (1964): 138–236; H. Hegermann, *Der Brief an die Hebräer,* THKNT 16 (Berlin: Evangelische Verlangsanstalt, 1988), 11 (not restricted to Rome, but Italy in general); F. Laub, *Bekenntnis und Auslegung: die paränetische Funktion der Christologie im Hebräerbrief* (Regensburg: F. Pustet, 1980), 18; A. Strobel, *Der Brief an die Hebräer: übersetzt und erklärt,* 13th ed. (Göttingen: Vandenhoeck & Ruprecht, 1991), 13; P. Vielhauer, *Geschichte der urchristlichen Literatur: Einleitung in das Neue Testament, die Apokryphen und die Apostolischen Väter* (Berlin; New York: Walter de Gruyter, 1978), 25. See H. Attridge, *Hebrews,* 410n79, for a list of places where the expression is used idiomatically to indicate place of origin rather than separation.

[110] Hebrews 2:3 makes it doubly difficult to argue for Pauline authorship, as he would probably never have referred to himself in that fashion. On other occasions, Paul does speak of himself as one who has seen the Lord, and claims apostolic authority on this basis. Neither the writer of Hebrews nor Luke claims apostolic authority. On the contrary, they disavow such a claim, as can be seen from Luke 1:1–4 and Heb 2:3–4.

[111] Drury, *Tradition and Design in Luke's Gospel,* 21.

[112] Ibid.

are all mentioned and illustrated throughout Acts. We might say that Heb 2:2–4 is a good summary of Luke's two-volume work; v. 2 summarizes the Gospel of Luke, while vv. 3–5 summarize Acts.[113]

When one collates the data from Hebrews that has a bearing on authorship—the style of writing, the theological depth, tightness, and intricacies of the argument—with the lexical, stylistic, and theological similarity between Luke-Acts and Hebrews, it becomes apparent that someone like Luke must have been the author. There is a certain academic training that Luke manifests in his two-volume work. The author of Hebrews likewise possessed an academic background. Hengel makes this observation in discussing the way the Synoptic writers handle their quotations of Ps 110:1. He notes that both Matthew and Mark change the last line of Ps 110:1 under the influence of Ps 8:7 (Mark 12:36; Matt 22:44); only Luke (Luke 20:42–43) corrects this change (as does the Byzantine text and the Old Latin version of Mark and Luke). Then Hengel comments, "As with the author of Hebrews the higher—one could say also the 'academic' training of the author Luke—is evidenced in such philological-historical 'minutia'."[114] Likewise, Trotter concludes that Hebrews "seems to have been written by someone trained in classical rhetoric and who used Greek with the ease of a native-born speaker and writer."[115] Krodel points out that Luke "never says everything at once, but expands and unfolds earlier themes as he moves step by step from one episode to another."[116] This is also the style of the author of Hebrews.

The work of Lukan scholars worldwide (through the Society of Biblical Literature and other groups and individuals) has produced over the past 35 years indisputable evidence that the author of Luke-Acts was an individual of remarkable literary and rhetorical skill. In the past, scholars often minimized the literary complexity of Luke-Acts,[117] but now the author of Luke-Acts is viewed by most as a writer of immense abilities and gifts. I do not see how it is possible to

---

[113] This was noted and argued by T. Jelonek, "Streszczenie dziel Lukaszowych w liscie do Hebrajezykow," *Analecta Cracoviensia* 13 (1981): 143–51. He later suggested that Luke was the author of Hebrews ("Chrystologia listu do Hebrajezykow," *Analecta Cracoviensia* 17 (1985): 253–57) and that he wrote in the name of Paul. Jelonek considers Hebrews to be a continuation of the Stephen speech in Acts 7.

[114] M. Hengel, *Studies in Early Christology* (Edinburgh: T&T Clark, 1995), 171–72.

[115] A. Trotter, *Interpreting the Epistle to the Hebrews* (Grand Rapids: Baker, 1997), 184.

[116] G. A. Krodel, *Acts*, ACNT (Minneapolis: Augsburg, 1986), 281.

[117] C. Mount, *Pauline Christianity: Luke-Acts and the Legacy of Paul* (Leiden/Boston: Brill, 2002), 67.

maintain any longer that the author of Luke-Acts is somehow "inferior" or "incapable" of having written a work such as Hebrews. This factor along with the way a theory of Lukan authorship can be historically reconstructed from the texts offers impressive evidence that points to the possibility of Lukan authorship of Hebrews.

Recipients of Hebrews

The question of the recipients of Hebrews, like the other matters of provenance, has engendered considerable discussion.[118] The internal evidence of the letter itself nowhere locates the readers, and thus the best one can do is to sift the evidence and see where it leads. It appears to me that the best solution was first offered in 1923 by J. V. Brown when he suggested the readers were a group of former Jewish priests mentioned in Acts 6:7 who had become Christians. This theory was later argued by Spicq in his work on Hebrews.[119] With the exception of Hughes's commentary on Hebrews, this suggestion has not been given the consideration it deserves in New Testament circles.[120]

---

[118] For a survey of the various theories, consult Guthrie, *New Testament Introduction*, 682–701, and Ellingworth, *Hebrews*, 21–29. Lindars, *The Theology of the Letter to the Hebrews*, 8–15, has argued that the crisis that precipitated the writing of Hebrews can be adduced from 13:7–16, where the practical aspects of the crisis are summarized. "The whole point at issue is a felt need on the part of the readers to resort to Jewish customs in order to come to terms with their sense of sin against God and need for atonement" (p. 10). The readers of Hebrews have lost confidence in the power of Christ's death to deal with their consciousness of sin. They have turned to the Jewish community, causing friction and division in the church (p. 12). Lindars's reconstruction would fit the theory that the recipients were former Jewish priests. The letter never contrasts Jews and Gentiles.

[119] Spicq, *L'Épître aux Hébreux* (Paris: Librairie Lecoffre, 1952–53), 1:226–31; Cf. J. V. Brown, "The Authorship and Circumstances of Hebrews—Again!" *BSac* 80 (1923): 505–38; M. E. Clarkson, "The Antecedents of the High Priest Theme in Hebrews," *AThR* 29 (1947): 89–95; and C. Sandegren, "The Addressees of the Epistle to the Hebrews," *EvQ* 27 (1955): 221–24. All of these argue for former Jewish priests as the likely recipients. Spicq later altered his view ("*L'Épître aux Hébreux*, Apollos, Jean-Baptiste, les Hellenistes et Qumran," *Revue de Qumran* 1 (1959): 365–90) to suggest the priests were members of Qumran. See also Yadin, Kosmala, Danielou, and more recently, B. Pixner, "The Jerusalem Essenes, Barnabas and the Letter to the Hebrews," in *Qumranica Mogilanensia*, ed. Z. Kapera (Krakow: Enigma Press, 1992), 6:167–78.

[120] P. E. Hughes, *A Commentary on the Epistle to the Hebrews* (Grand Rapids: Eerdmans, 1977), 10–15. Lindars called it a speculative reconstruction which "strains credulity." Lindars, *The Theology of the Letter to the Hebrews*, 4. R. Brown and J. P. Meier's critique of Spicq's proposal is primarily based on Spicq's suggestion that the converted priests remained in Jerusalem. R. Brown and J. P. Meier, *Antioch and Rome: New Testament Cradles of Catholic Christianity* (New York: Paulist Press, 1983), 143. The appeal to the Greek Bible (rather than Hebrew) and the tabernacle (rather than the temple) as arguments against former priests being the recipients are not a serious hurdle, as shown already. Guthrie is more optimistic when he says that this

Brown not only argued for priests as the recipients of Hebrews, but he also attributed part of the writing to Luke as a collaborator with Paul. He suggested that Paul was the "chief framer, planner and compiler" of the letter, but that Luke edited it.[121] Brown's theory concerning the author and recipients of Hebrews is the nearest to my own.

Brown was soon followed in his suggestion regarding recipients by Bornhauser in 1932, Clarkson in 1947, Ketter in 1950, Spicq in 1952, Braun and Sandegren in 1955, and then Rissi in 1987. Spicq revised his theory in 1958–59 and suggested that the priests had been influenced by the Qumran community. Spicq also followed Brown in noting a likeness between Hebrews and Stephen's speech in Acts 7. He proposes that parts of the book of Hebrews counter Qumranian speculations, and he concludes that Hebrews was written to Jewish priests who were Essene-Christians, some of whom were former members of the Qumran community.

This theory of Qumranian influence on the recipients of Hebrews was elaborated by Jean Danielou and Yigael Yadin. Danielou believed that converted priests were the most likely recipients. He thought John the Baptist had been influenced by Essene tendencies, and he accepted Cullman's idea that Stephen's speech contains several points similar to the Damascus Document, an Essene manuscript. Danielou posited that the Hellenists of Acts 6 were converted Essenes.[122]

Yadin argued that Hebrews was written to a group of Jews who had belonged to the Qumran sect and who upon conversion to Christianity continued to maintain some of their views.[123] Hughes favored the view that the recipients were former priests, but he found it unnecessary to assert that they had been former members of Qumran. He called this view the "best theory yet advanced to explain the occasion . . . of Hebrews."[124]

The Qumran connection has been exaggerated, and all that need be said is that the readers, if they were former priests, may have been

---

view must remain a conjecture, although a conjecture that deserves "careful consideration" (*New Testament Introduction*, 691).

[121] Brown, "The Authorship and Circumstances of Hebrews—Again!" 533–36.

[122] J. Danielou, *The Dead Sea Scrolls and Primitive Christianity*, trans. S. Attanasio (Baltimore: Helicon Press, 1958), 18–19.

[123] Y. Yadin, "The Dead Sea Scrolls and the Epistle to the Hebrews," in *Aspects of the Dead Sea Scrolls*, ed. C. Rabin and Y. Yadin (Jerusalem, Magnes, 1958), 38. See also H. Braun, *Qumran und das Neue Testament* (Tübingen, Mohr [P. Seibeck] 1966), 1:153–54.

[124] Hughes, *Hebrews*, 14.

influenced by some of the views of this sect of Judaism. However, a careful reading of the letter does not appear to indicate much influence, in my view.[125]

The suggestion that the recipients were former priests without necessarily a Qumran connection has plenty of evidence to support it, and merits reconsideration as one of the better solutions to the overall question. It seems to have greater explanatory power than any other theory. Josephus mentions there were 20,000 priests, while Jeremias says there were 7,200 priests attached to the temple in Jerusalem alone.[126] With the persecution raging in Jerusalem at the time of Stephen's martyrdom (Acts 8:1), these Jewish priests would no doubt have been forced out of Jerusalem along with Christians. The question is where they would have gone. Luke does not tell us what became of the former priests mentioned in Acts 6:7, probably out of concern for their safety. Perhaps this is why the recipients are never identified in the letter, although it is clear the author knew their circumstances. That Jewish-Roman relations were strained to the point of war would be reason to protect former priests likely to be viewed by the Roman government as potential leaders in the Jewish cause.[127]

Assuming Acts was written c. AD 63, the events narrated in Acts 6:7 ("So the preaching about God flourished, the number of the disciples in Jerusalem multiplied greatly, and a large group of priests became obedient to the faith") would have begun about 30 years earlier. Where might those priests have gone? One of the most likely (and safest) places would be Antioch in Syria.[128] There may have been a steady stream of converted priests leaving Jerusalem under persecution, and

---

[125] See the excellent discussion on the history of research on Hebrews and Qumran in P. E. Hughes, "The Epistle to the Hebrews," in *New Testament Criticism and Interpretation*, ed. D. A. Black and D. S. Dockery (Grand Rapids: Zondervan, 1991), 351–53. Also consult G. W. Buchanan, "The Present State of Scholarship on Hebrews," in *Christianity, Judaism and other Graeco-Roman Cults*, ed. J. Neusner (Leiden: Brill, 1975), 308–9.

[126] Jeremias, *Jerusalem in the Time of Jesus*, 198–207.

[127] This fact, along with the evidence that Hebrews was not written to an entire church but to a smaller group within a local church, contributes significantly to the reason there is no salutation and why the identity of author and recipients would become obscured in a relatively short time.

[128] Although exiled Jewish priests would not likely have relocated to Rome, J. V. Brown and J. P. Meier (*Antioch and Rome*, 154) suggested as much when they said that in the Christian community in Rome there may have been "elements of that levitical heritage" referenced in Acts 6:7. Brown critiqued Spicq's theory on the supposition that the converted priests were in Jerusalem. However, Spicq does not argue that they *remained* in Jerusalem, but were forced by persecution to move to some place such as Caesarea, Antioch, or Ephesus (*Hébreux*, 1:227). Brown is more open to this theory if the priests are somewhere other than Jerusalem, such as Rome. A Roman

most likely some would flee to Antioch. All three verbs in Acts 6:7 are in the imperfect tense, indicating action over a span of time. C. B. Williams translated this verse to bring out the force of the imperfects:

> So God's message continued to spread, and the number of the disciples in Jerusalem continued to grow rapidly; a large number even of priests continued to surrender to the faith.[129]

The use of *polus te ochlos*, "great company," makes it probable that several hundred, maybe even several thousand priests were included. As Spicq points out, Hebrews addresses itself to priestly thoughts, attitudes, and points of view.[130]

One of the preeminent themes of Hebrews is the high priesthood of Christ. Would not such a theme be of great interest to former priests? On one occasion the readers are exhorted to continue (in a figurative way) their priestly duties. In Heb 10:19–22, the readers are told to "enter the sanctuary" with their hearts "sprinkled clean from an evil conscience" and their bodies "washed in pure water." This is priestly language and would be immediately understood and appreciated by former priests but less applicable to the laity.

Apparently the primary recipients comprised not the entire church, but a group within it, as may be gleaned from Heb 5:12. They were addressed separately from their leaders as may be inferred from Heb 13:24. According to Downey's exhaustive work on Antioch, several groups of Christians were probably in Antioch, meeting in different locations. We may presume that at least on some occasions, the Jewish Christians and Gentile Christians met separately. Orthodox Jews probably still observed the law and did not eat with Gentiles. A hint of this is recorded in Gal 2:11–12, where Peter eats with the Gentiles until a delegation from James and the Jerusalem church comes to Antioch. Peter then separates himself from the Gentile Christians for fear of the Jerusalem delegation. Downey further suggests that subsequent history of the Antiochene Christians makes it probable there were a number of congregations and that they followed different teachings and practices.[131]

---

destination for Hebrews works just as well for Lukan authorship whether the recipients were former priests or not.

[129] C. B. Williams, *The New Testament: A Private Translation in the Language of the People* (Chicago: Moody, 1955).

[130] Spicq, *Hébreux*, 1:226.

[131] G. Downey, *A History of Antioch in Syria* (Princeton: Princeton University Press, 1961),

Given this background and the statements in Hebrews, it is easy to conceive of former priests, now a part of the church at Antioch, who may have found reasons to remain separate from the rest of the church.[132] Such an attitude could have sparked the exhortation in 10:24–25: "And let us be concerned about one another in order to promote love and good works, not staying away from our worship meetings, as some habitually do, but encouraging each other."

Of those following J. V. Brown and arguing for former priests as the recipients of Hebrews, Spicq presented the most effective case. Commentators on Hebrews often cite him as holding this view, but interaction with his evidence is rare. An exception is Ellingworth, who discusses six of Spicq's 12 arguments for priests and offers a brief rebuttal.[133] Since Spicq's work was produced over 50 years ago and has yet to be translated from French, it seems prudent to present his case again and add it to other arguments in this section in favor of former priests being the recipients of Hebrews.[134]

Spicq begins by noting that the depth of discussion in Hebrews demands a listener who is interested and able to understand it. He overstates the case when he says that "only the priests had enough intelligence" for someone to write to them in this way, but his point that the letter addresses itself to priestly thoughts, attitudes, and points of view is valid.[135]

Spicq then proceeds to list 12 arguments in favor of his view. First, the recipients were converted by the earliest disciples of the Lord

---

277–78. See also E. P. Sanders, *Judaism: Practice and Belief, 63 BCE–66 CE* (London: SCM; Philadelphia: Trinity Press International, 1992), 350–51. W. A. Meeks and R. L. Wilken, *Jews and Christians in Antioch in the First Four Centuries of the Common Era*, SBLSBS 13 (Missoula, MT: Scholars Press, 1978); I. Levinskaya, "Antioch," in *The Book of Acts in its Diaspora Setting*, ed. B. Winter (Grand Rapids: Eerdmans, 1996), 5:127–35.

[132] Why the group addressed in Hebrews was failing to meet regularly with the church we are not told. We know that historically, in the two centuries preceding the Maccabean revolt, many of the priests (especially those of the upper echelon) became open to Hellenistic influences in an attempt to attain Hellenistic citizenship for themselves in Jerusalem. See the discussion in N. Walter, "Hellenistic Jews of the Diaspora at the Cradle of Primitive Christianity," in *The New Testament and Hellenistic Judaism*, ed. P. Borgen and S. Giversen (Aarhus, Denmark: Aarhus University Press, 1995), 41. By the time of the early church, the Sadducean high priestly families were much more Hellenist than their Pharisee counterparts. If the recipients of Hebrews were former priests who had relocated to Antioch, perhaps there was some form of group conflict with others in the Antioch church. If the leadership of the church had become dominated by Gentiles, this could be a plausible factor.

[133] Ellingworth, *Hebrews*, 27.

[134] Spicq's arguments can be found in *Hébreux*, 2:226–31.

[135] Ibid., 226.

(Heb 2:3). They came into the church at the same time (Acts 6:7) and had been Christians for a long time (Heb 5:12; 10:32). Second, they may have known the Roman Jews living in Jerusalem at the time of Pentecost who were converted (Acts 2:10) and who, after going back to Rome, would add their greetings to those of the author of Hebrews (Heb 13:24).[136]

Third, they were strengthened in the faith by the Holy Spirit through the work of Stephen (Heb 2:4; Acts 6:8). Fourth, they should have been teachers (Heb 5:12), and this is commensurate with the teaching role the priests had, as indicated in the Old Testament (Hag 2:11; Zech 7:8; Mal 2:7) as well as the New Testament.[137]

Sandegren argues the same point, noting that an entire church would not be exhorted to be teachers. He speculates, like Spicq, that a smaller group within the larger church is being addressed. Sandegren further combines Heb 13:2, "Don't neglect to show hospitality," with 10:34, 'you . . . accepted with joy the confiscation of your possessions," and concludes that whatever else the recipients had lost through persecution, they still had their houses. He points out that according to the Mosaic law priests could not be deprived of their houses (cf. Lev 25:29–34).[138] This argument might be more applicable if the recipients were in Jerusalem rather than Antioch. It could also be argued that Sandegren overlooks the possibility that they may have lost their homes in previous persecution (in Jerusalem, for example) and now have homes in a new location such as Antioch.

Fifth, the present participle *anistatai*, "arising," in Heb 7:15 is reminiscent of Acts 20:17–18,28, and could have a hierarchical connotation. Such language would hardly have been applied to ordinary Christians, but would be consistent with priests who had the authority required to give counsel and make effective intervention. Sixth, the priests in Jerusalem had been used to the splendor of temple worship. As Christians, they lost their material and spiritual privileges as sons of Levi. They were separated from the temple and had been forced to give up their ministry. They were reduced to the status of ordinary people and were persecuted as members of a hated sect. Discouraged (Heb 12:12–13; 13:5–6), they were tempted to return to Judaism (Heb 3:12–14; 6:4–6; 10:39). The writer of Hebrews attempts

---

[136] Ibid., 227. Note that Spicq does not believe the recipients were in Rome.

[137] Ibid., 228.

[138] Sandegren, "The Addressees of the Epistle to the Hebrews," 222.

to transpose the material and visual aspect of temple worship into the domain of the conscience by highlighting the spiritual and inner nature of Christianity. For him, the loss of material goods leads to the acquisition of spiritual wealth. Although deprived of the symbols of worship, they received the reality of worship, namely, access into the presence of God. Spicq explains,

> To these converted Jewish priests, banned from the Temple, excommunicated from their nation, Hebrews brought back to mind their unique privilege: the confession of Christ as their High Priest . . . and proposed the permanent offering of a completely spiritual sacrifice . . . . Freed from the Law, they had grace; miserable on earth, they came resolutely into the heavenly Jerusalem. In this city of the living God, liturgy never ends.[139]

Seventh, Jewish priests were permitted by Mosaic law to eat a portion of the sacrifice. As Christians excluded from temple worship, they no longer had that right. But they did have a superior privilege: spiritual participation in the sacrificed Christ, from which their former brother priests were excluded (Heb 13:10). The wording here does not contrast Christians with Jews, but rather refers to two categories of priests: those who followed Moses and those who followed Christ. The temptation for these converted priests was to envy those who still served in the temple.[140]

Eighth, the conclusion of the doctrinal section (Heb 10:18), declared flatly that since Christ's sacrifice had taken away sins and brought forgiveness, sacrificial ritual was no longer needed. Jewish Christians generally would not be addressed in so terse and aggressive a fashion. The author is essentially saying that these converted priests no longer have any reason to practice their priesthood since Jesus' priesthood has taken care of it all.

Ninth, because he addresses priestly descendents of Levi, the author takes "psychological precautions" and uses doctrinal "circumlocutions" in order to denounce the foolishness of trying to perpetuate their priesthood. In an effort to show consideration for their feelings, he does not directly attack the temple priesthood in order to validate the priesthood of Jesus. Rather, he approaches the matter from the priesthood of Melchizedek as a priestly order that preceded and

---

[139] Spicq, *Hébreux*, 2:228–229.
[140] Ibid., 229.

supersedes the Levitical order, and which typifies the priesthood of Christ. This is the gist of the argument in Hebrews 7.[141]

Tenth, the vivid description of what the recipients were in danger of doing in Heb 6:6 ("recrucifying the Son of God and holding Him up to contempt") and 10:29 ("trampl[ing] on the Son of God, regard[ing] as profane the blood of the covenant by which he was sanctified, and insult[ing] the Spirit of grace") is better understood against the backdrop of readers who had taken part in the death of Jesus. The Gospels make it clear that the priests—especially the chief priests—were involved in masterminding the death of Jesus. The idea of crucifying Jesus again and showing contempt for Him was used by the author to motivate these converted priests to remain faithful to Jesus.

Eleventh, although the recipients of Hebrews had been victims of persecution, including loss of possessions (Heb 10:34), Spicq says they appear to be "rich" since they had enough to show generous hospitality (13:1–2), were tempted by greed (13:5–6), and were called upon to multiply their acts of kindness (13:16). To use the term "rich," as Spicq does, certainly goes beyond the evidence of the book, but the suggestion that they still had means—and maybe more than most—is justifiable. Most priests were Sadducees (Acts 5:17), who tended to be wealthy landowners. They were also, according to Acts, bitter adversaries of the Jerusalem church. Their anger would be directed especially to those of their own party who had become traitors by their allegiance to Jesus. The author's reference to the example of Moses who gave up the riches of Egypt to bear the reproach of Christ (Heb 11:24) would be appropriate to these circumstances.[142]

Twelfth, the traditional title given to the book, "To the Hebrews" (*pros Ebraious*; appearing as early as c. AD 200), suggests a homogeneous group. They were living in misfortune together, sharing trials. Brevard Childs's comment that the title construes the letter as addressing the problem of the two covenants would certainly support Spicq's theory since this issue would be of paramount importance to former priests. He notes Hebrews offers a programmatic statement of the theological relationship between the two covenants, which receives its content not from the historical setting in the first century, but rather from Scripture. If the author were writing before AD 70, or

---

[141] Ibid., 230.
[142] Ibid., 230–31.

even during the Jewish War, the best way of proceeding would not be a historical approach but a scriptural one, which is exactly what the author of Hebrews does.[143]

Each of these 12 arguments does not carry the same weight. Some are more substantial than others. But given the content and tone of Hebrews, one must admit that the theory of converted priests can account for a significant amount of the textual evidence.

Spicq offers another argument for converted priests from a comparison between Hebrews and Ezekiel:

> Both denounce the hardened heart and the refusal to listen to the Word of God (Eze. 2:4–8, 3:9?, 4[sic–3]:26–27, 12:2,25), weak hands and knees (7:17), the guilt of the ancestors (16; 20:27ff). They announce above all the conclusion of an eternal covenant (16:8, 60, 62; 34:25; 37:26), tied to the restoration of worship and a new priesthood (11:16; 37:28; 41:15ff). It is God who reveals the architecture of the new sanctuary (40:1ff). The sins are blemishes which God purifies (37:23). The Messiah is the shepherd of the sheep (34), etc.[144]

Ezekiel's being a priest makes these similarities noteworthy.

Horbury's discussion of the high priesthood in Hebrews furnishes at least two additional pieces of evidence that the recipients were former priests. First, he observes that the high priest is called an "apostle" of the elders and priests, *sheluhenu*, "our emissary," in *Yoma* 1.5, which compares to Heb 3:1b ("consider Jesus, the apostle and high priest of our confession"). He further states, "Hebrews on priesthood is not wholly detached from the real historical debates of the period of the First Revolt. The tithe belongs to the priest (7:5), and interestingly in AD 62, the Levites complained about it. Chapters 7 and 8 reflect the sacerdotal polity restored for a time during the First Revolt."[145] This is an argument for a pre-AD 70 date as well as for priests as recipients.

If the recipients of Hebrews were converted priests, what of their location? One logical suggestion that also may be supported with biblical evidence, especially if the author of Hebrews is Luke, is Antioch in Syria. We know from Josephus that Jews were numerous in Antioch, enjoying equal rights as citizens.[146] Furthermore, with a few

---

[143] Ibid., 231; B. Childs, *New Testament as Canon: An Introduction* (London: SCM, 1984), 415.

[144] Spicq, *Hébreux*, 2:226.

[145] W. Horbury, "The Aaronic Priesthood in the Epistle to the Hebrews," *JSNT* 19 (1983): 65, 67.

[146] Josephus, *Wars* 7.43. This was because of the proximity of Syria to Judea.

exceptions, there was not the level of persecution of Jews in Antioch as in other cities. However, in the third year of Caligula's reign (AD 40), there was an outburst of anti-Jewish violence. Details are sketchy for this period, and the extent of the violence cannot be known. When Claudius ordered the cessation of pogroms in Egypt in AD 41, a copy of his proclamation was sent to Antioch. This could be interpreted as proof that a similar situation existed in Antioch as in Egypt.[147] Even in AD 66 with the outbreak of the Jewish War, when relations between Jews and non-Jews became violent throughout the region of Syria, Josephus informs us that only Antioch, Sidon, and Apamea refused to kill or imprison a single Jew.[148] Probably one of the few cities of any size in AD 67 with a Christian population (both Jewish and Gentile) that could have been described as having not yet resisted unto blood (Heb 12:4) would have been Antioch.

Hebrews 6:10 mentions that the recipients had ministered to the saints. The Jerusalem offering given by the Antiochene church (Acts 11:27–30) may have been the referent of Heb 6:10. Of historical interest is Josephus's mention of the refusal by Antiochus to permit observance of the Sabbath rest in Antioch about AD 67–69.[149] Hebrews 4:1–10 speaks of the Sabbath rest to come, a subject that would have appealed to Antiochene Jews at that time. Another interesting point is the statement in Heb 13:12–14 that "here we do not have an enduring city; instead, we seek the one to come." How appropriate this statement would have been to exiled Jewish priests in Antioch, many of whom no doubt longed for Jerusalem and who needed to be reminded that their beloved city was not to be sought after.

The admonition of Heb 6:1–6 may have been given to counter pressure on these priests to return to Judaism and defend their nation against imminent peril from the Romans. The crisis of the Jewish War, like a powerful vortex, drew in sectarians of all sorts to defend their homeland. Even some from Qumran, a strict, isolationist sect, died at Masada while holding out against the Roman army. The same kind of pressure must have been brought to bear on many Jewish Christians. The possibility that some of their fellow countrymen would try to coerce them back into Judaism seems only natural under the

[147] Levinskaya, *The Book of Acts in its Diaspora Setting*, 132; Downey, *History of Antioch*, 192–93; Meeks and Wilken, *Jews and Christians*, 4; Brown and Meier, *Antioch and Rome*, 28–44.
[148] Josephus, *Wars*, II, 462–63.
[149] Josephus, *Antiquities*, XII, 120.

circumstances. These factors suggest Antioch as a possible location of the recipients of Hebrews.

More substantive evidence for Antioch is that Luke is associated both by Scripture and tradition with Antioch in Syria (see "The Identity of Luke" in chap. 6). According to the Anti-Marcionite prologue to Luke's Gospel (c. AD 160–180), Luke was a Syrian from Antioch. Eusebius (*Ecclesiastical History*) mentions "Luke who was born at Antioch, by profession a physician." While the accuracy of these traditions cannot be established beyond question, their early origin leads us to assume some factual basis for them. In Antioch was also a medical school where Luke may have received his training.

Scripture provides some verification for these traditions in that Luke is closely linked with Antioch. He had more than a passing interest in Antioch, as can be observed from statements in his Gospel and Acts. For example, in Luke 4:25–27, Jesus reminds His hearers that there were some in Syria who were helped by the earliest of Israel's prophets. In Luke 6:17, Phoenicia is mentioned as the home of some who heard Jesus preach the Sermon on the Mount.

Although Syria is not mentioned in Acts 2:9–11 in the table of nations having expatriates in Jerusalem at Pentecost, it is the geographic center of all the nations listed, and it is unusual that Syria is left out. In Acts 6:5, Luke points out that one of the seven Hellenists who was appointed as a deacon by the church at Jerusalem was from Antioch. Perhaps of most importance, Luke considers Antioch to be the starting point for the Gentile mission, and there are repeated references to it in Acts 11:20–13:16.[150] Acts 13:1 is a crucial text in this matter because it lists five leaders of the early church at Antioch. Since no equivalent list is given for any other missionary church in Acts, this would seem to point to the prominence given by Luke to the Antiochene church.

In this list of names appears Manaen, the foster brother of Herod. Glover highlights material about Herod that is unique to Luke's Gospel, and suggests that Luke's acquaintance with Manaen in the church at Antioch provides the source for much of this information.[151] He at least appears to have special knowledge of and interest in the affairs of the Antiochene Christians,[152] and this adds support to the possibility

---

[150] B. Reicke, *The Gospel of Luke*, trans. R. Mackenzie (Richmond: John Knox, 1964), 14–16.

[151] R. Glover, "'Luke the Antiochene' and Acts," *NTS* 11 (1964–65): 101.

[152] Cf. Harnack, *Luke the Physician*, 20–23.

that Luke wrote Hebrews and addressed it to Jewish Christians (former priests) there. Glover expresses curiosity as to why Luke should be so interested in Antioch but offers no explanation of how Christianity reached Alexandria, an equally important city.[153]

Dods also considers Antioch a possible location of the recipients: "Certainly they required some such exposition as is given in the Epistle, of the relation of Judaism to Christianity."[154] Rendall suggests Antioch as a likely destination for Hebrews, noting that "there alone existed flourishing Christian churches, founded by the earliest missionaries of the gospel, animated with Jewish sympathies, full of interest in the Mosaic worship, and glorying in the name of Hebrews; who nevertheless spoke the Greek language, used the Greek version of the Scriptures and numbered among their members converts who had, like the author, combined the highest advantages of Greek culture with careful study of the Old Testament and especially of the sacrificial law."[155]

Concerning the title, "To the Hebrews," we know it was not a part of the original text but a later addition.[156] It is usually interpreted to mean that the copyists, either because of content or tradition, considered the letter to have been addressed to Jewish Christians. That the term in early Christianity referred to "ritually strict Jewish believers . . . with a deep attachment to the ceremonial laws and to the Jerusalem temple,"[157] certainly would fit the situation of converted

---

[153] Glover, "'Luke the Antiochene' and Acts," 102. See also Franklin's argument that Luke-Acts may been written from Rome to the Antiochene church. E. Franklin, *Luke: Interpreter of Paul, Critic of Matthew*, JSNTSup 92 (Sheffield: JSOT Press, 1994), 388.

[154] M. Dods, "Epistle to the Hebrews," in *The Expositor's Greek Testament*, ed. W. R. Nicoll (Grand Rapids: Eerdmans, 1974), 4:223.

[155] F. Rendall, *The Epistle to the Hebrews* (London: Macmillan, 1888), 69. H. MacNeille, *The Christology of the Epistle to the Hebrews* (Chicago: Chicago University Press, 1914), 16, notes, "There is nothing incongruous in supposing the church at Antioch to be the recipient of the letter." E. Perdelwitz views Hebrews as written to Rome and Antioch. E. Perdelwitz, "Das literarische Problem des Hebräerbriefes," ZNW (1910): 59, 105.

[156] Some say the title *Pros Hebraious* could have been accidentally or deliberately changed by a copyist from its original *Pros Hieraious*. This latter form would be the verbal adjective "to the priestly men," but such a form is so far nonexistant. The similarity between the two titles can easily be seen, and the confusion of two letters at the beginning of the word is the kind of mistake not unknown in copying Scripture. Yet while a plausible explanation, it must remain in the realm of conjecture. J. V. Brown, "The Authorship and Circumstances of Hebrews, Again!" 538. On the manuscript evidence for Hebrews, see F. W. Beare, "The Text of the Epistle to the Hebrews in 𝔓⁴⁶," *JBL* 63 (1944): 379–96, and especially C. Spicq, *Hébreux*, 1:412–32.

[157] Ellis, *Making of the New Testament Documents*, 288.

priests. The title has often been viewed as indicating the recipients were in Palestine.[158]

The Date of Hebrews

Like everything else surrounding the background of this letter, the date is also unclear. Neither the internal evidence of the text nor the external historical data provide enough information for a dogmatic commitment to any of the theories that have been propounded, though a range of AD 60–100 is fairly certain.[159] Until recently the latest possible date was said to be AD 96 since Hebrews is quoted by Clement of Rome in his letter to the Corinthians (traditionally dated AD 96). However, both Clement's use of Hebrews and the traditional date for his letter have been questioned.[160] Attridge is probably correct that the wording in 1 Clement is a "sure sign of dependence on Hebrews,"[161] but the traditional date for Clement's letter is now

---

[158] Ibid. Ellis believes it was addressed to "various congregations" of strict Jewish Christians in Palestine. In light of recent studies of Hellenistic/Diaspora Judaism and Palestinian Judaism, the case for a Palestinian destination is strengthened.

[159] Attridge, *Hebrews*, 9. An early-second-century date has recently been argued by P. Eisenbaum, "Locating Hebrews Within the Literary Landscape of Christian Origins," in *Hebrews: Contemporary Methods*, ed. G. Gelardini (Leiden: Brill, 2005), 213–37. She suggests three reasons for her view: (1) Heb 2:3 indicates some distance between the time of Jesus and the author's audience; (2) Hebrews gives evidence of knowledge of one or more of the written Gospels; (3) Hebrews' affinity to some second-century writings (pp. 224–31). Of course, each of these points can be easily answered. Heb 2:3 does not specify just how much time may have elapsed between Jesus and the author's generation. It is impossible to tell. Eisenbaum assumes a late date for the canonical Gospels when there is ample evidence that all three Synoptic Gospels were penned prior to AD 70. The differences between Hebrews and second-century Christian literature outweigh the similarities. Her statement, "there is virtually no evidence tying Hebrews to the first century," is remarkable given the overall evidence.

[160] See the discussion in H. Attridge, *Hebrews*, 6–9; W. L. Lane, *Hebrews 1–8*, lxii–lxvi; W. L. Lane, "Social Perspectives on Roman Christianity during the Formative Years from Nero to Nerva: Romans, Hebrews, 1 Clement," in *Judaism and Christianity in First-Century Rome,* ed. K. P. Donfried and P. Richardson (Grand Rapids: Eerdmans, 1998), 196–244; and P. Ellingworth, *Hebrews*, 29–33. The question of the dating of 1 Clement was reopened by L. L. Welborn, "On the Date of First Clement," *BR* 24 (1984): 34–54. J. A. T. Robinson dates 1 Clement circa AD 70, largely because of his dependence on G. Edmundson, *The Church in Rome in the First Century* (London: Longmans, Green & Co., 1913). See D. A. Carson, D. Moo, and L. Morris, *An Introduction to the New Testament* (Grand Rapids: Zondervan, 1992), 398n22. First Clement's use of Hebrews is the decisive argument for K. Aland's thesis that Hebrews should be dated c. AD 70. K. Aland, "Corpus Paulinum bei den Kirchenvatern de Zweiten Jahrhunderts," in *Kerygma und Logos* (Göttingen: F. S. C. Andresen, 1979), 44. E. Ellis likewise accepts a pre-AD 70 date for 1 Clement. E. Ellis, *The Making of the New Testament Documents*, 286.

[161] H. Attridge, *Hebrews*, 7.

considered suspect by many and cannot be used as a firm peg for the
terminus ad quem for Hebrews.

There have been three major views relative to the dating of Hebrews: two of them date the book prior to the destruction of Jerusalem in AD 70 (pre-64 and 67–69) and the third toward the end of the
reign of Domitian (AD 96). These views are dependent on five primary matters: (1) the supposed author (if Paul, then a date after AD 67
is impossible), (2) location of the recipients, (3) the interpretation of
the internal evidence, (4) the correlation of internal and external data
(if a Roman destination, was the persecution mentioned in the letter
during Nero or Domitian?), and (5) theological factors.[162]

If Luke wrote Hebrews from Rome, then it was probably written
c. AD 67. As a member of the Pauline circle, it is highly unlikely that
Luke could have written as late as the last decade of the first century.
If the traditions surrounding his death are accurate, he died around
the middle of the 80s. I accept the traditional interpretation of the
scriptural evidence that indicates Luke was a member of the Pauline
circle and one of Paul's traveling companions. Since Luke is mentioned in 2 Timothy as being with Paul near the time of his death,
we may assume he was there when Paul died. Conventional Pauline
scholarship does not date Paul's death later than AD 67.

The evidence for a pre-AD 70 date outweighs the Domitian theory.[163] Porter's counsel is wise on the danger of using the present tense

---

[162] I will not go into all the arguments pro and con on these various views since they are
amply stated in the relevant literature. In addition to works listed above, see also Robinson's
Redating, 200–20 and Guthrie, *New Testament Introduction,* 701–5. P. Walker's "Jerusalem in
Hebrews 13:9–14 and the Dating of the Epistle," in *TynBul* 45 (1994): 39–71, is an incisive
argument for the pre-AD 70 date. Porter's article from a linguistic perspective on the use and
misuse of the present tense in Hebrews must be heeded by all of us who prefer a pre-AD 70 date.
S. Porter, "The Date of the Composition of Hebrews and Use of Present Tense–Form," in *Crossing
the Boundaries: Essays in Biblical Interpretation in Honour of Michael D. Goulder,* ed. S. Porter, P.
Joyce, and D. Orton (Leiden: Brill, 1994), 295–313. With respect to how one or more of these
five factors intertwine in the question of dating, consider the following example in Salevao who
proposed a date in the last quarter of the first century: "Hebrews does reflect a time when the
separation between Christianity and Judaism had become irrevocable. Hebrews was in fact a
calculated theological legitimation of the separation of a particular New Testament community
from Judaism." I. Salevao, *Legitimation in the Letter to the Hebrews: The Construction and Maintenance of a Symbolic Universe,* JSNTSup 219, ed. S. Porter (New York: Sheffield Academic Press,
2002), 108.

[163] Ellis critiqued the Domitian theory based on the evidence that Domitian's persecution was
not widespread enough to warrant the comments made in the New Testament documents. Ellis,
History and Interpretation in New Testament Perspective, 35.

regarding the temple cultus as an argument for a pre-70 date.[164] But the most important argument in favor of an earlier date for Hebrews is the deafening silence in reference to the fall of Jerusalem and the temple in AD 70. While related, the use of the present tense and the lack of reference to the destruction of Jerusalem are separate matters.

Those who would date Hebrews after AD 70 face the formidable task of explaining its silence on such a momentous event. How could the author have failed to use the only absolutely irrefutable argument in his attempt to show the passing nature of the temple cultus and Levitical system? Barton summarizes the problem:

> If the temple at Jerusalem had been destroyed decades before, as the hypotheses under consideration suppose, the fact would have been well known, and the employment of language which implied that its cult was still going on would have made the Epistle ridiculous in the eyes of its first readers. To refuse to be guided by this, the most tangible and definite of all the clues which exist for determining the date of Hebrews, is to throw away the key to the problem and open the door to fruitless speculation and confusion.[165]

Robinson is surely right that although the argument from silence proves nothing, it creates a very strong presumption in this case, which places the burden of proof on those who argue for a post-70 date.[166]

Nairne argues for a date shortly before AD 70. With the outbreak of the Jewish War, there may well have been a wave of patriotic nationalism that swept over Palestine and diaspora Judaism. This would have tempted Christian Jews to revert to Judaism and the stability of the Jewish cultus.[167] Moule agrees with Nairne's assessment:

> At such a time it is not only a fear of persecution and of being called traitors but also the human yearning for the ordered stability of an ancient system, with objective, tangible symbols, that will drive men back from the bold pioneering demanded by the Christian faith to the well-worn paths of the older way. It is to exactly such a temptation that the Epistle speaks, and it is thus, I think, that it becomes clearly intelligible.[168]

---

[164] Porter, "The Date of the Composition of Hebrews and Use of Present Tense-Form," 295–313.

[165] G. A. Barton, "The Date of the Epistle to the Hebrews," *JBL* 57 (1938): 200; See also Robinson, *Redating*, 200–20, on this point.

[166] Robinson, *Redating*, 205.

[167] A. Nairne, *The Epistle to the Hebrews*, CGTSC, ed. R. J. Parry (London: Cambridge University Press, 1922).

[168] C. F. B. Moule, "Sanctuary and Sacrifice," *JTS* 1 NS, no. 1 (1950): 37.

Nairne suggests that a date for Hebrews during the time of the Jewish War explains the language used in the letter concerning the second coming of Christ. "Like the Gospel of S. Luke this Epistle found in those fearful days an interpretation of the 'coming'."[169]

A further argument in favor of a date in the 60s can be adduced from the way Hebrews suggests that the tithe belongs to the priest (7:5). The argument that the tithe belonged to the priests and not to all the sons of Levi was apparently hotly debated at this time. Josephus notes that the high-priestly families during the reign of Felix (c. AD 52–60) and Albinus (c. AD 62–64) abused this practice, thus raising the ire of the Levites since their claim to share in the tithes went unnoticed.[170] In AD 62, the Levites demanded recognition over against the priests in this matter as Josephus chronicles.[171]

Horbury notes that the method of the writer of Hebrews in discussing these matters places this book within the historical debates that occurred during the period of the First Revolt (AD 66–70) and thus furnishes another argument in favor of c. AD 67.[172] In terms of the relationship of the church to Judaism, one must ask whether what we find in Hebrews suggests that the separation between the two had become all but complete, or whether the split was still in progress. Anderson suggests that the "assumptions" concerning the people and the law in Hebrews put the letter at an "early stage of the process" of disengagement.[173]

Those who wish to date Hebrews after AD 70 must also come to terms with Peter Walker's incisive argument for a pre-AD 70 date. He suggests that a pre-70 date is indicated not only by the author's treatment of the temple, but by his treatment of the earthly Jerusalem and its significance.[174] He argues that the key clue for dating the letter is the issue of the Jerusalem temple: was it still standing at the time Hebrews was written? He accepts the use of the present tense verbs at their face value and sees this as evidence for a pre-70 date, but his

---

[169] Nairne, *Hebrews*, 30.

[170] Josephus, *Antiquities*, 20.181.

[171] Ibid., 20.216–18; See also Horbury, "The Aaronic Priesthood in the Epistle to the Hebrews," 67–68.

[172] Ibid.

[173] C. P. Anderson, "Who are the Heirs of the New Age in Hebrews?" in *Apocalyptic and the New Testament: Essays in Honor of J. Louis Martyn*, ed. J. Marcus and M. Soards, JSNTSup 24 (Sheffield: Sheffield Academic Press, 1989), 273.

[174] Walker, "Jerusalem in Hebrews 13:9–14 and the Dating of the Epistle," 40.

article is not simply a rehash of the arguments for a pre-70 date based on the use of the present tense. His purpose is to "draw attention to other factors which support this straightforward interpretation [of the use of the present tense]."[175]

He lists and discusses five factors. First, in reference to Heb 10:39, the question is asked what tempted the readers to "draw back"? The answer comes later (13:9–14); the readers are called on to share in the "disgrace" that Jesus experienced. This disgrace was what they expected from their fellow Jews. Walker believes this favors a date before AD 70 for two reasons: (1) after AD 70 when Judaism had itself been "disgraced," the fear of incurring disgrace in the eyes of fellow countrymen would be less of a concern; (2) if the cause of the disgrace was their negative attitude toward the temple, all of Judaism was forced after AD 70 to develop a "spiritualizing attitude towards the role of the temple."[176]

Second, Hebrews gives the impression that the readers are not bereaved over the loss of Jerusalem and the temple, but are "tempted" [by its presence and dominance in Judaism]. "Such language makes far more sense if the Jewish alternative, based on the temple, was a viable and established system."

Third, the great care the author takes to convey his message is more likely to reflect a date before AD 70 when with "the looming clash between Jerusalem and Rome there would have been great sensitivities about the Temple and when such negative views as Hebrews espouses would indeed have been seen as almost treacherous."[177]

Fourth, the sense of expectancy could have been present because of a belief that there would soon be an "act of God" that would affect Jerusalem. Walker quotes F. F. Bruce's comment along these lines:

> We have evidence of a belief that God's dealings with Israel, which began with a probationary period of forty years, would be rounded off at the endtime by a probationary period of like duration; and (if this epistle was written shortly before AD 70), it was nearly forty years now since Jesus had accomplished his "exodus" at Jerusalem. Hence the urgency of the present appeal to the readers to take heed "so long as it is called Today."[178]

---

[175] Ibid., 58.

[176] Ibid., 59–60.

[177] Ibid., 60.

[178] Bruce, *Hebrews*, 65, cited in Walker, "Jerusalem in Hebrews 13:9–14 and the Dating of the Epistle," 62–63.

Walker notes that Heb 8:13 describes the old covenant as obsolete and soon to disappear. The disappearance of the old covenant must be tied to the contemporary locus of the tabernacle ritual which, of course, was the temple. Hence the author of Hebrews is, in prophetic fashion, announcing that the temple will soon be destroyed. Such an interpretation, he suggests, may shed new light on such passages as 10:25 ("all the more as you see the day drawing near") and 10:37 ("For yet in a very little while, the Coming One will come and not delay"), and 12:27 ("the removal of what can be shaken").[179]

Fifth, the emphasis in chap. 11 on the need for faith suggests a pre-70 date. Less faith would have been required to do what the author suggested had the temple been destroyed.[180]

Walker concludes that Heb 13:14 ("For we do not have an enduring city here; instead, we seek the one to come") is very similar to the words of Jesus in the Lukan Apocalyptic Discourse: "Then those in Judea must flee to the mountains! Those inside the city must leave it, and those who are in the country must not enter it" (Luke 21:21). "The historical and literary connection between Hebrews and Luke in this matter cannot here be pursued, but the parallel is suggestive. The author of Hebrews is saying something essentially similar."[181]

Although Lane locates the recipients in Rome, his date for the letter is during or just slightly before the beginning of the Jewish War. He dates Hebrews between AD 64 (after the fire in Rome) and AD 68 (before the suicide of Nero in June of that year).[182]

The historical and textual evidence supports a date before the destruction of Jerusalem in AD 70, possibly around AD 67.[183] The references to Luke in 2 Timothy, to "those who are from Italy" in Heb 13:24, and to Timothy both in 2 Timothy and Hebrews 13 can be easily explained by such a date.

For example, Ellis accepts a pre-AD 70 date for Hebrews by theorizing that Timothy responded to Paul's appeal (2 Tim 1:17) to come to Rome. Timothy arrived in the fall of AD 67 and was probably arrested. Timothy's release (Heb 13:23) would likely have occurred after the

---

[179] Walker, "Jerusalem in Hebrews 13:9–14," 63–64.

[180] Ibid., 65.

[181] Ibid., 71. See his discussion in *Jesus and the Holy City*, 227–34.

[182] Lane, "Social Perspectives on Roman Christianity," 215.

[183] This date was also advocated by Spicq, *Hébreux* 1:257–61, and Robinson, *Redating*, 215, among many others. See Lindars, *Theology of Hebrews*, 19–21, who believes a date later than AD 65–70 is not warranted by the evidence.

death of Nero in June of AD 68. Ellis dates 1 Clement in AD 69–70, and this suggests that a copy of Hebrews had been retained by the author or copied by the church and was available at Rome. This accounts for Clement's use of it in his letter. Furthermore, the language in Hebrews 8–9 concerning the superiority of the new covenant is, according to Ellis, "inconceivable" after AD 70. "Equally inconceivable" is the absence of reference to the events of AD 70.[184]

The preformed traditions of Hebrews (37 percent of the letter) also favor a date before AD 70, according to Ellis. They are mostly Old Testament expositions using midrashic technique and patterns that are absent from Christian literature (such as Barnabas, 2 Clement, and others) dated after AD 70.[185]

Excursus on Porter's "The Date of the Composition of Hebrews and Use of the Present-Tense Form"

Many scholars, including Hughes, Westcott, and Robinson, use the present tense form in Hebrews to support a pre-AD 70 date.[186] Even in more recent work on Hebrews, writers often exhibit little or no knowledge of the state of the discussion regarding verbal aspect in Greek.[187] As Porter notes, the assumption made is that the use of a particular verb tense implies reference to a particular temporal sphere. Hughes's list of examples includes several non-indicative verbs and verbals which are, according to many grammarians, exempt from temporal reference since they do not consider time to be one of the primary semantic categories attached to non-indicative verb forms.[188]

Porter laments the failure of recent commentators on Hebrews to specify the meaning of the Greek present tense where it may have been used in a variety of temporal contexts. He identifies three models used of the present tense in the Greek of Hebrews.

The *first* model retains temporal criteria for evaluating the use of the present tense form, but notes that one of these uses is the historic

---

[184] Ellis, *The Making of the New Testament Documents*, 285–88.

[185] Ibid., 286.

[186] Hughes, *Hebrews*, 30; B. F. Westcott, *The Epistle to the Hebrews* (London: Macmillan, 1892; repr., Grand Rapids: Eerdmans, 1977), xlii–xliii; and.Robinson, *Redating*, 300.

[187] One exception is Carson, Moo, and Morris, *An Introduction to the New Testament*, 399. They footnote a reference to Porter's work in this field.

[188] S. Porter, "The Date of the Composition of Hebrews and Use of Present Tense–Form," 296–97.

present and the other is the timeless present. Porter critiques Lane's assertion that the timeless present is unclear. He also notes Lane's statement regarding the aorist participle in Heb 1:3 contradicts his comments about the present tense. A *second* model is represented by F. F. Bruce, who says in reference to Heb 9:6–9 that the present tense could be explained as a "literary present." Porter discusses the problems with this model. The *third* model uses contemporary authors (usually Josephus) to show that they wrote about various aspects of the temple rituals in the present tense even though they were writing post-AD 70. Porter notes two problems with this model: (1) no definition of tense function is given, just the assumption that there is some underlying semantic category making this usage possible; (2) there is no consistency of application because there are no explicit criteria given to warrant this usage.[189]

Porter addresses this problem from the perspective of his verbal aspectual theory. Commentators on Hebrews err because they use outmoded grammars that perpetuate the equation of time and tense. Porter defines verbal aspect as a semantic category used to describe the meaningful oppositions in the Greek verbal system that express grammatically how a writer perceives a process or event.[190] He believes that Greek does not grammaticalize temporal reference in its verb forms. Rather, the language uses other means to establish temporal relations and reference.[191]

Discourse type appears to be the most significant category for establishing temporal reference. The crucial distinction is between narrative and description. The aorist tense serves as the default tense in narrative, and the present tense is used in descriptive or expositional material.

The important question regarding Hebrews is not whether Josephus or others used the present tense to refer to past events. Clearly they did. The important question is whether or not this is what is going on in Hebrews. Porter concludes, "On the basis of the most recent work in Greek grammar and linguistics, one cannot start with the individual verb tenses to establish extra-textual reference."[192]As a

[189] Ibid., 300–2.

[190] See S. Porter, *Verbal Aspect in the Greek of the New Testament, With Reference to Tense and Mood* (New York: Peter Lang, 1989), 88.

[191] S. Porter, "The Date of the Composition of Hebrews and Use of Present Tense-Form," 304.

[192] Ibid., 312.

result, the present-tense form alone cannot be used for establishing the date of Hebrews.

Conclusion

I have made the case that Luke, the traveling companion of Paul, was the author of the Gospel and Acts, which early church tradition attributed to him. He wrote both books while he was with Paul in his first Roman imprisonment c. AD 60–63. He may have written most or all of Luke before he arrived in Rome with Paul. The evidence for a pre-AD 70 date for Luke-Acts is strong, and on balance, more persuasive than post-AD 70 theories. Luke wrote for a single recipient, Theophilus, a former Jewish high priest who had been deposed by Herod Agrippa in AD 41.

Luke served as Paul's amanuensis for the Pastoral Epistles, which were written from Rome during Paul's second Roman imprisonment. Because of the nature of Paul's imprisonment, Luke was given greater latitude in the composition of the letters, hence the stylistic similarities to Luke-Acts. After Paul's death Luke remained in Rome, where he wrote the letter to the Hebrews c. AD 67–68. Hebrews 13:24 is best interpreted as "Those who are with me in Italy . . . ." This interpretation was the unanimous opinion of the church fathers, even when Pauline authorship was denied.

The recipients of Hebrews were former priests who had converted to Christianity and had relocated in Syrian Antioch, where they were part of the church. Acts 6:7 informs us that "a great company of the priests became obedient to the faith." No more is said about them in Acts or the rest of the New Testament. Based on the audience profile of Hebrews, several reasons were given substantiating the claim that these former priests would fit the profile well. Their location in the Antiochene church is a reasonable theory given its importance in the early history of the church, Luke and Paul's connection with it, and what we know about it from Acts. With a mixed congregation of Jews and Gentiles and a large and influential Jewish population, Antioch could create the kind of social/theological matrix that Hebrews addresses.

CONCLUSION

To revert to the courtroom analogy of my Introduction, I offer the following closing arguments. Based on all the evidence, I conclude that Luke himself (independently) wrote the Letter to the Hebrews from Rome c. AD 67. We may historically reconstruct the circumstances of writing: about five to seven years earlier, the Gospel of Luke and Acts were addressed to Theophilus, a former Jewish high priest in Jerusalem from AD 37–41. He was deposed by Herod Agrippa for unknown reasons. The Gospel of Luke was written in c. AD 60–61, and Acts in c. AD 62–63, while Luke was in Rome during Paul's first Roman imprisonment.

Luke wrote Hebrews from Rome shortly after Paul's death and addressed it to a group of former Jewish priests (Acts 6:7) who had relocated to Antioch in Syria. Evidence from Hebrews and the Pastoral Epistles was adduced that supports a date of composition c. AD 67 during the turbulent times of the Jewish War.

Chapter one presents early patristic evidence that some during that time believed Hebrews was Luke's translation of Paul's original Hebrew document or that Hebrews was the work of Luke as an independent author. Their view was based primarily on linguistic similarities between Hebrews and Luke's writings, and also on Luke's association with Paul. Clearly Luke was thought capable of writing Hebrews. None of the church fathers ever argued that Luke could not have written Hebrews because he was a Gentile, or even that he was a Gentile. The most reasonable reading of the evidence is that the early fathers considered Luke to have been Jewish. Then chapter one proceeds to outline the history of scholarship regarding Lukan authorship. I argue that the linguistic evidence noted by Delitzsch and collated by Alexander has not been given due weight by twentieth-century scholars, resulting in a rather tacit dismissal of the Lukan hypothesis.

Chapter two considers the evidence for and against Paul, Barnabas, and Apollos as potential authors of Hebrews. Since there are no extant writings of Barnabas and Apollos with which to compare Hebrews, it is simply not possible to make a linguistic comparison as with Paul. Furthermore, during the patristic era, only Tertullian proposed

Barnabas as the author, and Luther was the first to suggest Apollos. Some external evidence points to Pauline authorship, and some similarities in vocabulary between Hebrews and Paul's Letters supports this. Nevertheless, the early church fathers observed significant stylistic differences as well. The majority of New Testament scholars today reject Pauline authorship of Hebrews.

Chapter three presents the most significant evidence for Lukan authorship of Hebrews: the linguistic argument. Both the vocabulary and style of Hebrews are more like Luke-Acts than any other New Testament book. I have presented numerous examples of vocabulary and stylistic similarities that were heretofore undisclosed. Under the heading "textlinguistics," three comparative categories of evidence reveal a close similarity to Hebrews: the prologues, linguistic and semantic parallels between Acts 7 and Hebrews 11, and similarity in the use of chiasm and parallelism as an overarching framework for the entire discourses of Luke-Acts and Hebrews. Luke was as rhetorically capable a writer as the author of Hebrews.

Chapter four demonstrates a significant similarity of purpose between Luke-Acts and Hebrews. The Lukan emphasis on the concept of the "Word" and the "hearing of the Word" in Acts compares well to what we find in Hebrews. Hebrews—especially the warning passages—appears to have a similar purpose to that of Luke-Acts. Luke's pastoral concern revealed in his two-volume work is well known; the author of Hebrews exhibits a similar pastoral concern. Even though Luke wrote Luke-Acts as a narrative, he wrote with a pastoral purpose; such a purpose is also evident in Hebrews.

Chapter five compares the theological outlook of Luke-Acts and Hebrews and finds substantial agreement, especially in Christology, eschatology, and prophetic fulfillment. Several other areas of theological similarity also connect Luke-Acts with Hebrews. Luke clearly presented Jesus as the High Priest, especially in his Gospel. This is one of the most important links to Hebrews. Theologically, Hebrews is most like the writings of Luke in the New Testament. The linguistic, stylistic, and theological evidence clearly implies that Luke was the author of Hebrews.

The greatest objection to Lukan authorship of Hebrews is Luke's supposed Gentile background and mind-set. So chapter six careful considers his two-volume work and finds numerous examples of distinctively Jewish thought and interest. Our examination of Luke-Acts shows Luke to have been easily capable of writing a treatise such as Hebrews. As was sometimes suggested, Luke may have been a proselyte to Judaism, but the evidence seems to suggest that Luke was Jewish by birth. Furthermore, Luke's use of the Old Testament demonstrates his hermeneutical and exegetical abilities and skills. The way the Old Testament is used in Luke-Acts is also consistent with its use in Hebrews. Luke's use of the Old Testament is interwoven in a narrative framework. When we compare the Old Testament quotations (including the quotation formulae) used in Luke-Acts with Hebrews (an example of hortatory discourse given directly by the author to his readers), the similarities are remarkable.

The present state of Lukan studies on the issue of Luke's possible Jewish background renders it impossible to argue against Lukan authorship for Hebrews on the basis of the "Gentile" theory any longer. In the midst of a flurry of theories concerning the authorship of Hebrews in the past two centuries, the Lukan theory has much to commend it.

While thumbing through a commentary on Acts by one of my favorite preachers of a bygone era, G. Campbell Morgan, I ran across a passage I had marked several years earlier but had forgotten. In a comment on Paul's two-year imprisonment in Caesarea (Acts 24), Morgan briefly indicated his agreement with the suggestion that it was during this time that Hebrews was written. In a brief statement about the authorship of Hebrews, Morgan wrote,

> My own conviction is that Luke was the writer, but that he wrote what Paul had taught. Possibly during those two years Paul talked with Luke again concerning the things which Luke had so often heard him teach in those synagogues in Gentile cities; and then Luke wrote the thinking of Paul in this form of the Hebrew letter. . . . If we remember the Hebrew opposition at that time . . . we shall see that it argues exactly what he claimed before Felix, that the religion of "the Way" was the fulfillment of the Hebrew ideal.[1]

Although I think the circumstances were different, I believe the venerable British preacher was right about Luke's authorship of Hebrews.

The cumulative effect of the evidence implicating Luke is substantial. If the field of suspects for authorship is narrowed to include only those who are New Testament writers, then the evidence points to

---

[1] G. C. Morgan, *The Acts of the Apostles* (Revell: n.p., 1924), 506.

Luke. Having evaluated the available clues in this case of authorship attribution, I conclude that the missionary doctor, in Rome, with the aid of the Holy Spirit, wrote it.

SELECT BIBLIOGRAPHY

Alexander, Loveday. *The Preface to Luke's Gospel: Literary Convention and Social Context in Luke 1.1–4 and Acts 1.1.* SNTSMS 78. Cambridge: Cambridge University Press, 1993.

Alexander, William. *The Leading Ideas of the Gospels.* 3rd ed. London: Macmillan, 1892.

Alford, Henry. "Prolegomena and Hebrews." Vol. 4 of *Alford's Greek Testament: An Exegetical and Critical Commentary.* 5th ed. Cambridge: Deighton, Bell, & Co., 1875; reprint, Grand Rapids: Guardian Press, 1976.

Allen, David L. "An Argument for the Lukan Authorship of Hebrews." Ph.D. diss., University of Texas at Arlington, 1987.

———. "The Purposes of Luke-Acts and Hebrews Compared: An Argument for the Lukan Authorship of Hebrews." In *The Church at the Dawn of the 21st Century.* Edited by P. Patterson, J. Pretlove, and L. Pantoja. Dallas: Criswell Publications, 1989.

———. "The Discourse Structure of Philemon: A Study in Textlinguistics." In *Scribes and Scriptures: New Testament Essays in Honor of J. Harold Greenlee.* Edited by David A. Black. Winona Lake: Eisenbrauns, 1992.

———. "The Lukan Authorship of Hebrews: A Proposal." *JOTT* 8 (1996): 1–22.

———. "The Authorship of Hebrews: The Case for Luke." *Faith and Mission* 17.2 (2001): 27–40.

Andersen, Francis. "Style & Authorship." In *The Tyndale Lecture 1976,* Vol. 21, No. 2. Australia: Tyndale Fellowship for Biblical Studies, 1976.

Anderson, C. P. "The Epistle to the Hebrews and the Pauline Letter Collection." *HTR* 59 (1966): 429–38.

Anderson, R. Dean. *Ancient Rhetorical Theory and Paul.* Rev. ed. Leuven: Peeters, 1999.

———. "The Theoretical Justification for Application of Rhetorical Categories to Pauline Epistolary Literature." In *Rhetoric and the New Testament.* Edited by Stanley Porter and Thomas Olbricht. Sheffield: Sheffield Academic Press, 1993.

Anderson, Richard. "The Cross and Atonement from Luke to Hebrews." *EvQ* 71.2 (1999): 127–49.

———. "Theophilus: A Proposal." *EvQ* 69.3 (1997): 195–215.

Attridge, Harold. *The Epistle to the Hebrews.* Her. Philadelphia: Fortress, 1989.

———. "The Epistle to the Hebrews and the Scrolls." In *When Judaism and Christianity Began: Essays in Memory of Anthony J. Saldarini,* vol. 2. Edited by A. J. Avery-Peck, D. Harrington, and J. Neusner. JSJSup 85. Leiden: Brill, 2004.

———. "Parenesis in a Homily (προσ παρρακλησεως): The Possible Location of, and Socialization in, the 'Epistle to the Hebrews.'" *Semeia* 50 (1990): 210–26.

Barrett, C. K. "Attitudes to the Temple in the Acts of the Apostles." In *Templum Amicitae: Essays on the Second Temple Presented to Ernst Bammel.* Edited by W. Horbury. JSNTSup 48. Sheffield: JSOT Press, 1991.

———. "The Eschatology of the Epistle to the Hebrews." *The Background of the New Testament and its Eschatology: C. H. Dodd Festschrift.* Edited by W. D. Davies and D. Daube. Cambridge: Cambridge University Press. 1956.

———. *Luke the Historian in Recent Study.* London: Epworth, 1961.

———. "Theologia Crucis—in Acts?" In *Theologia Crucis—Signum Crucis: Festschrift für Erich Dinkler zum 70. Geburstag.* Edited by C. Andersen and G. Klein, 73–84. Tübingen: J. C. B. Mohr (Paul Siebeck), 1979.

Bates, William. "Authorship of the Epistle to the Hebrews Again." *BSac* 79 (1922): 93–96.

Bauckham, Richard, ed. *The Book of Acts in its Palestinian Setting.* Vol. 4 of *The Book of Acts in its First Century Setting.* Edited by Bruce Winter. Grand Rapids: Eerdmans, 1995.

Bechard, Dean. "The Theological Significance of Judaea in Luke-Acts." In *The Unity of Luke-Acts,* ed. J. Verheyden. BETL 142. Leuven: Leuven University Press, 1999.

Black, David. "On the Pauline Authorship of Hebrews (Part 1): Overlooked Affinities between Hebrews and Paul." *Faith and Mission* 16 (Spring 1999): 32–51.

————. "On the Pauline Authorship of Hebrews (Part 2): The External Evidence Reconsidered." *Faith and Mission* 16 (Summer 1999): 78–86.

————. "Who Wrote Hebrews?" *Faith and Mission* 18 (2001): 21.

Bock, Darrell L. *Luke 1:1–9:50.* BECNT, vol. 3a. Grand Rapids: Baker, 1994.

————. *Luke 9:51–24:53.* BECNT, vol. 3b. Grand Rapids: Baker, 1996.

————. *Proclamation from Prophecy and Pattern.* JSNTSup 12. Edited by David Hill. Sheffield: JSOT Press, 1987.

Bovon, Francois. *Luke the Theologian: Fifty-five Years of Research (1950–2005).* 2nd ed. Waco: Baylor University Press, 2006.

Bristol, L. O. "Primitive Christian Preaching and the Epistle to the Hebrews." *JBL* 68 (1949): 89–97.

Brown, J. Vallance. "The Authorship and Circumstances of Hebrews—Again!" *BSac* 80 (1923): 505–38.

Brown, Schuyler. *Apostasy and Perseverance in the Theology of Luke.* AnBib 36. Rome: Pontifical Biblical Institute, 1969.

Calvin, John. *The Epistle of Paul the Apostle to the Hebrews and the First and Second Epistles of St. Peter.* Edited by David W. Torrance and Thomas F. Torrance. Translated by William B. Johnston. Grand Rapids: Eerdmans, 1963.

Carpinelli, Francis Giordano. "'Do This as My Memorial' (Luke 22:19): Lucan Soteriology of Atonement." *CBQ* 61 (1999): 74–91.

Carson, D.A. and H. G. M. Williamson, eds. *It is Written: Scripture Citing Scripture: Essays in Honor of Barnabas Lindars, SSF.* Cambridge; New York: Cambridge University Press, 1988.

Clarkson, M. E. "The Antecedents of the High Priest Theme in Hebrews." *AThR* 29 (1947): 89–95.

Collison, Franklyn. "Linguistic Usages in the Gospel of Luke." Ph.D. diss., Southern Methodist University. Ann Arbor: University Microfilms International, 1977.

Cowles, Henry. *The Epistle to the Hebrews; with Notes, Critical, Explanatory and Practical, Designed for both Pastors and People.* New York: Appleton & Co., 1878.

Creech, Robert. "The Most Excellent Narratee: The Significance of Theophilus in Luke-Acts." In *With Steadfast Purpose: Essays in Honor of Henry Jack Flanders.* Edited by Naymond Keathley. Waco, TX: Baylor University, 1990.

Crump, David. *Jesus the Intercessor: Prayer and Christology in Luke-Acts.* Biblical Studies Library. Grand Rapids: Baker, 1992.

Cunningham, Scott Smith. *Through Many Tribulations: The Theology of Persecution in Luke-Acts.* JSNTSup 142. Edited by Stanley Porter. Sheffield: Sheffield Academic, 1997.

Dahms, John. "The First Readers of Hebrews." *JETS* 20 (1977): 365–75.

De Young, James. "A Grammatical Approach to Hebrews." Th.D. diss., Dallas Theological Seminary, 1973.

Delitzsch, Franz. *Commentary on the Epistle to the Hebrews.* Translated by Thomas L. Kingsbury. 2 vols. Grand Rapids: Eerdmans, 1871, 1952 reprint.

Denova, Rebecca. *The Things Accomplished Among Us: Prophetic Tradition in the Structural Pattern of Luke-Acts.* JSNTSup 141. Sheffield: Sheffield Academic, 1997.

Derrett, J. Duncan. "The Lucan Christ and Jerusalem: τελειοῦμαι (Luke 13:32)." *ZNW* 75 (1984): 36–43.

Dillon, Richard. *From Eye-Witness to Ministers of the Word: Tradition and Composition in Luke 24.* AnBib 82. Rome: Biblical Institute Press, 1978.

Doble, Peter. *The Paradox of Salvation: Luke's Theology of the Cross.* SNTSMS 87. Cambridge: Cambridge University Press, 1996.

Dods, Marcus. "The Epistle to the Hebrews." *Expositor's Greek New Testament,* vol. 4. Edited by Robertson Nicoll. Grand Rapids: Eerdmans, 1974.

Drury, John. *Tradition and Design in Luke's Gospel: A Study in Early Christian Historiography*. Atlanta: John Knox, 1976.

Eagar, Alexander. "The Authorship of the Epistle to the Hebrews." *Expositor* (6th series) 10 (1904): 74–80, 110–23.

Ebrard, J. H. A. *Exposition of the Epistle to the Hebrews*. Translated and Revised by A. C. Kendrick. Biblical Commentary on the New Testament. Edited by Hermann Olshausen. 6 vols. New York: Sheldon, Blakeman & Co., 1858.

Ellingworth, Paul. *Commentary on Hebrews*. NIGTC. Grand Rapids: Eerdmans, 1993.

Ellis, E. Earle. *Eschatology in Luke*. Facet Books. Biblical Series 30. Philadelphia: Fortress, 1972.

———. *The Gospel of Luke*. NCBC. London: Oliphants, 1977 reprint.

———. *History and Interpretation in New Testament Perspective*. Biblical Interpretation Series, vol. 54. Edited by R. Alan Culpepper and Rolf Rendtorff. Leiden: Brill, 2001.

———. *The Making of the New Testament Documents*. Biblical Interpretation Series, vol. 39. Edited by R. Alan Culpepper and Rolf Rendtorff. Leiden: Brill, 1999.

Evans, Craig A. and James Sanders. *Luke and Scripture: The Function of Sacred Tradition in Luke-Acts*. Minneapolis: Fortress, 1993.

Fitzmyer, J. A. *The Gospel According to Luke (I–IX): Introduction, Translation, and Notes*. AB 28. Garden City: Doubleday, 1981.

———. *The Gospel According to Luke (X–XXIV): Introduction, Translation, and Notes*. AB 28a. Garden City: Doubleday, 1985.

Ford, J. M. "The Mother of Jesus and the Authorship of the Epistle to the Hebrews." *TBT* 82 (1976): 683–94.

Ford, R. C. "St. Luke and Lucius of Cyrene." *ExpTim* 32 (1920–21): 219–20.

Franklin, Eric. *Christ the Lord. A Study in the Purpose and Theology of Luke-Acts*. London: SPCK, 1975.

———. *Luke: Interpreter of Paul, Critic of Matthew*. JSNTSup 92. Sheffield: JSOT Press, 1994.

Gardiner, F. "The Language of the Epistle to the Hebrews as Bearing upon its Authorship." *JBL* 7 (1887): 1–27.

Glover, Richard. "'Luke the Antiochene' and Acts." *NTS* 11 (1964–65): 97–106.

Godet, F. *A Commentary on the Gospel of Luke.* 4th ed. Translated by E. W. Shalders and M. D. Cusin. 2 vols. in one. New York: Funk & Wagnalls, 1887.

Goppelt, Leonard. *Theology of the New Testament.* Edited by Jürgen Roloff. Translated by John Alsup. 2 vols. Grand Rapids: Eerdmans, 1982.

Green, Joel. "The Death of Jesus, God's Servant." In *Reimaging the Death of the Lukan Jesus.* Edited by D. D. Sylva. BBB 73. Frankfurt am Main: Anton Hain, 1990.

———. "'Salvation to the End of the Earth' (Acts 13:47): God as Savior in the Acts of the Apostles." In *Witness to the Gospel: The Theology of Acts.* Edited by I. H. Marshall and David Peterson. Grand Rapids: Eerdmans, 1998.

———. *The Theology of the Gospel of Luke.* New Testament Theology Series. Edited by James Dunn. Cambridge: Cambridge University Press, 1995.

Guthrie, George. "The Case for Apollos as the Author of Hebrews." *Faith and Mission* 18 (2002): 41–56.

———. *The Structure of Hebrews: A Text-Linguistic Analysis.* Leiden: E. J. Brill, 1994.

Harnack, Adolph von. *Luke the Physician.* Translated by J. R. Wilkinson. London: Williams & Norgate, 1907.

——— . "Probabilia über die Addresse und den Verfasser des Hebräerbriefs." *ZNW* 1 (1900): 16–41.

Hemer, Colin. *The Book of Acts in the Setting of Hellenistic History.* WUNT 49. Edited by Conrad Gempf. Tübingen: J. C. B. Mohr (Paul Siebeck), 1989.

Hobart, William K. *The Medical Language of St. Luke: A Proof from Internal Evidence that 'The Gospel According to St. Luke' and 'The Acts of the Apostles' Were Written by the Same Person, and that the Writer Was a Medical Man.* Dublin: Hodges, Figgis, 1882; reprint, Grand Rapids: Baker, 1954.

Hoppin, Ruth. *Priscilla: Author of the Epistle to the Hebrews.* New York: Exposition Press, 1969.

Horbury, W. "The Aaronic Priesthood in the Epistle to the Hebrews." *JSNT* 19 (1983): 43–71.

Hughes, Graham. *Hebrews and Hermeneutics.* SNTSMS 36. Cambridge: Cambridge University Press, 1979.

Hurst, Lincoln. *The Epistle to the Hebrews: Its Background of Thought.* SNTSMS 65. New York: Cambridge University Press, 1990.

———. "Eschatology and 'Platonism' in the Epistle to the Hebrews." SBLSP. Edited by Kent H. Richards. California: Scholars Press, 1984.

Jervell, J. *Luke and the People of God: A New Look at Luke-Acts.* Minneapolis: Augsburg, 1972.

———. *The Theology of the Acts of the Apostles.* Cambridge: Cambridge University Press, 1996.

———. *The Unknown Paul: Essays on Luke-Acts and Early Christian History.* Minneapolis: Augsburg, 1984.

Jones, C. P. M. "The Epistle to the Hebrews and the Lucan Writings." In *Studies in the Gospels: Essays in Memory of R. H. Lightfoot.* Edited by D. E. Nineham. Oxford, Basil Blackwell, 1955.

Lane, William. *Hebrews 1–8.* WBC. Dallas: Word, 1991.

———. *Hebrews 9–13.* WBC. Dallas: Word, 1991.

———. "Hebrews: A Sermon in Search of a Setting." *SwJT* 28 (1985): 13–18.

Leonard, William. *Authorship of the Epistle to the Hebrews.* Rome: Vatican Polyglot Press, 1939.

Lindars, Barnabas. *The Theology of the Letter to the Hebrews.* Cambridge: Cambridge University Press, 1991.

Linnemann, Eta. "A Call for a Retrial in the Case of the Epistle to the Hebrews." Translated by David Lanier. In *Faith and Mission* 19/2 (2002): 19–59.

Maddox, Robert. *The Purpose of Luke-Acts.* Edinburgh: T&T Clark, 1982.

Manson, William. *The Epistle to the Hebrews: an Historical and Theological Reconsideration.* London: Hodder & Stoughton, 1951.

Marshall, I. H. *Luke: Historian and Theologian.* Exeter: Paternoster, 1970.

Mekkattukunnel, Andrews George. *The Priestly Blessing of the Risen Christ: An Exegetico-Theological Analysis of Luke 24, 50–53.* European University Studies Series 23, vol. 714. Bern: Peter Lang, 2001.

Moessner, David. "'The Christ Must Suffer,' The Church Must Suffer: Rethinking the Theology of the Cross in Luke-Acts." SBLSP. Edited by David Lull. Atlanta: Scholars Press, 1990.

———. "Jesus and the 'Wilderness Generation': The Death of the Prophet Like Moses According to Luke." In SBLSP. Edited by K. H. Richards. Chico, CA: Scholars Press, 1982.

———. *Lord of the Banquet: The Literary and Theological Significance of the Lukan Travel Narrative.* Minneapolis: Fortress, 1989.

———. "Paul in Acts: Preacher of Eschatological Repentance to Israel." *NTS* 34 (1988): 96–104.

———. "The 'Script' of the Scriptures in Acts." In *History, Literature, and Society in the Book of Acts.* Edited by Ben Witherington III. Cambridge: Cambridge University Press, 1996.

———. "Two Lords 'at the Right Hand'?: The Psalms and an Intertextual Reading of Peter's Pentecost Speech (Acts 2:14–36)." In *Literary Studies in Luke-Acts: Essays in Honor of Joseph B. Tyson.* Edited by Richard Thompson and Thomas Phillips. Macon: Mercer University Press, 1998.

———, ed. *Jesus and the Heritage of Israel: Luke's Narrative Claim upon Israel's Heritage.* Vol. 1 in *Luke the Interpreter of Israel.* Edited by David Moessner and David Tiede. Harrisburg, Penn.: Trinity Press International, 1999.

Neeley, Linda Lloyd. "A Discourse Analysis of Hebrews." *OPTAT* 3–4 (1987): 1–146.

Nolland. John. *Luke*. WBC, vol. 35. 3 vols. Dallas: Word, 1989–1993.

O'Reilly, L. *Word and Sign in the Acts of the Apostles: A Study in Lukan Theology*. Analecta Gregoriana 243. Rome: Editrice Pontificia Universita Gregoriana, 1987.

Parsons, M. C. *The Departure of Jesus in Luke-Acts: The Ascension Narratives in Context*. JSNTSup 21. London: Sheffield Academic, 1987.

Reicke, Bo. *The Gospel of Luke*. Translated by R. Mackenzie. Richmond: John Knox, 1964.

Rissi, Mathias. *Die Theologie des Hebräerbriefes: ihre Verankerung in der Situation des Verfassers und seiner Leser*. Tübingen: Mohr, 1987.

Robertson, A. T. *Luke the Historian in the Light of Research*. Nashville: Broadman, 1920.

Robinson, John A. T. *Redating the New Testament*. London: SCM, 1976.

Salmon, Marilyn. "Insider or Outsider? Luke's Relationship with Judaism." In *Luke-Acts and the Jewish People*. Edited by Joseph Tyson. Minneapolis: Augsburg, 1988.

Sandegren, C. "The Addresses of the Epistle to the Hebrews." *EvQ* 27 (1955): 221–24.

Spicq, C. *L'Épître aux Hébreux*. 2 vols. Paris: Librairie Lecoffre, 1952–53.

Stempvoort, P. A. "The Interpretation of the Ascension in Luke and Acts." *NTS* 5 (1958–59): 30–42.

Talbert, C. H. *Literary Patterns, Theological Themes and the Genre of Luke-Acts*. SBLMS 20. Missoula: Scholars Press, 1974.

————. *Reading Luke*. New York: Crossroads, 1983.

Thayer, J. H. "Authorship and Canonicity of the Epistle to the Hebrews." *BSac* 24 (1867): 681–722.

Tiede, David. *Prophecy and History in Luke-Acts*. Philadelphia: Fortress, 1980.

Tyson, Joseph. *The Death of Jesus in Luke-Acts.* Columbia: University of South Carolina Press, 1986.

————. *Images of Judaism in Luke-Acts.* Columbia: University of South Carolina Press, 1992.

————. *Luke-Acts and the Jewish People: Eight Critical Perspectives.* Minneapolis: Augsburg, 1988.

van Unnik, W. C. "The 'Book of Acts' the Confirmation of the Gospel." *NTS* 4 (1960): 26–59.

Walker, Peter. "Jerusalem in Hebrews 13:9–14 and the Dating of the Epistle." *TynBul* 45 (1994): 39–71.

————. *Jesus and the Holy City: New Testament Perspectives.* Grand Rapids: Eerdmans, 1996.

Wallis, Ethel. "Thematic Parallelism and Prominence in Luke-Acts." *NOT* 75 (1979): 2–6.

Wenham, John. "The Identification of Luke." *EvQ* 63 (1991): 3–44.

————. *Redating Matthew, Mark and Luke: A Fresh Assault on the Synoptic Problem.* Downers Grove, IL: InterVarsity, 1992.

Westcott, B. F. *The Epistle to the Hebrews.* Grand Rapids: Eerdmans, 1955 reprint.

Wolfe, Kenneth. "The Chiastic Structure of Luke-Acts and Some Implications for Worship." *SwJT* 22 (1989): 60–71.

NAME INDEX

SUBJECT INDEX

SCRIPTURE INDEX